The Holodomor Reader
A Sourcebook on the Famine of 1932–1933 in Ukraine

Compiled and edited by
Bohdan Klid and Alexander J. Motyl

The Holodomor Reader

A Sourcebook on the Famine of 1932–1933 in Ukraine

Compiled and edited by
Bohdan Klid and Alexander J. Motyl

Canadian Institute of Ukrainian Studies Press
Edmonton 2012 Toronto

Canadian Institute of Ukrainian Studies Press

University of Alberta
Edmonton, Alberta
Canada T6G 2H8

University of Toronto
Toronto, Ontario
Canada M5T 1N7

ISBN 978-1-894865-28-9 (bound).—ISBN 978-1-894865-29-6 (pbk.)

Library and Archives Canada Cataloguing in Publication

The Holodomor reader : a sourcebook on the Famine of 1932–1933 in Ukraine / compiled and edited by Bohdan Klid and Alexander J. Motyl.

Includes bibliographical references and index.

ISBN 978-1-894865-28-9 (bound).--ISBN 978-1-894865-29-6 (pbk.)

1. Ukraine--History--Famine, 1932–1933.

I. Klid, Bohdan, 1951- II. Motyl, Alexander J., 1953-

DK508.8377.H63 2012 947.7'0841 C2012-903012-0

Cover: Holodomor victims, Kharkiv, 1933. Photographs from the archive of Cardinal Theodor Innitzer (Vienna Diocesan Archives). Reproduced by permission of the Hordii Pshenychny Central State CinePhotoPhono Archives of Ukraine, Kyiv (items 5120, 5132, 5136).

The publication of this book has been funded by a generous donation from the estate of Edward Brodacky (1926–2007), who settled in London, England, after the Second World War.

A grant for this publication has also been provided by the Temerty Family Foundation.

Printed in Canada

LIST OF SHORT TITLES

The following sources, which occur repeatedly in this *Reader*, are cited by short title in the Table of Contents and in the text:

1. *XVII s"ezd Vsesoiuznoi Kommunisticheskoi partii (b)* (1934)
   XVII s"ezd Vsesoiuznoi Kommunisticheskoi partii (b) 26 ianvaria – 10 fevralia 1934 g. Stenograficheskii otchet (The Seventeenth Congress of the All-Union Communist Party [Bolshevik], 26 January–10 February 1934. Stenographic Record) (Moscow: Partizdat, 1934)

2. *The Black Deeds of the Kremlin: A White Book* (1953–55)
   The Black Deeds of the Kremlin: A White Book, ed. S. O. Pidhainy, 2 vols.
   Vol. 1. Toronto: Ukrainian Association of the Victims of Russian Communist Terror, 1953.
   Vol. 2. Detroit: Democratic Organization of Ukrainians Formerly Persecuted by the Soviet Regime in U.S.A., 1955

3. *Famine in Ukraine* (1934)
   Famine in Ukraine (New York: United Ukrainian Organizations of the United States, 1934)

4. *The Foreign Office and the Famine* (1988)
   The Foreign Office and the Famine: British Documents on Ukraine and the Great Famine of 1932–1933, ed. Marco Carynnyk, Lubomyr Y. Luciuk and Bohdan S. Kordan (Kingston, Ontario, and Vestal, N.Y.: Limestone Press, 1988)

5. *The Great Famine in Ukraine, 1932–33* (1988)
   The Great Famine in Ukraine, 1932–33 (Toronto: Ukrainian Orthodox Brotherhood of St. Volodymyr, 1988)

6. *Holod 1932–1933 rokiv na Ukraïni* (1990)
   Holod 1932–1933 rokiv na Ukraïni: ochyma istorykiv, movoiu dokumentiv (The Famine of 1932–33 in Ukraine through the Eyes of Historians and in the Language of Documents), comp. R. Ia. Pyrih et al. (Kyiv: Vydavnytstvo politychnoï literatury Ukraïny, 1990)

7. *Holod-henotsyd 1932–1933 rokiv v Ukraïni* (2005)
   Holod-henotsyd 1932–1933 rokiv v Ukraïni (The Famine-Genocide of 1932–33 in Ukraine), ed. Yurii Shapoval ([Kingston, Ontario]: Kashtan Press, 2005)

8. *Hołodomor 1932–1933* (2008)
   Hołodomor 1932–1933: Wielki Głód na Ukrainie w dokumentach polskiej dyplomacji i wywiadu (Holodomor 1932–33: The Great Famine in Ukraine in Documents of the Polish Diplomatic and Intelligence Services), comp. and ed. Jan Jacek Bruski (Warsaw: Polski Instytut Spraw Międzynarodowych, 2008)

9. *Holodomor 1932–1933 rokiv v Ukraïni* (2007)
   Holodomor 1932–1933 rokiv v Ukraïni: dokumenty i materialy (The Holodomor of 1932–33 in Ukraine: Documents and Materials), comp. Ruslan Pyrih (Kyiv: Vydavnychyi dim "Kyievo-Mohylians'ka Akademiia," 2007)

10. *Holodomor of 1932–33 in Ukraine* (2008)
    Holodomor of 1932–33 in Ukraine: Documents and Materials, comp. Ruslan Pyrih, trans. Stephen Bandera (Kyiv: Kyiv Mohyla Academy Publishing House, 2008)

    Documents excerpted from this source have been checked against the original texts, and the translations have been slightly revised in almost every selection.

11. *Holodomor v Ukraïni 1932–1933 rokiv* (2008)
    Holodomor v Ukraïni 1932–1933 rokiv za dokumentamy politychnoho arkhivu Ministerstva zakordonnykh sprav Federatyvnoï Respubliky Nimechchyna (The Holodomor in Ukraine in 1932–33 in Documents of the Political Archive of the Ministry of Foreign Affairs of the Federal Republic of Germany), ed. A. I. Kudriachenko (Kyiv: Natsional'nyi instytut stratehichnykh doslidzhen', 2008)

12. *Investigation of the Ukrainian Famine, 1932–1933* (1988)
    Investigation of the Ukrainian Famine, 1932–1933. Report to Congress (Washington, D.C.: United States Government Printing Office, 1988)

13. *Komandyry velykoho holodu* (2001)
    Komandyry velykoho holodu. Poïzdka V. Molotova i L. Kahanovycha v Ukraïnu ta na Pivnichnyi Kavkaz (Commanders of the Great Famine: The Journey of Viacheslav Molotov and Lazar Kaganovich to Ukraine and the North Caucasus), ed. Valerii Vasyliev and Yurii Shapoval (Kyiv: Heneza, 2001)

14. *Narodna viina* (2011)
    Roman Krutsyk, *Narodna viina. Putivnyk do ekspozytsiï* (The People's War: A Guide to the Exhibition) (Kyiv: Ukraïns'ka vydavnycha spilka, 2011)

15. *Natsiia v borot'bi za svoie isnuvannia* (1985)
    Mykhailo H. Marunchak, *Natsiia v borot'bi za svoie isnuvannia 1932 i 1933 v Ukraïni i diiaspori* (The Nation in the Struggle for Its Existence in 1932 and 1933 in Ukraine and in the Diaspora) (Winnipeg: Ukrainian Academy of Arts and Sciences in Canada, 1985)

16. *Pomór w "Raju Bolszewickim"* (2009)
    Pomór w "Raju Bolszewickim": Głód na Ukrainie w latach 1932–33 w świetle polskich dokumentów dyplomatycznych i dokumentów wywiadu (The Plague in the "Bolshevik Paradise": Famine in Ukraine in the Years 1932–33 in Light of Polish Diplomatic and Intelligence Service Documents), ed. Robert Kusznierz (Toruń: Adam Marszałek, 2009)

17. *Rozsekrechena pam'iat'* (2007)
    Rozsekrechena pam'iat'. Holodomor 1932–1933 rokiv v Ukraïni v dokumentakh GPU-NKVD (Declassified Memory: The Holodomor of 1932–33 in Ukraine in Documents of the GPU-NKVD), comp. Valentyna Borysenko, Vasyl Danylenko, Serhii Kokin, Olesia Stasiuk, and Yurii Shapoval (Kyiv: Stylos, 2007)

18. *Second Interim Report* (1988)
    Second Interim Report of Meetings and Hearings of and before the Commission on the Ukraine Famine Held in 1987 (Washington, D.C.: United States Government Printing Office, 1988)

19. *Soviet Ukraine Today* (1934)
    Soviet Ukraine Today (Moscow and Leningrad: Co-operative Publishing Society of Foreign Workers in the USSR, 1934)

20. *The Stalin-Kaganovich Correspondence 1931–36* (2003)
    The Stalin-Kaganovich Correspondence 1931–36, comp. and ed. R. W. Davies, Oleg V. Khlevniuk, E. A. Rees, Liudmila P. Kosheleva, and Larisa A. Rogovaya. Russian documents translated by Steven Shabad (New Haven and London: Yale University Press, 2003)

21. *Tragediia sovetskoi derevni* (2001)
    Tragediia sovetskoi derevni. Kollektivizatsiia i raskulachivanie. Dokumenty i materialy. Vol. 3, *Konets 1930–1933* (The Tragedy of the Soviet Village. Collectivization and Dekulakization. Documents and Materials. Vol. 3, Late 1930–1933), ed. I. Zelenin et al. (Moscow: Rosspen, 2001)

22. *We'll Meet Again in Heaven* (2001)
    We'll Meet Again in Heaven: Germans in the Soviet Union Write Their Dakota Relatives, 1925–1937. Translated, edited, and with an introduction by Ronald J. Vossler (Fargo, N.D.: Germans from Russia Heritage Collection, North Dakota State University Libraries, 2001)

TABLE OF CONTENTS

NOTE ON TRANSLITERATION

In this *Reader*, a modified version of the Library of Congress Romanization system has generally been used to transliterate Ukrainian and Russian personal and geographic names. Details of the system are posted on the Library of Congress website (http://www.loc.gov/catdir/cpso/roman.html). Names beginning with iotated vowels (Я, Є, Ї, Ю) are transliterated with an initial Y (Ya, Ye, Yi, Yu), and adjectival endings of masculine surnames (-ський, -ский) are simplified as -sky. The soft sign (ь, transliterated ') is indicated only in transliterated titles of publications. In texts translated for this *Reader* and selections published in recent decades, the spelling of personal and geographic names has been standardized according to Ukrainian usage (e.g., Dnipro, not Dnieper; Kosior, not Kossior; Kyiv, not Kiev).

A different approach has been taken with regard to English-language texts published at the time of the Holodomor and in decades immediately following it. These selections are grouped in the "Eyewitness Accounts and Memoirs" and "Survivor Testimonies, Memoirs, Diaries, and Letters" sections. Since there was no standard transliteration practice at the time, and Ukraine was conventionally treated as a region ("the Ukraine"), the imposition of modern standard forms would tend to undermine the authenticity of such writings. Consequently, personal names in these two sections are reproduced as originally published, with modern forms provided in brackets as necessary (e.g., Hatayevich [Khataevich]) on first mention in the selection. Personal names whose spelling does not differ greatly from the modern standard (e.g., Budyenny [Budenny], Marusya [Marusia], Petlyura [Petliura]) have been left as published. Older English forms of Ukrainian place-names, based mainly on Russian and French practice, have also been reproduced as published. In order to avoid the ubiquitous provision of bracketed modern forms, the principal place-names and variant spellings encountered in this *Reader* are given below for the reader's convenience.

Ukrainian place-name	*Variants*
Berdychiv	Berdicheff, Berdichev
Bila Tserkva	Byelaya Tserkov
Chernihiv	Chernigov
Dnipropetrovsk	Dniepropetrovsk, Dnipropetrowske
Donets (Basin, River)	Donetz
Kharkiv	Kharkiw, Kharkoff, Kharkov
Kyiv	Kieff, Kiev
Mykolaiv	Nikolayev
Myrhorod	Mirgorod
Odesa	Odessa
Zaporizhia	Zaporozhe

ACRONYMS, ABBREVIATIONS, AND TERMS

(Russian words and terms not used as English words in the text are *italicized*)

All-Union CP(B), AUCP(B) – All-Union Communist Party (Bolshevik)

CC – Central Committee
CCC – Central Control Commission
CEC – Central Executive Committee
Cheka – *Chrezvychainaia komissiia* (Extraordinary Commission): Soviet secret police
CP(B)U – Communist Party (Bolshevik) of Ukraine
CPC – Council of People's Commissars
CPSU – Communist Party of the Soviet Union
CPU – Communist Party of Ukraine

GPU – *Gosudarstvennoe politicheskoe upravlenie* (State Political Administration): Soviet secret police
GULAG – *Glavnoe upravlenie lagerei* (Chief Administration of Labor Camps)

KGB – *Komitet gosudarstvennoi bezopasnosti* (Committee for State Security): Soviet secret police
kolkhoz – *kollektivnoe khoziaistvo* (collective farm)
Komsomol – *Kommunisticheskii soiuz molodezhi* (Communist Youth League)
korenizatsiia – indigenization
krai – region
kraikom – regional committee
kulak – literally, "fist": highly elastic Soviet propaganda term for well-to-do peasant
kurkul' (Ukrainian) – kulak

Makhnovite – derogatory Soviet term for followers of Nestor Makhno, a Ukrainian peasant anarchist leader who fought both Bolshevik and White forces during the Civil War (1918–20)

NKVD – *Narodnyi komissariat vnutrennikh del* (People's Commissariat of Internal Affairs): Soviet secret police

obkom – *oblastnoi komitet* (oblast committee)
oblast – province
OGPU – *Ob"edinennoe gosudarstvennoe politicheskoe upravlenie* (All-Union State Political Administration): Soviet secret police
okrug – district, region

petliurovets – Petliurite: literally, a follower of Symon Petliura, president of the Directory of the Ukrainian People's Republic, 1918–20. Derogatory Soviet term for nationally conscious Ukrainians, as well as real or imagined anti-Soviet elements in Ukraine; *Petliurovshchina* – the Petliura movement

raion – county

RSFSR – Russian Soviet Federated Socialist Republic

Shumskyite – derogatory Soviet term for followers of Oleksander Shumsky, Ukrainian commissar of education (1924–27), accused by Stalin and Kaganovich of forcing cultural Ukrainization on the Russian proletariat

sovkhoz – *sovetskoe khoziaistvo* (state farm)

Sovnarkom – *Sovet narodnykh komissarov* (Council of People's Commissars)

stanitsa – Cossack town or settlement in the North Caucasus

SVU – *Spilka vyzvolennia Ukraïny* (Union for the Liberation of Ukraine)

Torgsin – *Torgovlia s inostrantsami* (All-Union Association for Trade with Foreigners)

TsK – *Tsentral'nyi komitet* (Central Committee)

UkrSSR – Ukrainian Soviet Socialist Republic

USSR – Union of Soviet Socialist Republics

VKP(B) – *Vsesoiuznaia Kommunisticheskaia partiia (bol'shevikov)* – All-Union Communist Party (Bolshevik)

ZAGS – *Otdely zapisei aktov grazhdanskogo sostoianiia* (Civil Registry Offices)

INTRODUCTION

Bohdan Klid and Alexander J. Motyl

The idea for this book came to both of us, separately, sometime during and after the seventy-fifth anniversary (2008) of the Holodomor—the murder by hunger of millions in the 1932–33 famine in Soviet Ukraine and the Kuban region of the North Caucasus, where Ukrainians formed a large percentage of the population.

Both of us were struck by the fact that, although the amount of material relating to the Holodomor was huge and steadily growing, there was no comprehensive sourcebook on the 1932–33 Ukrainian famine for English-language readers. As a result, finding basic information on the Holodomor and deepening one's understanding of this terrible tragedy required the kind of research that most nonspecialists have neither time nor energy to pursue.

The Holodomor Reader hopes to fill these gaps. Our goal was to compile a book of readings including a wide range of materials—survivor accounts, journalistic reports, scholarly studies, literary works, and documents—that would be of value both to students and scholars, who may not be familiar with the full extent of writings on the Holodomor and related events, and to nonspecialists, who need a thorough reference work on the Ukrainian genocide.

Our personal view of the Holodomor derives from the interpretation of genocide by Raphael Lemkin, who first coined the term. In his classic 1944 study, Lemkin wrote:

> Generally speaking, genocide does not necessarily mean the immediate destruction of a nation, except when accomplished by mass killings of all members of a nation. It is intended rather to signify a coordinated plan of different actions aiming at the destruction of essential foundations of the life of national groups, with the aim of annihilating the groups themselves. The objectives of such a plan would be disintegration of the political and social institutions, of culture, language, national feelings, religion, and the economic existence of national groups, and the destruction of the personal security, liberty, health, dignity, and even the lives of the individuals belonging to such groups. Genocide is directed against the national group as an entity, and the actions involved are directed against individuals, not in their individual capacity, but as members of the national group.[1]

In 1953, on the twentieth anniversary of the famine, Lemkin addressed the question of whether Soviet policies and actions in Ukraine constituted genocide:

> [P]erhaps the classic example of Soviet genocide, its longest and broadest experiment in Russification [is] the destruction of the Ukrainian nation....
>
> Ukraine is highly susceptible to racial murder by select parts and so the Communist tactics there have not followed the pattern taken by the German attacks against the Jews. The nation is too populous to be

1 Raphael Lemkin, *Axis Rule in Occupied Europe* (New York: Howard Fertig, 1973), p. 79. Reprint of 1944 edition.

> exterminated completely with any efficiency. However, its leadership, religious, intellectual, political, its select and determining parts, are quite small and therefore easily eliminated, and so it is upon these groups particularly that the full force of the Soviet axe has fallen, with its familiar tools of mass murder, deportation and forced labour, exile and starvation.[2]

Although Lemkin did not have access to the sources now available to scholars, his approach to the study and understanding of the Ukrainian famine was, in our view, sound. As he points out, the Ukrainian genocide encompassed the famine of 1932–33 as well as the destruction of Ukrainian intellectuals, writers, poets, musicians, and artists, the Ukrainian Autocephalous Orthodox Church, and the political elite. The genocide must therefore be viewed as the product of Joseph Stalin's revolution from above, in which Ukraine and Ukrainians were regarded as a fundamental obstacle to the realization of the communist leadership's ideological and state-building goals. Although the roots of the genocide reach into the failed national-liberation struggles of 1917–22, when Bolshevik forces, centered in Russia, crushed the Ukrainian drive for independence, Stalin's genocidal campaign began in 1929, reached its apogee in 1932–33, and ended sometime in the 1930s, perhaps as late as the Great Terror of 1937–38.

While there are scholars and policy makers who still dispute Lemkin's interpretation, it is our belief that expert opinion has begun decisively to shift—and will continue to shift—toward viewing the Holodomor as genocide. The opening of Soviet archives, the contributions of Ukrainian and Western scholars, the abandonment of formerly popular revisionist views of Stalin and Stalinism, and the unceasing efforts of Ukrainians in Ukraine and throughout the world have combined to produce that shift.

Consider where the famine was in the popular consciousness of the 1950s. The answer is: nowhere. Survivors, refugees, and émigrés wrote about it extensively, but primarily in Ukrainian, and their audience consisted largely of themselves. Although some Western journalists had written about the famine in the 1930s, their focus soon shifted to other stories, while Western scholars ignored the famine almost entirely. A Soviet history atlas compiled by the reputable historian Martin Gilbert in 1972, for instance, illustrates the "main area of the forced collectivization of over 5 million peasant holdings 1929–1938" and notes that "thousands of peasants were killed when they resisted (some by armed force)."[3]

Even in 1983, during the fiftieth anniversary of the famine, the regnant view of one of the great crimes of the twentieth century maintained that it was a minor tragedy at best and a consequence of agricultural policy gone awry at worst. It was not until 1986, with the publication of Robert Conquest's *Harvest of Sorrow*, that the Ukrainian famine first became more widely known to the scholarly community and the English-language reading public.

---

2 See "Soviet Genocide in Ukraine," pp. 79–81 in this volume.

3 Martin Gilbert, *Soviet History Atlas* (London and Henley: Routledge & Kegan Paul, 1979; first published in 1972 by Weidenfeld & Nicolson as part of the *Russian History Atlas*), p. 34.

The status of the famine as a nonevent or an émigré fantasy has thus changed by 180 degrees. No serious scholar or political figure now disputes that millions of Ukrainians starved to death in 1932–33. There is general agreement that the famine was avoidable and almost universal condemnation of it as a crime.

But will the view of the Holodomor as genocide gain the upper hand? We suspect that the answer is yes because expert opinion is formed on the basis of both evidence and the normative and political zeitgeist. As *The Holodomor Reader* demonstrates, the empirical evidence for regarding the Holodomor as genocide is overwhelming. If one is neutral, one is likely to be persuaded. If one is a diehard skeptic or has a political agenda, on the other hand, no amount of evidence will do the trick.

But to focus only on evidence is to misunderstand how academic expertise works in practice. Although scholars deny it, they are swayed as much, if not more, by real-world events as by dry evidence. No one today would deny the importance of women, even though the evidence—women—was always there. It took a women's movement to convince academics to see the obvious. By the same token, it was only after policy makers and business people began glorifying globalization some two decades ago that academics took notice.

In sum, experts, like all people, are swayed by life—by the zeitgeist. And the Holodomor-as-genocide thesis is just such an example of a zeitgeist-in-the-making. The currently undisputed status of the Holodomor as a mass killing will set the norm for future scholars without political agendas. As the diehards exit, their place will be taken by scholars who view the famine from the perspective of today's norm—and not yesterday's. As a growing number of experts come to regard the Holodomor as genocide, a tipping point will be reached, and scholars, like all rational beings, will accept the genocide interpretation simply because it is the zeitgeist and makes sense.

Naturally, to conclude that the Holodomor was genocide is not to diminish the suffering of other peoples who experienced genocide or to enhance the suffering of Ukrainians. It is only to call something by its right name and, as we suggest at the end of this introduction, to begin to think comparatively and practically about how such terrible events occurred and can be prevented from recurring.

Organization and Logic

Although some of the selections in this volume touch on the years before and after the Holodomor and on events not directly related to the famine itself, *The Holodomor Reader* focuses on the famine of 1932–33, both because the killings during this period reached into the millions—at the high point of the famine, some 25,000 Ukrainian peasants perished each day—and because the Holodomor is the central component of the genocide of Ukrainians. No less important, any book attempting to encompass the entirety of the genocide, along with its origins and consequences, would turn into a massive undertaking that would defeat the raison d'être of this volume: accessibility and comprehensiveness for specialists and nonspecialists.

The Holodomor Reader only tangentially addresses one of the central controversies among students of the Ukrainian famine—the number of victims.

Although readers interested in the demographic issues will find excellent guidance in the selections by Oleh Wolowyna and Jacques Vallin et al. included here, it was our conscious editorial decision not to delve into the question of numbers for two reasons. First, that question tends to be exceedingly technical and, as such, is better suited to a publication aimed at a narrow band of specialists, not a general readership. Second, we believe that the question of numbers—whether three million, six million, or more—is irrelevant to and a distraction from the far more important issues that the *Reader* addresses, namely, the existential reality of the Holodomor, the enormous suffering that its victims experienced, and the genocidal nature of Stalin's assault on Ukrainian peasants. There is, however, one point of contention that the *Reader* does resolve. As readers will note from the selections by Western journalists and others traveling to Ukraine in the 1930s, it was they who first suggested that the number of victims was six million or more, based on their conversations with Soviet officials.

Materials in the *Reader* have been organized into six sections: (1) Scholarship; (2) Legal Assessments, Findings, and Resolutions; (3) Eyewitness Accounts and Memoirs; (4) Survivor Testimonies, Memoirs, Diaries, and Letters; (5) Documents; and (6) Literature. A brief bibliographic note has been added as an aid to further reading and research. The texts for all six sections have been selected from a variety of published sources (one previously unpublished memoir and document also appear here). Many are easily available, many others are not, and some are known only to specialists. A large number of materials were translated into English expressly for the *Reader*. In most instances only excerpts have been provided. We have kept footnotes to a minimum in this introductory essay and have removed footnotes from the excerpts of scholarly writings in order to save space. Those interested in further study of these writings can consult the original works.

We chose materials for all six sections with three key aims in mind.

The first was to offer a broad picture of the Holodomor by presenting a large number and variety of sources and writings on the famine. These include scholarly literature and interpretations; Soviet Communist Party, government, and secret-police documents; diplomatic reports by representatives of four European countries; writings by outside observers and eyewitnesses to the famine, mainly journalists; accounts by famine survivors, such as testimonies, memoirs, diaries, and letters; appeals by contemporaries, such as Ukrainians living outside the USSR; legal assessments; and recent declarations, findings, or conclusions reached by governments and international bodies. The section on literature contains a variety of excerpts—most never before translated into English—from novels, stories, plays, and poems dealing with the Holodomor. Many of the writings are based on the personal experiences of the authors. Some of the works focus on the famine's most harrowing features, such as cannibalism; others dwell on mundane aspects—such as the difficulty of finding, cooking, and digesting food—that only accentuate the horror of the Holodomor. All the writings convey masterfully the pervasive sense of doom that became an everyday component of the Ukrainian peasantry's existence and nonexistence.

The second aim was to introduce readers to the context and consequences of the famine and to illustrate the many different ways in which it was perceived and treated by the international community, as well as by Ukrainian communities outside Soviet Ukraine. Although the 1932–33 famine was a catastrophic event of immense proportions and a historical event of international significance, it received surprisingly little attention in the world's leading newspapers. On the one hand, the Communist Party-controlled press in the Soviet Union suppressed news of the famine, while the Soviet authorities denied that it had taken place. This policy of denial continued until the late 1980s. To make the denial effective, the Soviet authorities banned foreign journalists from traveling to Ukraine and the North Caucasus in early 1933.

Although relatively few reporters witnessed what was taking place, some journalists, such as Malcolm Muggeridge and Gareth Jones, visited Ukraine illegally at the height of the famine and published reports about it. Some Western journalists, such as the *New York Times* correspondent Walter Duranty, reported on the famine in ways that belittled its scope and significance, thereby reinforcing the Soviet policy of silence and denial. Part of the reason for such biased reporting was the ubiquity of pro-Soviet sentiments among liberal and left-leaning Western intellectuals and journalists in the 1930s. While some left-wing journalists, such as Louis Fischer, continued to sympathize with the Soviet regime even after the famine, others, such as Harry Lang, published honest, unvarnished accounts of what they had witnessed.[4]

Other international factors worked against the famine's receiving the international attention it deserved. Official British, Italian, German, and Polish documents in this collection show that, although diplomats were fully aware of the famine and reported on it in detail, governments chose to remain silent. The Holodomor took place during the depths of the Great Depression and in a period of profound political crisis in Europe, which saw the rise of fascism and the coming to power of Adolf Hitler in Germany in early 1933. European governments, led by France, which supported the post-World War I Versailles settlement, were alarmed at Hitler's assumption of power and considered the Soviet Union a potential ally against a revanchist Germany. Moreover, shortly after coming to power, the Nazi government began enacting anti-Jewish measures, which drew the attention of the world's newspapers and shocked Europeans. At the same time, Western corporations were eager to sell machine tools to the Soviet Union, which was paying for them, in part, with grain exports at depressed prices. In late 1933 the United States government recognized the Soviet Union, and in 1934 the USSR was admitted to the League of Nations.

Our third aim was to highlight the national characteristics and consequences of the famine and its relation to nationalism and the nationality question in the Soviet Union. Those scholars who oppose the genocide interpretation generally argue that the victims of the famine were mostly peasants who died because of the social class to which they belonged, which bore no relation to their nationality, and that the famine was a pan-Soviet phenomenon. Even if it was particularly intense in Ukraine, Ukrainian peasants were not its only victims. Finally, they argue that Stalin and the Soviet leadership did not intend to destroy a nation or an ethnic group: in their view, the famine was largely the result or byproduct of mismanagement,

---

4 See excerpts from the writings of Louis Fischer and Harry Lang on pp. 117–35, 141-42 of this volume.

as well as of the chaos and brutality accompanying collectivization. In all these interpretations, the national—the specifically Ukrainian—dimension is incidental. We concur with Lemkin and many other scholars that the Ukrainian dimension was central to the Ukrainian famine.

As the United Nations Genocide Convention insists that genocide must entail the intent to destroy, at least in part, a national or ethnic group, a "national" interpretation of the Holodomor entails a demonstration that the famine affected Ukraine precisely because it was Ukrainian and that the decisions taken by the Soviet leadership with regard to Ukraine and Ukrainians before, during, and after the famine were based on that understanding. Since the main responsibility for the famine and the attacks on Ukraine's elites and cultural figures rests with Stalin, his pronouncements and actions are central to a genocide interpretation. As we argue below, Stalin's decision to embark on the intentional mass killing of Ukrainians was rooted, on the one hand, in his attempts to respond to and control critical events and achieve immediate or short-term goals and, on the other, in his understanding of communist doctrine, the nationality question, and the relation of class to nationality. By examining some of his pronouncements on these questions, we can observe how his thinking informed his decisions to attack Ukraine's political and cultural elites and intensify the famine in Ukraine and the Kuban.

Collectivization and Famine in the USSR and Ukraine

The years of the Great Depression and political instability in Europe coincided with the period in which Stalin consolidated his personal rule and turned the Soviet Union into a highly centralized totalitarian state. By 1929, at the onset of the Depression, he had succeeded in sidelining his main political rivals and secured his position as undisputed leader of the Communist Party. His position, though secure, was not yet unassailable.

Nineteen twenty-nine was also the second year of the first Five-Year Plan, during which rapid industrialization and forced collectivization of agriculture took place, radically changing the existing social and economic order of the Soviet Union. The creation of collective farms was especially problematic in Ukraine and in regions such as the Kuban in southern Russia, where individual farming practices were well entrenched and most peasants were independent subsistence or small-scale farmers. In the Kuban and some areas of Ukraine, such individualism was reinforced by memories of Cossack self-rule, the national-liberation movement and armed struggles, and general resistance to Bolshevik rule in the years 1917–21.

Collectivization was accompanied by a so-called dekulakization campaign (the expropriation and exile or imprisonment of supposedly rich peasants, called kulaks, but also of those who resisted collectivization) and grain-procurement campaigns (forced deliveries or requisitions of predetermined grain quotas to the state at low, fixed prices). The dekulakization operations and the fear of being labeled kulaks, coupled with the grain-procurement campaigns, which saddled individual farmers with ruinous quotas, were means of intimidating and coercing peasants to join collectives. The Soviet authorities often used coercion, violence, and deportations to intimidate and punish farmers who resisted joining the collective farms or failed to fulfill grain-procurement quotas.

Despite the risks, many Ukrainian peasants were reluctant to join the collective farms. Those who did so were in effect consenting to the expropriation of most of their private property in exchange for integration into a nascent system of state-run agriculture. Most peasants who joined collective farms thus became highly dependent and impoverished farmhands, a condition to which they sometimes referred as a second serfdom. Unsurprisingly, many peasants resisted, especially in Ukraine and the Kuban.

Their resistance was both passive and active, resulting at times in violent acts against state officials. In turn, it was not uncommon for the Soviet authorities to respond to mass protests with brute force. The result was not unexpected. The forced collectivization of agriculture and the accompanying grain-procurement and dekulakization campaigns, the arbitrary and heavy-handed actions of state authorities against the peasantry, and peasant resistance led to great waste and chaos in the countryside, which was disastrous for agriculture.

The Bolshevik leadership touted collectivization—an ideological goal integral to the building of socialism—as part of its countrywide campaign of economic modernization. But collectivization also served the more practical purpose of creating state-controlled enterprises that allowed the collective-farm leadership and other administrative/police bodies in the countryside to supervise and manage the peasantry. Collective farms were naturally considered more reliable than individual farms in meeting grain-procurement targets. Grain collected during the procurement campaigns was meant to help finance rapid industrialization through sales abroad and to provide cheap food for the swelling cities.

But the grain levies amounted to an extremely heavy burden on the Ukrainian farmers, as the republic was assigned exceedingly high—and effectively unrealistic—targets to meet. While the quota was fulfilled in 1930 owing to a bumper crop, unfavorable climatic conditions and the chaos and waste inherent in the collectivization drive resulted in a much lower harvest in 1931. Ukraine was thus unable to meet its target, but Soviet officials continued their grain-procurement campaigns. By December 1931 there was famine, and in the first half of 1932 deaths from starvation were observed in many parts of Ukraine.

This catastrophic situation caused alarm among Ukraine's officials, especially at the lower levels of the Party and government. In June 1932 two of Ukraine's leading communists and high-ranking government officials, Vlas Chubar and Hryhorii Petrovsky, wrote letters to Viacheslav Molotov, the head of the Soviet government, and Stalin, the head of the Communist Party, requesting relief and the reduction of grain-procurement targets for that year.[5]

Instead of taking measures to correct or reverse policies that had brought on the disaster and to avert an even greater catastrophe, Stalin reacted with scorn and anger to the Ukrainian leadership's plea for help. In a letter of 15 June to his lieutenant Lazar Kaganovich, Stalin insisted on maintaining the procurement targets, writing that "Ukraine has been given more than enough."[6] Moreover, he blamed the unfolding crisis on Ukrainian officials.

---

5 See excerpts from their letters on pp. 230–31 of this volume.

6 See excerpts from this letter on p. 232 of this volume.

In a letter of 11 August 1932 to Kaganovich (see excerpts in this volume on pp. 239–40), Stalin expressed concern over the opposition to grain-procurement targets in the Ukrainian Party and the overall reliability of Ukraine's Communist Party and leadership, noting the strength of nationalism in the country. Nationalists were referred to as Petliurites (followers of Symon Petliura, a political and military leader of the period of Ukrainian independence). Showing that he was following events in Ukraine closely, Stalin expressed fears that "[a]s soon as the situation gets worse," oppositional elements would coalesce, and Ukraine might be lost. Here, Stalin implicitly recognized the possibility of Ukraine's secession. Stalin also made known his intention to replace some of Ukraine's top leaders.

This letter was written four days after the promulgation of the so-called Five Ears of Corn Law, which declared all collective-farm property equivalent to state property and introduced draconian sentences, even death, for stealing state property. This meant that starving peasants now faced potential execution for taking grain to feed themselves and their families (see excerpts from the edict on p. 239 of this volume). While the 1932 grain levy for Ukraine was eventually lowered three times, the revisions were symbolic, as they did nothing to reduce the highly unrealistic quota to a level that would prevent mass starvation from breaking out in late 1932. Not only was the ruinous levy maintained, but in the second half of 1932 Stalin and the Soviet leadership took additional steps to coerce Ukrainian peasants into parting with their remaining grain. These included blockading entire villages and banning trade. Stalin also directed his wrath against those lower-ranking government and Party officials who tried to aid the starving peasantry. Many local officials and collective-farm administrators in Ukraine were removed from their posts; some were arrested and summarily executed.

In addition to applying pressure on Ukraine's lowest Party and administrative cadres, Stalin began replacing some of the country's mid- and upper-level leaders in September 1932. Earlier, in the first part of July, he had sent his lieutenants Molotov and Kaganovich to a plenum of the Communist Party of Ukraine called to discuss the agricultural crisis in order to pressure Party leaders to confirm the 1932 grain quota for Ukraine. In October 1932 he dispatched his two enforcers again—this time to Ukraine and the Kuban, heading special teams—to oversee and direct Communist Party and government officials during the grain-procurement campaigns.[7] Their primary task was to squeeze as much grain as possible from the malnourished, exhausted, and starving peasantry. To assist in the drive, thousands of communist cadres from Ukraine and Russia were mobilized to find grain that the peasants had stored in order to survive the winter and spring. Procurement teams often took all foodstuffs, not only grain, from peasant homes.

While famine also broke out in other parts of the Soviet Union in 1932–33, it was, unsurprisingly, especially intense in Ukraine and the Kuban. The large spike in Ukrainian deaths in late 1932 and the first half of 1933 was a consequence of the deliberate decisions and actions of Stalin and his close lieutenants Molotov and Kaganovich—decisions that pertained exclusively to Ukraine and the Kuban or were prompted in whole or in part as a response to developments there. Two of

---

7 Pavel Postyshev, who would soon be appointed Stalin's personal representative in Ukraine, headed a special team sent to the lower Volga region of Russia in December 1932.

these were particularly important: first, the resolution of 14 December 1932,[8] which revised and rolled back measures promoting the use of the Ukrainian language in Ukraine and the Kuban and criticized officials for improperly implementing cultural Ukrainization and facilitating nationalism, and, second, the order of 22 January 1933[9] that prevented peasants from leaving Ukraine and the Kuban for other areas of the Soviet Union to seek food. The resolution adopted by the Politburo of the AUCP(B) on 1 January 1933, threatening Ukraine's peasants with draconian punishments for "misappropriating and concealing grain," is also significant.[10]

By early 1933, at the height of the famine, the repressive machinery of the Soviet state had turned against Ukraine's Communist Party officials, who were accused of nationalism. On 24 January 1933 Stalin appointed his trusted lieutenant Pavel Postyshev as the Ukrainian Party's second secretary, a post that effectively allowed him to act as Stalin's plenipotentiary in Ukraine. Prior to Postyshev's appointment, Stalin had replaced Ukraine's secret-police chief with a more trustworthy and ruthless figure, Vsevolod Balytsky, who had held that position earlier. Postyshev immediately spearheaded a reign of terror against Ukraine's cultural and educational personnel and other communists. Mykola Khvyliovy, a leading communist writer, and Ukraine's most prominent old Bolshevik and champion of Ukrainization, Mykola Skrypnyk, committed suicide in protest in May and July 1933, respectively.

The intensification of the famine in Ukraine and the Kuban thus took place against the background of and in conjunction with the complete rollback of Ukrainization in the Kuban, the beginning of its revision and curtailment in Ukraine, and the start of a campaign of concerted attacks on Ukraine's autonomous-minded communist political and cultural elites. The result was their partial destruction and the loss of any meaningful cultural and political autonomy that Ukraine and its Communist Party still enjoyed. In the Kuban, residents of several Cossack towns (stanitsas) regarded as particularly incorrigible were deported north, and the entire region was subject to de-Ukrainization and Russification.

Stalin's Views on the Nationality Question

The period encompassing the attacks on Ukraine's elites and the famine coincided with Stalin's shift toward a more centralist and Russocentric state, which was accompanied by the promotion of Russian nationalism, messianism, and xenophobia. That shift was rooted in his long-standing views on the nationality question.

Stalin was the Bolshevik Party's acknowledged authority on the subject. In his early years as a revolutionary Marxist, Stalin, who was a Georgian, had witnessed the strength of nationalist sentiment among his compatriots, including Georgian Marxists, and was well aware of the potential implications of national feeling among the non-Russian peoples. He wrote theoretical works on the nationality question as it related to Russia dating back to prerevolutionary years and was responsible for nationality affairs in the first Soviet government.

---

8 See excerpts from this resolution on pp. 245–47 of this volume.

9 See excerpts from this order on p. 254 of this volume.

10 See excerpts from this resolution on p. 251 of this volume.

Given this orientation and responsibility, Stalin was well aware of developments in Ukraine during the revolutionary period and civil war of 1917–20, including the country's struggle for independence under the Central Rada and successive governments. Stalin participated in major decisions concerning Ukraine and wrote articles justifying Bolshevik policy toward it, including intervention by Bolshevik forces, and denounced the Central Rada.[11] To him, the peasantry and the independence movement were the main obstacles to the establishment of Bolshevik rule in Ukraine. Stalin was also fully cognizant that the Bolsheviks had a more solid base of support in Russia than in the non-Russian periphery of the former Russian Empire, including Ukraine.

Writing in October 1919, Stalin made the following observation on the geographic and economic bases of support for and opposition to the Bolsheviks, as well as their relation to nationality:

> As the civil war developed, the areas of revolution and counter-revolution became sharply defined. Inner Russia, with its industrial and cultural and political centres, Moscow and Petrograd, and with its nationally homogeneous population, principally Russian, became the base of the revolution. The border regions of Russia, however, chiefly the southern and eastern border regions, which have no major industrial or cultural and political centres, and whose inhabitants are nationally heterogeneous to a high degree—consisting, on the one hand, of privileged Cossack colonizers, and, on the other, of subject Tatars, Bashkirs and Kirghiz (in the east) and Ukrainians, Chechens, Ingush and other, Moslem, peoples—became the base of counter-revolution.[12]

At the Twelfth Congress of the Russian Communist Party (Bolshevik), held in April 1923, Stalin argued that questions of nationality and class were closely intertwined in the Bolshevik-ruled territories. "The class essence of the nationality question," he concluded, "consists in determining the interrelationship…between the proletariat of the former state nation and the peasantry of the formerly oppressed nationalities."[13] In 1925, in a polemic with a Yugoslav communist, Stalin again drew attention to the close interrelation between social status and the nationality question. Here he declared that "the peasant question is the basis, the quintessence, of the national question.… [T]here is no powerful national movement without the peasant army, nor can there be."[14]

In these three comments Stalin recognized that the class base of support for Bolshevik rule was in large part ethnically Russian and consisted primarily of the proletariat based in central or "Inner Russia," as he described it. Stalin also understood that largely peasant-based nations, such as Ukraine, could come into conflict with nations, such as Russia, where the Bolshevik regime's base of support lay with the

11 Several such articles appear in J. V. Stalin, *Works*, vol. 4 (Moscow: Foreign Languages Publishing House, 1953).

12 Stalin, "The Military Situation in the South," in *Works*, 4: 297–98.

13 See *Dvenadtsatyi s"ezd RKP(b) 17–25 aprelia 1923 goda. Stenograficheskii otchet* (Moscow: Izdatel'stvo politicheskoi literatury, 1968), p. 481.

14 Stalin, "Concerning the National Question in Yugoslavia. Speech delivered in the Yugoslav Commission of the E.C.C.I., March 30, 1925," in *Works*, vol. 7 (1954), pp. 71–72.

Russian proletariat. Moreover, Stalin recognized that an oppressed peasantry could be mobilized to form the central component of the armed forces of a national-liberation movement.[15]

The 1923 Congress of the Russian Communist Party, which discussed the nationality question at length, adopted the policy known as indigenization (*korenizatsiia*), intended as a means of building support for Soviet rule—fragile at the time—and as a concession to and regulator of the national aspirations and cultural needs of the non-Russians. In Ukraine, *korenizatsiia* resulted in linguistic Ukrainization and affirmative action in state hiring policies and recruitment to the Communist Party. Ukrainization was also seen as a means of attaining foreign-policy goals by showcasing cultural development in Soviet Ukraine to Ukrainians living under Polish rule, who suffered cultural and other forms of discrimination, with the aim of creating pro-Soviet sentiment among them. Earlier, in 1921, in an attempt to reconcile the peasantry to Soviet rule, the Communist Party had adopted the New Economic Policy, which allowed for private farming and the disposition of surplus grain on the market after farmers paid a tax in kind to the state. These economic and cultural/linguistic concessions reconciled most Ukrainians to Soviet rule.

Limited autonomy in cultural affairs and state support for the Ukrainian language and cultural development led, however, to a national self-assertiveness that alarmed Stalin. In 1926, in an important intervention that demonstrated his close attention to the implementation and consequences of nationality policy in Ukraine, Stalin chastised Oleksandr Shumsky, a communist leader who was then Ukraine's minister of education, and Mykola Khvyliovy, a prominent communist writer. In his reprimand, contained in a letter to Kaganovich (then Ukraine's first Party secretary) and other Ukrainian communist leaders, Stalin criticized Shumsky for seeking to Ukrainize the Russian proletariat in Ukraine by force and expressed concern that Ukrainization could "assume the character of a struggle to alienate Ukrainian culture and public life from general Soviet culture and public life, the character of a struggle against 'Moscow' in general, against the Russians in general, against Russian culture and its highest achievement—Leninism." This, Stalin claimed, was "becoming an increasingly real danger in Ukraine," even among some Ukrainian communists. Stalin next turned his invective against Khvyliovy: "At a time when the proletarians of Western Europe and their Communist Parties are in sympathy with 'Moscow,' this citadel of the international revolutionary movement and of Leninism, at a time when the proletarians of Western Europe look with admiration at the flag that flies over Moscow, the Ukrainian communist Khvyliovy has nothing better to say in favour of 'Moscow' than to call on the Ukrainian leaders to get away from 'Moscow' 'as fast as possible.'"[16]

The above passages demonstrate that Stalin was concerned not only with expressions of cultural autonomy by Ukraine's communist writers, such as Khvyliovy, and with some of Ukraine's political leaders, who were dissatisfied with the slow pace of de-Russifying Ukraine's cities. His comments reveal concern over the unity of the Soviet Union and indicate his support for Russian cultural supremacy as well

15 See the excerpt from an article by Andrea Graziosi (pp. 19–26 of this volume), who links the peasant and national questions.

16 See Stalin, "To Comrade Kaganovich and the Other Members of the Political Bureau of the Central Committee, Ukrainian C.P.(B.)," in *Works*, vol. 8 (1954), pp. 160–61.

as, implicitly, for Russian primacy in and leadership of the international communist movement. Stalin's criticisms represent an early manifestation of a fusion of Marxism and Russian nationalism, which becomes more evident in his pronouncements beginning in 1930. Stalin's intervention also presaged the possibility of his taking more decisive measures against Ukraine's political leadership and cultural figures, which actually began in 1929.

That year the Soviet authorities arrested scores of Ukrainian noncommunist intellectuals, some of whom were associated with Ukraine's independence-era governments, cultural workers, and members of the Ukrainian Autocephalous Orthodox Church, who were accused of belonging to a fictitious underground organization called the Union for the Liberation of Ukraine (Spilka vyzvolennia Ukraïny, SVU). They were indicted in the SVU show trial of 1930—the preparations for which Stalin followed, even providing a directive—and sentenced to imprisonment.[17]

In June 1930, in the wake of the trial, Stalin expressed his concern over the national assertiveness of non-Russians in a report to the Sixteenth Communist Party Congress. There he described "local nationalism" (the national assertiveness or nationalism of the non-Russians) as an attempt "to isolate and segregate oneself within the shell of one's own nation.... The danger of this deviation is that it cultivates bourgeois nationalism, weakens the unity of the working people of the different nations of the U.S.S.R. and plays into the hands of the interventionists.... The Party's task is to wage a determined struggle against this deviation...."[18]

Although Stalin continued to pay lip service to the notion that Russian chauvinism remained the greatest danger within the Party, his flagging of the danger of local nationalism proved ominous. These passages repeated themes contained in his criticisms of Shumsky and Khvyliovy, while the call for the Party to launch a "determined struggle" against "local nationalism" signaled that active measures against Ukrainian and other non-Russian nationalism would continue. In 1931 additional repressive measures were implemented against Ukrainian intellectuals. This time the arrested individuals were accused of belonging to the fictitious Ukrainian National Center, which allegedly maintained ties abroad (in the province of Galicia, then under Polish rule) with the Ukrainian Military Organization.

Stalin also began expressing Russian nationalist views more explicitly. In a letter of December 1930 to the writer Demian Bedny, he criticized the latter for expressing anti-Russian views and characterized Russia as the center of the world revolutionary movement. "In all countries," Stalin wrote, "the revolutionary workers unanimously applaud the Soviet working class, and first and foremost the *Russian* working class, the vanguard of the Soviet workers, as their recognized leader...." The leadership of workers' movements abroad, Stalin claimed, was "eagerly studying the highly instructive history of Russia's working class, its past and the past of Russia.... All this fills (cannot but fill!) the hearts of the Russian workers with a feeling of revolutionary

---

17 See Stalin's telegram to the Ukrainian Politburo in Terry Martin, *The Affirmative Action Empire: Nations and Nationalism in the Soviet Union, 1923–1939* (Ithaca and London: Cornell University Press, 2001), p. 253.

18 See his "Political Report of the Central Committee to the Sixteenth Congress of the C.P.S.U. (B.)," in *Works*, vol. 12 (1955), pp. 382–83.

national pride that can move mountains and perform miracles."[19]

Nationalist sentiments are also evident in Stalin's address of February 1931 to the First All-Union Conference of Managers of Socialist Industry. Elaborating on whether the tempo of accelerated industrialization should be moderated, Stalin argued that slowing the pace "would mean falling behind. And those who fall behind get beaten.... No, we refuse to be beaten! One feature of the history of old Russia was the continual beatings she suffered because of her backwardness...." Stalin further emphasized the achievement of statehood and its maintenance: "In the past we had no fatherland, nor could we have had one. But now that we have overthrown capitalism and power is in our hands, in the hands of the people, we have a fatherland, and we will uphold its independence. Do you want our socialist fatherland to be beaten and to lose its independence?"[20]

Stalin continued his praise of Russians, emphasizing the theme of Russia as a leading nation, in a speech given at a reception on 2 May 1933, following May Day celebrations. In his address Stalin characterized Russians as "the fundamental world nationality" that "first raised the Soviet flag against the entire world. The Russian nation is the most talented nation in the world."[21]

While Stalin was promoting Russian nationalism, the Communist Party of Ukraine declared at its November 1933 plenum that in Ukraine local nationalism constituted a greater danger than Russian chauvinism. This decision reversed the long-standing official line adopted by the Russian Communist Party at its 1923 congress, where Russian chauvinism, not local nationalism, was declared to be the greater danger in the realm of nationality relations. The 1933 plenum resolution made reference to the 14 December 1932 resolution of the Politburo of the All-Union Communist Party (Bolshevik) and the 24 January 1933 Politburo decision to replace members of Ukraine's top leadership.[22] Stalin himself declared Ukrainian nationalism the chief danger in Ukraine in his report of January 1934 to the Seventeenth Party Congress and stressed that under current circumstances it posed a danger to the Soviet state.[23] The shift in rhetoric obviously justified the assaults that had already taken place against so-called Ukrainian nationalists, now including Ukrainian communists, and presaged further repressions, which Stalin now implicitly linked to the defense and preservation of the Soviet state. The 1932–33 Ukrainian and Kuban famine raged, then, at the same time that Stalin was turning to Russian nationalism and conducting a campaign, begun in 1929, against Ukrainian nationalism.

Stalin's pronouncements in the 1930s effectively expanded the rhetorical boundaries of what was politically acceptable and correct. He could do so not only

---

19 Stalin, "To Comrade Demyan Bedny. (Excerpts from a Letter)," in *Works*, vol. 13 (1955), pp. 25–26.

20 "The Tasks of Business Executives. Speech Delivered at the First All-Union Conference of Leading Personnel of Socialist Industry, February 4, 1931," ibid., pp. 40–41.

21 V. A. Nevezhin, comp., *Zastol'nye rechi Stalina. Dokumenty i materialy* (Moscow and St. Petersburg: AIRO-XX, 2003), p. 44.

22 See the excerpt from "The Results and Immediate Tasks of the National Policy in the Ukraine. Resolution Adopted by the Joint Plenum of the Central Committee and Central Control Commission of the Communist Party of Ukraine on the Report of Comrade S. V. Kosior (November 22, 1933)" in this volume, pp. 264–65.

23 See Stalin's "Report to the Seventeenth Party Congress on the Work of the Central Committee of the C.P.S.U.(B.), January 26, 1934," in *Works*, vol. 13 (1954), p. 369.

because his firm grip on power allowed for some leeway but also because Russian nationalism already existed within the Communist Party and throughout much of Russian society. Russians could also feel a sense of pride in the achievements of industrialization during the first Five-Year Plan, which Stalin and the Soviet leadership accentuated. While consolidating personal power, building an industrial powerhouse, and collectivizing agriculture, Stalin was, according to his vision, also building socialism in one country. The Soviet socialist state he was building continued to retain the form of a federal, socialist state, but in content it was becoming increasingly centralized and Russian.

The Case for Genocide

The agricultural crisis in the Soviet Union came to a head by mid-1932. Up to this point, as noted by Andrea Graziosi (see p. 21 in this volume), the Ukrainian and Kuban famines can be regarded as part of a pan-Soviet famine caused largely by the general chaos associated with the collectivization drive, excessive grain-procurement quotas, and other accompanying measures. The result in Ukraine and the Kuban was a disastrous grain crop in 1932, which forecast the return of famine in the second half of 1932. It is at this point that the case for the specificity of the famines in Ukraine and the Kuban becomes obvious and the case for genocide becomes persuasive.

According to Graziosi:

> In those places where the "peasant question" was complicated—that is, strengthened and thus made more dangerous by the national one (let us remember that Stalin explicitly linked the two questions in his writings on nationalism, and that the Soviet leadership had seen this hypothesis confirmed by the Ukrainian countryside's great social and national revolts of 1919, repeated, albeit on a lesser scale, in early 1930)—the resort to hunger was more ruthless and the lesson much harsher....
>
> Famine thus took on forms and dimensions much bigger than it would have if nature had followed its course. It was less intense, in terms of both drought and the area it affected, than the 1921–22 famine (the 1932 crop, though quite low, was still higher than the 1945 crop, when there were no comparable mass hunger-related deaths), yet it caused three to four times as many victims—essentially because of political decisions that aimed at saving the regime from the crisis to which its very policies had led and at assuring the victory of the "great offensive" launched four years previously.
>
> The awareness that in Ukraine and Kuban the peasant question also was a national question determined the need to deal with and "solve" these questions together. In order to make sure that such a "solution" was there to stay, it was complemented by the decision to get rid of the national elites and their policies, which were suspected, as we know, of abetting peasants....
>
> These measures were accompanied, and followed, by a wave of anti-Ukrainian terror, which already presented some of the traits that were later to characterize the 1937–38 "mass operations." Thus ended

> the national-communist experiment born of the civil war, with the suicide in 1933 of important leaders such as Mykola Skrypnyk and writers such as Mykola Khvyliovy as well as the repression of thousands of its cadres.[24]

The crux of the matter is that the policies of Stalin and the Soviet leadership in the second half of 1932 and early 1933 knowingly deepened the famine. Stalin's view, as we have seen, was that questions of nationality and class could coincide, merge, or fuse, and that national and social groups could be virtually identical. Stalin's statements also demonstrate his awareness that the decisions he took in 1932 and in the first part of 1933 would intensify the famine in Ukraine and the Kuban, crush Ukrainian peasants and elites, and thereby help him attain a variety of important political and social goals.

As a potent center of resistance to Stalin's plans, Ukraine had to be crushed. Stalin destroyed, and clearly intended to destroy, a significant portion of Ukraine's most active cultural and political elite—especially the supporters of Ukraine's political and cultural rights—and terrorized the rest into conformity and passivity. Concurrently, he brought Ukrainization policies under central government control, thereby preparing the ground for their reversal in Ukraine and complete cancellation in the Kuban, which thereafter lost most traces of its Ukrainian roots. Throughout the 1930s, increasing state promotion of Russian language and culture was coupled with policies that served to reduce Ukrainian language and culture to second-rate or provincial status. In Stalin's view, the policies he was adopting facilitated and accelerated the consolidation of the Soviet state and society, whose dominant culture was to be Russian. The long-term goal was the total integration of the Kuban as a Russian territory and the eventual Russification of the Ukrainian people in order to deprive them of the potential to establish a state of their own with a full-fledged culture.

Stalin was also fully aware that resistance to collectivization and grain procurement policies was especially strong in Ukraine and the Kuban. The famine thus served as punishment of a recalcitrant, individualistic peasantry that resisted Stalin's collectivist vision of agriculture. By intensifying the famine, Stalin weakened the peasantry as a potentially disruptive social force. His Marxist suspicion of the peasantry as a class permeated with petty-bourgeois values was reinforced by the belief that Ukrainian peasants in particular could be disloyal to the Soviet state because of their resistance to Soviet forces in 1917–20, when they frequently gave strong support to Ukrainian nationalist leaders and opposed the imposition of Bolshevik rule. The Kuban Cossacks also strongly resisted Bolshevik rule and had shown support for the Ukrainian national cause.

Acts of resistance to Soviet rule continued throughout the 1920s and resumed with the onset of forced collectivization, dekulakization, and grain procurement in 1930. Particularly alarming to Stalin and the Soviet leadership was the potential of mass social discontent in the early 1930s to merge with or turn into a national-liberation movement at a time when the Soviet state was experiencing vast hardships and was not yet fully consolidated. Because the peasant nation

24 See pp. 23–24 of this volume.

resisted, while its intellectuals and political leaders abetted national deviations that provided a theoretical justification for Ukrainian autonomy, Ukraine took on particular importance in the plans of Stalin and the Soviet leadership. In addition, the Ukrainian elites, who could have risen to the defense of the Ukrainian peasantry, had to be silenced or cowed into submission. The agricultural crisis gave Stalin the opportunity to subdue the Ukrainian peasantry and consolidate his control over the autonomist wing and other unreliable elements in the Communist Party of Ukraine. The result was genocide—the intentional destruction of significant parts of the Ukrainian peasantry and the political, cultural, and religious elites—not because they were peasants and elites but because they were distinctly Ukrainian peasants and Ukrainian elites who resisted Stalin or stood in his way.

As Nicolas Werth argues:

> Up until the summer of 1932, the Ukrainian famine, already rearing its head, resembled the other famines that had started earlier elsewhere. However, from this point forward, the nature of the Ukrainian famine changed, with Stalin deciding to use hunger as a weapon, to aggravate the famine that was just beginning. Choosing to instrumentalize the famine, Stalin intentionally amplified it in order to punish the Ukrainian peasants who rejected the "new serfdom" and to break "Ukrainian nationalism," which he saw as a threat to his goal of constructing a centralized and dictatorial Soviet state. And while hunger hit the peasants harder than any other group, resulting in the death of millions in atrocious conditions, another form of repression, of a police nature, struck others in Ukraine at the same moment—the political and intellectual elites, from village teachers to national leaders, via the intelligentsia. Tens of thousands of Ukrainians were arrested and punished with camp sentences. In December 1932, two secret Politburo decrees put an end in Ukraine, and *only in Ukraine*, to the "indigenization" policy applied to Party cadres since 1923 in all of the federal republics: "Ukrainian nationalism" was firmly condemned....
>
> This specifically anti-Ukrainian assault makes it possible to define the totality of intentional political actions taken from late summer 1932 by the Stalinist regime against the Ukrainian peasantry as genocide. With hunger as its deadly arm, the regime sought to punish and terrorize the peasants, resulting in fatalities exceeding four million people in Ukraine and the northern Caucasus. That being said, the *Holodomor* was very different from the Holocaust. It did not seek to exterminate the Ukrainian nation in its entirety, and it did not involve the direct murder of its victims. The *Holodomor* was conceived and fashioned on the basis of political reasoning and not of ethnic or racial ideology. However, by the sheer number of its victims, the *Holodomor,* seen again in its historical context, is the only European event of the 20th century that can be compared to the two other genocides, the Armenian and the Holocaust.[25]

---

25 See pp. 49–50 in this volume.

Conclusion and Acknowledgments

Although the Holodomor occurred some eighty years ago, its consequences for Ukraine and Ukrainians are still very much in evidence. Kuban Ukrainians have ceased to exist as a separate national entity within Russia. Ukrainians in Ukraine, meanwhile, suffered devastating population losses (compounded by the brutal Nazi occupation of Ukraine during World War II) that affected later birth and mortality rates, economic development, and political culture. In particular, Ukrainians not only experienced a genocidal trauma, but in the decades that followed they were compelled to pretend that it had never happened—a form of denial that distorted the national mentality and produced or reinforced a variety of post-genocidal syndromes ranging from historical amnesia to substance dependence to broken families to dysfunctional gender relations. Although Ukraine today is an independent country, the long-term viability of the Ukrainian language and culture in Ukraine, and possibly of Ukraine's sovereignty itself, is still open to question—owing in no small measure to the terrible consequences of the Holodomor and the concurrent destruction of Ukrainian elites. No book can reverse history, but we trust and hope that *The Holodomor Reader* will promote understanding of the famine-genocide and, perhaps, help ameliorate some of its terrible consequences.

We also hope that *The Holodomor Reader* will spur specialists and nonspecialists to examine the Holodomor comparatively in relation to other genocides and other famines. We trust and hope that students of the Holodomor will increasingly investigate its origins, development, and consequences in comparison with other genocides, such as those that befell Jews, Armenians, Cambodians, Rwandans, Sudanese, and others. Comparative studies are always better served by a larger number of cases, and inclusion of the Holodomor can only enhance scholarly investigation of the dynamics of genocides. We also trust and hope that a greater understanding of the Ukrainian genocide will improve the effectiveness of measures taken against regimes that deliberately employ famine to destroy populations and bend them to their will. If we understand how and why genocides occur, we will be in a better position to prevent their recurrence.

A volume such as this can be produced only with the assistance of many people. In particular, we wish to thank Jars Balan, Laada Bilaniuk, Hennadii Boriak, Marco Carynnyk, Iryna Fedoriw, Roma Franko, Andrea Graziosi, Liudmyla Hrynevych, Vladyslav Hrynevych, Halyna Klid, Lubomyr Luciuk, Cheryl Madden, Rajan Menon, Maksym Motorenko, Alla Parkhomenko, Ihor Piddubny, Roman Serbyn, Myroslav Shkandrij, Lida Somchynsky, Myroslav Yurkevich, Larissa Zaleska Onyshkevych, and two anonymous reviewers for their assistance, suggestions, and criticism. The map showing the death toll of the Holodomor, reproduced by permission of the Kashtan Press (Kingston, Ontario, Canada), was redrawn for this volume by Wendy Johnson of Johnson Cartographics (Edmonton). Naturally, we assume full responsibility for the book's shortcomings, while hoping that they will spur others to correct them in subsequent works on the Ukrainian genocide.

To the memory of James Mace,
whose pioneering work on the Holodomor
brought the famine-genocide to the world's attention

1

SCHOLARSHIP

INTRODUCTION

The Scholarship section presents a broad selection of views on the famine by prominent scholars in North America, Europe, Ukraine, and Russia. Earlier works were usually based on eyewitness and survivor testimony; more recent writings are based largely on once-secret Soviet government and Communist Party documents that have supplemented the accounts of eyewitnesses and survivors. We have removed footnotes from the excerpts (with one exception) to save space.

The section opens with an article by the pioneering American scholar James Mace, who devoted much of his life and career to researching the Holodomor as genocide. The article, published in 1984 to much controversy, offers a summary of his views. Robert Conquest's *Harvest of Sorrow* details the Stalin regime's attack on Ukrainian intellectuals and civic leaders in the years 1929–32 and the resistance of Ukraine's communist leaders, especially Mykola Skrypnyk, a long-time Bolshevik who supported Ukrainian political and cultural autonomy. Liudmyla Hrynevych's article demonstrates that national sentiment was widespread in Ukraine before and during the famine and that it colored Ukrainian perceptions of Stalin's policies.

The section continues with a selection from the work of Terry Martin, who argues that the famine had a national dimension, but, like R. W. Davies, Stephen G. Wheatcroft, and Viktor Kondrashin, disputes the view that it was genocide. As Kondrashin writes, "Stalin's famine of 1932–33 was a general tragedy of the peoples of the former USSR, a tragedy of all the Soviet countryside, a crime of the Stalinist regime." The writings of these prominent scholars from the United States, Great Britain, Australia, and Russia provide an excellent counterpoint to the views of other experts in this section.

Four contributions by the French historian Nicholas Werth, the Italian historian Andrea Graziosi, the Ukrainian historian Yurii Shapoval, and the Canadian political scientist David Marples treat the Ukrainian-Kuban famine as distinctive within the context of the pan-Soviet famines of 1931–33. In contrast to Conquest and Mace, Werth, Graziosi, and Shapoval draw on recently uncovered archival sources. As Werth concludes, the "specifically anti-Ukrainian assault makes it possible to define the totality of intentional political actions taken from late summer 1932 by the Stalinist regime against the Ukrainian peasantry as genocide." Marples reaches the same conclusion as the others by means of a variable-centered political science analysis.

The question of death tolls is raised by two demographic studies, one by Oleh Wolowyna, an American of Ukrainian descent, and the other by the French demographer Jacques Vallin and his colleagues at the Institut national d'études démographiques in Paris. Wolowyna discusses the difficulties of establishing demographic losses caused by the Holodomor and concludes that they amounted to 4–5 million in Soviet Ukraine in 1932–34. Vallin and his colleagues arrive at a figure of 4.6 million.

Of particular historiographic interest is the selection by the senior Ukrainian historian Stanislav Kulchytsky. He began studying the Holodomor when he still shared the official viewpoint, but, after examining relevant archival documents, he became increasingly convinced that the famine was genocide. In his book *The Price of the Great Turning Point* (1991), Kulchytsky concluded that "Famine and genocide in the countryside were preprogrammed." His article ends with an assessment of the reasons why Russian historians and the Russian political establishment are opposed to the genocide definition of the Holodomor.

James E. Mace, "Famine and Nationalism in Soviet Ukraine"

Problems of Communism 33 (May–June 1984). Excerpts, pp. 44–49.

James E. Mace (1952–2004) was an American historian who specialized in Soviet Ukrainian history. He was one of the first Western scholars to focus on the Holodomor as genocide. In 1986–90, Mace served as executive director of the U.S. Commission on the Ukraine Famine. He was the author of *Communism and the Dilemmas of National Liberation: National Communism in Soviet Ukraine, 1918–1933* (1984).

The famine of 1932–33 came about primarily as a result of excessive grain procurements. Since the Ukrainian harvest of 1932 was better than that of the worst NEP year, it is clear that without the forced procurements of grain there would have been no starvation. The procurement quotas that were being imposed by Union authorities on Soviet Ukraine in conjunction with collectivization were clearly discriminatory....

The Ukrainian Party leadership appealed for lower quotas to the delegates from Moscow at the Third All-Ukrainian Party Conference in July 1932. [Lazar] Kaganovich and Viacheslav Molotov listened to one official after another tell of the hardships the quotas had caused. [Stanislav] Kosior, [Mykola] Skrypnyk, and Panas Liubchenko all told of villages where everything had been taken and where there was no longer anything to eat. Molotov responded that the quotas, which had already been lowered by 18 percent from the previous year (to 6.6 million tons), would remain in place, and the Party conference duly included the figure in its resolution. However, Ukrainian warnings about the dire consequences of what Kosior called the "mechanistic" enforcement of quotas, without regard for areas where the harvest had been poor, show that officials on the scene were giving Moscow ample warning of what was to come....

Stalin's public response was to disbelieve the reports....

Portraits of village life during succeeding months emerge from the files of the Harvard University Refugee Interview Project, which was conducted during the early 1950s. It should be stressed that the interviewers were not particularly interested in the famine and that the information was therefore given without any prompting while the respondents were relating their life experiences. One rather typical account (Case 128) is the following:

"...there was the famine in the Ukraine in 1933. We saw people die in the streets; it was terrible to see a dead man, when I close my eyes I can still see him. We had in our village a small church which was closed for services and in which we played. And I remember a man who came in there; he lay down with his eyes wide open at the ceiling and he died there! He was an innocent victim of the Soviet regime; he was a simple worker and not even a kulak. This hunger was the result of Soviet policy."

Other accounts are more graphic, as this one by a Russian woman (Case 373): "Well, in 1933–34 I was a member of a commission sent out to inspect wells. We had to go to the country to see that the shafts of the wells were correctly installed, and there I saw such things as I had never seen before in my life. I saw villages that not only had no people, but not even any dogs and cats, and I remember one particular incident: we came to one village, and I don't think I will ever forget this. I will always see this picture before me. We opened the door of this miserable hut and there... the man was lying. The mother and child already lay dead, and the father had taken the piece of meat from between the legs of his son and had died just like that. The stench was terrific, we couldn't stand it, and this was not the only time that I remember such incidents, there were other such incidents on our trip..."

Nor were such horrors confined to the countryside. Cannibalism occurred even in the cities, as a worker (Case 513) described: "I remember a case in 1933. I was in Kiev. I was at that time at a bazaar—the bazaar was called the Bessarabian market. I saw a woman with a valise. She opened the valise and put her goods out for sale. Her goods consisted of jellied meat, frozen jellied meat, which she sold at 50 rubles a portion. I saw a man come over to her—a man who bore all the marks of starvation—he bought himself a portion and began eating. As he ate of his portion, he noticed that a human finger was imbedded in the jelly. He began shouting at the woman and began yelling at the top of his voice. People came running, gathered around her and then seeing what her food consisted of, took her to the militsia (police). At the militsia, two members of the NKVD went over to her and, instead of taking action against her, they burst out laughing. 'What, what, you killed a kulak? Good for you!' And then they let her go."....

The All-Union Central Committee weighed in with two decrees, on December 14, 1932, and January 24, 1933, the first demanding that Ukrainization be carried out "properly" and that "Petliurists and bourgeois nationalists" be dispersed, the second declaring that Ukrainian authorities were guilty of laxity in failing to meet the procurement quotas. The January decree was tantamount to Moscow's taking direct control of the Ukrainian Party apparatus by appointing Pavel Postyshev (a non-Ukrainian former obkom secretary who had been transferred to Moscow some years earlier) as second secretary of the Ukrainian Central Committee and obkom secretary in Kharkiv.... This meant placing Ukraine directly under Moscow's control through the person of Postyshev, who acted as Stalin's viceroy....

While the published sections of the January decree referred only to the failure of the Ukrainian procurement campaign to meet its quota, Postyshev later indicated that the decree also dealt with nationality policy. Other Soviet officials never contradicted him on this. In any case, a campaign against an initially unidentified Ukrainian national deviation was begun, and it was conducted in a manner reminiscent of the campaign against a "right deviation" that had preceded attacks on Nikolai Bukharin in 1929. On February 28, 1933, a major government reshuffle was announced, transferring Skrypnyk from his post as commissar of education to that of deputy premier and head of the Ukrainian State Planning Commission.... Clearly, a final assault against Skrypnyk was being prepared. This came at the Ukrainian Central Committee's June plenum. Skrypnyk's speech was never published, but according to accounts that leaked out, he denied that hitherto loyal communists were guilty of national deviation and of intentionally sabotaging the grain procurement campaign. He asserted that opposition was the inevitable consequence of the policies imposed by Moscow, the restrictions on Ukraine's autonomy, and the famine, for which he laid the blame squarely at Moscow's door.

Postyshev's speech, on the other hand, was published under the telling headline: "We Are Mobilizing the Masses for the Immediate Delivery of Grain to the State." He defended the compulsory procurements policy and made it clear that it was Skrypnyk who had been the target of his campaign against "national deviations." He portrayed Skrypnyk as a leader of nationalist heretics, the protector of "nationalistic wreckers" responsible for the inadequate fulfillment of grain procurements. Interestingly, the only specific charge against Skrypnyk in Postyshev's stream of abuse was Skrypnyk's advocacy of orthographic changes tending to make Ukrainian spelling more distinct from Russian, something that "served only the annexationist designs of the Polish landlords."....

Skrypnyk, who committed suicide on July 6, 1933, was no longer alive when Nikolai Popov, a secretary of the Ukrainian Central Committee since March 1933, linked the struggle to extract grain to the struggle against Skrypnyk, both apparently being equally necessary to transform Ukraine into a model Soviet republic: "The task of raising our agriculture cannot be accomplished unless we correct errors which have been permitted in the national question, unless we purge our party, our state, cultural, agricultural, collective-farm and other institutions of bourgeois nationalists, without mobilizing the entire party mass to fight nationalism, without strengthening our efforts to bring the masses up in the spirit of internationalism.... Bolshevik nationality policy, most intimately connected with all our party's tasks... will be a mighty weapon for the consolidation of Soviet Ukraine as an indivisible part of the Soviet Union.... We face here and now the task of making Soviet Ukraine into a model Soviet republic."

By then Postyshev had already set about making Soviet Ukraine a model Soviet republic. In March 1933, the Ukrainian deputy secretary of agriculture and 22 others were shot for alleged attempts to sabotage agriculture. Other alleged conspiracies were connected with the old revolutionary Ukrainian parties, the Poles, and the underground Ukrainian Military Organization in Western Ukraine. Virtually all prominent communist dissenters from the past were arrested at this time in what become known as the "Postyshev terror." Arrests of writers became a wholesale process; and of the 259 Ukrainian writers whose works were published in Soviet Ukraine in 1930, only 36 had their works still printed after 1938.

Visible reminders of Ukraine's distinctiveness began to disappear. For example, Vasyl Ellan-Blakytny had been revered as a sort of founding saint of Ukrainian proletarian literature. His statue stood at a principal intersection in Kharkiv—until one day a truck ran into it. The statue was not replaced. As time passed, not only statues but also artistic and architectural monuments to the Ukrainian past either fell prey to trucks or were removed to make way for new projects, many of which never materialized.

In the remaining months of 1933 many of the organizations and individuals that had been central to Ukraine's intellectual life in the 1920s simply disappeared. Linguists, fiction writers, historians, poets—virtually everyone who had anything to do with creating a distinctly Ukrainian cultural scene in the 1920s—disappeared. Ukrainization became a dead letter. Concessions to Ukrainian national identity came to an end.

Robert Conquest, *The Harvest of Sorrow: Soviet Collectivization and the Terror-Famine*

(New York and Oxford: Oxford University Press, 1986). Excerpts, pp. 217–24.

Robert Conquest (b. 1917) is a British-American historian specializing in the history of Stalinism. He is a research fellow at the Hoover Institution, Stanford University. He is the author of many books, including *The Great Terror: Stalin's Purge of the Thirties* (1968, rev. ed. 1990, 40th anniversary ed. 2008), *The Nation Killers: The Soviet Deportation of Nationalities* (1970), *Inside Stalin's Secret Police: NKVD Politics, 1936–1939* (1985), *Reflections on a Ravaged Century* (1999), and *The Dragons of Expectation* (2005).

At the same time that Stalin made his move to crush the peasantry in 1929–30, he resumed the attack on the Ukraine and its national culture which had been suspended in the early 1920s....

...A great nation lay under Communist control. But not only was its population unreconciled to the system: it was also true that the representatives of the national culture, and even many Communists, only accepted Moscow's rule conditionally. This was, from the Party's point of view, both deplorable in itself and pregnant with danger for the future.

In 1929–30, having crushed the Right, and having embarked on a collectivization and dekulakization policy which hit the Ukraine with especial severity and met the strongest resistance there, Stalin was at last nearly ready to give effect to his hostility to all such centrifugal tendencies.

As early as April 1929, the OGPU was bringing charges of Ukrainian nationalist plotting against small groups. During the year there were public attacks on the most distinguished Ukrainian academics. In July mass arrests took place of some 5,000 members of an alleged underground organization, the Union for the Liberation of the Ukraine (SVU)....

From 9 March to 20 April 1930, a whole cycle of faked cases against Ukrainian personalities began with the set-piece public trial in the Kharkiv Opera House of forty-five alleged members of this organization. They were mostly former political figures of extinct parties, now engaged in work as scholars, critics, writers, linguists, with some students, lawyers, and especially priests, thrown in.

Their leading figure was Academician Serhii Yefremov, a linguistic scholar and lexicographer....

Another was Zinovii Margulis, a Jewish lawyer and member of the Ukrainian Academy of Sciences. The bulk of the other leading figures were academics or writers of the same background...men who had supported the independent Ukrainian Republic: such as the historian Yosyp Hermaize, the writers Mykhailo Ivchenko and Liudmyla Starytska-Cherniakhivska, the linguist Hryhorii Holoskevych, and others....

Confessions had been obtained, by the usual methods, and the accused were sentenced to long jail terms. It was announced in connection with the trial that the linguistic institutes of the Ukrainian Academy had been closed down and a number of scholars arrested. The charges in the SVU trial included, in addition to conspiring to seize power, that of working to make Ukrainian as distinct as possible from Russian. This was, in fact, much the same linguistic aim as that of [Mykola] Skrypnyk and other Ukrainian Communists....

In February 1931, a further series of arrests of leading intellectuals took place—mainly prominent figures who had returned from exile in 1924 or 1925. They had supposedly formed a "Ukrainian National Centre" with the country's most distinguished figure, the historian [Mykhailo] Hrushevsky, as leader, and [Vsevolod] Holubovych, former Premier of the independent Ukraine, among the major plotters.

...Most of the accused were sent to penal camps, though Hrushevsky himself was merely removed from the Ukraine under house arrest.

These moves were crucial in the assault on Ukrainization. They amounted to the crushing of that old intelligentsia which had become reconciled to the Soviet regime on a programme of Ukrainian cultural identity. In 1931 the Ukrainian Communist intelligentsia in turn came under attack....

This first assault on the Ukrainian intelligentsia preceded the general attack on the peasantry. Stalin clearly understood that the essence of Ukrainian nationhood was contained in the intelligentsia who articulated it, but also in the peasant masses who had sustained it over the centuries. The "decapitation" of the nation by removing its spokesmen was indeed essential.... But Stalin seems to have realized that only a mass terror throughout the body of the nation—that is, the peasantry—could really reduce the country to submission. His ideas about the connection between nationality and the peasantry are clearly put: "The nationality problem is, in its very essence, a problem of the peasantry." And in fact one of the aims of collectivization in the Ukraine had been officially stated as "the destruction of Ukrainian nationalism's social base—the individual land-holdings."

The SVU "plot" was...extended to the villages. Many village teachers are reported shot in connection with it. In one district the head of the Executive Committee, the District's chief doctor, and others including peasants were shot as SVU conspirators. And there are scores of such reports.

[Stanislav] Kosior was to sum up after the struggle: "the nationalist deviation in the Communist Party of the Ukraine...played an exceptional role in causing and deepening the crisis in agriculture." Or, as his Police Chief [Vsevolod] Balytsky is quoted as saying, "In 1933 the fist of the OGPU hit out in two directions. First at the kulak and Petliurist elements in the villages and secondly at the leading centres of nationalism."

Thus the kulak was blamed as a bearer of nationalist ideas, the nationalist as a sponsor of kulak attitudes. But in whichever capacity the Ukrainian peasant was considered, he had certainly proved particularly troublesome to the regime. Resistance to collectivization is always reported as stronger, or rather more militant, in the Ukraine than in Russia proper....

But it was not only the peasants who were inadequately subdued. The Ukrainian Communists, too, presented obstacles to Stalin. Even in 1929 the Ukrainian Party and Soviet organizations had been particularly stubborn in arguing against unrealistic grain targets, and particularly remiss in discovering kulaks....

In normal circumstances, the Ukraine and the North Caucasus had provided half of the total marketable grain. In 1926, the best harvest before collectivization, 3.3 million tons of grain (21% of the harvest), was taken from the Ukraine. In the good harvest of 1930 it was 7.7 million tons (33% of the harvest); and although the Ukraine only accounted for 27% of the total Soviet grain harvest, it had to supply 38% of grain deliveries.

In 1931 the same 7.7 million tons was demanded of the Ukraine, out of a harvest of only 18.3 million tons; that is, 42% (about 30% of the grain had been lost in the inefficiencies of collective harvesting)....

Only 7 million tons was actually collected. But this already meant that what amounted...to a famine was afflicting the Ukraine in the late spring of 1932: for only an average of c. 250 pounds of grain per capita was left for the Ukrainian rural population.

Needless to say, the lapses produced further Party purges.... Complaints about the whole Ukrainian position, as "disgracefully behind" and so on, became endemic in the central Moscow press. I note fifteen in *Pravda* alone between January and July 1932.

In July the vital decisions were taken which were to lead to the holocaust of the next eight months. Stalin had again ordered a delivery target of 7.7 million tons.... After considerable argument, the Ukrainians finally managed to get the figure reduced to 6.6 million tons—but this too was still far beyond the feasible.

This took place on 6–9 July 1932, at the "Third All-Ukrainian Conference" of the Ukrainian Communist Party, with Molotov and Kaganovich representing Moscow. Kosior opened the Conference. Some areas, he said, were already "seriously short of food"....

Skrypnyk told the Conference frankly that peasants had told him that "we had everything taken from us." And Kosior, Vlas Chubar, and others also argued that the grain targets were excessive....

However, Molotov called attempts to blame unrealistic plans for the failures "anti-Bolshevik," and concluded by saying, "There will be no concessions or vacillations in the problem of fulfillment of the task set by the Party and the Soviet government."....

So, on Stalin's insistence, a decree went out which, if enforced, could only lead to starvation of the Ukrainian peasantry....

Things were already bad in July 1932, and they got worse....

To enforce the decree on "the protection of socialist property"...watchtowers were now erected in the fields....

The towers were manned by guards armed, as a rule, with shotguns.

The first procurements were carried out in August, and in many areas by great effort the norms were met. But this virtually exhausted the countryside....

On 12 October 1932 two senior Russian apparatchiks were sent from Moscow to strengthen the local Party: [Ivan Alekseevich] Akulov, who had been Deputy Head of the OGPU, and [Mendel Markovich] Khataevich, earlier prominent in Stalin's collectivization on the Volga—a portent of more to come.

At the same time a second procurement was announced, though there was now almost nothing available....

People were already dying. But Moscow, far from relaxing its demands, now launched into a veritable crescendo of terror by hunger.

Terry Martin, *The Affirmative Action Empire: Nations and Nationalism in the Soviet Union, 1923–1939*

(Ithaca and London: Cornell University Press, 2001). Excerpts, pp. 302–8.

Terry Martin (b. 1963) is an American historian specializing in Russian, Soviet, and Central European history. He is George F. Baker III Professor of Russian Studies at Harvard University. He is coeditor of *A State of Nations: Empire and Nation-Building in the Age of Lenin and Stalin* (2001).

The National Interpretation of the Grain Requisitions Crisis

[Lazar] Kaganovich completed his second trip to the North Caucasus on November 25 [1932]. At the same time, [Viacheslav] Molotov completed his commission's work in Ukraine and also returned to Moscow. Molotov's commission had presided over an intensification of the grain requisitions terror in Ukraine, only slightly less severe than in Kuban. In the month of November and the first five days of December, under Molotov's supervision, the Ukrainian GPU arrested 1,830 individuals from the leadership of various collective farms. In addition, 327 communists were also arrested. By December 15, approximately 16,000 individuals had been arrested, including 435 Party members and 2,260 collective farm officials. Of these, 108 had been sentenced to be executed. After the return of Kaganovich and Molotov, the Politburo convened on December 14 and issued a secret decree on grain collection in Ukraine and the North Caucasus. This decree was the most important central intervention on nationalities policy since the 1923 decrees that first codified the Soviet nationalities policy. It marked the first time that the Soviet leadership officially declared that the 1923 policy of *korenizatsiia* [indigenization], as implemented in Ukraine and the North Caucasus, had not disarmed nationalist resistance as was intended, but rather had intensified it.

The December 14, 1932 Politburo decree articulated the national interpretation of the 1932 grain requisitions crisis. Ukraine and the North Caucasus were singled out for their lack of vigilance, which had allowed "kulaks, former officers, Petliurites and supporters of the Kuban *rada* [council] to penetrate the collective farm leadership." Likewise, their lack of vigilance empowered "the most evil enemies of the Party, working class and kolkhoz peasantry, the saboteurs of grain requisition with Party tickets in their pocket." In both Ukraine and the North Caucasus, the Politburo blamed this lack of vigilance on Ukrainization:

> TsK [Central Committee] and Sovnarkom [Council of People's Commissars] note that instead of a correct Bolshevik implementation of the nationalities policy, in many Ukrainian regions Ukrainization was carried out mechanically, without considering the specifics of each district, without a careful choice of Bolshevik Ukrainian cadres. This made it easy for bourgeois-nationalist elements, Petliurites and others to create a legal cover [*prikrytie*] for their counterrevolutionary cells and organizations.

The verdict on Ukrainization in the North Caucasus was much harsher:

> TsK and Sovnarkom instruct the North Caucasus *kraikom* [regional committee] that the light-headed [*legkomyslennaia*], non-Bolshevik "Ukrainization" of almost half the North Caucasus districts did not serve the cultural interests of the population, and with the total absence of surveillance by *krai* [regional] organs of the Ukrainization of schools and the press, gave a legal form to the enemies of Soviet power for the organization of opposition to Soviet power by kulaks, officers, re-emigrated Cossacks, members of the Kuban *rada* and so forth.

In short, the grain requisitions crisis was the product of resistance by traitors within the soviet and Party apparat, and many of them received their positions due to the policy of Ukrainization. This represented the national interpretation of the grain requisitions crisis.

Three series of events converged to produce this interpretation. First…an anti-*korenizatsiia* hard-line stance that maintained *korenizatsiia* was exacerbating rather than disarming nationalism gradually emerged in response to the perceived defection of national communists such as Oleksander Shumsky to a position of nationalism, the perceived influence of cross-border ethnic ties in causing such defections, as well as the cultural revolution terror campaigns against the national *smenovekhovstvo* [previously anti-Soviet] intelligentsia and the centralizing thrust of the socialist offensive. The December 14, 1932 Politburo decree represented the first central endorsement of the anti-*korenizatsiia* hard-line position that, at least in this one case, *korenizatsiia* had exacerbated rather than contained the threat of nationalist counterrevolution. Second…Ukraine's effort to annex neighboring RSFSR regions and to serve as the patron of the RSFSR Ukrainians both exacerbated central concerns about Ukrainian national communism and created a perceived political link between the Soviet Union's two most important grain-growing regions: Ukraine and the North Caucasus. Third, collectivization both elicited more violent resistance in the Soviet Union's non-Russian border regions, further exacerbating central concerns about national separatism, and resulted in a major political crisis in the fall of 1932 that made the perceived separatist threat in Ukraine intolerable.

The national interpretation, then, was not a cause of the grain requisitions crisis and famine. Rather, it emerged as a consequence of it. Although Ukrainization had lost momentum by 1932, there were no signals in Ukraine that the policy was being called into question in a fundamental way prior to December 14, 1932. In fact, on the eve of that decree, the Ukrainian Commissariat of Education had just launched another campaign to verify the implementation of Ukrainization. Likewise, as noted earlier, *Pravda* published an article in defense of Ukrainization in the North Caucasus only two days before Kaganovich's commission departed for Rostov. Most strikingly, in the available internal correspondence concerning grain requisitions in Ukraine, the national factor is mentioned only once prior to November 1932. From his letter to Kaganovich, we know that by August 11, Stalin had already linked Ukrainian nationalist infiltration of the Party with the grain requisitions crisis in Ukraine, but not yet with the crisis in Kuban and the North Caucasus. We have also seen that Kaganovich alluded briefly to counterrevolutionary sabotage by groups from Ukraine in a speech delivered on his arrival in Rostov on November 1. However, aside from that stray comment, Kaganovich overwhelmingly blamed the crisis on the kulaks, the Kuban Cossacks, and rural communists.

The available evidence suggests that the national interpretation emerged in full form and received central sanction after the initial missions of Molotov and Kaganovich to Ukraine and the North Caucasus in early November. Molotov and Kaganovich both returned to Moscow for extensive consultation with Stalin from November 12 to 16. After these meetings, Molotov returned to Ukraine and Kaganovich traveled to both Ukraine and the North Caucasus. During these repeat visits, the Ukrainian question received much greater emphasis. On November 18, Molotov told the Kharkiv Party *aktiv* that, "you must fight with those remnants of bourgeois nationalism in the form of Petliurites and half-Petliurites; one must understand that not only is the internal enemy at work here, but also...the enemy from across the border." The same day, two Ukrainian TsK decrees both referred to the need to fight the *Petliurovshchina* and "to liquidate kulak and Petliurite nests." Likewise, as noted earlier, Kaganovich began to emphasize the role of Ukrainian counterrevolutionaries in Kuban. The Ukrainian factor provided a convenient explanation for why Ukraine and the North Caucasus (and, above all, Kuban) were the Soviet Union's two most delinquent grain-producing regions. Nor was this interpretation unpopular with local communists in the North Caucasus, who eagerly seconded Kaganovich's attacks on Ukrainian counterrevolutionaries. As we have already seen, they greatly resented Ukrainian attempts to annex their territory and to promote RSFSR Ukrainization. Moreover, they were relieved that central terror was now being deflected somewhat on to national targets. Likewise, the 1933 nationalities terror in Ukraine focused on Ukrainian cultural and educational institutions, as well as on political émigrés from Galicia, and away from rank-and-file communists.

The Politburo's development of a national interpretation of their grain requisitions crisis in late 1932 helps explain both the pattern of terror and the role of the national factor during the 1932–33 famine. The 1932–33 terror campaign consisted of both a grain requisitions terror, whose primary target was the peasantry, both Russian and non-Russian, and a nationalities terror, whose primary target was Ukraine and subsequently Belorussia. The grain requisitions terror was the final and decisive culmination of a campaign begun in 1927–28 to extract the maximum possible amount of grain from a hostile peasantry. As such, its primary targets were the grain-producing regions of Ukraine, the North Caucasus, and the Lower Volga, though no grain-producing regions escaped the 1932–33 grain requisitions terror entirely. Nationality was of minimal importance in this campaign. The famine was not an intentional act of genocide specifically targeting the Ukrainian nation. It is equally false, however, to assert that nationality played no role whatsoever in the famine. The nationalities terror resulted from the gradual emergence of an anti-*korenizatsiia* hard-line critique combined with the immediate pressures of the grain requisitions crisis in Ukraine and Kuban, whose particularly intense resistance was attributed to Ukrainization. The December 14 Politburo decree formalized this national interpretation and authorized an additional nationalities terror against Ukraine and Kuban. A second Politburo decree, on December 15, formally abolished Ukrainization throughout the entire RSFSR. A third Politburo decree, a day later, extended the nationalities terror to Belorussia as well.

My analysis explains why the 1932–33 grain requisitions terror embraced both Russian and Ukrainian territories and also why the terror was worse in Kuban and Ukraine than in the Lower Volga. The Lower Volga was visited by an extraordinary Politburo commission headed by Pavel Postyshev in December 1932, which did unleash a wave of terror against both the peasantry and local communists, but the level of terror never reached that of Ukraine and Kuban. By March 1933, as a result of the grain requisitions terror, there were 90,000 individuals in Ukraine's jails and concentration camps, 75,000 in those of the North Caucasus, and 29,000 in those of the Lower Volga. These numbers understate the actual difference, since 30,000 individuals had been transferred out of the North Caucasus camps in January, and Ukraine's camp population had already been reduced in late November.

Above all, my analysis explains why Ukraine and the Kuban were singled out in a January 22, 1933 TsK circular that called for the closing of the Ukrainian and North Caucasus borders to peasant out-migration:

> TsK VKP/b/ and Sovnarkom have received information that in the Kuban and Ukraine a massive outflow of peasants "for bread" has begun into Belorussia and the Central-Black Earth, Volga, Western, and Moscow regions. TsK VKP/b/ and Sovnarkom do not doubt that the outflow of the peasants, like the outflow from Ukraine last year, was organized by the enemies of Soviet power, the SRs and the agents of Poland, with the goal of agitation "through the peasantry" in the northern regions of the USSR against the collective farms and against Soviet power as a whole. Last year the Party, Soviet, and Chekist organs of Ukraine were caught napping by this counterrevolutionary trick of the enemies of Soviet power. This year we cannot allow a repetition of last year's mistake.
>
> First, TsK VKP/b/ and Sovnarkom order the kraikom, krai executive committee, and OGPU of the North Caucasus not to allow a massive outflow of peasants from the North Caucasus into other regions or the entry into the North Caucasus from Ukraine.
>
> Second, TsK VKP/b/ and Sovnarkom order TsK KP/b/U, the Ukrainian Sovnarkom, as well as [Vsevolod] Balytsky and [Stanislav] Redens not to allow a massive outflow of peasants from Ukraine into other regions or the entry into Ukraine of peasants from the North Caucasus.

> Third, TsK VKP/b/ and Sovnarkom order the OGPU of Belorussia and the Central-Black Earth, Middle Volga, Western and Moscow regions to immediately arrest all "peasants" of Ukraine and the North Caucasus who have broken through into the north and, after separating out the counterrevolutionary elements, to return the rest to their places of residence.
>
> Fourth, TsK VKP/b/ and Sovnarkom order the OGPU to give a similar order to the OGPU transport organs.
>
> 65Sh. Molotov, Stalin

This directive once again points to Stalin's concern over the political impact of Ukrainian out-migration. It is impossible to determine how many Ukrainian and North Caucasus peasant lives might have been lost due to this directive, but it clearly shows that Ukraine and Kuban were singled out for special treatment specifically because of the national interpretation of the famine....

Conclusion: The Aftermath of the December 1932 Politburo Decrees

In retrospect, it is clear that the December 14, 1932 Politburo decree marked a decisive turning point in the evolution of the Soviet nationalities policy. At the time, however, this was not at all clear. The decree did not condemn Ukrainization wholesale, but rather its "mechanical" implementation and the failure to make "a careful choice of Bolshevik Ukrainian cadres." The suggested solution was not russification, but rather "serious attention to the proper implementation of Ukrainization" and "the careful choice and education of Bolshevik Ukrainian cadres." Only time would tell what exactly the shift to "Bolshevik" Ukrainization would mean. It is true that the December 15 Politburo decree abolished Ukrainization throughout the entire RSFSR, and this was an unambiguous policy innovation. However, given the high levels of assimilation among the RSFSR Ukrainians, it could easily have been understood as a single exception that proved the rule (as it in fact was for four years). Moreover, the decree was issued in the midst of a major political crisis, which involved a large-scale year-long terror campaign. That campaign was officially brought to a halt on May 8, 1933. At that point, the December 14 decree could easily have been allowed to lapse, especially since it was never published. This did not occur. Instead, the December 14 decree initiated a series of far-reaching changes in the Soviet nationalities policy, the onset of Soviet ethnic cleansing and the emergence of the category of the "enemy nation"; a fundamental revision, but not abolition, of *korenizatsiia;* a shift from ethnic proliferation to ethnic consolidation, accompanied by an administrative russification of the RSFSR; and, finally, the rehabilitation of the Russians and traditional Russian national culture as part of the process of establishing a revised Soviet national constitution, whose organizing metaphor would be the Friendship of the Peoples.

Liudmyla Hrynevych, "Stalins'ka 'revoliutsiia zhory' ta holod 1933 r. iak faktory polityzatsiï ukraïns'koï spil'noty" (Stalin's "Revolution from Above" and the Famine of 1933 as Factors in the Politicization of Ukrainian Society)

Ukraïns'kyi istorychnyi zhurnal (Ukrainian Historical Journal, Kyiv), 2003, no. 5. Excerpts, pp. 50–53, 56–63.
Translated by Maksym Motorenko and Bohdan Klid.

Liudmyla Hrynevych (b. 1962) is a Ukrainian historian specializing in Soviet Ukrainian history. She is a research associate of the Institute of Ukrainian History at the National Academy of Sciences of Ukraine (Kyiv). She is the compiler of *Khronika kolektyvizatsiï ta Holodomoru v Ukraïni 1927–1933*, vol. 1, 1927–1929 (A Chronicle of Collectivization and the Holodomor in Ukraine, 1927–1933, vol. 1, 1927–1929; Kyiv, 2008).

...[T]he determining factors in the politicization of Ukrainian society were the forced collectivization of agriculture initiated by the Stalin leadership at the end of the 1920s and the Holodomor of 1933. This successive "agricultural experiment" of the Bolshevik leadership was at the same time an imperious offensive against the foundations of the very existence of the Ukrainian ethnos, causing it actively to resist the political regime in place to the extent that this was possible, given the existence of the Communist Party dictatorship and total terror....

...[A]ctions of mass protest in Ukraine had their own specificity, which consisted in the closest intertwining of social and national motives.... [A]lmost all the social cataclysms that accompanied Bolshevik rule in Ukraine were assessed by a large section of Ukrainian society through the prism of national feelings and national interests.

In March 1928 the leader of the [Ukrainian] republic's Party organization, Lazar Kaganovich, speaking at the plenum of the Central Committee of the Communist Party (Bolshevik) of Ukraine, had to admit that the beginning of the grain-procurement campaign in Ukraine had caused a "strengthening of chauvinism," moreover, "not only from the upper strata, but from the lower ones as well.".... And indeed, such "inconvenient" questions for the rulers as "Where did they take the grain harvested in Ukraine?"; "Why is the grain-growing republic starving now?"; "Who is guilty of the ongoing robbery of the Ukrainian village and the rapid impoverishment of the town?" were not only being most actively discussed among various strata of the population but also, on the level of social consciousness, were sharply raising the problem of the direct and extremely close connection between Ukraine's impending tragedy and its existence as a component of the USSR, a republic wholly dependent on the Union center (Moscow)....

..."It would be better if Ukraine separated from Russia. We would live better—but now, give bread to Russia, and Russia sells it abroad. So it turns out that Ukraine is like a milch cow"; "...It would be better for the peasantry if Ukraine were independent. Then we ourselves would direct our country and people"; "The USSR is agitating for the Soviet Union because it is afraid of losing Ukrainian bread"; "...Why would we need socialism if Ukraine could be independent?"... "[Symon] Petliura's administration really struggled for the interests of Ukraine, but now all instructions come from Russia, which is living at Ukraine's expense," some peasants said. "Petliura did not have enough time to manifest himself, and nobody knows how things would have turned out had he stayed in power." "If we had had Petliura, there would have been enough of everything in Ukraine," insisted others.

As the food situation in the republic deteriorated sharply, particularly in the famine conditions of 1928–29, national feeling among the Ukrainian masses grew ever more acute, and manifestations of national discontent spread not only in villages but in towns as well. In May 1928, at factories in the Odesa region, workers could be heard saying such things as: "The government ships bread abroad, but we are starving"; "Moscow eats white bread, which it takes from Ukraine."....

The beginning of the authorities' resort to violence objectively called forth a tendency toward the consolidation and self-organization of the Ukrainian peasantry.... This tendency did not go unnoticed by the GPU of the Ukrainian SSR, whose head, Vsevolod Balytsky, in a memorandum of July 1928 addressed to Lazar Kaganovich, the general secretary of the Central Committee of the Communist Party (Bolshevik) of Ukraine, titled "On the Revival of the Ukrainian Counterrevolution," noted "the appearance of new anti-Soviet activists directly among peasant elements and, especially lately, among youth.".... It was extremely telling that the national and political platform of all neutralized groups did not derive from the idea of achieving equality for Soviet Ukraine within the USSR but was based on an understanding of the need to establish an independent Ukrainian state on the model of the Ukrainian People's Republic....

The tendency toward the consolidation of Ukrainian society and the activation of its mobilizing forces made itself apparent, in particular, in the sharp increase of anti-Soviet leaflets in the villages. A significant number of them appealed precisely to the national feelings of Ukrainians, calling on them to rise up against social and national oppression. If in the course of 1928 only 150 leaflets of this type were discovered in Ukraine by the security services, during the period from 20 November 1929 to 7 April 1930 there were 349 leaflets (834 copies); from 20 November 1929 to 1 January 1930, 29 (34 copies); from 1 January to 1 March 1930, 86 (111 copies); from 1 to 7 March 1930, 39 (48 copies); from 7 to 17 March, 72 (121 copies); and from 17 March to 7 April, 123 (472 copies).

The central theme of the nationalist leaflets was the accusation that the ruling Party and the Union center were ruining "Mother Ukraine" and an appeal to fight for its liberation from "foreign rule."....

The activities of "counterrevolutionary groups," whose numbers kept increasing in the villages at this time, were imbued with efforts to incite the peasant masses to armed struggle against the Stalin regime. According to information from Balytsky, between 21 January and 9 February 1930 11,865 men were arrested in the Ukrainian countryside, and 334 "counterrevolutionary organizations and groups" were liquidated, members of which "were capable of playing the role of 'ideologues' and organizers of counterrevolutionary actions." We should note that, according to the report of the head of the GPU of the Ukrainian SSR, the main slogans of the liquidated insurgent organizations were of a "Ukrainian chauvinist" and "Petliura" type....

Mass arrests of "kulak-Petliura elements" conducted at the beginning of 1930 and the deportation to the north of tens of thousands of "kulak families" weakened the anti-Soviet peasant movement, largely depriving it of its organizational base. However, the fact that, despite the arrests and deportations, the security services recorded 1,716 mass peasant actions in 41 districts of Ukraine between 20 February and 2 April 1930 indicated that this movement still had significant potential....

The fact that the ideology of the Ukrainian national-liberation movement resonated in the collective consciousness of Ukrainian society was also confirmed in a number of districts by the appearance of farmers opposed to Soviet rule, armed with pitchforks, axes, and sawed-off rifles, singing the national anthem [*Shche ne vmerla Ukraïna* (Ukraine Is Not Yet Lost)]....

An extremely interesting phenomenon that testified to the actualization in public consciousness of the idea of reestablishing an independent Ukrainian People's Republic, as well as the ongoing spontaneous self-organization of anti-Soviet activists, was the voluntary, demonstrative support of peasant participants in various anti-Soviet actions for the "Union for the Liberation of Ukraine," which had been "uncovered" by the GPU and whose alleged members had been tried in Kharkiv from 9 March to 19 April 1930....

...[O]n 30 March 1930 the head of the GPU of the Ukrainian SSR, Vsevolod Balytsky, reported in a letter to Stanislav Kosior, general secretary of the Central Committee of the Communist Party (Bolshevik) of Ukraine, that mass peasant disturbances under the slogans "Long live the SVU [Union for the Liberation of Ukraine]" and "Although the SVU has been arrested, its mission lives on" had been observed in several villages of the Tulchyn, Berdychiv, Shepetivka, Vinnytsia, and other districts.

Although in spring 1930 the Stalin regime managed to extinguish the flames of peasant uprisings in Ukraine and relieve the existing political tension in the Ukrainian countryside, it was unable to do so in society at large.... Observing the mass arrests of rebellious peasants, workers at one of the factories in the Kyiv district were heard to say: "...The tsar drove Ukrainians to Siberia, and the Soviet authorities to the Solovets Islands...." In the countryside, assessments of the Soviet authorities' offensive against Ukrainian "kulaks" were even harsher. Peasants from the village of Stupychne in the Mokro-Kalihorsk raion, Shevchenko district, declared that "The *katsapy* [literally billy-goats, a derogatory term for Russians] have made a plan to enslave Ukraine...".... Although all repressive actions of the Soviet authorities were officially conducted under the watchword of struggle against "kulaks," the populace was not misled by this tactical measure. "...Conscious Ukrainians are being persecuted by the GPU services, which accuse them of being 'kulaks' or 'bourgeois'": such was the categorical conclusion about the situation in Ukraine voiced by a worker who was lucky enough to make his way from Podilia to Czechoslovakia at the end of 1930....

Further destruction of the Ukrainian village and the resulting famine, which had already claimed tens of thousands of victims by the spring of 1932, produced a new outburst of negative political attitudes connected with the problem of Ukraine's colonial status. One of the concrete factors provoking this was the mass exodus of Ukrainian peasants to Moscow, Leningrad, Minsk and other industrial centers, which, being better supplied, contrasted with the situation in Ukraine. There the Ukrainian peasant could buy a life-saving loaf of bread.... Many letters addressed to the authorities were full of surprise, indignation, and protest against such injustice. One 23-year-old worker, who did not give his name, wrote to the Zaporizhia city Party committee: "You have destroyed Ukraine, bringing it to the point where Ukrainians travel for bread to Petrograd and Moscow, from which there was always an influx for our bread."….

Sensing the approach of disaster, the Ukrainian village fought desperately for its life.... In the course of protest actions, as in previous years, national slogans resounded alongside social ones.... The situation was also tense in the cities at this time.... Letters to the political leadership from outraged workers attest to the growth of national discontent among the proletarian masses. "...In the Russian part of the USSR, the system of food supply is good...workers are even given white bread, and there is no talk of lack of bread for families there," wrote one of the depot workers in Liubotyn to Kosior. "Among Ukrainian workers national hatred is becoming evident.... We can now say with confidence that 99 percent of the Ukrainian population has become anti-Soviet."....

…On 23 December 1932 Balytsky sent a report to Stalin about the activities of numerous Petliurist elements and groups in sixty-seven counties of Ukraine—both in the countryside (on collective farms, state farms, and even machine-tractor stations) and in the towns, among the "chauvinistically inclined intelligentsia."....

In winter–spring 1933, Ukraine was in agony from the terrible famine. At the same time, the GPU services continued a most active struggle against "kulaks" and "Petliurism." On 16 January 1933 the Politburo of the Central Committee of the All-Union CP(B), meeting in closed-door session, decided to approve a proposal from Kaganovich and Balytsky to deport 500 "kulak families" from the Odesa oblast; a proposal from Kosior to deport 300 families from the Chernihiv oblast and 400 families from the Kharkiv oblast; and a proposal from the CC of the CP(B) of Ukraine to deport 700 families from the Dnipropetrovsk oblast. Finally, in March 1933, the CC of the All-Union CP(B) voted by secret ballot to propose that the OGPU deport all "Petliurite elements" from the Kyiv oblast—about a thousand families....

…[F]rom the fall of 1932, a wide-ranging offensive against "Ukrainian nationalism" was undertaken in the republic. It was officially proclaimed the "principal threat," indicating that the Stalin regime clearly understood the risk posed by the rapid politicization of Ukrainian society to its retention of power in general and the successful communization of the Ukrainian countryside in particular. Attempting to overcome this threat, the Stalin regime resorted to suppressing the national movements in Ukraine, and terror by hunger became one of its most effective instruments. The rejection after 1933 of previous concessions on the nationality question…became a logical extension of this type of power politics.

R. W. Davies and Stephen G. Wheatcroft, *The Years of Hunger: Soviet Agriculture, 1931–1933*

(New York: Palgrave Macmillan, 2004). Excerpts, pp. 431–36, 439–41.

R. W. Davies (b. 1925) is professor emeritus of Soviet economic studies at the University of Birmingham. He is the author and editor of many books, including *Soviet Economic Development from Lenin to Khrushchev* (1998); *Crisis and Progress in the Soviet Economy, 1931–1933* (1996); *The Stalin–Kaganovich Correspondence, 1931–1936* (2003); *The Soviet Collective Farm, 1929–1930* (1980); *The Soviet Economy in Turmoil, 1929–1930* (1989). He collaborated with E. H. Carr on vols. 9 and 10 of *The History of Soviet Russia*. Stephen G. Wheatcroft (b. 1947) is professor in Russian and Soviet history at the University of Melbourne. He is one of the main editors of the major Russian publication of archival materials, *The Tragedy of the Soviet Village, 1927–1939*. He is the author of *The Economic Transformation of the Soviet Union, 1913–1945* (1994, with R. W. Davies and M. Harrison) and of *Challenging Traditional Views of Russian History* (2002).

...In the second half of the 1920s, the Soviet Union embarked on rapid industrialisation, enforced through the consolidation of the centralised planning system....

The first five-year plan, approved by the Party and government in the spring of 1929, sought to increase the production of food and consumer goods *pari passu* with the growth of capital goods.... This policy failed completely, as the example of grain illustrates (million tons):

	1927/28 Actual	1932/33 Plan	1932/33 Actual (from grain budget IV)	1932/33 Actual (from grain budget III)
Grain production	73	106	56.8	62.6
Extra-rural grain	8	20	15.2[a]	15.4[a]
Remainder in countryside	65	86	41.6[a]	47.2[a]

Note: [a] Grain collections plus sales on kolhoz market amounted to 19.3 million tons (190.5 in grain budget III), but 4.1 million tons of this was returned to the countryside as seed and food loan, allocations to timber, peat and fisheries, and special allocations to agriculture.

The amount retained by the peasants for food in 1932/33 was estimated...at between 20 million and 25 million tons, compared to 27 million tons in 1927/28. The lower figure is much more plausible, as is confirmed by the data on food consumption. The grain consumption per head of the rural population declined substantially; and the consumption per head of meat and dairy products declined even more rapidly.

The state also failed to secure adequate food for the towns....

...[T]he absolute lack of food was the background to the famine. Shortage of grain and other foods in the towns resulted in widespread malnourishment; the acute shortage of grain in the countryside resulted in widespread starvation....

The fundamental cause of the deterioration of agriculture in 1928–33 was the unremitting state pressure on rural resources. Following the grain crisis in the winter of 1927–28, investment in industry, which already exceeded the pre-war level, approximately doubled between 1927/28 and 1930.... Simultaneously, state grain collections increased from 11 million tons after the 1927 harvest to 16 million tons after the 1929 harvest, even though the 1929 harvest was lower than the harvest of 1927.... To obtain this increase, an elaborate system of coercion was established. The removal of grain from the countryside was a major factor in the decline in livestock, which began in 1929 and continued until 1933....

...In 1929, against the background of the tension between peasant and state, the Soviet authorities concluded that the implementation of the industrialisation programme would be impossible if agriculture was not brought under firm control....

Collectivisation, coupled with dekulakisation, brought agriculture under state control. But its introduction brought with it enormous difficulties.... The difficulties were made worse by the inability of most communists, from Stalin to the Party members sent into the countryside, to understand agriculture and the peasants, and offer sensible means of coping with the transformation of the countryside. In 1930, collectivisation proceeded at a breakneck pace, and impracticable schemes were enforced for the wholesale socialisation of livestock as well as grain.... Most agricultural difficulties were not attributed to mistakes in policy, or even treated as a necessary cost of industrialisation. Instead, the machinations of kulaks and other enemies of the regime were blamed for the troubles, and the solution was sought in a firmer organization of agriculture by the state and its agencies.

The chaos in administration and in agriculture, and the demoralisation of many peasants, were the context in which grain production deteriorated.

...In 1930, the year in which collectivisation was launched, the weather—and the harvest—were particularly favourable. The good harvest in a year of turmoil undoubtedly strengthened the illusion among the political leaders that agricultural difficulties would easily be overcome....

Confronted by the poor harvest of 1932, the Soviet authorities were in great difficulty. Even before the harvest, their partial recognition of the parlous state of agriculture led in May 1932 to the introduction of the policies known as 'neo-Nep,' including a reduction in the grain collections below the amount planned for 1931. At this time the Soviet leaders followed their usual practice of overestimating the harvest. But as early as the end of June 1932 they already conceded that it would amount to only about 75 million tons.... This was far below the 90 million tons planned in January 1932, and still further below the five-year plan target of 106 million tons. This put the reduced collection plan of May 1932 in jeopardy. Our work has confirmed...that the grain campaign in 1932/33 was unprecedentedly harsh and repressive.... In response to pressure from the local authorities and the peasants, the Politburo reluctantly made large, though insufficient, reductions in planned collections between August 1932 and January 1933, amounting to as much as 4 million tons. Eventually, 5 million tons less than planned were collected....

...[T]he amount of grain available for internal use was still substantially less in 1932/33 than in the previous year. The Politburo decided that the grain must be concentrated on the hungry towns, and ruled firmly that no allocations from the state collections would be made available to the countryside for seed, food or fodder. But, in fact, in a very large number of piecemeal Politburo decisions, nearly 2 million tons were issued for these purposes, including 330,000 tons for food (about 194,000 tons of which was for Ukraine).

In spite of the reduction in the collections, and the issue of grain to the countryside, the grain available in Ukraine, the North Caucasus and the Volga regions was not sufficient to prevent the deaths of several million people from famine....

Our study of the famine has led us to very different conclusions from Dr. Conquest's. He holds that Stalin 'wanted a famine,' that 'the Soviets did not want the famine to be coped with successfully,' and that the Ukrainian famine was 'deliberately inflicted for its own sake.' This leads him to the sweeping conclusion: 'The main lesson seems to be that the Communist ideology provided the motivation for an unprecedented massacre of men, women and children.'[1]

We do not at all absolve Stalin from responsibility for the famine. His policies towards the peasants were ruthless and brutal. But the story which has emerged in this book is of a Soviet leadership which was struggling with a famine crisis which had been caused partly by their wrongheaded policies, but was unexpected and undesirable. The background to the famine is not simply that Soviet agricultural policies were derived from Bolshevik ideology, though ideology played its part. They were also shaped by the Russian pre-revolutionary past, the experiences of the civil war, the international situation, the intransigent circumstances of geography and the weather, and the *modus operandi* of the Soviet system as it was established under Stalin. They were formulated by men with little formal education and limited knowledge of agriculture. Above all, they were a consequence of the decision to industrialise this peasant country at breakneck speed.

Andrea Graziosi, "The Soviet 1931–1933 Famines and the Ukrainian Holodomor: Is a New Interpretation Possible, and What Would Its Consequences Be?"

Harvard Ukrainian Studies 27 (2004–5): 97–115. Excerpts.

Andrea Graziosi (b. 1954) is an Italian historian specializing in Soviet, Russian, and Ukrainian history. He is professor of history at the Federico II University of Naples, Italy. He is the author of *The Great Soviet Peasant War: Bolsheviks and Peasants, 1918–1934* (1996), *L'Urss di Lenin e Stalin: Storia dell'Unione sovietica, 1914–1945* (2007), and *L'Urss dal trionfo al degrado: Storia dell'Unione sovietica, 1945–1991* (2008).

Between the end of 1932 and the summer of 1933, famine in the USSR killed, in half the time, approximately seven times as many people as the Great Terror of 1937–38. It was the peak of a series of famines that had started in 1931, and it constituted the turning point of the decade as well as Soviet prewar history's main event. With its approximately five million victims (I am not including the hundreds

1 Conquest (1986), 344. In correspondence Dr. Conquest has stated that it is not his opinion that 'Stalin purposely inflicted the 1933 famine. No. What I argue is that with resulting famine imminent, he could have prevented it, but put "Soviet interest" other than feeding the starving first—thus consciously abetting it' (September 2003).

of thousands, possibly more than a million, who had already died in Kazakhstan and elsewhere since 1931), compared to the one to two million victims of 1921–22 and 1946–47, this also was the most severe famine in Soviet history and an event that left its mark for decades. Its effect was felt in countries inhabited by immigrant communities from the Russian Empire and the USSR, and its importance, political as well as historical, is still strong today. Since 1987–88, the rediscovery and interpretation of the Famine have played a key role in Ukraine in discussions between supporters of the democratization process and those who still adhere to a procommunist ideology. The *Holodomor* (the word coined to mean hunger-related mass extermination, implying intentionality) thus moved to the center of the political and cultural debate, becoming part of the process of state and nation building in Ukraine.

Yet until 1986, when Robert Conquest published his *Harvest of Sorrow*, historians had almost completely ignored this extraordinary event....

That is why Conquest's book, the outcome of the Harvard Ukrainian Research Institute project, has been of crucial importance: it forced a reluctant profession to deal with a fundamental question, and it did so by stressing the connection between famine and the national question, while properly differentiating the Kazakh case. It can thus be maintained that historiography on the famines and the Holodomor starts with Conquest, even though other authors, such as Sergei Maksudov or Zhores Medvedev, were by then seriously dealing with these events. The book's significance is even greater in light of the polemics that it raised. Because their level was much superior to that of previous polemics, they grew into a positive phenomenon, which may be viewed as part of the process through which historians finally became aware of these events' extraordinary human and intellectual dimensions. This process was, and still is, especially painful because it took and is taking place *after* a historical judgment had already been made and a "collective memory" had set in, all *without* the Soviet famines entering the picture. This was both a consequence of the successful Soviet attempt at concealment and a manifestation of one of the European twentieth century's key features—the logic of "taking sides" that dominated the discussion. Therefore, the famines had to, and today still have to, be brought into our representation of the past at the price of a complete restructuring of commonly held beliefs.

Then came the 1991 archival and historiographical revolution. It allowed the accumulation of new knowledge and caused a leap in the quality of polemics, which, with few exceptions, then grew into serious controversies. True scholarly spirit and a firm moral commitment, born of an awareness of the immensity of the tragedy they deal with, animate the two camps in which it is possible to group today's existing positions at the price of some simplification and much schematization. One can thus contemplate these past few years, during which Conquest's conclusions have been integrated and in part surpassed, with a sense of satisfaction and find in them some reason for optimism.

By means of yet more simplification, the positions of these two camps may be summed up in the following way (I am paraphrasing from a letter that a brilliant young Ukrainian scholar recently sent me). On one side there are what we could call "A" people. They support the genocide thesis and see in the Famine an event artificially organized in order to: (a) break the peasants and/or (b) alter (destroy) the Ukrainian nation's social fabric, which obstructed the transformation of the USSR into a despotic empire. On the other side we have "B" people, who, though fully recognizing the criminal nature of Stalin's policies, deem it necessary to study the Famine as a "complex phenomenon," in which many factors, from the geopolitical situation to the modernization effort, played a role in Moscow's intentions and decisions.

I believe that today we have most of the elements needed for a new and more satisfactory interpretive hypothesis, capable of taking into account both the general and complex Soviet picture and the undeniable relevance of the national question. This hypothesis can be put together using the excellent works of Ukrainian, Russian, and Western scholars as building blocks, thus breaking the wall that still partially separates their efforts....

In order to formulate this new interpretation, we need first to define the object of our investigation. As should be clear by now, we are in fact dealing with what it would be more correct to call, on a pan-Soviet level, the *1931–33 famines*, which had, of course, common causes and a common background, but included at least two very different and special phenomena: the Kazakhstan famine-*cum*-epidemics of 1931–33 and the Ukrainian-Kuban (the latter area, though belonging to the Russian republic's province of the Northern Caucasus, being mostly inhabited by Ukrainians) Holodomor of late 1932 to early 1933.

Many past misunderstandings have been caused by the confusion between these two *national* tragedies and the general phenomenon that provided their framework. In a way, it is as if students of Nazism would confuse Nazi repression in general with quite specific and crucial cases, such as the extermination of Soviet prisoners of war, or that of Poles and Gypsies—not to mention the Holocaust, an exceptional phenomenon that cannot be explained simply as an aspect or element of Nazi killings at large, and yet certainly was also a part of them. Both Nazi repression in general and such "specific" tragedies existed, and both must be studied, as in fact they are, in and of themselves as well as in their connections.

A very clear distinction between the general phenomenon and its republic-level or regional manifestations should therefore be introduced in the Soviet case. However, most "A" supporters are in fact speaking specifically of the Holodomor, while many of the "B" proponents think on a pan-Soviet scale. If we analytically distinguish what they are doing, we end up discovering that in many, albeit not all, ways they are correct in their respective domains.

The second step toward a new interpretation consists of yet another analytical distinction. We must separate the 1931–32 "spontaneous" famines—they too, of course, were direct, if undesired, consequences of choices made in 1928–29—from the post–September 1932 Famine, which took on such terrible features not least because of human decision. (Events in Kazakhstan followed an altogether different pattern and I will therefore only make some passing references to them.) Finally, the third step we need to take is to gather and combine useful elements from both "A" and "B" and drop their unsatisfactory parts.

"A" people are right in drawing our attention to the national question. Anyone studying the Soviet Union should be acutely aware of its importance, as Lenin and

Stalin themselves were (after all, the former decided not to call the new state Russia, and the latter, who initially opposed such a choice, never reversed the decision in later years). One should be equally aware of the Ukrainian primacy in this matter. In late 1919 Lenin started the shift towards indigenization (*korenizatsiia*), until that time considered to be a request of "extreme nationalists," because of the Ukrainian Bolsheviks' defeat of 1919, and Stalin gave a new spin to *korenizatsiia* in late 1932 because of the Ukrainian crisis. But in Ukraine, at least up to 1933, the national question *was* the peasant question. This is what both Lenin and Stalin thought, and rightly so. "A" people seem instead to be wrong in thinking that the "Famine" (meaning also the pan-Soviet one) was organized ("planned") to solve the Ukrainian national, or rather peasant, problem.

"B" people give us a detailed reconstruction of the causes and wider context of the Famine on a pan-Soviet scale, with all its complexity, and are thus able to criticize convincingly the simplistic views of the "A" camp. However, they seem unable to fully understand or accommodate the national factor; that is, to "descend" from the pan-Soviet to the republic level. "B" people also do not always seem capable of seeing that Stalin, even when he did not initiate something willfully, was always very quick to take advantage of "spontaneous" events, giving them a completely new turn.... One can thus use good "B" data for the development of the pan-Soviet crisis, stressing however that at this level, too, Stalin at a certain moment decided to *use* hunger to break the peasants' opposition to collectivization. For a number of reasons, such opposition was stronger in non-Russian areas, where events soon started to follow their own course....

What can therefore be said? From 1931 to 1933 scores, perhaps hundreds, of thousands of people died of hunger throughout the USSR. In Kazakhstan, Ukraine, the Northern Caucasus, and the Volga basin (Povolzh'e), however, the situation was completely different. But for Western Siberia, these were the country's most important grain-growing regions, where the post-1927 state-village conflict over the crop was strongest. Since 1918–19, moreover, the war between the regime and peasants and nomads there had been particularly brutal because of the intensifying role of national and religious factors, and in the Volga because of both the Russian peasant movement's strong traditions and the presence of German colonists.

Except in Kazakhstan, the phenomenon's causes were *similar* across these areas: the devastating human toll, as well as the toll on the capacity for production, taken by dekulakization—a de facto nationwide, state-led pogrom against the peasant elite; forced collectivization, which pushed peasants to destroy a large part of their inventories; the kolkhozes' inefficiency and misery; the repeated and extreme requisition waves originated by a crisis-ridden industrialization, an urbanization out of control, and a growing foreign debt that could be repaid only by exporting raw materials; the resistance of peasants, who would not accept the reimposition of what they called a "second serfdom" and worked less and less because of both their rejection of the new system and hunger-related debilitation; and the poor weather conditions in 1932. Famine, which had started to take hold sporadically already in 1931 (when Kazakhs were dying in mass), and had grown into solid pockets by the spring of 1932, thus appears to have been an undesired and unplanned outcome of ideology-inspired policies aimed at eliminating mercantile and private production.

Based on the results of the 1920–21 war communism policy, the Famine should not have been difficult to foresee. Yet if one analyzes the Famine's origins and pre-autumn 1932 developments on a pan-Soviet level, it seems arduous to claim that famine was the conscious goal of those policies, as it is maintained by those who support the hypothesis that famine was willfully implemented to break the peasant resistance or to execute a Moscow- (sometimes meaning Russian-) planned Ukrainian genocide.

However, the intensity, course, and consequence of the phenomenon, which new studies and new documents allow us to analyze, were undeniably and substantially *different* in different regions and republics. Out of the six to seven million victims (demographers now impute to 1930–31 part of the deaths previously imputed to 1932–33), 3.5 to 3.8 million died in Ukraine; 1.3 to 1.5 million in Kazakhstan (where deaths reached their peak in relation to the population size, exterminating 33 to 38 percent of the Kazakhs and 8 to 9 percent of the Europeans); and several hundred thousand in the Northern Caucasus and, on a lesser scale, in the Volga, where the most harshly hit area coincided with the German autonomous republic.

If we consider annual mortality rates per thousand inhabitants in the *countryside*, and make 1926 equal to 100, we see them jump in 1933 to 188.1 in the entire country, 138.2 in the Russian republic (which then still included both Kazakhstan and the Northern Caucasus), and 367.7—that is, *almost triple*—in Ukraine. Here life expectancy at birth dropped from 42.9 years for men and 46.3 for women registered in 1926 to, respectively, 7.3 and 10.9 in 1933 (it would be 13.6 and 36.3 in 1941). Also, in Ukraine there were 782,000 births in 1932 and 470,000 in 1933, compared with an average of 1.153 million per year in the period from 1926 to 1929. The extreme figures for Ukraine are explained by the Famine's different course there, for which different Moscow policies were largely responsible....

In those places where the "peasant question" was complicated—that is, strengthened and thus made more dangerous by the national one (let us remember that Stalin explicitly linked the two questions in his writings on nationalism, and that the Soviet leadership had seen this hypothesis confirmed by the Ukrainian countryside's great social and national revolts of 1919, repeated, albeit on a lesser scale, in early 1930)—the resort to hunger was more ruthless and the lesson much harsher. According to demographic data, in Ukraine, too, mortality depended on residency, urban or rural, and not on nationality, meaning that people living in the countryside suffered independently of their ethnic background. Yet one cannot forget that, as everybody knew, in spite of the previous urbanization-*cum*-Ukrainization, villages remained overwhelmingly Ukrainian, while cities had largely preserved their "alien" (Russian, Jewish, Polish) character. In Ukraine, therefore, the countryside was indeed targeted to break the peasants, but with the full awareness that the village represented the nation's spine....

Famine thus took on forms and dimensions much bigger than it would have if nature had followed its course. It was less intense, in terms of both drought and the area it affected, than the 1921–22 famine (the 1932 crop, though quite low, was still higher than the 1945 crop, when there were no comparable mass hunger-related deaths), yet it caused three to four times as many victims—essentially because of political decisions that aimed at saving the regime from the crisis to which its very policies had led and at assuring the victory of the "great offensive" launched four years previously.

The awareness that in Ukraine and Kuban the peasant question also was a national question determined the need to deal with and "solve" these questions together. In order to make sure that such a "solution" was there to stay, it was complemented by the decision to get rid of the national elites and their policies, which were suspected, as we know, of abetting peasants....

...These measures were accompanied, and followed, by a wave of anti-Ukrainian terror, which already presented some of the traits that were later to characterize the 1937–38 "mass operations." Thus ended the national-communist experiment born of the civil war, with the suicide in 1933 of important leaders such as Mykola Skrypnyk and writers such as Mykola Khvyliovy as well as the repression of thousands of its cadres.

The adoption of the term Holodomor seems therefore legitimate, as well as necessary, to mark a distinction between the pan-Soviet phenomenon of 1931–33 and the Ukrainian Famine *after* the summer of 1932. In spite of their undeniable close relationship, the two are in fact profoundly different. The same applies to the famines' consequences, which also were partially similar yet essentially different. Whereas throughout the USSR the use of hunger broke peasant resistance; guaranteed the victory of a dictator whom people feared in a new way and around whom a new cult, based on fear, started to develop; opened the door to the 1937–38 terror; marked a qualitative change in the lie that had accompanied the Soviet regime since its inception; allowed, by means of the subjugation of the most important republic, the de facto transformation of the Soviet federal state into a despotic empire; and left a dreadful legacy of grief in a multitude of families that were prevented from dealing with it (Gorbachev too lost three paternal uncles then) because of the Famine taboo and the dogma about life having become "more joyous"—in Ukraine and in Kazakhstan famine dug even deeper....

The number of victims makes the Soviet 1931–33 famines into a set of phenomena that in the framework of European history can be compared only to later Nazi crimes. The course of events in Ukraine and the Northern Caucasus, and the link this course had to both Stalin's interpretation of the crisis and the policies that originated from this interpretation, reintroduce, in a new way, the question of its nature. *Was there also* a Ukrainian genocide?

The answer seems to be *no* if one thinks of a famine conceived by the regime, or—this being even more untenable—by Russia, to destroy the Ukrainian people. It is equally *no* if one adopts a restrictive definition of genocide as the planned will to exterminate *all* the members of a religious or ethnic group, in which case only the Holocaust would qualify.

In 1948, however, even the rather strict UN definition of genocide listed among possible genocidal acts, side by side with "killing members of the group, and causing serious bodily or mental harm to members of the group," *"deliberately inflicting on members of the group conditions of life calculated to bring about its physical destruction in whole or in part"* (emphasis mine). Not long before, Raphael Lemkin, the inventor of the term, had noted that, "generally speaking, genocide does not necessarily mean the immediate destruction of a nation.... It is intended rather to signify a coordinated plan of different actions aiming at the destruction of essential foundations of the life of national groups."

Based on Lemkin's definition—if one thinks of the substantial difference in mortality rates in different republics; adds to the millions of Ukrainian victims, including the ones from Kuban, the millions of Ukrainians forcibly Russified after December 1932, as well as the scores of thousands of peasants who met a similar fate after evading the police roadblocks and taking refuge in the Russian republic; keeps in mind that one is therefore dealing with the loss of approximately 20 to 30 percent of the Ukrainian ethnic population; remembers that such a loss was caused by the decision, unquestionably a subjective act, to use the Famine in an anti-Ukrainian sense on the basis of the "national interpretation" Stalin developed in the second half of 1932; reckons that without such a decision the death count would have been at the most in the hundreds of thousands (that is, less than in 1921–22); and finally, if one adds to all of the above the destruction of a large part of the republic's Ukrainian political and cultural elite, from village teachers to national leaders—I believe that the answer to our question, "Was the Holodomor a genocide?" cannot but be positive.

Between the end of 1932 and the summer of 1933:

1. Stalin and the regime he controlled and coerced (but certainly not Russia or the Russians, who suffered from famine too, even though on a lesser scale) consciously executed, as part of a drive directed at breaking the peasantry, an anti-Ukrainian policy aimed at mass extermination and causing a genocide in the above-mentioned interpretation of the term, a genocide whose physical and psychological scars are still visible today.
2. This genocide was the product of a famine that was not willfully caused with such aim in mind, but was willfully maneuvered towards this end once it came about as the unanticipated result of the regime policies (it seems that the even more terrible Kazakh tragedy was "only" the undesired, if foreseeable, outcome of denomadization and colonial indifference towards the natives' fate).
3. It took place within a context that saw Stalin punishing with hunger, and applying terror to, a number of national and ethnosocial groups he felt to be actually or potentially dangerous. As all the quantitative data indicate, however, the scale of both punishment and terror reached extreme dimensions in Ukraine for the reasons I listed, thus growing into a qualitatively different phenomenon.
4. From this perspective, the relationship between the Holodomor and the other tragic punishments by repression of 1932–33 do in a way recall the already-mentioned relationship between Nazi repressions and the Holocaust. The Holodomor, however, was much different from the Holocaust. It did not aim at exterminating the *whole* nation, it did not kill people *directly*, and it was motivated and constructed theoretically and *politically*—might one say "rationally"?—rather than ethnically or racially. This different motivation at least partially accounts for the first two differences.
5. From this perspective, the Holocaust is exceptional because it represents the purest, and therefore qualitatively different, genocide imaginable. It thus belongs in another category. Yet at the same time it represents the apex of a

multilayered pyramid, whose steps are represented by other tragedies, and to whose top the Holodomor is close.

Stanislav Kulchytsky, "Why Did Stalin Exterminate the Ukrainians? Comprehending the Holodomor. The Position of Soviet Historians"

The Day Weekly Digest (Kyiv), nos. 35 and 37, 8 and 22 November 2005. http://www.day.kiev.ua/152116; http://www.day.kiev.ua/153028/.

Stanislav Kulchytsky (b. 1937) is a Ukrainian historian and economist specializing in twentieth-century Ukraine. He is professor of history and deputy director of the Institute of Ukrainian History at the National Academy of Sciences of Ukraine (Kyiv). He is the author, in Ukrainian and Russian, of 62 books and coauthor, in Ukrainian, of *Stalinism in Ukraine, 1920s–1930s* (1991).

...I spent 11 years working at the Institute of Economics of the Academy of Sciences of the Ukrainian SSR, where I studied the history of the nation's economy, moving from one time period to the next. I then transferred to the Institute of History to prepare a doctoral thesis within the framework of the so-called interwar period: from 1921 to 1941. When I received my doctorate and was appointed to chair the Department of Interwar History, my scholarly specialty and position required me to study the 1933 famine once it became a widely discussed topic.

Other people in the department were studying the history of the peasants before and after collectivization, while I specialized in the problems of industrialization and the history of the working class. Like everybody else, I knew about the famine. Moreover, I had access to demographic data that was locked away in special repositories and knew that the Ukrainian countryside had lost millions of people, and that this loss could not be attributed to urbanization. But I could not understand the causes of the famine. Even in my worst nightmare I could not imagine that the Soviet government was capable of exterminating not only enemies of the people (at the time I never questioned the legitimacy of this notion), but also children and pregnant women....

Before the worldview transformation caused by my study of the Holodomor, I was a *Soviet* scholar like everyone else. That is, I looked at history from the class point of view, viewed capitalism and socialism as socioeconomic formations, considered uncollectivized peasants to be representatives of the petty bourgeoisie, believed that collective ownership of production facilities was a viable option and that collective farms were the peasants' collective property.

I considered it a normal thing that there were special repositories in libraries and archives, i.e., I accepted the division of information into classified and public. But for this very reason I could not understand why the 1933 famine was a forbidden topic. Since there was no one in Ukraine who didn't know about it, why did this information have to be classified? An older colleague, who also chaired a department at the Institute of History of the Academy of Sciences of the Ukrainian SSR, confided in me that in his village everybody knew who had eaten whom. They spent the rest of their lives with this knowledge.

When some important individuals on the staff of the CPU's Central Committee, whom I knew well, got word of a US congressional commission on the Ukrainian famine, they went into a state of continuing stress. The Feb. 11, 1983, report by the Central Committee's secretary in charge of ideology and the Ukrainian KGB chief contained a recommendation addressed to our specialists abroad: Do not enter into polemics on the famine. It was clear that this polemic would be a losing proposition under any circumstances. At the time, however, they could no longer bury their heads in the sand.

In the fall of 1986 the CC CPU formed a so-called "anti-commission." I found myself among its members. We scholars were expected to produce studies that would "expose the falsifications of Ukrainian bourgeois nationalists."

I had worked in special repositories before but received clearance to access "special files" of CPU committees only once I began working as a member of the commission. Soviet archives had one special characteristic: a researcher could have access to 99.9 percent of all files, yet all crucial information relating to the history of this totalitarian state was contained in the 0.01 percent of inaccessible files.

After six months of working in the archives, I learned about the agricultural situation in the early 1930s. After this, some causes, which I had taken for granted since my school years, changed places with consequences. The new cause-and-effect relationships often coincided with what I got to read in the so-called "anti-Soviet" literature.

While I was working in the archives, the commission's work was proving fruitless. Perhaps those upstairs realized that the scholars had been given an unrealistic assignment. I sent an analytical report under my own name to the Central Committee with a proposal that the famine be officially recognized.

Now I understand that I was demanding something impossible from the Central Committee.... How could they possibly admit that Stalin had succeeded in using the system of government, which everybody called "people's rule," to exterminate the people, i.e., to commit genocide? In exposing famine, the rhetoric about Stalinist vices would not hide the organic flaws of the Soviet government behind the great chieftain's broad back.

I remember writing that report at a time when I still had not given up many stereotypes of the official concept of history. Now I understand that this helped me formulate my arguments in such a way that my report would not appear too explosive to those in a position to make the political decision to recognize the famine.

I think this report was only about recognizing the fact that famine had really occurred. While I, an expert on the history of the interwar period, still could not interpret this mysterious famine as genocide in 1987, our chiefs in the Party committees were even farther from such an interpretation. Granted, we knew that books had been published in the West in which the victims of the 1933 famine said that the government had intended to destroy them. But such stories were always rejected in the USSR as anti-Soviet propaganda.

While rereading the text about the ability or inability of our government officials of the time to recognize the fact of the famine, I caught myself in a contradiction: while I state that I was demanding the impossible of the members of the Central Committee, I am insisting that they could not identify the famine with genocide....

I think, however, that even people who are not expert historians but have enough life experience can recall exactly what they thought about the 1933 famine a decade and a half ago, and how their views have changed now that thousands of horrifying documents have been published.

Those who were in power in the late 1980s had access to such documents even in those days. I dare say, however, that they could not evaluate them properly because they were not Stalin's contemporaries and did not contribute to his crimes. Like me, they were products of the Soviet school....

Thus, I am certain that none of the CPU leaders realized the true essence of the events of 1933, but they all knew that something horrible and monstrous had happened. On the other hand, they felt that the Stalinist taboo on the word famine could no longer continue.

For several months my report wandered from office to office at the Central Committee. Finally, they allowed me to submit it as a scholarly article to *Ukraïns'kyi istorychnyi zhurnal* [Ukrainian Historical Journal], but only once a political decision to recognize the famine as a historical fact was publicized. That event was scheduled for Dec. 25, 1987, when Volodymyr Shcherbytsky, the first secretary of the CC CPU, was slated to deliver his report on the 70th anniversary of the Ukrainian SSR.

In the meantime, the liberalization of the political regime, which started with Gorbachev's announcement of his policy of perestroika, was becoming more and more pronounced. The conspiracy of silence surrounding the famine began to disintegrate by itself. On July 16, 1987, the newspaper *Literaturna Ukraïna* [Literary Ukraine] carried two articles that mentioned the famine matter-of-factly as a well-known fact. Discussions of the famine began in Moscow. On Oct. 11, 1987, the famous scholar Viktor Danilov of the Institute of Soviet History at the Academy of Sciences of the USSR, who had already experienced much unpleasantness within the Party organs for his "distorted" portrayal of Soviet agrarian history, published a statement in the newspaper *Sovetskaia Rossiia* [Soviet Russia], stating that famine had claimed a huge number of lives in the winter and spring of 1933. In his short article entitled "How Many of Us Were There Then?" published in the December issue of the magazine *Ogonek*, the Moscow-based demographer Mark Tolts blew the lid off the suppressed union-wide census of 1937, revealing that its organizers had been repressed for malicious underestimation of the population. Tolts pointed to the 1933 famine as the cause of this "underestimation."

On Nov. 2, 1987, CPSU Secretary General Mikhail Gorbachev delivered a report in the Kremlin pegged to the 70th anniversary of the October Revolution. Aleksandr Yakovlev recalled that the conservatives and liberals on Gorbachev's team prepared several versions of the same report. A conservative version of this assessment of the country's historical path got the upper hand, and Gorbachev did not mention the famine.

Volodymyr Shcherbytsky could not follow his Moscow patron's example because what had raged in Ukraine was not merely famine but manmade famine, or the Holodomor. Moreover, the US congressional commission was about to announce the preliminary results of its investigation. For this reason Shcherbytsky's anniversary report contained six or seven lines about the famine, which was allegedly caused by drought. For the first time in 55 years a CPSU Politburo member broke the Stalinist taboo on the word "famine." This created an opportunity for historians to study and publish documents on the Holodomor.

My article, "Concerning the Evaluation of the Situation in Agriculture of the Ukrainian SSR in 1931–33," was published in the March 1988 issue of *Ukraïns'kyi istorychnyi zhurnal*. Its abridged version had already been published in January 1988 in two Soviet newspapers for Ukrainian emigrants: the Ukrainian-language *Visti z Ukraïny* and the English-language *News from Ukraine*. In May 1988 the Foreign Ministry of the Ukrainian SSR received the materials of the US congressional commission via the Soviet Embassy in the US and passed them on to the Institute of History of the Academy of Sciences of the Ukrainian SSR. The English-language version of my article was almost entirely quoted and analyzed. James Mace concluded, "The scale of the famine is minimized, the Communist Party is depicted as doing its utmost to improve the situation, while the actions of the Communist Party and the Soviet state, which exacerbated the famine, have been ignored."

This is an objective conclusion, for I had deliberately excluded materials that had already been discovered in Party archives from this article, which in fact was my report to the CC CPU. I could not afford to make things difficult for Shcherbytsky to render a decision that was coming to a head under the conditions of increasing glasnost and which was necessary in the face of the investigation being pursued by the US Congress.

Meanwhile, Ukrainian writers were bringing the subject of the famine to the forefront of civic and political life. On Feb. 18, 1988, *Literaturna Ukraïna* published Oleksa Musiienko's report to a meeting of the Kyiv branch of the Writers' Union of Ukraine. Welcoming the new CPSU leadership's policy of de-Stalinization, Musiienko accused Stalin of orchestrating a brutal grain procurement campaign in the republic, which resulted in the Holodomor of 1933. The word "Holodomor" used in this report was coined by the writer Ivan Drach.

In early July 1988 the writer Borys Oliinyk addressed the 19th CPSU conference in Moscow. Focusing on the Stalinist terror of 1937, he surprised those present with his conclusion: "Because repressions in our republic started long before 1937, we must also determine the causes of the 1933 famine, which killed millions of Ukrainians; we must list the names of those who are to blame for this tragedy."

In a November 1988 interview with the Moscow weekly *Sobesednik* [Interlocutor], the writer Yurii Shcherbak, the founder of the Green movement in Ukraine, devoted much attention to the problem of the famine. He was convinced that the 1933 famine was the same kind of method for terrorizing peasants who opposed collective farm slavery as dekulakization. At the same time, he was the first to speculate that Stalin's policy of repressions in Ukraine was also aimed at forestalling the danger of a large-scale national liberation movement. The peasantry, he said, was always the bearer of national traditions, which is why the 1933 famine was a blow aimed against the peasants. In the summer of 1993 James Mace published his analytical article "How Ukraine Was Permitted to Remember" in the American journal *The Ukrainian Quarterly*. In describing the process of how the Holodomor was understood, I have followed this article to some extent and in separate instances, while making independent evaluations. I cannot agree with one of his statements.

In July 1988 the Writers' Union of Ukraine instructed Volodymyr Maniak to prepare a memorial book comprised of testimonies of Holodomor survivors. Mace wrote that Maniak was not allowed to address the famine eyewitnesses in the press; this mission was entrusted to me. In December 1988 I appealed to the readers of *Sil's'ki visti* [Village News] and published a questionnaire.

In fact, neither Maniak nor I were instructed to prepare a memorial book. This problem did not concern the republican leadership. The initiative was Maniak's. After enlisting the support of the Writers' Union, he came to the Institute of History at the Academy of Sciences of the Ukrainian SSR with a proposal to join forces. At the time we were actively searching for documents relating to the famine, which had been amassed in the archives of Soviet government agencies. We collected so many sensational materials that we processed them in parallel form: memoirs *and* documents. We could not immediately publish the manuscripts we had prepared. Radians'kyi Pys'mennyk [Soviet Writer] published the colossal book of recollections, *Famine '33: The People's Memorial Book* compiled by Maniak and his wife, Lidiia Kovalenko, only in 1991. In 1992 and 1993 Naukova Dumka [Scholarly Thought] published a collection of documents from the Central State Archive of the Highest Organs of Government and Administration of Ukraine, compiled by Hanna Mykhailychenko and Yevheniia Shatalina.

In the meantime, the substance and even the words from my article that appeared in *Ukraïns'kyi istorychnyi zhurnal* became the target of harsh criticism in the press immediately after its publication in March 1988. Only one year after its publication society was viewing the fundamental questions concerning Soviet reality in a completely different way.

In 1988 I wrote a brochure for the Znannia [Knowledge] Society of the Ukrainian SSR. While the brochure was being prepared for publication, I obtained permission from the society to publish it in *Literaturna Ukraïna*. At the time this newspaper was most popular among radical intellectual circles and in the diaspora. The text, published in four issues of the newspaper between January and February 1989, was the product of 18 months of archival work. Complete with photographic evidence, the story of Viacheslav Molotov's extraordinary grain procurement commission shocked the public.

In June 1989 Znannia published 62,000 copies of my brochure entitled *1933: The Tragedy of the Famine*. Surprisingly, it was published as part of a series entitled *Theory and Practice of the CPSU*. The art editor designed an original cover depicting a cobweb with the brochure's title centered in red and white lettering. As I reread it now, I can see that it is an accurate portrayal of the socioeconomic consequences of forced collectivization of agriculture, the major one being famine in many areas of the USSR. However, at the time I still did not understand the specifics of the Ukrainian famine. In particular, the brochure listed all the clauses of the Nov. 18 decree of the Central Committee of the Communist Party (Bolshevik) of Ukraine and the Nov. 20 decree of the Council of People's Commissars of the Ukrainian SSR, both of which were approved as dictated by Molotov. These decrees were the spark plug of the Holodomor. The brochure also cited the most disturbing clause, calling for the imposition of penalties in kind (meat, potatoes, and other foodstuffs). However, at the time I still had no facts about the consequences that stemmed from that clause. For this reason the Ukrainian famine was considered the result of a mistaken economic policy, not a deliberate campaign to seize food under the guise of grain procurements....

A detailed analysis of my own brochure was necessary to provide background to the story about the major accomplishment of the Soviet period, which was being quickly consigned to the past. I am speaking about the book *The Famine of 1932–1933 in Ukraine: Through the Eyes of Historians and the Language of Documents*. The book was published in September 1990 by Politvydav Ukraïny [Political Publishers of Ukraine] as an imprint of the Institute of Party History at the CC CPU. It contained four articles, including one of mine, but I will discuss the documents from the archival funds of the Central Committee of the All-Union Communist (Bolshevik) Party and the CP(B)U. The documentary section was compiled by Ruslan Pyrih, head of the team of compilers that included A. Kentii, I. Komarova, V. Lozytsky, and A. Soloviova. The official pressrun was 25,000, but the real number of published copies was ten times smaller. When it became clear that the book would be published, somebody decided to turn it into a bibliographic rarity.

I saw the documents discovered in the Party archives of Moscow and Kyiv by Pyrih's team one year before their publication. Some of them are reason enough to accuse Stalin of committing the crime of genocide....

A battle over this manuscript broke out at the highest political level in the republic—in the Politburo of the CC CPU. The Politburo meeting in January 1990, to which I was invited as an expert, took a long time to discuss the expediency of publishing this book. I got the impression that those present heaved a sigh of relief when Volodymyr Ivashko, the first secretary of the CC, assumed responsibility and proposed publishing the documents.

Why did the Politburo decide to publish such explosive documents? There are at least two reasons. First, in 1988–89 the originally bureaucratic perestroika was already evolving into a popular movement. Constitutional reform had divested the ruling Party of its power over society. In order to remain on top of the revolutionary wave, Party leaders had to distance themselves from Stalin's heritage. Second, the US congressional commission had already completed its work and published a conclusive report that contained many impressive details. The Politburo members were familiar with the specific results of the work carried out by Mace's commission. I am so sure of this because I have this particular volume, 524 pages, published in Washington in 1988, in my own library. The book's cover bears the red stamp of the CC CPU's general department, identifying the date of receipt as Sept. 5, 1988. I obtained the book during the transfer of Central Committee documents to the state archive after the Party was banned (as material foreign to the compiler of the funds).

The above-mentioned Politburo meeting of Jan. 26, 1990, approved a resolution "On the 1932–1933 Famine in Ukraine and the Publication of Archival Materials Relating to It." The Politburo identified the immediate cause of the famine as the grain procurement policy that was fatal to the peasants. Yet this statement did not correspond to the truth, much like Shcherbytsky's statement about the drought.

Mace came to Ukraine for the first time in January 1990. He brought me a computer printout of the famine survivors' testimonies recorded by the US congressional commission. The three volumes of testimonies on 1,734 pages were published in Washington only in December 1990. In the first two weeks of that month the journal *Pid praporom leninizmu* [Under the Banner of Leninism] published my article "How It Happened (Reading the Documents of the US Congressional Commission on the 1932–33 Ukraine Famine"). My own experience of analyzing archival documents and the testimonies recorded by the American researchers enabled me to reach the following conclusion: "Alongside grain procurements and under their guise, a repressive expropriation of all food stocks, i.e., terror by famine was organized." Now the conclusion about genocide was no longer based solely on the emotional testimony of Holodomor eyewitnesses but on an analysis of archival documents.

March 1991 saw the publication of my summary volume *Tsina velykoho perelomu* [The Price of the Great Turning Point]. The final conclusion was formulated in no uncertain terms: "Famine and genocide in the countryside were preprogrammed" (p. 302)....

Reviewing the book a decade and a half later, I have reconsidered its merits and shortcomings. Its merit lay in the detailed analysis of the Kremlin's socioeconomic policy that resulted in an economic crisis capable of disrupting the political equilibrium. This explained why Stalin unleashed terror by famine against Ukraine in one particular period—a time when the economic crisis was at its peak. The monograph's shortcoming was the lack of an analysis of the Kremlin's nationality policy. Without such an analysis the conclusion of genocide was suspended in midair.

In those distant years Mace and I often engaged in sharp polemics. However, these polemics were disinterested, i.e., they concerned problems, not specific persons. I criticized him for his inadequate attention to the Kremlin's socioeconomic policy, and he criticized me for my inattention to its nationality policy. Time has shown that establishing that the Holodomor was an act of genocide requires an equal amount of attention to both the socioeconomic and nationality policies.

However, Mace had an advantage in this polemic. He did not have to change his worldview the way I had to change mine, one that was inculcated in me by my school, university, and my entire life in Soviet society, and to do so posthaste in the face of irrefutable facts. He saw in me an official historian, which in fact I was. However, in the above-mentioned article, "How Ukraine Was Permitted to Remember," Mace concluded the chapter on the evolution of my worldview with these words: "He approached the development of the topic [of the famine] as a Soviet historian whose works were as political as they were scholarly. When the possibilities for studying archives expanded, he stopped being a Soviet historian and became simply a historian."....

Discussions with Russian Scholars

The attitude of the Russian public and government to the events of 1932–33 is another important issue. Even if we substantiate with facts that the 1932–33 famine in Ukraine was an act of genocide, we will have to face a different interpretation of our common past at the international level....

For many years I have been conferring with a small community of scholars in Russia and the West who are studying the Ukrainian Holodomor, and I know their way of thinking. For this reason I have to offer a thought-out and clear position on the subject of genocide....

These discussions were touched off by the May 1993 informational and analytical conference organized by the Ukrainian Embassy in Moscow, which was entitled "The Holodomor of 1932–33: Tragedy and Warning." Both sides were represented by scholars, politicians, and journalists. We spoke about terror by famine, which the Kremlin used against Ukraine, while they claimed that the Stalinist repressions had no national component. Only Sergei Kovalev, a former dissident who in 1993 chaired the Human Rights Commission in the Russian parliament, summoned the courage to say "Forgive us!" while addressing the Ukrainian side.

Then a Moscow newspaper carried an article by the journalist Leonid Kapeliushny, who wrote it after reading the book by Volodymyr Maniak and Lidiia Kovalenko, *33: Holod: narodna knyha-memorial* [Famine '33: The People's Memorial Book]. In the book the journalist saw "eyewitness testimonies that have legal force, testimonies of genocide witnesses."

Kovalev's "Forgive us" and Kapeliushny's conclusion were reinforced by papers presented at the international scholarly conference "The Holodomor of 1932–33 in Ukraine: Causes and Consequences," which took place in Kyiv on Sept. 9–10, 1993 and was attended by the president of Ukraine. While President Kravchuk blamed the tragedy of the Ukrainian nation on the Stalinist government, Ivan Drach, who took the floor after him, placed this problem in a different dimension. "It is time to fully understand once and for all that this was only one of the closest to us—surviving and now living Ukrainians—stages in the planned eradication of the Ukrainian nation. Intolerance of this nation is deeply rooted in the descendants of the northern tribes, to whom our people gave its own faith, culture, civilization, and even its name," Drach said.

The Russian experts on the problems of collectivization and famine—Ilia Zelenin, Nikolai Ivnitsky, Viktor Kondrashin, and Yevgenii Oskolkov—wrote a collective letter to the editors of a historical journal of the Russian Academy of Sciences, expressing their concern over the fact that most conference participants insisted on "a certain exceptionality of Ukraine, a special nature and substance of these events in the republic as opposed to other republics and regions in the country." They claimed that the famine in Ukraine was no different from famines in other regions, whereas the anti-peasant policy of the Stalinist leadership had no clearly defined national direction.

In an attempt to substantiate their position, the Russian colleagues emphasized the socioeconomic aspects of the 1932–33 famine, quoting my paper presented at that conference. Without a doubt, the Kremlin's economic policy did not distinguish among the national republican borders, and in this respect their arguments were flawless. However, the rejection of the Ukrainian specifics of the famine led the Russian colleagues, whether they wanted to or not, to state that the Kremlin had no nationality policy or repressive element of such a policy....

In recent years the Institute of Ukrainian History has established cooperation with the Institute of General History of the Russian Academy of Sciences, and through it with experts at other Russian institutions as part of the Russian-Ukrainian Commission of Historians (co-chaired by the Ukrainian academician Valerii Smolii and the Russian academician Aleksandr Chubarian). On March 29, 2004, Moscow hosted the commission's meeting, attended by numerous prominent Russian experts on agrarian history. They discussed the book *Holod 1932–1933 rokiv v Ukraïni: prychyny ta naslidky* [The Famine of 1932–33 in Ukraine: Causes and Consequences], published in 2003 by the Institute of Ukrainian History to coincide with the 70th anniversary of the Holodomor. Thirty authors collaborated on this large-format volume of 888 pages supplemented with a 48–page section of illustrations.

Several copies of the book were sent to Moscow long before the commission's meeting. Yet it failed to convince the Russian historians. Soon after that meeting Viktor Danilov and Ilia Zelenin publicized their views of the problem discussed in an article that appeared in *Otechestvennaia istoriia* (History of the Fatherland, no. 5, 2004). The gist of their position is reflected in the title of their article: "Organized Famine. Dedicated to the 70th Anniversary of the Peasants' Common Tragedy."...

Summing up the results of our meeting on March 29, 2004, Danilov and Zelenin came to the following conclusion: "If one is to characterize the Holodomor of 1932–33 as 'a purposeful genocide of Ukrainian peasants,' as individual historians from Ukraine insist, then we must bear in mind that it was in equal measure a genocide of Russian peasants." The Ukrainian side can accept such a conclusion. After all, we are not saying that only Ukrainians were Stalin's victims....

In Ukrainian society only marginal right-leaning politicians insist that present-day Russia is responsible for the Ukrainian Holodomor and demand moral or even financial compensation. However, the fact that Russia has been recognized as the legal successor of the USSR does not burden it with responsibility for the crimes of the Bolsheviks, White Guards, or any other regimes that controlled Russian territory in the past. Even the attempts of the Kremlin leadership to associate itself with certain attributes of the former Soviet Union, as evidenced by the melody of Russia's state anthem, are not reason enough to put forward such claims. After all, nostalgia for the Soviet past is equally present in Ukrainian and Russian societies, mainly in the older generations.

Russia is freely publishing documentary collections that reflect the state crimes of the Stalinist period. In fact, it has become possible to build the concept of the Ukrainian Holodomor as an act of genocide only on the basis of documents publicized in Moscow. At the same time, Russia's attempts to inherit the achievements of the Soviet epoch, especially the victory in World War II, are forcing Russian officials to throw a veil over Stalin's crimes as much as this can be done in the new conditions of freedom from dictatorship. This applies particularly to the crime of genocide, even though the Dec. 9, 1948 Convention does not place responsibility on the legal successors of criminal regimes.

Naturally, if Russia wants to inherit the accomplishments of the Soviet epoch, it must also inherit its negative aspects, i.e., the obligation to utter Kovalev's "Forgive us." The European Parliament hinted at this "liability" in 2004, when it found the deportation of the Chechens to be an act of genocide. However, few would like to inherit moral responsibility for the crimes of previous regimes, unless absolutely necessary.

This is why Russia is a decisive opponent of recognizing the Ukrainian Holodomor as an act of genocide. In August 2003 Russian Ambassador to Ukraine Viktor

Chernomyrdin said in an interview with BBC's Ukrainian Service: "The Holodomor affected the entire Soviet state. There were no fewer tragedies and no less pain in the Kuban, Ural, and Volga regions, and Kazakhstan. Such expropriations did not happen only in Chukotka and the northern regions because there was nothing to expropriate." Russia's official representatives at the UN did everything possible to have the definition of the Holodomor as an act of genocide excluded from the Joint Statement of 36 nations on the 70th anniversary of the Ukrainian Holodomor....

Yurii Shapoval, "Understanding the Causes and Consequences of the Famine-Genocide of 1932–1933 in Ukraine: The Significance of Newly Discovered Archival Documents"

Originally published in *Famine in Ukraine, 1932–1933: Genocide by Other Means*, ed. Taras Hunczak and Roman Serbyn (New York: Shevchenko Scientific Society, USA, 2007), pp. 84–97; revised text online at http://faminegenocide.com/print/resources/shapoval.htm. Excerpts.

Yurii Shapoval (b. 1953) is a Ukrainian historian specializing in twentieth-century Ukrainian history. He is director of the Center for Historical Political Studies at the National Academy of Sciences of Ukraine (Kyiv). He is the editor of *The Famine-Genocide of 1932–1933 in Ukraine* (2005) and coeditor of *Commanders of the Great Famine* (2001, in Ukrainian). He is the author, in Ukrainian, of *The CHEKA-GPU-NKVD in Ukraine: People, Facts, Documents* (1997) and *Ukraine in the Twentieth Century: People and Events in Difficult Times* (2001).

...Newly discovered archival documents provide grounds for the following conclusion: it was the meticulous organization of the execution of Ukrainian peasants that invested the Holodomor, i.e., forced starvation, in Ukraine with the character of a genocide....

Thanks to recently uncovered archival documents, scholars are now able to picture in a more systematic fashion, without simplification or onesidedness, the exact methods that were used to strike a "decisive blow" against Ukrainian villages.

Fines in kind. These penalties were introduced by a resolution "On Measures for Intensifying Grain Procurements," passed by the Central Committee of the Communist Party (Bolshevik) of Ukraine on 18 November 1932. In particular, the resolution authorized the levy of fines in kind from independent homesteads not fulfilling the grain delivery plan: these took the form of a fifteen-month quota of meat deliveries and a yearly quota of potatoes, on top of grain deliveries.

On 20 November 1932 the Council of People's Commissars of the Ukrainian SSR approved a decision to introduce fines in kind for collective farms that "had allowed the theft of collective farm grain and were maliciously wrecking the grain procurement plan." These fines in kind appeared to be "additional tasks" requiring a fifteen-month quota of meat deliveries that a given collective farm was to supply in the form of both collectivized cattle and cattle belonging to collective farm members. In other words, the principle of both individual and collective responsibility was being introduced here. As one Ukrainian researcher has precisely noted, "In Soviet Communist Party resolutions on fines in kind, only meat, fatback, and potatoes are mentioned." They made no mention of long-storage products. Yet within two months after the publication of the 18 November resolution "malicious debtors" were issued fines in kind in full. Holodomor survivors have confirmed this. With the exception of 1,500 farms, all the collective farms in Ukraine were branded as "malicious debtors."

Ban on trading food. On 1 December 1932 the Council of People's Commissars of the Ukrainian SSR banned the trade in potatoes in raions that were maliciously refusing to fulfill their contract duties and the inspection of current stores of potatoes on collective farms. Twelve raions in the Chernihiv region and four raions each in Kyiv and Kharkiv oblasts were listed. On 3 December trading in meat and animals was banned in a number of raions in Ukraine. In keeping with a resolution of the Central Committee of the Communist Party (Bolshevik) of Ukraine and the Council of People's Commissars of the Ukrainian SSR of 6 December 1932, these villages began to be entered on so-called "blacklists."

Stoppage of deliveries of manufactured goods. As early as 30 October 1932 Molotov wrote in a telegram to Stalin: "We are using manufactured goods as an incentive, and the deprivation of a portion of manufactured goods as repression of collective farms, particularly independent homesteads." Sources confirm that no detail was too small for Stalin's premier. For example, on 20 November 1932 Molotov sent a telegram to Stanislav Kosior from Henychesk: "Until now the order concerning the sale of matches, salt, and kerosene has been in effect in all raions. There is a telegram about this from Bliakher, dated 9 November. It is necessary to rescind it immediately and make sure that this is carried out."

On 15 December 1932 the Central Committee of the Communist Party (Bolshevik) of Ukraine confirmed a list of eighty-two raions where deliveries of manufactured goods had been suspended because these raions had not carried out the grain procurement plan.

Ban forbidding peasants to flee the famine. In the fall of 1932 and the winter of 1933 a food blockade was set up on the borders of Ukraine, which was enforced by Interior troops and the militia. The blockade prevented peasants from leaving the Ukrainian SSR, thereby dooming them to death by starvation. At the same time there was a ban on food "reverses," i.e., private individuals were forbidden to bring food from Russia into Ukraine without the state's permission.

On 22 January 1933 Stalin and Molotov sent a directive to Party and Soviet organs, which emphasized that the migration processes that had begun among the peasantry as a result of the famine were being organized by "enemies of the Soviet government, S[ocialist] R[evolutionarie]s, and agents of Poland with the goal of conducting agitation against the collective farms and generally against the Soviet government 'through the agency of the peasants' in the northern raions of the USSR."

In this connection governmental and GPU organs of the Ukrainian SSR and the Northern Caucasus were ordered to prevent mass departures of peasants to other raions. Appropriate instructions were issued to the transport departments of the OGPU USSR.

One detail is striking: the famine did not affect any Russian oblasts bordering Ukraine. This is why starving Ukrainian peasants—those who were able to cross the designated borders—traveled there to barter and buy bread.

Introduction of the passport system. On 15 November 1932 the Politburo of the Central Committee of the All-Union Communist Party (Bolshevik) approved a decision "On the Passport System and Relieving Cities of Superfluous Elements," which noted that with the goal of "relieving Moscow and Leningrad and other large urban centers of the USSR of superfluous elements not connected to manufacturing and institutions, as well as of kulak, criminal, and other anti-civic elements that are hiding in the cities," it was essential to introduce a single passport system throughout the USSR with the concomitant elimination of all other types of identification.

On 27 December 1932 the Central Executive Committee and the Council of People's Commissars of the USSR approved a joint resolution "On the Creation of a Single Passport System throughout the USSR and the Obligatory Registration of Passports." A few days later, on 31 December, the All-Ukrainian Central Executive Committee and the Council of People's Commissars of the Ukrainian SSR passed a congruent resolution.

On 28 April 1933 the Council of People's Commissars of the USSR passed a resolution on the issuing of passports to Soviet citizens residing everywhere on the territory of the USSR. The resolution declared, "citizens who reside permanently in rural areas do not obtain passports." Registration of the population in these areas was carried out according to settlement lists of villages and village councils controlled by raion administrations of the militia. In this manner the Soviet regime in fact "bound" the peasants to this or that territory, transforming them into neo-serfs.

Purchase of valuables from peasants. The All-Ukrainian Bureau TORGSIN, i.e., the All-Union Association for Trade with Foreigners, was created on 29 June 1932. The system of TORGSIN stores was in operation earlier. Besides foreigners, it catered to citizens of the USSR: for hard currency, they could purchase food products and other items. Gradually the objective of the TORGSIN system was made more exact: these stores were relied on to extract gold and valuables from the population, and the network of stores was expanded accordingly. By October 1933 in the Ukrainian SSR there were 263 such stores consisting of a system of shops, receiving points, and branches.

In 1931, the TORGSIN system generated 6 million currency *karbovantsi* (rubles) for the Soviet treasury; in 1932, nearly 50 million, and in 1933—107 million. Peasants would bring to the TORGSIN stores the crosses they wore around their necks, rings, earrings, family valuables, etc. In one working day some receiving points purchased up to 800 kilograms of gold, which they would accept according to a single standard and then record a different standard in the registry books.

Eighty-six out of the above-mentioned 107 million *karbovantsi* collected in 1933 represented internal revenue. In addition, the TORGSIN stores were a type of "litmus test" for the GPU: if peasants brought in gold coins, they were immediately detained. The Chekists also demanded lists of "gold suppliers" with their addresses and surnames. Directors of TORGSIN stores were obliged to remit currency valuables to the fund for industrialization.

Actions of the communist special service in villages. Archival documents provide evidence that this service crushed genuine peasant resistance in the places where it was occurring, and also fabricated various types of cases as a preventive counteraction to the peasant discontent. At the same time the GPU was the very structure that knew the truth about the realities of the famine. On 16 February 1933 a Party-state directive was issued: "Categorically forbid any kind of organization to record cases of famine-related swelling and death, with the exception of the GPU organs." Village councils were instructed not to indicate the cause of death in the registers. In 1934 a new instruction was issued: all Registry Office books concerning the registration of deaths for the period 1932–33 were to be sent to special sections, where they were most probably destroyed....

What made the situation in Ukraine radically different from what was happening, say, in Russia or Kazakhstan, were changes in nationality policy. On 14 December 1932 Stalin and Molotov signed a resolution of the CC of the All-Union Communist Party (Bolshevik) and the Council of People's Commissars of the USSR in connection with the execution of the grain procurement campaign. This document stipulated the "correct implementation of Ukrainization" in Ukraine and beyond its borders in regions densely settled by Ukrainians. The document also included a categorical imperative to wage a struggle against Petliurite and other "counter-revolutionary" elements. This spelled the end of the limited policy of "Ukrainization" and the beginning of anti-Ukrainian purges.

This was confirmed by the events of 1933, when cadre changes took place in the Party-state leadership of the Ukrainian SSR. The most important change was the appointment of Pavel Postyshev as second secretary of the Central Committee of the Communist Party (Bolshevik) of Ukraine and first secretary of the Kharkiv oblast Party committee of the CP(B)U. Postyshev simultaneously retained his post as secretary of the CC of the All-Union Communist Party (Bolshevik). Newly discovered archival materials indicate that throughout 1933 Postyshev and his "team" (his closest associates, as well as Party workers who had come from Russia for "support") implemented the Kremlin's economic line for obtaining grain, and carried out a large-scale purge of Petliurites and Ukrainian nationalists from all social spheres. The latter were soon accused of organizing the famine.

In his speech at the joint Plenum of the CC and the Central Control Commission of the CP(B)U in November 1933 Postyshev drew up a political summary of the events of 1932–33. Underlining the fact that collective farms in Ukraine had been turned into Bolshevik ones, he also emphasized that "errors and shortcomings committed by the CP(B)U in implementing the Party's nationality policy were one of the chief causes of the decline in Ukrainian agriculture in 1931–32. There is no doubt that without the liquidation of errors in the implementation of the Party's nationality policy, without the crushing defeat of nationalistic elements that had lodged themselves in various areas of social construction in Ukraine, it would have been impossible to liquidate the lag in its agriculture."

The Plenum approved a resolution that noted, "[A]t the present moment the chief danger is local nationalism that is uniting with imperialist interventionists." This "present moment" would be extended over a period of many years, thus legitimizing the rollback of the Ukrainization policy and the beginning of the campaign of mass repressions, which in Ukraine began as early as 1933, in time becoming an organic part of the history of Yezhov's "Great Terror" of 1936–38.

To summarize, archival documents that have been uncovered in the last few years incontrovertibly attest to the fact that the famine-genocide was a desirable and effective device for transforming Ukraine into a "model republic," to use Stalin's euphemism. According to these new documents, the actions of the Stalinist regime reveal special anti-Ukrainian accents whose significance and profound consequences will serve to expand the range of scholarly discourse on the Holodomor.

Nicolas Werth, "The Great Ukrainian Famine of 1932–33" in *Online Encyclopedia of Mass Violence*, 18 April 2008

Online at http://www.massviolence.org/The-1932-1933-Great-Famine-in-Ukraine. Excerpts.

Nicolas Werth (b. 1950) is a French historian specializing in the history of the Soviet Union. He is director of research of the Institut d'histoire du temps présent at the Centre national de la recherche scientifique in Paris. He is the author of fourteen books on Soviet history (with a focus on Stalinism), including *La Terreur et le désarroi. Staline et son système* (2007) and *L'ivrogne et la marchande de fleurs. Autopsie d'un meurtre de masse, 1937–1938* (2009). He is coauthor of *Cannibal Island: Death in a Siberian Gulag* (2007) and *The Black Book of Communism: Crimes, Terror, Repression* (1999).

Over four million people starved to death between the fall of 1932 and the summer of 1933 in Ukraine and the Kuban, an administrative unit of the Russian Republic in the northern Caucasus populated largely by Ukrainians. Up until Gorbachev's *perestroika*, this tragedy was never spoken of in the USSR. The 1932–33 famine was officially recognized in Ukraine only in December 1987 during a speech given by Volodymyr Shcherbytsky, the First Secretary of the Ukrainian Communist Party, on the 70th anniversary of the establishment of the Ukrainian Republic. Since then, the opening up of once inaccessible archives has brought to light a number of documents that have made it possible to analyze and better understand the political mechanisms behind the genesis and aggravation of the famine in Ukraine and the Kuban, and the role of the Soviet leadership in this process. These sources include secret resolutions passed by the Politburo or the Central Committee of the Ukrainian Communist Party, Stalin's correspondence with his closest collaborators, [Viacheslav] Molotov and [Lazar] Kaganovich, and secret police reports on the situation in the countryside, in particular at the "collection fronts." The documents also help to delineate the particular characteristics of the Ukrainian famine vis-à-vis other famines that ravished a slew of regions in the USSR in 1931–33, including Kazakhstan, where between 1.1–1.4 million died (or almost one-third of the indigenous Kazakh population), and western Siberia and the Volga area, with several hundred thousand victims....

The Mechanisms of a Murderous Famine: Prologue (First Half of 1932)

In 1931, Soviet state collection agencies managed to extract a record quantity of grain (almost twenty-three million tons) from a very mediocre national harvest (sixty-nine million tons), five million of which was exported. Owing to poor harvests in western Siberia and Kazakhstan, the three most important grain-producing centers of the country, i.e., Ukraine, the northern Caucasus and the central black earth region, were targeted for particularly heavy contributions that year. Thus in

1931, more than 42 percent of Ukraine's total harvest was taken, an exceptionally large levy that would disrupt a production cycle already seriously shaken by the forced collectivization and de-kulakization begun the year before. Many kolkhozes were forced to give up some of the seed required for the following year's crop, seriously undermining future yields. Beginning in February–March 1932, reports by the Secret Political Department of the OGPU sent to the chief Soviet leaders mentioned "isolated sites of food problems." These reports were confirmed by [Stanislav] Kosior, the First Secretary of the Ukrainian Communist Party, in a letter to Stalin on April 26, 1932. According to Kosior, these "isolated cases of starving villages" were the result of "excesses and deviations by local officials who had gone a little too far in the last collection campaign…." He added, "One must categorically reject all talk of a supposed 'famine' in Ukraine."

In the course of the following weeks, which coincided with the traditional "gap" between two harvests, the food shortage deteriorated to such an extent that [Hryhorii] Petrovsky, the President of the Executive Committee of Ukrainian Soviets, and Vlas Chubar, the head of the Ukrainian government, decided to each address a long letter to Stalin and Molotov on June 10, 1932. Both letters described the now critical situation in the Ukrainian countryside: "At least 100 districts (as opposed to sixty-one in May) need emergency food assistance," wrote Chubar, adding, "I visited many villages and I saw people starving everywhere… Women were crying, even the men sometimes." Criticism was pointed: "Why have you created this artificial famine? We had a harvest, why did you confiscate it all? Even under the old regime, no one would have done this!" Like Petrovsky, Chubar blamed the situation on "excesses" and the "giddiness of success" among local officials, remaining silent on the fact that these officials were simply obeying specific orders to fulfill the plan at all costs. Both warned of danger ahead: If the *muzhik* [peasant] was too weak to work, the 1932 harvest would be catastrophic. Chubar asked for emergency assistance, albeit modest, of one million poods (16,000 tons) of grain. Petrovsky boldly requested a little more, one and a half million poods (24–32,000 tons).

These requests met with no response. Addressing an assembly of top Party officials on June 12, 1932, Molotov, the head of the Soviet government, declared: "Even if we are confronted today with the specter of famine, mostly in the grain-producing zones, the collection plans must be fulfilled at all costs." A week later, on June 18, Stalin shared his opinion with Kaganovich. In Stalin's view, the situation in Ukraine was the product of a "mechanistic approach to the last collection plan…. The real situation of each kolkhoz had not been considered." He explained that it was out of the question, however, to ease the 1932 plan. On June 21, Stalin and Molotov sent a very firm telegram to the leadership of the Ukrainian Communist Party, reminding it that "no decrease in deliveries owed by the kolkhozes and the sovkhozes will be tolerated, and no extension of the deadline is granted."

The Mechanisms of a Murderous Famine: The Second Phase (July–October 1932)

At the Third Conference of the Ukrainian Party, which assembled in Kharkiv between 6–10 July, the vast majority of speakers (secretaries of district or regional committees) deemed Moscow's collection plan "unachievable." Nevertheless, the delegates ratified the 1932 plan, under pressure from Molotov and Kaganovich, who had been rushed to Kharkiv for the occasion. The two intervened brutally in the debates, not hesitating to declare that "any attempt to ease the plan is fundamentally anti-Party and anti-Bolshevik." Ukraine was required to provide 356 million poods of grain, or about six million tons. However, in July 1932, the first month of the new "levy," "grain is not coming in," and at the end of July, barely 48,000 tons were delivered, or seven times less than the year before! The opposition demonstrated by the Ukrainian chiefs did not, of course, go unnoticed by Stalin, as his recently published correspondence with Kaganovich shows: on August 11, Stalin sent Kaganovich a long letter that helps to illuminate the history of the Ukrainian famine. According to Stalin:

> The most important thing now is Ukraine. The current situation in Ukraine is terribly bad. It's bad in the Party. They say that, in two regions in Ukraine (Kyiv and Dnipropetrovsk), some fifty district committees have spoken against the collection plan, declaring it unrealistic. Things are no better in the other district committees. What does it sound like? It's no longer a party, it's a parliament, a caricature of a parliament. Instead of leading, Kosior has been maneuvering between the directives of the Party Central Committee and the requests of the district committees: now he's squeezed into a corner. Things are bad with the soviets. Chubar is not a leader. The situation with the GPU is not good. [Stanislav] Redens is not up to leading the struggle against the counter-revolution in a republic as large and particular as Ukraine. If we do not immediately take charge of straightening out the situation in Ukraine, we could lose Ukraine. Bear in mind that [Józef] Piłsudski never rests, his espionage capabilities in Ukraine are much stronger than Redens and Kosior realize. And remember too that, in the Ukrainian Communist Party (500,000 members, ha ha!), we find no few (no, no few!) rotten types, conscious and unconscious "Petliurites," as well as direct agents of Piłsudski. As soon as things get worse, these elements will lose no time in opening up a front within (and outside) the Party, against the Party. The worst of it is that the Ukrainian leaders are oblivious to these dangers.

Continuing, Stalin proposed that Kaganovich take charge of the Ukrainian Party, that [Vsevolod] Balytsky replace Redens at the head of the GPU, and Chubar be dismissed. The letter ended with: "Ukraine must be transformed as soon as possible into a true fortress of the USSR, into a truly exemplary republic. Spare no effort. Without these measures (economic and political reinforcement of Ukraine, firstly in the border districts, etc....), we risk losing Ukraine."

For Stalin, Ukraine was vulnerable, but not because of the imminent famine that threatened to kill millions of Ukrainians. It was vulnerable politically, the weak link in the system. Stalin had not forgotten that, two years earlier, the Soviet regime had lost control for several weeks of some 100 border districts along the Polish frontier, following the greatest wave of consecutive peasant uprisings against forced collectivization; that Ukraine alone had been the site of almost half of the some 6,500 peasant riots and disturbances reported by the OGPU in the course of the single month of March 1930; that the peasant insurgents had demonstrated under explicit banners proclaiming *Shche ne vmerla Ukraïna!* [Ukraine Is Not Yet Lost]. The situation had to be reined in through the submission of the Ukrainian peasantry to the demands of the global development of the USSR. In the immediate term, that meant the fulfillment, within set deadlines, of the First Five Year Plan, which depended largely on a program of agricultural exports. Commenting on the situation, Sergei Kirov...observed that, in this context, the annual collection campaign was "the touchstone of our strength or our weakness, of the strength or weakness of our enemies."

On the collection front, September and October 1932 were catastrophic. In September, only 32 percent of the monthly target was reached in Ukraine and 28 percent in the northern Caucasus. In October, deliveries shrank again: On October 25, only 22 percent of the mandatory levy fixed for that month was collected in Ukraine, and 18 percent in the northern Caucasus. The confidential reports of the Secret Political Department of the OGPU throw light on the various strategies employed by the peasants, often in complicity with the kolkhoz administration, to withhold some of the harvest from the state: grain, barely harvested, buried in "pits," hidden in "black granaries" (secret storage sites scattered around village lines), ground the traditional way in "hand mills," overturned on the way to silos or at weighing points; children, women and the elderly—"who the peasants thought might enjoy some lenience before the law"—sent, often by cover of darkness, to cut down some stalks (they were referred to in the countryside, with some derision, as "the barbers"). It was these acts of resistance, this "kulak sabotage," that the Politburo set out to break when it decided, on October 22, to send out two "plenipotentiary commissions" to Ukraine and the northern Caucasus—one headed by Molotov, the other by Kaganovich.

The Mechanisms of a Murderous Famine: The Third Phase (November 1932–January 1933)

During the course of three decisive months (end of October 1932–end of January 1933), these commissions, involving the highest-level chiefs of the OGPU (notably [Genrikh] Yagoda, the head of the Soviet secret police), played a critical role in aggravating the famine. Crucial documents, now declassified, vividly elucidate the political and ideological arguments advanced by Stalin's envoys, the escalation of repressive measures, and the increasingly resolute use of hunger as a weapon to crush the resistance of the Ukrainian peasantry: telegrams sent to Stalin by his two "plenipotentiaries," dispatches exchanged between the chiefs of the Ukrainian Communist Party, speeches given by Molotov and Kaganovich before local assemblies of Party movers as well as before kolkhozes, and the travel journal of Kaganovich—taken together, they paint the picture of the unfolding famine.

Before leaving for Rostov-on-the-Don on October 29, Kaganovich presented a "resolution project" to the Politburo outlining the goals of his mission to the northern Caucasus. Notable among these was "the intensification of the levies, i.e., to take all measures to break the sabotage of the collections and of the sowing campaign by kulak counter-revolutionary elements." Upon arriving in Rostov on November 1, Kaganovich announced to the local regional Party chiefs that "it is useless to try and give me a precise account of grain reserves. This can only lead to all sorts of deceit and amounts essentially to a rejection of the collection plan. The problem can only be resolved by crushing the kulak counter-revolutionary elements." On November 5, Kaganovich wrote to Stalin from Krasnodar:

> The counter-revolutionaries are strongly entrenched. The dreadful work of the local Party organizations, of liberalism, opportunism and sloppiness have paved the way for the rise of the counter-revolution... Our main task today is to break sabotage, sabotage that is organized and led by a single center. I'm leaving Krasnodar today for the *stanitsy* (Cossack towns). I'll head to the most rebellious, Poltavskaia, which is home to no fewer than 400 teachers, doctors, technicians, Cossack officers, etc....

The missions of Kaganovich and Molotov (the latter expressing much of the same upon his arrival in Kharkiv and during the course of his expedition in the Odesa and Dnipropetrovsk regions) resembled veritable military campaigns against insurgents. Hundreds of detachments consisting of "activists" and "plenipotentiaries" with vague mandates, supported by agents of the OGPU, were sent into the countryside to "take the grain."

Among the first measures taken by Molotov and Kaganovich was to halt the supply of all manufactured products to those districts that had not fulfilled the plan. The most "rebellious" towns were "placed on the blackboard," signifying the removal of all products, both manufactured goods *and food*, from stores, a complete stoppage in trade, immediate repayment of all active credits (individual and collective), a special levy (i.e., basically the total confiscation of the peasants' last remaining food reserves), and massive arrests of all the "saboteurs of the collection plan." The number of arrests in Ukraine and the northern Caucasus skyrocketed: 20,000 in November for leading the "sabotage of collections" and more than 30,000 for the "theft of social property" (punishable, under a new law promulgated on August 7, 1932, by ten years in a prison camp or even death). In December, 72,000 were arrested in total. During the search-and-arrest missions carried out by the "collection detachments," thousands of "grain pits" were unearthed. However, as Balytsky (the new head of the Ukrainian GPU) admitted, the "total haul" was pathetic—barely 10,000 tons of grain, or 0.2 percent of the collection plan!

It is clear that the Ukrainian countryside was deprived of its last food reserves during the fall of 1932, the village store shelves stripped bare of their paltry supply of products. The final stage in the escalating repression was the collective deportation of all the inhabitants of "rebellious" villages that had "waged war against Soviet power," as Kaganovich declared to the villagers of Medvedovskaia *stanitsa* on November 6, 1932. A few weeks later, all of the inhabitants of three large *stanitsy* in the Kuban (Medvedovskaia, Umanskaia and Poltavskaia), totaling more than 45,000 people, were collectively deported to Siberia, the Urals, and Kazakhstan for failing to fulfill the unrealistic collection plan that had been imposed on them. These coercive measures were also designed to break the final resistance of a certain number of Ukrainian communist chiefs, compelling them to fully yield on the collection plan at all costs. The correspondence between Molotov and [Mendel] Khataevich, the First Secretary of the Dnipropetrovsk region, sheds some light on this point. In his letter of November 23, 1932, Khataevich tried to explain to Molotov that it would be economically irrational to seize the last reserves held by the kolkhozes: "If production is to go up in future to meet the needs of the proletarian state, we must take into account the minimal needs of the kolkhozes and their members, otherwise there will soon be nobody left to plant the crop and harvest it." Molotov's reply the same day is revealing:

> Your position is profoundly incorrect, non-Bolshevik. We Bolsheviks cannot place the needs of the State—minimal needs that have been precisely defined and on numerous occasions by the resolutions of the Party—in tenth or even in second place in order to satisfy the needs of the kolkhozes. A true Bolshevik must place the needs of the State first.

It was in the second half of December 1932 that the fatal measures were taken condemning tens of millions of Ukrainian peasants to starvation. On December 19, the Politburo demanded "a radical break in the collection pace." Kaganovich, seconded by tens of upper Party chiefs and by the OGPU, was dispatched again as "plenipotentiary" to Ukraine, empowered to "occupy strategic regions and adopt all measures to fulfill the collection plan before January 15, 1933." A few days later, in a letter sent to Stalin from Odesa, he proposed the annulment of a resolution passed by the Ukrainian Communist Party stipulating that only the Regional Executive Committee of Soviets could authorize, in special circumstances, the confiscation of kolkhoz "seed stores" and their inclusion in mandatory state levies. With Stalin's enthusiastic support, Kaganovich imposed this measure on the leadership of the Ukrainian Communist Party on December 29. The local leadership also bowed at this time to another critical tactic: kolkhozes that failed to fulfill the "collection plan" would have five days to hand over their "so-called seed stores" (*tak nazyvaemye semennye fondy*), the last reserves ensuring the next harvest, even the most minimal, or some final assistance to starving kolkhoz members. Three days later, on January 1, 1933, the Ukrainian Communist Party heads adopted a resolution calling for all kolkhoz members and individual peasants caught with "hidden stocks" to be included among "thieves of socialist property" and judged "with all the severity of the law of August 7, 1932." The repression had crossed a new threshold.

Between January 7–12, 1933, an important plenum of the Central Committee took place in Moscow, a great annual reunion bringing together Party leaders from around the country. Stalin acknowledged that, despite an overall better harvest in 1932 than the year before, the collection campaign had encountered more difficulties. He blamed these on "sabotage" perpetrated by "kulak infiltrators within the kolkhozes," the "criminal nonchalance of the rural communists," their "non-Marxist attitude towards collective agriculture." Like all the speakers, the leaders of the Ukrainian Communist Party, some of whom had tried to withstand Moscow's pressure, celebrated the "triumph of socialism" and the "spectacular successes of the First Five Year Plan, completed in four years and three months," remaining silent on the real situation in Ukraine.

While the plenum progressed in Moscow, the peasant exodus from the famine zones intensified. For the chiefs of the OGPU, these departures were "consciously organized by counter-revolutionary organizations." "In one week, our services have stopped 500 hardened instigators who were pushing the peasants to leave," Balytsky wrote to [Genrikh] Yagoda, the head of the OGPU. On January 22, 1933, Stalin himself drafted a key secret directive ordering an immediate halt to the massive peasant exodus from Ukraine and the Kuban "on the pretext of searching for bread." Stalin wrote:

> The Central Committee and the Council of People's Commissars have evidence that this exodus from Ukraine, even that of the year before, has been organized by the enemies of Soviet power, the socialist-revolutionaries, and Polish agents. Their goal is propaganda, to use the peasants fleeing towards the regions of the USSR north of Ukraine to discredit the kolkhoz system and, in particular, the Soviet system in general.

The same day, Yagoda sent a circular to the regional leaders of the OGPU ordering that special patrols be set up, especially in stations and on the roads, to intercept all the "runaways" from Ukraine and the northern Caucasus. Once those stopped had been "filtered," the "kulak and counter-revolutionary elements," the "individuals spreading counter-revolutionary rumors on supposed food problems," as well as all those who refused to return home were to be arrested and deported to "special villages" (or, in the case of the most hardened, sent to camps). The other runaways would be "sent back home," i.e., to villages ravaged by famine, and left to fend for themselves without any food assistance at all. This, in effect, was a death sentence.

The following day, on January 23, 1933, Stalin's directive against peasant flight (as well as the spread of news about the famine) was put into motion by the imposition of various restrictions, beginning with a suspension of the sale of train tickets to peasants. On January 25, to "prevent the production of false departure authorizations," officials forbade rural soviets and kolkhoz directors from providing peasants with the usual certificates permitting kolkhoz members to travel. During the last week of January, some 25,000 runaways were intercepted. Two months after the start of the operation, more than 225,000 people had been apprehended, 85 percent of whom were sent back to their villages. The weekly reports of the OGPU "on the measures taken to stop the massive exodus of peasants" addressed directly to Stalin and Molotov made no mention, of course, of the physical condition of those apprehended.

The Famine at its Height (February–July 1933)

During February–July 1933, the period marking the height of the famine, the higher officials of the Ukrainian GPU drafted a few documents (very few, in fact) on what was actually happening in the starving Ukrainian countryside that help supplement the accounts provided by survivors in later years. Thus, in one revealing communication, Balytsky instructed his subordinates:

> Provide information on the food problems only to the First Secretaries of the regional committees of the Party and only orally, after carefully checking the reports. This is to ensure that written notes on the subject do not circulate through the *apparatus*, where they might stir rumors... Do not write specific reports for the Ukrainian GPU. It is sufficient for me to be personally informed by personal letters from the leaders addressed to me directly.

It is interesting to compare the rare sources unearthed from the central archives of the secret service agencies of the former Soviet Union (the forerunners of the KGB, now the FSB) to other more loquacious internal reports written by officials in various administrations that show quite clearly that the "secret" famine was no secret at all. They also convey an aloof police vision of the "food problems," which were attributed to "sabotage perpetrated in the agriculture of Ukraine by kulak and counter-revolutionary elements [that had] infiltrated the kolkhozes, sovkhozes, and some of the villages." This attitude emerges starkly in the details provided by [Jan] Krauklis, the head of the regional department of the Dnipropetrovsk GPU, concerning the autopsies performed under his authority. In attempting to determine the "exact causes of death" of those who had starved (Did these individuals *really* die of hunger? Were these not cases of "enemy provocation"?), or investigating cannibalism and necrophagia, Krauklis reported in the manner of the detached ethnologist describing the "savage customs" of a "primitive tribe." A similar tone is apparent in a communication sent by [Aleksandr] Rozanov, the head of the Kyiv GPU, to Balytsky:

> One might even say that cannibalism has become a habit. There are some who were suspected of cannibalism last year and are now backsliding again, killing children, acquaintances, even strangers on the street. In the villages that are affected by cannibalism, every passing day strengthens people's belief that it is acceptable to eat human flesh. This idea is particularly widespread among the starving and children.

The reports of the OGPU chiefs also reflect very clearly the dread of a mass uprising of starving peasants, whose anti-Soviet talk was systematically noted, especially in the "reports-compilations" of letters written by peasants and seized by a highly vigilant postal surveillance. With the famine raging stronger than ever, the deportation of tens of thousands of starving peasants continued and "grandiose" plans were laid for the deportation of millions of "kulak, counter-revolutionary, and socially harmful elements." At the same time, the powers of the *troiki* (special courts) were further tightened for fear of peasant insurrections. Police reports show too how hazardous it is to determine the number of famine victims, given that the officials of the rural soviets—often decimated themselves when entire districts were subject to a complete blockade as "punishment" for having failed to fulfill their "sacred obligations before the State"—no longer kept up the civil register (births, deaths, marriages). Moreover, the dead were not always buried anymore, while others were simply dumped into communal pits. It is estimated that barely 32 percent of the four million deaths were recorded by the state authorities at the peak of the famine.

The new documents also throw some light on the question of food assistance provided in the final hour to certain districts hit by the famine. As recent studies have shown, between January–June 1933, when the famine reached its greatest height and reach, the central authorities passed no fewer than thirty-five resolutions on aid to regions affected by "food problems." Assistance rose to about 320,000 tons, which, applied to the some thirty million people hit by the famine, amounts to only ten kilos of grain per person, or scarcely 3 percent of a peasant's average annual consumption! In 1932, the USSR exported 1,730,000 tons of grain and another 1,680,000 tons in 1933. In addition, at the beginning of 1933, state reserves reached more than 1,800,000 tons. As for the paltry food aid, no doubt only a small portion

Political Geography of the Holodomor (1932–33)

Map reproduced by permission from *Holodomor: Reflections on the Great Famine of 1932–33 in Soviet Ukraine* (Copyright Kashtan Press, Kingston, ON, 2008).

actually reached the villages, since the cities of Ukraine and the northern Caucasus were also severely hurt by the famine (Kharkiv lost more than 120,000 inhabitants in one year alone, while medium-sized cities like Krasnodar or Stavropol lost 40,000 and 20,000 respectively) and absorbed most of the emergency food.

Instructions sent by Balytsky on March 19, 1933 "on the measures to be taken in connection with the food problems" specify that the emergency food supplies, accorded "on a class basis," were exclusively for the benefit of "those who deserved them, i.e., in order of priority, kolkhoz members with a significant number of work days, brigadiers, tractor operators, families with a least one member in the Red Army, kolkhoz members and individual peasants who had chosen to join the kolkhoz." Balytsky's circular in fact focused on the repressive measures that were to be taken against the "kulak, counter-revolutionary, parasitical, and enemy elements of all kinds that sought to exploit the food problems for their own counter-revolutionary purposes, spreading rumors about the famine and various 'horrors,' purposely leaving the dead unburied."

In the spring of 1933, the reports of the Ukrainian GPU reveal another major preoccupation, namely how to ensure the working of the fields for the next harvest in the regions ravaged by the famine. As we saw earlier, in November 1932, the Second Secretary of the Ukrainian Communist Party, Khataevich, had warned Molotov that, "Soon there will be nobody left to sow and prepare for the next crop!" A few months later, officials were faced with this very scenario. Given their weakened state, surviving kolkhoz members were hard pressed to rebuild their work force, as those reporting realized, albeit not without some cynicism: "The very few who still work are unable to fulfill quotas. Consequently, they do not receive enough bread and begin to bloat." In an attempt to deal with the dramatic loss of rural labor, the authorities, backed up by the military, began by mobilizing a part of the urban population, which was sent to the fields. The Italian consul in Kharkiv reported what he witnessed: "The mobilization of the urban forces has assumed enormous proportions... This week, at least 20,000 people were sent to the countryside... The day before yesterday, they surrounded the market, seized all able persons, men, women, and adolescents, transported them to the station under GPU guard, and shipped them to the fields." Later, officials resorted to mass transfers of "colonists" from other parts of the USSR: more than 200,000 peasants were displaced in 1933–34 towards the areas devastated by the famine, most as soon as they had completed their military service.

The OGPU reports on conditions in the countryside in Ukraine and the northern Caucasus also speak of the incredible repression and brutalization that accompanied the hunger and starvation. Rural banditry soared and, more generally, society witnessed a rise of extraordinary violence on a daily basis in a world traumatized and overwhelmed by a relentless permanent hunger: lynched thieves, including children caught on trains trying to pinch a few vegetables, summary judgments (*samosudy*) administered by the peasants themselves, tortures, brutalities, exactions of all kinds, child abandonment, cannibalism and necrophagy... The extreme violence committed by the regime and its representatives against the population ended by driving people to the same in their everyday lives.

Accounts by survivors, gathered at several points (in the 1950s among the émigrés of the "second wave," and in the 1990s in Ukraine itself, after the fall of the USSR) constitute another invaluable source for understanding the famine, not only from the inside but from the perspective of its victims. All describe the incredible fury and determination of the "activist brigades," made up of policemen and local Party chiefs, but often also of people from outside the village. Together, they systematically confiscated the peasants' last food reserves. Their exactions, which often resembled a mass plundering (anything having the slightest market value was confiscated, in addition to food products) demonstrate that their objective was not only to "fulfill the grain collection plan at all costs," but also to "punish" the peasants who were hostile to the kolkhoz system, which they perceived as a "second serfdom." These peasants tried to survive by gleaning ("stealing," according to the authorities) a few stalks or some potatoes in the collective fields, hiding a chicken, or growing a tiny vegetable garden ("at the expense of collective labor"). The testimonies also paint a terrible picture of the slow agony of death by starvation, the progressive dehumanization of the victims, and the multiplication of transgressions against others (anthropophagy, the mass abandonment of young children, collective suicides).

Not all segments of the population were affected to the same extent, however. The accounts show that the Ukrainian countryside paid a higher price than the cities, which were inhabited by a strong minority of non-Ukrainians (Russians, Poles, Jews); and ordinary peasants were more vulnerable than kolkhoz members or the "specialists" (technicians, tractor-operators). In the end, the surviving testimonies underline the sense of total abandonment felt by the inhabitants of the rural zones left to starve, trapped in their village, deprived of even the slightest food aid, in a word—condemned to death.

The Famine: A Genocide?

Since the late 1980s, the "rediscovery" of the 1932–33 famine has played a crucial role in Ukrainian political life, in the confrontation between those advocating a break with the USSR (and then with Russia) and others who prefer to maintain close ties with the "big Russian brother." The *Holodomor* (from *holod*/hunger, *moryty*/ killed by privation, starved, exhausted), as Ukraine now calls the intentional mass extermination of its population, has not only been the centre of political and cultural debate but has become an integral part of the process of state and national reconstruction in post-Soviet Ukraine. It is within this context that, following lengthy discussions, the Parliament of the Republic of Ukraine officially recognized the 1932–33 famine as a genocide perpetrated by Stalin's regime against the Ukrainian people. Six months later, on the 70th anniversary of the *Holodomor*, the United Nations General Assembly drafted a declaration recognizing that "the great famine of 1932–33, the result of a cruel policy of a totalitarian regime...constituted a national tragedy for the Ukrainian people." The declaration did not, however, equate the famine with a genocide.

The question of whether the 1932–33 famine constitutes a genocide is a matter of disagreement among historians studying the calamity, whether Russians, Ukrainians, or their Western counterparts. There are basically two schools of thought. Some historians see the famine as an artificially organized phenomenon, planned since 1930 by the Stalinist regime to break the particularly strong resistance of Ukrainian peasants to the kolkhoz system. In addition, this plan sought to destroy the Ukrainian nation, at its "national-peasant" core, which constituted a serious obstacle to the transformation of the USSR into a new imperial state dominated by Russia. According to this view, the famine was a genocide. At the other end of the analytical spectrum are scholars who recognize the criminal nature of the Stalinist policies but believe that it is necessary to assess all of the famines that took place between 1931–33 (in Kazakhstan, Ukraine, western Siberia and Volga regions) as part of a complex phenomenon shaped by numerous factors, from the geopolitical context to the demands of an accelerated industrialization and modernization drive, in addition to Stalin's "imperial objectives." From this perspective, the 1932–33 famine in Ukraine and the Kuban was not a genocide.

The Italian historian Andrea Graziosi, a specialist on Ukrainian history, recently proposed a "fusion" of these two arguments on the basis of a comparative analysis of the various Soviet famines that took place in the early 1930s and an in-depth study of the chronology of events. According to this view, the famines that hit the USSR beginning in 1931 were the direct, but not foreseen or planned, result of the ideologically driven policies implemented since late 1929—forced collectivization, dekulakization, the imposition of the kolkhoz system, and excessive grain and livestock levies. Up until the summer of 1932, the Ukrainian famine, already rearing its head, resembled the other famines that had started earlier elsewhere. However, from this point forward, the nature of the Ukrainian famine changed, with Stalin deciding to use hunger as a weapon, to aggravate the famine that was just beginning. Choosing to instrumentalize the famine, Stalin intentionally amplified it in order to punish the Ukrainian peasants who rejected the "new serfdom" and to break "Ukrainian nationalism," which he saw as a threat to his goal of constructing a centralized and dictatorial Soviet state. And while hunger hit the peasants harder than any other group, resulting in the death of millions in atrocious conditions, another form of repression, of a police nature, struck others in Ukraine at the same moment—the political and intellectual elites, from village teachers to national leaders, via the intelligentsia. Tens of thousands of Ukrainians were arrested and punished with camp sentences. In December 1932, two secret Politburo decrees put an end in Ukraine, and *only in Ukraine*, to the "indigenization" policy applied to Party cadres since 1923 in all of the federal republics: "Ukrainian nationalism" was firmly condemned.

Two fundamental issues need to be considered in defining the Ukrainian famine of 1932–33 as a genocide, along lines set by the December 1948 United Nations Convention: intention and the ethnic-national targeting of a group (Article II of the Convention recognizes only national, ethnic, racial, and religious groups, not social or political). In the case of Ukraine, sufficient evidence exists to demonstrate intention. A crucial document on this point is the resolution of January 22, 1933 signed by Stalin, ordering the blockade of Ukraine and the Kuban, a region of the Caucasus with a majority Ukrainian population. The blockade intentionally worsened the famine in Ukrainian-populated areas *and in these areas alone*. On the question of target group, i.e., whether Stalin viewed the peasants of Ukraine and the Kuban as peasants or as Ukrainians, which is key to justifying use of the term genocide, scholars disagree. For some historians, the famine's primary objective was to break peasant rather than national resistance. Others argue that the peasants of Ukraine and the Kuban were targeted first as Ukrainians: For Stalin, the Ukrainian peasant question was "in essence, a national question, the peasants constituting the principal force of the national movement." By crushing the peasantry, one was breaking the most powerful national movement capable of opposing the process of the construction of the USSR. As the famine decimated the Ukrainian peasantry, the regime condemned the entire policy of Ukrainization underway since the early 1920s: the Ukrainian elites were rounded up and arrested.

This specifically anti-Ukrainian assault makes it possible to define the totality of intentional political actions taken from late summer 1932 by the Stalinist regime against the Ukrainian peasantry as genocide. With hunger as its deadly arm, the regime sought to punish and terrorize the peasants, resulting in fatalities exceeding four million people in Ukraine and the northern Caucasus. That being said, the *Holodomor* was very different from the Holocaust. It did not seek to exterminate the Ukrainian nation in its entirety, and it did not involve the direct murder of its victims. The *Holodomor* was conceived and fashioned on the basis of political reasoning and not of ethnic or racial ideology. However, by the sheer number of its victims, the *Holodomor*, seen again in its historical context, is the only European event of the 20th century that can be compared to the two other genocides, the Armenian and the Holocaust.

Viktor Kondrashin, "Hunger in 1932–1933—A Tragedy of the Peoples of the USSR"

Holodomor Studies 1, no. 2 (2009): 16–21. Excerpts.

V. V. Kondrashin (b. 1961) is professor and chair of the Department of History, Penza State Pedagogical University. He specializes in the history of the Russian peasantry in the twentieth century. He is the author, in Russian, of *The Peasant Movement in the Volga Region, 1918–1922* (2001); *The Years 1932–1933 in the Soviet Village (Based on Materials of the Volga, Don, and Kuban Regions)* (coauthor, 2002); *The Famine of 1932–1933 in the Russian Village* (2003); and *The Famine of 1932–1933: A Tragedy of the Russian Village* (2008).

Russian researchers began writing about the famine of 1932–33 in the second half of the 1980s.... They argued that the famine was a tragedy for the whole Soviet peasantry, and that it was the result of the implementation of the Stalinist model of forced industrialization, which entailed forced collectivization and forced collection of agricultural products, especially of grain. Collections were aimed at increasing grain exports and satisfying the needs of a growing level of industry....

Numerous sources prepared by Russian researchers...conclusively point to the inextricable link between the Famine of 1932–33 and Stalin's industrialization. The famine can be classified as "an organized famine" resulting from the policy of the Stalinist leadership....

...The grain procurements were a direct result of Stalin's leadership in forcing industrialization, which required grain exports. And in order to get as much grain as possible mass collectivization was introduced in 1930 in the main grain-producing regions.

Immediately there was a sharp increase in grain procurement plans. In 1930 the government collected twice as much grain as in 1928....

...[I]n 1930 the USSR began pursuing a policy of returning to Tsarist Russia's status of being Europe's main grain exporter.... This presented the best prospects for the USSR to receive large amounts of foreign currency needed to support industrialization. But it required the forced collection and export of huge amounts of grain. It was precisely for this purpose that collective farms were introduced in grain surplus regions of the USSR....

The vast majority of victims of hunger were concentrated in the major grain areas, which had become zones of mass collectivization. These were the traditional regions for growing wheat and rye for export as well as to meet the needs of the urban population. The lion's share of grain exported in 1930 (70 percent) came from two regions—[the] Uk[rainian] SSR and North Caucasus *Krai*, and the rest came from the lower Volga and Central Black Earth Region. A similar situation was repeated in 1931....

The economic specialization of the separate regions directly affected the way that these regions experienced the tragedy: the grain regions that had already experienced forced collectivisation and forced grain procurements suffered most. In 1932–33 mass deaths from famine occurred in Ukraine, North Caucasus, Volga, Central Black Earth Region, Urals, Western Siberia and Kazakhstan.

The Stalin leadership group did not want famine but created it by its policy of planning obligatory state procurement of agricultural produce from the collective, state and individual farms, as well as by its actions to fulfill these plans.... The grain collection plans were clearly excessive in terms of the productive capabilities of the collective farms and of the entire agricultural sector. The fulfillment of these plans using administrative and repressive measures destroyed agriculture, undermined the interest of the peasants towards carrying out conscientious work, caused them to resist through grain theft, unauthorized migration, and neglect of work. In addition, collectivization undermined livestock farming, thereby aggravating the food situation in the country....

...Emergency Committees of the Politburo for 1932 grain collections were created almost simultaneously in Ukraine, Kuban and the Volga region. "Black boards" for *raions* that did not comply with the grain collection plans were introduced in Ukraine, North Caucasus, Volga and other regions. The confiscation of all food from the peasants for not fulfilling grain collection plans occurred in 1932–33 in many grain areas....

In 1933, it was not only Ukraine but also Russia's regions that experienced the horror of mass death from famine....

The primary responsibility for the tragedy of 1932–33 is borne by the top leadership of the Soviet Union and by Stalin personally. They consciously chose and pursued the anti-peasant policy of collectivization and grain procurement that destroyed the country's agricultural sector. But local authorities also played a negative role in the organization of the famine. Not only did many local leaders unquestioningly fulfill the orders of Stalin and the Central Committee, but they also initiated repression against the peasants, failed to report to Moscow the real extent of the famine, and concealed their own failures and mistakes with "triumphant relativism."....

The responsibility of [Stanislav] Kosior, secretary of the Ukrainian Central Committee of the CP(B), for the tragedy in Ukraine is not in doubt....

The scale of the tragedy was directly proportional to the share of the regions in grain collections and grain exports. In all of the USSR at least 7 million people died from famine in 1932–33. A comparative analysis of the 1926 and 1937 censuses shows the following level of decline of rural population in separate famine-affected areas: Kazakhstan 30.9 percent, Volga region 23 percent, Ukraine 20.5 percent, North Caucasus 20.4 percent....

Stalin's famine of 1932–33 was a general tragedy of the peoples of the former USSR, a tragedy of all the Soviet countryside, a crime of the Stalinist regime.

David R. Marples, *Holodomor: Causes of the 1932–1933 Famine in Ukraine*

(Saskatoon: Heritage Press, 2011). Excerpts, pp. 95–98, 100–104.

David R. Marples is Distinguished University Professor in the Department of History and Classics, University of Alberta, and director of the Stasiuk Program for the Study of Contemporary Ukraine at the Canadian Institute of Ukrainian Studies. He is the author of thirteen individually authored monographs, including *Heroes and Villains: Creating National History in Contemporary Ukraine* (2008) and *Russia in the Twentieth Century: The Quest for Stability* (2011).

Arguably, there were two famines that affected Ukraine and Ukrainian-ethnic territories of the North Caucasus: a general famine that was common to a number of areas of the Soviet Union, including the Russian Federation, and a second one caused more directly by measures applied most specifically to the villages of Ukraine in late 1932, which resulted in the *Holodomor* by the spring and summer of 1933.... Discussion of the causes of the Famine in Ukraine has been somewhat overwhelmed by the debate as to whether it constituted a genocide, which entails discussion of the definition of that term, how it originated under Raphael Lemkin and why the United Nations was obliged to accept ultimately such a broad definition to secure the assent of the Soviet Union. Suffice it to say the 1948 definition of genocide can certainly be applied to Ukraine....

...[L]et us consider the reasons for the famines that pervaded the Ukrainian SSR in 1932 and 1933.

1. Stalin's mass collectivization, accompanied by a dekulakization campaign, sometimes described as a war in the countryside or the Second Bolshevik Revolution. The resulting chaos, accompanied by slaughter and losses of livestock, as well as deportations of many of the better farmers from villages, affected agriculture in all grain-growing regions of the Soviet Union, of which Ukraine was an important component.
2. Reorganization of the administrative structure, which eliminated the former system of *okrugs* and created new oblasts and made it difficult to monitor the situation in individual raions and villages. To make matters worse, it is evident that Stalin and Kaganovich in particular lacked respect for the local republican leadership, Stanislav Kosior and Vlas Chubar in particular, and proved unwilling

to allow the Ukrainian leaders to deal with problems alone. From August 1932 onward the two Ukrainian leaders fall under suspicion. The degree of confusion and helplessness at the republican level is manifest from the proceedings of the Party Conference of July 1932. The deployment of figures like Kaganovich, Molotov, and Postyshev, as well as secret police officials Vsevolod Balytsky and Stanislav Redens from the OGPU, exacerbated an already tense situation, and also indicated that the Moscow authorities had taken control of the situation away from their counterparts in Kharkiv.

3. The grain procurement campaign harkened back to the situation of the USSR under War Communism. It paid little heed to the real situation in the villages and imposed unrealistic targets on the Ukrainian SSR, even after the totals were lowered. The consequences of the first two points above were that the population of Ukraine was simply not in a position to comply with all-Union demands, and the new kolkhozes and individual farms were likewise incapable of meeting state targets. The Soviet government prioritized the supply of food to the towns, army, and for export rather than feeding the farmers who produced the grain.
4. The 7 August 1932 decree on the protection of state property which marked the beginning of a terror campaign in Soviet villages. It became evident that the campaign to remove "kulaks" or anti-Soviet elements from agriculture had failed. Likewise such peremptory measures could only alienate the villages and create hostility toward the Soviet regime. Linked to this decree, Stalin's letter to Kaganovich four days later about the danger of losing Ukraine was a clear signal that this republic was of priority concern and should be subjected to special measures. Thus within the general picture, the specific focus on Ukraine can be ascertained.
5. The forming of the Commissions under Molotov and Kaganovich in Ukraine and the North Caucasus (although Postyshev headed a commission in the Volga region, it did not act as harshly). In Ukraine, this led directly to the two major decrees of 11 November and 18 November 1932, which imposed additional quotas on Ukrainian villages in meat, potatoes, and other products. The deliberate removal of remaining supplies of food condemned the peasants to starvation, and the imposition of the "blackboard" worsened the situation by curtailing movement and ostracizing select villages and collective farms. The later decree authorized the OGPU to carry out purges and repressions of the villages, which was formalized by the operational order of 5 December "On measures for liquidating sabotage of grain procurements."
6. The decree of 14 December, which effectively ended Ukrainization and rendered Ukrainian cultural activists effectively "Ukrainian bourgeois nationalists." Mass arrests followed, undertaken under the leadership of Balytsky and Redens, who linked opposition to procurements directly to the supposed national uprising planned for the spring of 1933 across Ukraine.
7. The ban on travel outside the villages of Ukraine on 23 January 1933, together with the closure of the borders of the republic, deprived the starving peasants of any hope of relief. Either arrested or returned to their villages, they had no further hope of survival.

Other than the imposition of the "blackboard," points 5 to 7 above pertain directly to Ukraine—or to Ukraine and the North Caucasus—as distinct from other parts of the Soviet Union. Only these two areas among the key grain-growing areas were believed to be troublesome, even to the extent in Ukraine of plans for alleged mass uprising. They were subjected to the harshest measures and ultimately depopulated, as a result of both fleeing farmers and the effects of starvation. Throughout the period there was a political dimension to the economic policies applied. Underlying the decrees adopted was the sentiment that Ukraine and the essentially Ukrainian-populated North Caucasus were politically unreliable areas permeated by nationalists and anti-Soviet elements that had found a natural ally in the kulak. That explains why punitive measures in Ukraine were applied using officials from outside and answerable directly to Stalin. The goal was without doubt to ensure that Ukraine fulfilled the reduced procurements quota, but there was an underlying second goal, namely to bring a republic to heel through the application of harsher punishments than were applied elsewhere....

...Procurements, deportations, and a general assault on the village had resulted in mass deaths from forced famine from which it would take Ukraine decades to recover both demographically and in terms of cultural and social development. It was not a premeditated event or even an attempt to destroy all Ukrainians—the Albanians and other groups, for example German and Jewish colonies, were also caught up in the upheaval. By late 1932, however, official reprisals originating in Moscow were very clearly directed at the Ukrainian republic as well as the intelligentsia and cultural leadership linked to ethnic Ukrainians living outside Ukraine, especially those living in Poland. Measures applied to all rural regions of the Union were expanded and deepened in Ukraine into a campaign to eliminate both real and alleged hostile national forces.... [T]he famines that developed across Soviet grain-growing regions in 1932 resulted from collectivization, a campaign to remove kulaks, and excessive grain requisitions; the catastrophe that occurred in Ukraine in 1933, however, went considerably further. It was an attempt to subdue through punishment—starvation and alienation—the second largest Soviet republic; to denationalize an emerging nation and bring it into the Soviet fold, no matter what suffering was entailed in the process.

Jacques Vallin, France Meslé, Serguei Adamets, and Serhiy Pyrozhkov, in "The Great Famine: Population Losses in Ukraine," *Holodomor: Reflections on the Great Famine of 1932–1933 in Soviet Ukraine*, ed. Lubomyr Y. Luciuk with the assistance of Lisa Grekul

(Kingston, Ontario, Canada: Kashtan Press, 2008). Excerpts, pp. 35–46.

Jacques Vallin (b. 1941) is research director emeritus of the Institut national d'études démographiques (INED, Paris). His main fields of research are population growth in developing countries, mortality and causes of death in developed countries, and historical demography. He is the author or coauthor of some thirty books. France Meslé is director of research at INED; Serguei Adamets is a researcher at INED; and Serhiy Pyrozhkov is the founding director of the Kyiv Institute of Demography and Social Sciences.

Is it possible to estimate the demographic consequences of the *Holodomor?*

It seemed to us that more precise estimations can be done by using all available data and trying to correct them after a detailed discussion of their quality. Such an approach not only leads to a new estimation of the global losses more strictly focused on the two years of the crisis (1932–33), it also opens the door to distinguishing between (1) direct losses attributable to excess mortality and (2) indirect losses linked to the fall in fertility and to outward migration. In order to do this, a return to population change statistics is required, even if this means hypothesizing about under-registration. We think, along with most previous authors, that we can rely on the 1926 and 1939 censuses (after necessary corrections), but that vital statistics can also be used with rather modest adjustment for the years in between (with the exception of 1932 and 1933, years which certainly suffered from under-registration). Migration flows are more problematic, but even for them existing data marks a starting point.

Indeed, vital statistics give a quite plausible picture of the history of Ukrainian mortality for the years before and after the crisis (see Figure 1). Firstly, in relation to the 28.9 million inhabitants recorded in the 1926 census, the 519,000 deaths for that same year provide a crude death rate of 18 per thousand that is fully compatible with what we know about the country's state of health at that time.... If there was under-registration of deaths during this period, it was probably not very significant—except during the crisis where the registration services really seem to have been "snowed under" (or perhaps manipulated to minimize the extent of the crisis). In spite of the fact that vital statistics show a very sharp increase in mortality in 1932–33, registration of deaths could have deteriorated significantly then. It is essentially the extent of this "crisis under-registration" that must be assessed. As for the rest, classical corrections for under-registration of infant deaths and deaths among the oldest should be quite satisfactory.

Figure 1. Annual change in numbers of births and deaths by sex, from 1924 to 1939

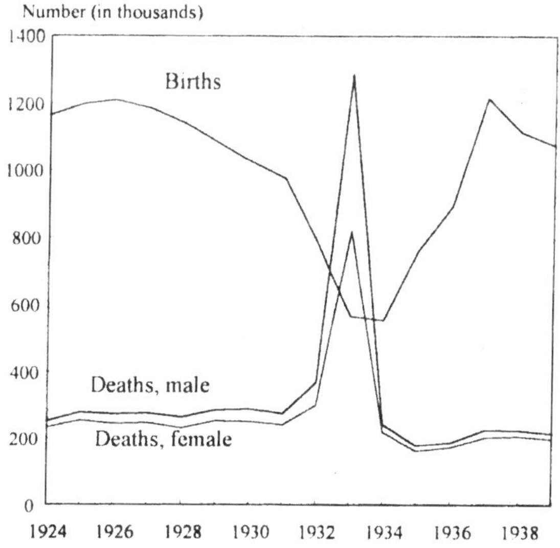

In terms of fertility, with a crude birth rate of 42 per thousand in 1926, it is hard to imagine a large under-registration of births, although the number of births declines in the late 1920s. The crisis obviously led to an abrupt fall, but it was less severe than the rise in mortality, followed by a catch-up peak....

To estimate the global losses due to the Great Famine, we followed the same general principle as in previous studies: to calculate an expected population by projecting the 1926 population until 1939 on the basis of fertility, mortality and migration rates that would have prevailed without crisis, and to compare it to the observed 1939 population. But unlike previous attempts, we decided that using vital statistics for the years before and after the crisis (after correction for under-registration) would be much more effective than referring to theoretical models for hypothesizing fertility rates throughout the period....

...[A]fter necessary corrections, existing data enabled us to calculate two life tables, or the start and the end of the period, relying on the 1926 and 1939 censuses and on the death statistics by sex and age available for 1926–27 and 1938–39. Between these two pillars, we interpolated survival probabilities by age for the period 1928 to 1938, assuming that in the absence of crisis, mortality rates would have decreased regularly from their 1926–27 levels to the 1938–39 ones. These probabilities were then applied, year by year from 1927 to 1939, to the generations involved in the 1926 census, in order to obtain an estimate of survivors, if there had been no crisis, on 1 January of each year from 1928 to 1939.

Then, to complete the projection, we estimated the numbers of births that would have occurred without the crisis.... [W]e deliberately chose the simplest hypothesis possible: through the whole period 1932–39, the general fertility rate was maintained at its 1931 level. A birth series was obtained that combines births registered by ZAGS [Civil Registry Offices] from 1924 to 1931 (corrected for under-registration) and estimated non-crisis births for 1932 to 1938. The projection was completed by applying the probabilities of survival if there had been no crisis affecting these births, which finally resulted in an *expected 1939 population*. While a total population of 35.5 million was expected at the time of the 1939 census, only 30.9 million were actually observed: 4.6 million Ukrainians were missing.

How to distinguish excess mortality from birth deficit and migration effect?....

1. *The role of the birth deficit*

   The easiest task is to estimate the role of birth deficit. Redoing the same population projection for 1939 and replacing the estimate of non-crisis births with registered births (corrected for under-registration of infant deaths) leads to a 1939 population of 34.4 million instead of 35.5.

   Conversely, the difference of 3.5 million between the second projection and the population actually observed in 1939 gives us a measure of the extent of losses attributable to both excess mortality and outward migration.

2. *Role of migration*

   Indeed, migration effects certainly are the most difficult to estimate, but not impossible if the various pieces of the puzzle are taken into consideration. Two types of migration have to be identified: forced migration, which has been carefully documented, and voluntary flight from the crisis, which is more difficult to assess.

For the first type of migration...[w]e ended with 400,000 Ukrainian people deported to camps outside of Ukraine during the years 1930 to 1938 and 530,000 to the *Gulag*: a total of 930,000 forced migrations of whom 563,000 were male and 367,000 were female.

It is much harder to make an assessment of voluntary migration.... Of course, the famine led some Ukrainians to flee the disaster zone, to Russia and Belarus, but most of these refugees had to return to Ukraine quickly since their illegal migration status (linked to the passport requirement imposed in 1932) prevented them from living and working outside Ukraine. Therefore, we have preferred to accept the balance of voluntary migration as almost nil and to confine ourselves to forced migration alone, while acknowledging that net outward migration may thus be underestimated. Thus, migration effect could account for 0.9 million.

3. *Estimating crisis mortality effect and under-registration of crisis deaths*
Finally, when subtracting from the 4.6 million global losses initially estimated the (1) 1.1 birth deficit effect and the (2) 0.9 outward migration effect, the remaining 2.6 million arises from the excess mortality of the crisis (see Table 1).

If we compare these 2.6 million deaths resulting from the excess mortality of the crisis to the 1.7 million difference observed between deaths registered and total numbers of deaths expected without the excess mortality arising from the crisis, we obtain the total number of deaths that escaped registration (0.9 million). However, among these, some are the result of the ordinary under-registration...which was taken into account in correcting the 1926–27 and 1938–39 life tables that we used to estimate non-crisis mortality by interpolation. There finally remain 530,000 deaths that escaped registration because of the crisis and acts of concealment by the regime....

Table 1. Contributions of excess mortality and of birth deficit to overall losses in the 1930s crisis, by sex

	Total numbers (thousands)		
Population (observed and expected) and losses	**Males**	**Females**	**Total**
Observed in the census (1)	14,753	16,193	30,946
Expected, given non-crisis mortality & fertility (2)	17,373	18,142	35,515
Expected, given non-crisis mortality and after correction of registered births (3)	16,833	17,625	34,458
Losses			
Total (2) - (1), of which	2,620	1,949	4,569
due to forced outward migration	563	367	930
due to excess mortality (or to voluntary outward migration) resulting from the crisis (3) - (1) - (4)	1,517	1,065	2,582
due to the birth deficit (2) - (3)	540	517	1,057

An Exceptional Fall in Life Expectancy

Given these hypotheses on the under-registration of deaths, an attempt can be made to estimate the annual change in life expectancy during the 1920s and 1930s, distinguishing the crisis years from other years....

While from 1927 to 1931, life expectancy was almost stable, with a few oscillations—going from 43.3 years to 43.5 for males and from 46.8 to 47.9 for females (see Table 2 and Figure 2)—it fell very abruptly with the crisis, losing almost 9 years in 1932, then another 28 years in 1933. In that year, it was just over 10.8 years for females and 7.3 for males.

This result may appear exaggerated, but we do not think that is the case.... [R]elying on the estimates given by Evgenii Andreev et al. for Russia (15.2 years for males and 19.5 years for females) and by the same authors, repeated by Alain Blum, for the whole USSR (10.3 years for males and 13.0 for females), it might be expected that life expectancy in Ukraine, which, of all the republics of the USSR, suffered most from the famine, would be significantly below 10 for males and around 10 for females.

Table 2. Estimate of annual change in life expectancy from 1927 to 1939

Year	Males	Females	Year	Males	Females
1927	43.3	46.8	1934	37.6	42.1
1928	44.6	48.7	1935	46.3	52.7
1929	42.8	46.7	1936	47.6	53.0
1930	42.5	46.9	1937	46.2	51.9
1931	43.5	47.9	1938	47.9	52.7
1932	34.5	39.4	1939	47.7	52.5
1933	7.3	10.9			

Calculated transversally, life expectancy measures the extent of the immediate circumstances of the crisis....

Figure 2. Change in life expectancy at birth between the wars, annually

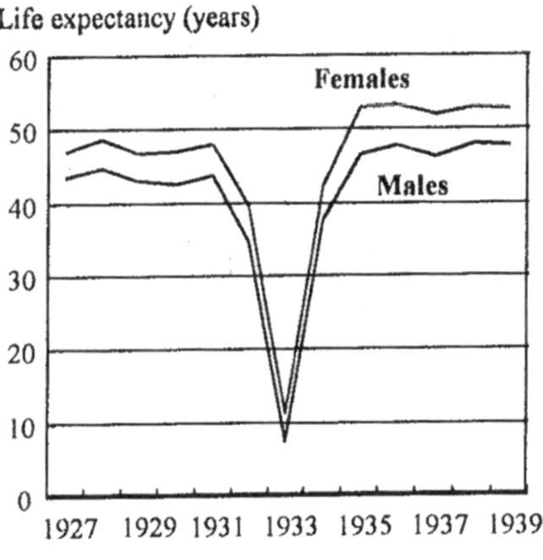

Conclusion

When precisely calculated by using all existent reliable data, total Ukrainian population losses strictly due to the *Holodomor* appear to be of 4.6 million people. This is significantly less than indicated by several previous studies.... Out of these 4.6 million losses, 1.1 million were due to the crisis birth deficit, 0.9 to forced outward migration, and 2.6 to the excess mortality. Here again, our 2.6 million estimate is much less than the levels currently available through the media, which vary from 4 to 10 million. Such a difference is mainly due to the fact that the results of studies on global losses are taken as the proper effect of excess mortality, and also that some authors attribute to Ukraine losses of the whole USSR.... There is no need to use incredible estimation when one can easily demonstrate that the crisis was so severe that it immediately reduced life expectancy at birth to 7 years for males and 10 years for females. The Great Ukrainian Famine of 1932–34 was far more brutal than the last great famine in Europe, which occurred in Finland in 1868. And the most astonishing is that such a famine resulted from deliberate human action, not from climatic hazard.

Oleh Wolowyna, "The Famine-Genocide of 1932–33: Estimation of Losses and Demographic Impact"

Originally published under the title "Demographic Dimensions of the 1932–33 Famine in Ukraine" in *Famine in Ukraine, 1932–1933: Genocide by Other Means*, ed. Taras Hunczak and Roman Serbyn (New York: Shevchenko Scientific Society, USA, 2007), pp. 98–114. Text revised for this publication.

Oleh Wolowyna (b. 1939) is an American demographer and statistician who specializes in Ukraine, the Ukrainian diaspora, and international development. He is a research fellow at the Center for Slavic, Eurasian and Eastern European Studies at the University of North Carolina-Chapel Hill, director and founder of the Center for Demographic and Socio Economic Research of Ukrainians in the US at the Shevchenko Scientific Society, and president of the Ukrainian Association of North Carolina.

Background

The number of losses due to the 1932–34 Famine in Ukraine (Famine losses were also recorded in 1934) has been the subject of many studies and controversies. The different estimates vary from around 2.6 million to more than 10 million. The figure of 10 million, extensively used by the government of Ukraine and some Ukrainian diaspora leaders, seems to be based on statements attributed, among others, to Stalin and the Moscow correspondent of the *New York Times*, Walter Duranty, who in his official reports to the *Times* denied the existence of the Famine, as well as on preliminary estimates made before key statistical data became available to researchers.

Before presenting the evidence for a more accurate estimate, it is essential to define what is meant by Holodomor losses. This definition needs to address four dimensions or issues: a) time period; b) territory; c) which deaths should be counted; d) whether lost births should be counted. Regarding the time period, although the brunt of the Famine took place in 1933, its effects started sometime in

1932 and continued through part of 1934; thus the period to be used for estimating the losses should be 1932–34. As for territory, the logical answer is the Ukrainian Socialist Soviet Republic (SSR). The inclusion in this estimate of losses during 1932–34 in other parts of the Soviet Union, such as the heavily Ukrainian-populated Kuban region, or of all Ukrainians in the Soviet Union, is problematic. This would require an estimate of Famine losses throughout the Soviet Union by ethnicity, i.e., losses among all Ukrainians (as well as other ethnic groups) on the territory of the Soviet Union as a whole or in specific regions of the Russian SFSR, such as the Kuban. No such estimates have been produced to date.

While Ukrainians as an ethnic group were not specifically targeted by official policies that caused the Famine, the historical record shows that the Ukrainian republic, as well as the Kuban region, with its large concentration of ethnic Ukrainians, were specifically targeted during the Famine years, resulting in much larger losses than elsewhere in the Soviet Union.

For historical and statistical reasons, it makes more sense to restrict the calculation of Holodomor losses to the territory of the Ukrainian SSR. Once a thorough estimate of Famine losses is made for the Kuban, one may consider adding them to the category of Holodomor losses.

Estimation of Losses

One of the sources of confusion about Holodomor losses is the lack of a universally accepted definition of this concept. We define "Holodomor losses" as deaths caused by the 1932–33 Famine, that is, deaths due directly or indirectly to starvation. Deaths due to other causes, such as political repression or deportation of kulaks, are not included in this concept. Strictly speaking, this definition makes it practically impossible to estimate the number of deaths caused by famine, as one would need a classification of all deaths during the Famine period by cause. A practical way of determining the number of these deaths is to try to separate "normal" deaths, i.e., deaths that would have occurred had there been no Famine, from deaths caused by the Famine. This can be done by estimating all the deaths that occurred during this period and then subtracting the "normal" deaths expected to have occurred had there been no Famine. This difference has been called "direct losses" or "excess deaths."

A related question is whether the estimate of Holodomor losses should also include "indirect" deaths caused by the Famine. "Indirect" deaths are defined as births lost during the Famine period as a direct cause of the Famine. As in the case of direct losses, they have to be estimated indirectly as the difference between the expected births had there been no Famine and the actual number of births during the Famine years. There has been a fair amount of discussion in the literature about the inclusion of these "indirect" deaths in the number of Holodomor losses. We argue that they should be included. The Famine was directly responsible for lost births owing to several mechanisms: a) reduced sexual activity; b) diminished male and female fecundity; c) higher levels of miscarriage; d) births lost owing to the death of potential parents. These lost births are thus a direct consequence of the Famine and should be included in the number of Holodomor losses.

Estimates of Holodomor losses may be divided into four types: a) subjective estimates by politicians and journalists during or shortly after the Holodomor;

b) estimates based on a variety of methods before key data (the 1937 and 1939 censuses, vital statistics, and data on migration) became accessible to researchers; c) estimates based on two contiguous censuses; d) more recent estimates based on demographically sophisticated methods that reconstruct annual populations by age and sex. Estimates of the first type are not credible because of their subjective nature, and estimates of the second type are problematic because key information was missing, and the estimates had to be based on unverifiable assumptions.

Estimates of the third type, based on the Soviet censuses of 1926, 1937, and 1939, were a significant improvement on those that preceded them, but one of their flaws is that they include all losses occurring between the two census dates (1926–37 or 1926–39). Besides the Holodomor losses of 1932–34, they include losses sustained during other years of these longer intercensal periods, and they almost certainly overestimate the number of Holodomor losses, which should be confined to the years 1932–34.

A very important factor in the estimation of Famine losses is net migration, i.e., the difference between out- and in-migration during a certain time period on a specified territory. The problem is that the actual census population (in 1937 or 1939) includes net migration during the intercensal period, which should be excluded from the estimate, as net migration has a direct bearing on the estimate of direct losses.

Our discussion is based on two recent studies that provide the most detailed estimates of Holodomor losses using the population reconstruction method. The first study is: J. Vallin, F. Meslé, S. Adamets, and S. Pyrozhkov, "A New Estimate of Ukrainian Population Losses during the Crises of the 1930s and 1940s," *Population Studies* 56, no. 3 (November 2002). The second study is: E. M. Libanova, I. O. Kurylo, N. M. Levchuk, O. M. Palii, N. O. Ryhach, O. P. Rudnytsky, V. S. Steshenko, L. I. Sliusar, P. I. Shevchuk, H. I. Bryker, N. V. Kulyk, and V. O. Sharapova, *Demohrafichna katastrofa v Ukraïni v naslidok Holodomoru 1932–1933 rokiv: skladovi, mashtaby, naslidky* (Demographic Catastrophe in Ukraine Owing to the 1932–33 Holodomor: Elements, Scope, and Consequences; Kyiv: Institute of Demography and Social Studies, 2008).

The population reconstruction method applied in both studies consists in making two detailed population reconstructions using the cohort-component population projection method. Starting with the initial 1926 census population disaggregated by age and sex, annual trends in fertility, mortality, and net migration are specified, and the cohort-component projection method calculates annual populations by age and sex (for the years 1926–37 or 1926–39). The first projection is based on the assumption that there was no Famine, i.e., historical trends in fertility and mortality are extrapolated and assumptions are made about net migration trends as if there had been no Famine. For the second projection, the annual population by age and sex is estimated as it actually occurred. For this purpose one needs to estimate the actual number of annual births by sex, the actual number of annual deaths by age and sex, and the annual number of net migrants by age and sex. Differences between the two projections allow us to estimate, on an annual basis, the number of excess deaths by age and sex, as well as the number of lost births by sex.

The population reconstruction method has several advantages over estimation methods used previously: a) Famine losses can be calculated on an annual basis, and thus for the Famine years (1932–1934); b) separate estimates are provided for excess deaths and for lost births; c) estimated excess deaths can be disaggregated by age and sex, and lost births by sex; d) the very useful indicator of life expectancy at birth by sex is also estimated.

The 2002 study provides the following estimates of Holodomor losses during the years 1932–34: excess deaths 2.6 million and birth losses 1.0 million, for a total loss of 3.6 million. The results of the 2008 study are as follows: excess deaths 3.6 million and lost births 1.1 million, for a total of 4.7 million. Based on these studies, we have a range of 2.6 to 3.6 million for direct losses and about 1 million for lost births, with a range of 3.6 to 4.7 million for total losses.

There are problems associated with the estimates derived by the 2002 study. First, estimates of lost births and net migration are for the 1926–39 intercensal period, while a more correct estimate should be limited to the years 1932–34. Second, it is assumed that the data for the 1926 and 1939 censuses were correct, and they were used without any adjustments. Third, as it is very difficult to estimate net migration because of serious data problems, the 2002 study made some estimates of net migration based on records of forced migration and assumed that voluntary net migration during the intercensal period was zero.

The 2008 study made estimates of lost births and net migration for the 1932–34 period and tried to make a more precise estimate of net migration. It also documented serious problems with the 1926 and 1939 censuses and made the necessary adjustments before proceeding to estimate Famine losses. Thus the estimates of Famine losses in the second study are likely to be more precise than those in the first study.

Both studies were restricted to Ukraine. In order to capture the complete migration dynamics between Ukraine and the rest of the Soviet Union, the analysis should be expanded to include all Soviet republics. Preliminary results from a more comprehensive study currently under way, which includes all the republics of the Soviet Union, provide what are probably more definite results: 3.9 million excess deaths and 600,000 lost births, for a total of 4.5 million losses. We see that, compared with the 2008 study, the estimate of direct losses is somewhat higher, while the estimate of indirect losses is significantly lower.

Given the nature of the data available, it is unlikely that one can determine estimates of Famine losses with great precision; it is more reasonable to state the results in terms of ranges. Thus, based on the more credible 2008 study and preliminary results from the more comprehensive study under way, one can state that direct Famine losses for Ukraine were close to four million, and that indirect losses were likely between 600,000 and one million, resulting in a range of 4.5 to 4.7 million total losses. These results can be put into better perspective by comparing them with the total population. If we assume that the population of the Ukrainian SSR in the early 1930s was about 30 million, Holodomor losses represent around 15 percent of the total population.

Although our proposed definition of Holodomor losses excludes losses outside the Ukrainian SSR, let us evaluate the claim that Ukrainians lost a total of seven million persons owing to the Famine. If approximately four million Holodomor victims died in Ukraine proper, this leaves 3 million Holodomor losses outside the Ukrainian SSR. Most of these losses occurred in the Kuban region, where Ukrainian settlements were targeted with starvation policies similar to those in Ukraine.

According to the 1926 census, the total population of the Kuban region was 3.3 million, and the proportion of ethnic Ukrainians was estimated at 60 percent, or 2 million persons. If we assume that losses due to the Famine constituted about 15 percent of the Kuban's total population (as in Ukraine) and affected exclusively Ukrainians (an extreme assumption), then the number of Holodomor losses in the Kuban would be about 300,000 (15 percent of 2 million). This would leave 2.7 million direct losses of Ukrainians in the rest of the Soviet Union (outside Ukraine and Kuban). As Ukrainians in the Soviet Union outside these two areas numbered 6.3 million according to the 1926 census, this means that more than 40 percent of them were victims of the Holodomor, clearly an unrealistic result.

Summary and Conclusions

Careful demographic analysis based on the most complete set of data available and using a sophisticated estimation methodology shows that the number of direct Holodomor losses in the Ukrainian SSR was close to four million, and the number of lost births an additional 0.6 to 1.0 million, for a total loss ranging between 4.5 and 4.7 million. This represents 15 percent of the total population of the country. These are staggering figures, unique in the history of twentieth-century Europe.

The impact of the 1932–34 Famine is further aggravated by differential mortality effects on various age groups. These effects are captured by the indicator "life expectancy at birth," which is usually calculated separately for males and females. This indicator is defined as the average number of years a person born in a specific year is expected to live, assuming that mortality conditions prevailing in that year remain constant throughout the person's lifetime.

Life expectancy at birth can also be interpreted as the weighted average of mortality levels at different ages. During years previous to the Famine, life expectancy at birth in Ukraine was about 42 years for males and about 45 years for females. According to the analysis by Libanova et al., in 1933 these values dropped to 4.4 years for males and 6.5 for females. These extremely low values are due to the fact that half of all deaths caused by the Holodomor in Ukraine in 1933 claimed persons under 25 years of age, and that 40 percent of all newborns died during their first year of life. (The respective life expectancies at birth estimated by the 2002 study were somewhat higher but equally dramatic: 7.3 years for males and 10.8 years for females.)

In order to put these life-expectancy values in perspective, we offer two comparisons: a) with average values of life expectancy at birth for West European countries in 1933; b) with respective values for Ukraine in 1942, the worst year in terms of World War II casualties. In 1933 the average life expectancies at birth for West European countries were 56.1 years for males and 58.7 for females, compared to 4.1 and 7.3 years for Ukraine, respectively; that is, in 1933 the average life span in Western Europe was from 9 to 12 times longer than the expected life span in Ukraine, assuming that Holodomor mortality conditions continued to prevail at the 1933 level. In 1942 these values were 17.7 years for males and 25.6 for females, that is, more than three times higher for males and about four times higher for females, compared with the 1933 values. The comparisons with West European figures provide a mortality standard that Ukraine was expected to reach some years later, while the comparisons with 1942 illustrate the age-specific mortality impact of the

Holodomor. Although in absolute numbers mortality in Ukraine was higher in 1942 than in 1933, a majority of these deaths were among army personnel, while in 1933 the Famine had a disproportionate effect on infants and children. This explains the significantly smaller values for life expectancy at birth during the Holodomor than during World War II.

The number of Holodomor losses remains a controversial subject, fueled by lack of understanding of the technical problems involved in these estimates, as well as by ideological and political considerations. In this article we have attempted to explain the challenges researchers face when making these estimates, and we summarize the results of the technically most reliable and objective research on this problem. Hopefully this will contribute to reaching a consensus on realistic figures for Holodomor losses and help channel efforts to achieve a better understanding of the details of this tragedy.

2

LEGAL ASSESSMENTS, FINDINGS, AND RESOLUTIONS

INTRODUCTION

This section begins with an excerpt from the United Nations Genocide Convention, which provides the definition of genocide recognized under international law. Readers may also wish to look at articles 6 and 7 of the Rome Statute of the International Criminal Court, not included in the *Reader*, which define genocide and crimes against humanity.

The section continues with statements by two commissions that studied the famine before the release of many important Soviet archival documents. In 1988 the Commission on the Ukraine Famine reported to the U.S. Congress that "Joseph Stalin and those around him committed genocide against Ukrainians in 1932–1933." In 1990 the International Commission of Inquiry into the 1932–33 Famine in Ukraine was unable to reach a consensus on the issue of genocide but did state that "in all probability, the grain procurements, collectivization, dekulakization and denationalization pursued a common, if not exclusive, goal and may not be radically disassociated when analyzing the causes of the famine." Professor Jacob Sundberg, who headed the commission, did find that the Ukrainian famine was genocide.

There follow official resolutions and statements by governmental and international bodies. In 2003, on the seventieth anniversary of the famine, the Ukrainian parliament stated that "the Holodomor of 1932–33 was deliberately organized by the Stalin regime and should be publicly condemned by Ukrainian society and the international community as one of the largest acts of genocide in world history by virtue of the number of its victims," while the UN joint statement recognized it as "a national tragedy for the Ukrainian people." The Law of Ukraine of 28 November 2006 declared the Holodomor "an act of genocide against the Ukrainian people resulting from deliberate actions of the repressive totalitarian Stalin regime aimed at the annihilation of part of the Ukrainian people and other peoples of the former USSR." Partly in response to the Ukrainian law, the Russian Duma declared that the famine "does not and cannot have the internationally established characteristics of genocide and should not be the subject of present-day political speculation." The Parliamentary Assembly of the Council of Europe noted that Ukraine "suffered the most" of all the regions of the USSR affected by famine.

On 13 January 2010 the Kyiv Court of Appeal issued a ruling in which it found the Soviet regime headed by Stalin guilty of genocide. The decision has symbolic value as the only legal ruling ever to have been made against Stalin and the Soviet leaders for the crimes they committed, even though the accused are long dead. The historian Timothy Snyder wrote a critique of the court's decision that readers can access at http://www.nybooks.com/blogs/nyrblog/2010/feb/03/ukraines-past-on-trial/.

This section ends with legal assessments of the famine. Raphael Lemkin, who pioneered the concept of genocide, argues that the famine constituted an essential part of "perhaps the classic example of Soviet genocide." Roman Serbyn, a Canadian historian of Ukrainian origin, analyzes the Holodomor through the prism of the UN Genocide Convention and concludes that it was genocide. Volodymyr Vasylenko, a Ukrainian legal scholar and diplomat, measures the Soviet authorities' decisions, actions, and failure to act against international criminal law and concludes that "planning the confiscation of excessive quantities of farm produce from the peasants is tantamount to planning the Holodomor."

Finally, the human-rights activist Yevhen Zakharov argues that until November 1932 the famine in Ukraine was similar to famines in other regions of the USSR. By February 1933, however, "death took on a mass character" in Ukraine. "Mass famine," he concludes, "was combined with political repression against the intelligentsia and national communists in 1933, as well as with the cessation of the policy of Ukrainization. Death from starvation...and from political repressions should be regarded as a crime against humanity and as the crime of genocide."

Convention on the Prevention and Punishment of the Crime of Genocide

Adopted by Resolution 260 (III) A of the United Nations General Assembly on 9 December 1948.
Text online at http://www.hrweb.org/legal/genocide.html.

Article 1

The Contracting Parties confirm that genocide, whether committed in time of peace or in time of war, is a crime under international law which they undertake to prevent and to punish.

Article 2

In the present Convention, genocide means any of the following acts committed with intent to destroy, in whole or in part, a national, ethnical, racial or religious group, as such:

(a) Killing members of the group;
(b) Causing serious bodily or mental harm to members of the group;
(c) Deliberately inflicting on the group conditions of life calculated to bring about its physical destruction in whole or in part;
(d) Imposing measures intended to prevent births within the group;
(e) Forcibly transferring children of the group to another group.

Article 3

The following acts shall be punishable:

(a) Genocide;

(b) Conspiracy to commit genocide;
(c) Direct and public incitement to commit genocide;
(d) Attempt to commit genocide;
(e) Complicity in genocide.

Article 4
Persons committing genocide or any of the other acts enumerated in Article 3 shall be punished, whether they are constitutionally responsible rulers, public officials or private individuals.

Article 5
The Contracting Parties undertake to enact, in accordance with their respective Constitutions, the necessary legislation to give effect to the provisions of the present Convention and, in particular, to provide effective penalties for persons guilty of genocide or any of the other acts enumerated in Article 3.

Article 6
Persons charged with genocide or any of the other acts enumerated in Article 3 shall be tried by a competent tribunal of the State in the territory of which the act was committed, or by such international penal tribunal as may have jurisdiction with respect to those Contracting Parties which shall have accepted its jurisdiction....

Commission on the Ukraine Famine, "Findings"

in *Investigation of the Ukrainian Famine, 1932–1933* (1988), pp. vi–viii.

Based on testimony heard and staff research, the Commission on the Ukraine Famine makes the following findings:

1) There is no doubt that large numbers of inhabitants of the Ukrainian SSR and the North Caucasus Territory starved to death in a man-made famine in 1932–33, caused by the seizure of the 1932 crop by Soviet authorities.
2) The victims of the Ukrainian Famine numbered in the millions.
3) Official Soviet allegations of "kulak sabotage," upon which all "difficulties" were blamed during the Famine, are false.
4) The Famine was not, as is often alleged, related to drought.
5) In 1931–32, the official Soviet response to a drought-induced grain shortage outside Ukraine was to send aid to the areas affected and to make a series of concessions to the peasantry.
6) In mid–1932, following complaints by officials in the Ukrainian SSR that excessive grain procurements had led to localized outbreaks of famine, Moscow reversed course and took an increasingly hard line toward the peasantry.
7) The inability of Soviet authorities in Ukraine to meet the grain procurements quota forced them to introduce increasingly severe measures to extract the maximum quantity of grain from the peasants.

8) In the Fall of 1932 Stalin used the resulting "procurements crisis" in Ukraine as an excuse to tighten his control in Ukraine and to intensify grain seizures further.
9) The Ukrainian Famine of 1932–33 was caused by the maximum extraction of agricultural produce from the rural population.
10) Officials in charge of grain seizures also lived in fear of punishment.
11) Stalin knew that people were starving to death in Ukraine by late 1932.
12) In January 1933, Stalin used the "laxity" of the Ukrainian authorities in seizing grain to strengthen further his control over the Communist Party of Ukraine and mandated actions which worsened the situation and maximized the loss of life.
13) [Pavel] Postyshev had a dual mandate from Moscow: To intensify the grain seizures (and therefore the Famine) in Ukraine and to eliminate such modest national self-assertion as Ukrainians had hitherto been allowed by the USSR.
14) While famine also took place during the 1932–33 agricultural year in the Volga Basin and the North Caucasus Territory as a whole, the invasiveness of Stalin's interventions of both the Fall of 1932 and January 1933 in Ukraine are paralleled only in the ethnically Ukrainian Kuban region of the North Caucasus.
15) Attempts were made to prevent the starving from traveling to areas where food was more available.
16) Joseph Stalin and those around him committed genocide against Ukrainians in 1932–33.
17) The American government had ample and timely information about the Famine but failed to take any steps which might have ameliorated the situation. Instead, the Administration extended diplomatic recognition to the Soviet government in November 1933, immediately after the Famine.
18) During the Famine certain members of the American press corps cooperated with the Soviet government to deny the existence of the Ukrainian Famine.
19) Recently, scholarship in both the West and, to a lesser extent, the Soviet Union has made substantial progress in dealing with the Famine. Although official Soviet historians and spokesmen have never given a fully accurate or adequate account, significant progress has been made in recent months.

International Commission of Inquiry into the 1932–33 Famine in Ukraine, *Final Report*

(Stockholm: International Commission of Inquiry into the 1932–33 Famine in Ukraine, 1990). The Stockholm Institute of Public and International Law, no. 109. Excerpts, pp. 38–43.

...*The Commission is unanimous* in finding the existence of a famine situation in Ukraine between approximately August–September, 1932, and July, 1933. As to the number of famine victims, the Commission agreed that it was unable to choose between one or other figure given by experts in different estimates. However, the Commission arrived at the conclusion that the number of victims in Ukraine was at least 4.5 million....

As causes of the famine, the *Commission majority* has identified (a) the grain procurements; (b) collectivization; (c) dekulakization; and (d) denationalization, and advances the following reasoning:

The Commission majority finds beyond doubt that the immediate cause of the 1932–33 famine lay in the grain procurements imposed upon Ukraine from 1930 onwards. It finds it also indisputable that the dreadful effects of the excessive grain procurements were considerably aggravated by the Soviet authorities trying to carry out the forced collectivization of agriculture, to eliminate the kulaks and to snuff out those centrifugal Ukrainian tendencies which threatened the unity of the Soviet Union. The ensuing disorders magnified the catastrophic consequences of a shortfall of cereals out of all proportions. The famine was certainly man-made in the sense that its immediate origin lies in human behaviour. No decisive evidence of a necessary connection between grain procurements, collectivization, dekulakization, and denationalization was put to the Commission. Nonetheless, it is very likely that these policies, pursued at the same time, were part of the same plan. The Commission believes that, in all probability, the grain procurements, collectivization, dekulakization and denationalization pursued a common, if not exclusive, goal and may not be radically disassociated when analyzing the causes of the famine.

Likewise, the Commission majority found it beyond doubt that the Ukraine was severely hit by famine in 1932–33 and that the Ukrainian and Soviet authorities were aware of the dire food shortages of the population....

The Commission majority observed that the Soviet authorities adopted various legal measures which amplified the disastrous effects of the famine....

However, the Commission majority found itself unable, with the information now at its disposal, to affirm the existence of a preconceived plan to organize a famine in the Ukraine in order to ensure the success of Moscow's policies. The Commission majority believes that the Soviet authorities, without actively wanting the famine, most likely took advantage of it once it occurred to force the peasants to accept policies which they strongly opposed.

In conclusion, the Commission majority does not believe that the 1932–33 famine was systematically organized to crush the Ukrainian nation once and for all; nonetheless it is of the opinion that the Soviet authorities used the famine voluntarily, when it happened, to crown their new policy of denationalization.

In his dissenting opinion, the President, Prof. [Jacob] *Sundberg,* followed a different line of reasoning. In his opinion, following the paper trail, you arrive at a number of manifest, non-controvertible causes which certainly have contributed to the famine and which allow placing responsibility squarely on the shoulders of particular individuals, but which have not been the only causes....

The Commission majority proceeds by finding that responsibility for the famine almost certainly lies with the authorities of the Soviet Union. The Commission majority has no doubt as to this responsibility; it suffices that the famine occurred and grew worse as the normal outcome of the measures adopted by the authorities....

Attempting to find which persons should bear the brunt of the responsibility for the famine in Ukraine, the Commission majority found itself generally unable to verify allegations referring to particular officials; except that all available materials—testimonies, documents, studies—attribute key responsibility to J. Stalin. So, it is he who first and foremost bears responsibility for the Ukraine famine of 1932–33. The Commission majority finds it reasonable to maintain that this responsibility must be shared by the other members of the Politburo, although the precise role that these other members played cannot easily be determined....

In his dissenting opinion, the President, Prof. *Sundberg*, again followed a different line of reasoning. In his opinion, the evidence shows that the famine situation was well-known in Moscow from the bottom to the top. Very little or nothing was done to provide some relief to the starving masses. On the contrary, a great deal was done to deny the famine, to make it invisible to visitors, and to prevent relief being brought....

In the opinion of Prof. Sundberg, industrialization, collectivization and suppression of nationalism were all, essentially, different sides of one and same problem created by the particular philosophy of the Party State. He thus finds the issue to be a matter of *aims within aims*. On the basis of this reasoning, Prof. Sundberg arrives at the conclusion that the statutory intent includes an intent to kill, and that this intent covers also major groups of people. On the basis of the same reasoning, Prof. Sundberg is inclined to dismiss all objections to the effect that the individuals in question may have been unaware of the conditions that resulted from the grain requisitions, in particular, the massive mortality. He find[s] that the lethal intent was directed at the Ukrainian nation as such—as it was directed at other nations as such within the big multi-nation empire that was the USSR—because this targeting was an aim within the overriding aim of establishing a new world of Socialism/Communism....

The Commission majority—Professors [Joe] Verhoeven, [John P.] Humphrey and [Ricardo] Levene—deems it plausible that the constituent elements of genocide were in existence at the time of the famine although the Genocide Convention was not created until 1948....

Prof. [Covey T.] Oliver does not feel convinced that the Petitioner has made a technical, legal case for genocide under the facts....

Prof. [Georges] Levasseur concurs partly with the statements in the majority opinion, but thinks that a qualification of the facts found should establish crimes against humanity and not genocide....

Prof. Sundberg states that his findings are such as to coincide with what is called genocide in the Genocide Convention.

"Resolution of the Verkhovna Rada of Ukraine no. 789–IV of 15 May 2003 on the Appeal to the Ukrainian People from Participants in the Special Session of the Verkhovna Rada of Ukraine on 14 May 2003 to Honor the Memory of the Victims of the Holodomor of 1932–1933"

Vidomosti Verkhovnoï Rady Ukraïny (News of the Verkhovna Rada of Ukraine, Kyiv) 2003, no. 30, p. 262.
English translation online at http://www.artukraine.com/famineart/ukr_speaks.htm, amended by Bohdan Klid.

...We, the participants in the Special Session of the Verkhovna Rada of Ukraine, guided by the ideals of humanism and social justice, upholding human and civil rights from the standpoint of values common to all humanity, appeal to the Ukrainian people, citizens of Ukraine of all nationalities, in this year of a tragic date in our history—the 70th anniversary of the Holodomor organized by the totalitarian Stalin regime.

The national and international community are commemorating the 70th anniversary of this Ukrainian national catastrophe in which, probably for the first time in human history, confiscation of food products was used by the state as a weapon of mass destruction of its own people for a political aim. The Holodomor of 1932–33, which became an inhuman means of liquidating millions of Ukrainians, confirms the criminal nature of the political regime of that time.

The brutal seizure of the 1932 harvest and its shipment beyond the borders of Ukraine, the confiscation of all food products from every peasant family, the destruction of temples and churches, mass repressions of the Ukrainian intelligentsia and clergy—all this was aimed at undermining the Ukrainian national spirit, eradicating its elite, and liquidating the economic independence of the peasantry.

The total extermination of millions of Ukrainian farmers by means of an artificially created famine was a deliberate terrorist act of the Stalinist political system. The social foundations of the Ukrainian nation, its ancient traditions, were ruined; its spiritual culture and ethnic uniqueness were undermined. For many decades, the tragedy of the Holodomor of 1932–33 in Ukraine was not only suppressed but also officially denied by the ruling political elite of the USSR. Its causes, nature, mechanism of organization, and scale were carefully concealed not only from the international community but also from several generations of our compatriots. But attempts to suppress the truth about the Holodomor of 1932–33 forever and drown it in the flow of time and history failed. The West has known and written about this Ukrainian Catastrophe since 1933. In 1988 the US Congress officially recognized the Holodomor of 1932–33 as genocide of the Ukrainian people, as did the International Commission of Jurists.[1]

As for the citizens of Ukraine, the truth about the events of 1932–33 began to be revealed to them on the eve of the collapse of the USSR. It was then that a breakthrough first occurred in the official suppression of these tragic facts of history.

It can now be said with certainty that the first words of truth about the Holodomor of 1932–33 played a notable role in the national renaissance and became one of the important factors contributing to the attainment of the independence of Ukraine.

Concomitantly, we believe that in the conditions of an independent Ukraine the terrible truth about those years must be made public officially by the state, as the Holodomor of 1932–33 was deliberately organized by the Stalin regime and should be publicly condemned by Ukrainian society and the international community as one of the largest acts of genocide in world history by virtue of the number of its victims.

---

1 The members of the International Commission of Inquiry were unable to reach a consensus on the question of genocide. See the preceding document. (Editors)

We, the participants in the Special Session of the Verkhovna Rada of Ukraine of May 14, 2003, do so today by recognizing the Holodomor of 1932–33 as an act of genocide against the Ukrainian people by the evil design of the Stalin regime.

We believe that designating this Catastrophe of the Ukrainian nation as genocide is of fundamental significance for stabilizing sociopolitical relations in Ukraine; is an important factor for restoring historical justice and moral healing of several generations from terrible social stress and evidence of the irreversibility of the process of social democratization; and is a severe warning against any attempt to establish a new dictatorship in Ukraine or violating the most basic of human rights—the right to life.

Having considered the question of the Holodomor as an act of genocide at a special session of the Verkhovna Rada of Ukraine, we have to a degree fulfilled our civic and patriotic duty to the memory of millions of people and to younger generations.

At the same time, we are deeply aware that it is only after making an official political and legal assessment of this social Catastrophe in the history of our Fatherland at the highest level of state authority and on behalf of all branches of government in Ukraine, holding an appropriate annual commemoration of its countless victims, and apprising the international community of the fact that this Holodomor was genocide against the Ukrainian people—only after doing this can we call ourselves a full-fledged civilized Nation.

In the name of the future, let us not forget the past!

Joint Statement on the Great Famine of 1932–33 in Ukraine (Holodomor) on Monday, November 10, 2003 at the United Nations in New York. By the delegations of: Azerbaijan, Bangladesh, Belarus, Benin, Bosnia and Herzegovina, Canada, Egypt, Georgia, Guatemala, Jamaica, Kazakhstan, Mongolia, Nauru, Pakistan, Qatar, The Republic of Moldova, The Russian Federation, Saudi Arabia, The Sudan, The Syrian Arab Republic, Tajikistan, Timor-Leste, Ukraine, The United Arab Emirates, and The United States of America on the seventieth anniversary of the Great Famine of 1932–33 in Ukraine (Holodomor)

Online at http://www.un.int/ukraine/Ukr-UN/Holodomor/N0360402.pdf.

In the former Soviet Union millions of men, women and children fell victims to the cruel actions and policies of the totalitarian regime. The Great Famine of 1932–33 in Ukraine (Holodomor), which took from 7 million to 10 million innocent lives and became a national tragedy for the Ukrainian people. In this regard we note activities in observance of the seventieth anniversary of this Famine, in particular organized by the Government of Ukraine.

Honouring the seventieth anniversary of the Ukrainian tragedy, we also commemorate the memory of millions of Russians, Kazakhs and representatives of other nationalities who died of starvation in the Volga River region, Northern Caucasus, Kazakhstan and in other parts of the former Soviet Union, as a result of civil war and forced collectivization, leaving deep scars in the consciousness of future generations.

Expressing sympathy to the victims of the Great Famine, we call upon all Member States, the United Nations and its special agencies, international and regional organizations, as well as non-governmental organizations, foundations and associations to pay tribute to the memory of those who perished during that tragic period of history.

Recognizing the importance of raising public awareness on the tragic events in the history of mankind for their prevention in future, we deplore the acts and policies that brought about mass starvation and death of millions of people. We do not want to settle scores with the past, it could not be changed, but we are convinced that exposing violations of human rights, preserving historical records and restoring the dignity of victims through acknowledgement of their suffering, will guide future societies and help to avoid similar catastrophes in the future. We need that as many people as possible learn about this tragedy and consider that this knowledge will strengthen effectiveness of the rule of law and enhance respect for human rights and fundamental freedoms.

Law of Ukraine "On the Holodomor of 1932–33 in Ukraine" no. 376–V of 28 November 2006

Vidomosti Verkhovnoï Rady Ukraïny (News of the Verkhovna Rada of Ukraine, Kyiv) 2006, no. 50, p. 504. Unofficial translation online at http://www.ukremb/canada/en/26651.htm, amended by Bohdan Klid.

The Verkhovna Rada of Ukraine resolves:

Honoring the memory of millions of compatriots who became victims of the Holodomor of 1932–33 in Ukraine and of its consequences;

Respecting all citizens who endured this terrible tragedy in the history of the Ukrainian people;

Realizing its moral duty to past and future generations of Ukrainians and recognizing the need to restore historical justice and affirm the unacceptability of manifestations of violence in society;

Noting that for many decades the tragedy of the Holodomor of 1932–33 in Ukraine was officially denied by the authorities of the USSR;

Condemning the criminal acts of the totalitarian regime of the USSR directed toward organizing the Holodomor, which resulted in the annihilation of millions of people and the destruction of the social foundations of the Ukrainian people and of its centuries-old traditions, spiritual culture, and ethnic distinctiveness;

Sympathizing with the other peoples of the former USSR who sustained losses as a result of the Holodomor;

Highly valuing the solidarity and support of the international community in condemning the Holodomor of 1932–33 in Ukraine....

Proceeding from the Recommendations of parliamentary hearings on honoring the memory of the victims of the Holodomor of 1932–33, approved by Resolution no. 607–IV of 6 March 2003 of the Verkhovna Rada of Ukraine, as well as from the Appeal to the Ukrainian People from Participants in the Special Session of the Verkhovna Rada of Ukraine on 14 May 2003 to Honor the Memory of the Victims of the Holodomor of 1932–33, approved by Resolution no. 789–V of 15 May 2003 of the Verkhovna Rada of Ukraine, in which the Holodomor was recognized as an act of genocide against the Ukrainian people resulting from deliberate actions of the repressive totalitarian Stalin regime aimed at the annihilation of part of the Ukrainian people and other peoples of the former USSR;

Recognizing, in accordance with the Convention on the Prevention and Punishment of the Crime of Genocide of 9 December 1948, the Holodomor of 1932–33 in Ukraine as an intentional act of mass destruction of people, hereby adopts this Law.

Article 1. The Holodomor of 1932–33 in Ukraine is genocide of the Ukrainian people.

Article 2. Public denial of the Holodomor of 1932–33 in Ukraine shall be regarded as desecration of the memory of the millions of victims of the Holodomor and denigration of the dignity of the Ukrainian people, and shall be unlawful.

Article 3. Organs of the national government and local authorities shall undertake, according to their competence:

> to take part in the formation and realization of government policy in the sphere of restoring and preserving the national memory of the Ukrainian people; to promote the consolidation and development of the Ukrainian nation, its historical consciousness and culture, dissemination of information about the Holodomor of 1932–33 in Ukraine among citizens of Ukraine and the international community; to provide for study of the tragedy of the Holodomor in the educational institutions of Ukraine; to take measures to perpetuate the memory of the victims and casualties of the Holodomor of 1932–33 in Ukraine, including the erection in populated areas of memorials and the installation of commemorative plaques to the victims of the Holodomor; to facilitate, according to established procedure, the access of scholarly and public institutions and organizations, scholars, and individuals studying problems of the Holodomor of 1932–33 in Ukraine and its aftermath to archival and other materials on questions regarding the Holodomor.

Article 4. The state shall ensure conditions for research on the Holodomor of 1932–33 in Ukraine and the commemoration of its victims on the basis of an appropriate national program, making annual provision for its financing from the state budget of Ukraine.

Article 5. Final provisions

1. This Law shall take effect on the date of its publication.
2. The Cabinet of Ministers of Ukraine shall:
   1) determine the status and functions of the Ukrainian Institute of National Memory and provide for its financing from the state budget as a specially authorized central executive body in the sphere of the restoration and preservation of the national memory of the Ukrainian people;
   2) within three months of the effective date of this Law:
      - submit proposals for consideration by the Verkhovna Rada of Ukraine on the harmonization of legislative acts of Ukraine with this Law;
      - harmonize its normative and legal acts with this Law;
      - ensure the revision and cancellation by executive organs of their normative and legal acts that do not conform to this Law;

3) resolve according to established procedure, together with the Kyiv Municipal State Administration, the issue of erecting in the city of Kyiv a Memorial to the victims of holodomors in Ukraine by the 75th Anniversary of the Holodomor of 1932–33 in Ukraine.

President of Ukraine
V[iktor] Yushchenko

State Duma of the Federal Assembly of the Russian Federation, Fifth Convocation. Declaration of 2 April 2008 "In Memory of the Victims of the Famine of the [19]30s on the Territory of the USSR"

Online at http://ntc.duma.gov.ru/bpa/searchrun.phtml?idb=1&ogu1=&nm=262-5+%C3%C4&sort=1.
Translated by Bohdan Klid.

The State Duma of the Federal Assembly of the Russian Federation shares the sorrow of the peoples of the former USSR on the occasion of the 75th anniversary of a terrible tragedy—the famine of the 1930s—that encompassed a considerable portion of the territory of the Soviet Union.

Archival documents studied by modern historians reveal not only the scope of the tragedy but also its causes. Extraordinary methods were used to attain the following aims: to destroy small property owners, carry out the forced collectivization of agriculture, and drive peasants from the village in order to obtain an army of workers for the rapid industrialization of the country.

As a result of the famine brought about by forced collectivization, there was suffering in many regions of the Russian SFSR (the Volga region, the Central Black Earth region, the North Caucasus, the Urals, the Crimea, part of Western Siberia), Kazakhstan, Ukraine, and Belarus. About seven million people died there in 1932–33 from starvation and diseases related to malnutrition.

The peoples of the USSR paid a heavy price for industrialization—for the huge economic breakthrough that occurred in those years. The Dniprohes, the Magnitogorsk and Kuznetsk metallurgical combines; the metallurgical giants of Ukraine: Zaporizhstal, Azovstal, and Kryvorizhstal; the large coal mines of the Donbas, Kuzbas, Karaganda, the Kharkiv Tractor Plant, the Moscow and Gorky automobile factories—in total, more than 1,500 industrial enterprises, many of which provide even now for the economic development of the independent states on the territory of the former Soviet Union—stand as an eternal monument to the heroes and victims of the thirties.

In an effort to resolve at any price problems of food supply to the rapidly growing industrial centers, the leadership of the USSR and the Soviet republics used repressive measures to secure grain requisitions, greatly aggravating the severe consequences of the poor harvest of 1932. However, there is no historical evidence that the famine was organized along ethnic lines. Its victims were million of citizens of the USSR representing different peoples and nationalities living largely in agricultural areas of the country. This tragedy does not and cannot have the internationally established characteristics of genocide and should not be the subject of present-day political speculation.

The State Duma confirms its commitment to the assertions of a joint statement of delegations of a number of UN member states adopted at the 58th session of the UN General Assembly in 2003 expressing sympathy for the millions of victims of the tragedy, irrespective of nationality.

The deputies of the State Duma, paying tribute to the victims of the famine of the 1930s on the territory of the USSR, resolutely condemn the regime that disregarded people's lives for the sake of achieving economic and political goals and declare as unacceptable in the states formerly part of the USSR any attempts at a revival of totalitarian regimes disregarding the rights and lives of their citizens.

Commemorating the victims of the Great Famine (*Holodomor*) in the former USSR. Resolution 1723 of the Parliamentary Assembly of the Council of Europe. Adopted on 28 April 2010

Online at http://assembly.coe.int/Mainf.asp?link=/Documents/AdoptedText/ta10/ERES1723.htm.

...3. One of the most tragic pages in the history of the peoples of the former Soviet Union was the mass famine in grain-growing areas of the country which started in the late 1920s and culminated in 1932–33.

4. Millions of innocent people in Belarus, Kazakhstan, Moldova, Russia and Ukraine, which were parts of the Soviet Union, lost their lives as a result of mass starvation caused by the cruel and deliberate actions and policies of the Soviet regime.

5. In Ukraine, which suffered the most, the peasantry was particularly hit by the Great Famine, and millions of individual farmers and members of their families died of hunger following forced "collectivisation," a ban on departures from the affected areas and confiscation of grain and other food. These tragic events are referred to as *Holodomor* (politically-motivated famine) and are recognised by Ukrainian law as an act of genocide against Ukrainians.

6. In Kazakhstan, too, millions fell victim to the mass famine, and the ratio of the dead to the whole population is believed to be the highest among all peoples of the former Soviet Union. Traditionally nomads, the cattle-raising Kazakhs were forced to settle down and were deprived of livestock. The Great Famine is remembered as the greatest tragedy of the Kazakh people.

7. In the grain-producing areas of Russia (the Middle and Lower Volga, the North Caucasus, the Central Black Soil region, the Southern Urals, Western Siberia and some other regions), the famine caused by "collectivisation" and dispossession of individual farmers took millions of lives in rural and urban areas. In absolute figures, it is estimated that the population of Russia had the heaviest death toll as a result of the Soviet agricultural policies.

8. Hundreds of thousands of farmers also died in Belarus and the Republic of Moldova.

9. While these events may have had particularities in various regions, the results were the same everywhere: millions of human lives were mercilessly sacrificed to the fulfilment of the policies and plans of the Stalin regime.

10. The Assembly honours the memory of all those who perished in this unprecedented human disaster, and recognises them as victims of a cruel crime of the Soviet regime against its own people.
11. It strongly condemns the cruel policies pursued by the Stalin regime, which resulted in the death of millions of innocent people, as a crime against humanity. It resolutely rejects any attempts to justify these deadly policies, by whatever purposes, and recalls that the right to life is non-derogable.
12. It welcomes the efforts aimed at revealing the historical truth about, and at raising the public awareness of, these tragic events of the past. Such efforts should seek to unite, not divide peoples.
13. The Assembly welcomes the important work already done in Belarus, Kazakhstan, the Republic of Moldova, Russia and in particular in Ukraine in order to ease access to archives, and calls on the competent authorities of these countries to open up all their archives and facilitate access thereto to all researchers, including from other states.
14. It further calls on other Council of Europe member states to make their national archives open and accessible.
15. The Assembly calls on historians of all countries of the former Soviet Union which suffered during the Great Famine, as well as historians from other countries, to conduct joint independent research programmes in order to establish the full, unbiased and unpoliticised truth about this human tragedy, and to make it public.
16. It urges the politicians in all Council of Europe member states to abstain from any attempts to exert political influence on historians and prejudge the outcome of independent scientific research.
17. It welcomes the decision by the Ukrainian authorities to establish a national day of commemoration of the victims of the Great Famine (*Holodomor*) in Ukraine, and encourages the authorities of other countries which also suffered to do the same with regard to their own victims.
18. It furthermore encourages the authorities of all these countries to agree on joint activities aimed at commemorating the victims of the Great Famine, regardless of their nationality.

Kyiv Court of Appeal Ruling of 13 January 2010 on the Famine of 1932–33 in Ukraine

Ukrainian text posted at http://www.reyestr.court.gov.ua/Review/9470003. Excerpts from English translation, pp. 1, 3, 12–13, 57–58. Translated by Victor Rud, Myroslaw Smorodsky, and Volodymyr Vasylenko. Amended by Bohdan Klid.

UKRAINE
KYIV COURT OF APPEAL
2-A Solomianska Street
Kyiv

RULING
IN THE NAME OF UKRAINE
13 January 2010, Kyiv

Judge V. M. Skavronik of the Criminal Chamber of the Kyiv Court of Appeal, in the presence of M. S. Bondarenko, secretary, with the participation of O. M. Dotsenko, prosecutor of the Kyiv Prosecutor's Office, carried out a preliminary examination of criminal case No. 1–33/2010, initiated by the Security Service of Ukraine pursuant to Article 442, section 1 of the Criminal Code of Ukraine, based upon the fact of the crime of genocide committed in Ukraine during the years 1932–33....

The pretrial investigation established that in 1932–33, on the territory of the Ukrainian SSR, the leadership of the Bolshevik totalitarian regime committed genocide of part of the Ukrainian national group: [the leadership consisting of] Joseph Vissarionovich Stalin (Dzhugashvili), general secretary of the Central Committee of the All-Union Communist Party (Bolshevik)/CC AUCP(B); Viacheslav Mikhailovich Molotov (Skriabin), member of the CC AUCP(B), head of the Council of People's Commissars [of the USSR]; Lazar Moiseevich Kaganovich, secretary of the CC AUCP(B); Pavel Petrovich Postyshev, secretary of the CC of the AUCP(B), second secretary of the CC Communist Party (Bolshevik) of Ukraine/CP(B)U, first secretary of the Kharkiv Oblast Committee of the CP(B)U; Stanislav Vikentiiovych Kosior, member of the CC AUCP(B), general secretary of the CC CP(B)U; Vlas Yakovych Chubar, member of the CC AUCP(B), member of the Politburo of the CC CP(B)U, head of the Council of People's Commissars of the Ukrainian SSR; Mendel Markovich Khataevich, member of the CC AUCP(B), second secretary of the CC CP(B)U....

[T]he pretrial investigation established irrefutable evidence that during the years 1932–33 J. V. Stalin, V. M. Molotov, L. M. Kaganovich, P. P. Postyshev, S. V. Kosior, V. Ya. Chubar, and M. M. Khataevich organized and perpetrated genocide in Ukraine by creating conditions of life calculated to bring about the physical destruction of part of the Ukrainian national group, using the following mechanisms and means:

- imposing on Ukraine a grain-procurement quota set at such a high level as to make its implementation unrealistic, and where it was fulfilled, only through the use of force with repressive measures and total confiscation from peasants of their grain and seed grain reserves;
- "blacklisting" of raions, population centers, collective farms, and village councils, that is, blockading them with military forces, preventing the population from leaving these territories, and the total confiscation of foodstuffs and prohibition of trade;
- isolating the territory of Ukraine with special task forces, military units, and militia;
- preventing peasants from freely traveling in search of food and banning correspondence;
- imposing "fines in kind";
- instituting constant searches with the confiscation of grain, sowing seed reserves, chattels, clothing, all foodstuffs, and cooked food;
- strengthening measures of criminal repression, including the execution of people who showed resistance to the authorities during the confiscation of meat, potatoes, sunflower seeds, and other foodstuffs.

The conclusions of the forensic judicial expert demographic assessment of the Institute of Demography and Social Research of the National Academy of Sciences of Ukraine, dated 30 November 2009, state that 3,941,000 people died as a result of the genocide perpetrated in Ukraine. Of these, 205,000 died in the period from February to December 1932; in 1933, 3,598,000 people died, and in the first half of 1934, the number of dead was 138,000....

Furthermore, according to the conclusion of the pretrial investigatory body, the guilt of J. V. Stalin (Dzhugashvili), V. M. Molotov, L. M. Kaganovich, P. P. Postyshev, S. V. Kosior, V. Ya. Chubar, and M. M. Khataevich in organizing and perpetrating genocide in 1932–33 against part of the Ukrainian national group is confirmed by factual data contained in...testimony....

[G]uided by Article 6, section 1, par. 8 and Articles 240 and 248 of the Code of Criminal Procedure of Ukraine, the Court of Appeal

Rules

To close the criminal case owing to the deaths of Joseph Vissarionovich Stalin (Dzhugashvili); Viacheslav Mikhailovich Molotov (Skriabin); Lazar Moiseevich Kaganovich; Pavel Petrovich Postyshev; Stanislav Vikentiiovych Kosior; Vlas Yakovych Chubar; and Mendel Markovich Khataevich, who, according to the conclusion of the pretrial investigatory body—the Chief Investigation Department of the Security Service of Ukraine—for the purpose of suppressing the national-liberation movement in Ukraine and preventing the restoration and consolidation of an independent Ukrainian state, deliberately organized the genocide of part of the Ukrainian national group by creating conditions of life calculated to bring about its destruction through the planned Holodomor of 1932–33, which resulted in the destruction of 3,941,000 people, that is, they directly perpetrated the crime as defined in Article 442, section 1 of the Criminal Code of Ukraine....

V. M. Skavronik
JUDGE
Criminal Chamber
Kyiv Court of Appeal

Raphael Lemkin, "Soviet Genocide in Ukraine"

Journal of International Criminal Justice 7 (2009): 123–30. Excerpts.

Raphael Lemkin (1900–1959) was a Polish-Jewish scholar who coined the term "genocide" and played a large role in the adoption of the United Nations Convention on the Prevention and Punishment of the Crime of Genocide. He was the author of *Axis Rule in Occupied Europe: Laws of Occupation – Analysis of Government – Proposals for Redress* (1944), where the word "genocide" first appeared in print. The text excerpted here is an address that he delivered at the Ukrainian Famine commemoration in New York in 1953.

The mass murder of peoples and of nations that has characterized the advance of the Soviet Union into Europe is not a new feature of their policy of expansionism, it is not an innovation devised simply to bring uniformity out of the diversity of Poles, Hungarians, Balts, Romanians—presently disappearing into the fringes of their empire. Instead, it has been a long-term characteristic even of the internal policy of the Kremlin—one which the present masters had ample precedent for in the operations of Tsarist Russia. It is indeed an indispensable step in the process of "union" that the Soviet leaders fondly hope will produce the "Soviet Man," the "Soviet Nation" and to achieve that goal, that unified nation, the leaders of the Kremlin will gladly destroy the nations and the cultures that have long inhabited Eastern Europe.

What I want to speak about is perhaps the classic example of Soviet genocide, its longest and broadest experiment in Russification—the destruction of the Ukrainian nation....

As long as Ukraine retains its national unity, as long as its people continue to think of themselves as Ukrainians and to seek independence, so long Ukraine poses a serious threat to the very heart of Sovietism. It is no wonder that the Communist leaders have attached the greatest importance to the Russification of this independent member of their "Union of Republics," have determined to remake it to fit their pattern of one Russian nation. For the Ukrainian is not and has never been, a Russian. His culture, his temperament, his language, his religion—all are different. At the side door to Moscow, he has refused to be collectivized, accepting deportation, even death. And so it is peculiarly important that the Ukrainian be fitted into the Procrustean pattern of the ideal Soviet man.

Ukraine is highly susceptible to racial murder by select parts and so the Communist tactics there have not followed the pattern taken by the German attacks against the Jews. The nation is too populous to be exterminated completely with any efficiency. However, its leadership, religious, intellectual, political, its select and determining parts, are quite small and therefore easily eliminated, and so it is upon these groups particularly that the full force of the Soviet axe has fallen, with its familiar tools of mass murder, deportation and forced labour, exile and starvation.

The attack has manifested a systematic pattern, with the whole process repeated again and again to meet fresh outbursts of national spirit. The first blow is aimed at the intelligentsia, the national brain, so as to paralyse the rest of the body. In 1920, 1926 and again in 1930–33, teachers, writers, artists, thinkers, political leaders, were liquidated, imprisoned or deported....

Going along with this attack on the intelligentsia was an offensive against the churches, priests and hierarchy, the "soul" of Ukraine. Between 1926 and 1932, the Ukrainian Orthodox Autocephalous Church, its Metropolitan ([Vasyl] Lypkivsky) and 10,000 clergy were liquidated. In 1945, when the Soviets established themselves in Western Ukraine, a similar fate was meted out to the Ukrainian Catholic Church. That Russification was the only issue involved is clearly demonstrated by the fact that before its liquidation, the Church was offered the opportunity to join the Russian Patriarch at Moscow, the Kremlin's political tool....

These attacks on the Soul have also had and will continue to have a serious effect on the Brain of Ukraine, for it is the families of the clergy that have traditionally supplied a large part of the intellectuals, while the priests themselves have been the leaders of the villages, their wives the heads of the charitable organizations. The religious orders ran schools, and took care of much of the organized charities.

The third prong of the Soviet plan was aimed at the farmers, the large mass of independent peasants who are the repository of the tradition, folklore and music, the national language and literature, the national spirit, of Ukraine. The weapon used against this body is perhaps the most terrible of all—starvation. Between 1932 and 1933, 5,000,000 Ukrainians starved to death, an inhumanity which the 73rd Congress decried on 28 May 1934.... The method used in this part of the plan was not at all restricted to any particular group. All suffered—men, women and children. The crop that year was ample to feed the people and livestock of Ukraine, though it had fallen off somewhat from the previous year, a decrease probably due in large measure to the struggle over collectivization. But a famine was necessary for the Soviet and so they got one to order, by plan, through an unusually high grain allotment to the state as taxes....

The fourth step in the process consisted in the fragmentation of the Ukrainian people at once by the addition to the Ukraine of foreign peoples and by the dispersion of the Ukrainians throughout Eastern Europe. In this way, ethnic unity would be destroyed and nationalities mixed. Between 1920 and 1939, the population of Ukraine changed from 80% Ukrainian to only 63%. In the face of famine and deportation, the Ukrainian population had declined absolutely from 23.2 million to 19.6 million, while the non-Ukrainian population had increased by 5.6 million. When we consider that Ukraine once had the highest rate of population increase in Europe, around 800,000 per year, it is easy to see that the Russian policy has been accomplished.

These have been the chief steps in the systematic destruction of the Ukrainian nation, in its progressive absorption within the new Soviet nation. Notably, there have been no attempts at complete annihilation, such as was the method of the German attack on the Jews. And yet, if the Soviet programme succeeds completely, if the intelligentsia, the priests and the peasants can be eliminated, Ukraine will be as dead as if every Ukrainian were killed, for it will have lost that part of it which has kept and developed its culture, its beliefs, its common ideas, which have guided it and given it a soul, which, in short, made it a nation rather than a mass of people.

The mass, indiscriminate murders have not, however, been lacking—they have simply not been integral parts of the plan, but only chance variations. Thousands have been executed, untold thousands have disappeared into the certain death of Siberian labour camps....

What we have seen here is not confined to Ukraine. The plan that the Soviets used there has been and is being repeated. It is an essential part of the Soviet programme for expansion, for it offers the quick way of bringing unity out of the diversity of cultures and nations that constitute the Soviet Empire. That this method brings with it indescribable suffering for millions of people has not turned them from their path. If for no other reason than this human suffering, we would have to condemn this road to unity as criminal. But there is more to it than that. This is not simply a case of mass murder. It is a case of genocide, of destruction, not of individuals only, but of a culture and a nation....

Roman Serbyn, "The Ukrainian Famine of 1932–1933 and the United Nations Convention on Genocide"

in *Famine in Ukraine 1932–1933: Genocide by Other Means*, ed. Taras Hunczak and Roman Serbyn. (New York: Shevchenko Scientific Society, USA, 2007). Excerpts, pp. 34–35, 37–44. Online at http://www.holodomorsurvivors.ca/Roman%20Serbyn.html.

Roman Serbyn (b. 1939) is a Ukrainian-Canadian historian specializing in nineteenth- and twentieth-century Ukrainian history. He served as associate professor of history at the University of Quebec (Montreal). He is the editor of the journal *Holodomor Studies* and coeditor of *Famine in Ukraine, 1932–1933* (1986) and *Famine in Ukraine 1932–1933: Genocide by Other Means* (2007).

The historicity of the Ukrainian famine of 1932–33 is no longer challenged. What is still disputed is the number of victims, the reasons for the catastrophe, and its nature.... The question of the Ukrainian famine has always had academic and political dimensions. And today, it still elicits partisan feelings among scholars and politicians.

The Ukrainian famine has not yet been recognized as genocide by the United Nations. When the 70th anniversary of the event was commemorated in November 2003 by the UN General Assembly, a declaration signed by some 60 countries stated that "the Great Famine of 1932–33 in Ukraine" took seven to ten million innocent lives, and explained that these people were victims of "the cruel actions and policies of the totalitarian regime." The catastrophe was called "a national tragedy for the Ukrainian people," but there was no allusion to genocide. The declaration erroneously attributed the cause of the famine to "civil war and forced collectivization" and misleadingly merged the Ukrainian catastrophe with the "millions of Russians, Kazakhs and representatives of other nationalities who died of starvation in the Volga River region, North Caucasus, Kazakhstan and in other parts of the former Soviet Union." The Ukrainian delegation agreed to this watered-down version out of fear that Russia would block a more strongly worded declaration. Ambassador Valerii Kuchynsky of the Ukrainian Mission to the UN later stated that it was, nevertheless, "an official document of the General Assembly" whose importance resided in the fact that "for the first time in the history of the UN, the Holodomor was officially recognized as a national tragedy of the Ukrainian people caused by the cruel actions and policies of a totalitarian regime." The recognition did constitute a precedent, and the Ukrainian Ambassador took advantage of it to return to the famine two years later. During the General Assembly discussion of the resolution on the International Holocaust Day, Kuchynsky recalled the Holodomor and urged the audience that it was "high time that the international community recognized that crime as an act of genocide against the Ukrainian nation."....

Generally speaking, opponents of the Ukrainian genocide thesis have a tendency to fall back on the UN Convention in their denial of the genocidal nature of the Ukrainian famine....

Advocates of the recognition of the Ukrainian famine have not yet succeeded in convincing the international community of the justice of their claim. Yet Andrea

Graziosi, a recognized expert in the field, has come to the conclusion that this will happen, due to new information revealed by new documents. What the Italian historian does not say is whether he believes that this claim can be made on the basis of the UN Convention. I think it can. In this paper I shall argue the following three points:

1. The Ukrainian famine was genocide.
2. Documents show that deliberate starvation was directed against Ukrainians.
3. The evidence meets the criteria set by the 1948 UN Convention on Genocide.

The UN Convention on Genocide

The Convention on the Prevention and Punishment of the Crime of Genocide was adopted by the UN General Assembly on 9 December 1948 and came into force on 12 January 1951. Soviet Ukraine became a signatory of the Convention on 16 June 1949 and ratified it on 15 November 1954. Independent Ukraine continues to respect the international Convention and has inscribed "Article 442. Genocide" into its own Code of Criminal Law.

The term "genocide" was coined in 1943 by Raphael Lemkin (1900–1959) "from the ancient Greek word *genos* (race, tribe) and the Latin *cidere* (to kill). In its composition it thus corresponds to such words as tyrannicide, homicide and infanticide." A Polish Jew born in what today is Lithuania, Lemkin studied law at the University of Lviv, where he became interested in crimes against groups and, in particular, the Armenian massacres during the First World War. In October 1933, as lecturer on comparative law at the Institute of Criminology of the Free University of Poland and Deputy Prosecutor of the District Court of Warsaw, he was invited to give a special report at the 5th Conference for the Unification of Penal Law in Madrid. In his report, Lemkin proposed the creation of a multilateral convention making the extermination of human groups, which he called "acts of barbarity," an international crime.

Ten years later, Lemkin wrote a seminal book on the notion of genocide. The author's approach was much broader than the one later adopted by the UN, as the following excerpt from his book shows: "Generally speaking, genocide does not necessarily mean the immediate destruction of a nation, except when accomplished by mass killings of all members of a nation. It is intended rather to signify a coordinated plan of different actions aiming at the destruction of essential foundations of the life of national groups, with the aim of annihilating the groups themselves. The objectives of such a plan would be disintegration of the political and social institutions, of culture, language, national feelings, religion, and the economic existence of national groups, and the destruction of the personal security, liberty, health, dignity, and even the lives of the individuals belonging to such groups."

The annihilation of a national group did not necessarily imply physical extermination of the whole group; the killing of individual members of the group and the destruction of the group's national foundations were sufficient to constitute genocide. Lemkin's book became a guiding light for the framers of the UN Convention on Genocide.

The Convention voted by the UN General Assembly contains 19 articles, dealing mainly with the problems of the prevention and punishment of genocidal activity. Most relevant to our discussion is the preamble and the first two articles. The preamble acknowledges that "at all periods of history genocide has inflicted great losses on humanity," while the first article declares that genocide is a crime under international law "whether committed in time of peace or in time of war." The all-important definition of genocide is contained in Article II: "In the present Convention, genocide means any of the following acts committed with intent to destroy, in whole or in part, a national, ethnical, racial or religious group, as such." The delegates of various countries who sat on the drafting committees arrived at this definition after much discussion. It was a compromise, which satisfied few people and continues to be criticized by legal experts, politicians and academics. However, it remains the only legal definition sanctioned by the UN General Assembly and operative in international courts.

A major objection to the definition is the restricted number of recognized genocide target groups. Coming in the wake of the Second World War and informed by Lemkin's work and the evidence of the Nazi concentration camps, the definition was necessarily tailored to the Jewish Holocaust. Jews fit all four categories: national, ethnic, racial and religious. They did not form a distinct political or social group, but this was not the reason for the exclusion of the two categories, which, after all, were part of Lemkin's concern. The exclusion of social and political groups from the Convention...was the result of the Soviet delegation's intervention. Today, the limitation of the definition to the four categories of victims implies that one cannot argue for the recognition of a specific Ukrainian genocide if its victims are identified only as peasants. Since it is clear that of the four human groups listed by the Convention, the Ukrainians did not become victims of the famine because of their religious or racial traits, this leaves the two other categories, "national" and "ethnic(al)," on which the case for genocide must be built.

There has always been a certain ambiguity about the distinction between the two groups labeled "national" and "ethnic(al)" by the Convention. William Schabas, internationally recognized legal expert on genocide, believes that all four categories overlap, since originally they were meant to protect minorities. He argues that "national minorities" is the more common expression in Central and Eastern Europe, while "ethnic minorities" prevails in the West. But if both terms were used to designate the same group then there would be redundancy, a fact that Schabas fails to account for.

A recent court case cited by Schabas provides, in my opinion, a more appropriate interpretation of "national group": "According to the International Criminal Tribunal for Rwanda, the term 'national group' refers to 'a collection of people who are perceived to share a legal bond based on common citizenship, coupled with reciprocity of rights and duties.'" What we have here is a "civic nation" formed by all the citizens of a given state, regardless of their ethnic, racial or other differentiation, as distinct from "ethnic nation," or people belonging to the same ethnic community, who may or may not live within the same state. Relevant to this discussion is a statement made in 1992 by a Commission of Experts, applying the Genocide Convention to Yugoslavia: "a given group can be defined on the basis of its regional existence...all Bosnians in Sarajevo, irrespective of ethnicity or religion, could constitute a protected group." The "regional" group is thus analogous to a civic nation. Such a clarification of the terms "national" and "ethnical" in reference to the term "group" used by the UN document removes all ambiguity and redundancy in the Convention. It also helps our understanding of the role of the government-induced starvation during the Ukrainian genocide, a policy directed against the Ukrainian peasants as citizens of the Ukrainian SSR and a specific ethnic group in the UkrSSR and RSFSR.

According to the UN Convention, the decisive element in the crime of genocide is the perpetrator's intent to destroy a human group identified by one of the four traits mentioned above. When applying this notion in concrete cases, certain aspects of the question of intent must be taken into consideration. First, it is not an easy task to document intent, for, as Leo Kuper pointedly remarked, "governments hardly declare and document genocidal plans in the manner of the Nazis." This is particularly true with reference to the totalitarian Communist regime. Yet, documents, which directly reveal Stalin's criminal intent, have survived in Soviet archives and are now available; furthermore, there is also a large body of circumstantial evidence which points in the same direction.

Secondly, contrary to a common misapprehension, the Convention's definition of genocide is not predicated on the intent to destroy the whole group; it is sufficient that the desire to eliminate concern only a part of the group. The Convention thus implies the possibility of victim selection within the designated group. Practical application to the Ukrainian case would mean the recognition of the probability that the choice of victims was limited to a sizable portion of the Ukrainian peasants and the more nationally conscious elements of the Ukrainian cultural and political elites, both in Ukraine and in the RSFSR. Most of the victims of the genocide were starved to death, but others were executed or perished in the Gulag.

Thirdly, the Convention (Article II) lists five ways in which the crime is executed:

1. Killing members of the group;
2. Causing serious bodily or mental harm to the members of the group;
3. Deliberately inflicting on the group conditions of life calculated to bring about its physical destruction in whole or in part;
4. Imposing measures intended to prevent births within the group;
5. Forcibly transferring children of the group to another group.

It should be noted that while the first and the third points specify physical annihilation, the other three speak of weakening the group, or what Lemkin referred to as the destruction of essential foundations of the life of the national group. All of these acts can be documented in the Ukrainian experience.

Fourthly, the Convention does not demand the establishment of the motive behind the crime, even though knowing the reasons for a crime can help to establish the criminal's intent. The Soviet delegate contested this omission during the framing of the Convention, arguing that "a crime against a human group became a crime of genocide when that group was destroyed for national, racial, or religious motives." A compromise was found, and to the enumeration of the four victim groups the committee added the qualifier "as such." The lack of precision was convenient, for it allowed each country to give its own interpretation to the clause. The Soviet side explained this addition as recognition that "in cases of genocide, the members of a group would be exterminated solely because they belonged to that group." This interpretation became part of the Soviet definition of genocide and has persisted in post-Soviet Ukraine until the present day. The online *Great Ukrainian Dictionary* defines genocide as "destruction of distinct groups of population for racial, national or religious motives." This explains why Ukrainian scholars today focus on the question "*why* Stalin destroyed?", while the Convention demands proof of Stalin's *intent* to destroy.

The analysis offered by Schabas is close to that of the old Soviet position. While admitting that "there is no explicit reference to motive in article II of the Genocide Convention" and pointing out that "intent and motive are not interchangeable notions," Schabas nevertheless focuses on the expression "as such," and insists that the crime of genocide must be "motivated by hatred of the group." To a large extent this is so. With the help of a criminal ideology, perpetrators of genocide can transform a targeted group into an object of blind hate, which then, in itself, becomes a motive for total or selective destruction of members of that group. In other words, members of a group "X" become singled out for destruction because they are members of that group. As Lemkin wrote: "Genocide is directed against the national group as an entity, and the actions involved are directed against individuals, not in their individual capacity, but as members of the national group."....

Two Canadian scholars with long experience in genocidal studies have divided genocides into four groups according to the objectives of the perpetrators:

To eliminate a real or potential threat;

To spread terror among real or potential enemies;

To acquire economic wealth; or

To implement a belief, a theory or an ideology.

All these aims were present in the Ukrainian genocide: a) to avert the threat to the integrity of the Soviet empire from the Ukrainian national revival; b) to terrorize the Ukrainian people into submission to Stalin's will; c) to seize Ukrainian grain to feed Soviet industrial centers and export abroad; d) to eradicate the vestiges of capitalist economy and consolidate socialism....

Volodymyr Vasylenko, *The Ukrainian Holodomor of 1932–33 as a Crime of Genocide: A Legal Assessment*

(Kyiv: Olena Teliha Publishing House, 2009). Excerpts, pp. 5–8, 10–15, 39–43.

Volodymyr Vasylenko (b. 1937) is a Ukrainian legal scholar, jurist, and diplomat. A professor of international law at the Kyiv Mohyla Academy National University and the Diplomatic Academy of Ukraine, he has served as ambassador to the Benelux countries, the United Kingdom, and Ireland; as representative of Ukraine to the European Union, the North Atlantic Co-operation Council, the International Maritime Organization, and the UN Commission on Human Rights (since 2006, the UN Human Rights Council); and as judge ad litem of the International Criminal Tribunal for the Former Yugoslavia.

Distinctive Features of Genocide

...Some researchers of the Holodomor often criticize the legal definition of genocide for its imperfection, and the 1948 Convention for its drawbacks.... Moreover, some of them conclude that only the Holocaust meets the Convention's legal criteria and that such criteria still "do not provide a 100 percent guarantee that all cases of mass destruction of people will be identified as genocide".... Such assessments of the 1948 Convention are erroneous from at least two perspectives.

First, the legal criteria of the Convention were not designed to qualify *all* cases of the mass destruction of people as genocide. Pursuant to article II of the Convention, the term genocide means certain criminal acts committed against any national, ethnic, racial or religious group as such, and not simply cases of mass destruction of people....

Secondly, while the criteria of the 1948 Convention were formulated under the impact of the tragic events of World War II, they remain the rules of general international law. Thus, this document and only this document may be used to determine whether certain criminal acts meet the legal definition of genocide.

The Convention on the Prevention and Punishment of the Crime of Genocide reflects the historical context in which it was elaborated. Whether or not one likes the final version of the Convention signed on 9 December 1948, it remains an authentic and legally valid instrument of international law. No state [n]or the international community as a whole has challenged the authority of the 1948 Convention, as was convincingly confirmed fifty years later when article II, which defines the *corpus delicti* of genocide, was repeated word for word in article 6 of the Rome Statute of the International Criminal Court.

In light of the above, any attempt to interpret the provisions of the 1948 Convention in order to "improve" it or adapt it to the specifics of "Soviet genocide" would be counterproductive. The researchers who take such an approach present theses which, from a legal point of view and contrary to their good intentions, provide grounds for denying the genocidal nature of the Holodomor.

On the other hand, attempts by researchers, politicians and political scientists of certain countries to deny the genocidal nature of the Holodomor by consciously distorting the provisions of the 1948 Convention are inadmissible.

In accordance with the principles of the law of international treaties, the 1948 Convention should be accepted just as it is and applied to qualify criminal acts as genocide in strict conformity to the *corpus delicti* set forth exclusively by the Convention, and not to arbitrarily selected criteria for the sake of convenience.

The essence of the crime of genocide is defined in the introductory part of article II of the 1948 Convention as "...acts committed with intent to destroy, in whole or in part, a national, ethnical, racial or religious group, as such." It is well recognized in the theory of international law and confirmed by practice that for a criminal act to constitute genocide, one must prove that the perpetrator had a special intent (*dolus specialis*) to destroy a group specified in the Convention, and that the criminal behavior was committed against the defined group as such.

Actions that lack both of the aforementioned essential elements do not constitute an act of genocide even if they resulted in a group's extermination. Genocide differs from other crimes against humanity, first, in the nature of the intent rather than the number of victims. Secondly, it is committed, not against people in general, but against a clearly defined group. Thirdly, genocide is not directed just against individual members of the group but primarily against the group as such.

In other words, a distinctive feature of genocide is that members of the groups defined in the 1948 Convention—national, ethnic, racial or religious—are exterminated, in whole or in part, because of their very affiliation to a respective group.

A decisive factor in qualifying certain behavior as the crime of genocide is the proof of a special intent to destroy a particular national, ethnic, racial or religious group and demonstrating that this intent specifically related to that group, rather than asking why, when and where was the crime committed or concentrating on the so-called quantitative threshold, that is, the number of victims....

Proof of Intent to Organize the Holodomor

To prove the genocidal nature of the Holodomor, it is first of all necessary to demonstrate that Stalin's totalitarian communist regime intended to organize the man-made famine in Ukraine. Those who deny that the Holodomor was an act of genocide ask whether this intent was documented and whether there existed a premeditated plan as evidence of this intent....

Given the above, it should be emphasized that the 1948 Convention does not require a document to be produced as evidence of the existence of a criminal plan or the intent to commit a crime: it only requires that such intent be proven.

Moreover, it is highly unlikely that a document containing a plan for the destruction by starvation of the Ukrainian peasantry will ever be found. Given the proclivity to secrecy instilled in the minds of Bolshevik leaders and their desire to cover up a horrifically criminal and inhuman act, the existence of such a document is problematic in principle. Even in Nazi Germany with its officially approved racist policy, the genocide committed against the Jews was implemented under the guise of a "final solution to the Jewish question."

Today those who deny that the Ukrainian Holodomor was an act of genocide agree that the famine in Ukraine and elsewhere in the USSR was precipitated by the arbitrary confiscation of grain and other produce grown by the peasants, in compliance with the government's excessive grain procurement plans as ordered by higher Party organs. The implementation of such plans doomed the inhabitants of rural areas to an inevitable death by starvation. Hence, planning the confiscation of excessive quantities of farm produce from the peasants is tantamount to planning the Holodomor. It can therefore be said that the plan for exterminating Ukrainian peasants was disguised in the form of the state's excessive grain procurements.

All of the plans for excessive grain procurements served criminal purposes but only the grain procurement plans of 1932 and 1933 became plans for the genocidal extermination of the Ukrainian peasantry....

There can be no doubt that the Bolshevik leaders fully understood that the continuous practice of such procurement plans would precipitate a large-scale famine and doom millions of peasants to death by starvation....

Thus, the Ukrainian Holodomor planned by Stalin's regime commenced with the implementation of the 1932 plan for grain procurement. In light of this, it is erroneous to assert that the Holodomor-genocide started in Ukraine in 1933. Such a conclusion is based upon the presumption that the crime of genocide requires a certain quantitative threshold related to the number of victims. This is clearly incorrect, as the 1948 Convention does not make the number of victims a legal element of the crime. It is not difficult to imagine instances where the number of victims of genocide could be quite limited, involving not even thousands of people, but only hundreds, as in the destruction of a small tribe or ethnic minority.

Killing by starvation occurred in Ukraine and the Kuban both before and during 1933. The difference between the two periods consisted only in the quantitative scale of the crime. While in 1932 hundreds of thousands of people were starved to death, the death toll in 1933 was already in the millions. However, the famine of 1932–33 in both Ukraine and the Kuban—unlike in other regions of the USSR, where many also perished of hunger—was an act of genocide because it was deliberately directed against the Ukrainian nation as such.

In the critical situation that developed in Ukraine, a civilized solution to the crisis would have been to drastically reduce the excessive grain procurement plans, stop the barbarian plundering of rural areas, declare the famine-struck areas as zones of humanitarian catastrophe, and immediately provide large-scale assistance.

Instead, Stalin's totalitarian communist regime continued to implement excessive grain procurement plans and, to ensure their unconditional fulfillment, also undertook unprecedented repressive measures against the Ukrainian peasants, accompanied by the confiscation of all food products....

The strict and widespread application of exceedingly cruel and repressive measures in order to fulfill the excessive grain procurement plans, such as the arbitrary confiscation of all food supplies, should be convincing proof of the intent of the totalitarian regime to precipitate a famine in Ukraine as the instrument for the premeditated extermination of the Ukrainian peasantry *as part of the Ukrainian nation*.

An analysis of the behavior of the communist leaders reveals a body of circumstantial or indirect evidence that convincingly proves the existence of the special intent required for the crime of genocide.

First, at the height of the Holodomor Ukrainian peasants were prohibited from leaving Ukraine.... This restriction deliberately deprived starving peasants of access to life-saving food beyond the borders of famine-struck Ukraine, thereby condemning them to death.

Second, Party and Soviet leaders at all levels who disagreed with the excessive grain procurement plans and who wished to help the starving peasants with collective-farm produce reserves were systematically and ruthlessly repressed.

Third, the sizable quantities of grain that had been accumulated in the state reserves of both the Inviolable and Mobilization Funds were not used to help Ukraine....

Fourth, while millions of Ukrainian peasants were starving to death, large quantities of grain and other Ukrainian food products were being exported to other regions of the USSR and abroad....

Fifth, Stalin's regime denied the existence of a famine in Ukraine and therefore refused to accept the aid offered by many foreign non-governmental organizations and, in particular, by the Ukrainian communities abroad. Such assistance would have substantially reduced the scale of the tragedy, if not preventing it altogether. This policy of denial and the refusal of international humanitarian aid is additional convincing evidence of the regime's intention to use famine for exterminating the Ukrainian peasantry *as part of the Ukrainian nation*.

Hence, the communist regime had sufficient resources to prevent both the Holodomor in Ukraine and starvation in other regions of the USSR. However, instead of using these resources, a well-devised system of repressive measures was deliberately implemented to deprive the peasants of all food because Kremlin leaders intended to use a man-made famine as an instrument of genocidal extermination.

The regime's obvious ability to "control" the famine in 1932–33 confirmed the artificial nature of the Ukrainian Holodomor and its deliberate use for killing the Ukrainian peasants. By the middle of 1933 the mortality rate due to starvation began to drop in Ukraine. In the following year the famine actually ended, even though the 1934 harvest was a mere 12.3 million tonnes and much smaller than the harvests of 1932 and 1933, which totaled 36.9 million tonnes....

The regime's "efficiency" in both organizing and ending the Holodomor is evidence of the fact that the intent to exterminate the Ukrainian peasants was implemented within the strict time limits that the regime had set for itself....

Guilt and Healing

Qualifying the Holodomor of 1932–33 as the crime of genocide also raises the issue of responsibility. From a legal point of view, this responsibility rests with the USSR as the Party state, and with all persons who participated in organizing and committing this crime, regardless of their position, status, or ethnic origin.

The Party state ceased to exist with the collapse of the USSR. All of the former union republics had become its successor states. However, the Russian Federation, contrary to international law, has declared itself to be the "state continuator of the USSR." In any case, Ukraine has repeatedly stated that it does not link recognition of the Holodomor as genocide with the international responsibility of the Russian Federation. Ukraine will therefore make no claims in that regard. Of course, this does not preclude individuals—the descendants of Holodomor victims—from claiming against the Russian Federation, as it considers itself the state continuator of the USSR. However, in practical terms the successful realization of such claims would be problematic.

The terrible circumstances of the crime make it impossible to state the exact number of victims and, in many cases, to determine their identities. It would also be very difficult to find witnesses for concrete cases, as the crime was committed several decades ago. Finally, one should also take into account the jurisdictional difficulties associated with the fact that perpetrators of the crime at the republic level were officials of the UkrSSR, who in many cases acted on their own initiative and in compliance with the republic's legislative and regulatory acts. However, it must be remembered that the UkrSSR, as a constituent republic of the USSR, was subordinated to the "Party state" dictatorship.

It is relatively simpler to establish the responsibility of the main organizers and perpetrators of the crime at both the union and republic levels. However, their punishment would be impossible because some of them—in particular, [Joseph] Stalin, [Lazar] Kaganovich, and [Viacheslav] Molotov—died natural deaths. By far the larger part—among them [Stanislav] Kosior, [Vlas] Chubar, [Pavel] Postyshev, [Vsevolod] Balytsky, [Stanislav] Redens, and [Mendel] Khataevich, and heads of all regional committees of the CP(B)U—were eliminated during Stalin's purges. It is rather ironic that this larger group was punished, but not for their participation in the Holodomor.

It should be noted that the various ethnic affiliations of the ideologists, organizers, participants, perpetrators and accomplices of the Holodomor cannot, of course, be used to accuse their respective peoples—Georgians, Russians, Jews, Poles, Latvians and others—of having a role in the crime.

In political terms, responsibility for the Holodomor-genocide in Ukraine and the extermination of peasants by famine elsewhere in the USSR should rest with Stalin's communist regime. This explains why representatives and followers of the Communist Party of Ukraine, which is the ideological successor to the All-Union CP(B) and then CPSU, attempt to deny the genocidal nature of the Ukrainian Holodomor, and often deny that there was even famine in the former USSR.

Russian Federation officials have actively opposed international recognition of the Ukrainian Holodomor as the crime of genocide. This is not surprising, given that the principal organizer of the crime, Stalin, is regarded today by Russia's ruling elite as a "strong politician" and "successful manager." What is surprising and incomprehensible, however, is that recognition of the Holodomor as genocide is viewed by various officials of the Russian Ministry of Foreign Affairs as an insult to the memory of the victims in other regions of the former USSR.

Qualifying the Ukrainian Holodomor as a crime of genocide should not be taken as a denial of the criminal nature of the actions of Stalin's regime against the peasants of Russia, Belarus, Kazakhstan, Bashkortostan and others. Ukraine does not oppose honoring the memory of those victims, nor is it against condemning the other crimes of Stalinism. In fact, the real insult to the memory of those victims is not the position taken by Ukraine, but the glorification of the person most responsible for the crimes of the communist regime.

The Russian political establishment's hysterical reaction to historical truth can be easily explained. The revelation about the causes of the Holodomor and its consequences undermines the position of anti-Ukrainian elements in both Ukraine and abroad, and calls for action aimed at strengthening national statehood, developing democratic institutions, and moving further towards Ukraine's integration into European and Euro-Atlantic structures.

The majority of the Russian political establishment still regards Ukraine as a part of Russia, sharing with it a common history and fate. Hence, the Russian leadership wishes to impose on Ukraine and the world its own version of Ukrainian history. Denying Ukraine the right to its own history is a covert form of denying its right to independence.

It is now obvious that the underlying causes of the Holodomor were rooted in Ukraine's loss of independence and its domination by a regime subordinated to the Kremlin leadership and hostile to its nationhood. This fact alone should expressly warn Ukraine about the deadly threat to its statehood by neo-imperialistic plans for the restoration of a "Unified Greater Russia" that includes Ukraine....

The tragedy of the Holodomor should compel one to resolutely oppose the Kremlin's neo-imperialistic plans. This may also explain why the revelation and dissemination of the historical truth about the Ukrainian Holodomor has met with such rejection and opposition on the part of official Russia.

James Mace concluded that the Holodomor left Ukrainian society in a state of post-genocidal trauma. To a considerable degree, this remains true today. Therefore the immediate task is to politically condemn the crimes of Stalin's totalitarian communist regime. This should be accompanied by a systematic study of the Holodomor's devastating consequences and the undertaking of comprehensive measures for the revival of the Ukrainian nation, the rehabilitation of Ukrainian society, and the democratic development of an independent Ukrainian state....

Yevhen Zakharov, "Pravova kvalifikatsiia Holodomoru 1932–1933 rokiv v Ukraïni ta na Kubani iak zlochynu proty liudianosti ta henotsydu" (Opinion: Legal Classification of the Holodomor of 1932–33 in Ukraine and in the Kuban as a Crime against Humanity and Genocide)

Online at http://khpg.org.ua/en/index.php?id=1221299499.
Translated by the Kharkiv Human Rights Protection Group and Alexander J. Motyl.

Yevhen Zakharov (b. 1952) is a Ukrainian human-rights activist. He is a board member of the Ukrainian Helsinki Human Rights Union, co-chair of the Kharkiv Human Rights Group, and board member of the International Memorial Society. He is the author and editor of many articles and studies of human rights in Ukraine.

This Opinion attempts to demonstrate that the Holodomor of 1932–33 in Ukraine and the Kuban has the features of a crime against humanity in accordance with the Rome Statute of the International Criminal Court (hereafter RC ICC), adopted on 17 July 1998, and of genocide according to the Convention on the Prevention and Punishment of the Crime of Genocide (hereafter the Convention), adopted on 9 December 1948....

When speaking of the famine of 1932–33, it is necessary to differentiate among three different types of hunger, each of which has, in addition to common features, its own specific causes, characteristics, and consequences that vary in scale. The famine of the first half of 1932 was caused by nonfulfillment of the grain-requisition quotas for the 1931 harvest and the Kremlin's policy toward rural areas in connection with this nonfulfillment. That famine was stopped by the return from ports of some of the grain intended for export, as well as by the purchase of grain from abroad. In the third quarter of 1932, famine occurred again as a result of the nonfulfillment of the grain-requisition quotas for the 1932 harvest. It must be stressed that the nature of the famine in Ukraine up to November 1932 was the same as in other agricultural regions of the USSR. *Starvation during the famine of the first and second periods should be considered a crime against humanity.*

The third type of famine was caused by the confiscation of bread and all other food products, which was carried out only in the rural areas of Ukraine and the Kuban. Confiscation was partial in November–December 1932 and total in January

1933. Moreover, owing to measures adopted by the Party and state leadership of the USSR and the Ukrainian SSR, people were prohibited from leaving in search of food or from receiving it from outside. Left without any food, the peasants died of starvation. From February 1933, death took on a mass character: from February to August millions of peasants died of starvation in Ukraine, and hundreds of thousands in the Kuban. According to demographic statistics, the direct losses to Ukraine from the famine of 1932–33 constituted 3–3.8 million according to some data and 4–4.8 million according to other data. Mass famine was combined with political repression against the intelligentsia and national communists in 1933, as well as with the cessation of the policy of Ukrainization. *Death from starvation during the famine of the third type and from political repressions should be regarded as a crime against humanity and as the crime of genocide.*

Death from Starvation during the Period from January to October 1932—A Crime against Humanity

...[T]he grain-requisition quota for 1930 was already excessive, but the Soviet leadership increased it still further from 440 to 490 million poods; moreover, the 1930 quota was fulfilled only in the spring of 1931 by taking away all grain reserves.... The grain-requisition quota for 1931...again significantly exceeded Ukraine's capacity, amounting to 510 million poods. At the end of the year the quota had been met by 79 percent. To fulfill the "first commandment"—first meet the quota and only then pay people for their labor—on Molotov's instructions, grain began to be confiscated in January 1932, which led to famine in the first half of 1932. As a result of the grain confiscations, 144,000 peasants in Ukraine died of starvation during this period. It was only at the end of April 1932 that the state began providing food aid to the starving.

...[T]he Soviet leadership had a purely functional attitude to the villages, seeing them as only a source of grain supplies for accelerating industrialization. Furthermore, the food produced on collective farms was considered just as much state property as the products of state farms. But state-farm employees received wages, while collective-farm workers were supposed to be paid in kind for their labor. Since all the grain had been handed over to the state to meet the quota, and almost nothing remained, the collective-farm workers were working for nothing. According to Stanislav Kosior, half of Ukraine's collective farms paid people nothing for their labor in 1931.

In their letters to Stalin and Molotov at the beginning of June [1932], Hryhorii Petrovsky and Vlas Chubar wrote of famine in the villages resulting from the impossibility of meeting an unrealistic quota and the need to increase food aid. The response was an irritated reaction from Stalin and the cessation of food imports into Ukraine. Despite the Ukrainian Party organization's request that the grain-requisition quota for 1932 be decreased and the presentation at the Third All-Ukrainian Party Conference on 6–7 July of graphic accounts of cases of starvation and criticism of policy in the villages, Molotov and Kaganovich forced the conference to adopt the Kremlin's unrealistic quota....

Stalin and Kaganovich stopped food aid and initiated the draconian "five ears of corn law"—the resolution "On the protection of property of state enterprises, collective farms, and cooperatives, and the consolidation of socialist property"—according to which theft of collective-farm and cooperative property carried the death penalty and the confiscation of all property, with the possibility of commuting this to a prison term of no fewer than ten years in the presence of mitigating circumstances.

One may conclude that Stalin's policy in the villages amounted to deliberately depriving collective-farm workers and independent farmers of access to the grain they had grown in case they failed to fulfill the grain-requisition quota, which led part of the population to die of starvation. This part of the population was destroyed as a result of the conscious policy of the Soviet state. *The death of part of the population thus took place as a result of their knowingly being deprived of access to food products, which constitutes a crime against humanity.* The state policy of grain requisitions applied to all rural regions of the USSR; therefore this conclusion relates to all those who died of starvation on the territory of the USSR during that period.

The Holodomor of 1932–33—A Crime of Genocide

An analysis of demographic statistics undertaken by Ukrainian and foreign researchers indicates that the direct losses to the Ukrainian people as a result of the Holodomor of 1932–33 constitute 3–3.8 million people according to some data and 4–4.8 million according to other data. The largest number of deaths took place during the period under consideration (November 1932–August 1933), while tens of thousands died of starvation during the period from January to October 1932. In any case, the number of people who died of starvation during the period in question is not less than 10 percent (according to other figures, 15 percent) of the total population of Ukraine. This portion of the Ukrainian people is considerable and can be considered the object of the crime of genocide according to the 1948 Convention on Genocide.

It should be stressed that the secret resolutions of the Central Committee of the All-Union Communist Party (Bolshevik) of 14–15 December 1932 totally changed the policy of Ukrainization and placed responsibility for the food crisis on both the peasants and the leaders of Ukrainization, marking the beginning of the elimination of Ukrainian national communists. The many representatives of the cultural, economic, and political elite who were repressed at this time were of great importance to the development of the Ukrainian people. That is why it is necessary to supplement the peasants who died of starvation with those who died as victims of political repression....

...[T]he Ukrainians of the Kuban...[also] became the object of the crime of genocide....

The Ukrainization of territories with compact settlements of ethnic Ukrainians had been the official policy of the USSR. According to the all-Union census of 1926 there were 915,000 Ukrainians in the Kuban, or 62 percent of the total population. They had generally retained their language and culture: 729,000 said that Ukrainian was their native language. In some areas of the Kuban Ukrainians made up 80 or even 90 percent of the population, while overall in the North Caucasus there lived 3,106,000 Ukrainians.

The policy of Ukrainization was supported by the Ukrainian population of the North Caucasus.... However, the secret resolution of the Central Committee of the All-Union Communist Party (Bolshevik) of 14 December 1932 put an end to the policy of Ukrainization. Ukrainian cultural life in the Kuban was repressed.... Another secret resolution of the Central Committee of the All-Union Communist Party (Bolshevik) of 15 December also put an end to Ukrainization in other regions where there were compact settlements of Ukrainians.

The Elements of the Crime of Genocide

The mass death from starvation of millions of Ukrainian peasants, as well as hundreds of thousands of peasants in the Kuban, was caused by the following actions of the Party-Soviet-economic leadership of the USSR:

1. The deliberate forced imposition of an unrealistic grain-requisition quota on the 1932 harvest, despite the protests of Ukrainian leaders.
2. The passing on 7 August 1932 by the Central Executive Committee and the Council of People's Commissars of the USSR of the resolution "On the protection of property of state enterprises, collective farms, and cooperatives, and the consolidation of socialist property."
3. The directive of 29 October adopted by the Central Committee of the Communist Party (Bolshevik) of Ukraine at the initiative of Molotov and the telegram of 5 November from Molotov and Khataevich on intensifying repressive measures.
4. The resolutions of the Central Committee of the Communist Party (Bolshevik) of Ukraine of 18 November and of the Council of People's Commissars of the Ukrainian SSR of 20 November "On measures to increase grain requisitions," prepared by the Molotov Commission, and the resolutions of the Bureau of the North Caucasus Territory Committee of the All-Union Communist Party (Bolshevik) of Russia, prepared by the Kaganovich Commission, which ordered the confiscation of previously distributed grain and the introduction of fines in kind.
5. The creation of "troikas" and Special Commissions, which were given the power to carry out accelerated examinations of "grain cases" and to apply the death penalty.
6. The practice of placing villages and collective farms on "blacklists" at Kaganovich's initiative, first in the Kuban (by means of a resolution of the Bureau of the North Caucasus Territory Committee of the Communist Party (Bolshevik) of Russia of 4 November), and then in Ukraine (by means of a resolution of the All-Ukrainian Central Executive Committee and the Council of People's Commissars of the Ukrainian SSR of 6 December).
7. Blanket searches of peasant farmsteads in December 1932 in order to find "squandered and stolen grain" on the basis of the resolutions of 18 and 20 November 1932, and the intensification of repression over "grain cases" in Ukraine and the Kuban.
8. The secret resolutions of the Central Committee of the All-Union Communist Party (Bolshevik) of 14 and 15 December on intensifying repression against "saboteurs with Party tickets in their pockets" and ending Ukrainization in the Kuban and other regions of the USSR with compact Ukrainian settlements. These resolutions set in motion the repression of national communists.

9. Deportations to the north of more than 62,000 Kuban peasants for "sabotage."
10. The decision of 29 December 1932 of the Central Committee of the Communist Party (Bolshevik) of Ukraine on confiscating seed funds, passed under pressure from Lazar Kaganovich.
11. Stalin's telegram of 1 January 1933, which demanded that grain be handed over and threatened to repress whoever did not comply.
12. The directive of 22 January of the USSR Council of People's Commissars and the Central Committee of the All-Union Communist Party (Bolshevik) imposing a blockade on those starving in Ukraine and the Kuban and introducing patrol units at railway stations and roads.
13. A government resolution of 17 February 1933, initiated by Mendel Khataevich and Pavel Postyshev, which stipulated that the collection of seeds be carried out by means of grain requisitions, and that the grain confiscators be given part of what they collected.
14. A resolution of the Central Committee of the All-Union Communist Party (Bolshevik) of 31 March 1933, initiated by Postyshev, which stipulated that food aid be provided to those capable of working.
15. The political repressions of 1933 against the intelligentsia and the national communists, initiated by Pavel Postyshev, and the campaign against "Skrypnykism" [so-called national deviations associated with Commissar of Education Mykola Skrypnyk, a key figure in Ukrainization].
16. The total destruction of all ethnocultural forms of existence of Ukrainians in the Kuban.

In their totality, the actions listed here amounted to *deliberately inflicting on the group conditions of life calculated to bring about its physical destruction in part, which constitutes the crime of genocide* (Article II (c) of the Convention)....

The presence of intent to destroy is also proven by the continuation of grain exports, even though the USSR leadership was fully aware of the extent of the famine, as well as by the storing of grain reserves (they would have sufficed to save the starving) and the refusal to accept international assistance. Another indicator of intent is the rapidity with which the famine was ended in the second half of 1933, after the "crushing blow" had been delivered....

General Conclusions

1. The death from starvation of close to 150,000 people in Ukraine from January to October 1932 was the result of a crime against humanity organized by the Party-Soviet leadership of the USSR. This conclusion applies to all those who died of starvation on the territory of the USSR in this period.
2. The death from starvation of millions of people in Ukraine and the political repressions during the period from November 1932 to August 1933 correspond to the definition of the crime of genocide as per the UN Convention on the Prevention and Punishment of the Crime of Genocide, adopted on 9 December 1948, in particular Article II (c): "Deliberately inflicting on the group conditions of life calculated to bring about its physical destruction in whole or in part."

3. The death from starvation of hundreds of thousands of people and the political repressions in the Kuban during the period from November 1932 to August 1933 correspond to the definition of genocide in the UN Convention of 9 December 1948 as per Article II (c): "Deliberately inflicting on the group conditions of life calculated to bring about its physical destruction in whole or in part" and (e) "forcibly transferring children of the group to another group."
4. The Holodomor was the result of the totalitarian Soviet regime's deliberate and systematic actions for which there is historical and documentary evidence and which, in James Mace's words, were aimed at "the destruction of the Ukrainian people as a political factor and as a social organism."
5. The horrible consequences of the Holodomor of 1932–33 require that the Holodomor be legally classified as a crime of the totalitarian regime of the USSR.
6. Some researchers consider it possible to apply the 1948 UN Convention on the Prevention and Punishment of the Crime of Genocide toward a legal classification of the Holodomor of 1932–33 as a crime of genocide, while others deny this. In the author's opinion, such a classification will be appropriate if Article 58 of the Constitution of Ukraine is amended in accordance with Article 7 of the 1950 European Convention on the Defense of Human Rights and Fundamental Freedoms.
7. In order to establish the legal classification of the Holodomor as a crime, it is also proposed that an International Tribunal be established to adopt a legal classification of the famine of 1932–33 as a crime of the totalitarian regime of the USSR. The decision to create such a tribunal could be approved by interstate organizations—the UN, the Council of Europe, and the Organization for Security and Co-operation in Europe.

3

EYEWITNESS ACCOUNTS AND MEMOIRS

INTRODUCTION

This section contains descriptions, reports, and memoirs of the famine by eyewitnesses and contemporaries.

In *Kapoot*, Carveth Wells, a world traveler and writer, notes that "the farther we penetrated into the Ukraine" in July 1932, "the less food there was and the more starvation to be seen on every side." This is followed by one of the first reports of 1933 about the famine, filed by Gareth Jones: it was immediately disputed by the *New York Times* reporter Walter Duranty. Two other journalists, Malcolm Muggeridge and William Chamberlin, both saw the famine as a struggle between the Soviet state and the peasantry and blamed the authorities for it.

The French journalist Suzanne Bertillon interviewed Martha Stebalo, an American citizen of Ukrainian origin who had visited famine-stricken Ukraine in July–August 1933. She concludes that the Kremlin organized the famine to destroy Ukrainian hopes of self-rule.

Harry Lang, a journalist with the Yiddish-language *Jewish Daily Forward* (New York), provides horrific details of the famine, notes the resistance of Ukraine's peasants to collective farming, likens a village to "cemeteries of houses," and recognizes that the famine was man-made. He visits a model Jewish collective farm, noting that aid from Jews living abroad helped save its members from starvation.

Whiting Williams, who traveled in Ukraine in 1933, describes how peasants hoped to save their children by abandoning them in Kharkiv. He was told that these "wild children" would be "unloaded out in the open country—too far out for it to be possible to walk back to town."

Eugene Lyons describes how Western journalists downplayed or failed to report on the famine. A onetime fellow traveler, Lyons directs his ire at the Pulitzer Prize winner Duranty of the *New York Times*. Ewald Ammende's *Human Life in Russia*, the first major study of the famine, gives a scathing analysis of the staged visit to Ukraine in the late summer of 1933 by the former French prime minister Edouard Herriot, who denounced reports of the famine as Nazi propaganda.

Victor Kravchenko and Lev Kopelev both took part in the grain-requisition campaigns. Kravchenko describes how one of Stalin's emissaries, Mendel Khataevich, insisted that grain be requisitioned mercilessly from the peasantry. Kopelev admits to a fanatical belief in the regime at the time of the famine.

Accounts by four Western ex-communists follow. Freda Utley notes that the famine was particularly intense in Ukraine and was caused by Soviet policies, which "deliberately left the peasants to die of starvation." Describing a visit to a lifeless village near Kharkiv, Fred Beal states: "I have seen dead people who had died naturally, before. But this was from a cause and a definite one. A cause which I was somehow associated with, which I had been supporting." Adam Tawdul, who went to the USSR to work as an engineer in 1931, met the Ukrainian minister of education, Mykola Skrypnyk, who told him that eight million had died in Ukraine. The secret-police chief Vsevolod Balytsky told Tawdul that the number was eight to nine million. The well-known writer Arthur Koestler describes seeing starving men, women, and children, whom his traveling companions dismissed as kulaks.

Two selections deal with the reaction to the famine on the part of Ukrainians living in Poland. Stepan Baran, a politician and journalist, describes how hungry Ukrainians trying to flee to Poland and Romania were shot by Soviet border patrols. Milena Rudnytska, a political leader and feminist, reports that although the Council of the League of Nations did not deny the existence of the famine, it did no more than instruct its president to turn to the International Red Cross. Thus, according to Rudnytska, "[T]he League of Nations, under the pretext of procedural impediments, washed its hands in the manner of Pilate."

This section concludes with comments by the post-Stalin Soviet leader Nikita Khrushchev and by Viacheslav Molotov, a principal organizer of the Holodomor. Khrushchev attributes the lack of information about the famine to fear of Stalin, while Molotov denies that it ever occurred.

Carveth Wells, *Kapoot: The Narrative of a Journey from Leningrad to Mount Ararat in Search of Noah's Ark*

(New York: Robert M. McBride and Company, 1933). Excerpts, pp. 113–16, 120–22.

Grant Carveth Wells (1887–1957) was an explorer, world traveler, and writer who described his travels in the following books: *Six Years in the Malay Jungle* (1925), *Let's Do the Mediterranean* (1928), *In Coldest Africa* (1931), *Adventure* (1931), *Exploring the World* (1934), *Bermuda in Three Colors* (1936), *Panamexico* (1937), *North of Singapore* (1940), *Introducing Africa* (1944), and *The Road to Shalimar* (1952).

The extraordinary thing was that the farther we penetrated into the Ukraine, which used to be the "Granary of Russia," the less food there was and the more starvation to be seen on every side. Hour after hour the train passed through country that looked very much like North Dakota or Saskatchewan except that it was covered with weeds as far as the eye could see.

Farm houses were in ruins everywhere, roofs gone, fences broken down, wagons without wheels, farming implements lying about in every stage of *kapootness* while wretched-looking peasants with rags tied around their feet were to be seen wandering about aimlessly and watching the train go by without a smile on their faces.... None of us knew what tragedies had been enacted here as a result of trying to force the people to join collectivized farms and the liquidating of the Kulaks. Once or twice a day we would pass a long freight train that had been shunted into a siding to permit our passage, loaded with so-called Kulaks who were being transported to Siberia, where they would be liquidated by Nature or by the bullet of a taskmaster in a lumber camp.

The sight of these poor people, riding behind the bars of cattle trucks, was pitiful....

Packed like sardines, without any sanitary arrangements whatever and with only the food and water that the people themselves may have thought of bringing, thousands and thousands of helpless human beings have been transported from their homes to the worst districts of Russia's arctic regions....

We ourselves happened to be passing through the Ukraine and the Caucasus in the very midst of the famine in July, 1932. From the train windows, children could be seen eating grass. The sight of small children with stomachs enormously distended is not at all uncommon in Africa or other tropical countries, but this was the first time I had ever seen white children in such a state.

Although we did not know it, there happened to be in Russia about the same time as we were, two American girls, Miss Alva Christensen and Miss Mary Degive of Atlanta, Georgia. Describing one of the scenes they witnessed, these two young explorers of the Soviet Union state:

"At one table sat five Soviet officials, partaking of expensive liqueurs and chocolate cakes covered with rich cream. This does not coincide with Communists' stories of sacrifice for the sake of the masses. We thought of that little incident many times when we saw the swollen bellied Russian children on all fours eating grass like so many sheep!"....

Here is an extract from Zetta's [his wife's] diary....

> ...We have arrived at the station. My God! What a sight! I shall never forget it. Poverty, filth, disease and hunger everywhere. Women in rags and tatters are lying about in the dust and dirt half asleep with emaciated little babies sucking at their empty breasts. The people's clothes are actually tied on with bits of string and they look as if they had lived in them for years without taking them off. I can see one poor woman with four small children. The smallest looks about a week old and is nursing at one breast while another about year old is tugging at the other. Now she has moved the year old baby and is nursing a two year old and pushing the oldest child away. She is nursing all three children while she herself is chewing on a small cucumber. There are pieces of old watermelon rind on the ground about her. I see a little girl who looks about ten years old to judge from her skinny little body but her face looks like that of a woman thirty years old.
>
> She is taking care of a tiny baby whose face is purple with the cold.
>
> Even I am cold at this hour of the morning. I smiled at the child but she didn't smile back; I'm wondering if she has ever learned to smile.

[Reuters], "Famine in Russia. Englishman's Story. What He Saw on a Walking Tour"

Manchester Guardian, 30 March 1933. Online at http://colley.co.uk/garethjones/soviet_articles/walking_tour.htm.

Gareth Jones (1905–35) was a journalist and foreign-affairs adviser to Prime Minister David Lloyd George of Great Britain. In early 1933, following a trip to Germany, he traveled to Russia and Ukraine. On his return to Berlin in late March he issued a press release on the famine that was published by many newspapers. Walter Duranty of the *New York Times* tried to discredit Jones's report in his article "Russians Hungry, But Not Starving," published on 31 March 1933. Banned from returning to the Soviet Union, Jones left in late 1934 for the Far East, where he was killed, apparently by bandits, in August 1935.

Berlin, March 29

"Russia to-day is in the grip of famine, which is proving as disastrous as the catastrophe of 1921, when millions died," said Mr. Gareth Jones, formerly one of Mr. Lloyd George's political secretaries, when he arrived in Berlin this morning on his way to London after a long walking trip through the Ukraine and other districts of the Soviet Union.

Mr. Jones, who speaks Russian fluently, is reporting to the Institute of International Affairs to-morrow. In an interview with the New York "Evening Post," Mr. Jones said that famine on a colossal scale was impending. It meant death to millions by hunger and the beginnings of serious unemployment in a land which has hitherto prided itself of every man having a job. This summed up Mr. Jones's first-hand observations.

The arrest of the British engineers in Moscow is a symbol of panic, and is a consequence of conditions worse than in 1921, when millions died of hunger (declared Mr. Jones). The trial, beginning on Saturday, of the British engineers is merely a sequel to the recent shooting of 35 prominent workers of agriculture, including the vice commissar in the Ministry of Agriculture, in an attempt to check the popular wrath at the famine which haunts every district of the Soviet Union.

I walked alone through villages and twelve collective farms. Everywhere was the cry, "There is no bread; we are dying." This cry came to me from every part of Russia. In a train a Communist denied to me that there was a famine. I flung into the spittoon a crust of bread I had been eating from my own supply. The peasant, my fellow-passenger, fished it out and ravenously ate it. I threw orange peel into the spittoon. The peasant again grabbed and devoured it. The Communist subsided.

A foreign expert returning from Kazak[h]stan told me that one million out of five million have died of hunger. I can believe it. After Stalin the most hated man in Russia is Bernard Shaw; to many of those who can read and have read his descriptions of plentiful food in their starving land the future is blacker than the present. There is insufficient seed. Many of the peasants are too weak to work the land. The new taxation policy, which promised to take only a fixed amount of grain from the peasants, will fail to encourage production because the peasants refuse to trust the Government.

In short, the Government's policy of collectivisation and the peasants' resistance to it have brought Russia to the worst catastrophe since the famine of 1921 swept away the population of whole districts. Coupled with this, the prime reason for the breakdown is the lack of skilled labour and the collapse of transport and finance.

Walter Duranty, "Russians Hungry, But Not Starving. Deaths From Diseases Due to Malnutrition High, Yet the Soviet Is Entrenched. Larger Cities Have Food. Ukraine, North Caucasus and Lower Volga Regions Suffer From Shortages. Kremlin's 'Doom' Denied. Russian and Foreign Observers in Country See No Ground for Predictions of Disaster"

New York Times, 31 March 1933.

Online at http://colley.co.uk/garethjones/soviet_articles/russians_hungry_not_starving.htm.

Walter Duranty (1884–1957) was a journalist who served as Moscow bureau chief for the *New York Times* from 1922 to 1936 and received the Pulitzer Prize in 1932 for his reporting on the Soviet Union. Some of Duranty's writings on the Soviet Union have been deemed controversial, especially those on the famine, the severity of which he downplayed, and for which he has been posthumously criticized. In addition to his many articles on the Soviet Union, Duranty authored several books on the USSR, among them *Red Economics* (1932); *Duranty Reports Russia* (1934); *The Kremlin and the People* (1941); *USSR: The Story of Soviet Russia* (1944); and *Stalin & Co.: The Politburo, The Men Who Run Russia* (1949).

***Special Cable to* The New York Times**

MOSCOW, March 30.—In the middle of the diplomatic duel between Great Britain and the Soviet Union over the accused British engineers there appears from a British source a big scare story in the American press about famine in the Soviet Union, with "thousands already dead and millions menaced by death from starvation."

Its author is Gareth Jones, who is a former secretary to David Lloyd George and who recently spent three weeks in the Soviet Union and reached the conclusion that the country was "on the verge of a terrific smash," as he told the writer.

Mr. Jones is a man of a keen and active mind, and he has taken the trouble to learn Russian, which he speaks with considerable fluency, but the writer thought Mr. Jones's judgment was somewhat hasty and asked him on what it was based. It appeared that he had made a forty-mile walk through villages in the neighborhood of Kharkov and had found conditions sad.

I suggested that that was a rather inadequate cross-section of a big country, but nothing could shake his conviction of impending doom.

Predictions of Doom Frequent.

The number of times foreigners, especially Britons, have shaken rueful heads as they composed the Soviet Union's epitaph can scarcely be computed, and in point of fact it has done incalculable harm since the day when William C. Bullitt's able and honest account of the situation was shelved and negatived during the Versailles Peace Conference by reports that Admiral [Aleksandr] Kolchak, White Russian leader, had taken Kazan—which he never did—and that the Soviet power was "on the verge of an abyss."

Admiral Kolchak faded. Then General Denikin took Orel and the Soviet Government was on the verge of an abyss again, and General [Nikolai] Yudenich "took" Petrograd. But where are Generals Denikin and Yudenich now?

A couple of years ago another British "eyewitness" reported a mutiny in the Moscow garrison and "rows of corpses neatly piled in Theatre Square," and only this week a British news agency revealed a revolt of the Soviet Fifty-fifth Regiment at Dauria, on the Manchurian border. All bunk, of course.

This is not to mention a more regrettable incident of three years ago when an American correspondent discovered half the Ukraine flaming with rebellion and "proved" it by authentic documents eagerly proffered by Rumanians, which documents on examination appeared to relate to events of eight or ten years earlier.

Saw No One Dying.

But to return to Mr. Jones. He told me there was virtually no bread in the villages he had visited and that the adults were haggard, gaunt and discouraged, but that he had seen no dead or dying animals or human beings.

I believed him because I knew it to be correct not only of some parts of the Ukraine but of sections of the North Caucasus and lower Volga regions and, for that matter, Kazak[h]stan, where the attempt to change the stock-raising nomads of the type and the period of Abraham and Isaac into 1933 collective grain farmers has produced the most deplorable results.

It is all too true that the novelty and mismanagement of collective farming, plus the quite efficient conspiracy of Feodor M. Konar and his associates in agricultural commissariats, have made a mess of Soviet food production. [Konar was executed for sabotage.]

But—to put it brutally—you can't make an omelette without breaking eggs, and the Bolshevist leaders are just as indifferent to the casualties that may be involved in their drive toward socialization as any General during the World War who ordered a costly attack in order to show his superiors that he and his division possessed the proper soldierly spirit. In fact, the Bolsheviki are more indifferent because they are animated by fanatical conviction.

Since I talked to Mr. Jones I have made exhaustive inquiries about this alleged famine situation. I have inquired in Soviet commissariats and in foreign embassies with their network of consuls, and I have tabulated information from Britons working as specialists and from my personal connections, Russian and foreign.

Disease Mortality Is High.

All of this seems to me to be more trustworthy information than I could get by a brief trip through any one area. The Soviet Union is too big to permit a hasty study, and it is the foreign correspondent's job to present a whole picture, not a part of it. And here are the facts:

There is a serious food shortage throughout the country, with occasional cases of well-managed State or collective farms. The big cities and the army are adequately supplied with food. There is no actual starvation or deaths from starvation, but there is widespread mortality from diseases due to malnutrition.

In short, conditions are definitely bad in certain sections—the Ukraine, North Caucasus and Lower Volga. The rest of the country is on short rations but nothing worse. These conditions are bad, but there is no famine.

The critical months in this country are February and March, after which a supply of eggs, milk and vegetables comes to supplement the shortage of bread—if, as now, there is a shortage of bread. In every Russian village food conditions will improve henceforth, but that will not answer one really vital question—What about the coming grain crop?

Upon that depends not the future of the Soviet power, which cannot and will not be smashed, but the future policy of the Kremlin. If through climatic conditions, as in 1921, the crop fails, then, indeed, Russia will be menaced by famine. If not, the present difficulties will be speedily forgotten.

Gareth Jones, "Reds Let Peasants Starve. Famine Found Even in Large City in Ukraine"

New York American / Los Angeles Examiner (and other Hearst syndicated papers), 14 January 1935. Online at http://colley.co.uk/garethjones/soviet_articles/hearst3.htm.

"The Communists came and they seized our land, they stole our cattle and they tried to make us work like serfs in a farm where nearly everything was owned in common"—the eyes of the group of Ukrainian farmers flashed with anger as they spoke to me—"and do you know what they did to those who resisted? They shot them down ruthlessly."

I was listening to another famine-stricken village further down the icy railroad track along which I was tramping and the story I now heard was one of real warfare in the villages.

The peasants told me how in each village the group of the hardest-working men—the kulaks they called them—had been captured and their land, livestock and houses confiscated, and they themselves herded into cattle trucks and sent for a thousand or two thousand miles or more with almost no food on a journey to the forests of the north where they were to cut timber as political prisoners.

In one village which was inhabited by German colonists—and what a spotlessly clean and well-kept place it was!—they told me trainloads had left the district packed full of wailing farmers and their families.

Torn [a]way from their homes, prisoners of the heartless secret police and of the hated land army, which exists to drive the peasants to work, these formerly well-to-do farmers had as their only crime the fact that they had worked all day and into the night, had had little more land and had accumulated one or two more cows than others.

Ninety Children Die on the Train

Some months later the news arrived in the district about the exiled colonists, and it was this: NINETY CHILDREN HAD DIED OF HUNGER AND DISEASE ON THE WAY TO SIBERIA.

The Communists I spoke to did not deny that they had ruthlessly exiled the hardest working farmers.

On the contrary they were proud of it and boasted that they would show no mercy to those who wanted to own their own land.

"We must be strong and crush the accursed enemies of the working class," the Communists would say to me, "let them suffer now. We have no place for them in our society."

Nor did they deny the shootings that had gone on in the villages.

"If any man, woman or child goes out into the field at night in the Summer and picks a single ear of wheat, then the punishment according to law is death by shooting," the Communists explained to me.

And the peasants assured me that this was true.

The greatest crime in Russia is the taking of socialized property and murder is regarded as a mere relic of capitalist upbringing and comparatively unimportant compared with the sin of the mother who goes out to the field at night to gather ears of grain in order to feed her children.

Betrays Mother: He Is a Hero!

One child who denounced his mother to the secret police for plucking wheat at night was made into a great hero throughout Russia.

His praise was lauded in all the schools as the boy who was noble enough to betray his mother for the good of the state!

Tramp! tramp! tramp! on I went from village to village, hearing all this news. Everywhere the same tale of hunger and terror.

In one place the folk whispered how some miles away the peasants had refused to give up their land and cows and form a Communist collective farm.

"So they sent the Red army soldiers to force them," they told me. "But the soldiers would not shoot upon their fellow peasants.

What did they do? They called the YOUNG COMMUNISTS in from the town and THEY shot down all the peasants who would not give up their land and their cows."

Throughout Russia there have been these small revolts, but they have been easily and bloodily crushed.

My shoes were becoming worn out by plodding along on the mixture of grit and stones and ice on the railroad track and each step brought a new cold squelch of hardened snow or a new stone through the soles.

But I was buoyed up by the desire to solve a problem—why was there a famine in one of the richest wheat growing countries in the world? And to each peasant I asked; "Potchemu golod?—why is there a famine?"

Famine Is No Fault of Nature

The peasants replied: "It is not the fault of nature. It is the fault of the Communists.

"They took away our land. Why should we work if we have not our own land?

"They took away our cows. Why should we work if we have not our own cows and if we have to share what is our own with all the drunkards and lazy fellows in the village? They took away our wheat. Why should we work, if we know that our wheat will be taken away from us?

"The Communists have turned us into slaves and we shall not be happy until we have our own land, our own cows and our own wheat again."

Suddenly, however, there came a stop to my investigations. It happened in a small station, where I was talking with a group of peasants: "We are dying," they wailed and poured out the old story of their woes. A red-faced, well fed OGPU policeman in uniform approached us and stood listening for a few moments.

Then came the outburst, and from his lips poured a series of Russian curses. "Clear away, you! Stop telling him about hunger! Can't you see he's a foreigner?"

He turned to me and roared: "Come along. What are you doing here? Show me your documents."

A Welcome Anti-Climax

Visions of a secret police prison darted before my mind. The OGPU man looked at my passport and beckoned to one of the crowd, whom I had taken to be an ordinary passenger, but who obviously was in the secret police.

He came to me and in the most polite and respectful terms bade me follow him. "I shall have to take you to the nearest city, Kharkov."

At this moment a train came and we entered it.

Throughout the journey I impressed him with the fact that I had interviewed Lenin's widow, and a number of commissars and great panjandrums of the Soviet régime, and by the time we reached Kharkov I believed he was thoroughly convinced that any real arrest of myself would plunge Russia and Europe and the United States into a world war.

For he decided to accompany me to a foreign consulate in Kharkov and he left me at the doorstep, while I, rejoicing at my freedom, bade him a polite farewell—an anti-climax but a welcome one.

My journey through the villages was over and I was in the chief city of the Ukraine, where all I saw confirmed my views of the Russian famine.

In the streets there were peasant beggars from all parts of the country who had fled from the hunger of the villages to seek food in the towns, and their pale children stood with outstretched hands crying: "Uncle, give us bread!"

I spoke with workers who told me that they had been dismissed from the factories, because the factories were slowing down their work, and when they were thus made unemployed they had their bread cards taken away from them and were ordered to leave the towns.

I saw a bread line of over a thousand nerve-wrecked people.

"We have been waiting here for nearly two days," one of the women in the queue said to me, "and perhaps the supply will run out before we reach the first place."

In another street I saw police driving away a hundred ragged men and women who had formed a bread line outside a store.

"We want bread," they cried. "There is no more bread left," yelled the police, but the crowd did not give up hope and would not.

Hundreds of Homeless Boys

The most terrible sight, however, was the homeless boys, who wandered about the street in filthy rags, who were covered with the sores of diseases, and whose features were depraved and criminal.

Three hundred of them had been rounded up and were homed in the station, where I glanced at them through a window and noticed some lying on the bare ground in a severe state of typhus.

Those have been some of the results of the Soviet regime which I witnessed MYSELF.

Can it be wondered at that there has been a feeling of revolt among the population and that there have been plots within the Communist party itself?

The opposition is too weak to overthrow the regime which is powerfully entrenched, but nevertheless the disillusion and the despair of the masses of the Russian people, typified by the scenes which I have described in the Ukraine, are the real reason why Stalin was forced this Christmas and New Year to inaugurate a new reign of terror in the land of the Soviets.

Malcolm Muggeridge, "The Soviet's War on the Peasants"

Fortnightly Review (London) 133 n.s. (1933). Excerpts, pp. 558–61, 564.

Malcolm Muggeridge (1903–90) was an English journalist and writer who wrote extensively on the Soviet Union, communism, and Christianity. He became the *Manchester Guardian*'s Moscow correspondent in 1932. He was the author of many books, including *Winter in Moscow* (1934), *The Thirties, 1930–1940, in Great Britain* (1940), *Jesus Rediscovered* (1969), and *Conversion: The Spiritual Journey of a Twentieth-Century Pilgrim* (1988).

With that inspired cynicism that characterized most of his slogans, Lenin defined revolutions as the conquest of bread. "Il a compris," M. [Henry] Rollin says in his very remarkable book, *La Révolution Russe:*

> que les révolutions n'étaient point une question de doctrine, mais un drame de la faim, et que la conquête du pain en réglat le cours, en dictait la tactique, en imposait les dogmes, suivant l'époque et les circonstances [that revolutions were by no means a question of doctrine but a drama of hunger, and that the conquest of bread determined their course, dictated their tactics, and imposed their dogmas, depending on the era and the circumstances].

The struggle for bread in Russia has now reached an acute stage. All other questions are superfluous. It is war between the Government and the peasants, and this year's spring sowing will be a—perhaps the—decisive battle. After fifteen years of Bolshevik rule, large areas, some the most fertile, notably the North Caucasus, the Ukraine, and the Volga districts, are quite without bread; the population is, in the most literal sense, starving; even in the large towns the food-shortage is acute, and every day grows more acute. More serious, the soil itself is impoverished, choked with weeds; at least 70 per cent of live-stock and horses have been killed to eat or have died of starvation; and the peasantry everywhere hate and distrust the Government. The Communist Party, using its familiar weapons, hysterical propaganda and brutal coercion, is making a desperate effort to deal with this situation. On the success of its effort depends the whole future of the Soviet regime.

The Bolsheviks achieved power mainly by giving the land to the peasants; thereby, however, they created a problem, an internal conflict which, far from being settled, has steadily grown more acute. Their dreams and plans were essentially urban; proletarian Big Business; Marx-Ford Bourneville; and depended for their fulfilment on a working class aristocracy being able, like the Tsarist aristocracy before it, to exploit the peasantry, to use them, as Stalin put it once, as "reserves of the proletariat." On the other hand, as long as the peasants owned their land and worked it as independent proprietors the "reserves of the proletariat" were unrealisable; and to take away the land from them meant a battle between the Soviet Government and the major part of the population of Russia. Or, put another way, the Soviet Government had to choose between famine and the abandonment of its plans, between Nep (the New Economic Policy) and Socialism, between yielding to the individualistic instincts of the peasants and building a new social order in a desert....

...It soon became apparent that something would have to be done about the "reserves of the proletariat," or the old difficulty, the difficulty against which every revolutionary government has sooner or later run its head, the difficulty of famine, would arise. To meet this difficulty, the policy of collectivization was introduced. Thousands of stalwart Communists were sent into the villages to cajole, or more often to coerce, the peasants into joining collective farms....

The Bolshevik mind found in collectivization a perfect solution to its difficulties. Farms should be like factories; peasants should read newspapers and be a proletariat; tractors should replace horses; food production, like coal production, should be planned; the "reserves of the proletariat," like the proletariat itself, should be brought into a form in which propaganda and the G.P.U. could conveniently get at them, make them into material for building Socialism. It was rather like the dreams of Victorian philanthropists; inconceivable and horrible to anyone having even a remote connection with earth, with the seasons, with the labour of sowing and the joy of harvest; plausible enough in some stuffy café or committee room.

In any case, collectivization was a colossal failure. The ten thousand stalwart Communists proved to be vigilant and effective on the "kulak front," and grossly incompetent, sometimes corrupt, on "the agricultural front." Agriculture went completely to pieces. Last year the Government had to reduce its exports of grain practically to nothing and, despite military measures in many districts, was unable to collect enough food to feed the town populations. Shooting and exiling thousands of peasants (nicknamed kulaks), some even of the stalwarts and unfortunate agronomes sent to advise them, has not helped to repair the consequences of two years of incompetence and neglect. This year began with starving and resentful peasants; unploughed, unweeded fields; a desperate lack of cattle and of transport; town rations reduced to a pound and a half of bread, nothing else, and that, in the case of the unemployed and of many workers' dependents, withdrawn....

On a recent visit to the North Caucasus and the Ukraine, I saw something of the battle that is going on between the Government and the peasants. The battlefield was as desolate as in any war, and stretches wider; stretches over a large part of

Russia. On the one side, millions of peasants, starving, often their bodies swollen with lack of food; on the other, soldiers, members of the G.P.U. carrying out the instructions of the dictatorship of the proletariat. They had gone over the country like a swarm of locusts and taken away everything edible; they had shot and exiled thousands of peasants, sometimes whole villages; they had reduced some of the most fertile land in the world to a melancholy desert. The conquest of bread, like the conquest of glory, seemed a vain pursuit.

Now the same soldiers and members of the G.P.U. have been entrusted with the task of producing abundance out of the desert they have themselves made. If they succeed, it will be by organizing a kind of slavery beside which serfdom was riotous freedom; if they fail, it will mean sooner or later, and sooner rather than later, the end of the dictatorship of the proletariat.

Stepan Baran, "Z nashoï tragediï za Zbruchem" (About Our Tragedy beyond the Zbruch)

Dilo (Lviv), 21 May 1933, p. 1. Translated by Bohdan Klid.

Stepan Baran (1879–1953) was a lawyer, journalist, and political figure in Galicia before World War I and during the interwar period. In 1918–19 he was a member of the National Council of the Western Ukrainian People's Republic and secretary for rural affairs in its first government. In 1914–18 he served as editor in chief of the weekly *Svoboda* (Liberty), the organ of the Ukrainian National Democratic Party, and in the interwar period worked as a journalist for the newspaper *Dilo* (Deed). In addition to his many articles, Baran was the author of four books.

We do not often receive direct news from beyond the Zbruch [River] about the greatest tragedy that our people has ever undergone during the course of its thousand-year history. There are no personal ties at all between our countrymen in Galicia or in Volhynia and our conationals in the Dnipro region [of Ukraine] today. Those excursions that some of our people made from time to time over the past several years on the occasion of various jubilees and gatherings have also ceased. And they did not explain anything to us about events taking place in Greater Ukraine, for those unsympathetic to the Bolsheviks were not allowed to see anything with their own eyes, while sympathizers of the Red regime presented everything in the best light. All this has now ended.... Despite all the efforts of the State Political Administration (GPU—formerly the Cheka), Sovietophilism today is not making any headway in our circles....

A reason for this is the echoes of the [seemingly] inhuman groans of martyred victims, millions of our peasants, that break through to us from time to time across the dense Bolshevik border. More than one victim who attempted to break out of the Bolshevik hell has been covered forever by the waves of the Dnister [River]. More than one has died from the bullets of the Muscovite Red Army. And those—not very many, after all—who managed to break through to us—our everyday people—relate horrors that remind one of Dante's Inferno.

Not long ago, during the winter months, when the waters of the Dnister were frostbound, masses of our refugees tried to cross to the Bessarabian side, to Romania. Almost all of them lost their lives. Only a few reached Bessarabia alive, most of them with bullet wounds. The European press has given some coverage to this tragedy of Dnipro [Ukraine]. Some of its correspondents even went to the scene, spoke with the tormented victims, and described them. And that was all. The conscience of Western Europe was not moved, as it has its own worries and often falls under the influence of Red propaganda in the press. Obviously, hope of trade interests with the communist East exerts its own influence.

An unprecedented famine, thoroughly reminiscent of the days of 1922, now extends across the fertile Ukrainian black earth. Ukrainian peasant farmers, who with the work of their hands and the bounty of their fertile soil fed the vast lands of Europe—to say nothing of the hungry of Muscovy—and lived in relative affluence themselves, are now dying of hunger. This is not being caused by flood or drought, nor by any other natural disaster, but only by the mad experiments of today's leaders of the Red regime. The peasants of Greater Ukraine, as basically everywhere in the Soviet Union, have been expropriated. State farms and collective farms have turned them into serfs, casting them into poverty unknown in history by any other serfdom. From the Zbruch to the endless steppes, one hears the groans of millions of dying peasants who are wasting away in despair, seeing no assistance of any kind, even moral, from any quarter. For the most part churches have been closed, the priesthood destroyed, and those remaining are without rights.

The Ukrainian national movement has been smothered by shootings, [imprisonment or exile in] the Solovets [Islands], prisons, and [exile to] Siberia. Its formal remains are also being liquidated. Moscow is attaching itself even more firmly [to Ukraine] than under Peter and Catherine....

...Now, the Red Kremlin has gone even further. Our peasants near the Polish border are being [uprooted and] resettled in the depths of Muscovy or Siberia to make room for Muscovite peasants and turn them into a barrier against Ukrainian influences from the west. The border [area] has been planted thickly with an army of Muscovite origin. The eastern side of the Zbruch now looks like a real military line that is difficult for a civilian to cross even at night, as in wartime. We are informed of this by refugees who recently managed to wade across the Zbruch, for most of them died from bullets or fell into the hands of the Bolshevik guards. They arrived as living skeletons because the famine there is terrible. Even dogs are being killed, and today's slaves of the collective farms are being fed dog meat, for in fertile Ukraine neither bread nor potatoes are to be had. The Commune has taken everything from the village, and the Ukrainian village is perishing helplessly. Salvation is to be found by fleeing across the Zbruch....

...[I]f it were not for the extraordinarily strong Bolshevik border guard details, armed with machine guns and field artillery, Eastern Galicia and Volhynia would be flooded with tens of thousands of our peasants from beyond the Bolshevik border posts....

Suzanne Bertillon, "L'effroyable détresse des populations de l'Ukraine" (People of Ukraine in Terrible Distress)

Le Matin (Paris), 29 August 1933, p. 1. Translated by Iryna Fedoriw.

Suzanne Bertillon (1891–1980) was an anti-Soviet French journalist and writer, a participant in the French resistance during World War II, and a niece of the famed French criminologist Alphonse Bertillon. She was the author of many books, including *Le paradis en IIIe classe (au pays des Soviets): choses vues* (1935), *Vie d'Alphonse Bertillon, inventeur de l'anthropométrie* (1941), and *La tentation chimérique* (1953).

American country folk of Ukrainian origin who, after a twenty-year absence, received special permission from the Soviet authorities to spend a month in their home country, provide moving descriptions of the pitiful state of the villages and their emaciated compatriots.

Where cases of cannibalism appear but the harvest is good

From every corner of the world, one hears alarming echoes of the situation in Soviet Ukraine.

The official press of the USSR admits that foreign journalists and tourists are prohibited from entering Ukraine without special authorization. What horrible event could be taking place in the country once known as the "breadbasket of Europe"? This is revealed by two travelers who returned from Ukraine on August 12 after their one-month stay.

Martha Stebalo and her husband (the two travelers in question) emigrated from Ukraine, their native land, in 1913 to settle in the United States. They were ordinary peasants. In 1918 they adopted American citizenship but continued to maintain ties with their relatives, who had stayed behind. I shall allow Martha Stebalo to explain:

"The letters from Ukraine were rare but more and more pressing; they begged us to send supplies and money. We satisfied the demands. I would send money to our family on a regular basis; in return, the Soviet authorities notified us that the money had been delivered safely.

On July 1, 1933, as members of a tourist group who wanted to visit the USSR, we boarded a cruise ship in New York for Europe; we wanted to see our family and our native land again. On July 14 we disembarked in Leningrad and started for Moscow. In Moscow we asked permission to go to Ukraine. We would learn later that all other tourists were refused such authorization, but it was granted to us, doubtless because we are uneducated peasants. Moreover, two days prior to our return we were given an offer to take charge of a collective farm.

In Moscow, those friends who knew of our intention to go to Ukraine warned us that it might be difficult to obtain necessary supplies there, so we would do well to bring nonperishable provisions. In a Torgsin (a store servicing foreigners only), we bought two hundred pounds of flour, ten pounds of cheese, and four pounds of herring, sausage, and smoked salmon. In fact, food is rationed in Moscow, but the citizens are able to find necessary provisions. In addition, we had nine poods (228 kilos) of clothes brought as part of our luggage.

After a two-day trip in a grimy train car, we arrived in Kyiv. We found the city little changed, but in the outskirts we were surprised by the way people looked. Most of them stayed on the ground, unable to move, their legs swollen. They seemed feeble and ill. Others walked bent over, their eyes wide and staring. Nobody spoke.

Ruin, hunger, and silence

We left Kyiv to go to the surrounding villages where we had left relatives. How surprised we were to see, instead of the pretty and jolly villages we used to know, gloomy ruins, not a flower to be seen, torn-down fences, leafless trees, hopeless silence, no more dogs barking or poultry running, and an atmosphere of death. With heavy hearts we arrived in our native village, got off the train, and saw people coming toward us. The people looked large in size. "Oh, well," I thought, "We were misinformed. These people are fat, so they must be well-fed." But when they approached us, we realized that their stoutness was due to the swelling of their limbs. Their bodies were covered with leaking sores and gave off a rotten smell; in place of clothes they wore rags.

The word spread that the Americans had arrived. My husband asked to see his mother, whom he had not seen for twenty years. Alas, she had not escaped the lot of the others. She was like the rest of them, swollen and covered with sores. And when she finally realized that we were her children, she put her hands together and started to cry, unable to say a word. I learned that for more than a year she had not received any of the money or provisions I had sent her, contrary to what the Soviet authorities told us.

Then I asked whether there was some sort of epidemic that was making everyone suffer from abscesses and swelling. They were afraid to answer, as they were constantly spied on; every denunciation that proved true was rewarded with a bit of food—and what one would not do to receive a piece of bread! In short, I learned that, forced by hunger to put something into their stomachs, they had been eating tree leaves, scraping tree trunks and eating the bark, and trying to make a mixture of sawdust and grass. I learned that everyone was dying, and though the harvest was good, no one could touch it, as the fields were under surveillance by guards on watchtowers with orders to shoot anybody approaching them.

I left this miserable village to go to Podilia, where my mother and my brothers lived in Pysarivka. I found the same desolation there. Our house was empty. I asked whether my relatives had moved out.

"No, they are dead…"

"But that is impossible. I received a letter from them only a month ago."

"They've been dead since then. They died of hunger. We are all going to die. In this village of eight hundred people, one hundred fifty have already died since last spring, even though during the war only seven of ours were killed. No births this year either, except for one stillborn baby. Ah! If only someone could help us."

"But is there any authority to which you could appeal?"

"Nobody. It's the authorities themselves who are most relentlessly set on our destruction. They want us to perish. This is an organized famine. The harvest has never been so rich, but we are forbidden to touch it. If we are caught cutting a few stalks, it's either jail or the firing squad, and in jail you will die of starvation by the third week."

Famished

So I opened my packages of flour and herrings. They started grabbing the food with their bare hands, swallowing it as fast as they could. It was a horrifying spectacle to watch these poor people stuff themselves in this manner.

"Wait," I said, "you are going to choke. You are not used to eating so much at once. You need to cook the flour."

"No, no! We want to eat. Ah! To have something in the stomach. Let us eat. You don't know what it is like to want to eat."

Alas, two of them died during the night. Their stomachs were no longer accustomed to digesting food. I was told that the only survivor of my family was a 22-year-old boy. He was only as tall as a child, covered with sores and ulcers, and so weak that he could hardly stand.

"But," I said to him, "can't you work? Don't they need anybody to gather the harvest?"

"I am too weak. There are still some who can work. They are employed from three o'clock in the morning to eleven o'clock at night, and they are given a bushel of grain as payment. They are the luckiest. Nobody needs us. We cannot belong to the Komsomol or any other organization. We are regarded as sons of kulaks because Ukraine used to be rich at one time."

I went a few miles outside the village to see some friends of mine who were still alive. It was late when I arrived there, and night was falling. They begged me to stay with them.

"It's too dangerous for you to be outside at this hour. You can get killed. There isn't a crime that people would not commit to find something to eat."

I didn't sleep a wink at night. Often the children would wake up, crying, "Hliba, hliba, holodni" (Bread, bread. We are hungry). Their parents would shut them up, but two minutes later the crying would resume.

Scenes of horror

"Is it true," I asked their parents, "the misery is such that there are cases of cannibalism?"

"That is why we didn't want you to go out at night. People who venture out at this hour run the risk of being killed as grub for these unfortunates. The dead are not buried in coffins. The bodies are covered with a few spadefuls of dirt and then dug up at night. The Kripaks in the village of Chahiv ended the lives of their two children and ate them afterwards. A few days later they learned that a child had just died; they went and dug it up."

In a village near Odesa, a woman from Kyiv came to visit her godson, a seven-year-old boy. On entering the house, she saw both parents slumped in their chairs, with a strange, stupefied look on their faces.

"Where is my godson?"

No answer. After a long silence they took her to the cellar, and there in a barrel she saw quarters of salted meat. Ah, who will help us and relieve us of this misery? What have we done to deserve such suffering?

In 1931, when I visited the Museum of the Revolution in Stalingrad, I saw photographs of the famine of 1921. Ten years later, the Soviets agreed to accept the truth of the facts. The photographs displayed skeletal figures covered with rags, their bones protruding through the skin. The interpreters assured us that at that time in the Samara region people had eaten human flesh.

Suzanne Bertillon, "La Famine en Ukraine" (Famine in Ukraine)

Le Matin (Paris), 30 August 1933, p. 1. Translated by Iryna Fedoriw.

Ukraine has a territory of 680,000 sq. km. (France, 542,000) and is populated by 31 million inhabitants. It is one of the richest countries in the world on account of its legendarily rich soil, as well as what is beneath the soil.

It has large deposits of iron in Kryvyi Rih, the Donets coal basin, and manganese mines, to mention only the most important raw materials.

Cultivated land represents 53 percent of the territory (France, 56 percent) and produces grain, sugar, grapes, fruit, and 86 percent of the famous Russian cigarettes. In addition, its population contributed 4 million soldiers to the tsarist army.

This is what attracts the "robbers of the homeland." This is the country that the Soviet government wants to destroy systematically.

Alas, too often in history the strongest have lived to the detriment of the weakest; neither the tsarist nor the Soviet government showed restraint in dealing with Ukraine. Both fully applied the formula "might makes right."

After the war, this barbaric rule was countered by Wilson's noble dogma of "the right of nations to self-determination," which the Soviet government abused in Machiavellian fashion to instigate troubles in our colonies, without ceasing to torment Ukraine for all that. The Soviet constitution of 1923 appeared to give full autonomy to Ukraine, Georgia, Azerbaijan, Turkestan, etc. That was only in theory, so as to produce a favorable effect on foreign countries; in reality, they never ceased to treat these territories as conquered lands, much more harshly than any European nation ever treated its colonies.

Ukrainian and Russian

They left these peoples with hardly anything but the right to speak their own language; hence one can establish that the Ukrainian language is completely different from the Russian language. There is as much difference between a Ukrainian and a Russian as there is between a Pole and a Russian. A nation's autonomy is not real until its people obtain political and economic freedom, and yet Ukraine does not benefit from any of its riches. It is under the exclusive sovereignty of Moscow and, against its will, under the communist regime.

Moreover, it is in order to destroy all irredentist elements that the Soviet government has systematically organized the horrifying famine that is currently raging, in hopes of completely destroying a whole nation whose only fault is its aspiration to freedom.

The famine is confined to Ukraine and the North Caucasus; in other parts of the USSR food is rationed, but people manage to survive, and the Soviet press just recently printed in *Pravda*: "Peace and order prevail throughout the country; hundreds of collective farms delivered their grain requisitions; the standard of living is very high.... Russia is making great strides toward the wonderful life that Stalin has predicted for it...."

Yet the stories of travelers returning from there contradict this statement completely. I return to the account of Martha Stebalo (an American countrywoman of Ukrainian origin who has just come back from her trip).

Komsomol members

After having described the hideous destitution of the population in *Le Matin* yesterday, she continued on the same note:

"Very often it is Komsomol members, brigades of fanaticized young people, who are in charge of agricultural work in Ukraine. They may have undergone very intense political training, but they have only a rudimentary knowledge of agriculture, so insufficient that they want to husk millet seed before sowing it.

The taxes imposed on the population of this unfortunate country in preparation for the famine are devastating. I can give you a few examples: the regular tax is 35 rubles per person per year, as well as other taxes in kind, which vary. For example, when they still had cows, they had to pay 100 rubles per year per cow and provide the government with 175 liters of milk. In the same measure, taxes were imposed on anything owned. If they were not paid on time, they would be doubled and even, in case of a second failure to pay, tripled. If a peasant remains unable to pay, his possessions are confiscated: this is what has happened throughout Ukraine.

On top of these mandatory taxes, there are so-called "voluntary" ones to allow the government to purchase planes, tractors, etc. Recently a "voluntary" tax to promote world revolution was abolished.

Those unable to pay the taxes are pronounced "class enemies," "saboteurs," and "bandits"; they are often deported to unknown destinations.

Eat to survive

This regime has swiftly reduced the country to its present condition. Having no more poultry or livestock, people started to kill cats and dogs for food; then horses became weaker and weaker, dying in their turn. To prevent rotting and the outbreak of disease, authorities butchered the dead horses, covered them with carbolic acid and lime, and then buried the carcasses. At night people would come and dig up the carcasses; they would immerse pieces of meat in water, dry them, and eat. There are not even any horses there today.

Sometimes, in the country, one sees a group of houses with black banners, meaning that the village is empty. Everyone has died of hunger.

Other accounts

Here are some clippings from the foreign press that confirm Martha Stebalo's story.

Chas (Time), Romania, August 19:

> The accounts of two Czechoslovakian workers who have just returned from the USSR and shared their impressions at the Prague Socialist Club:
>
> "The famine in Kyiv is terrible. People sit on the ground in the street, drinking water from a used can. They stay this way for several days, having no strength to pick themselves up, and they end up dying right there. At the marketplaces in Kyiv there are eight to ten corpses every night, quickly stripped of their clothing. In the morning, wagons arrive to take them to the burial grounds. In streets far from the city center, corpses remain until they decompose completely. Often two or three corpses of persons who have died on board streetcars are carried out. In the main street, groups of children beg for a piece of bread and, at the same time, steal anything within reach."

The pamphlet *Brüder in Not* [Brothers in Need] (Berlin). A sample excerpt from an eyewitness account:

> "The famine of 1921 was significant, but the current situation is beyond any comparison. In many villages 50 percent of the inhabitants are dead. Many houses remain empty and fall into ruin."

M. Auchagen, a professor at the Oriental Institute, says on the basis of testimony from German settlers returning from the USSR:

> "Famine reigns in southern Ukraine and the North Caucasus, more terrible than that of 1921. In Kharkiv, corpses remain on the ground. In the Taganrog district, a woman killed her three children to feed herself. In Kryvorizhia, a woman was arrested because she had killed her husband. In Sofiivka, a village in the Stavropol district, almost half the inhabitants have died of hunger."

Excerpts from the memorandum of Dr. Otto Schiller, who visited the North Caucasus this spring:

> "Since the autumn of 1932, the food situation in the whole region has become catastrophic. The population is being reduced by deportations and numerous deaths from hunger. Villages are becoming depopulated, and cases of cannibalism are frequent.
>
> ...The number of deceased will increase by next autumn. Nobody is offering any help to the population; the authorities are completely indifferent. This famine is much more severe than that of 1921, when five million people died of hunger. The starving population could be saved if it had access to the grain that the Soviet government has exported abroad. The present crisis can end only with the death of most of the population."

The appeal of Cardinal [Theodor] Innitzer, archbishop of Vienna, published in the *Reichspost* and widely reprinted in the foreign press, requests that an emergency aid mission be sent to the regions suffering from starvation. He relies on the testimony of Gareth Jones, a former secretary of Lloyd George (*Manchester Guardian*), and above all on an extremely detailed memorandum by Dr. Ewald Ammende, who, having already contributed to the humanitarian action of 1921 (the Nansen mission and the American Relief Committee), is now trying to achieve the same result.

The Stockholm *Aftonbladet* writes on August 14:

> "The mysterious measures taken with regard to foreign newspaper correspondents in Moscow to prevent them from traveling far from the capital are about to be explained. Ukraine and the neighboring regions are in revolt. All railways are being patrolled by troops. Trains are packed with soldiers dispatched to the endangered regions. Details are unavailable for the time being, but we are certainly on the brink of disastrous events."

Harry Lang, "Seen and Heard in the Villages of the Ukraine"

Jewish Daily Forward (New York), 27 December 1933.

In *Holodomor Studies* 2, no. 2 (Summer-Autumn 2010): 218–19, 221–28. Excerpts. Translated by Moishe Dolman.

Harry Lang (1884–1970) was a journalist, writer, and activist in the labor and socialist movements in the United States. Lang was a writer and labor editor of the Yiddish-language *Jewish Daily Forward (Forverts)*, published in New York, when in the summer and early fall of 1933 he and his wife, Lucy (Robbins), traveled in the Soviet Union, including Ukraine. Upon his return to the United States, Lang wrote a series of some thirty articles about the trip that appeared in the *Forward* from late November 1933 to February 1934. In 1935 Lang wrote several articles based largely on his earlier accounts for a Hearst newspaper, the *New York Journal*. Following their publication, Lang was expelled from the Socialist Party and almost lost his job at the *Forward*.

Our automobile speeds along.... Before our eyes, fields spread out both near and far. Everywhere we see piles of raked-up grain—here corn, there wheat, somewhere else plain hay fodder. The grain has been cut down from the fields, but no one has taken it away to thresh. The hay has not been taken away to the stables. The piles of grain and hay are already soaked and have begun to rot....

No people are to be seen in the fields. We've traveled throughout the Ukraine, to Ukrainian villages. The world has heard—and has not heard—that over the course of the year these villages were the site of a terrible famine....

...[L]ast spring and summer a curtain descended over Soviet Russia, her provinces and districts, as well over the separate Soviet republics. On the face of it, it would seem that the Soviet government felt it necessary that no one from the outside world should come near, peep in or hear a sound.

Voices have nevertheless broken through—indeed voices from the Ukraine. When it proved impossible to completely stifle these voices, statements were issued to the effect that these voices only came from certain places, insignificant corners of the great country, in which there had occurred an incidental hunger, the result of a crop failure in the local fields.

If there was "something else" at play in addition to this crop failure, and if this "something else" actually maintains a grip on the greatest part of the country, the authorities have used all their strength to keep it hidden from the world.

In Russia itself, however, they have not been able to conceal it. They cannot use walls to block the cities from the villages, so in the cities people are aware of what was happening in the villages. Moreover, it was even government policy that the city *should* know. It was written in the cities that the peasants wished to starve them. They, the peasants, had earlier refused to sow the fields, and subsequently refused to gather the grain that had been sown. What's more, the city was sorely needed. Young and old were sent from the city to work in the fields. Factories were shut down and industrial workers were sent to overnight become agricultural labourers. People in the city have thereby become very familiar with what was happening in the fields. But to allow foreign correspondents there was not in Moscow's interests.

When I informed a colleague, an American journalist in Moscow, that the itinerary of my voyage included the Ukraine and White Russia [Belarus], he exclaimed:

"They won't let you travel there..."

And when I told him that everything was ready and that I was to depart the next day, his eyes bulged as he examined my passport. Yes indeed, it stated my profession: journalist.

The situation of the foreign journalists in Moscow thus became clear to me....

I travelled to Ukrainian villages before I arrived in Kiev. With me was a person who was interested that I should receive a full understanding of everything that has taken place, and what a Soviet village with *kolkhozy* and *sovkhozy* now represents....

In the world it is proclaimed that Stalin's collectivization has prevailed.... In the Ukraine, it is said to be self-evident. The Ukraine is covered with *kolkhozy*. This is the case according to the statistics. The world believes in statistics; but beneath statistics there always lies something else. What is underneath the statistics concerning the *kolkhozy*? What happens in the *kolkhozy*? The dissatisfied peasants who were forced into them have not yet become satisfied. They have invented the most diverse forms of sabotage, from inflicting harm upon the fields to inflicting damage upon the field machinery, all so that the *kolkhozy* should be of no benefit to anyone.

In hundreds of villages the beginning of each sowing season is accompanied by a direct strike. The peasants refuse to do anything; should a strike during the sowing season be broken, they attempt a new one during the gathering of the grain. But a strike is easily broken: The authorities arrest an entire village of peasants, together with their wives and children. They set them to work in a *sovkhoz*, a government-owned farm where the peasants work like factory labourers, or they make them toil in mines (as coal diggers), or they send them to work on the roads, or to be woodcutters in the forests, and so forth. The whole process is a system of prison labour.

Still, the peasants' taste for struggle against the imposed "collectivization" does not end with strikes. They permit the establishment of a *kolkhoz*, but take to sabotaging it. Last spring a popular method of sabotage involved the kernels that are thrown into the tilled soil. The peasants slit their own throats this way. Like everything else, these kernels are, of course, purchased from the government.

A *kolkhoz* buys these kernels and pays the government one way or the other—if not from its revenues, then from its own produce. Moreover, the *kolkhoz* operates according to "piecework." The measure of the work each person does is calculated. Subsequently, this measure is tabulated according to hours and days, and, in proportion to the day's work, each peasant receives bread, other articles and, from time to time, small amounts of money. When someone ruins the kernels, the *kolkhoz* becomes a debtor. It must pay for the ruined kernels as well. Atonement falls on everybody's head. Each member of the *kolkhoz* thereby becomes a debtor to the government. He becomes its body-and-soul slave, together with all the members of his household. This does not stop the peasants. They are not bothered by what will happen to them in the future; that's how embittered they are.

Every act of sabotage brings death. People are shot on the spot. This, too, does not frighten the peasants.

Another form of sabotage consists of damaging tractors....

For damaging a tractor the penalty is death....

Last summer, cutting stalks was a widespread tactic employed throughout Russia. Further episodes of famine had been expected; the wish was to conceal something for oneself. In the *sovkhozy*, even more stalks had been cut down than in the *kolkhozy*. This represented direct theft from the government. The Soviet newspapers designated such stalk-stealers *striguni* and did not cease to write about them. For shearing stalks the penalty is death. This, of course, did not lead the peasants to discontinue the practice.

There are also *striguni* in the Ukrainian village in which I was now staying. Officials have arrived in order to completely dissolve the *kolkhoz*, confiscate the entirety of its possessions as well as all the fields and establish a *sovkhoz*.... The officials have not come to listen to the opinions of the peasants; the latter have been condemned in advance. The officials have come to take an accounting of the village, the entirety of which has to all intents and purposes been placed under arrest.

The officials who have arrived are from Soviet institutions specializing in village life. The authorities bustle about in boots and short leather coats. They are accompanied at all times by soldiers in long great-coats, rifles perched on their shoulders. The peasants wear rags[1] wrapped around their feet. Their *rubashkas* [shirts] and coats are no better. The officials and soldiers go around constantly carrying pieces of black bread. They have brought these with them from the places from whence they had come; you can't get any in the village. The village receives a fixed amount of bread and no more....

We depart for more distant villages....

Our automobile again drives through heaps of soaked, rotting grain....

Heaps of wheat have been raked up haphazardly. No peasant hands have come into contact with them.

And this is the cause of the famine which struck the country throughout the year and which can soon return. This famine did not stem from a poor harvest in the

1 I assume here a typographical error of one Yiddish letter in the original, which not changing would have us reading that the peasants wore shovels or spatulas (and not rags) wrapped around their feet.

fields, but from a harvest of party manoeuvres and a harvest of peasant mistrust of the state. Everyone here knows this, and the present situation confirms it.

During spring, Stalin turned to the villages with the following appeal:

"Sow and you will have!"

This should have been an encouragement to the peasants: that they might sow the fields and profit thereby. The government would not torment them with new "experiments." There was no great reverberation, so Stalin subsequently made the following appeal:

"Render the *kolkhoznik* a man of means!"

There was laughter throughout the country, so he added:

"This time we mean business."

As such, during the summer the villages became virtual prison camps. This started as soon as the cutting began. And I am a witness: fields under the watchful eye of rifles....

Driving from village to village we come upon a village of death...

Several dozen little houses, the doors nailed up, not a single creature inside, not a single creature in the gardens and fields surrounding dead chimneys on the roofs, dead windows.

A human figure appears in the distance. A soldier's great-coat shuffles along from a road to our side.... He arrives at the spot where we have stopped, carrying two loaves of black bread under his arms. He answers my escort:

"Yes, more than half the people died of starvation. Those that survived left..."

And he indicates two nearby villages:

"Same thing over there."

"And in another area, just over there, also... It was a horrible year."

Cemeteries of houses.

What is he doing here?

He's been placed on guard duty.

He watches over death...

We approach several houses. It's frightening. We want to look at these tombs....

He leads us to a place, a piece of sunken clay earth like a shallow grave, and points:

"Here lie the masters of the village..."

There is no shape of a grave. The dead were buried there with no nearby marker.

The piece of empty ground in which they lie is directly opposite and not far from the little houses where they lived. Others lie right next to the doors of their little houses. Members of a family would bury each other. The soldier tells us of a girl who looked on as her mother buried her father. Later it happened that the girl buried her mother and her little brother. And then she went away from there. She is somewhere in Kiev....

He indicates to us two small houses where bodies were lying, certainly for a couple of weeks, until soldiers were sent into the village to gather all the dead. His speech becomes more and more difficult; he is getting all choked up.

Of course he knows how it came to be that so many starved to death. He makes no mention of crop failure in the fields. He talks about what it was like earlier in the villages: The peasants refused to do anything, so no bread was delivered to them.

In other words, it was a revolt: revolt by starvation, revolt by swollen bellies and revolt by mass death....

In this village there was, in fact, a *kolkhoz*, but even with a *kolkhoz* the peasants did not want to work. They did not want the *kolkhoz*.... [T]he *kolkhoz* never functioned.

Something still remains in the dead *kolkhoz* amidst the dead little houses: the bell which had been suspended on a fence in the middle of the village....

A bell to call the dead...

Bells to rouse people to work can be found in all *kolkhozy*. The peasants were accustomed to waking up in the morning when the cocks would begin to crow. O, how the peasants were accustomed! They would sing at work. This is something you don't hear now. It goes without saying that the Ukrainian song of the field, of the steppe, has become famous throughout the world. In the Ukraine itself, however, the song is silent. There is no singing in the Ukrainian fields.

On a holiday in the Ukraine, the peasant women used to dress up in flowery dresses, with ribbons and beads of all colours and embroidered jackets. Now you don't see this. Now, you only see Ukrainian peasant clothes at a masked ball in New York...

Leaves from the trees have fallen over the dead village. An autumn wind has carried them over the dead houses. We bid farewell to the soldier. He glances at the two loaves of black bread under his arm as if to say: "This is what I have to show for my guard duty over this extinct village."

We leave him, alone, amidst the dead little houses and amidst the leaves from the trees which are falling upon them. Great flocks of birds drift over the piles of rotted wheat. We hear their cry. Leaving the dead village, we again come to a gate with two red, but broken-off flags and a Soviet star next to them and a photograph of Stalin... There is something symbolic in this picture...

Harry Lang, "A Trip to the Jewish *Kolkhozy* of Ukraine and White Russia"

Jewish Daily Forward (New York), 30 December 1933.

In *Holodomor Studies* 2, no. 2 (Summer-Autumn 2010): 229–40. Excerpts. Translated by Moishe Dolman.

...Several miles from Kharkov...you wind up on a gravel side-road. This brings you to a gate with a Yiddish inscription: *Royteh Shtern*....

Upon entering Royteh Shtern, I beheld this little scene: A quiet war was taking place between a horse and a tall Jew in big boots. The Jew sought to drive the horse into a stream, but the horse would have none of it. The Jew stood on the bank. He wanted to wash the horse. Meanwhile, the horse went into the stream, took a few steps deeper into the water, but then soon turned back. The Jew drove him again and again; the horse refused to be "disciplined." Ducks were sitting near the stream. They seemed to be waiting for the Jew to finish with the horse so as to go in and give a real swimming lesson. It was an idyllic little country scene. I thought—I hoped—that here in Royteh Shtern I would find a peaceful, happy life, the peace of the country and the happiness of "socialized" Jews on the land, of Jewish kolkhozniki.

Although it is only six years old, through labour and economy Royteh Shtern has become a successful settlement.... Altogether in this kolkhoz there are approximately four hundred souls....

This kolkhoz strictly complies with all the Soviet kolkhoz regulations, turning over to the government its percentage of grain, paying its taxes punctually and participating in the government "loan" campaigns....

Who are they, these Jewish kolkhozniki?....

All came from cities and towns, this one from the Vinnytsia district, that one from Nikolayev, another from Berdichev. Some are from the Khersonschina, in Ukraine, where there had been Jewish villages or settlements as far back as Czarist times.... For the most part, though, they are new hands on the field. They are former *lishentsy*[2] from the very recent past, town-dwelling families who until the revolution lived from trade with peasants from the neighbouring village and who after the revolution found themselves déclassé.

This chapter of déclassé Jews contains tragedies which have not yet been revealed to the outside world....

In the yard of the kolkhoz, at the midpoint between the houses and the stables, I encountered the tall Jew with the big boots who had previously been driving the horse to the stream.... Speaking with him, I made a remark about "better times." He shrugged his shoulders and muttered:

"Sure, if you can sleep through a night of woe, in the morning things become easier... Your troubles are still there, but you get used to them..."

He examined his boots.

"They cost me a year of work," he continued, showing me a calculation explaining how he could afford the boots.

He had totalled the extra days' work in the kolkhoz he and his wife had squeezed in over the course of the year and the food they acquired in consequence. To this he added what they didn't get because it was unobtainable, as well as the food they did not consume so as to save up a little something in order that he might indeed be able to get a pair of boots....

A kolkhoz may not provide bread for itself; it must depend upon the "centre"; it must be under the control of the regime.

An absurd state of affairs ensues, even when the government eventually pays for the grain it takes from the kolkhoz. It gives the kolkhoz the cheapest price. Afterwards the kolkhoz has to pay for the baked bread it takes in. It soon notices that the money received for the grain is not sufficient for the bread baked from the same grain.

The whole cooperative set up in Russia—the inland Soviet trade between institutions—is subject to the severest curses from every kolkhoz throughout the land.

---

2 Those disenfranchised by the Soviet Constitution for, among other reasons, unacceptable political or class personal histories.

Nor may a kolkhoz decide to make for itself a festival and, let's say, slaughter a calf for everyone. The person, as well as the calf, is under government control.

It is existence under police surveillance, in fact under a whole chain of police. There are kolkhoz committees which are responsible to higher committees, and the whole twisted committee system with police powers peers into your house and casts its eyes upon your table.

It feeds the people the way you feed cattle in the stable.

Sixty per cent of earnings are paid out at the halfway point of the year, the remainder at the end. But very often you discover at the end of the year that on the one hand the kolkhoz must give a "loan" to the government and on the other hand that it is in debt to the government.

The people have no faith in these "loans." They know that these are not really loans, but rather another form of taxation. The debts owed by the kolkhoz to the government, however, are another matter. Try to buy certain products for the field in the various government institutions and you realize that a debt is a debt. This debt falls upon every member of the kolkhoz, and every individual becomes collateral....

Kolkhozniki give the impression of being oppressed convicts toiling in some field. They lie there, burying themselves in the ground. They bury themselves deeper and deeper, and over them stands the police "administration," watching, counting, guarding....

In order to avoid persecution for something petty, in order to avoid attacks from the government committees, Jewish kolkhozy must profess to be "godless."[3] That is to say, they must pass themselves off as made up of non-believers, as having nothing to do with anything of a religious nature.

For Jews, this however means more than expunging religion. It also means smashing the folk traditions of home life....

That *Royteh Shtern* is "godless" causes woeful heartache for the older kolkhozniki. On the eve of every Jewish holiday, all the kolkhozniki must assemble to hear a *drosheh*[4] from a party propagandist. This drosheh is replete with vehement curses heaped upon every Jewish movement in the world. As such, it seems that whatever bread the Jewish kolkhozniki of Royteh Shtern actually do sometimes receive comes at a price: helping to vituperate other Jews....

There is a Jewish school in Royteh Shtern; after all, it is a Jewish village. But the children are not interested, and the school is poorly attended.... The teachers have no eagerness to pursue their work because they are severely harassed by Party commissions. Every so often a blemish is discovered on this one or that one indicating some deviation from the "Stalinist line." Nor do the children want the schools; there is no place for them in the children's hearts. What, indeed, do these schools teach them? Everything which may be connected to Jewish intellectualism has been wiped out; after all, the latter represents "bourgeois justice." Such is the interpretation of the Jewish-Communist course of study.... [T]he Jewish parents have concluded that it is better to send their children to the Ukrainian and Russian schools....

---

3 In Russian: bezbozhnik. In Yiddish, this word connotes a generalized attribute of shamelessness.

4 Yiddish/Hebrew: (religious) sermon. Here used ironically.

...What is the mood in the Jewish kolkhozy with regards to religion? Are there outbreaks of protest as in the non-Jewish kolkhozy?

A kolkhoznik from the Nay-Zlatopol [Novozlatopil] district speaks about this at a get-together of friends in a house in Kharkov. I gather from his words that it is bad for Jews to be protestors and rebels and it is bad for them to be quiet and compliant.

Should a protest occur in a Jewish kolkhoz, all soon receive a warning that they are former lishentsy,[5] and it is better for them to remain silent. This warning serves as another signal that the Jews should be content just to be permitted on the soil. Yet at the same time, Christian peasants come to the Jewish villages and hint that they, the Jews, should not remain aloof from some plan or other to drive away certain officials from the area. These hints are bitter, because they are accompanied by other insinuations to the effect that "the whole regime is in Jewish hands."

In light of this, the Ukrainian Jews remember the frightful pogroms they endured during the years of civil war.

In short, the Jewish village has no inner peace, and events in the area are always portents of yet more cause for apprehension.

By means of help from relatives in America, the Jewish kolkhozniki managed to somehow tide over the famine which during the course of the year struck the whole countryside. Consequently, the Christian villages looked upon the Jews with a bitter envy.

But the kolkhoznik from the Nay-Zlatopol district spoke of wholly different encounters between Jewish and non-Jewish country people.

Several villages of Ukrainian peasants were arrested and exiled to Novo Seversk to mine for coal. Dozens came to Jewish villages to bid farewell. There were scenes of drama. The Ukrainian peasants wept. Many came to implore the Jewish villagers not to go should "the authorities" wish to send them to kolkhozy on land taken from those banished. Still others came to plead with the Jews to indeed go and to write the exiled about what becomes of everything...

Yes, to go or not to go: this has truly become a moral question for the Jews. But then who in Russia can decide for themselves whether to go or not to go?....

In the Nay-Zlatopol district there is a Jewish kolkhoz by the name of "Shock Worker." It was a functioning kolkhoz. Entire families worked: the women like the men, children like their parents. They worked year after year, day-in day-out, without rest, without holiday. Results, with respect to field crops, were great. So were achievements in the stables and in the production of grain and milk. But it was not so for the kolkhozniki. They alone were constantly exhausted and emaciated as a result of little food and a lot of government "manoeuvres."....

The managers of the kolkhoz were also members of the Party. Hence they were like landlords, and when it came to the distribution of food, they first accommodated those closest to them, people from their families....

I inquired of every Jewish kolkhoznik whose company I shared, whether in Ukraine or White Russia, as to the "national significance" of the Jewish kolkhozy. We know that this is a subject of discussion in foreign lands and indeed among ourselves in America. I got a lot of smiles. Others spoke with agitation:

5 See note 2 above.

> "Do you people actually know what is happening to us? National significance? That rings hollow! So do we live as a distinct, integral nationality? So do we have proper Jewish schools for our children? Do they let us have a book, religious or secular? What do you mean, 'national significance'? Is not our national tragedy that you, in foreign lands, do not know what is happening to us?"

Their tragedy is also our own. One peek at the so-called Jewish country life in Soviet Russia and a chill travels through your every limb; a painful sadness begins to tug at your heart.

Harry Lang, "Writer Quotes Soviet Official: '6 Million Died of Hunger'"

New York Evening Journal, 15 April 1935, pp. 1–2. Excerpts.

...Says Russian Famine Was Man-Made

It may be news to the wide American public to learn that the Jewish press in this country is much better informed on Russia than the English language press, and that the *Forward* has for years supplied its readers with complete and unvarnished information on the tragedy of the Russian people under Bolshevism.

Even the shock-proof world of today would shudder if it were to learn all the details of the famine in Russia, especially in the southern, once fertile, territory of the Ukraine. It was a famine that did not spring from drought, from floods, from any act of nature. It was a man-made famine, a planned famine.

While traveling in Soviet Russia, I often asked myself, "What has happened to civilization? We have a press boasting of its far-flung system of facilities unsurpassed in history. We have the technical marvels of telegraphy and radio, which in a few minutes bring the news of the least event in a remote corner of the globe to the whole wide world. And yet we have also developed systems of modern dictatorship which can prevent the starvation of millions of people, such as has occurred in Soviet Russia, from becoming known."....

Article One

I went to Soviet Russia as a freelance writer. I had no assignments, no duties to perform, no promises to fulfill. From country to country I traveled with one aim—to observe how people lived, to see where there is pain and where there is joy. I LOOKED FOR JOY IN SOVIET RUSSIA.

I am a Jew, and harbored nothing but hatred for the Russia of the Czars where my people had suffered so much. Full of hope I was now going to the new Russia to see the system which is trying to remake the entire world.

My Americanism had influenced me sufficiently to enable me to look at Soviet Russia with all the tolerance that the principles of American democracy stand for. My familiarity with the theories and practice of the labor movement equipped me especially to judge correctly what was going on under the Communist flag....

"Eating Dead Children Is Barbarism," Says Poster Distributed in Villages

In the office of a Soviet functionary I saw a poster on the wall which struck my attention. It showed the picture of a mother in distress, with a swollen child at her feet, and over the picture was the inscription: "EATING OF DEAD CHILDREN IS BARBARISM."

I wondered. What was the purpose of such a poster? The Soviet official explained to me:

"It is one of our methods of educating the people. We distributed such posters in hundreds of villages, especially in the Ukraine. We had to."

"Is the situation that bad?" I asked in astonishment. "Are people really in such a condition as to eat their children's corpses?"

The official was silent. It was a painful, disturbing silence.

"Not all our people are enlightened," he remarked a little later.

Again I shuddered.

But I went down to the Ukraine and saw with my own eyes the destruction wrought there, the wreckage of a great country. I might have gone back to America after seeing Moscow and Leningrad. I had obtained a sufficient grasp of what life is under a dictatorship. I had seen the chasm between the Russia as she is painted abroad by the Soviet propaganda machine and the true Russia, unhappy, tortured, bleeding.

Goes to Inspect "Barred Land"

But I felt it my duty to myself to go beyond that stage, to look into the heart of the land. After all, the two great cities were but shadows of an immense country. I decided to drink the bitter cup to the end....

Told Six Million Died of Hunger

Only when I came to the Ukraine did I understand why Moscow kept foreign journalists out of it. A high Ukrainian Soviet official confidentially told me that 6,000,000 people had perished from famine in that territory alone, once the granary of Russia.

What I saw there made me think again and again:

"Why does not a new Jeremiah arise to lament in a voice that would make the whole world tremble the millions that are perishing on this soil? Why? Why?"

The harrowing facts I discovered in the Ukraine will be described in the following articles.

Harry Lang, "Red Soldiers Turn Bandit to Avenge Fate of Kin"

New York Evening Journal, 16 April 1935, pp. 1–2.

Article Two

We arrived in Kharkoff, then the capital of the Ukrainian Soviet Republic. The first street scenes I saw spoke their own language. Men and women were returning at sunset from the great tractor plant and other factories.

Their clothes were old, dirty strips of sacking. Their shoes were of shriveled leather or rotten rubber, full of holes.

Many women were carrying infants in their arms. There are no baby carriages in Soviet Russia.

Ukrainian Soviet at Odds with Moscow

And all, men and women alike, thousands of them, had lumps of black bread under their tattered sleeves. On the way, they nibbled at the bread and swallowed every crumb. The hand of hunger was sticking out from the mutilated chunks of bread.

A high official of the Ukrainian Soviet, with whom we established contact, confidentially advised me to take a trip to the villages. Only there, he said, would I see the full handiwork of the famine. And he added:

"Six million people have perished from hunger in our country in 1932-33." Then he paused, and repeated: "Six million."

Why should this Ukrainian official be interested in conveying that information to an American visitor? The answer is that the Ukrainian Soviet, the Ukrainian nationalists, are constantly at odds with Moscow.

The suggested trip cost me $50 a day for the use of an automobile. The Ukrainian official accompanied me. We had a chauffeur. The road was grey gravel for stretches, and sticky yellow clay for other stretches.

'Impossible to Conceal Truth in Russia'

No people were to be seen in the fields. On all sides were heaps of grain, corn or wheat, and ordinary hay. Although it was late in the Fall, the hay had not been stored. The grain had not been threshed and the shocks, soaked through and through, were already rotting.

It was morning. A vapor was rising from the damp and putrid shocks and heaps. It looked as if the fields were on fire. There were miles and miles and miles of such landscape.

My escort wanted me to see what the collectivized villages looked like. His heart was rent by the destruction of his people. Did the world know?

The previous Spring and Summer a curtain had been dropped over certain provinces and regions of Soviet Russia. Yet within Russia, it was impossible to conceal the truth. It was impossible to erect walls between the cities and the villages.

The very political interests of the Soviet Government demanded that a cry should be raised in the cities that the peasants were seeking to starve the urban population. The Communist cry was that the peasants had refused to plow the fields, or to harvest crops. Factories were stopped and industrial workers were transformed overnight into agricultural laborers.

The city people, therefore, knew only too well what was going on in the country. But foreign correspondents were a different matter. It was vital to the Soviet government that the outside world should not be able to penetrate to the countryside, and to hear the voice of the people. And now the curtain was lifting before me.

We were approaching the first village. The entrance was in the form of a crude gate made of stocks and stripped tree branches. The Soviet emblem, a star designed from sticks, was over the gate. In the center of the star, under glass, was a photograph of Lenin. Over it two red flags were hanging so as to form a crooked cross. One of the flags was tattered.

A soldier wearing a long army coat, with a rifle on his shoulder, was seated near the gate, his head partly sunk between his shoulders, his face buried in the collar of his coat. He was dozing. His bayonet, rising over his huddled figure, pointed straight upward.

Officials Investigating 'Sabotage' Bring Their Own Food to Farm

An investigation was going on when we arrived. Soldiers with rifles slung across their shoulders were standing at the doors of a couple of cabins. Other soldiers with fixed bayonets were on an army truck.

The investigation had to do with damaged tractors. The village had been collectivized, the peasants had been forced to join a kolkhoz—a collective farm. And now it was charged that the peasants had been "sabotaging," a high crime indeed.

Officials in boots and short leather jackets were snooping about accompanied by soldiers. All the officials and soldiers carried chunks of black bread. They had brought their food supply along. They knew that in the villages it was impossible to obtain bread.

Mother Drops Sick Child in Roadway

With bated breath I was watching the Soviet investigators at work. Suddenly something else caught my eye. A peasant woman, dressed in something like patched old sacks, appeared from a side path. She was dragging a child of three or four years old by the collar of a torn coat, the way one drags a heavy bag-load. The woman pulled the child into the main street. Here she dropped it in the mud.

Everybody saw the scene, but no one made a move. My escort explained that he had long since grown accustomed to such sights. The peasant woman was the mother. The child's little face was bloated and blue. There was foam around the little lips. The little hands and tiny body w[ere] swollen. Here was a bundle of human parts, all deathly-sick, yet still held together by the breath of life.

The mother left the child on the road, in the hope that somebody might do something to save it.

My escort endeavored to hearten me. Thousands and thousands of such children, he told me, had met a similar fate in the Ukraine that year.

Comes to Village Inhabited by Dead

We visited one wretched village after another, until we came to the village of the dead.

Before us was a settlement of a few score houses. The doors were boarded up. Not a living creature in the gardens and the adjacent fields. Dead chimneys on the roofs, dead windows stared at us.

And then the image of a human stirred in the distance. The long overcoat of a soldier was dragging its way towards us....

"Here is where most of the inhabitants lie," the soldier observed.

It did not look like a grave. There were no signs over it. The dead had simply been dumped into the ditch. How many were buried there? The soldier started to figure, and replied:

"A few dozen."

2 Red Soldiers Become Bandits to Avenge Parents' Starvation

The common grave was near the houses of the dead. Some of those who had perished were buried at the doors of their homes. Such was the case when a family buried one member after another. The soldier named a girl who had seen her mother bury her father, and who then had to bury her mother. Later the girl buried her little brother next to her parents. Then she fled to Kieff. But before leaving her native village, she set fire to a stable full of army horses.

The soldier had two comrades in the Red Army. They were brothers from a neighboring village. They served in separate regiments, in different localities.

One of them heard reports of famine at home and obtained leave to visit his native village. When he arrived his parents were already gone, expired from hunger. He went off to bring his brother to show him their deserted homestead. When the two men completed their service terms they became bandits, roving the countryside at night, getting their revenge.

Collective Farm Foisted on Village

The soldier pointed out two houses where corpses had lain for weeks until soldiers were sent to the village to gather up the dead.

My escort knew all the facts given by the soldier, but he wanted me to get it direct from the source. It seems that a kolkhoz (collective farm) had been foisted on the village.

The soldier pointed out to us the house which had belonged to the peasant who acted as chairman of the kolkhoz. Nominally, the chairman had been a Communist. But he had ikons in his home, and the peasants would come there to kneel and to pray. The chairman was then expelled from the Communist party.

"Stalin Enthroned Over Dead World"

But there was a monument among the deserted houses to the dead kolkhoz. It was a bell used to awaken the peasants, to call them to work. The bellman was a loyal adherent of the kolkhoz. The peasants kept away from him. When half the village was already dead from hunger, he would still rise at dawn and ring the bell—as if to call the dead.

As we left the village of the dead, we passed a gate over which were waving two red flags with broken poles. There was the customary Soviet emblem over it—the star.

A picture of Stalin was in the center. There was something symbolic about the photograph: Stalin enthroned over a dead world.

Harry Lang, "Street Bands in Kiev Steal Food from Starving Women"

New York Evening Journal, 17 April 1935, pp. 1–2.

Article Three

We were shaken by the scenes of famine in the Kharkov zone of Russia where we saw the village of the dead, its residents starved. But the Ukraine has a population of more than 30,000,000. What were conditions in the other sections? We proceeded upon our trip of investigation, and went to Kiev, the ancient capital of Russia, now capital of the Ukraine.

The main street of the city, the famous Krestchatik [Khreshchatyk], told a harrowing tale of famine at first glance. It was early in the morning. The sidewalks were crowded, thousands marching to work carrying their rations of coarse black bread. It was their breakfast—at which they nibbled on their way. Hunger was the standard of living in Soviet Russia.

Woman Slumps To Ground—Dead

Suddenly I saw a woman, still young, drop to the ground. She had an empty basket in her hands, and the basket rolled down the sidewalk. Her arms were convulsed for a moment, then they stretched out. Her eyes opened wide once or twice, then they closed. Her head shook fitfully, then it hit the stone pavement, and relaxed into stillness.

The passersby kept marching. Not one of them turned around. My first thought was that the woman had slipped and fallen by accident. I made a move to help her rise. With me was a man from my hotel. He quickly stopped me:

"Don't! Under no circumstances should you go! It is not fitting for you, a visitor, a foreigner, to interfere."

It appeared that this tragedy was a common occurrence. People enfeebled by starvation just collapsed in the streets and died. But why did it not attract attention? Were all those passersby heartless? Far from it. But everybody knew his own helplessness, that the dead were better off than the living.

Haunted by Vision of Clutching Hands

I was haunted for a long time by the vision of those outstretched still hands, that convulsed head, that empty basket rolling on the sidewalk.

I became a prey to conflicting moods. Now I felt crushed, almost paralyzed. Now I felt the impulse to run and to shout from the house-tops.

It was the season of the Jewish new year. I visited the central synagogue. It was crowded with thousands of worshippers, despite the threats of persecution by the Communist godless society.

There is a special Jewish prayer which enumerates all the known forms of death. Its text contains a reference to death from famine. While I was in the synagogue, the man officiating at the services recited that prayer. When he came to the words, "And he that dies from hunger," he repeated the last word three times with burning anguish. Thousands of Jews sobbed and cried after him:

"Hunger, hunger, hunger!"

I went down the Basin st., the Bowery of Kiev. In the United States I had heard many stories of the excellent care taken by the Soviets of homeless children. All over Russia I heard references to the "bandits"—the homeless children of the civil war period that had now reached maturity. Their number was legion in Kiev. Many of these street wolves were already in their twenties.

Basin st. was the headquarters of these "bandits." It also was the stamping ground of veterans of the Red Army, a ghastly collection of cripples and invalids pursuing unsavory affairs. The two parties were in alliance. The cripples acted as spotters, the street wolves carried out the open robberies.

I saw a woman carrying away food from the "open market" in Basin st. The street wolves prefer to attack women. One of them swooped down upon her and bit her arm. She dropped her food, and shrieked. The "bandit" snatched his loot and fled. A crowd formed quickly, but no one even tried to catch the thief. The policeman who came up to comfort the woman remarked:

"It's the hunger that's driving them on."

Robbery Gets No Attention With Hunger in Every Throat

And hunger was the immediate subject of conversation in the crowd. The woman was holding her wounded arm. Some distance away, the crippled soldiers laughed leeringly. No one talked of the robbery. The word famine was on everybody's lips. Indeed, it was not banditry, it was calamity which filled the air.

I went to one of the Kiev cemeteries which had a special famine section. As far as the eye could see, hundreds of new graves stretched before me. They held the victims of starvation of part of 1932 and part of 1933. They were like the graves which follow a war or an epidemic. There were no headstones, only wooden sticks with numbers.

During the critical famine months, there were scores of daily burials. Sometimes the corpses would lie in the open on the grass for days until their turn came to be interred. Mourning relatives stood watch over their dead ones day and night. Huge armies of crows and ravens circled over the corpses and rent the air with their calls.

Cemeteries Hold Many Living Dead

One of the grave-diggers came up to me and started a conversation.

"You are looking at our fresh graves?" he said. "You see, Kiev has also made its contribution to the second five-year plan. Tell my brothers in America about it."

Cemeteries in Soviet Russia are seldom if ever visited by foreign correspondents. Yet what testimony they have to offer! For there are living people among the graves.

In the Kiev cemetery I saw hundreds of people scarified by the GPU, bearing the marks of torture from persecution and hunger. They stood over the graves of their dear ones and begged the dead for bread.

It was a damp day. The old trees in the cemetery were dripping. The cemetery fence had been removed to complete the construction of a factory. Its stones, boards, nails all had gone into the five-year plan. Even some of the headstones had been removed as building material.

I walked along until I came to a woman sobbing and crying aloud.

"What shall I tell you, my dear sister? You are well off. You see nothing, you hear nothing. Mother wanted to come and join you today. But she hasn't the strength. We have nothing to eat at home, dear sister. Do you remember the beautiful home which we once had?" She was talking to the dead.

Young Mother Pleads For Death

A young man, with his eyes half-closed, was addressing himself to two graves over which stood one headstone:

"Can you do nothing for me? Nothing? How long must I continue to suffer?"

A young woman dressed coarsely was sitting on the ground at the foot of a fine monument. Her sleeves were torn. Against the shining marble, she formed a striking contrast. It was her mother's grave. She murmured something in Russian about mama taking her away. At her side was a boy. He wore a cap with a Soviet star. In his hands was a piece of black bread. He tried to bite at it, but tears were in his eyes.

The entire cemetery was peopled with such scenes.

Harry Lang, "Peasants in Russia Burn Wheat Fields in Hunger Revolt"

New York Evening Journal, 20 April 1935, pp. 1–2. Excerpts.

Article Five

We took a motor trip from Kieff, the present capital of the Ukraine, into the country, and came upon a new sight. A field, with the crops still lying on it, was burning. As in other zones, the grain in the province of Kieff had also been left to perish. But sunshine had dried the stacks and, to prevent the Government from saving the wheat, rebel peasants had set it on fire at night.

As far as the eye could reach, the bread field was in flames. Troops had been called out to combat the conflagration, but they were helpless. Groups of soldiers were struggling to remove the stacks from the path of the fire.

'Rather Death Than Slavery'

Other soldiers were seated on two army lorries, wearily watching the weird spectacle. Peasants driving by in their carts did not even turn to look at the burning field. They feigned indifference.

Here was a new form of revolt. Its silent slogan was: Destroy everything and perish from hunger! There are times when people would rather have death than slavery.

In Soviet Russia, bayonets and hunger march side by side. Frequently, as our car passed through wooded zones, I observed muddy side roads leading into the forest.

There I saw parties of peasants, surrounded by armed soldiers, doing forced labor. Some of the convicts were women with infants in their arms. My escorts, including the chauffeur of the Soviet-owned car, explained that the prisoners were rebels, strikers, who refused to join in *Kolkhoz* (collective farm) work.

Woman Carries Dead Child to Cemetery

We arrived in a town about 60 miles from Kieff. Here I witnessed a singular funeral procession. It was the Jewish Sabbath, on which day no burials are allowed by the Mosaic law.

A Jewish woman, carrying a dead child in her arms, was making her way to the cemetery. The child, about three years old, had died the night before. The mother, who shared quarters with other families having children, could not keep the little corpse at home.

All the other children were bloated from hunger. The mother was going to stay with her dead child at the cemetery until sundown, when she would dig a little hole in the ground and bury him.

Not a single person accompanied the woman. When I stopped her, she hugged the little corpse. She talked in a voice that snapped in the middle of words. A month earlier she had buried in the same fashion another child of hers. Both children had died from hunger.

I wanted to know about her husband. Yes, she had had one, a worker, but he had been sent down to Odessa. For a while he had sent her a little money.

Then she received a notice from the Odessa Soviet that her husband was dead.

It was just like a war notice. She wanted to investigate, but could not get permission to leave. Perhaps her husband had been shot. She did not know.

I obtained the services of a man to perform the rites of an undertaker and grave-digger. Only when the dead child was removed from her arms, to be put away until nightfall, did the woman break down. She cried:

"There are still people with hearts left in the world."

And I, a stranger from faraway America, wept with her.

Berdicheff Now Town Of Mudholes

We continued on our journey until we came to Berdicheff, once a lively Jewish trading center in the sugar-beet district. The city now seemed to sink in mud holes.

Soldiers and police were driving the townspeople to work in the fields, as the peasants in the country had refused to dig the beets. The whole region was in a state of terror.

People would rather [have] *died from hunger than labor in the fields. Why? Because they demanded bread for their toil. Some wanted more bread, better bread, not the coarse black stuff baked with straw, which the Soviet supplied.*

A large modern bakery had been installed some months earlier in Berdicheff. The Communist managers and the bakers, it was revealed, had formed an alliance to steal flour and bread from the Government bakery.

Here was a new sidelight on the famine—bakers going hungry and forced to steal bread! Yet they knew that their crime involved more than theft, that they would be charged with a conspiracy against the state. The main cause of all Soviet crime is hunger, but the Soviet Government is not interested in the cause of crime....

Finally, we left the Ukraine and started for the Soviet Republic of White Russia. We were passing through fields flooded by Autumn rains.

In the middle of the night armed soldiers boarded our train. We learned from them that the entire territory was under martial law. The peasants had refused the orders of the local Soviets to dig ditches and drain the roadways. They demanded bread. Troops had been called to drive them to the task.

Says All Roads Led To Famine

The woman conductor on our train warned me to watch my things.

"People are hungry," she said. "Look out, when the train stops at stations somebody might get on board and steal your provisions."

It became clear that all the roads of the land led to famine.

Harry Lang, "Soviets Seized Cash Sent by U.S. Kin to Starving Russians"

New York Evening Journal, 23 April 1935, pp. 1–2. Excerpts.

My trip to Soviet Russia was part of a world's tour which took a year and included 19 countries. As a Socialist, as a lover of freedom, and as a Jew, I went to Russia full of fervent expectations.

I came out crushed, shell-shocked. Nowhere did I see suffering on such a titanic scale. Nowhere did I find the tragedy of a great people so effectively concealed behind a conspiracy of silence.

That conspiracy hid from the eyes of the world not only the famine of millions, but also the iron shadows of that famine, which strangled the cries of the victims. They were the shadows of inquisition which followed in the wake of the famine.

Dollars Sent by U.S. Kin Seized

The first of these shadows was the "Dollar Inquisition." Before I left the United States, I knew that the Jews of this country were aroused by numerous reports of a system of extortion and torture practiced by the G.P.U. on relatives of American immigrants.

The latter, replying to appeals for help from their starving kinsmen in Russia, sent them small money orders. The famine had impoverished the Soviet State treasury. The coffers of the G.P.U. were empty. The G.P.U. then launched an organized campaign to extort the American dollars as a source of government revenue.

This "Dollar Inquisition" caused the American Jewish Congress, led by Rabbi Stephen S. Wise, to call meetings of protest.

The Hebrew poet laureate in Palestine, Chaim Nachman Bialik, had gathered a mass of authentic evidence proving conclusively that the G.P.U. was terrorizing all the Jewish communities in Russia, imprisoning people just because they had relatives in America, and holding them as hostages until ransom arrived....

Behind the appalling scenes of the famine that I had witnessed stretched the second iron shadow of the Russian tragedy.

There was revealed before me a spontaneous general strike of millions of peasants.

Peasants Resist Collectivization

Hundreds of villages, without leadership, were offering resistance to the Stalin system of collectivization, which forced them to turn their homes, cattle, fields and implements into government-operated enterprises. The peasants who had made the revolution in order to gain the land now found themselves deprived of their gains.

Millions resisted passively. Others resorted to sabotage. Beneath the cloak of the famine a grim and silent war was being waged. It was waged with arson, with theft, with crafty means of vengeance.

Peasants joined collective farms in order to wreck them from within. They destroyed their livestock, neglected their fields and stubbornly marched to death. It was a war for bread, perhaps the most gruesome war that has ever been fought....

The third shadow of the famine reached as far as America. It is still in our midst. While the Soviet propaganda machine would have the American people believe that the Russian people are happy, another arm of the Soviet Government gathers and solicits American dollars for victims of hunger in Russia.

Every year hundreds of thousands of immigrants in this country send to their relatives in Russia food parcels and money orders through the Torgsin. The advertisements of the Torgsin appear in our press....

We are told that everybody in Russia is employed. Yet the records of the Soviet Torgsin and its innumerable agencies will show how many unemployed immigrants in America keep their employed relatives in Russia alive.

Most of these immigrants are Jewish workers. I interviewed hundreds of their relatives in Russia.

Russian Workers Envy U.S. Freedom

All of them gave me the same message to bring home, namely, that the workers of Russia envy American freedom, American democracy. More than once I was told:

"Tell American labor not to be misled by the false friends of the Soviet Union. They are the enemies of the Russian people. Many of them are big industrialists and promoters who seek to make money doing business with the Soviet Government.

"These Wall Street friends of Bolshevism think that we are different from other human beings, that the Russian people like their oppressors. Tell them in America the truth about us."

Appalled as I was by the excruciating sights of the famine, I was even more appalled by the task of conveying the truth, conveying a picture of the monster which created the famine—the monster of dictatorship.

Whiting Williams, "My Journey Through Famine-Stricken Russia"

Answers (London), 24 February 1934. Excerpts, pp. 16–17, 28.

Charles Whiting Williams (1878–1975) was a writer and lecturer on labor-management relations. On the basis of his observations of working conditions and workers' attitudes in various countries, Williams wrote books and articles, including *What's on the Worker's Mind, by One Who Put On Overalls to Find Out* (1920), *Full Up and Fed Up: The Worker's Mind in Crowded Britain* (1921), *Horny Hands and Hampered Elbows: The Worker's Mind in Western Europe* (1922), *Mainsprings of Men* (1925), and *America's Mainspring and the Great Society: A Pick-and-Shovel Outlook* (1967). His experiences are described in Daniel A. Wren, *White Collar Hobo: The Travels of Whiting Williams* (1987).

...[D]uring the last twelve months, in one European country, millions of people have died of starvation.... Dying in a land which was formerly one of the richest of all the peasant states....

"Only the strong will see next summer's sun," said the chambermaid in a Soviet hotel in which I stayed at the beginning of the tour which took me through the length and breadth of the Russian Ukraine. I laughed at her.

Travelling by rail to Kharkov, the capital of this great agricultural and industrial province, I talked in German to an engineer who was in the same coach.

"You know that starvation has been killing off people here by the millions?" he said....

"Nonsense," I said. "The thing's crazy! If there were anything like that happening, the whole world would be ringing with it and organising relief."

He shrugged his shoulders.

"Well, let's ask the conductor," I said. He was passing through the coach just then.

"My own daughter died of hunger just three months ago to-day," he said simply, when we put the question to him.

Even then I could hardly believe that there had been anything beyond, perhaps, a few isolated deaths in remote villages. But as I went through the country, and particularly in the Donetz Basin, I found that the engineer had not lied....

...Once I was off the beaten track which the tourists follow I saw with my own eyes the victims of famine. Men and women who were literally dying of hunger in the gutter.

Have you ever seen a human being in the last stages of starvation? If you have done so once, you can never mistake the signs. The swollen faces and ankles which follow the breakdown of the body's normal functioning set the final seal of famine upon the emaciation of long-continued want....

...[T]he worst memory I have brought out of Russia is the children. There was one youngster I saw in Kharkov. Half-naked, he had sunk, exhausted, on the carriage-way, with the kerbstone as a pillow, and his pipe-stem legs sprawled out, regardless of danger from passing wheels.

Another—a boy of eight or nine—was sitting among the debris of a street market, picking broken eggshells out of the dirt and examining them with heartbreaking minuteness in the hope of finding a scrap of food still sticking to them. His shrunken cheeks were covered with an unhealthy whitish down that made me think of those fungoid growths that sprout in the darkness out of dying trees.

I saw him again in the same place the next day—motionless now with his head sunk between his knees in a piteous abandonment.

While eating in a restaurant in the same town I saw a girl of twelve run up the steps towards a veranda table from which a customer had just risen. For a moment she hesitated; shrank back as if in fear as she saw the man look at her. Finally, reassured by his expression, she darted boldly forward, gathered the scraps he had left on his plate in her fingers, then turned and ran down the steps with her prize.

For all the world she was like a wild bird driven by a hard winter to a town garden. There was the same suspicion, the same holding back, and the same momentary boldness followed by headlong flight. Something, also, perhaps, of the same grace and beauty. I shall never see her again, but I cherish the hope that she will survive.

There are hordes of those wild children in all the towns. They live—and die—like wild animals.

Where do they come from? I made inquiries about them, and learned that last winter, when food supplies began to fail, large numbers of peasants left their villages and came into towns with their families, hoping that there they might get a chance to work—and eat.

There was neither work nor bread for them, and under a new regulation that required every adult in the towns to show papers to prove his right to be there, they were driven back to their foodless villages.

They believed they were returning to certain starvation. So they left the children behind. In the villages, they said, the little ones would inevitably die—in the towns, their chance of life might be slender, but it was at least a chance.

Something like 18,000 children were abandoned in this manner—abandoned because that was the only way in which their parents could help them—in Kharkov alone....

I saw some of the wild children of this winter being rounded up. A horse-drawn wagon lumbered along the street, with two or three policemen marching beside it. When they saw one of the little Ishmaels the police gave chase. If the youngster was caught, he was placed among the others already in the wagon....

Once, when the wagon stopped and a chase was in progress, two of the lads previously captured saw their chance, scrambled to the ground, and made off as hard as they could into a maze of narrow alley-ways.

I felt rather sorry for these youngsters, running back to the hardship and hunger of their life in the gutter, when, as I thought, they would have been fed and clad and educated in the institution to which they were being taken. But when I mentioned this to a Russian acquaintance he just stared at me.

At first I could not believe what he told me. Then I spoke to a number of other people. They all said the same thing.

These children were not sent to homes. Bread was too scarce. They were put into railway wagons and unloaded out in the open country—too far out for it to be possible to walk back to town.

And once, at least, three wagons filled with youngsters were shunted into a siding and forgotten for three days. When, at the end of that time, someone found them, not one of the children remained alive.

I don't pretend, of course, that this was a typical case. But what chance have children dumped out in the open country?...

William Henry Chamberlin, *Russia's Iron Age*

(London: Duckworth, 1935). Excerpts, pp. 82–89.

William Henry Chamberlin (1897–1969) was an American historian and journalist who specialized in Russia, the Soviet Union, and the Cold War. He served as Moscow correspondent of the *Christian Science Monitor* and the *Manchester Guardian* from 1922 to 1934. His most influential books include *Soviet Russia: A Living Record and a History* (1930), *Russia's Iron Age* (1934), and *The Russian Revolution 1917–1921* (1935).

Rumors of wholesale starvation in the villages, especially in the southern and southeastern provinces of European Russia and in Central Asia, began to filter into Moscow in the early spring. A clear intimation that things were happening in the country districts which the Soviet censors very definitely wished to conceal from the outside world was the unprecedented action of the authorities in forbidding several foreign correspondents to leave Moscow, and the establishment of a new ruling to the effect that no foreign correspondent could travel in the countryside without submitting a definite itinerary and obtaining permission to make the trip from the Commissariat for Foreign Affairs.

No such permissions were granted until September, when the new harvest was largely gathered in, the corpses had all been buried, the trucks which, during the late winter and early spring, made regular rounds in Poltava, Kiev, and other centres of the famine region, picking up the corpses of refugees from the country districts, had ceased to function, and conditions were generally more normal. After the prohibition had been lifted, I visited three widely separated districts of the Soviet Union—Kropotkin, in the North Caucasus, and Poltava and Byelaya Tserkov, in Ukraina. I talked at railroad stations with peasants ranging from the southeast corner of Ukraina, in the Donetz Basin, to the northwestern part of Chernigov Province. On the basis of talks with peasants and figures supplied not by peasants, who were often prone to exaggeration, but by local Soviet officials and collective-farm presidents, whose interest was rather to minimize what had taken place, I have no hesitation in saying that the southern and southeastern section of European Russia during the first six months of 1933 experienced a major famine, far more destructive than the local famines which occurred, mostly on the Volga, in exceptionally bad drought years under Tsarism, second in the number of its victims probably only to the famine of 1921–22.

The first thing that struck me when I began to walk about in the Cossack villages in the neighborhood of Kropotkin was the extraordinary deterioration in the physical condition of what had once been an extremely fertile region. Enormous weeds, of striking height and toughness, filled up many of the gardens and could be seen waving in the fields of wheat, corn, and sunflower seeds. Gone were the wheaten loaves, the succulent slices of lamb that had been offered for sale everywhere when I visited the Kuban Valley in 1924. At that time every Cossack settlement had its large number of fierce, snapping dogs, trained to guard sheep and cattle; now there was an almost ghostly quiet; the bark of a dog was never heard. "The dogs all died or were eaten up during the famine," was the general explanation of their disappearance.

In the first house which I entered, quite at random, in the *stanitsa*, or Cossack settlement of Laduzhskaya, southwest of Kropotkin (the Cossack *stanitsa* is usually much larger than the typical peasant village), I encountered a grim episode of what would officially be called "class struggle on the agrarian front." A handsome young Cossack woman, who had just given birth to a baby and who lived in the house with her mother, her husband being away on military service, told me how her brother, with some companions, had beaten a grain collector so badly that he died; and how he returned from serving a term in prison, where he received nothing but water and very little bread, so weakened that he, with his wife and five children, had all died of hunger and exhaustion in the spring....

In another *stanitsa,* Kazanskaya, which is picturesquely situated on a high bluff above the Kuban River, I called on the president of the local Soviet, Mr. Nemov, in an effort to obtain some official information about the mortality rate during the preceding winter and spring. Nemov scouted the stories of the peasants that a third or a half of the inhabitants had perished. "The population declined from about 8,000 to about 7,000," he declared. "About 850 died and another 150 were deported because they sabotaged the government's programme of grain collection." Mr. Nemov showed me mortality statistics for four months—January, February, March, and April. They indicated how the curve of death mounted upward as the peasants' last reserves of grain were exhausted toward spring. Thus 21 persons died in January, 34 in February, 79 in March, and 155 in April. This upward tendency most probably continued during May and early June, until early vegetables provided some relief.

Regarding the causes of the famine, the accounts of Mr. Nemov and of the peasants tallied fairly closely.... [I]t was the general testimony of the peasants that they could have pulled through if the local authorities had not swooped down with heavy requisitions. The last reserves of grain, which had been buried in the ground by the desperate peasants, were dug up and confiscated. A man named Sheboldaev, with a reputation for cruelty in "liquidating" kulaks in the lower Volga district, was made President of the North Caucasus, where the passive resistance was doubtless stiffer than in other sections of the country, because a considerable part of the population consisted of Cossacks, who had enjoyed a higher standard of living than the mass of the peasants before the Revolution and who had mostly fought on the side of the Whites during the civil war. Under Sheboldaev's orders whole communities, such as Poltavskaya, in the Western Kuban, were deported *en masse* to the frozen regions of the north in the dead of winter. Other villages which did not fill out the grain quotas that were demanded from them were "blockaded," in the sense that no city products were allowed to reach them. Local officials who protested against the pitiless repression were deposed, arrested, in a few cases shot.

Sheboldaev's methods, which were, of course, applied with the knowledge and approval of the central authorities in Moscow, squeezed out of the North Caucasus the full amount of grain which Moscow demanded.[6] But they turned what would otherwise perhaps have been a hunger into a famine, and they left a diseased and weakened population (there was a tremendous epidemic of malignant malaria in the Kuban Valley in 1933) and a ravaged and devastated countryside which will require years of reconstruction before it can hope to regain its former prosperity.

In the villages around Poltava, a charming Ukrainian town built on a hillside with an abundance of leafy trees along its streets, and in the vicinity of Byelaya Tserkov, a small town southwest of Kiev, largely inhabited by Jews, I found much of the same situation as in the North Caucasus.... [P]eople often broke down and wept when they described what they and their relatives and friends had experienced during the preceding winter and spring. "No war ever took from us so many people," exclaimed one woman with whom I talked in Poltava. And in one veritable Village of Death (its name was Cherkass), some eight miles south of Byelaya Tserkov, I had it on the authority of the secretary of the local Soviet, Mr. Fishenko, that about 600 of the village's former 2,000 inhabitants had perished. Hundreds of others had fled. Fishenko's figure found abundant confirmation in the stories of the famine survivors and in the grim mute evidence of the numerous abandoned houses, with their weed-grown gardens and gaping doors and windows.

Two noteworthy features of the famine were that far more men died than women and far more *edinolichniki* (individual peasants) than members of collective farms. If in many districts 10 per cent of the collective farmers died, the percentage of mortality among the individual peasants was sometimes as high as 25. Of course not all who died passed through the typical stages of death from outright hunger, abnormal swellings under the eyes and of the stomach, followed in the last stages by swollen legs and cracking bones. The majority died of slight colds which they could not withstand in their weakened condition; of typhus, the familiar accompaniment of famine; of "exhaustion," to use the familiar euphemistic word in the death reports. Here and there one heard dark stories of cannibalism; in Poltava it was said that a trade in human flesh had been going on until the authorities discovered it and shot the participants. But apparently cannibalism had not been widespread. The famine area, so far as I could observe and learn from reliable information, included Ukraina, the North Caucasus, a number of districts in the middle and lower Volga, and considerable sections of remote Kazak[h]stan, in Central Asia. Northern and Central Russia and Siberia suffered a good deal of hardship and undernourishment, but not actual famine. The number of people who lived in famine areas was in the neighborhood of sixty million; the excess of deaths over a normal mortality rate can scarcely have been less than three or four million.[7]

---

6 How ruthlessly the fertile North Caucasus was plundered under the regime of collectivization is evident from the following figures, which Sheboldaev cited at the last Party Congress. The amount of grain realized by the state in the North Caucasus was as follows: 1928, 56,000,000 poods (a pood is about three-fifths of a bushel); 1929, 92,000,000 poods; 1930, 123,000,000 poods; 1931, 187,000,000 poods; 1932, 112,000,000 poods; 1933, 133,000,000 poods. In other words, the state, during the last three hungry years, has been regularly taking from the North Caucasian peasants two or three times as much as the peasants gave up in 1928, when the situation with meat and dairy products was vastly better.

7 The average mortality rate which I found with monotonous regularity in the districts I personally

There is something epically and indescribably tragic in this enormous dying out of millions of people, sacrifices on the altar of a policy which many of them did not even understand. The horror of this last act in the tragedy of the individual peasantry is perhaps intensified by the fact that the victims died so passively, so quietly, without arousing any stir of sympathy in the outside world. The Soviet censorship saw to that.

Of the historic responsibility of the Soviet Government for the famine of 1932–33 there can be no reasonable doubt. In contrast to its policy in 1921–22, it stifled any appeal for foreign aid by denying the very fact of the famine and by refusing to foreign journalists the right to travel in the famine regions until it was all over. Famine was quite deliberately employed as an instrument of national policy, as the last means of breaking the resistance of the peasantry to the new system where they are divorced from personal ownership of the land and obliged to work on the conditions which the state may dictate to them and deliver up whatever the state may demand from them.

Louis Fischer, *Soviet Journey*

(New York: Harrison Smith and Robert Haas, 1935). Excerpts, pp. 170–72.

Louis Fischer (1896–1970) was an American journalist who served as Moscow correspondent for *The Nation* from 1923 to 1938. Originally a communist fellow traveler, he eventually became a critic of communism and the Soviet Union. He was the author of *Oil Imperialism: The International Struggle for Petroleum* (1926), *The Soviets in World Affairs* (1930), *The War in Spain* (1937), *Stalin* (1952), and *Lenin* (1964).

I had spent the month of October, 1932, traveling through the Ukraine. All over the countryside I saw grain which the peasants had left on the fields. It had rotted. It was their winter's food. Then those same peasants starved. They had been practising passive resistance against the government....

The peasants brought the calamity upon themselves. Yet one can understand what prompted this suicidal action. The Bolsheviks had launched the ambitious Five Year Plan. It had to be financed.... The worker paid in the form of reduced consumption goods. The peasant paid in the form of huge taxes. In many cases, the government took thirty, even fifty, indeed even sixty per cent of his crop....

It was a terrible lesson at a terrific cost. History can be cruel. The Bolsheviks were carrying out a major policy on which the strength and character of their regime depended. The peasants were reacting as normal human beings would. Let no one minimize the sadness of the phenomenon. But from the larger point of view the effect was the final entrenchment of collectivization. The peasantry will never again undertake passive resistance. And the Bolsheviks—one hopes—have learned that they must not compel the peasantry to attempt such resistance.

visited was about 10 per cent. If one makes allowance for normal mortality and also for the fact that the towns suffered much less than the country districts, the excess of three or four million still remains.

In the final analysis, the 1932 famine was a concomitant of the last battle between private capitalism and socialism in Russia. The peasants wanted to destroy collectivization. The government wanted to retain collectivization. The peasants used the best means at their disposal. The government used the best means at its disposal. The government won.

Adam J. Tawdul, "10,000,000 Starved in Russia in Two Years, Soviet Admits"

New York American, 18 August 1935, pp. 1–2. Excerpts, p. 2.

Adam J. Tawdul (1894–1976) was born in Omsk, Russia. He attended the Tomsk Polytechnical Institute and became involved in revolutionary activity in tsarist Russia. In 1913 he fled to the United States, where he became an active communist. On being hired by Amtorg as an engineer, he returned to the USSR in 1931 and worked at the Kharkiv Tractor Plant. Disillusioned with what he saw, he returned to the United States in 1934.

...The acid test of all news from the Soviet Union remains to this day the suppression of the fact that at least 10,000,000 people perished from famine in that country in 1932-33. This figure was disclosed to me by high Soviet officials in confidential conversations.

There are Communist and pro-Communist publications in this country which specialize in telling the "truth" about Russia—the Stalin truth. I was myself a voracious reader of these publications and a zealous believer in their "truth"—until I went to live in Soviet Russia and saw the reality....

Now I was a high Communist official in Russia, I mixed with the upper crust of the Soviet aristocracy, and none of them ever denied the facts of the widespread famine which their government officially suppressed from a gullible world.

Indeed, many of these Soviet potentates gave me data as to the extent of the catastrophe, and some of them even justified it as prudent policy for the solution of the agricultural problem....

The case of Nikolai Skrypnik [Mykola Skrypnyk], Stalin's most trusted commissar in the Ukraine, attracted attention abroad. In 1933, after a stormy session with Stalin, Skrypnik returned to the capital of the Ukraine, Kharkov, where, according to an official announcement, he committed suicide. According to unofficial information, he was assassinated.

Officials Justified Famine

Skrypnik knew me as a child in Siberia. When he was a fugitive from the Czarist police, my father kept him in hiding in our home in Tomsk. He was a native Ukrainian, and I recognized him at the all-Ukrainian trade union congress, where I was present as a delegate, in spite of a lapse of many years. He was deeply moved when I introduced myself.

"So you are Adka!" he exclaimed, and vividly recalled my father, my home, and his own conversations with me when I was a lad. I became a friend of the Skrypnik household, and through it entered the highest Communist circles on a social basis, a rare privilege for even a foreign Communist in Russia these days.

"At least 8,000,000 people have already perished from the famine in the Ukraine and the Northern Caucasus alone," Skrypnik told me one evening early in 1933, in the course of our many intimate conversations on the famine.

He was at that time insisting that Stalin change his policy and was even in favor of an understanding with the socialists and of a democratization of the Soviet system. According to Skrypnik, Stalin was ready to make peace with the socialist and liberal elements under the threat of the famine within and of Japan without.

"If Europe does not come to our aid now, we will go down, and the cause of the revolution will be lost for many generations," Skrypnik told me. He had argued along the same lines with Stalin and was under the impression that Stalin was ready to institute reforms. He was quickly disillusioned, in spite of his past loyalty to Stalin, when he discovered that the Kremlin was cynical about the devastation wrought by the famine in his native Ukraine.

I was staggered by the figure of 8,000,000 deaths from starvation coming from such an authoritative source as Skrypnik, but I pursued my inquiries on the subject in other high quarters, only to find that Skrypnik's figure checked with all official estimates of the victims of the famine.

Adam M. [*sic*] Tawdul, "Russia Warred on Own People"

New York American, 19 August 1935, pp. 1–2. Excerpts.

The Soviet Government published no statistics of the famine. Indeed, as far as the Soviet press was concerned the famine did not exist.

Everybody in Russia knew, however, that ENTIRE PROVINCES in the South and in the East were being depopulated by starvation and epidemics....

"From 8,000,000 to 9,000,000 people have already perished in the Ukraine alone," I was told in 1933 by [Kliment] Voroshilov's right hand man in Kharkov, Balinsky [Vsevolod Balytsky] who hold [*sic*] the rank of a general in the Red Army.

"This is the figure that we have submitted to the boss [Stalin], but it is approximate, as none of us knows the exact numbers."....

Balinsky's figure may be regarded as the most authoritative official estimate available of the victims of the famine in the Ukraine, as Balinsky is a member of the executive council of the G.P.U. of the Soviet Union and was the representative of that all-powerful organization in the Ukraine....

The famine in the Ukraine and the North Caucasus mowed down from eight to nine million souls, but there was also fearful devastation by hunger in the Ural and Western Siberian zone....

"More than one million people died from hunger in the Urals, in the trans-Volga region and in western Siberia in 1932–1933," I was told by [Kazimir Petrovich] Lovin, the director of the Cheliabinsk tractor plant....

"The great majority of the deaths were among the non-Russian natives," Lovin observed, "such as Tartars, Kirghiz, Bashkirs and other nomads. The famine among these races coincided with the Soviet drive to settle permanently in collectives the native tribes and to consolidate thereby the Russian domination of the area."

Lovin, a relative of Stalin's last wife, was the czar of the Urals. His name was awe and his word was law to the local population. He discussed frankly with me the policies which made for the famine, and did not conceal the POLITICAL CONSIDERATIONS which the Kremlin entertained in connection with the disaster.

On the basis of Balinsky's and Lovin's official estimates submitted to Stalin, a total of at least TEN MILLION PEOPLE PERISHED FROM HUNGER in the Soviet Union in 1932–33….

Adam J. Tawdul, "Soviet Traded Lives for Power, Says Ex-Aide"

New York American, 20 August 1935, p. 4. Excerpts.

…"The famine must be artificially aggravated and actively exploited as a means of 'finishing with the Kulak' once for all," were the whispered views which I heard expressed more than once among the superior G.P.U. functionaries in Kharkov….

Said Comrade Lovin:

"The famine has been of great benefit to us in the Urals, in Western Siberia and in the Trans-Volga. In these regions the losses from starvation have mostly affected the alien races. Their place is being taken by Russian refugees from the central provinces.

"We are, of course, no nationalists. But as realists in politics we cannot overlook this advantageous fact. The Slav population in the borderlands is COMPELLED, for its own self-protection, to support the Soviet Government."….

If those Communist apologists in America who prattle about the freedom of nationalities in Russia could have heard Lovin's cold-blooded statement of Russian imperialism and subjection of the minority races by the scourge of famine, they might have gained an insight into the real nature of the Soviet Government….

Adam J. Tawdul, "Official Murder in Soviet"

New York American, 21 August 1935, p. 4. Excerpts.

…Early in the Fall of 1933 I returned to Kharkov on the way from the North Caucasus. A little party was arranged for me at the village of Chuhuyevo [Chuhuiv], where certain functionaries of the Kharkov tractor plant and other Communist leaders were wont to stage drinking bouts behind lines of sentries, far from the eyes of the hungry population.

The party lasted a couple of days. Among those present was Tolmachev, the chief of the Communist Party control in Kharkov.

Killed Own Children

"The damned Kulaks are destroying their own children out of hatred for the Soviet Government," Tolmachev began to relate his experiences to me as the head of a punitive expedition when our celebration was already in its second day and tongues wagged more freely.

"There was a wholesale anti-Kulak drive on in the province," he continued. "I was in command of a detachment of 15 Communists sent down to supervise the operation, as Moscow had received reports that the local authorities were too soft in their actions.

"Our expedition worked smoothly and there was no resistance. Of course, the women and children were wailing without let-up. We discovered some concealed grain, made the necessary requisitions, evicted the Kulaks from their homes, arrested some and sent them off by the prison route to exile.

"Then we came upon a peasant who was strangely quiet, not only when we made an inventory of all his house and barn belongings, but even when we discovered a sack of rye under a pile of manure in the garden.

"The peasant's wife, holding an infant at her breast, was moaning all the while, and pleaded especially with us to leave them the cow and a chest packed with garments.

"We went about our job and were on the point of taking the cow away when the peasant, although under guard of a soldier, suddenly jumped up, seized the infant out of his wife's arms, and swung it against the corner of the house, killing it instantly.

"For a second I was dazed. Then I pulled out my revolver and shot him on the spot. The mother, with a frightful cry, threw herself upon me. I had to shoot her down too."....

Tolmachev told me of the episode after he had been drinking for a couple of days. It seemed to me for a moment that, in spite of his hardened exterior, he felt the need of pouring out his "soul." But he narrated it in a tone of indignation at the "Kulak," and emphasized that he had been justified in his act....

Special detachments were assigned to gather corpses in city streets, at railway stations and along the railways where human bodies thrown off trains would be found. These squads of grave-diggers kept no records and left no traces. They dug "fraternal" graves and buried all the dead without bothering to identify them....

How many were buried in the villages without any formalities during the famine can never be established....

Yet the horrors observed in the cities were but the remote reverberations of the quake which shook the countryside where the famine raged like an unchecked pestilence.

Ewald Ammende, *Human Life in Russia*

(London: Allen and Unwin [1936]; repr. Cleveland: John T. Zubal, Inc., 1984).
Excerpts, pp. 223–29, 231–32, 243–45, 252–56.

Ewald Ammende (1892–1936) was a Baltic German businessman, human-rights activist, and champion of national rights. He participated in international relief efforts during the famine of 1921–22 in Ukraine and Russia. He was the founder and secretary general of the Congress of Organized National Groups in the States of Europe, which first met in 1925 and was based in Geneva. He was the author of *Die Nationalitäten in den Staaten Europas* (1931) and *Muß Rußland hungern? Menschen- und Völkerschicksale in der Sowjetunion* (1935; published in translation as *Human Life in Russia* in 1936).

Among Moscow's guests of honour a special place must be assigned to the former French Prime Minister, Edouard Herriot; not only because his journey was a political event of the first importance which initiated a complete change in France's attitude towards Soviet Russia, but also because it was M. Herriot's ambition to give to his Russian journey and to the publication of its results the character of "a visit for purposes of study by an experienced administrator." .... M. Herriot's categorical declaration that there was no famine in Russia naturally made the very greatest impression throughout Europe....

...His action has had a disastrous influence upon the incipient will to bring relief to Russia which was beginning to make itself felt in a number of countries.... M. Herriot...not only disputed the existence of any famine in Russia; he went on to say generally that people who talked about a famine could be doing so only in the interests of a definite anti-Russian policy, of separatist tendencies, or the like....

It is significant that although M. Herriot was supposed to be travelling for information and in a private capacity, he was accompanied not only by French journalists and Soviet officials, but also by the French Ambassador, M. Alfan. One may fairly ask whether a journey undertaken to obtain the truth about Russian conditions could reasonably require the presence of the French representative accredited to the Kremlin.

...On August 26 M. Herriot arrived at Odessa in the Soviet vessel *Chicherin* after a "delightful journey."....

A few miles away from Odessa and Belyaevka [Biliaivka] is the site of the formerly flourishing German Black Sea settlements—now a scene of death and destruction. Dozens of letters on this point may be seen at the offices of the "Brethren in Distress" dating precisely from the period of M. Herriot's visit. The contrast is striking. In a later article (*Pester Lloyd,* October 1) M. Herriot confidently declares: "Nowhere did I find a sign of distress, not even in the German villages, which had been described as suffering from famine." According to the latest figures 140,000 Germans died in Russia in 1932–33....

After this first great piece of stage-management M. Herriot and his suite had completed their studies of Odessa and the surroundings and proceeded...to Kiev, the second stage of the visit to the Ukraine. Kiev is, of course, next to Kharkov, the town in the south most severely afflicted by the famine and its attendant phenomena. M. Herriot was now in the centre of the agricultural district of the Ukraine, the best place from which to undertake a serious study of the position....

But what did the ex Prime Minister and skilled administrator do? The report published in *Pravda* on September 27 is so characteristic of the activities of M. Herriot and his suite...that I quote it at length.

"This morning M. Herriot arrived at Kiev, accompanied by his secretary Serlen, and the deputies Julien and Marcel Ray, former chefs de cabinet of the ex Prime Minister. M. Alfan, the French Ambassador, also arrived. They were accompanied by Helfand;[8] the deputy president of the Ukrainian Chamber of Commerce, Velitchko; the representative of the *Petit Parisien,* Lucien; the special correspondent of *Izvestia,* Gari; and the special correspondent of the Tass agency. At the station the

8 A former official of the Ogpu well known for his activities.

guests were met by the president of the regional Ispolkom [executive committee], Vassilenko, the deputy president of the Gorsoviet [municipal council], the agent of the Narkomindel [foreign commissariat], Shenshev, and representatives of the Moscow and the local press. After an exchange of greetings M. Herriot and his companions proceeded to their hotel, and after a brief rest went on to the Ukrainian Academy of Sciences."

This was the second grand deception. After the achievements of Ukrainian agriculture, the visitors are now presented, in accordance with Moscow's plan, with evidence of the care devoted to Ukrainian culture and science. The report says: "On the way to the Academy M. Herriot expressed the wish to visit St. Sophia's [Cathedral], with its historically valuable mosaics.[9] M. Herriot was then received at the Ukrainian Academy of Sciences by a number of members headed by the president Palladin, who explained the work of the various departments. A long stay was made at the Geological Museum, with its many valuable exhibits. Later the Ukrainian model town was visited, where the work of the museum for historical relics in the religious field and the valuable Potocki collection were studied."

Thus, at the moment when the dictator [Pavel] Postyschev [Postyshev] was exterminating every trace of Ukrainian cultural individuality, and a few days after Lenin's friend and co-founder of the Soviet State, the Ukrainian Communist [Mykola] Skrypnik [Skrypnyk], had shot himself, when even Ukrainian Bolshevists were protesting against the starvation of their countrymen, the Pan-Ukrainian academicians were enlightening M. Herriot about the splendid work done to promote the cultural endeavours of the Ukraine. At this very moment the Moscow delegate was speaking openly of the danger inherent in the activities of the Academy and other similar organizations: and a few days after the guests had left Kiev the members of another similar institute were expelled or arrested....

Other delights awaited the guests after their study of cultural movements in the Ukraine and the promotion of these by the central authority. The report says: "Comrade Vassilenko, the President of the District Executive Committee, gave a luncheon in honour of the guests." The report is silent as to the menu of the lunch; but Ukrainian cooking has a good reputation, and it may be assumed that during his fortnight in Russia M. Herriot was one of the best-fed people in the country. No unpleasant interludes marred the feast, and none of the guests was reminded that during the summer thousands of innocent people had perished in that ancient metropolis. First-hand reports from foreign observers tell how in the summer of 1933 starving persons were collapsing in the streets of Kiev, and were often buried before they died. The common graves at Kiev speak eloquently of the tragedy which visited that city, like Kharkov, Odessa, Rostov and many other towns during the months preceding the 1933 harvest....

Early on August 28 the illustrious travellers arrived at Kharkov, which at that time was the official capital of the Ukraine....

M. Herriot was particularly favourably impressed by Kharkov; his later articles expressed the view that it was "one of the best administered of cities." Apparently

---

9 This interest in Tsarist church art had presumably not been anticipated in the programme; hence the *Izvestia* report ascribed this whim to the historical importance of the mosaics.

he did not know that at Kharkov, as at Kiev, starving people were lying in the streets until just before his arrival, and that almost every other house was the scene of dreadful tragedies owing to passport and other Government regulations....

The preparation and execution of M. Herriot's expedition must be admitted to be a masterpiece of Soviet propaganda, and any states arranging similar trips for foreign guests of honour could learn much from this collaboration of all Soviet officials in arranging the different stages of M. Herriot's Russian journey....

The chief object was to get M. Herriot to deny the existence of the famine and the disastrous position of the Ukrainian population when he was actually in such centres as Odessa, Kiev, etc.; this would be in August, i.e. before the beginning of the League [of Nations] Assembly meeting, and at a time when news of the catastrophe was just beginning to spread in the West and in America and Cardinal [Theodor] Innitzer was initiating the Russian relief work in Vienna. Accordingly the ablest journalists had been sent from Moscow to meet M. Herriot at Odessa, their function being to wait for utterances from the French statesman. Nor did they have long to wait; after the impressive experiences at Kiev Herriot was "ripe" for making statements. His denial of the famine and of the sufferings of the Ukrainians made at the station at Kiev amounted to a striking success for the Soviet regime, and further declarations about the idyllic state of things in the Ukraine were not wanting. Daily the Russian correspondents were able to telegraph to Moscow, with appropriate comment, the written and spoken dicta of M. Herriot, and thence they were distributed throughout the world. The French journalists who accompanied M. Herriot and took part in the proceedings rendered valuable auxiliary service, some intentionally, others unintentionally....

M. Herriot cannot be conceded the right publicly to deny the existence of famine in the Ukraine and to represent it to be "propaganda by political fanatics." His assertions that on the present occasion when "travelling through" the Ukraine "in various directions" he saw "nothing of the kind" (contrary to his experience ten years previously) are meaningless.... [H]e did not take the trouble, as a serious investigator, on whom the eyes of the world were fixed, should have made it his duty to do, to follow up the visible traces of one of the greatest human tragedies of the present day, a tragedy which had reached its climax in the days preceding the new harvest, immediately before his arrival. Such an investigation would have meant leaving his special coach, escaping his Moscow guides, and putting an end to the whole official mystification which was practised upon him during his five days' visit, hour by hour, from morning to night, over a stretch of nearly 2,000 miles....

But there is another and more regrettable aspect of M. Herriot's proceedings. Embarrassed by the controversy on the Russian position and especially on the famine in the Ukraine, he made the following statement in the lecture given in the Vichy Casino (*Journal des Débats*): "La famine russe, qu'on agite comme un épouvantail, n'est que le produit suspect de la propaganda hitlérienne."[10] And in another connection he plainly declares that the Ukraine was not so much endangered by hunger as by separatist machinations enjoying the support

10 The Russian famine that we shake like a scarecrow is nothing but the suspect product of Hitlerite propaganda.

of German National Socialism.... In view of the tragic struggle now in progress between Moscow centralization and the various peoples living in the Soviet Union and anxious to preserve their individuality, it is perhaps unnecessary to insist on the arbitrariness of M. Herriot's interpretation of present events in the Ukraine. Of course there will always be interested parties willing and ready to exploit every current of feeling and every divergency of view. Such elements may be observed at work in a great many different countries. But to believe that real convulsions within or between the nations can be initiated by the work of 'agents' or 'propagandist machinations' implies a complete misconception of the real conditions in most European countries, and reveals an entire misapprehension of the problem of nationalities.

...[E]ven papers which cannot be suspected of being under National Socialist influence or of being anti-French vigorously oppose M. Herriot's thesis. Thus the *New York Herald-Tribune* (October 22, 1933) expresses doubts of M. Herriot's reliability.... Impartial observers, the paper added, had found that there was famine in the Ukraine, but had found no traces of National Socialist propaganda. M. Herriot's claim, therefore, must be either a sensational 'stunt' by a talented amateur writer or else a testimonial to the efficiency of Communist stage management.

M. Herriot is indignant at the alleged "campaign of defamation"...but is apparently not aware that his own account of the causes of recent developments in the Ukraine is a defamation of wide circles of an entire people, uttered at a moment when this people, deserted by the entire world, is fighting desperately for its future, for its nationhood, and perhaps for its bare existence.

Fred E. Beal, *Proletarian Journey: New England, Gastonia, Moscow*

(New York: Hillman-Curl, Inc., 1937). Excerpts, pp. 305–7, 310–12.

Fred E. Beal (1896–1954) was a communist labor organizer who was arrested and convicted, along with several others, for the murder of the Gastonia, North Carolina police chief during labor disturbances there in 1929. Skipping bail, he fled to the Soviet Union, where he lived for three years (1930–33), with Kharkiv as his last place of residence. Returning to the United States, he lived underground for several years, during which he wrote his autobiography, *Proletarian Journey*, before surrendering to authorities to serve his sentence. Beal was also the author of *The Red Fraud: An Exposé of Communism* (1949).

In the spring of 1933, when the last of the winter snows had melted away, I made a random visit to a Ukrainian collective near the village of Chekhuyev [Chuhuiv]. In company with a Russian-American comrade from the factory, I took the train from our little station of Lossevo and rode for two hours to Chekhuyev. From this place, we walked east for several miles. We met not a living soul....

The village we reached was the worst of all possible sights. The only human there was an old woman who passed us on the village street. She hobbled along with the aid of a stick. Her clothes were just a bunch of rags tied together. When she came close to us she lifted the stick as if to strike us but the movement petered out in weakness. She spat at us and mumbled something incoherent, something my friend could not make out, though he knew the language well. Her feet were dreadfully swollen. She sat down and pricked her swollen feet with a sharp stick, to let the water out of the huge blisters. There was a large hole in the top of her foot from continuous piercing of the skin. She was stark mad. She laughed when she sat down and screamed with pain when she squeezed her foot. She spat again at us. We moved on.

There was no other life. The village was dead. Going up to one of the shacks, we looked into a window. We saw a dead man propped up on a built-in Russian stove. His back was against the wall, he was rigid and staring straight at us with his faraway dead eyes. I shall always remember that ghastly sight. I have seen dead people who had died naturally, before. But this was from a cause and a definite one. A cause which I was somehow associated with, which I had been supporting. How that deathly gaze pierced me! How it caused me to writhe in mental agony! As I look back, I think that unforgettable scene had more effect than any other in deciding me to do what I could do to rectify my horrible mistake in supporting the Stalinists of Russia and the Third International.

We found more dead people in what had been their homes. Some bodies were decomposed. Others were fresher. When we opened the doors, huge rats would scamper to their holes and then come out and stare at us.

At one house, there was a sign somehow printed on the door in crude Russian letters. My friend read it: "God bless those who enter here, may they never suffer as we have." Inside two men and a child lay dead with an icon alongside of them....

Many of the houses were empty. But, in the rear, the graves told a story of desolation and ghastly death. More signs were stuck up on these graves by those who buried them:

I LOVE STALIN. BURY HIM HERE AS SOON AS POSSIBLE!

THE COLLECTIVE DIED ON US!

WE TRIED A COLLECTIVE. THIS IS THE RESULT!

I had seen enough of villages and collectives and communes. On our way back, near the station, people told us that *that* village was to be burned. Three or four others in the vicinity had already been burned. Not a trace of the houses or of the dead bodies in them was left....

In 1933, I had the occasion to call on [Hryhorii] Petrovsky, the President of the Ukrainian Soviet Republic, in his office in Kharkov. I was accompanied by [Isadore] Erenburg, my superior in the cultural-propaganda work at the [Kharkiv] Tractor Plant. "Comrade Petrovsky," I said, "the men at our factory are saying that millions of peasants are dying all over Russia. They see poverty and death all about them. They say that up to five million people have died this year, and they hold it up to us a challenge and a mockery. What are we going to tell them?"

"Tell them nothing!" answered President Petrovsky. "What they say is true. We know that millions are dying. That is unfortunate, but the glorious future of the Soviet Union will justify that. Tell them nothing!"

Now the Ukraine is known as the bread-basket of Europe. Its soil is as rich as that of Nebraska, Iowa, and Kansas. That black earth will grow anything, given only the seed and care. What then was the cause of this general starvation? One of the answers is Stalin's forced collectivization. The peasants stubbornly fought the campaign ordered from the Kremlin. Their seeds were confiscated and distributed only to collective and state farms. Their horses and cows were expropriated. The right of disposing of their crops was denied the individual peasants. Farm implements were made unavailable to them. Heavy taxes were placed upon peasant holdings and collected at the point of a gun. Scores of thousands were killed outright because they refused to go into the collectives. Red Army detachments were sent into the villages for that purpose. The inhabitants of hundreds of villages literally died in their tracks and, in thousands of other villages, the peasants abandoned their homes after the forcible seizure of from 60 to 90 percent of their grain. Great numbers took to the roads, flocked to the cities, and wandered as far as their legs could carry them. The tragedy of these living corpses, who were often without even the customary rags in the coldest weather, was more gruesome than the tragedy of the dead.

Heart-rending was the condition of the great swarms of homeless children let loose by the Stalin policy. It should be remembered that this new crop of waifs was not inherited from the Tsarist regime, from the early period of the Revolution. The Stalinists have a way of blaming the Tsar and the World War of nearly two decades ago for the latest wave of homeless children. These youngsters hated the Soviet factories, the G.P.U. and all the government institutions and restrictions. They preferred to ride the freight trains, to beg, to steal. Their parents had been starved to death, shot, sent to concentration camps far away, or were still roaming over the land lost to their children forever. All the stations and railroads of the country were infested with these waifs. They had a way of getting through the cordons of guards despite the vigilance of the G.P.U. officials.

On a trip that I made to Moscow from Kharkov and back, I encountered many little derelicts pleading for food. I was on board the International train and ate in the restaurant car. Across from me sat a characteristic Soviet bureaucrat with shaven head. He carried a brief case. Into this he put the remains of his meal, such as pieces of bread. Outside the window a dirty-faced kid, wearing a cap much too big for him, appealed to the bureaucrat: *"Dyadya, dai kusok khlieba!"* (Uncle, give me a piece of bread.)

"Go to work. You ought to be arrested for begging!" the bureaucrat said.

I gave the youngster my bread. The bureaucrat, who could speak English, told me that I should not spoil the waifs by giving them food.

"He is too young to work," I answered, estimating the boy's age to be about twelve.

"He could go to a Soviet institution," was the retort.

"But perhaps he does not want to go to an institution," I replied, thinking of the disgraceful Gorky Commune near Kharkov where the children received very little food and plenty of discipline.

"Well, he ought to be made to go! He and the rest are a nuisance to the government!"

Indeed, the more I saw of Russia the more convinced I became that not only the homeless children but all the common people of the country were a nuisance to the Soviet Government.

Eugene Lyons, *Assignment in Utopia*

(New York: Harcourt, Brace and Co., 1937). Excerpts, pp. 572–75, 577–78.

Eugene Lyons (1898–1985) was an American journalist and writer who, after some time as a fellow traveler of the Communist Party, became highly critical of the Soviet Union. He served as United Press International correspondent in Moscow (1928–34). His major works include *Modern Moscow* (1935), *Assignment in Utopia* (1937), *Stalin, Czar of All the Russias* (1940), and *The Red Decade: The Stalinist Penetration of America* (1941).

"There is no actual starvation or deaths from starvation but there is widespread mortality from diseases due to malnutrition."

This amazing sophistry, culled from a New York *Times* Moscow dispatch on March 30, 1933, has become among foreign reporters the classic example of journalistic understatement. It characterizes sufficiently the whole shabby episode of our failure to report honestly the gruesome Russian famine of 1932–33.

The circumstance that the government barred us from the afflicted regions may serve as our formal excuse. But a deaf-and-dumb reporter hermetically sealed in a hotel room could not have escaped knowledge of the essential facts....

...Not a single American newspaper or press agency protested publicly against the astonishing and almost unprecedented confinement of its correspondent in the Soviet capital or troubled to probe for the causes of this extraordinary measure.

The New York *Times*, as the foremost American newspaper...was certainly not alone in concealing the famine. The precious sentence quoted above was prefaced with its correspondent's celebrated cliché: "To put it brutally—you can't make an omelette without breaking eggs." A later dispatch enlarged upon the masterpiece of understatement and indicated how the eggs were being broken. Asserting that "in some districts and among the large floating population of unskilled labor" there "have been deaths and actual starvation," he catalogued the maladies of malnutrition as "typhus, dysentery, dropsy, and various infantile diseases." The maladies, in short, that always rage in time of famine.

Not until August 23 did the *Times* out of Moscow admit the famine. "It is conservative to suppose," it said, that in certain provinces with a total population of over 40,000,000 mortality has "at least trebled." On this basis, there were two million deaths more than usual. In addition, deaths were also "considerably increased for the Soviet Union as a whole." This dispatch came one day behind an uncensored cable to the New York *Herald Tribune* by Ralph Barnes, in which he placed the deaths in his ultra-conservative fashion at no less than one million. The Barnes story was front-paged and the *Times* could no longer ignore the subject. Its own admission followed, raising Barnes' ante. By a singular twist of logic, the *Times* story introduced the admission of famine with this remarkable statement:

"Any report of a famine in Russia is today an exaggeration or malignant propaganda. The food shortage which has affected almost the whole population in the last year and particularly in the grain-producing provinces—the Ukraine, North Caucasus, the lower Volga region—has, however, caused heavy loss of life."

The dividing line between "heavy loss of life" through food shortage and "famine" is rather tenuous. Such verbal finessing made little difference to the millions of dead and dying, to the refugees who knocked at our doors begging bread, to the lines of ragged peasants stretching from Torgsin doors in the famine area waiting to exchange their wedding rings and silver trinkets for bread.

These philological sophistries, to which we were all driven, serve Moscow's purpose of smearing the facts out of recognition and beclouding a situation which, had we reported it simply and clearly, might have worked up enough public opinion abroad to force remedial measures....

All of us had talked with people just returned from the famine regions....

The truth is that we did not seek corroboration for the simple reason that we entertained no doubts on the subject. There are facts too large to require eyewitness confirmation—facts so pervasive and generally accepted that confirmation would be futile pedantry. There was no more need for investigation to establish the mere existence of the Russian famine than investigation to establish the existence of the American depression. Inside Russia the matter was not disputed. The famine was accepted as a matter of course in our casual conversation at the hotels and in our homes....

The first reliable report of the Russian famine was given to the world by an English journalist, a certain Gareth Jones, at one time secretary to Lloyd George. Jones had a conscientious streak in his make-up which took him on a secret journey into the Ukraine and a brief walking tour through its countryside....

On emerging from Russia, Jones made a statement which, startling though it sounded, was little more than a summary of what the correspondents and foreign diplomats had told him. To protect us, and perhaps with some idea of heightening the authenticity of his reports, he emphasized his Ukrainian foray rather than our conversation as the chief source of his information.

In any case, we all received urgent queries from our home offices on the subject. But the inquiries coincided with preparations under way for the trial of the British engineers. The need to remain on friendly terms with the censors at least for the duration of the trial was for all of us a compelling professional necessity.

Throwing down Jones was as unpleasant a chore as fell to any of us in years of juggling facts to please dictatorial regimes—but throw him down we did, unanimously and in almost identical formulas of equivocation. Poor Gareth Jones must have been the most surprised human being alive when the facts he so painstakingly garnered from our mouths were snowed under by our denials....

I was not the first Moscow observer to remark that God seems to be on the side of the atheists. What the Kremlin would have prayed for, had it believed in prayer, was perfect weather, and that is what it received that spring and summer: perfect weather and bumper crops. The fields had been planted under the aegis of the newly established *Politotdyels* (Political Departments) with unlimited authority over the peasants. Food rations barely sufficient to sustain life had been distributed only to those actually at work in the fields. Red Army detachments in many places had been employed to guard seed and to prevent hungry peasants from devouring the green shoots of the new harvest. In the midst of the famine, the planting proceeded, and the crops came up strong and plenteous. The dead were buried—for the living there would be bread enough and to spare in the following winter.

Belatedly the world had awakened to the famine situation. We were able to write honestly that "to speak of famine *now* is ridiculous." We did not always bother to add that we had failed to speak of it or at best mumbled incomprehensibly *then*, when it was not ridiculous. Cardinal Innitzer, Archbishop of Vienna, made the first of his sensational statements about Soviet agrarian conditions on August 20, when those conditions were already being mitigated. Certain anti-Soviet newspapers in England and America began to write about the famine at about the time it was ended, and continued to write about it long after it had become history: their facts were on the whole correct, but their tenses were badly mixed. The most rigorous censorship in all of Soviet Russia's history had been successful—it had concealed the catastrophe until it was ended, thereby bringing confusion, doubt, contradiction into the whole subject. Years after the event—when no Russian communist in his senses any longer concealed the magnitude of the famine—the question whether there had been a famine at all was still being disputed in the outside world!

In the autumn, the Soviet press was exultant. Lazar Kaganovich was given most of the credit for the successful harvest. It was his mind that invented the Political Departments to lead collectivized agriculture, his iron hand that applied Bolshevik mercilessness. Now that a healing flood of grain was inundating the famished land, the secrecy gradually gave way. Increasingly with every passing month Russian officials ceased to deny the obvious. Soviet journalists who had been in the afflicted areas now told me personally such details of the tragedy as not even the eager imaginations of Riga and Warsaw journalists had been able to project. They were able to speak in the past tense, so that their accents were proud boasts rather than admissions.

The Kremlin, in short, had "gotten away with it." At a cost in millions of lives, through the instrumentalities of hunger and terror, socialized agriculture had been made to yield an excellent harvest. Certain observers now insisted in print that the efficacy of collectivization had been demonstrated; nothing, of course, had been demonstrated except the efficacy of concentrated force used against a population demoralized by protracted hunger.

Freda Utley, *The Dream We Lost: Soviet Russia, Then and Now*

(New York: John Day, 1940). Excerpts, pp. 50–57, 86–87.

Winifred (Freda) Utley (1899–1978) was a scholar and writer. Her books include *Lancashire and the Far East* (1931); *Japan's Feet of Clay* (1937); *Japan's Gamble in China* (1938); *China at War* (1939); *The High Cost of Vengeance* (1948); *Last Chance in China* (1948); *The China Story* (1951); *Will the Middle East Go West?* (1956); and *Odyssey of a Liberal* (1970). A member of the British Communist Party from 1927 to 1930, she lived and worked in the Soviet Union and the Far East from 1928 to 1936. She left the USSR after her husband, Arkadii Berdichevsky, was incarcerated by the Soviet authorities in 1936.

In November 1929, Stalin announced the end of individual farming, ordered the "liquidation of the Kulaks as a class," and the establishment of collective farms everywhere and for everyone. Stalin had decided to solve the agricultural problem "in a socialist sense" by violence and terror....

There began that terrible murder of the Kulaks by the state, which is almost unparalleled in history for its cruelty. I use the word murder deliberately, for although the Kulaks were not lined up and shot, they were killed off in a manner far more cruel. Whole families, men, women, children, and babies, were thrown out of their homes, their personal possessions seized, even their warm clothing torn off them; then, packed into unheated cattle trucks in winter, they were sent off to Siberia or other waste parts of the Soviet Union. A few of the men survived to start life again and build farms in the waste lands into which they had been exiled. The women and children perished. Hundreds of thousands of other peasants were herded off to the timber prison camps in the Arctic regions, to die like flies from hunger and cold and exhausting labor, whipped by the O.G.P.U. guards and treated like the slaves of Pharaoh or some other Asiatic tyrant....

Fear of reprisals by the desperate, starving, expropriated peasants drove the Party to attempt to exterminate all their victims. "We must destroy our enemies until not one is left," was the cry. An orgy of cruelty raged in the countryside. One must go back to the days of the Mongol hordes who swept across Asia and eastern Europe in the thirteenth century, or to the massacres by the Assyrians in biblical times, for an historical parallel with the communist "class war" on the Russian peasants....

Who were the Kulaks now declared enemies of the state? In theory they were the exploiting peasants, those who rented extra land and employed hired labor, or who advanced money or seed at high rates of interest to the poorest peasants. Kulak means a fist, and the word meant an exploiter and a usurer. Under Stalin the word came to mean any peasant who dared to oppose collectivization....

...[S]ince in many parts of the country real Kulaks who "exploited" other peasants were hard to find, the designation was applied to every peasant who was a little better off than his neighbors, to anyone who owned two horses and two cows, or had managed in some way to lift himself a little above the miserably low general standard of life in the Russian village. It meant that hard work and enterprise were penalized wherever they were found....

Stalin, having at last decided upon collectivization, thought he could force it through by a terror exercised against the whole peasant population. He did it, but in doing it he laid waste the countryside and caused the death of millions from starvation....

Soviet morale has never recovered from those terrible years which were my first years of residence in the U.S.S.R. The Communist party and the Comsomols ("Young Communist League") became the expropriators of the people, an army of occupation in the countryside. Decent young men and women sent down to the villages were persuaded that it was their duty as Socialists to stifle all humanitarian scruples while driving the bewildered, sullen, and resentful peasants into the collective farms, and levying grain, milk, and meat from men and women whose children were to starve to death in consequence. Those who could not perform the terrible deeds expected of them were expelled from the Party as "rotten liberals." Both duty and hopes of a career compelled the Party member and the Comsomol to utter ruthlessness and inhumanity. Many of the young people became hardened and cynical careerists prepared to commit any atrocity commanded by Stalin. The war on the peasants was more brutalizing than war against another nation, for the peasants were unarmed and defenseless....

During my first winter in Russia (1930–31) it was believed that if once the peasants could be forced into the collective farms, the food problem would be solved.... Since they now no longer owned the land, since intensive industrialization and concentration on the production of capital goods meant that the state had even less to sell them than before in the way of manufactured goods, and since the state virtually confiscated the grain by taking it at nominal prices, the collectivized peasants worked less than ever before. They opposed to the government the same passive resistance as before the N.E.P. had been introduced, and sowed and reaped just enough to feed themselves. This fact, coupled with drought in the Black Soil region, reduced the harvest to a much smaller amount than in previous years. But the government nevertheless enforced its full demands, telling the peasants that it was their own fault if they were short of food, and leaving them to die of starvation. A terrible famine set in, especially severe in the rich corn-bearing lands of the Ukraine. This time there was no relief from abroad, since the Soviet Government denied that there was a famine and deliberately left the peasants to die of starvation.

Foreign journalists were not allowed to visit the South. All Russia knew what was happening; but the hacks of the foreign press, obedient to Stalin for fear of losing their jobs, sent out no word. Only a few brave and honest foreigners like Eugene Lyons of the United Press and Malcolm Muggeridge of the *Manchester Guardian* told the truth and were expelled from Russia, or put in a position in which they were forced to leave. The others followed the lead of Duranty of the *New York Times* and denied the existence of a famine, until years afterwards.

Foreign visitors, carefully shepherded by Intourist, and given huge meals in the hotels of the starving land, went home to deny the rumors of famine....

Arcadi [Berdichevsky, Freda Utley's husband] finally broke down when he went on a *Komanderofka* [Russ. *komandirovka*, business trip] to Odessa in April 1932. He came back white and miserable and shaken. Down there he had seen the starving and the dead in the streets. At each railway station en route there had been hundreds and hundreds of starving wretches, emaciated women with dying babies at their milkless breasts, children with the swollen stomachs of the starving, all begging, begging for bread. In station waiting rooms he had seen hundreds of peasant families herded together waiting transportation to the concentration camps. Children dying of starvation and typhus, scarecrows of men and women pushed and kicked by the O.G.P.U. guards. It sickened even those who were hardened to the sight of suffering in the Far East.

Arcadi had relatives in Odessa. From them he heard the facts of the Ukrainian famine. The picture he painted for me, a picture which had seared him to the soul and shattered the optimistic view he had until then insisted upon preserving, bore out all the rumors we had heard—was in fact worse. What perhaps shocked Arcadi most of all was to find that the train guards, conductors, and attendants were all speculators. They were buying food in Moscow, always better provided for than other cities, and selling it at fantastic prices down in the stricken southern land.

Starving children are the most pitiful sight on earth. There were enough of them in Moscow to make one's heart ache, but in the Ukraine they were legion.

Bodies of the starving lay in the streets, and pitiful wrecks of humanity, with great watery blisters and boils on their feet, legs, and arms, dragged themselves from place to place till they died in the vain quest for work and food.

In the summer of 1932 we went on a holiday to the Crimea, taking with us my mother, who had just come from England. We left Moscow well provided with food for the long journey. But by the end of the first day my mother had given it all away to the starving wretches at the country stations. With tears streaming down her face she called my attention to one wretched beggar after another, especially to the pitiful children. That journey was an ordeal I shall never forget. It was a sea of misery which the few bits of food we had could do nothing to assuage.

Totia dai Kleb, Totia dai Kleb ("Auntie, give bread"), will always ring in my ears as the national song of "socialist" Russia.

As in China, so in Russia, one hardened oneself to the sight of suffering in order to live. But at least in China the government does not hold it a crime to give aid to the starving. In Russia it tells you that the starving are Kulaks or counter-revolutionaries not to be aided, whereas in reality they are bewildered, ignorant, powerless wretches sacrificed to the insensate ambitions and fanaticism of a man and a party.

It was the contrasts which were always so appalling. The fat officials in the dining car, the well-fed callous O.G.P.U. guards, and the starving people. We and they, we and they, rulers and ruled, oppressors and oppressed.

In the Rest Home in the Crimea, where we had got places, there was abundant food. So abundant that bread and fruit, ices and cake were thrown away when left on the plates of the guest, or when too much had been provided. This place belonged to the Central Committee of the Soviets of the Crimean Republic.... It was so very "upper class" that we really had no business there, but it gave us an insight into the life of the Party aristocracy. The sight and sound of the starving was shut out from these former palaces and country houses of the Russian nobility, now as in the past. Only now there was a new aristocracy. That seemed to be the main difference.

Victor Kravchenko, *I Chose Freedom: The Personal and Political Life of a Soviet Official*

(New York: Charles Scribner's Sons, 1946). Excerpts, pp. 91–92, 111–13, 118–19, 130.

Victor Kravchenko (1905–66) was a high-ranking Soviet official who arrived in Washington, D.C., in August 1943. On 4 April 1944 the *New York Times* announced Kravchenko's defection and published his sensational statement denouncing the brutal crimes of the Soviet regime. Kravchenko's memoir, *I Chose Freedom* (1946), was the most searing indictment of Stalinism of its time. An international bestseller, it contains a chapter, "Harvest in Hell," devoted to the famine. In 1949 Kravchenko successfully sued the pro-communist French newspaper *Les Lettres françaises*, which had called his book a fraud. The trial, which became a cause célèbre in Western Europe, is described in his second book, *I Chose Justice* (1950). After being granted asylum, Kravchenko lived in the United States and South America under a pseudonym. His death in 1966 was ruled a suicide. Victor Kravchenko's son, Andrew, has recently completed a book about his father, the secret family, and his parents' relationship. A biography by Gary Kern, *The Kravchenko Case: One Man's War on Stalin*, appeared in 2007.

...Through the Party office of the Institute I was instructed to report at the Regional Committee. The purpose: mobilization of Party brigades for work in the villages....

...We were being sent into the farm districts to help collect grain and speed up the final phase of the harvest. But we felt and behaved as if we were about to plunge into the thick of a bloody war.

Comrade [Mendel] Hatayevich [Khataevich], a member of the Central Committee of the Party, made a speech....

..."[I]t is absolutely necessary to fulfill the government's plan for grain delivery. The kulaks, and even some middle and 'poor' peasants, are not giving up their grain. They are sabotaging the Party policy. And the local authorities sometimes waver and show weakness. Your job is to get the grain at any price. Pump it out of them, wherever it's hidden, in ovens, under beds, in cellars or buried away in back yards.

Through you, the Party brigades, the villages must learn the meaning of Bolshevik firmness. You must find the grain and you *will* find it. It's a challenge to the last shred of your initiative and to your Chekist spirit. *Don't be afraid of taking extreme measures.* The Party stands four-square behind you. Comrade Stalin expects it of you. It's a life-and-death struggle; better to do too much than not enough."....

The first dividends of collectivization were death. Although not a word about the tragedy appeared in the newspapers, the famine that raged throughout southern Russia and Central Asia was a matter of common knowledge. We denounced as "anti-Soviet rumors" what we knew as towering fact.

Despite harsh police measures to keep the victims at home, Dniepropetrovsk was overrun with starving peasants. Many of them lay listless, too weak even to beg, around railroad stations. Their children were little more than skeletons with swollen bellies. In the past, friends and relatives in the country sent food packages to the urban districts. Now the process was reversed. But our own rations were so small and uncertain that few dared to part with their provisions....

Everything depended on the new harvest. Would the starving peasantry have the strength and the will to reap and to thresh in the midst of million-fold death? To make sure that the crops would be harvested, to prevent the desperate farmers from eating the green shoots, to save the *kolkhozes* from breaking down under mismanagement, to fight against enemies of collectivization, special Political Departments were set up in the villages, manned by trusted Communists—military men, officials, professionals, N.K.V.D. men, students.... I was among those mobilized.

Three hundred of us from various city organizations gathered at the Regional Committee headquarters. The head of the committee and one of the foremost Communists of the Ukraine, Comrade Hatayevich, made the principal speech.

Again and again he referred to the "purge" of the Party scheduled for later in the year. The hint was too clear to be missed. Upon our success or failure in the famine regions would depend our political survival.

"Your loyalty to the Party and to Comrade Stalin will be tested and measured by your work in the villages," he declared ominously. "There is no room for weakness. This is no job for the squeamish. You'll need strong stomachs and an iron will. The Party will accept no excuses for failure."

Armed with a mandate from the Regional Committee, I set out for the Piatikhatsky district in the company of a schoolmate who was also my friend, Yuri. The local officials of that district, we found, were unnerved by what they had lived through. We questioned them about the new crops, but they could talk only of the mass hunger, the typhus epidemics, the reports of cannibalism.

Yes, they agreed, we must prepare to reap and to thresh the new grain; but how to get started seemed beyond their paralyzed wills. The police stations and jails were jammed with peasants from surrounding villages, arrested for unauthorized reaping of grain—"sabotage" and "theft of state property" were the official charges.

We arrived at the large village of Petrovo towards evening. An unearthly silence prevailed. "All the dogs have been eaten, that's why it's so quiet," the peasant who led us to the Political Department said. "People don't do much walking, they haven't the strength," he added. Having met the chief of the Political Department, we were conducted to a peasant hut for the night.

A feeble "smoker" provided the only light in the house. Our hostess was a young peasant woman. All feeling, even sadness and fear, seemed to have been drained from her starved features. They were a mask of living death. In a corner, on a narrow bed, two children lay so quietly they seemed lifeless. Only their eyes were alive. I winced when they met mine.

"We're sorry to intrude," Yuri said. "We'll be no trouble to you and in the morning we'll leave." He spoke in an unnatural subdued voice, as if he were in a sick-room or a cemetery.

"You're welcome," the young woman said, "and I'm only sorry I cannot offer you anything. We haven't had a crust of bread in this house for many weeks. I still have a few potatoes but we daren't eat them too fast." She wept quietly. "Will there ever be an end or must my children and I die like the others?"

"Where is your husband?" I asked.

"I don't know. He was arrested and probably banished. My father and brother were also banished. We have surely been left here to die of hunger."

Yuri said he wanted to smoke and left the house precipitately. I knew that he was afraid of breaking down and crying before this stranger.

"Don't give way to despair, my dear," I said to the woman. "I know it's hard, but if you love your children you will not give up the struggle. Bring them to the table. My comrade and I have some food from the city, and you will all dine with us."

Yuri returned. We put all our provisions on the table and ate sparingly ourselves so that there would be more for the others. The children looked at the slab of bacon, the dried fish, the tea and sugar with startled eyes. They ate quickly, greedily, as if afraid that it would all vanish as miraculously as it had appeared. After she had put the children to sleep, our hostess began to talk.

"I will not tell you about the dead," she said. "I'm sure you know. The half-dead, the nearly-dead are even worse. There are hundreds of people in Petrovo bloated with hunger. I don't know how many die every day. Many are so weak that they no longer come out of their houses. A wagon goes around now and then to pick up the corpses. We've eaten everything we could lay our hands on—cats, dogs, field mice, birds. When it's light tomorrow you will see the trees have been stripped of their bark, for that too has been eaten. And the horse manure has been eaten."

I must have looked startled and unbelieving.

"Yes, the horse manure. We fight over it. Sometimes there are whole grains in it."

It was Yuri's first visit to the village. Afraid that the initial impact of the horror might unnerve him, I interrupted the woman's story and insisted that we all retire for the night. But neither Yuri nor I slept much. We were glad when morning came....

What I saw that morning, making the rounds of houses with Chadai, was inexpressibly horrible. On a battlefield men die quickly, they fight back, they are sustained by fellowship and a sense of duty. Here I saw people dying in solitude by slow degrees, dying hideously, without the excuse of sacrifice for a cause. They had been trapped and left to starve, each in his home, by a political decision made in a far-off capital around conference and banquet tables. There was not even the consolation of inevitability to relieve the horror.

The most terrifying sights were the little children with skeleton limbs dangling from balloon-like abdomens. Starvation had wiped every trace of youth from their faces, turning them into tortured gargoyles; only in their eyes still lingered the reminder of childhood. Everywhere we found men and women lying prone, their faces and bellies bloated, their eyes utterly expressionless.

We knocked at a door and received no reply. We knocked again. Fearfully I pushed the door open and we entered through a narrow vestibule into the one-room hut. First my eyes went to an icon light above a broad bed, then to the body of a middle-aged woman stretched on the bed, her arms crossed on her breast over a clean embroidered Ukrainian blouse. At the foot of the bed stood an old woman and nearby were two children, a boy of about eleven and a girl of about ten. The children were weeping quietly and repeating in a plaintive peasant chant, "Mama, dear little mama." I looked around and my eyes rested on the swollen, inert body of a man lying on the shelf of the oven.

The nightmarishness of the scene was not in the corpse on the bed, but in the condition of the living witnesses. The old woman's legs were blown up to incredible size, the man and the children were clearly in the last stages of starvation. I retreated quickly, ashamed of my haste.

In the adjoining house we found a man of about forty sitting on a bench, repairing a shoe. His face was swollen. A tidy looking little boy, reduced to little more than a skeleton, was reading a book, and a gaunt woman was busy at the stove.

"What are you cooking, Natalka?" Chadai asked her.

"You know what I'm cooking," she answered, and in her voice there was a murderous fury.

Chadai pulled me by the sleeve and we went out.

"Why did she get so angry?" I asked.

"Because—well, I'm ashamed to tell you, Victor Andreyevich.... She's cooking horse manure and weeds."

My first impulse was to return to the house and stop her, but Chadai held me back. "Don't do it, I beg of you. You don't know how starving people feel. She might kill you in despair if you take away the contents of her pot."

After we had been in a dozen homes, I yielded to Chadai's urging that we stop the inspection. "It's the same everywhere. Now you know enough," he said.

My course seemed to me clear. The situation was too desperate for half-measures. Whatever the consequences to myself, I would ignore laws and orders. Unless I restored the strength of these peasants, everything would be lost. Returning to Chadai's home, I wrote a letter to Comrade Somanov, chief of our Political Department, and dispatched it by messenger. Toward evening the messenger returned with an answer:

"I am well aware of the conditions. I urge you to think the matter over again and to weigh all considerations. What you propose is a serious breach of our definite orders. If you see no other way out, however, you may do what you deem necessary...."

The answer satisfied me. At least he did not say no. What I proposed was to reap some oats to feed the horses and to mow a little barley at the sides of the fields for the population. Such premature reaping was being denounced, in the [Soviet central government newspaper] *Izvestia* spread before me, as "theft of state property" and "kulak sabotage." Peasants were being arrested and deported for such "crimes."....

A few days later, while I was inspecting one of the fields, I suddenly heard the honk of an automobile. I was astounded to see several big, handsome cars coming down the road.... They stopped and half a dozen men stepped out. One came towards me. I recognized Comrade Hatayevich....

"Comrade Kravchenko...who gave you permission to cut the oats and barley and to divert government milk supplies?"...

"Comrade Hatayevich," I answered calmly, "I could not do otherwise. Children were dying. Horses were dying. The collective farmers hadn't the strength to do any harvesting."....

Hatayevich took my arm. He pressed it in a friendly way that belied his harsh tones. Apparently he was making a scene "for the record." He began to stroll out of earshot of his associates and guards.

"You're a future engineer, I'm told, and a good Party man. But I'm not sure that you understand what has been happening. A ruthless struggle is going on between the peasantry and our regime. It's a struggle to the death. This year was a test of our strength and their endurance. It took a famine to show them who is master here. It has cost millions of lives, but the collective farm system is here to stay. We've won the war."

Arthur Koestler, *The Invisible Writing: An Autobiography*

(New York: Macmillan, 1954). Excerpts, pp. 51, 55–56.

Arthur Koestler (1905–83) was a Hungarian-born Jewish journalist, novelist, and essayist who wrote extensively about the Soviet Union, Europe, and contemporary affairs. A communist turned anticommunist, he was the author of numerous works of fiction, including *Darkness at Noon* (1940), his classic novel of totalitarianism, and nonfiction, such as *Von weißen Nächten und roten Tagen* (1934), *The Yogi and the Commissar* (1945), *Promise and Fulfillment: Palestine 1917–1949* (1949), and an essay in *The God That Failed* (1949).

The train puffed slowly across the Ukrainian steppe. It stopped frequently. At every station there was a crowd of peasants in rags, offering ikons and linen in exchange against a loaf of bread. The women were lifting up their infants to the compartment windows—infants pitiful and terrifying with limbs like sticks, puffed bellies, big cadaverous heads lolling on thin necks. I had arrived, unsuspecting, at the peak of the famine of 1932–33 which had depopulated entire districts and claimed several million victims. Its ravages are now officially admitted, but at the time they were kept secret from the world. The scenes at the railway-stations all along our journey gave me an inkling of the disaster, but no understanding of its causes and extent. My Russian travelling companions took pains to explain to me that these wretched crowds were *kulaks*, rich peasants who had resisted the collectivisation of the land and whom it had therefore been necessary to evict from their farms.

Another incident was so slight that I only registered it half-consciously. As our train was approaching a river across which a bridge was being built, the conductor came walking down the corridor with an armful of square pieces of cardboard and blocked up all the windows. When I asked why this was done, my travelling companions explained with smiles that bridges were military objectives, and that this precaution was necessary to prevent anybody from photographing them. It was the first of a series of equally grotesque experiences which I put down as examples of revolutionary vigilance....

Less amusing, because difficult to contemplate without a feeling of constriction in the throat, was the bazaar. This was a permanent market held in a huge, empty square. Those who had something to sell squatted in the dust with their goods spread out before them on a handkerchief or scarf. The goods ranged from a handful of rusty nails to a tattered quilt or a pot of sour milk sold by the spoon, flies included. You could see an old woman sitting for hours with one painted Easter egg or one small piece of dried-up goat's cheese before her. Or an old man, his bare feet covered with sores, trying to barter his torn boots for a kilo of black bread and a packet of mahorka tobacco. Hemp slippers, and even soles and heels torn off from boots and replaced by a bandage of rags, were frequent items for barter. Some old men had nothing to sell; they sang Ukrainian ballads and were rewarded by an occasional kopeck. Some of the women had babies lying beside them on the pavement or in their laps, feeding; the fly-ridden infant's lips were fastened to the leathery udder from which it seemed to suck bile instead of milk. A surprising number of men had something wrong with their eyes: a squint, or one pupil gone opaque and milky, or one entire eyeball missing. Most of them had swollen hands and feet; their faces, too, were puffed rather than emaciated, and of that peculiar colour which Tolstoy, talking of a prisoner, describes as 'the hue of shoots sprouting from potatoes in a cellar.' .

The bazaar of Kharkov was one of those scenes one imagines one could paint from memory, even after twenty years. Officially, these men and women were all *kulaks* who had been expropriated as a punitive measure. In reality, as I was gradually to find out, they were ordinary peasants who had been forced to abandon their villages in the famine-stricken regions. In last year's harvest-collecting campaign the local Party officials, anxious to deliver their quota, had confiscated not only the harvest but also the seed reserves, and the newly established collective farms had nothing to sow with. Their cattle and poultry they had killed rather than surrender it to the *kolkhoz*; so when the last grain of the secret hoard was eaten, they left the land which no longer was theirs. Entire villages had been abandoned, whole districts depopulated; in addition to the five million *kulaks* officially deported to Siberia, several million more were on the move. They choked the railway stations, crammed the freight trains, squatted in the markets and public squares, and died in the streets; I have never seen so many and such hurried funerals as during that winter in Kharkov. The exact number of these 'nomadised' people was never disclosed and probably never counted; in order of magnitude it must have exceeded the modest numbers involved in the Migrations after the fall of the Roman Empire.

Officially the famine did not exist. It was only mentioned in the terms of veiled allusions to 'difficulties on the collectivisation front.'

Milena Rudnytska, "Borot'ba za pravdu pro velykyi holod" (The Struggle for Truth about the Great Famine)

in idem, *Statti, lysty, dokumenty* (Articles, Letters, Documents) (Lviv: [Misioner], 1998). Excerpts, pp. 421–30. Originally published in *Svoboda* (Jersey City), 5–8 August 1958. Translated by Bohdan Klid.

Milena Rudnytska (1892–1976) was a journalist, politician, and feminist activist. During the interwar period she was a leading figure in the women's movement in western Ukraine, serving from 1929 to 1938 as president of the Union of Ukrainian Women. As a political figure she was a cofounder and executive member of the Ukrainian National Democratic Alliance, and was elected to the Polish Diet in 1928 and 1930 as a member of that party. Besides numerous articles, she wrote four books, one of which deals with the Soviet occupation of western Ukraine in World War II.

Before Ukrainian representatives waged the main battle on the grounds of the League of Nations, they raised the issue of the Famine at the Congress of European Nationalities....

Such congresses were held annually, mainly in Geneva, on the eve of the September session of the League of Nations.... In 1933, the congress took place in Berne, the capital of the Swiss Federation, from 16 to 19 September....

The goal of the Congresses of Nationalities was to fight for better international protection of minorities and to defend their interests against the abuses of the ruling nations....

At the congress of 1933 there were four Ukrainian delegates. Bukovynians [Ukrainians under Romanian rule] were represented by Senator Volodymyr Zalozetsky and Deputy [Yurii] Serbeniuk [Serbyniuk]; the delegates from Galicia [Polish-ruled territory in western Ukraine] were Z[enon] Pelensky and M[ilena] Rudnytska.

In mid-September, when we arrived in Berne, the issue of the Famine was not on the congress agenda.... The president of the organization, Dr. Josip Vilfan, a Slovene from Trieste, spoke against the Ukrainian proposal, arguing that events in the Soviet Union were outside the competence of the Congress of Nationalities. However, we had an ally in the secretary, Dr. [Ewald] Ammende: as director of Cardinal [Theodor] Innitzer's Vienna committee, he had already become actively engaged in the issue of the Famine. The Ukrainian proposal to introduce the Famine as a subject of debate at the congress was supported at a presidium meeting by delegates of the numerous German groups, since German colonists in Ukraine and the North Caucasus were also suffering from hunger. But it was not just considerations of national solidarity with their starving kinsmen that motivated the German delegates.... In Germany the first anti-Semitic laws had just been proclaimed. It was easy to foresee that that this issue would be raised at the congress and would attract the attention of the world community. Consequently, the Germans were interested in toning down the uproar over the anti-Semitic course of German policy by means of some other more acute issue. And this was the Famine, and only the Famine.

Thus, owing to a confluence of circumstances and behind-the-scenes bargaining, we achieved our goal: the Congress of Nationalities...would discuss the Famine.

This happened immediately at the inaugural session of the congress, on the afternoon of 16 September 1933....

Immediately after the opening of the congress by the president, Dr. [Josip] Vilfan, who specified in his opening remarks that the congress could address the Famine not from the political viewpoint but only from the humanitarian one, the floor was given to the "elder brother," the Russian delegate M. Kurchinsky, representing the Russian group in Estonia.... In a long address on the Famine, he did not even once mention Ukraine or say a single word about the causes of the catastrophe, nor did he even hint at collectivization and the nationality policy of the Soviet government....

I was given the floor following the Russian delegate. Without softening or passing over anything in silence, I explained [to the delegates] the calamitous famine that had struck the Ukrainian people and the criminal policy of Moscow that had caused the calamity, as well as the policy of the Great Powers, who, for the sake of good relations with the Soviet government, were closing their eyes to its crimes in Ukraine and thus also becoming co-responsible for them....

...[T]he international press picked up the main Ukrainian theses on the Famine, and the congress passed a separate resolution on the matter, directing the presidium to submit it directly to the president of the League of Nations....

...Whenever a session of the Council [of the League of Nations] was prepared, its agenda was confirmed in advance by the Secretariat, speakers on the various agenda points already designated, and questions to be brought before the Council studied by various committees and subcommittees long in advance. In that [situation], introducing the issue of the Famine into a Council session at the last minute through regular channels was out of the question.

And who was to do this? Only the governments of states that were members of the League of Nations had the right of initiative. It was hopeless to think that in the international situation of that time any state would want to scrap with the Soviet Union and take on the role of champion of the issue of the starving.... To gain access to the League of Nations through its Secretariat was therefore hopeless. Another way had to be sought.

The incoming president of the League of Nations Council in the autumn of 1933 was to be the prime minister of Norway and its minister of foreign affairs, Dr. Joh[an] L. Mowinckel. This presented us with a great opportunity, for the leadership of the League...was passing to a representative not of a Great Power, who would be held back by the demands of "high policy," but of a small country, to wit, Norway. Norway was proud of the tradition of Fridtjof Nansen, the organizer of assistance to the starving in [the Soviet famine of] 1921–22 and protector of political refugees. The issue, then, was how to find a way to Minister Mowinckel.

The permanent representative of the Norwegian government at the League of Nations was Rolf Andvord....

I immediately contacted Andvord, explained to him the matter at hand, and asked him to take me to his superior. Prime Minister Mowinckel received me the very next day....

...We could not have hoped for a better defender of our interests. By the end of the first long conversation he had already promised to do all he could. I asked him to place the issue of the Famine on the agenda of the Council of the League of Nations and persuade it to adopt a resolution on the organization of international aid under the auspices of the League of Nations.

Those Ukrainian delegates present in Geneva naturally did all they could to supply Minister Mowinckel with materials to help him with his planned presentation in defense of starving Ukraine.... Over the next few days, Minister Mowinckel received several dozen telegrams and letters asking him to urge intervention on the part of the Council of the League of Nations on behalf of starving Ukraine....

But the Secretariat of the League of Nations firmly resisted placing the issue of the Famine on the agenda of the Council session. The general secretary pointed out that, according to regulations, a question pertaining to a country that was not a member of the League could not be put forward for discussion, and, further, that the League's customs did not allow intervention in the "internal affairs" of states, and so on. There was no question that procedural regulations were against us.

However, there was one regulation in the League's statutes that left the gate open for our noble Norwegian. A sitting League president had the right to place before it any question that he, in his own opinion and preference, considered especially important. President Mowinckel wished to make use of this regulation....

...Informing me of his plan, he said: "Help me. See to it that a respected international organization addresses an appeal to me, as president of the

League Council, on the issue of the Famine. That will give me the moral right to bypass procedural regulations, notwithstanding the opposition of the secretary general."....

At this very time, the Liaison Committee of Women's International Organizations, composed of representatives of the ten largest international women's organizations, together representing tens of millions of organized women, was meeting in Geneva. This was a time when women's organizations had great authority and extensive influence in international circles, particularly Geneva circles. The Lviv headquarters of the Ukrainian Women's Union had been a full-fledged member of one of these women's federations for many years, and we maintained semiofficial ties with two others. I had many acquaintances among the activists at the Liaison Committee meeting....

Following my conversation with Minister Mowinckel, I immediately contacted the president of the International Alliance [of Women for Suffrage and Equal Citizenship], Mrs. [Margery] Corbett Ashby.... Explaining the situation to her, I asked her to convince international womanhood to intervene, which would allow Minister Mowinckel to speak on the issue of the Famine. Mrs. Corbett Ashby asked me to attend a meeting of the Liaison Committee, where I gave a presentation about the matter the following morning. The Liaison Committee unanimously passed a resolution in favor of my request....

President Mowinckel kept his word. Already on 29 September he called a meeting of the Council to consider the catastrophic famine in Ukraine. True, the meeting was not open to the public but "private," that is, confidential. On this alone he had to yield to the secretary general.... Only representatives of the governments of those countries that had a permanent or temporary seat on the Council were present. By this means the secretary general wanted, obviously, to avoid publicity, unpleasant for the Great Powers to which he was beholden, as well as for the Soviet Union....

The secret session soon became an open secret. Here is what the general public learned about it. The meeting of the Council was long and heated. Representatives of all fourteen countries then making up the Council were present. When the head of the Council explained the situation, no one, in essence, denied the fact of the famine. However, representatives of the countries that saw their interests lying in political and economic cooperation with the Soviet Union indicated formal obstacles to an official reaction on the part of the League of Nations concerning the Famine. They referred to the fact that the matter pertained to a country that did not belong to the League of Nations and apparently had not expressed its own wishes [on the matter]. Mowinckel himself spoke four times. He tried to convince his colleagues of the need to come to the aid of Ukraine or at least make some gesture on its behalf. He declared that his small and poor Norwegian people was ready to make the greatest sacrifice to help the starving. He called on the Great Powers to speak out boldly and act generously. The president of the League was supported by the representatives of Ireland, Germany, and Spain. But most members were of the opinion that the Council of the League could not act directly. In the end, it was decided to refer the matter to the International Committee of the Red Cross and appeal to it to organize international relief for Ukraine....

Thus the League of Nations, under the pretext of procedural impediments, washed its hands in the manner of Pilate....

On 6 October Minister Mowinckel paid a visit to the president of the International Committee of the Red Cross, Professor Werner, to pass on material about the Famine and inform him personally of the position of the Council. The Presidium of the International Committee of the Red Cross immediately held a meeting and, after a long discussion, decided to consider the matter referred to it by the League of Nations. It was necessary to begin by confirming the "practical possibilities" for organizing assistance, that is, to turn to the Soviet government with a proposal to grant permission to organize international relief for the starving in Ukraine....

...After a while, a reply was received from Moscow: there was no famine, and no relief action of any kind was required. The letter was extremely insulting in form.

Khrushchev Remembers

(Boston: Little, Brown and Company, 1970). Excerpts, pp. 73–74. Translated by Strobe Talbott.

Nikita Khrushchev (1894–1971) was first secretary of the Communist Party of Ukraine from 1938 to 1949, during which time he oversaw the implementation of the Great Terror, the Soviet anti-German resistance, postwar reconstruction, and the destruction of the Ukrainian nationalist underground. After the death of Joseph Stalin in 1953, Khrushchev served as first secretary of the Communist Party of the Soviet Union (1953–64). His "secret speech" at the Twentieth Congress of the CPSU on 25 February 1956 denounced Stalin and introduced de-Stalinization in the USSR. He was the author of a memoir translated under the title *Khrushchev Remembers* (1970).

Subsequently the word got around that famine had broken out in the Ukraine. I couldn't believe it. I'd left the Ukraine in 1929, only three years before, when the Ukraine had pulled itself up to prewar living standards. Food had been plentiful and cheap. Yet now, we were told, people were starving. It was incredible.

It wasn't until many years later, when Anastas Ivanovich Mikoyan told me the following story, that I found out how bad things had really been in the Ukraine in the early thirties. Mikoyan told me that Comrade [Mykola] Demchenko, who was then First Secretary of the Kiev Regional Committee, once came to see him in Moscow. Here's what Demchenko said: "Anastas Ivanovich, does Comrade Stalin—for that matter, does anyone in the Politbureau—know what's happening in the Ukraine? Well, if not, I'll give you some idea. A train recently pulled into Kiev loaded with corpses of people who had starved to death. It had picked up corpses all the way from Poltava to Kiev. I think somebody had better inform Stalin about this situation."

You can see from this story that an abnormal state of affairs had already developed in the Party when someone like Demchenko, a member of the Ukrainian Politbureau, was afraid to go see Stalin himself.

Lev Kopelev, *The Education of a True Believer*

(New York: Harper & Row, 1980). Excerpts, pp. 224–26, 248–50, 256, 259, 267–68, 278–79, 283–86.
Translated by Gary Kern.

Lev Kopelev (1912–97) was a writer and Soviet-era dissident who emigrated to West Germany in 1980. A communist idealist, he served as a Party agitator during the collectivization of agriculture in Ukraine. Kopelev was arrested and sentenced to ten years' imprisonment in 1945 for criticizing fellow Red Army soldiers for their inhumane and brutal treatment of the German civilian population. Released in 1954, he was stripped of his Party membership and expelled from the Writers' Union in 1968 for protesting the treatment of Soviet dissidents and for denouncing the Soviet invasion of Czechoslovakia. Kopelev's three volumes of memoirs were translated into English as *To Be Preserved Forever* (1977), *The Education of a True Believer* (1980), and *Ease My Sorrows* (1983).

The Mirgorod district had not fulfilled its plan of grain collections in December 1932. The oblast committee dispatched a visiting delegation of two newspapers, the *Socialist Kharkov Register* and our *Locomotive Worker*, to issue news sheets in the lagging villages. There were four of us: two lads from Mirgorod—a typesetter and a printer; and two from Kharkov—my assistant Volodya and myself....

In the village of Petrivtsy [Petrivtsi] the district GPU official related:

"There are counterrevolutionary elements in the villages here.... [T]hey went after us with weapons, they spilled our blood.... [W]e've got figures to show that weapons are hidden in a hundred fifty households.... The district is jam-full of people like that, people who never planted a day in their lives, but who fought under Petlyura, Makhno, Marusya, the Angel. In the Civil War there were as many bands of soldiers as Spot has fleas."

We believed him without reservation....

The grain front! Stalin said the struggle for grain was the struggle for socialism. I was convinced that we were warriors on an invisible front, fighting against kulak sabotage for the grain which was needed by the country, by the five-year plan. Above all, for the grain, but also for the souls of these peasants who were mired in unconscientiousness, in ignorance, who succumbed to enemy agitation, who did not understand the great truth of communism....

I have always remembered the winter of the last grain collections, the weeks of the great famine....

How could all this have happened?

Who was guilty of the famine which destroyed millions of lives?

How could I have participated in it?...

We were raised as the fanatical adepts of a new creed, the only true *religion* of scientific socialism. The party became our church militant, bequeathing to all mankind eternal salvation, eternal peace and the bliss of an earthly paradise. It victoriously surmounted all other churches, schisms and heresies. The works of Marx, Engels and Lenin were accepted as holy writ, and Stalin was the infallible high priest....

Many things then began to be called a struggle....

We deliriously sang out the refrain of the "Budyenny March," one of the most popular songs in those years: "And all our life is but a struggle!"

For what, against whom and how exactly we should struggle at any given moment was determined by the party, its leaders. Stalin was the most perspicacious, the most wise (at that time they hadn't yet started calling him "great" and "brilliant"). He said: "the struggle for grain is the struggle for socialism." And we believed him unconditionally....

Our party, our state, waged war on the peasantry.

In August and September 1932, *Pravda* wrote that the peasants in the Ukraine were not delivering enough grain; they were "bazaaring" it, harbouring it.

Molotov and Kaganovich came to our factory. At a meeting held outdoors after the first shift, they spoke of "mistakes committed in the Ukraine in the grain collection policy.".... What they said about mistakes and shortcomings didn't alarm anybody. The tone was not ominous. And they didn't name any "concrete bearers of evil."

But now, looking through the newspapers and journals of those years, I realize that by the beginning of September 1932, one could have felt the underground tremors of the approaching catastrophe....

The struggle *for grain* had begun in 1932 with a strategic retreat. This was the situation in May and June.

But in August a sharp turn was taken. And the state launched a hectically disordered full-scale attack.

All the means of propaganda, all the powers of the regional administration, the party and Komsomol apparati, the courts, the procurator's office, the GPU and the police were enlisted to strive for one goal—the acquisition of grain.

Our traveling newspaper was one of the countless number of hastily mobilized military units—or better, subunits—of the panicking grain front....

Today I am convinced that no victories or attainments, neither the rout of Hitler's forces nor the flights of the cosmonauts, can exonerate us, can even be considered "mitigating circumstances."

And even less forgivable are all the intellectual and emotional factors which led to my guilt, my participation in those fateful grain collections, be they explained or predetermined by sociohistorical objectivity or purely personal subjectivity.

This sin cannot be prayed away. No one can pray it away. And it cannot be expiated by anything. It remains only to live with it as seemly as possible. For me this means: not to forget, not to cover over, but to try to tell as much truth as I can as precisely as I can....

In February 1933 I was sick. The comrades who came to see me told of train stations packed with crowds of peasants. Whole families with youngsters and elders were trying to get away somewhere, fleeing from the famine. Many were roaming the streets, asking for handouts.

Every night trucks covered with tarpaulins gathered up the corpses at the train stations, under the bridges, in the doorways. They cruised the city during those hours before anyone had come out of his house. Other trucks of the same kind rounded up the homeless on the streets. The completely wasted were driven to the hospitals. All the infirmaries in the city were filled to overflowing. The morgues too.

Children left without parents were sent to reception centers. But all those who were sturdier than the others were simply driven somewhere distant from the city and left there....

On February 19, 1933, Stalin delivered a long speech at the all-union conference of kolkhoz shock workers. He spoke of the famine of 1918–19....

By this time hundreds of thousands of peasants were already dying. They were dying in deserted villages, on the roads, in city streets. Famine was raging through the Ukraine, the Kuban, the Volga area.

But Stalin declared that it wasn't worth "serious discussion."

And so we did not discuss it.

Not only because it was already dangerous to doubt, let alone criticize, Stalin's speeches. And not only because one of the terrible marks of mass starvation was the feeling of helplessness, of preordained doom....

No, we did not discuss it, we did not object, because we were convinced that the disaster was not so much the fault of the party and state, as the result of inexorable "objective" circumstances. We were convinced that the famine was caused by the opposition of suicidally unconscientious peasants, enemy intrigues and the inexperience and weakness of the lower ranks of the workers.

In the same speech Stalin solemnly promised "to make all the kolkhozniks well-to-do."

After this all the public speakers, orators, lecturers, newspapermen and propagandists repeated his promises every which way. Praises to the leader and predictions of forthcoming kolkhoz benefits sounded in those days when people were starving to death by the hundreds of thousands. This dismally monotonous clamor served to drown out the moaning and groaning....

In the spring the village shops and kolkhoz storehouses distributed relief once or twice a week: little bags of flour, peas, groats, preserves, sometimes baked bread.

Women with kerchiefs wrapped over their fur and velvet jackets stood and sat in line. They were still cold, even on sunny days. Edematose faces, dull, apparently unsighted eyes. The men were fewer. Skinny, bent, they looked even more emaciated next to the swollen, wrapped-up women.

The silence of these lines was frightening. Both old and young conversed little, with weak voices. Even the most shrewish squabbled quietly and somehow without passion.

The chairman of the village soviet, very skinny, pale yellow, a mummy come to life, tried to buck up his spirits as he related to the big shots:

"For today we have a reserve improvement. Neither yesterday, nor the day before, was there any fatality. All this week only four were buried, and two of them were from various illnesses. They caught cold, and they were old people besides. But those from insufficiency of nourishment—that's definitely down to a few. And you could even say some of them are doing it from lack of social conscience. Soon as they started getting relief, soon as the first grass came up, the first green shoots, they started eating like mad. But their health is weak. You have to do it a little at a time, go slow. But some of 'em, even though they're fullgrown daddies, they're worse than kids. Soon as they saw borscht or kasha, be it a potful or a bucketful, they wouldn't leave off till they had downed the whole thing. And then their guts don't turn over the way they're supposed to. Just like a horse: if it eats too much clover or drinks too much cold water, it gets a belly like a mountain and kicks out its hoofs for good.... Or it happens that the old boy got fresh-baked bread for the whole family, a loaf and a half, or twice as much, and while he's carrying it home he gobbled it all up. The kids cry with hunger, and he's clutching his belly, groaning his groan. And then he ain't breathing no more. That's how they're dying—not from hunger but from stupidity. This is mostly the muzhiks. The women—they're more conscientious, you could say, about nourishment. Or more patient. And of course, they're sorrier for the kids. The women don't die that way."

Not that way, but all the same the women died too. Even in May, when the weeding of the vegetables began. The work best suited for women.

A hot afternoon in May. The women weeders move down the dark furrows between the rows of bright green young leaves. They take heavy steps. Bend over slowly. Even more slowly stand back up. Some can only crawl on all fours. Dark and dingy clumps amid the fresh, gay greenery.

One has stopped. She didn't exactly lie down, didn't exactly sit down. An hour later someone notices.

"Oy, woe, Auntie Odarka, she's up and died! And I thought her's just taking a rest."

But in the spring they were able to bury them in separate graves. And in coffins.

They were dying less and less often. In the second half of May there were no burials for weeks.

A day in June. The district agit brigade drove in to the kolkhoz field camp. Young lads in embroidered shirts, wide blue trousers; young lasses in ribboned garlands, blouses with even more variegated embroidery, multicolored skirts with petticoats, fancy dress boots.

Lunch break. Women behind wooden tables spooning up thick gruel from earthen pots. Cauldrons steaming on the fireplace under a canopy. The rich aroma of cooked millet.

The women are hot: they are wearing white kerchiefs, bright jackets or linen undershirts. And therefore their faces and hands, blackened by the smoke, become even darker. No edematose faces. Almost all the women are thin, dried up, hardened, like old bark on logs.

And they are no longer silent: even though they have worked since sunup—"checked" the sugar beets, banked the potatoes, burned off the weeds in the cabbage field. The young people laugh to one another, looking at the rigged-up visitors.

The agitators lined up in front of a table. The musical director, in a little pea jacket, announced in a rather hoarse tenor:

"In honor of the shock workers of the socialist fields, our choir will perform folk songs."

> ...I gaze at the heavens
> Their riddle to ponder...

They sang full volume, in one voice. And right away you could tell they were not from the city. They sang not in neatly rounded melodies, as on the stages and music hall platforms, but way up high, in long, drawn-out, sonorous phrases. The way they sing in the villages—at friendly get-togethers, at weddings.

The women leave the pots, put aside the spoons. Stand fixed to the spot. Some lean on each other, press into little clusters.

And suddenly one breaks out crying. And then another. Crying softly. Covering their faces with their bandannas.

The choir falters. The director looks around. Whispers. A slender young woman in a garland strikes up a merry tune:

> Oy, beyond the grove,
> Grove so green, so green...

The choir picks it up quickly, in a slapdash manner:

> Here plowed a little lassie
> With bull so keen, so keen...

But the women keep crying. And another. And now another. First those who are older, then the young ones. And now they are crying openly, sobbing out loud.

> She plowed, she plowed,
> Worked till she could scream,
> So she hired a little Cossack
> To play on his violin...

The singers begin to lose their places. The dressed-up girls in the choir wipe their eyes and wet cheeks. The director looks around anxiously.

"What is this, good, women, comrades? What's wrong? Who's making you sad? We're trying to make things more merry."

The women's crying is broken by a shout:

"It's not you, not you! Oy, good people! It's we ourselves. We will never sing again.... Oy, how we used to sing! We don't even hear those songs in our sleep anymore.... We've buried everything.... We ourselves are already dead.... Oy, Mamochka my own, where are your bones? Oy, children, my own little dears, my own little darlings, I didn't cry over your little graves.... I handed you over to a stranger to bury without any coffins."

Another, and still another, began to scream, to lament.

The singers bunched together. And several of the young women in garlands began crying out loud.

The director rushed to the brigade leader, who was standing to the side with the drivers who had brought the guests. The men were smoking roll-your-owns, looking off to the side. The cook sat down on the ground, covered her face with her bandanna. Her shoulders shook.

The brigade leader, a broad, almost square man with a reddish tan and a rusty stubble of many days growing up to his cheekbones, waved off the director irritably:

"Just take it easy, dear comrade.... Let the women have their cry.... Their tears have welled up.... They're crying for everyone now. Don't interfere. They'll cry it out, then things'll be better."

Molotov Remembers: Inside Kremlin Politics. Conversations with Felix Chuev

ed. Albert Reis (Chicago: Ivan R. Dee, 1993). Excerpts, pp. 243–44.

Viacheslav Molotov (1890–1986), whose real family name was Skriabin, was a long-standing, high-ranking Communist Party and Soviet government official who held important posts during the Stalin era. In government he served as Soviet head of state (1930–41) and as minister of foreign affairs (1939–49; 1953–56); in the Communist Party he was a member of its Central Committee (1921–57) and Politburo (1926–57). In 1931–32 Molotov was deeply involved in managing the collectivization and grain-procurement campaigns. Together with Lazar Kaganovich, he served as one of Stalin's trusted emissaries and enforcers during this period.

Famine, 1933

Among writers, some say the famine of 1933 was deliberately organized by Stalin and the whole of your leadership.

Enemies of communism say that! They are enemies of communism! People who are not politically aware, who are politically blind.

No, in collectivization, you can be sure, hands must not tremble, you must not quake in your boots, and if anyone begins to shiver—beware! We get hurt! That's just the point. Now everyone demands everything ready-made! You are like children. The overwhelming majority of present-day communists come to us hands outstretched. They just demand that everything good we have be handed them on a silver platter. They act as if that is the meaning of life. But it is not.

People will be found who understand this. Such people will come along. The struggle against the petty bourgeois heritage must be merciless. If life does not improve, that's not socialism. But even if the life of the people improves year to year over a long period but the foundations of socialism are not strengthened, a crack-up will be inevitable.

But nearly twelve million perished of hunger in 1933....

The figures have not been substantiated.

Not substantiated?

No, no, not at all. In those years I was out in the country on grain procurement trips. Those things couldn't have just escaped me. They simply couldn't. I twice traveled to the Ukraine. I visited Sychevo in the Urals and some places in Siberia. Of course I saw nothing of the kind there. Those allegations are absurd! Absurd! True, I did not have occasion to visit the Volga region. It is possible that people were worse off there. Of course I was sent where it was possible to procure grain.

No, these figures are an exaggeration, though such deaths had been reported of course in some places. It was a year of terrible hardships.

4

SURVIVOR TESTIMONIES, MEMOIRS, DIARIES, AND LETTERS

INTRODUCTION

The fourth section of the *Reader* consists of testimonies, memoirs, and letters by famine victims. Most are by ordinary folk and are usually of a personal nature. At the same time, they provide a plethora of oftentimes painful and gut-wrenching details about the fate of family members and particular villages. Interestingly, several testimonies emphasize the limitation of the famine to Ukraine, noting that conditions just across the border in Russia were significantly better. A letter from German settlers in southern Ukraine to their relatives in North Dakota illustrates the fate of the German minority in Ukraine during the famine.

Some testimonies were given before U.S. government-sponsored investigative bodies. Some, such as those published in *The Black Deeds of the Kremlin*, were collected and published by Ukrainian émigrés and Holodomor survivors at the height of the Cold War. This made it easy for those holding pro-Soviet views to dismiss them as anticommunist propaganda. A noteworthy personal account is that of Maria Zuk, who emigrated from southern Ukraine to western Canada to join her husband in the late summer of 1933, when she gave her interview to journalists working for a Ukrainian-language newspaper in Winnipeg. Another is Miron Dolot's *Execution by Hunger*, published by a major American press in 1985.

This section also contains materials from non-peasants: Fedir Pigido-Pravoberezhny, who worked as an engineer in Ukraine; Yurij Lawrynenko and Mykola Prychodko, both literary scholars; and Vladimir Keis, an urban worker at the time of the famine who retained strong ties with the Ukrainian village. Lawrynenko states that repressive measures against the Ukrainian intelligentsia, carried out while the famine raged in the villages, constituted "a double blow delivered against Ukraine." Pigido-Pravoberezhny describes the degenerate behavior of those sent by the Kremlin to extort grain from the Ukrainian peasants. Prychodko describes "the miserable hulks of humanity dragg[ing] themselves along on swollen feet, begging for crusts of bread or searching for scraps in garbage heaps, frozen and filthy," in Ukraine's cities. Finally, Keis notes that "The horror of death by starvation hung like a dark shadow all over Ukraine. The moaning and sobbing spread throughout our land. Some villages died out completely. All those people died a martyr's death at the hands of the vicious executioner in Moscow. Whoever witnessed it knows that I am telling the truth."

Letter from Yu. Shvets, a collective farmer from the Lenin's Testament collective farm, village of Horozhene, Bashtan district, to the head of the All-Ukrainian CEC, Hryhorii Petrovsky, about the unjust grain-procurement plan for the collective farm and the starvation of collective farmers

In *Holod-henotsyd 1932–1933 rokiv v Ukraïni* (2005). Excerpts, pp. 115–16.
Translated by Maksym Motorenko and Bohdan Klid.

13 September 1932

Comrade Petrovsky,

In 1931 our cooperative had 2,400 hectares of land and was completely sown, but as we have a good deal of land close to the river, and it is useless, the district [authorities] directed our cooperative to use this land for particular agricultural needs—growing vegetables, raising cattle and pigs....

Our cooperative has 1,052 people to be fed, and here, in 1931, most of our cooperative members—poor peasants—were starving, beginning in December. In this year of 1932, the cooperative sowed 600 hectares of grain crops....

When the District Executive Committee apportioned the grain-procurement plan, our cooperative was obliged to fulfill a grain-procurement plan of 2,400 poods of grain. But, Comrade Petrovsky, if we stretch it considerably, perhaps there will be enough [grain] to fulfill the established plan, but there will be absolutely nothing left for food....

So please explain to me: has full agreement been reached with our district authorities to leave our village and cooperative hungry for the whole year, or have former landowners perhaps joined the ranks of the authorities and begun to take vengeance for their [lost] estates? Or, perhaps, it is the state of affairs to be hungry under Soviet rule?.... When the grain-procurement plan was being discussed at cooperative and executive meetings, and someone says that the plan is very great and that there would be nothing left to eat, our village board immediately threatens us with the police and the GPU....

Yu. R. Shvets....

"Zhinka z Ukraïny opovidaie pro holod i liudoïdstvo" (A Woman from Ukraine Tells of Famine and Cannibalism)

Ukraïns'kyi holos (Ukrainian Voice, Winnipeg), 13 September 1933. Excerpts, pp. 1, 5. Translated by Alexander J. Motyl.

The wife of Ivan Zhuk, a farmer in Consort, Alberta, came to him from the Pervomaisk district near Odesa, Ukraine. On the way, she made a stop in Winnipeg for a few days and was brought to the editorial offices of *The Ukrainian Voice* by some good people. We have to admit that it was interesting to see this woman; she seemed like someone from another world. Her poor clothing showed that she had not come from prosperous conditions. It will be best to convey our conversation in the form of questions and answers.

Q: *When did you leave home?*
A: On August 5.
Q: *How were people living in Ukraine at that time?*
A: There was a terrible famine. People were dying of hunger like flies.
Q: *Did many die of hunger?*
A: As far as I could learn, 25 versts [ca. 17 miles] in either direction about one-quarter of the population survived. Three-quarters died.
Q: *Are people suffering the famine quietly, or are they rebelling?*
A: How are they to rebel, and what will they achieve by rebelling? They suffer because they have lost all hope. They walk like the blind, and they fall wherever death strikes them. No one pays attention to the corpses lying on the streets. People either step over or sidestep them and keep on walking. From time to time they are collected and buried in common pits. Seventy and more people are buried together.
Q: *Have you heard anything about instances of cannibalism?*
A: Why not? It happens all the time. There have been cases of a mother starving with her children and then killing and eating them when she sees that they are about to die. Or you are walking along the street and you see a corpse. You look around to see whether anyone is watching, and you cut off a piece of flesh and then bake or cook it.
Q: *What is the reason for the famine? Has there been a drought or a bad harvest, or are you not sowing anything?*
A: There has been a harvest, we sow and we plant, but as soon as anything grows, they take it all away and pack it off to Moscow. We had a good harvest this summer, but so what? They sent in the machines, cut everything, threshed it, and left not a kernel behind. They took everything. People were weeping. They asked, "What will we eat?" But the Chekists [members of the secret police] laughed and answered: "You'll find something." What will people not do in order to hide some grain for themselves! They hide it in their hair, they hide it in their mouth, beneath their tongue, but they [the Chekists] search it out and take it too.
Q: *Do people on the collective farms live better?*
A: At first they had it better, but now they take everything from them as well. I myself was on a collective farm, and if I have not died so far and could leave, it is only because my husband in Canada sent me money, and I could buy things in the Torgsin shops [state-run hard-currency stores].
Q: *Do people not expect something better in the future?*
A: They used to, but now things get worse and worse with every year. And now they have reached the limit. No one expects anything any more; everyone just expects death. Even the officials do not know what the future holds and only shrug their shoulders. Some tell the people, "Rebel, and we will join you." And the people respond: "You rebel first."
Q: *How did you come to Canada? Through Romania?*
A: No, that is impossible. You have to go through Moscow.
Q: *And how do people live in Moscow? In the Moscow region? Is there also a famine there?*

A: No, there is no famine there. There is enough of everything. When I arrived in Moscow, I could buy everything I wanted at the bazaar—bread and meat and vegetables.

Q: And how much did your passport to Canada cost?

A: 283 dollars.

Q: Rubles or dollars?

A: No, dollars, American dollars. My husband had to send them from Canada. If someone wanted to earn them, it could never be done. See these slippers on my feet? They cost me 90 rubles last year. I had to work three months in order to buy them.

Q: They take your wheat and grain, and you have no bread, but may you keep your animals? Cows, horses, chickens, pigs?

A: The famished people ate everything. If anyone still has a horse or cow, they guard it like the greatest treasure. People caught field mice and ate them like the greatest delicacies. The cats and dogs have been eaten long ago. Some collective farms still have pigs, but the Chekists guard them and seize and take them away as soon as they grow fat. People have already forgotten how pork tastes....

Petro Shovkovytsia, "Zhakhlyva diisnist'" (Terrible Reality)

Chas (Time, Chernivtsi), 18 March 1933, p. 3; 19 March 1933, pp. 2–3. Excerpts. Translated by Bohdan Klid.

Petro Shovkovytsia, a journalist for the Chernivtsi paper *Chas*, wrote this article on the basis of a conversation with the head of the Kryzhanivsky family, who had recently escaped with his family from Soviet Ukraine, crossing the Dnister River to what is now Chernivtsi oblast (then part of Romania).

...It was here that I saw with my own eyes the lucky ones from the Soviet heaven: two men, two women, and five children. The older man [surname Kryzhanivsky] was over 60, the younger past 30. The women were approximately the same age. These were not people, but rather shadows of people. Cut them with the dullest of knives, and you will not get blood to flow from them: beaten, tortured, exhausted.... The younger man is talking, answering questions, and narrating, while the older one falls silent ever more, replying only rarely, on occasion, with utter hopelessness etched into his eyes and face.

For some unknown reason, it was just the older man with whom I wanted to talk, so I began to address him personally from a distance. A bit later, I sat down closer to him, conversing with him about their extremely miserable outer appearance.

"Eh, young man, we've recovered a bit, thank God," he replied. "We have been on this side for more than twenty days—let the merciful Lord thank for us the good people who are feeding us. We are all eating—knock on wood—not badly at all. Whatever we are given by the good folk is all eaten to the last morsel. At first we were careful, so as not to fall ill. You should have seen, young man, what we looked like when we crossed over to this side—what we were like then.

So how could we resemble people, when [we had no] lard—God be witness to this—from [the Feast of] Cosmas and Damian [14 November] we had only sugar beets to eat? I myself would have been the first to disbelieve this if someone were to have told it to me twenty years ago, but now I believe it, having lived through this reality, and I implore the whole Christian world to believe it.

We ourselves are more or less fine, but what about these unfortunate children? There, you see, are two of mine, and three of my daughter's. They were the ones in real trouble. We at least knew that disaster had come, but the dear ones did not understand that, and when they began their 'Mom, I want to eat; Mom, I want to eat; Mom, I want to eat,' it seemed that a sharp knife through the heart would have been less painful than that 'Mom, I want to eat.' Believe me, when we crossed the Dnister—for in the village we have distant relatives who, having learned of this, were the first to bring us a package of bread and lard—not one of the children knew what lard was. All of them said that it was soap. And, in the way children converse with one another, they expressed amazement that there was such tasty soap here. And that smallest boy—he is three years old—when we were taken from the riverbank by soldiers to their base, and one of the soldiers gave him a piece of bread before the others, the poor soul ate half that piece and gave his mother the other half, telling her to put it away for the next day, for what, he said, am I going to eat tomorrow?

The merciful Lord has turned his face away from us, and such a hard misfortune the blessed earth has never seen before. Here is my daughter, and those are her three children (pointing to three of the children). Shortly before Christmas, some three or four days previously, in the evening, when it had already gotten quite dark, she comes to me, sits down, we talk about this and that. And later she admitted to the old woman [his wife] that she had fired up the oven, put the children to sleep, closed the damper [to the chimney], and come to me to stay until she was certain that the [closed] damper had suffocated the children [that they had died of carbon monoxide poisoning]. She could no longer listen to that 'Mom, I want to eat.' The old woman, screaming, relayed this to me. For fear of God, child, I told her, what are you doing? If we are to die, then let it start with us, the older ones. We ran immediately and saved the poor souls."

Hearing this, both the old woman and the young one began to cry.

After a moment of silence, I again asked the old man: How could it happen that in autumn, that is, right after threshing, you were already hungry? I gather that you sowed at least a small amount of something? And if your brother, knock on wood, is such a good farmer, then I gather that you are not some kind of oaf who does not know how or does not want to think about himself and his family, so that they do not go hungry.

"Yes, dear sir, we sowed," replied the old man. "We both had sown a dessiatine [2.7 acres] of rye and a dessiatine of spring wheat. But, you see, we were individual farmers (not collectivized), so, you see, we were given the worst type of land, pure gravel. All the individual farmers got this. The better lands were taken for the collective farms. So we managed to thresh 14 poods of wheat per dessiatine and up to 8 poods of rye [per dessiatine], but according to the *rozverstka* [procurement plan], we were supposed to supply 70 poods of wheat and 55 of rye each. My son-in-law was able to grind one pood each of wheat and rye, but I was not. They came and took [all the grain] from both of us to the last kernel."

"Couldn't you hide at least a third of this grain?" I asked. "What are you talking about, dear sir? They will find it underground. And then a special court will be sent to sentence you. They will sentence you in your own home. They will sentence you to a *dopr* [forced-labor colony], to exile in Siberia, and sometimes you are taken away, and God knows where you will end up. By themselves, they would not always be able to find [hidden grain], but the collective farmers report to them. It is hard to hide from your neighbor, especially there, among the Bolsheviks, where half the population, for sure, are secret informers." "Well, the collective farmers are also subject to the procurement plan, are they not? Or, if they are assessed, then perhaps less [than individual farmers]? Or why are they such faithful dogs?"

"They are assessed, dear sir, as well—a bit less, it is true. But they are also dying of hunger. And that is precisely why the [practice of] secret informing is increasing, as well as informing by others. If I am to die, say I, then let him die as well. That is the kind of life all the unfortunate folk live there."

"And now, having left your home, did you leave anything alive in the yard—a lamb, a cow, a horse, or something else? Or did you sell everything that was there?

"There was nothing to sell and no one to buy. I left a rooster in the home, and my son-in-law left a one-and-a-half-year-old colt on the veranda. I left it a sheaf of straw that I tore from the roof. Nobody has anything. We were ordered to kill even the dogs, skin them, and give them the hides. My son-in-law and I already did this in the spring [of 1932]."

"Tell me, please, how you crossed the border with such small children. Did this have to be done quickly and quietly?" "It was impossible to do it quickly under any circumstances, but we managed to do it quietly. When there was still daylight we told the children that we were going to Romania, and that uncle would give them bread there, but that if any one of them started to cry or cough, that one would be thrown into the water. Of course, the children believed this, and when we were climbing down [to reach the riverbank] and walking atop [the ice] on the Dnister, not one of them even peeped. Believe me, that smallest one—the poor thing was running and only breathing heavily. But by this riverbank a Bolshevik dog saw us and fired two or three times, but we were no longer afraid of those shots."

"Could you please tell me one more thing: Does the population expect someone to rescue them?" "Yes, they are waiting, but they themselves do not know who it will be. There appeared some Yakhromiv who wanted to liberate the people. They awaited him. What has become of him, God knows... People say that someone else was shot by firing squad in his place, and that he was freed by some band.

If only [Symon] Petliura were to show up now! Everyone would pick up not a rifle but even a skeleton [anything that could be used as a weapon] and would run to assist him. People on this side say that even he is no longer on earth, but God knows whether this is true or not."....

From the diary of the teacher Oleksandra Radchenko

In *Rozsekrechena pam'iat'* (2007). Excerpts, pp. 542–43, 545–48. Translated by Bohdan Klid.

Thursday, 26 February 1931

We Ukrainians are living through an exceptional moment in history. When you read Leo Tolstoy, you always understand his outrage over the vile acts committed by the government in that disgusting time. But now those horrors appear miserly in comparison with what is going on at the present time. There is no justice. Sticks and whips. Besides sticks and whips, there is much more. They say that during interrogations at the militia station, the accused are beaten. They are forced to place their fingers between the door and the frame, and they are squeezed until the person suffering, enduring inhuman torture, either confesses or reveals his accomplices.

Why are hundreds of thousands of completely innocent people suffering? Children are suffering because their parents were capable, energetic workers.

This is how "dekulakization" is taking place. About three years ago a peasant had two cows, a horse, a sower, and a thresher. This was the "first kulak." Everything is taken from him, and he is driven out within a three-day period. Most recently, he is thrown out of the house in winter within 24 hours. Most often the parents are taken to prison.

Most recently the following methods of "dekulakization" are also being employed. Meat procurement takes place. The "kulak" (and the "kulak" has only one horse and one cow) is obliged to deliver 20 poods of meat and 400 rubles in cash to the state. This has to be fulfilled in 24 hours. Obviously, the peasant cannot meet this levy. The result is known.

The peasant is driven out of his home, and everything is taken from him. There are 600 households in the village of Khotimlia, 80 of which have been designated for "dekulakization." There are 600 households in the village of Velyka Babka. The village has been assessed a meat-procurement levy of 400 head of cattle.

One peasant said: "If the Soviet government cared about the future, it would not enter anyone's head to impose such meat-procurement levies." Taking so many cattle means removing half of all that is in the village. The situation is so tense that one can hardly imagine it. Terrible dissatisfaction and rancor are spreading throughout almost all strata of society. Anyone who says that life is good now (and that is only one in a thousand) is laughed at straight to his face. The stores are empty. We do not receive rations. Sugar is again not freely available. They say that only in Kharkiv can one buy sugar at 6 rubles a kilogram. Ilinka has stomach flu. She often falls ill. There is no white bread, of course. There is nothing at all to be had. We eat potatoes most of all. We have milk for the time being.

We can receive nothing from abroad. My sister tried several times to send a parcel. But parcels either were not admitted or were returned. "We do not have any hungry people" was written on one of the parcels. What impudence! Headscarves and shoes were stolen from a parcel in Moscow, and the parcel was returned....

Tuesday, 12 January 1932

Our life is becoming ever more difficult in economic terms. The flour has run out. Where to get it? How to obtain it? These thoughts give one no rest. The peasants continue to be swept clean. All are astonished and indignant, talking of an inevitable famine to come, but no one will tell this to "the powers that be." The most idiotic show trials continue to be held of people who did not have enough grain; they are subject to extortion and deprived of freedom for 2–3–5–6 years.

Wednesday, 10 February 1932

Today I was told by peasants that they saw...two children freezing along the road to Chuhuiv. The children were still alive. Why did the passersby not pick up those children? How cruel people have become. My God, what is going on? They were obviously children of plundered peasants, brought to ruin by the authorities. Yesterday a frozen adult male was brought to the hospital at Khotimlia. Today they went for the body of a murdered carpenter from Khotimlia whose name I do not recall; he was killed on a farm near Burluk. In Khotimlia M. Bozhko could not take it any longer and threw himself on the grain-procurement brigadier with an axe; the brigadier ran off.

Horrific thievery has developed. I fear famine so much; I fear it for the children. God protect us and have mercy on us.

It would not be so offensive if there were a poor crop, but the grain has been taken away and an artificial famine created...

Tuesday, 5 April 1932

Famine, artificially created famine is taking on a nightmarish character. No one can understand why they are pumping out grain to the last kernel, and now, having seen the results of such pumping out, they nevertheless continue to demand grain for sowing and sowing material in general. And when the indignant peasant exclaims that all his grain was taken for the grain procurement, he receives a question in reply: "Why did you give everything; you should have realized that you would have to sow with something," and the endless negotiations begin. And the children go hungry, worn out, emaciated, tormented by tapeworms, as they eat only sugar beets—and those will run out soon—and the harvest is still four months away. What will become of us?

A beggarly way of life is gradually turning people into rude, cruel, unbridled creatures ready to turn to crime....

Wednesday, 6 April 1932

...The famine is beginning to rage everywhere, bringing all the miseries that one could possibly imagine. Criminality is developing especially rapidly. Anger at the authorities has grown to such an extent that it seems if a match is lit, a fire will erupt, uncontrollable, terrible, as in a summer drought with windy weather. I am tormented by the thought of peasant children swollen with hunger, and my anger grows. The poor things, and it is for them that socialism is being prepared. Funny—some kind of comedy.

Thursday, 2 June 1932

How difficult it is to live, desperately difficult. In general the times are exceptional, unknown in history. All are suffering from malnutrition or famine, and generally from a half-indigent way of life. There is a terrible and oppressive indifference to everything....

Monday, 24 October [1932]

...I received 3 dollars from Nina. With this V[asia] bought 6 kg of wheat flour, 2 kg of sugar, 3 or 4 of rice and 1 kg of wheat groats at the Torgsin. What a great help to us....

Monday, 9 January 1933

...The horrors of famine are developing in Kharkiv. Children are being stolen and sausage made of human flesh is being sold. Adults (the better-fed ones) are lured by tricks under the pretext of selling them footwear. Even the papers wrote about this, calming people that measures are being taken, but...children are still disappearing.

Thursday evening, 23 March 1933

...I saw awfully much human misery this day. I returned home with heavy impressions. Along the road to Zarozhne, in a field by the roadside, we saw a deceased old man, in tatters, thin, without boots. Obviously, he became enfeebled and froze or died right away, and someone took his boots. Returning, we again saw the old man, who was unneeded by anyone. When I told the Babchanka village council that the body should be taken away, the chairman asked, smiling: "And how was he lying, with his feet in our direction or toward Zarozhne? If toward Zarozhne, then let the Zarozhne village council take him away."

Upon entering Babka, we came up to a 7-year-old boy. My co-passenger yelled out, but the boy staggered on as if he had not heard; the horse overtook him; I shouted; the boy unwillingly turned from the road; I was drawn to look him in the face. And it was unbearably horrible. The expression on that face left an everlastingly indelible impression. Obviously, that expression in the eyes can be found in people when they know that they will soon die but do not want to die. But this was a child. My nerves could not take it. "For what? For what, children?"

I cried quietly, so that my co-passenger would not see. The thought that I could do nothing; that millions of children were perishing from starvation; that this was elemental, reduced me to total despair....

April 1933

Facts of the famine

It is already three o'clock in the morning, meaning that today is 27 April. I am not sleeping. The last days have been filled with a terrible apathy. The whole horror of the situation that has been created has affected my health. Although we are not starving, we are not eating as we should.

People are dying by handfuls each day in every village, and this throughout Ukraine. Yesterday a member of the collective, Leontii Petrovych Tkachev, came. His leg is hurting. He is swollen from hunger. He implored me to give him something to eat. We gave him whatever we could. I complained to him that I am feeding a hunting dog, once expensive, but no one needs it now, as there is nothing with which to feed it. He asked me for it, saying that they would eat it. The roofer Korzhev regularly maintains his family with dog meat....

From the diary of Dmytro Zavoloka

In *Rozsekrechena pam'iat'* (2007). Excerpts, pp. 553–58, 560–61, 566–67. Translated by Bohdan Klid.

...14.III.1932

At twelve o'clock midnight I am to drive to Barash.... These collective farmers are completely without bread, even without potatoes. And that is why, in a number of collective farms of the district (Barash, Novyi Yablonets, Usoluiasia, Bobrytsia, Kyianne, and others), collective farmers steal even food meant for pigs (mixed fodder), bake flat cakes from this, and eat it. In some of the collective farms seed grain is [being] eaten.... And the general impression is as if the country were suffering through a difficult famine, or on the eve of mass starvation....

The methods of grain procurement were overly leftist. For the most part, naked administrative methods were used: mass searches, arrests, and, in general, completely unjustified arbitrariness was allowed.... The population, beginning with the well-to-do kulak stratum and ending with the poor collective-farm peasant, was intimidated and terrorized. In the resolutions of the District Party Committees there were various preemptive resolutions of the authorities against "leftist" excesses and lawlessness, but in fact no struggle was undertaken against such manifestations. Moreover, even the DPC went down the road of naked administrative methods, forming an operative troika under the direction of the DPC secretary, before which the full complement of the delegated village council and the administration of the collective farm were summoned for a chastening, accompanied by arrests, intimidation, and so on. As a result of all this work, the district, for all that, fulfilled only 66–69 percent of the grain-procurement plan.

At present the state of preparation of seed stocks is especially dangerous. Across the whole district 40 percent have been prepared. There is almost no hope of significantly increasing this amount. Hence the danger that almost 50 percent of the fields for sowing will remain unplowed in the spring.... [E]ven if the whole seed stock were available, there is still the danger that many of the collective farmers will not go to work, as they have no food.... That is today, and what will happen when the harvest is to be gathered? Then there will be even fewer food resources than there are now. And again there will be the danger that the sown fields will not be harvested in time, or that a portion will perish completely. To what end was such a tense situation created in the village? And especially in the collective-farm sector? Could this undesirable confrontation have been avoided? Clearly, it could have. There should have been greater attention to the needs of the populace, above all to their need for food....

19.III.1932

Mother was already here yesterday. But only today did we have a frank conversation. The situation at home is especially difficult. For several months there has been no bread in the house. They live on potatoes and potato pancakes. The children are developing acute anemia (Misha, Kolia, Vitia), and they often complain of dizziness. Bread appears in the house only when Mother returns from Kyiv and brings "presents." Earlier, when Mother would begin to talk about her affairs and bring up hunger and malnutrition, I did not believe it. I did not listen attentively to these conversations and said: "Mama, why are you falling for enemy agitation and blabbering about all sorts of kulak 'frights'?" And I would turn the conversation to jokes and assure her that nothing terrible could take place; that the state and the Party would not allow it. But today, when she again began to talk to me about this, and her voice quivered near weeping, while her face showed tearful spasms and her eyes glistened with tears, I could not but feel that heavy, hopeless state in which our household is living....

I did not know how to respond to her words. I was helpless to cheer her up in any way and only managed to say that this situation would not last long. It could not be that the Party was taking no notice of the way people all around were living, and if there were instances of hunger, this would soon be corrected. I do not know whether she believed me or not.... She is constantly perturbed whether in fact it will come to placing one's hopes only on those seed funds that the people have and on the food available for spring work.... According to Mother's words, the collective farmers do not have anything at all....

22.IV.1932

We conversed almost the entire evening. Mother and I. She had come to buy bread for "the holidays"....

We talked a great deal, but I heard nothing of any good thought or event. And this was not really a conversation but, in essence, Mother's narrative about current village life and her own, of course.... According to her words, "The peasants have never before lived as they do now. Never have the people suffered as they do now. The peasants are oppressed to the uttermost, and that is why they are living as they do; may our enemies never live this way, and it is also bad for the workers"....

To the question of how the sowing campaign was proceeding, there was also a reply that paints an unhappy picture. "The people are working but moving as if barely alive. They gather at nine in the morning, but then, by the time tasks are assigned, before they begin to work, give them something to eat. And for food they give three quarters of the type of bread that you cannot force down your gullet. Well, and with bread they boil hot broth once. As for those who stay home—the little ones, the elderly, the sick—do not even mention them: they are left on their own, even to die."....

Yes, it is extremely difficult to hear and learn about the condition of the peasantry. And we, the Party, have consciously brought this about with our line, our behavior, our leadership....

12.VI.1932

Only 2,417,367 hectares of the spring fields have been sown, or 57.1 percent of the plan. This is as of 10.VI.... The possible time for sowing has passed. Sowing after 10 June is more hopeless for germination, and even more so for yield. This means that in Kyiv oblast alone almost two million hectares of unsown fields remain.... As of 10.VI, only 314,170 hectares of potatoes have been planted, which constitutes 56.7 percent fulfillment [of the plan]. The results of spring sowing are more than catastrophic. In the aftermath of the newspaper observations, a comrade commented: "I HEARD THAT WHEN MOLOTOV WAS IN OUR OBLAST, HE SAID: 'Through our mistakes this year we have set back the agricultural economy of Ukraine a number of years.' What he said was absolutely true if one believes that it was he who said this, but he was also present precisely when the grain procurements were in full swing and our mistakes were at their worst." I was unable to object to this but only thought how profoundly true were the words spoken by Molotov or someone else to the effect of "setting back our agricultural economy a number of years." And that pertains not only to the unsatisfactory state of sowing this year but to all the ruination that has occurred in agriculture.

Almost 40–50 percent of the horse herd has died. The number of horned cattle has decreased more than twice. Pigs are decreasing in number. Smaller livestock is almost wiped out. The peasants from the villages have dispersed and scattered to the four corners—if not all, then a considerable portion.

Political confidence in the Soviet government has been catastrophically shaken, and it is strange that in all these matters the fault remains that of "DISTORTIONS AT THE LOCAL LEVEL," which "THE CC OF THE PARTY INDICATED" in timely fashion. And certainly there will be no quick re-release of the outstanding historical explanations of the Party "chief," Comrade Stalin, concerning the reasons for the distortions and the next steps for dealing with them. Just as it was with regard to the question of collectivization in 1930, when the guilty were whoever you please, but not the CC.

For the latter "indicated more than once" the danger of "dizziness with success." How despicable to engage in self-criticism and not admit to one's own mistakes!

What is the use of a leadership that cannot see the destruction resulting from its own deeds, is unable to prevent catastrophe in timely fashion, and then does not have the courage and decency to admit its own mistakes?

Letter from Adam and Rosina Ketterling to Johann and Dorothea Ketterling

In *We'll Meet Again in Heaven* (2001). Excerpts, pp. 194–95.

May 18, 1933
Wishek Nachrichten

Kassel, South Russia [Komarivka, Ukraine]
April 23, 1933

A nice greeting and kiss to you, my beloved friends, in the wide distant world, brother Johann Ketterling and Dorothea and all of your children....

...We are, thank God, healthy and still among the living. But for how long, we don't know, for it looks so sad and sorrowful in our lives. Many people are dying of hunger. They swell up and then die. It is such a terrible time that I can hardly write about it.... I must let you know that our brother died on March 8. He had to leave his house, and then he lived with his daughter, and there was nothing to eat. It is awfully hard. He starved and then died....

Meat I haven't seen for a long time, much less eaten. Anything fried, or fat or oil, it has been three months since we had anything like that....

A pud [pood] of corn costs 200 rubles, but there is no money. A pud of potatoes and also of beans costs 70 rubles. We eat anything we can. Potato peels, grape seeds, and roots. We put it all together and cook it in water, and that keeps us alive, if there is enough of it. If there is grass, we cook grass.... This is the third letter I've written you, and also probably the last. If it continues as it is now, then we will soon find our end.

You might want to know what work I do. I work in the vineyards by cutting and pruning, and each night I must stand watch at a house in which are stored fruit, potatoes and corn. Many people in Kassel get help from their relatives in America. That is good for our people, otherwise many more of them would starve. Starvation is a terrible death. People swell up so much....

My dear brother Johann and Dorothea, and all friends and acquaintances, I would like to ask all of you, if it is in your good will, to please help us out some. If you can't help much, I'll be satisfied with a little. If I don't get help, then everything is lost. Then we must go to the ground, to our deaths. I must close and give you another heartfelt greeting. We hope for a very quick answer from you.

Adam and Rosina Ketterling

Unsigned letter

In *We'll Meet Again in Heaven* (2001). Excerpts, pp. 196–97.

June 8, 1933
Wishek Nachrichten

[Probably] Kassel [Komarivka, Ukraine]

Dear Friends,

We want to let you know that we got your gift, which saved us from certain death. We send you a loving heartfelt thank you for that. But worst of all is how our people are afflicted, always with death before their eyes. The higher authorities have sent 150 men here to our village, whose job it is to plague us half to death. At our community gatherings at least several leaders, the commandants, have told us, "Now that we have grown in power over you, you will see that wherever you destructive insects have settled in our land, that we have you in our hands, and no God will drop manna from heaven to help you, and nowhere will anyone hear your miserable complaints. Hangings, shootings, starvation, and freezing—all of those will be done to you if you don't work to exactly meet the requirements of the predetermined Plan."

But who can work? People are so weak that they fall over. So it has been for a while. When they can hardly move anymore, they are sent to the forest to work. Even old people must work. They have ordered everyone from 13 to 100 years in age to work in the forests, there in the deepest snow, in the grimmest of cold. They must cut trees and get wood.

Men and women must arise early, at 6 a.m., and before, go to the collective kitchen to eat a piece of bread and a little soup, and after that try to work—if they can. And if you don't work, you don't get paid. Whoever has no money to pay is tossed out and must lie there without food until it is 10 o'clock at night. So many of the people fall over dead, up to six people each day, with hardly anyone left to bury them in the snow. The husband lies in his final resting place, while the wife must still work. He falls dead on the way, but the others must let him lie there and go on to their work. If someone lies dead at home, the others must still work. Still others, who try to get help and find food, fall along the way and just lie there. Until now our God has not been pacified with all this death.

I just don't know what will happen in the future. Every day I think: only God knows if my husband will come home alive. Almost everyone who has worked with him is already dead. With your gift we bought the cheapest food: gruel, flour, and a little fat. It has been over half a year since we've seen anything cooked with fat. You can just imagine how we thank our loving God whenever we do have food. Now, live well with the Lord. We'll meet again in heaven.

[Unsigned]

Letter from the collective farmer Mykola Reva to Joseph Stalin about the Famine of 1933 in Ukraine

In *Rozsekrechena pam'iat'* (2007). Excerpts, pp. 573–75, 576. Translated by Bohdan Klid.

---

1 May 1940....

Dear Joseph Vissarionovich,

You are, it would seem, our friend, teacher, and father, so the bold idea occurred to me of writing to you with the whole truth....

The dark reaction of the hungry year of 1933, when people ate tree bark, grass, and even their own children, when hundreds of thousands of people died of starvation, and <u>all this before the eyes of the communists, who drove their cars across our bodies and impudently praised life</u>....

...[T]he people were dying of hunger not because there was a poor harvest but because the state took their grain, and that grain lay in the Zahotzerno [Grain Procurement] warehouses in elevators and was being distilled into alcohol for intoxication, while people were dying of hunger.... [I]n 1933, when hungry people gathered grains of corn by the Zahotzerno warehouse at the Khorol station, they were shot like dogs; a detachment of mounted police was dispatched from the town of Khorol, and like lions, with sabers drawn, they pursued us hungry ones, and there was grain in the warehouses, there was flour, but people were dying of hunger, which means that all this was carried out deliberately by the state, and the state knew about this....

The village council does not issue death certificates for 1933 because mortality in that year was so great that in more than fifty years so many people did not die as in that year. Whoever was left alive, having endured such difficulties—that person is already ruined because, as I know from my own experience, we collective farmers were swollen from hunger, we fell on our feet, we lost our ability to think, we lost a certain percentage of our eyesight, there is no health, no strength, a general weakness of the bodily organism, and a great incidence of hospital visits and many sick people in those areas where the year 1933 made itself felt. All this took place before the eyes of the communists—how can they not be sorrowful and ashamed that they could not besiege the higher authorities and sound the alarm about this misfortune, so that it would not exist.... [T]he communists cared more for their own skins, for if anyone endeavored to stand up for the people with a mere word, his fate would be settled along with ours. That is how we are valued, Joseph Vissarionovich....

N. Reva

V. Maly, *Selo Druha Korul'ka* (The Village of Druha Korulka)

(Munich: Suchasna Ukraïna, 1952). Excerpts, pp. 19, 21–22. Translated by Alexander J. Motyl.

After the famine of 1932–33, Russians from Russian territories were brought into the village—twenty-five families—and settled there. A little while later, another seven Russian families arrived. In this manner Moscow filled the gaps that emerged in the Ukrainian village as a result of "dekulakization" and the planned famine. All these Russian families occupied the farms of those who had been dekulakized or had died of hunger.

They did not need to build their own houses! After a while the Russians occupied all the key "leadership" positions on the village collective farm.... The Russians also began to compose the cadre of the Korulka village soviet....

About 1938–39 I got to know one A. Kulish in Sloviansk. He used to live in the Poltava region. In 1930 Kulish had been "dekulakized"; he and his family then settled on Russian territory, where he lived in the village of Kastorna, about a hundred kilometers from Voronezh....

At the beginning of 1933, in the winter, the NKVD issued an order in Kastorna, where many dekulakized Ukrainian refugees lived, instructing all Ukrainian "kulaks" to present themselves within twenty-four hours at the train station nearest their place of residence. Several NKVD agents were sent to Kastorna, where they collected all the Ukrainian inhabitants and led them to the Krasnaia Dolina station. These NKVD agents said openly that the Ukrainian "kulaks" hiding on Russian territory would be sent to the Urals, that is, in fact, to Siberia....

While waiting for space on some train to Siberia, many Ukrainians died of hunger and cold at the station. The NKVD gave the arrested people nothing to eat. It was cold at the station, and people sat and lay helplessly on the bare cement floor. The wailing of children and women could be heard incessantly. The NKVD simply threw these Ukrainian prisoners—children, sick women, and old people—into the fully packed freight cars of some train. Once a car was packed tight with people, they would slide the door shut and lock it. The eyewitness A. Kulish said that some unfortunates would tear their clothes and hair and go mad.

Mykola Prychodko, "The Year 1933 in Soviet Ukraine"

In *The Black Deeds of the Kremlin* (1953–55). Excerpts, vol. 1, pp. 234–38.

Mykola Prychodko (Prykhodko, 1904–80) was a Ukrainian literary scholar and writer. He was imprisoned in a Soviet concentration camp in 1938–41. After World War II he settled in Canada. He was the author, in English, of the novels *Stormy Road to Freedom* (1968) and *Good-Bye Siberia* (1976); the concentration-camp memoir *One of the Fifteen Million* (1952); *Moscow's Drive for World Domination* (1961), and *Ukraine and Russia* (1953).

Through the streets of Kiev, Kharkiw, Dnipropetrowske, Odessa and other cities, the miserable hulks of humanity dragged themselves along on swollen feet, begging for crusts of bread or searching for scraps in garbage heaps, frozen and filthy. Each morning wagons rolled along the streets, picking up the emaciated remains of the dead. Often even the undershirt had been stripped from the corpse, to be exchanged for a slice of bread.

Those who were lucky enough to reach Moscow had a better chance for survival. Here were more scraps of bread, made of Ukrainian wheat, on the dumps; here one could also buy a little food on the black market.

The difficulty was to get there. On the trains and in the stations the GPU, in their red and blue caps, halted every traveller, demanding his official travelling permit. Those who could not produce them were arrested.

At this time my friend S. was working as an assistant in the October Revolution Hospital. Having completed his medical studies in 1931, he now worked in the surgical division. One evening he invited me to visit him in the hospital, promising me an unusual spectacle. When I arrived he took me to a large garage in the yard. A guard unlocked the door and we entered. S. switched on the light and I beheld an unforgettable picture of horror.

Piled like cord-wood against the walls, layer upon layer, were the frozen corpses of the victims picked off the streets that morning. Some of the bodies, I later learned, were used for dissection and experiments in the laboratories. The rest were simply buried in pits, at midnight, in nearby ravines out of sight of the people.

"This, my friend," S. whispered softly, "is the fate of our villages."

I was too unnerved to utter a word. With unbelieving eyes I could only stare at the hundreds of outstretched frozen hands which still seemed to be begging for bread, begging for life.

S. turned out the lights and we departed without a word. The guard slammed the door and locked it behind us. Slowly we walked home, speechless and shaken, but with mutual understanding between us....

There is another unforgettable incident which I witnessed in that year of 1933. It happened in the spring, as I was riding on the train from Kiev to Uman. At the Monasteryshche station 12 farm laborers came aboard, their faces bloated with starvation, tattered and dirty, all on their way to work on a state farm. With them was a young lad, about 14, his hands tightly pressed against his chest, inside the shirt.

Like a pack of wolves, the men gathered around the boy, their hungry eyes glued to the hand at his bosom. The lad tightened his grip upon his possession—a slice of black bread—and stared back with frightened eyes at the fierce, unshaven, swollen caricatures of human faces around him. To a man, they were urging and pleading with him to share the bread with them. Tomorrow, they promised, there would be boiled potatoes at the farm, maybe even bread!

The hungry boy stoutly refused. His mother, he explained, had somehow procured that one slice for him and had admonished him to save it for tomorrow.

The tragic scene ended when the twelve men, as though electrified by a command, fell upon the lad and tore away the bread which crumbled and scattered over the floor. The starving, snarling human beasts tore the crumbs out of each other's fingers, scratched them out of crevices, as though in a paroxysm of insanity. The hungry youngster sobbed bitterly, but for the men he had already ceased to exist.

J. Chmyr, "Speak Russian or Starve"

In *The Black Deeds of the Kremlin* (1953–55). Excerpts, vol. 1, pp. 272–74.

I had an opportunity to observe the life of the "muzhiks" [peasants] in the Russian villages. It was different from life in the Ukrainian villages. Each farmer had, on the average, 4 horses, 6 cows, sheep and pigs, while in Ukraine the people had been deprived of all their possessions and were starving. The Russians had bread, meat, and potatoes were rotting in the farm yards. No one dreamed of any famine here!

I worked here for a year. Towards the end I lived in a Moscow suburb, and saw Ukrainians come to buy bread, which they tried to take back to their dying families in Ukraine.

I left Moscow on April 20, 1933, after having provided myself with 79 pounds of bread. When about to leave I met two women from my native village who had come to Moscow to buy bread. Our journey was uneventful until we reached Bakhmach on the Russian-Ukrainian border. Here, all the passengers were ordered by the NKVD to go to the customs office, where the officials took away my bread, leaving me only 9 pounds. This was in consideration of the fact that I had been working in Moscow, but my countrywomen were not only robbed of their bread but were themselves detained for "taking" bread away from Russia.

These two unfortunate women left hungry children at home. Their husbands died from hunger, and the children were alone. They never came back.

After my arrival in my native village I was ordered by the village soviet chairman, a Moscow henchman, Klym Komiychenko, to oversee a brigade of women, swollen from hunger, whose task it was to sow and weed sugar beets. Practically all the people in the village were suffering and swollen, many were already dead from hunger. The work these hungry women were doing was too hard for them, and they would fall down and die. It was terrible to look at them, the skin cracked and water oozed out. The peak of mortality was reached just before the harvest.

Then another man and I were ordered to roam over the village and gather up the corpses. Cannibalism raised its ugly head, mothers ate their children and wives their husbands. Nastya Kyzyma ate her husband, Andriyan, and one child, and then she and her remaining five children died. Osadchy's wife ate him when he died, and then told the neighbours that she had buried his bones behind the cottage. The hot weather hastened the decomposition of the bodies, and the stench in the village was unendurable. About twenty people died every day, and there was no one to bury them. Four men were steadily employed at the cemetery, digging graves. We brought in the dead on the wagon like logs. No one lamented their deaths because their families or relatives lay sick or were already dead. The NKVD agent, a Russian, was telling us what to do. People were buried worse than cattle. If I should, by some miracle, return to my native village I would be able to find all those holes where more than half the people in the village were buried.

I worked at this collection of the dead for two months, and then myself swelled with hunger. All I had to eat during that time was 3 ½ ounces of bread and a small potato a day, and lack of other foods, especially meat and fats, began to affect my body. I ate nettles, lambs quarters, locust flowers and drank water. My body swelled so badly that I could walk no longer, I could only crawl along.

But luckily for me, the ears of rye began to fill with a milky substance. I greedily sucked the ears and the swelling abated. In Moscow I had weighed over 200 pounds, but now I was only 106. Slowly my strength returned. I could walk, and in four weeks was out of danger, thanks to the ears of rye.

Fedir Pigido-Pravoberezhny, *The Stalin Famine: Ukraine in the Year 1933*

(London: Ukrainian Youth Association in Great Britain, 1953). Excerpts, pp. 44–45, 50–51.

Fedir Pigido (pseud. Pravoberezhny, 1888–1962) was a Ukrainian economist, publicist, and civic activist. Born to a peasant family, he completed medical training in Kyiv and served in the main medical administration of the Ukrainian People's Republic (1917–20). After obtaining a degree in economics (1935), he worked as a construction engineer. He spent World War II in German-occupied Ukraine. In 1949 he joined the émigré Ukrainian Revolutionary Democratic Party and became one of its leading figures. His major work is *Velyka Vitchyzniana viina* (The Great Patriotic War, 1954, repr. 2007).

Hunger increased ever more until it assumed huge proportions. The divisional, district and national leaders acted as if they saw nothing. But that was not all: anyone who lived at that time in Ukraine will surely remember the dissolute orgies which were being arranged during the dreadful spring of 1933 by the Party bosses. I shall mention only one of them, the "Paradise Evening" arranged in May, 1933, in the city of Zaporozhe [Zaporizhia], to take place—if I am not mistaken—in the "Intourist" hotel. In arranging that Party the following persons were particularly active: the secretaries of the Divisional Party Committee, Budny and Leibeson; Rohachesky, director of the Zaporozhe Steel Works; Kuryluk, secretary of the Steel Works Party Committee; Porokhnia, secretary of the Construction Works Party Committee, and others. Through the open window of the hotel there flowed out into the streets and to the ears of those sleeping in a hungry stupor the drunken songs and wild laughter of the leaders of the city as well as of the famous Party nymphs who, naked as on the day they were born into this world, were dancing gracefully on the tables among the bottles of champagne. It was possible for the ruler of the Dniepropetrovsk region, the notorious M. N. Chatayevich [Mendel Khataevich], secretary of the Party District Committee, to be ignorant of this "Paradise Evening Party," but as he was whirling at that same time in drunken fox-trots somewhere else, he did not want just then to hear anything about the "Paradise Party." Not until 1937, during the so-called [Nikolai] Yezhov period, when it was necessary for reasons unknown to the public to "settle" with the above named Party secretaries, were the details of the "Paradise Party" dragged out into the glare of publicity.

It is interesting to note that one evening, when the Zaporozhe leaders were amusing themselves in a "cultural" way, as described above, dozens of peasants in the village of Mala Lepetykha in the neighbourhood of Zaporozhe were shot down like so many mad dogs. This is how it happened: in March 1933 a horse died in the local kolhosp [collective farm]. As was learned later, the cause of the horse's death was glanders. The horse was buried, but the hungry peasants, unaware at that time of the cause of death, dug out the corpse, and a whole section of the village tasted the horsemeat. After a short time several cases of glanders appeared among them. The Zaporozhe authorities investigated the matter and found out that the sick people had eaten horsemeat. It was decided to liquidate all those who had consumed the dead horse. It is not known how or in what minutes' book of a meeting that decision was written down, but the results, at least, are known. One evening that section of the village was surrounded by a detachment of N.K.V.D.; a few N.K.V.D. men went then from house to house and all people—young and old—were shot to death. That job was entrusted to first class specialists, amongst whom was Alexander Rezenov, the inspector of "Workers' and Peasants' Militia," well-known for his foaming rages. In that fearful spring of 1933, when masses of people were dying of hunger each day, when on the streets and in houses thousands of corpses were lying for days and days without being carried out for burial by anyone, at such a time no-one paid any attention to the "little" affair in the village of Mala Lepetykha....

To the accompaniment of the drunken, savage shouting of the leaders, the last act of the tragedy of the starving Ukrainian villages was taking its course. People walked through the streets as if half-asleep, supporting themselves on sticks or leaning upon walls of stables or upon fences—wherever any of these were still standing. Most of them had swollen legs that looked like heavy logs of wood, as well as swollen hands and faces. Very often the swelling would burst, and then a white fluid would flow out. Legs and hands were covered with numerous tumours; they were strange tumours, and people called them "hunger tumours." Those who had died lay on the very spot where death had overtaken them; they would lie there, side by side with those yet living, for days and days, sometimes for over a week.

Once a week, and sometimes more than once, men and women were driven to a burial ground to dig common graves. Waggons passed through the streets of the village picking up the corpses and carrying them to the common graves. From twenty to a hundred corpses were thrown, like so many pieces of wood, into each grave, which was then covered with earth. These was no Christian burial for them—these victims—they were tossed away like animals, not human beings. In any Ukrainian village you will be shown dozens of such common graves, stacked up with corpses and then covered with earth in the year 1933.

Members of the kolhosps were buried separately from the "indus" (individual farmers). In Hermaniwka [Hermanivka], a large village about 60 km (about 40 miles) north of Kiev, not far from my village, the corpses were being carried one day to the burial ground and piled up by the grave. When about sixty corpses had been thus piled up, they were thrown into the grave. At dinner-time comrade Nikiforow [Nikiforov], the head of the local village council, happened to come to the burial ground, and, seeing the corpse of an "indus" in the grave of a peasant who during his lifetime had refused stubbornly to join the kolhosp, he ordered the corpse to be thrown out as not being worthy to lie in the same grave as members of the kolhosp. By Nikiforow's order a man was lowered into the pit to bind a rope to the foot of the poor "indus," who then was pulled out of the kolhosp grave and thrown aside; there he lay for a week or so before that notorious village satrap would allow anyone to throw him into an indus grave.

"Testimony of Yurij Lawrynenko, Through the Interpreter, Roman Olesnicki"

In *Eighth Interim Report of Hearings before the Select Committee on Communist Aggression, House of Representatives, Eighty-Third Congress* (Washington, D.C.: United States Government Printing Office, 1954). Excerpts, pp. 114–15, 116, 117–18.

Yurij Lawrynenko (Lavrinenko, 1905–87), a Ukrainian literary scholar, critic, and publicist, was born in Khyzhyntsi near Cherkasy. He was imprisoned in the Norilsk concentration camp (1935–39) and then exiled. He settled in the United States in 1950. He was the editor of the anthology *The Executed Renaissance* (1959) and the author, in Ukrainian, of *Socialism and the Ukrainian Revolution* (1949), *At the Test of the Great Revolution* (1949), *The Stump and Its Offshoots* (1971), *Vasyl Karazyn* (1975), and the memoir *The Black Blizzard* (1985). He also compiled *Ukrainian Communism and Soviet-Russian Policy toward the Ukraine: An Annotated Bibliography, 1917–1953* (1953).

Mr. McTigue: All right; Mr. Lawrynenko, you were testifying as to what happened in your village.

Mr. Lawrynenko: My native village originally consisted of about 2,000 inhabitants, and I know personally that at least 700 of them died of starvation. I also know that this year was a normal one as far as harvests were concerned.... All the grain and other food products produced by this village were confiscated by force. At first the food was stored in the local church, and later it was transferred to the nearest railroad station. Searching parties went around the village looking for food and looking even into the pots in the kitchens. On the one hand, the confiscated grain was transported to Moscow and—

Mr. Feighan: When you referred to searching parties, you meant the Russian Communists?

Mr. Lawrynenko: Special brigadiers were at that time dispatched from Leningrad and other Russian cities and the total of these brigadiers was in excess of 20,000 people, and their task was to search and confiscate the grain in the Ukrainian villages. And they could call upon the Red Army to help them.

On the one hand the confiscated grain was transported to Russia where it was stored in railroad stations and sometimes out in the open. The other part of that grain was being transported to Odessa and other parts of the Black Sea, and from there it was transported to foreign lands.

My wife's family escaped from Poltava to the city of Voroniezh, which is in Russia, and there they were able to save themselves from starvation because at the railroad stations of Russia grain was plentiful. Kharkov is the main railroad center of the Ukraine, and in that city I myself saw whole trainloads of grain being dispatched to Russia day by day during the famine and the ravaging of the Ukraine. This was a mass phenomenon. Many of my friends and colleagues undertook trips as far as Moscow and Leningrad in order to buy bread there which they brought along in suitcases back to their families, and in this manner they were able to save their families from starvation.

Mr. McTigue: Did you personally feel the effects of this terrible famine?

Mr. Lawrynenko: I lived in the capital, and personally I felt it to a lesser extent than people in smaller cities felt it. There were many times when I went hungry.

Mr. McTigue: Why do you think, Mr. Lawrynenko, that the Russians staged this terrible famine of grain in a year when crops were plentiful?....

Mr. Lawrynenko: The famine was organized in order to break the opposition which the Ukrainians were displaying to the policy of colonial exploitation of the Ukraine by the Russians from Moscow.

There was a double blow delivered against Ukraine, one against the basic population element of the Ukraine which is the agricultural element of the peasants. The other was against the educated people of the Ukraine, that is, the intelligentsia.

According to my personal observations I have come to the conclusion that during the period of the famine at least 6 million people died in the Ukraine as a result of it, and about 80 percent of the Ukrainian intelligentsia, that is, the classes of the Ukrainian leadership, also perished during this period....

I myself was arrested and declared a bourgeois nationalist, an enemy of the people, merely because of the fact that as a student in the course of intellectual discussions I defended the position that the Ukrainians formed a part of the Western European culture and that therefore Ukraine is alien to Russian culture which the Moscow rulers were attempting to impose upon Ukraine....

Mr. Feighan: Are the Ukrainians called bourgeois nationalists because they are patriotic and they love their country and their culture, and because they have a national spirit? Also, because they want to have a country with their own sovereignty and independence and also because they oppose Russian imperialism?

Mr. Lawrynenko: Yes; absolutely. For example, in the year 1933 such was the method of terror applied against the Ukrainians that merely the persistent use of the Ukrainian language was sufficient reason to be classified as a bourgeois nationalist.

Mr. Feighan: Bourgeois nationalism then is a very common crime, a most common crime in Ukraine?

Mr. Lawrynenko: Every day and every hour the term "bourgeois nationalist" is on every page of every newspaper, and at every meeting that term is employed to castigate those with whom the ruling class is dissatisfied. But this term "bourgeois nationalist" is applied only to Ukrainians, Byelorussians, Caucasians, and other non-Russian nationalities. During the whole time that I was in the Soviet Union I never heard the term "bourgeois nationalist" applied to Russians, ethnic Russians. There are all shades of bourgeois nationalists, Ukrainians, Byelorussians, Caucasians, but there does not exist a Russian bourgeois nationalism....

Mr. Feighan: Mr. Lawrynenko, were you in Kharkov during the time of the manmade famine, when Edouard Herriot, the French diplomat, came to make an investigation?

Mr. Lawrynenko: In the summer of 1933 Edouard Herriot arrived at the Kharkiv Airport.

Mr. McTigue: In an airplane?

Mr. Lawrynenko: Yes. The route which M. Edouard Herriot was supposed to take from the airport to downtown Kharkov was especially prepared for that occasion. Buildings and fences were painted, the many corpses that had been lying in the streets, the people who had died from starvation, were removed, and the whole place was especially staged for the trip which he was to take through the city.

Edouard Herriot in an interview declared that the Ukraine was a most prosperous and flowering country, and this was one of the most horrible personal blows that I had ever experienced because I knew that this was far from the truth.

Mr. Feighan: Was this the same year in which over 6 million Ukrainians died because of the forced famine?

Mr. Lawrynenko: The same year. This was the same year when 6 million people died of starvation. That is why it was so difficult for me to reconcile the statement made by Herriot with the real conditions then prevailing.

Vira P-ko, "It Happened in 1933"

In *The Black Deeds of the Kremlin* (1953–55). Excerpts, vol. 2, pp. 641–44.

Then began the most difficult time of our student days. It is with great sorrow that I recall this harrowing period of famine in the Ukraine.

On the farm to which we were sent there had been quite a number of workers, but only a third of them were still alive. The following was a daily occurrence: In the morning, bullock-carts full of yet-living people were transported to work. Some were so dried up, only the eyes glittered as a sign of life; their arms were skinny and long, their legs likewise, their noses protruded, their clothing was tattered, they were unkempt, unwashed, the men unshaven, their eyes avid with hunger. Others were distended, their arms and legs like logs, their bellies huge; their legs were particularly horrible. When they moved them the skin cracked, a fluid seeped out, the sunlight caused festering sores to form, on which flies alighted and soon larvae developed.

So they proceeded, transporting both the lean and the swollen to work, and in the evening the bullock-carts would collect two-thirds of them from the fields and take them to the previously prepared "fraternal" graves; sometimes even those still living were picked up and buried. It was rare for members of the family to come to claim their dead; they, too, were deep in the clutches of starvation.

Like hungry wolves lying in wait for their prey, the workers of the State Farm lay in wait for the assorted kitchen refuse which was thrown or poured out beside the students' mess, and indeed, there was not much to be thrown out, except potatoes or beet peelings or some smelly bone. They precipitated themselves in a heap at these leavings, retrieving them from the pit, in which everything was in a state of decay and larvae flourished. The poor hungry people, having lost all feelings of disgust, ate all that they could lay their hands on and died of stomach ailments in the bushes close by.

Once I happened to be a witness to such a ghastly, unheard-of occurrence. Not far from the students' quarters lay the latrine. After lectures, during our dinner-hour, my friends and I often used to see someone who always, in the greatest heat of the summer day, used to wander in that filth, seeking something and putting it in his mouth. What could he possibly find there, we often wondered? A feeling of dread and horror assailed us. How could we prevent this abomination? Even though we ourselves had nothing to spare, receiving, on the completion of our quotas, 200–300 grams of incompletely baked bread, we resolved to save this individual.

We approached in a group and observed the following: Out of the human offal the man was picking cherry stones, apple and pear seeds, and other such things which became visible after the sun dried out the vile stuff in which they were embedded. We were seized by an unheard-of horror. How should we approach this person, who was perhaps mentally deranged? He might attack us. A burning pain enveloped us, our hands and feet trembled, ants crawled up and down our spines. Then one of the boldest, Larissa M—h, approached to a certain distance and shouted, "Come to us. We have bread!" The figure straightened out and began to flee but our group blocked the way. The man halted. It is difficult to describe that frenzied expression in his eyes, which gazed with complete sanity out of the skeleton-features.

Without questioning him at all, we put down the pieces of dry bread which we had earlier prepared for him, and shouted to him to come again to this place at the same time the next day. We did not expect to see him the following day, for we doubted whether he had understood us, but he did come; we again gave him some bread and some clothing, having made a collection among the students. On leaving him we told him to wash and put on the clean clothing. We were curious to know whether the man had understood us and whether he would obey. On the third day we were all there again. A shocking scene ensued. This time we approached closer with the bread. Before us stood a clean young person, who, even in that old clothing, looked almost normal. Gently swaying with exhaustion, he approached us, stretching out his hand toward the bread when suddenly he swayed backwards, his large protruding eyes assumed a frightfully death-like appearance, he fell backwards and died in a convulsive fit.

Later we discovered that this was Vasil [Vasyl] Kuchma from the village of Babanka, whose starving wife had killed and eaten their five-year-old daughter. He had been working at the State Farm, saving every last crumb and bringing it home to save his beloved daughter from a hungry death. Heavy labor and hunger compelled him to seek additional means of subsistence. He went out into the harvested fields to glean ears of grain and was arrested the next day, but, strangely enough, was not sentenced. They kept him in prison for a week, beat him, then set him free. It was obvious that his end was near.

After returning from prison he noticed that his little Marika was not at home. He asked his wife where she was. The wife replied that she had taken her to her mother's at Talne, in the hope that she might escape starvation there. He believed her and was glad that his daughter would be safe. He sustained himself by cooking chaff, burdocks, and other weeds. However, uncertain thoughts tormented him. Was Marika really at his wife's mother's? Or was she elsewhere? Sometimes, on returning home with some sort of food for himself and wife, he smelled the odor of meat. He searched but found nothing. However, once when he came home he discovered a horrifying sight. In the middle of the floor lay his deranged wife, dead, tightly clasping the severed head of her child. He crossed the threshold and collapsed. He was found, still alive, by some people. In a confused state he left his home, whereupon the fate already known to the reader overtook him.

It might also be in order to mention here certain facts concerning the students. Twenty-five of them died at this time, unable to bear the hunger and excessively hard labor.

I. Hannych, "The Living Grave"

In *The Black Deeds of the Kremlin* (1953–55). Excerpts, vol. 2, pp. 585–87.

This event occurred during the peak of the famine in 1933, in the village of Mykailiwka [Mykhailivka], Neforoshchanske district, Poltava region. A farmer named Marko Klymenko lived in this village. He was not very poor, but neither was he rich. He had a horse, a cow, a few simple farm implements and a nice orchard and vegetable garden beside the house. But his most valuable possession was a beautiful tract of land, twelve acres of highly fertile black loam.

With the beginning of collectivization the whole countryside was infested with Russian Communist workers and "25-thousanders," armed with pistols and unlimited power to crucify Ukrainian farmers. No sooner was the threshing completed than the Komsomol [Communist Youth League] shock brigade, under the leadership of a "25-thousander," appeared in the village under the grain-collecting plan, diligently searching out and seizing every kernel of grain. The grain poured in a steady stream into the railroad stations and thence on to Moscow.

Those who had refrained from joining the collective farms were branded as kurkuls [well-to-do peasants]. And this is what happened to Marko Klymenko. Several times he had been summoned by Urbanov, who beat him with his pistol and demanded his signature on the application form, but Marko withstood the brutality and refused to sign. Then Urbanov ordered the grain-collecting commission to seize all the grain Marko had and even the buckwheat, millet and potatoes. Again they pressed him to join the collective farm, threatening him with deportation if he refused, and again he remained resolute.

Then he was declared a kurkul and dispossessed of all his property. The livestock and machinery were appropriated by the collective farm and everything else by the government. He was arrested and sentenced to Siberia with about ten others. As he was taken away he resisted strongly, and the GPU beat him so badly that he could not stand on his feet. Every inch of his body was bruised and covered with blood. In this condition he was taken to the district prison, while his wife and three children were left without even a crust of bread in the cold, empty house.

The deliberate appropriation of grain by the Soviet government soon brought the inevitable results. In the first months of 1933 people ate mice, oil-cake, bark and almost everything imaginable. By spring hundreds were swollen from starvation. Dead bodies littered the streets and market places, ignored by everyone. Soon, though, an order was issued that all the dead must be promptly buried because the decay was causing disease which threatened the GPU, "25-thousanders" and other Communist officials. Because none of the farmers were fit to dig graves, Urbanov called a GPU detachment from the district headquarters for this task. They dug a huge pit where once every three days dead bodies were dumped, after being collected by the village active [*aktiv*, Party activists] and Komsomol group, and covered with a thin layer of earth.

Urbanov himself took an active part in the burial. He distinguished himself by throwing into the pit people who, though they were motionless, were still living, and burying them. This happened when one day he came to the home of Marko Klymenko and found his wife and three children lying on the floor, swollen and unable to move from starvation. Urbanov ordered them to be taken to the pit and buried. When some of his commission members protested that it did not seem right to bury people who were still alive, Urbanov answered that it made no difference, that today or tomorrow they would die and have to be buried anyway.

When the woman and the children were brought to the edge of the pit, she seemed to realize what was about to happen. Summoning all her remaining strength and raising her head, she spoke in a pleading voice: "Please do not bury us. We are still alive and, God willing, we may yet get well again."

In answer Urbanov kicked her on the chin with his heavy boot and with the words, "You did not want to join the collective farm, so now you die," he threw her and the children into the almost full grave and buried them.

That is why this grave was called the "living grave" by the people.

Miron Dolot, *Execution by Hunger: The Hidden Holocaust*

(New York and London: W. W. Norton, 1985). Excerpts, pp. 203–8.

Miron Dolot (pen name of Simon Starow, 1916–98) was born in a village of Cherkasy oblast. After World War II he settled in the United States and worked as a language teacher in California. He was the author of *Who Killed Them and Why?* (1984) and of articles and brochures about the famine published in Switzerland and Germany. He wrote this memoir in the 1950s.

I cannot find the words to describe what my eyes saw in the spring of 1933, but since those awesome memories still haunt me, I shall endeavor to convey my recollections of the sufferings and deaths of my fellow Ukrainians.

World War II was a reality, and I was a part of it. I saw the multitude of dead and mutilated bodies; I heard the cries of despair, and the moans of agony all around me. Day after day, I felt cold and hunger. I was constantly in fear of death. But all of that is now seen through the mist of time. In the haziness of those memories, I see a dim spark of light. This spark is the recognition that those sufferings were caused by war, that I and others at that time had a chance to fight for our lives, to defend ourselves no matter how slim those chances might be. Above all, I realized that while fighting in the war, I had not been completely abandoned. The military was always there with daily food rations, no matter how deficient in quantity and quality. We were also clothed (after a fashion), and barracks as such for sleep when possible were provided. The sufferings of war pale in comparison with the events in our village, all of which remain in my memory as absolute in horror.

Those of us who were still alive harbored a secret and final hope that the coming of the spring of 1933 would bring us some relief. We thought that the new vegetation would help us live through the long months of waiting for the new bread. Nourished by this hope, we were able to carry on until we saw the first signs of green. Sadly, however, many of the villagers were no longer alive by the time the long-awaited spring finally arrived. And many of those who lived long enough to see the passing of winter found their death in the very vegetables and grasses they were so hopefully and patiently awaiting.

That spring of 1933 in Ukraine was unusually cold. In our region, the spring weather usually set in around the beginning of April. The snow would melt quickly, and the green blanket of vegetation would immediately appear in its place. But in 1933, snow was still visible everywhere in mid-April. An icy-cold wind blew continually. It would often bring heavy clouds of rain or snow, or both, and the village would sink deep into mud and slush again. Then a freeze would turn all that into knobs of dirty ice.

Starvation in our village now reached a point at which death was a desirable relief. Many houses around us had already been standing for a long time with no signs of life. As the snow slowly melted away, human corpses were exposed to view everywhere: in backyards, on roads, in fields. Those dead bodies constituted a pathetic problem for the living. As the weather warmed, they started to thaw and decay. The stench which resulted plagued us, and we could do nothing about it. The villagers who survived were unable to bury the dead, and no one from the outside seemed in a hurry to do it, so the bodies were just left wherever they happened to die. Those in the fields or in the forest fell prey to wild animals; those in their homes became the prey of countless rats.

For the third time, the village was stricken with panic. Those who were fortunate enough to remain alive were in the depths of despair. The resources they possessed had been used up long ago. They all finally had to face the shocking truth that there was nothing to eat, and no hope of getting any help: that death from starvation was their imminent fate.

Most of these desperate villagers reconciled themselves to this fact. They stayed at home, and their conditions were indescribable. They were unkempt and haggard, and so weak that they could hardly drag one foot after the other. They just sat, or lay down silently, too feeble even to talk.

The bodies of some were reduced to skeletons, with their skin hanging grayish-yellow and loose over their bones. Their faces looked like rubber masks with large, bulging, immobile eyes. Their necks seemed to have shrunk into their shoulders. The look in their eyes was glassy, heralding their approaching death.

The bodies of others were swollen, a final stage of starvation. Their faces, arms, legs and stomachs resembled the surfaces of plastic balloons. The tissues would soon crack and burst, resulting in the fast deterioration of their bodies.

The thaw brought with it a new wave of beggars. Those who still had strength enough to move left their dwellings and took off in search of food. Old and young, mostly women and children, slowly moved from house to house dragging their rag-covered feet. They pleaded for food: a potato, or a piece of bread, or at least a kernel—a single kernel!—of corn. At the onset of the famine, I remember how the emaciated would come to the doorstep, often sobbing, and would ask for some spare food. If refused, they would excuse themselves politely and go away, apologizing for bothering us.

But this spring's beggars presented an entirely different picture. These desperate people, numbed by cruelty and injustice as well as hunger, were no longer the modest, honorable small farmers they had been before. Their fear of starvation was so great that they lost all semblance of self-control, becoming more like wild, hungry beasts in their search for food. They no longer distinguished friends from enemies and were ready to commit even murder for a mere scrap. Their clothes had long ago turned to rags, and they themselves were worn out and exhausted to the point of collapse.

With protruding frightened eyes and outstretched hands, they would approach someone, but this time they did not plead: they were voiceless; they just cried. Often their heavy tears were mixed with fluid slowly oozing out of the cracks in their swollen faces. They whispered and begged for a crumb of bread.

Another sign of almost imminent death from starvation was the body lice, those small, flat, wingless, parasitic insects who were the constant companions of the wretched and impoverished. The starving villagers were no longer able to take care of their sanitary needs, nor had they the strength to fetch water, let alone heat it in order to bathe themselves, or wash their clothes and their bedding. Those who still had strength could do some washing, but not properly because they had no soap. For a few years now, not a single bar of soap had been seen in the village. But, even if soap had been available, we could not buy it. First, we had no money; second, we were prohibited from buying any merchandise in the stores as our grain quotas had not been met. As a result, all of us were dirty and infected with lice.

As the limbs of a starving person turn cold with the approach of death, the lice begin to migrate to the warmer facial areas such as the eye sockets, ears, mouth corners, and nostrils. When this happened, it was an unmistakable sign that the starving person's sufferings would soon come to an end.

The plight of the children was one of the most heartbreaking experiences for me during that time, and their pathetic faces, parched or swollen, and streaked with tears, will remain in my memory forever.

They could not understand why they couldn't get a piece of bread or something else to eat. They were not able to comprehend what was going on in their own small world. Thinking of them still makes me tremble with horror. God is my witness that as I write these words, the paper is wet with my tears.

Not many children in our neighborhood had survived the terrible winter, but those who had were reduced to mere skeletons, too weak to cry. The heads on their small thin necks looked like inflated balloons. Their small bony arms and legs were like sticks protruding from their little bodies. Their stomachs were bloated to unusual proportions, and water flowed uninterruptedly from their genitals. Those childish faces looked prematurely aged and twisted. They resembled old folks: wrinkled, listless, and very, very sad. At their stage of starvation, they were in a constant stupor which is peculiar to those who suffer from extreme hunger. It seemed as if nature itself had conspired with the Communist regime to add a final touch of pathos and horror to the sufferings the children had to endure. Hair had started to grow on the faces of some, mainly on their foreheads and temples. I saw a few such children and they looked so strange to me—like creatures from another planet, and they left me with a feeling of helplessness and doom.

Often starvation would sweep away an entire family. The adult members would die first, leaving the children alone in a cold house, half-naked and hungry, to fend for themselves. One can imagine what happened to such hopeless children: these orphans, scantily clad and feet wrapped in rags, joined the rest of the beggars. Struggling in the snow, they would first go to their nearest neighbors only to find that they too were dead. Then they would go to another house and yet another farther away. Compassionate villagers who were still alive would let a child or two stay with them only to watch them slowly die.

Yet miraculously, some children managed to survive. These were mostly boys and girls between ten and fifteen years of age. With the coming of spring, they saw their chances of survival in terms of leaving home, and going to the city. A few, but *very* few, children managed to do just that and were fortunate in finding help and understanding from some of the urban dwellers. Others, less fortunate, were picked up by the militia and locked up in the Children's Detention Home. These children had a better chance of surviving the famine, although we heard that many of them also died. And then, there were those whose fate it was to join the ranks of the city's juvenile criminals. God alone knows what happened to them. Finally, there were those who neither reached the city nor were picked up by the militia. They lay dead wherever they had fallen for days or even weeks, until someone would drag them out of sight into some ditch like a dead animal.

I saw many tragic events in which children were the innocent victims, but one episode in particular emerges from my memories of that spring as a symbol of humanity gone completely mad. It was sometime at the onset of April. One early morning while we still lay in our beds, we heard a child's cry and a weak knocking on the door. I was the first to jump out of bed. As I opened the door, I saw a small girl of about four. She stood trembling from the cold and exhaustion with streams of tears flowing down her famished little cheeks. We knew her! It was Maria, the daughter of our neighbor Hana, who also had a seven-year-old son and lived about half a mile from us. Hana's husband, a young and industrious farmer, had been arrested like many others, for no apparent reason, and exiled somewhere to a concentration camp about two years before. Hana was left alone with her two children to struggle for food, like all the rest of us. However, as winter came and starvation struck us, we lost track of her.

I let the child into the house.

"My mommy won't wake up!" the child announced, wiping away the tears with the sleeve of her dirty coat.

Mother and I glanced at each other. A short while later, my brother Mykola and I were on our way to Hana's home. When we entered the house, our fears were confirmed. Hana was dead, lying on her back on the sleeping bench. Her bulging glassy eyes seemed to be looking at us. Her widely opened mouth still seemed to be gasping for air. We could see that she had met her death not too long before Maria had knocked on our front door. On Hana's cheek we could still see the traces of her tears; we could also see the lice moving back and forth like ants, in search of a warm spot. Next to her, wrapped in some cloth, lay her dead son. The one-room house was empty and dirty. There was no furniture except for two benches, and no trace of food. The mud floor had been dug up all over, and there were holes in the walls. The chimneys of the cooking and heating stoves were totally ruined. We recognized immediately the work of the Bread Procurement Commission. There was no doubt that they had been there recently, searching for "hidden" foodstuffs.

Mykola and I stood there aghast. I felt the impulse either to run away screaming, or to sit down next to their dead bodies and hold their cold hand in mine in sorrow and sympathy, but I did neither. I just stood there petrified, and looking at the dead mother and her young son, I asked the question:

"Why? Why did they have to die?"

We left the bodies in the house hoping that soon the kolhosp [collective farm] burial brigade would pick them up on their daily search for bodies. This brigade was set up about two months before for the purpose of collecting and burying the corpses of the starved villagers.

Little Maria survived the famine. She stayed with us for a while until her relatives, who lived in one of the cities, took her into their family.

Anastasiia Lysyvets, *Spomyny* (Memoirs)

(Kyiv: K.I.S., 2008). Excerpts, pp. 28–30. Translated by Alexander J. Motyl.

Anastasiia Ivanivna Lysyvets (1922–2011) was born into a peasant family in the village of Berezan, Kyiv oblast. She lost her parents, sister, and brother in the Holodomor. During World War II she was taken to Germany for forced labor. After returning to Ukraine, she received a degree in philology from Kyiv State University and then worked as a schoolteacher in the village of Kuianivka, Sumy oblast. This memoir was written in the 1970s.

Father died at night, before daybreak. Mother's screaming and weeping woke up Halka and us and drove us off the oven. We jumped up and looked at our dead father. Mother ordered us to kiss Father's head and hands. We kissed them, trembling with fear and grief... The neighbors brought what they could, as we had nothing of our own; out of respect for Father, our relatives and neighbors wanted to bury him according to custom....

Everyone saw that famine was approaching; that this spring would be terrible. Grandfather Nykypor sold a cow in order to pay the tax and buy grain. Uncle Lavrentii placed his hopes on the hospital, where he was often called to do various things, and for which he accepted payment only in food. He also had a cow. At Uncle Mykhailo's they were waiting for a cow to give birth to a calf before Easter. Uncle Petro had no expectations, for things were no better with him than with us. Besides, his wife took absolutely no pity on him. Uncle Petro knew that when death by starvation came to his family, he would have to die first, then his mother-in-law, and then his elder daughter, since his wife looked after his younger daughter and herself. Everyone saw this but remained quiet, as they could do nothing about it. There was nothing to eat. Yudykha, the Hopkal family, Lazar Lysyvets, and many other people, both non-collective farmers and collective farmers, also had nothing to eat. Everyone prayed and concealed a hope known only to him in the depths of his soul....

The second day after Father's funeral, everyone started to go away. Everyone told Mother to take care of herself above all, not to kill herself with grief, for that was the only way she could somehow save her children from death by starvation. Some suggested she go to the head of the collective farm, Semen Kozatsky, and ask to be admitted to the collective farm.

Grandfather Nykypor and Aunt Motria were stubbornly quiet and waited until everyone had gone home. But even then a terrible silence hung over the house. Finally, Mother asked Grandfather Nykypor and my aunt:

"Papa, Motria, can you help me somehow?"

"Just how? How can we help you? We have no bread, no cow; we'll give you three or four small buckets of potatoes. We don't know ourselves whether we'll survive the spring. We've placed our hope in God and Dunka and Palazhka. Let them go and find a job for some bread. If they don't, we'll die... We still won't go into the collective farm, but you, daughter, do as you wish... Go to Mykhailo for help..."

"What, Papa—to Mykhailo? Everyone's going to him for help, but he can't save everybody. And then there are Maria's relatives; they're all starving, all looking to be saved... I thought that maybe you would take in at least one of my children and save him. And if Mykhailo also took one, I'd somehow manage with two..."

Grandfather was silent, as was my aunt. And Mother spoke again: "Why are you silent? I'm asking you. Will you take one of my children? At least one... Whichever one you like..."

"No, we won't. If they die with you, Oksana, no one will say anything... Even God will not say anything... But if they die with us, then all the people will talk, as will God... We can't take a child, daughter... If we get a slice of bread or some potatoes, we'll share, and if we don't, then all of us will die, if God wills it."

Grandfather Nykypor crossed himself and again began to read the psalms. We prayed for the repose of the soul of God's servant Ivan, for the heavenly kingdom. Soon an oppressive gloom and a horrible silence descended on the house, which smelled of incense, wax, oil, smoke, and hunger...

When I recall my relatives today and analyze their actions, their characters, and their words, I cannot say who of them was better and who worse. They all sympathized with us and shared our grief. Everyone wanted to live, and no one wanted to go to the grave in place of another. Who wants to go to the grave for anyone, even the person closest to you? Only a mother could do that for a child, and not always even then. Everyone looked after himself; everyone wanted to survive the hard times. There began a terrible struggle for existence and salvation from death by starvation. It was like this all over Ukraine, in the villages and towns, within families, between unrelated and related families, between friends and acquaintances, between old and young. It was a terrible year of struggling against death and for a chance to breathe the air, walk the earth, see the sun and sky, speak to people, and see people—and yourself among them.

Pavlo Makohon, *Svidok. Spohady pro Holod 33-ho roku* (Witness: Memoirs of the Famine of 1933 in Ukraine*)*

(Toronto: Anabasis Magazine, 1983). Excerpts, pp. 20–21. Translated by Alexander J. Motyl.

...Our village was becoming increasingly emptier because some of the peasants had been "dekulakized" and transported to Siberia, while others had abandoned everything and fled at night so as to avoid Siberia. The remaining peasants were forced to join the collective farm. The activists had taken the bread from all the houses. Horrible times were approaching, as there was nothing to eat. Famine had begun. Winter was approaching. Our house became sad because all of us were hungry. Father tried everything possible to find something to eat, but his attempts produced almost nothing. I, too, ran about wherever I could, looking for food. People began to swell up. In a short time the famished people had eaten all the village's dogs, cats, hedgehogs, and birds. I, too, would bring hedgehogs home—I even caught somebody's dog—and we cooked and ate them.

Afterwards, the horses also began to die of hunger in the collective farmyards. Everybody, including me, fell upon the dead horses, but the authorities did not want the people to eat them and dug pits. They poured carbolic acid on the dead meat and threw it into the pits so as not to give it to the people. But the people did not care; they dug up the pits, and everyone cut off a piece of meat. They were not afraid of the carbolic acid, for starving people have no fear.

Freezing winter came, and total famine set in. People began to die of hunger. All of us were already swollen. The first to die in our house was my mother's mother, while the others were barely able to move. A rumor spread throughout the village that some woman in the fifth brigade had eaten her two children, but that rumor was quickly hushed up. Then the district militia arrived and closed the case, so that I do not know exactly what happened. But famine encompassed the whole village, and people began to die en masse. The authorities sent the stronger men to the cemetery, where they dug mass pits, while special wagons went from house to house, collecting dead people and taking them to the cemetery. All of them were thrown into one pit without coffins, and when it was full, they dug another one.

Many people tried to leave the village to find something to eat, but they died along the way, as they had no strength to go farther. The village became sad.

I was still able to move a bit and was therefore able to walk and see everything that happened. When evening or night approached, there was no one to be seen in the village any more. A hungry deathliness reigned, and it was terrible to walk through one's own village, for there was no longer any voice—either that of a dog, or a cat, or a human. I saw it all and mulled over all those horrors. I concluded that my days were also numbered. But our family was saved from death for some time by the fact that our father had managed to hide some bread from those who were searching it out, and we could therefore live a little longer than the others.

But a sad and tragic time also came for our family and our house. I saw my brothers die of famine—a famine artificially created by Moscow in order to break the Ukrainian people and use death by hunger to drive it into collective farms.

"Testimony of Mr. Ivan Kasiianenko of Los Angeles, California"

In *Second Interim Report* (1988). Excerpts, pp. 10–12.

In 1932 the harvest was a normal one. It was brought in before anyone suspected what was to happen. It was winter when they came in to take the grain that had already been ground into flour and was sorted in bags. They came and seized all of this grain, not only from us but from all the villagers. And ours was a large village—6,000 people lived there.

The sound of crying was everywhere. Those who seized the grain carried out their orders without mercy. I remember as if it were yesterday how a man ran away, leaving behind a wife and three children. They took absolutely everything: cows, pigs, everything. There was nothing left for the wife to do. She sent her children away to fend for themselves, set fire to the house, and hanged herself.

Things were a little different in my family. My father was always on the run during the day and would only come at night. We had nothing; they had taken everything from us. They came with their pikes, poked around, asked questions, and grabbed my mother by the hair. They tore off my mother's earrings and her cross. We children cried, but nothing helped. No one paid any attention to our tears.

They locked our mother in the basement. So there we were, five of us children with me the oldest, and our father nowhere to be found. They came back to see if they had missed anything and found one egg that had not been taken. They took it away.

Father would sometimes be able to bring us a little flour, sometimes a little grain, anything that had not been seized. But protecting the food was impossible because our house was under constant surveillance, and he could not get to us every night. They took everything, even our clothes. We did not even have a blanket. We were poor as church mice. We huddled together at night to keep warm.

After two weeks they let mother out of the basement. But what could she do when there was nothing to eat? In March or April, 1933, they took our cow. The first to die was my youngest sister, then another sister. Then my brother and a third sister died at the same time. Father died and was buried on Holy Thursday. Mother died two days later, and they threw her in a hole on Easter Sunday. I remember how a neighbor came and comforted me, saying that although my parents had gone, they had died on holy days, Holy Thursday and Easter. It was a terrible time for me. I was starving myself to such an extent that I could not walk. Before he died, my father had asked one of the teachers to take me under his wing. I was only in the first grade at the time, and it was only thanks to this teacher that I survived. He took me to a hospital. I don't remember who the doctor was or anything about the place. I only remember that my skin was shiny and transparent like glass. The doctor cut me open in several places and let the liquid under my skin run out. It smelled like dead flesh. When I left the hospital, I had no strength to walk and sat in the sun. The teacher picked me up and saved my life. But many who had owned everything they needed now died like flies.

It was hard. While still swollen, I would go to the point to catch fish and frogs. I tore them up and ate them raw.

After my family died, I lived alone in the empty house until the same teacher came and took me to live with him. Usually, people took no interest in small children. Typhus was very widespread then. But whether they were sick or starving, they would be put on open trucks like sheaves of wheat and taken away. The people who took the children said that they were being driven to a hospital, but none of these children were ever seen or heard from again.

A horrifying silence settled over the village. I can still remember going to my neighbors' houses to see if anyone was alive. I remember going into one house and seeing the blind son sitting in one corner. His skin was grey. He had been dead perhaps a week or two. And he wasn't the only one. Starving people on the verge of death, sometimes even mothers, sometimes lost their sanity and turned into animals who smothered their own children and ate them. It happened, for example, to one of my acquaintances. His name was Ivan Ostapenko. His mother put a noose around his neck and tried to strangle him, but he was stronger than she was and managed to break her hold. But he kept the marks the rope left on his throat for a long time.

I went to another neighbor's house. They were young people. I looked in the window and saw the mother and father lying dead on the floor. Their infant son was lying in the middle, still alive, and sucking its mother's dry breast. I took him to a retention place for such children, and he was saved. As long as I stayed in the village, he was like a brother to me, and I watched over him. When they took us to the orphanage, we went together. Children whose parents had died of starvation were not treated well. They were not allowed to light the stove to keep warm or to wear warm clothing. We were told that we were parasites, capitalists, vestiges of the *kulaks* [well-to-do peasants] and exploiting classes.

These weren't orphanages; they were houses of torture. The children had nothing to eat. It was impossible to keep clean. We were literally eaten by lice. But nobody cared. We were the progeny of the defeated class enemy.

"Testimony of Mr. Mykola Kostyrko of Sacramento, California"

In *Second Interim Report* (1988). Excerpts, pp. 6–8.

The famine started—that is, when they took away all the meager reserves from the Ukrainian peasants. Those who had some clothing or other articles came to the city, to the market, to sell it and buy bread. But bread was sold by ration cards. A black market emerged, and the high prices did nothing to resolve the hunger problem. Starving, ragged peasants staggered through the city. On the streets, especially on the outskirts of town, lay the bodies of those who died of starvation.

The government did all it could to make sure no one saw this, because many foreign vessels came to Odessa's ports to take the "surplus" Ukrainian grain and other merchandise abroad. They exported everything in order to get foreign capital for the "needs of the state"—to buy tractors and for propaganda abroad, among other things. The city "cleaned up" the corpses every morning. A special club was created for foreign sailors to prevent them from going into the city and seeing what they could not have missed. At the club they were entertained and distracted, even with girls.

I also had the opportunity to witness the "show of prosperity" staged to pull the wool over the eyes of the French minister [Edouard] Herriot, who was invited to the Ukraine to convince him that there was no famine. (He was undoubtedly convinced when he received a number of rare paintings from museums.) As proof that life was absolutely normal, they escorted him along streets that had been especially prepared for him. Police were stationed around these streets and did not admit people who were poorly dressed or had shabby-looking vehicles. I walked along the main street and was amazed to see that the storefront windows were full of all sorts of merchandise. In those days all the stores were empty, and one could buy only poor quality cheesecakes and tooth powder. I went into one store where I knew the sales clerk and asked if I could buy something. He told me that nothing was for sale. For what, then? Maybe they were filming a movie...

At that time, there were only a few personal cars in the city. They belonged to the government and were used by big party bosses. These automobiles were cruising back and forth to create the impression that our streets were as busy as any abroad. A few weeks later I learned that this had been a sham, a stage play of "the good life," especially arranged for a few hours for Mr. Herriot's visit. This spectacle had a historical precedent—the "Potemkin village" of Catherine the Great's time.

If the villages were condemned to die of starvation, then the city was half starved. The retail stores were empty. Rationed bread was doled out in meager doses. Only heavy laborers got one kilogram per day. Civil servants got 400 grams, and dependents received from one to two hundred grams. That bread, black as earth, moldy with all sorts of additives, was the staple food.

Many in the city died of starvation. They were old, single pensioners. They received a very small pension—thirty rubles per month—on which one could live maybe one or two days. The state started selling the so-called "commercial bread" at forty rubles for two-and-one-half pounds.

The "dekulakization" [expropriation of kulak property] of the urban population progressed hand-in-hand with that of the village. The only difference (between the city and the village) was that the city dwellers were allowed to hang on to their lives, while the peasants were put to death by this criminally organized starvation....

I witnessed yet another tragic phenomenon. Starving mothers brought their children into the city and left them on the streets, hoping that they would be saved if someone picked them up. There was a pediatric clinic not far from the place where I lived. On my way to work I passed by this clinic. During the famine I saw small children at the gate of this clinic. When the famine first started, there were five or six children there each day, but with each day more children appeared. They looked horrible. They sat on the ground, emaciated, with strained, suffering faces. Many of them were bleeding from their intestines. Heartsick women from the local area knocked at the gate, shouting at the clinic to take these children. But the medical personnel were in no hurry to do this. But, when I returned home from work, these children would be gone. They took them in after all. On subsequent days, the scene was the same, and the number of abandoned children increased.

A sort of defensive protection was organized around the children. No one gave them bread or anything to eat, because, in the state these poor children were in, it was understood that this could kill them. And the bread at the time was of such poor quality that it was harmful, even for adults.

In those days I had to go for a short time to Kharkiv, then the capital of the Ukraine. A conference of all the high-ranking employees of the industrial cooperatives was being held. As I noted, all craftsmen were forced into collectives also, just like the peasants. The "commercial bread" was already on the market at that time, at very high prices. There were enormous lines for it. The starving peasants tried to stand in the lines, but they were not allowed. I heard from the locals that the police took the living, the half-dead and the dead together out of the city in freight trucks and threw them into the snow.

F. P. Burtiansky, "The Famine: A Pogrom of the Ukrainian Peasantry"

In *The Great Famine in Ukraine, 1932–33* (1988), pp. 96–101. Excerpts.
Online at Memoirs of the Famine, http://faminegenocide.com/resources/memoirs/pogrom1.html.

My family lived in Selevyna, a village in the Odessa province. It consisted of about two hundred households and was considered prosperous. During the struggle for national liberation, during the rule of the Ukrainian People's Republic, my father was chosen the (assistant) vice county chief of Lovshyn. When Ukraine lost the war with the Russian communists, and the latter came to power, my father was arrested by the Cheka and summarily shot....

By 1932, virtually all peasants had been inducted into collective farms, and so the grain consignment plans were applied to the latter. In applying the plan to the collective farms, the government dictated that the state quotas were to be satisfied first, and then the needs of the individual collective and its workers dealt with. However, the grain consignment plan was so unrealistic that even entire collective farms were unable to meet them, let alone provide enough for the needs of its members. The cruelty of the Communist Party in its dealings with communized farmers offered no hope for compromise between the two parties. The defenceless collective farm workers were thrown to the mercy of fate, and were thus destined for famine. Nobody stood up for them, and there were no laws that protected the collective farms from such robbery. The Party and the government were like bandits stealing not only grain, but also all food. As a result of this, people managed to find food during the summer, but by fall and early winter, the famine began in earnest. My God. What a terrifying word that is, and how much more of a terrifying sight.

My wife and I had already fled to [the] Donbas to escape the famine. Here I found a job and received my food ration as a worker. These rations saved the three of us from a death by starvation. But not everyone survived: our infant son could not endure, and left us for a better world.

In the spring of 1933, my wife and I both worked in a mine, and we both received food rations. I filed for leave from work because I had decided to visit the village of my brothers and sisters, and to provide my in-laws with some assistance. While still on the train, I wondered at the fact that all of the windows were covered. Later, I found out that these were coverings put in place to prevent anyone from seeing what was going on outside. When I arrived at Zinovievsk (now Kirovohrad) I found a real hell. The station was empty, and all around swollen, starving people begged everyone who had arrived for but one crust of bread. The dead lay in the street—they were only taken away at night. Those who were still moving and those who were already dead were all village people, I could tell by their clothing.

As I passed through the city, I noticed the building of the local government administration. There was a Torgsin (Soviet Foreign Trade) shop on the first floor. I steeled my courage and dared to look inside. Everything you could desire was in that store, but only for gold or silver. This was ostensibly free trade, and yet all communists, higher officials and OGPU operatives benefited from outfitters not open to the public called "zakritie raspredy" (closed outlets).

I went to a bazaar that was located near an alcohol distillery and saw a terrible sight. On one side of the plant, waste and still mash were pouring into the Inhul River. People were falling into this waste, drinking it, and dying slowly. No one made any effort to prevent them from doing this; no one tried saving their lives. On the plant grounds, cisterns full of clean mash stood under armed police guard—intended for feeding pigs and other livestock.

In the bazaar, it was possible to buy bread, but a half kilo piece cost forty to fifty karbovantsi [rubles].

I hurried on my way to the village, and arrived in the evening. Here I had spent my childhood and my tempestuous youth, but I could not recognize the place. It was all in gloom; everything was dead; no dogs barked, no birds chirped, no children shouted. I shuffled through the weed-covered streets until I reached my sister Onila's house. The yard was overgrown with briars, and I was afraid to go into the house: was anyone alive in there? Both my sister and her husband were in fact alive, but they were both emaciated by hunger. They told me what was happening in the village and listed off the people who had already died of hunger. Only those who managed to come to work in the collective farm were surviving, because they could eat in the mess hall, as they did.

I stayed with my sister overnight and then moved on to Reimentarivka, where my in-laws lived. On the way, I passed through the Rozpashka farm. It stood empty. The once luxurious orchards were reduced to stumps overgrown with nettles and brambles, and collapsed houses seemed to stare up at the sky with their crumbling chimneys. People from Redchyna and Zashchyta told me that some of the villagers had been dekulakized and deported somewhere, and those who remained had died of starvation. The last residents of the farm, the father and his two sons, had been imprisoned, apparently for cannibalism.

When I reached Reimentarivka, I went to the village council building to register my arrival. The head of council was a relative of my wife's, Ivan Hudzenko. He related the events of the recent past in the village to me and said that seven hundred people had perished of hunger.

On my way back to [the] Donbas, I stopped in on my sister once again. She told me that in Selevyna over three hundred people had died of hunger. It was only June at the time, two months of waiting until the next harvest.

Vasyl Zaiika [Zaïka], "The Secrets of the Famine (Where the NKVD-OGPU Buried Thousands of Bodies)"

In *The Great Famine in Ukraine, 1932–33* (1988), pp. 86–87. Excerpts. Online at Memoirs of the Famine, http://faminegenocide.com/resources/memoirs/secrets1.html.

During the tragic years of the famine orchestrated by Moscow, I worked in the Donbas region in Mine 4–6 Maksymivka, as a coal quality inspector. My responsibility was to take samples of coal as it was loaded onto freight cars, and send these samples to the laboratory for testing. I then took the results of these tests to the chief inspection bureau.

In terms of work-time, my job was not regulated by norms, because the railyards supplied freight cars both day and night, and I had to appear at the time they arrived, whatever the time of day. The main street in Kadiivka, a town that I walked through each day, was Torhova Street. Virtually all of the administrative and commercial buildings were located on this street. There were various shops, a factory kitchen, a cafeteria for the workers of the "Illich" mine, a restaurant, and, at one end of the street, a bazaar that everyone called the "tolkuchka." During the spring of 1933, famine was raging in the countryside. Peasants were trying to save themselves by escaping to the cities and towns in droves, because there at least some food was being issued by ration card. However, most of the peasants got neither jobs nor food and died in the street.

The chief inspection bureau was located behind a school park across from Torhova Street. Thus, every day I walked along it and saw hundreds of people, emaciated by hunger, as they lolled all swollen on the sidewalks, and saw the dead and dying among them.

One night in May 1933, I was walking to the bureau on business and witnessed how drunken policemen or NKVD (OGPU) [secret police] operatives, aided by some criminal elements (who always seemed to hang around the police), loaded the dead and half-dead onto trucks. The criminals, who were also drunk, paired up, took the bodies by the legs and arms and then threw them onto the trucks as if they were firewood. They always did this at night, in order that local residents not know where the bodies were taken or what was done with them. I too wondered about these secret burials many a time.

Once, also in May 1933, a messenger from the mine came to me at around one or two o'clock in the morning. He was a boy of about sixteen or seventeen, and he told me that the coal was being loaded at the mine. I dressed quickly, and we set out toward it. In order to get there more quickly, we did not pass through the town but cut across a field behind, following a path that led from the Parkom mine, past the no. 31 mine to the Maksymivski mines. There were a number of auxiliary mineshaft exits along the way that were used for ventilation and as emergency outlets in case of collapse of one of the tunnels. These exits, or "shufry" as they were called, were excavated about two hundred to three hundred metres away from the main shaft, and when the coal in the mine was exhausted they were fenced off and then covered over.

The path we followed wound about eight to twelve metres past one of these "shufry" that had fallen into disuse. As we drew nearer to it, we saw a truck pull up. Some NKVD (OGPU) men got out, turned off the light in the truck, rolled back the fences around the exits, and then the criminals began to throw the corpses and the dying into the shafts. We could hear the groans and cries of the unfortunate victims of this wantonness.

We could see the cargo of this "shipment" with complete clarity because the moon came out from behind a bank of clouds and lit up the sight of this unspeakable crime. It was obvious that the NKVD (OGPU) had given the order to use this place as a burial ground: the police would not have dared. When we got to about thirty or forty metres away from the "shufr" a voice from the truck stopped us: "Halt! Who goes there?"

We stopped and a drunken NKVD (OGPU) man came up to us. We could now see his uniform. He drew his gun and said: "Who are you and what are you doing walking around here so late?" I had my certificate of place of work, so I showed it to him, explaining that I was on my way there, and that the boy was a messenger who was sent to me. I also said that we had taken a short cut to the mine to get there more quickly.

"What did you see or hear?" he asked sternly. I played stupid and replied: "We met nobody on the way, and we saw nothing and we heard nothing." All the while, two more NKVD (OGPU) men got off the truck and one of them said: "Maybe you want to go down there too?" and pointed to the "shufr." "I've already been in there," I replied. "I worked in the mine for a couple of years, and now I've got another job."

The NVKD (OGPU) men said nothing in return and turned back to the truck, speaking in Russian, and left two of the criminals standing beside us like guards. I recognized one of them—he was a pickpocket everyone called "Lafa." The NKVD (OGPU) men came back up to us and told us to get on our way to work. Then one of them, apparently the chief, said: "If you breathe a word of this anywhere, one word, about this night, then we'll see that you come back here."

We left, and the two of us promised each other not to tell anyone, any time, not a word. However, rumours were already circulating among the people, because many had seen bodies of those who had died in the famine buried in these "shufry." Mainly the no. 5 Semenivka shaft and the no. 8 Maksymivka shaft were used for this. Later all shafts so used were filled in and razed to the ground. Then they were divided into lots and sold to workers as gardens....

"Survivor Transcript: Victor Tkacz"

In *The Great Famine in Ukraine, 1932–33.*
Online at http://www.theage.com.au/multimedia/ukrainefamine/transcripts/transcript_viktor.pdf.

Mine are a child's experiences, but they are so vivid—the (mental) pictures I have are so vivid they have been with me all the time.

I remember fear. Fear of losing my parents, because I had seen what was happening. There was famine, and there was another disaster—collectivisation, Stalin's idea.

Both my grandfathers were arrested and taken away to Siberia. My father, he was going to be next, he was told. So he ran away to [the] Caucasus. It was freer up there, because the communists had not as much control as they did in our area of Ukraine.

We didn't know where he was. He just ran away, and he couldn't write letters. He used to come home and bring food. We had been put in this category, kulaks [well-to-do peasants], therefore we had to pay what they called contribution, heavy taxes. They come in and they take all the food away.

And this was also where my fear was—there was nothing to eat! Mum had hidden somewhere bags of dried bread. It was dangerous to hide food. She used to bring it into the house little by little.

So it is winter time, and we're still alive. And so they come in and say, "How come (you are still alive)?" And so they search the place again. Father knew we would perish if he didn't help us. He had come in two or three nights before, and there was half a loaf of bread.... They knew it wasn't locally baked, he had brought it from another city, and they immediately recognised it. They said, "Ha! Look what they eat. They are well fed!" And they took the half-loaf, it was the only thing they could find.

Later on, as they were going through the house, someone picked up a cooking pot and in it there were some dry beans hidden away. And they said, "Ah, here it is! Give us the bag. Bring out the bag." And I've got this vivid picture of them throwing the dry beans and they go on the floor as well. To me, that is the food that we cherish, and that was gone.

We were tossed out in the street. It was deep snow. Mum had run away because we got a message they were coming. She had gone to a neighbor's, because they were going to arrest her. She was watching from there.

My grandmother was the only one in the house with us at the time, so we run away and are standing on the other side of the street, watching what is going on in our yard. They are taking everything of ours on their carts—clothes and bedding. And they took grandmother out and shook her out of her coat and into the snow. To me that was a horrible picture.

After this, mum took us to the train. At night, because she knew they were waiting at the station to catch her. She got us on the train, not from the platform side, but from the other side somehow.

I don't know how she did this. She dragged us through the snow, two small boys—my brother was completely in the snow! It was like a cat taking her kittens. Anyway, we had to crawl under a stationary train, then she threw us on to another train that was already moving, and she got on.

The grain stores were all locked up and full of grain, and yet the people were starving. In this same place! The grain was guarded by police or military, with weapons. As a small child, I could roam and see these mountains of grain. People who pinched some, they were sent to Siberia. It was very strict.

You know the cobs, when they take the corn off? Then they use the cobs for fuel for the fires. But we were rubbing them one against the other to get anything at all that was left on these cobs, these husks. Mum used to boil that and give it to us as gruel.

We had to be very careful not to say where we were from. Father spoke very good Russian—undetectable, in fact—but us others, we lived in constant fear of being discovered.

I remember a big panic to run away again, because my father thought he had been recognised by someone who knew him back in Ukraine.

This is the fear in which we lived.

Vladimir Keis, "Moi zhiznennyi put' i zhiznennye perezhivaniia moei molodosti na rodnoi ukrainskoi zemle do 1929 goda i Vtoraia Mirovaia Voina" (My Life and Youthful Experiences in My Native Ukrainian Land up to 1929 and the Second World War)

Unpublished memoir. Excerpts, pp. 6-8. Translated by Alexander J. Motyl.

In 1933 I left the city of Sochi.... I bought a ticket for the express train to Mykytivka. I figured that I would be a welcome guest in my native land and would relate where I had been and what I had seen. I would relate how I had spent my youthful years on my own.

I arrived in Mykytivka, got off the train, and entered the station. There was a large number of people in the building, more than in Sochi. But they looked the same: hungry, cold, and unfortunate. Women were looking for men, while men were looking for women. At that time many people had fled to the Donbas.

One man told me how to get to the No. 19–20 Mine. That evening I found Barracks No. 2, where the miners and their families lived. My family lived on the second floor. I knocked on the door. They said to come in. I walked into the room: there stood my mother. She threw herself at me with the cry: "Where have you been, my son?" Everyone wept for joy. My five-year-old sister, Nadia, and my three-year-old brother were in the room. Mama said that my father would soon arrive from work in the mine. She also said they were very fortunate to have avoided the famine.

Father received one kilogram of bread a day, while Mama and the children received 300 grams. I asked Mama where our Niura, who was then twelve years old, was. Mama said that, when they were separated, Niura stayed with her godmother, my father's sister. Her last name was Zvonar. Mama also said that she had heard that Niura was living with people like them in Krasnyi Lyman. They were living near a bread factory in the barn of a repressed peasant. My father soon came from work and was very happy to see his prodigal son at home.

We all sat down to the table to eat supper. We did not eat as much as we talked. We ate some kind of black herb soup and bread. Mama said we should eat less bread and more soup because there was little bread and much soup. Father spoke of his fate: how the activists had plundered and thrown him out of his home. I spoke of my adventures: of where I had been and what I had seen. I stayed a few days with my parents. We agreed that I would go to find my sister Niura. This was in January 1933. A very cold winter had set in. My mother and father saw me off. I spent the whole night waiting in line for a ticket at the Mykytivka station. I managed to leave for the city of Sloviansk only in the morning. I had frozen and was very hungry.

Mama had given me nothing for the road because they themselves did not have enough food. I arrived in the city of Sloviansk. I very much wanted to eat. I had a little money, but there was nothing to buy. I bought a ticket for the train that took workers to the city of Krasnyi Lyman. I arrived in Krasnyi Lyman late in the evening. I was very cold and decided to spend the night in the station. When I awoke in the morning, I saw that I had fallen ill. Exiting the station, I asked people how to get to the bread factory. They told me which way to go. But I just stood and could not move: I felt ill and was shaking. I thought that I had found death, and not my sister.

Suddenly I saw a young girl approaching me. She came up to me and asked: "Is that you, Volodia?" That is how my sister Niura and I met. Tears flowed from my eyes. When I asked her what she was doing there, Niura said that she was going from house to house of the workers of state security and begging for food. I said that Mother and Father had sent me to find her. She said we should go together and gave me a piece of bread. I did not want to eat, as I had become quite ill. And so it happened that I did not find my sister, but she found me. She took me to the place where she lived. Next to the bread factory stood a house formerly inhabited by a rich peasant. Next to it stood a barn where they kept the sheep.

The dreadful smell of manure was pervasive. We entered the barn. Two old people were sitting inside—a man and a woman. Inside the barn was a small oven with coal burning, as well as three wooden beds on which they slept. After greeting me, the old man with a large beard came up to me and asked me why I had come. I said that my sister had brought me to them. Niura then broke into tears and said that I really was her brother. At that point the old woman, Oksana, joined the conversation. They allowed me to stay with them. The old woman, Oksana, gave me soup to eat. I ate a bit and fell asleep. I recovered in a month. They said I had had typhus, and that a doctor had even come to see me. All that time those elderly people took care of me as one of their own. As it turned out, they too had been subjected to repressions. In very difficult times those people had saved me and my sister from death by starvation.

After the mass persecutions of peasants in 1929–31, a terrible famine took place in Ukraine. The communist authorities took everything they could find in homes, even from inadequately supplied peasants. They went from house to house and searched for hidden grain. They even took the beans that were being dried in the garrets for planting. The famine began in the winter, and in the spring of 1932 terrible things began to happen. People began to die in large numbers. The mass flight of peasants to cities began. But there was not enough to eat in the cities either. At that time they confiscated all poultry from the peasants. At the beginning of 1933 a full-scale famine set in. Millions of Ukrainians died of starvation. All the horrors of famine began to appear: cannibalism and the eating of corpses. I lack the words to convey the horror of the famine caused by the despots in Moscow. Mountains of corpses turned black on the roads. People were dying at train stops, in train stations, and in the fields where collective-farm grain was growing. Wherever you went, you would see the dead. When walking past the dead, people crossed themselves and said: "May the heavenly kingdom be yours." The dead were buried in pits that were not even covered with earth. Thousands of crows circled above those pits. The problem was that during the very cold winter there was no one to dig graves and bury the dead.

The horror of death by starvation hung like a dark shadow all over Ukraine. The moaning and sobbing spread throughout our land. Some villages died out completely. All those people died a martyr's death at the hands of the vicious executioner in Moscow. Whoever witnessed it knows that I am telling the truth.

Tetiana Nykytiuk, "A Candle Lit in Memory and Hope"

The Day Weekly Digest, no. 10, 2003. Edited excerpts. Online at http://www.day.kiev.ua/260363/.
Original Ukrainian text: "Svichka pam'iati ta nadiï," *Den'* (Kyiv), 20 March 2003.

Why does my heart ache so whenever I recall that old story? I heard it from my mother when I was a little girl. Perhaps I was in a bad mood and did not want to clean my plate. In such cases parents, back in the 1950s, would say, "You must eat everything on your plate, for your dad and mom..." I do not remember, but I clearly remember what my mother told me. It happened in her youth, and the story would have a lasting impact on my mentality...

My mother, Antonina Tkachuk, was fortunate to be born in Kyiv. Although the famine after the Russian Revolution did not discriminate among its victims, it was not as ruthless in the big city. However, my mother's famished childhood, when a boiled beet and no bread was considered a festive treat in winter, would take its toll in the form of countless ills as she grew older.

After school she enrolled in an agricultural technical school in Kyiv. Together with other happily young and enthusiastic Komsomol [Communist Youth League] girls, she would be sent to neighboring villages for her academic practice. It was in 1933, and food was a problem in Kyiv, so the girls expected to be better off on the collective farms.

Somehow, my mother, then 16, went to the village assigned her alone. She had to walk 60 kilometers. She had long eaten the small slice of bread she had taken from home. Her young system vigorously protested an empty stomach, and she strained her eyes, trying to spot a village by the road. If and when she found one, she thought she would be sure to have something to eat; there were no people anywhere in the world as friendly and hospitable as those in the Ukrainian countryside.

Finally, she saw a village. It looked strange. No dogs barking, no chickens cackling, no children playing and shouting. There was no one in sight. As she reached the place, she found it deserted and frighteningly quiet, every home standing like an old blind beggar, all the windows hastily boarded up, the boards blackened with rain and snow. And then she noticed a cabin with its door ajar. Tentatively she stepped inside. "Anyone here?" Something moved in the rags on top of a big stove. She heard a faint woman's voice, "What do you want, little girl?" My mother looked closer and recoiled, horrified. A living skeleton was looking at her, eyes glinting in a face all skin and bones. Stammering, she explained that she was on her way to such-and-such a village and that she had hoped to find a place to rest and have something to eat; that this place looked so weird, so dead. "You're right, the place is dead. Some died of hunger, others left for the city to stay alive," the woman whispered and then told my mother something she refused to believe. No one of sound mind, with healthy instincts, above all that of self-preservation, demanding food and drink, would believe it. "See that small chunk of bread on the table? Take it. You're young, you need it. I don't. It won't help me anyway. I am dying." The woman did not ask her to give her bread but to take it and eat it!...

My mother took it and ate it (it was hard as stone, made from goosefoot, weeds, and acorns) as she went on her way. She ate and wept for that woman with such a big heart and because there was nothing she could do to help, for she could not understand what was happening. No one heard her... Like so many others, she knew nothing about the man-made famine, the Holodomor. She knew that one of her friends had been told by a well-wishing chairman of a collective farm to go home because she looked too healthy for her own good. One morning in Kyiv she had seen several dead emaciated bodies in country clothes by a bakery. A woman nearby had whispered that they had eaten fresh bread on an empty stomach....

Tamara Orlova, "My Beloved Unhappy Mother a Murderer?"

The Day Weekly Digest, no. 10, 2010. Edited excerpts. Online at http://www.day.kiev.ua/292315#.
Original Russian text: "Moia dorogaia neschastnaia mama... ubiitsa?" *Den'* (Kyiv), 12 February 2010.

"Tomochka, do you remember anything from your past, I mean that horrible famine seven years ago?" my mother asked me back in 1940.

"I do, Mom, I remember everything," I replied. My mother looked at me and remained silent for a couple of minutes; then she said quietly, as though unsure of what she was about to tell me: "Please listen to me carefully and do as I say. There is one thing that you must promise me. Do you remember the man who bit your leg during the Holodomor? You started shrieking with pain. I heard you, dashed out of the cabin, and grabbed him by the throat to protect you. I couldn't stop strangling him with my hands until the man died. Please keep this secret as long as you live. Please swear to me this will remain between the two of us!" Mom started crying, and I told her no one would ever learn of this secret, cross my heart and hope to die.

Arriving at my twilight years, I am tortured by my oath of secrecy; I cannot tell the horrifying story about what we—and other Ukrainians—went through during the Holodomor period, and how we survived. I am still amazed that my mother and I did, with families dying of hunger around us. Few people survived the Holodomor in our village, although I remember that the year was marked by good harvest yields....

In 1932, our family was subject to dekulakization [expropriation of kulak property]. They [the NKVD] came and robbed us mercilessly. I believe it happened in October 1932. Seven men came, and two wearing militiamen's uniforms, with four horse-driven carts, and told us that they were acting on orders from "upstairs"; that they had to divest us of all our property, evict us from our home, and send us into exile because we were "hostile elements." That included elders and children. They spent three days robbing our household; they even confiscated our winter clothes, as well as our two horses, two cows, pigs, poultry, grain, and kitchenware. My father was thrown behind bars in Berezna; my grandfather made himself scarce. My elder brother was placed in the care of my old maternal grandmother in the village of Shabalyniv; my paternal grandmother succeeded in staying with her daughter, whose husband was a Party member. This left my mother and me in our plundered home, with no clothes or food. We were downright beggars. Mom told me later that she had spotted two men wearing our clothes—members of the dekulakization team that had invaded our home. In fact, our home was turned into the office of the local collective farm. Mom and I were shown the door and told to go wherever we wanted. We had nowhere to go and kept sitting in our courtyard, knowing that no one in the village would have anything to do with a dekulakization victim, for such were the Soviet authorities' instructions. Eventually, one of the local kolkhoz functionaries walked over and told us that we could live in a cabin, but we alone. He added, "If I find anyone else living with you, I will throw all of you out; you'll have to live in the street." The cabin in which we were allowed to live was actually my grandmother's windowless pantry, where she had kept all kinds of trash. However, this cabin was a godsend for us. Mom brought an armful of dry straw—there was a sheaf at the back of the barn-cum-stables—and made our abode somewhat warmer, for there was no heating. We survived. How? I went out to answer a call of nature one evening (in early November). It was dark outside, and as I stepped out someone grabbed me by the leg. I fell and felt a terrible pain. I started yelling and saw Mom dash out of the cabin. She looked like a zombie—I could not even recognize her. She ran over and pounced on what turned out to be a man on top of me. She grabbed him by the throat and did not let go. She started yelling that she could not get her hands off his throat. We were both screaming. Then she managed to get her hands off the man's throat. She stood up, grabbed the man by his clothes, and dragged him behind the barn. She returned to the cabin, washed the blood off her hands, then washed my knee wound, applying a clay bandage (she used the clay that grandma had used to polish the floor). My wound did not heal until the summer. I still have a scar left from where the man bit me. As it was, Mom and I left our cabin the next morning to meet Maria Shablykha, a woman who lived next door. She asked about the yells she had heard the previous night. We went over to the barn and saw a boy dressed in rags, with blood spots on his chest. Shablykha said he was between 12 and 13 years old. His mouth was open, with just one front tooth left. Mom and I were crying. Shablykha was saying this was the werewolf who had bitten a three-year-old boy the previous night in Azarovychky. He had sucked his blood, and the boy died shortly after. This was God's punishment. My mother changed afterwards: she was like a living skeleton, with shaking limbs. I remember thinking she was not the Mom I remembered. Famine had changed her beyond recognition, and I became afraid of her. Even decades later, I still cannot figure out how we survived; we had no food, just water. Mom kept saying that the situation would change for the better; that there would be grass in the spring, along with leaves, bark, and roots.

We heard a knock on our cabin door early in the morning. It was early March, and the frost was murderous. Mom opened the door and let in a man who looked horrible, dirty, unshaven, and dressed in rags. His feet were wrapped in rags for want of shoes. Mom was scared, but the man said, "Have no fear, Dunia; I'm your father-in-law; please let me spend at least an hour in your home, for I can't survive in the woods. I'm on the militia's wanted lists; they want to exile me to the north of Russia." He was an intelligent man, proud of his Cossack heritage—a well-to-do and hard-working individual reduced to enemy-of-the-people status. What had he done to deserve such a lot? He and his family had worked hard from dawn to dusk. None of his family had wronged any fellow villagers. Mom was afraid he had been spotted by a kolkhoz activist or militiaman; that we would be thrown out of our cabin and left to die in the street. As it was, my grandfather spent a day with us. In the evening he told Mom he was leaving. Mom kept walking around the room, wringing her hands, racking her mind for a way to save her father-in-law. In the end, her fear for her baby got the upper hand. If and when discovered, both of us would be thrown into the street, and no one would dare to take care of us, for there was a decree from "upstairs" that no one was to accommodate a dekulakized character on pain of harsh punishment. And so my grandfather left. His frozen naked body was discovered the next morning by the dam. That same day a militia officer visited Mom and asked if she had accommodated the "old Bannyk" the previous night. Without waiting for her answer, he faced me: "Hey, little one, did your granddad visit you last night?" I replied in the negative (I understood the situation even then). The man told Mom: "I'll have you evicted if I find your testimony to be false. You're allowed to live here because you have a child. We found his frozen body by the dam; we'd been hunting him down for half a year, only to find him right under our nose."

Mom told me later the weather would get better; God willing, we would survive this horrible period and settle in Russia, following in the footsteps of many, for in Russia we would not have to experience the horrors we did in Ukraine. Vain hopes of a horror-stricken people. We lived through every painful day, hoping for warmer weather, so as to walk all the way to Russia to find salvation. In the depths of poverty we lived on hope alone, as did all those around us. But there was one living skeleton, our former villager, who told my mother—and all the other starving villagers who were dreaming of salvation in Russia—that their dreams would never come true. He said he had been on the Russian border and was nearly killed there, for there were too many people trying to cross it, and soldiers and armed civilians kept them from doing so. Some Ukrainians tried to cross the border anyway: they were hit with rifle butts, and some were shot on the spot. He had seen bodies being carted away, so he returned to Ukraine's living hell.

5

DOCUMENTS

INTRODUCTION

The Documents section is divided into subsections containing Soviet, British, German, Italian, Polish, Ukrainian Galician, European, American, and Ukrainian diaspora documents.

The first subsection begins with Soviet government and Communist Party documents. Their generally matter-of-fact bureaucratic tone stands in shocking contrast to the accounts of extreme human suffering elsewhere in the *Reader*. Yet these documents are a more terrible indictment of the Stalin regime's policy than any overt denunciation. In the words of the perpetrators themselves, they show to what lengths the regime was prepared to go in order to "knock sense" into the Ukrainian peasantry, as Stanislav Kosior expressed it. The Soviet leaders focus relentlessly on compelling Ukrainian officials, functionaries, and peasants to meet the grain-procurement quotas assigned to them and take "measures to strengthen grain procurement," no matter what the human cost, and on eliminating resistance to that goal by whatever means necessary.

The first document is a letter of August 1931 from Stalin to his lieutenant Lazar Kaganovich. It shows Stalin to have been well aware that excessive grain requisitions could lead to famine. The GPU document of 28 December 1931 shows that grain-procurement quotas were widely recognized as excessive and unrealistic, likely to result in the depletion of seed stock and famine. Nevertheless, the CP(B)U resolution of 29 December 1931 (in effect, a dictate from Stalin's envoy Viacheslav Molotov) enjoins the Ukrainian communist leadership to extort ever more grain from an already famished peasantry.

A letter from a young Russian worker to the newspaper *Izvestiia* (sent before 31 March 1932) tells of hungry Ukrainian peasants flooding into Russia's neighboring Central Black Earth province in search of food in early 1932. This is followed by a memorandum from the USSR deputy commissar of agriculture dated 3 May 1932. On the basis of a fact-finding visit to one Ukrainian raion, he describes the catastrophic conditions, including starvation, the mass exodus of the most capable farmers, and the loss of more than half the draft animals.

The two letters from the Ukrainian communist leaders Hryhorii Petrovsky and Vlas Chubar, sent to Stalin in June 1932, are particularly important. Both write of the existence of famine, asking for assistance and a reduction of the grain-procurement quota for Ukraine. It is here that Stalin's animus against Ukraine and the Ukrainian leadership starts to become apparent. In a letter to Kaganovich written soon afterward, he expresses displeasure with these entreaties, stating his intention to take a hard line against Ukraine's leadership. The resolution of 7 August 1932 goes further, authorizing draconian measures, even summary execution of anyone caught gleaning, of "stealing" even a minuscule amount of grain.

This exchange of letters took place on the eve of an important conference of the Communist Party of Ukraine on 6–7 July 1932 to which Stalin sent his emissaries Molotov and Kaganovich (see their correspondence of 2 and 6 July 1932 with Stalin). Mykola Skrypnyk's speech at that conference shows that this prominent Ukrainian communist leader bent dutifully to the will of the Party's central authorities, even as he mentioned a case of famine that he had witnessed. The OGPU report of late July 1932 reveals the extent of the agricultural catastrophe, including cases of starvation, cannibalism, and suicide. The report notes the strength of resistance in Ukraine and the formation of anti-Soviet insurgent groups, including those of a national character.

Stalin's letter to Kaganovich of 11 August 1932 deserves special attention. The Soviet leader vents his dissatisfaction with Ukraine's leaders and suggests that they be replaced by his trusted lieutenants. Importantly, he twice expresses fear of losing Ukraine and associates that possibility, as well as resistance to grain-procurement quotas, with Ukrainian nationalism and Polish efforts to promote the secession of the Ukrainian SSR. Stalin exhorts Kaganovich to turn Ukraine into "a fortress of the USSR, a real model republic, within the shortest possible time." This was a green light for repressive measures against the peasants and the Ukrainian leaders alike. Ukrainians clearly understood that Stalin's policies were anti-Ukrainian, as evidenced by a secret-police report of 10 September 1932 on the attempt of two young scholars at the All-Ukrainian Academy of Sciences to inform Ukraine's foremost historian, Mykhailo Hrushevsky, of the famine. They believed that the famine was directed against Ukraine and its people—"to break the Ukrainian nation once and for all as the only national force capable of serious resistance."

As the crisis deepened in the autumn of 1932 and it became clear to the Soviet leadership that Ukraine would fall far short of its grain-procurement quota, Stalin appointed Molotov and Kaganovich to head special commissions (see the document of 22 October) to extort even more grain from Ukraine and the Ukrainian-populated North Caucasus. One result of Molotov's involvement was the CP(B)U resolution of 18 November reaffirming procurement policies and the instituted bans, fines, and punishments for noncompliance on collective and individual farms. The CC AUCP(B) resolution of 14 December 1932 sanctioned purges of Party organizations in Ukraine and the Kuban and ordered a complete rollback of policies promoting the use of the Ukrainian language, known as Ukrainization, in the Kuban region, and a partial rollback in Ukraine. This resolution also authorized the deportation of the entire Kuban Cossack settlement Poltavskaia *stanitsa* and its repopulation with reliable elements from the Red Army. On 15 December Ukrainization was halted in other parts of the USSR outside Ukraine. Other documents of late November and December 1932 show that the Soviet leadership was becoming increasingly concerned with political and nationalist (in Soviet parlance, "Petliurite") resistance in conjunction with the deepening crisis and the deteriorating food situation. It responded by closing loopholes, making threats, increasing repression, and continuing to take food from an already famished and plundered countryside.

In early 1933 the Soviet leadership continued its punitive measures. The Kremlin Politburo resolution of 1 January, based on a telegram from Stalin to the Ukrainian leadership dated the same day, threatened Ukraine's farmers "who stubbornly insist on misappropriating and concealing grain" with application of the draconian resolution of 7 August 1932. In his speech of 11 January to the Central Committee of the AUCP(B), Stalin blamed peasant resistance to grain collection on collective-farm leaders who had come under the sway of anti-Soviet elements, including Ukrainian nationalists (Petliurites), and authorized further repressive measures against them.

Two other brutal measures followed in January. First, an order of 22 January authorized barring peasants from Ukraine and the North Caucasus from searching for food in areas where it was available, such as central Russia and Belarus. Second, a resolution of the Central Committee of the AUCP(B) dated 24 January made Stalin's trusted lieutenant and opponent of Ukrainization Pavel Postyshev second secretary of the CP(B)U (effectively, Stalin's plenipotentiary in Ukraine). The resolution signaled the start of purges of Ukrainian communists, whom *Pravda* accused in an editorial of 10 March of engaging in "distortions of Leninist nationality policy in Ukraine" and of "underestimating the unbreakable link between the national and peasant questions."

A GPU report of 12 March 1933 shows that the secret police was fully aware of the extent of death from starvation. The memorandum of the CC CP(B)U to the CC AUCP(B), dated 15 March and signed by the Ukrainian Party's first secretary, Stanislav Kosior, is particularly cynical. Kosior admits to widespread famine but attributes it to "poor management and an unacceptable attitude toward the public good (losses, stealing, and waste of grain)." The peasants, he claims, are no longer blaming the famine on grain requisitions by the authorities but on "themselves for poor work, for not safeguarding grain, for allowing it to be pilfered." Even so, Kosior concludes, "starvation has not yet knocked sense into the heads of a great many collective farmers."

Another speech by Kosior, delivered in November 1933 at a CP(B)U plenum, blames the problems in the agricultural sector on Ukrainian communists who neglect the dangers of Ukrainian nationalism. He links kulaks with Ukrainian nationalists, treating them as almost identical enemies of Soviet rule. Skrypnyk, who had committed suicide earlier that year in protest against the Kremlin's policies, is condemned. The resolution adopted at the plenum links the social and class struggle with the struggle against Ukrainian nationalism, now identified as "the principal danger" in Ukraine. The resolution marked a subtle but important shift toward establishing the Soviet state on a Russian national foundation: in the 1920s, Russian chauvinism had been designated the greatest danger to the Party and Soviet society.

The subsection of Soviet documents ends with excerpts from three speeches—by Postyshev, Kosior, and Stalin—delivered at the Seventeenth Congress of the AUCP(B), dubbed "the Congress of Victors," in January 1934. Postyshev emphasizes the link between class-based anti-Soviet activities and Ukrainian nationalism, reminding delegates that "the Ukrainian kulak underwent a lengthy schooling in struggle against Soviet power, for in Ukraine the civil war was especially fierce and lengthy, given that political banditry was in control of Ukraine for an especially long period." This passage indicates the Soviet leadership's recognition that the Ukrainian peasantry's fierce resistance to Soviet power in the years 1919–24, often under the national banner, might be reviving. Kosior dwells on Ukrainian nationalism not only in society but in the CP(B)U itself, which, he claims, "played an exceptional role in creating and intensifying the lag in agriculture." Referring to Stalin's view of the interconnectedness of the class and nationality questions in Ukraine, Kosior notes that "the national flag plays an exceedingly important role for the class enemy. Moreover, the predominant coloring of the class enemy, with which he masks himself, is above all the national flag, nationalist clothing." Finally, Stalin reaffirms the designation of nationalism as "the chief danger" in Ukraine and denounces it as a danger to the Soviet state.

The next subsection contains five documents from the British Foreign Office. The first is a report by the agricultural expert Andrew Cairns on his trip to Ukraine and the North Caucasus in the late spring and early summer of 1932. This is followed by a brief report on conditions in the Kuban and in Ukraine. The next item is a report from the German agricultural expert Otto Schiller on his trip to the North Caucasus in the spring of 1933. Schiller describes famine conditions, expulsions, deportation of the Kuban Cossacks, and Young Communist confiscations of hidden stores of grain. The fourth document contains a report by William Strang, a counsellor at the British embassy in Moscow, on famine conditions in Ukraine in the summer of 1933 and mass deaths from starvation. In the fifth item, Strang forwards the *New York Times* correspondent Walter Duranty's description of his trip to Ukraine and the North Caucasus in the late summer of 1933. In contrast to his published articles, in which he downplayed the famine, Duranty here estimates population loss in Ukraine at four to five million and comments that "Ukraine had been bled white." He estimates total losses in the Soviet Union at ten million.

The two documents from the German Foreign Office are of particular interest for their analysis of the nationality question in relation to the famine. The first specifically discusses "The Ukrainian Question," noting the commonly held view in Ukraine that the government had brought the famine about "to force the Ukrainians to their knees." The report concludes that Ukraine is now guided by "Great Russian communist chauvinism." The second document is a report on a trip through Ukraine in 1936. The author begins with the startling assertion that "Ukrainian Ukraine has been destroyed." He estimates human losses at six million. Of particular interest are his descriptions of Russification and of the chauvinist attitudes of Russians and Russian speakers he met in Kyiv. He concludes that "the Ukrainian people's moral spine was broken in the terrible years of 1932 and 1933."

Italian Foreign Office documents follow the German reports. The first report of April 1933 describes the limitations on peasant mobility and the consequences for blacklisted villages in the North Caucasus. The second report, "The Famine and the Ukrainian Question," was written by the Italian consul in Kharkiv in May 1933. He argues that the famine was "contrived" in order to "teach the peasants a lesson" and concludes: "The current disaster will bring about a preponderantly Russian colonization of Ukraine. It will transform its ethnographic character. In a future time, perhaps very soon, one will no longer be able to speak of a Ukraine, or a Ukrainian people, and thus not even of a Ukrainian problem, because Ukraine will become a *de facto* Russian region." His report of 19 July 1933 relays an apocryphal but deeply symbolic account of Skrypnyk on his deathbed telling Postyshev that the greatest danger to communism is Russian imperialism. The last Italian document is a letter from the consul in Odesa, who writes: "The persecutions conducted against the Ukrainian intellectuals...the suicide of Skrypnyk...the withholding of the grain reserves from the peasants...[have] turned Ukraine...into the site of an unprecedented famine, which according to reliable evidence has sent 7,000,000 people to their deaths; all of these things betoken the Moscow Government's intention to use every means at their disposal to crush every last vestige of Ukrainian nationalism." Appended to this subsection is a news item (reproduced from a recent collection of documents from the Vatican archives) describing the reaction of Pope Pius XI to a report on the famine.

The next subsection of documents comes from Polish Foreign Ministry and Intelligence Service offices. In a document of 8 May 1933 the consul in Kharkiv reports on economic policy and the resultant famine as seen through the prism of the nationality question. He notes that ruthless grain collections "stripp[ed] bare the Ukrainian countryside" and calls the famine a result of the Kremlin's "predatory management," concluding that "the economic policy of the central government with regard to Ukraine has been much more ruthless and predatory than toward the neighboring provinces of the RSFSR, with the sole exception of the North Caucasus." The same consul, reporting on a car trip from Kharkiv to Moscow on 5 May, describes the stark difference in conditions in the Ukrainian and Russian countryside as akin to crossing "from the land of the Soviets into Western Europe."

The report of the Polish journalist Berson on his conversation with Karl Radek, Stalin's adviser and envoy on Polish affairs, shows that Soviet propaganda is prepared to equate or link any expression of concern over the famine with sympathy for or collaboration with Nazi Germany and its foreign-policy objectives. A document of 6 November 1933 contains an excerpt from a report by the Polish ambassador in Turkey on a conversation with Stalin's confidant Kliment Voroshilov. While official Soviet rhetoric trumpeted the equality of nations in the USSR, Voroshilov's remarks clearly indicate that the Soviet leadership was anti-Ukrainian. Commenting in the wake of an attack by a Ukrainian nationalist on the Soviet consulate in Lviv in Polish-ruled western Ukraine, he told the Polish ambassador that Poland was lenient with Ukrainians, whereas "in Soviet Russia they are kept on a tight leash."

An article of 10 October 1933 in a bulletin intended for diplomats, *Poland and the Outside World*, notes that the Communist Party has taken control of Ukraine by breaking the resistance of the peasantry and destroying "the decentralizing nationalist tendencies of the Ukrainian intelligentsia." Reporting on 6 January 1934, the Polish consul in Kharkiv analyzes the reversal of Bolshevik nationality policy in Ukraine, stressing that this suits the Soviet leadership's long-term goal of making the USSR a great power: "[T]hey are becoming more and more great-power politicians, strengthening their regime and the borders of their state, sacrificing to that end the ideals hitherto upheld by the Communist International." Finally, a letter from a Polish student notes that the famine has produced antipathy toward the Soviet state and promoted Ukrainian nationalist and separatist tendencies.

The next subsection of documents focuses on reaction to the famine by Ukrainian organizations and non-governmental bodies outside the Soviet Union, including the Polish-ruled province of Galicia. An appeal by leaders of the Ukrainian Catholic Church, headed by Metropolitan Andrei Sheptytsky, characterizes the Soviet state-run economy as a "cannibalistic system of state capitalism." The signatories accuse the Soviet leadership of abandoning religion, suppressing liberty, turning free farmer-citizens into slaves and starving them. Another declaration is signed by the most influential western Ukrainian political and civic leaders, who claim that the Soviet authorities intend to exterminate Ukrainians and Ukrainian national life.

An appeal by Cardinal Innitzer of Vienna calls on non-governmental and religious organizations to create an inter-faith committee to organize famine relief. This is followed by a letter from Margery Ashby, a feminist leader, on behalf of the international coordinating body of the worldwide feminist movement—the Liaison Committee of Women's International Organizations—to Johan Mowinckel, president of the League of Nations. The letter urges Mowinckel, who was also Norway's prime minister, to raise the famine as an issue at a meeting of the League's Council in order to press for "League action in any form which you may think wise."

In their letter to Prime Minister R. B. Bennett of Canada, the leaders of the Ukrainian National Council, an umbrella group uniting Ukrainian organizations in that country, accuse the Kremlin authorities of systematically starving the population of Soviet Ukraine. In their memorandum to President Franklin Roosevelt opposing the recognition of the USSR by the United States, the president of the United Ukrainian Organizations of the United States and several other Ukrainian civic leaders conclude: "We are firmly convinced that the famine in Ukraine is not the result of poor crops or drought, but on the contrary, is a result of the political and cultural conflict between Ukrainian nationalistic aspirations and Moscow's imperialistic and centralizing designs.... The famine is the culmination of that unremitting and ferocious persecution of the Ukrainian people by [the] Moscow dictatorship." There follows a draft resolution of the U.S. House of Representatives sponsored by Congressman Hamilton Fish. The document accuses the Soviet central government of being aware of the famine and of having complete control of food supplies but failing to take relief measures. Instead, the regime used famine "as a means of reducing the Ukrainian population and destroying the Ukrainian political, cultural, and national rights."

The final subsection contains official Soviet denials of the famine. In his letter of 3 February 1934 to U.S. Congressman Herman Koplemann, the Soviet counsellor B. Skvirsky writes that the death rate in Soviet Ukraine was the lowest of the seven constituent republics comprising the Soviet Union. Skvirsky makes reference to articles by Duranty. The last official, and quite lengthy, denial was issued by the Soviet embassy in Ottawa on 28 April 1983. It is reproduced here in its entirety.

SOVIET GOVERNMENT, COMMUNIST PARTY, AND SECRET POLICE DOCUMENTS

Letter from Stalin to Kaganovich on grain-procurement policy and famine in Georgia

In *The Stalin-Kaganovich Correspondence 1931–36* (2003). Excerpts, pp. 53–54.

[Later than 11 August 1931]
Greetings, Comrade Kaganovich....

6) It is now clear to me that Kartvelishvili and the secretariat of the Georgian CC, with their reckless "grain-procurements policy," have brought a number of districts in western Georgia to the point of famine. They do not understand that the Ukrainian methods of grain procurement, which are necessary and expedient in grain-surplus districts, are unsuitable and damaging in grain-deficit districts, which have no industrial proletariat whatsoever to boot....

From a summary report by the UkrSSR GPU "On the Course of Grain Procurement in Ukraine"

In *Tragediia sovetskoi derevni* (2001). Excerpts, pp. 218–19, 221–23. Translated by Bohdan Klid.

28 December 1931
Top Secret

Since September, the course of grain procurement in Ukraine has been characterized by systematic nonfulfillment of the plan.

If in July and August the monthly quotas were fulfilled with some surpluses, in the following months there was a sharp decline....

In September, 62.6 percent of the monthly quota was met.

In October, 53.9 percent of the monthly quota was met.

In November, 43.5 percent of the monthly quota was met,

As of 1 December, 74.1 percent of this year's plan was fulfilled....

This year's grain-procurement campaign is taking place in the context of widely held opinions that the plans are unrealistic and cannot be fulfilled....

In many villages, despite their not fulfilling the plan, not only the village councils but also a number of representatives of raion organizations, succumbing to prevailing references to the absence of grain, have completely stopped working on grain procurement....

In Berdiansk raion (formerly the Mariupol district), where 76.9 percent of the grain-procurement plan had been fulfilled by 20 December...the [p]lenipotentiary... of the R[aion] E[xecutive] C[ommittee], Shcherbyna, announced in conversations with workers that "We will not fulfill the grain-procurement [quota], as the plan is unrealistic. We already see that there is not enough grain for the peasants."....

Reports coming in during the most recent period from individual counties tell us that in the course of fulfilling the grain-procurement [plan], some collective farms have delivered part of their seed grain.

In Novo-Ukraina raion (Steppe Region), the Pishchanobrody village council forced four collective farms to give up almost all their seed stocks in order to fulfill the plan....

As a result of such unsatisfactory planning, some collective farms delivered, along with their marketable grain, the portion that should have remained for distribution [as payment in kind] for workdays. The surrender of a substantial portion of the above-mentioned seed stocks has already produced some threat of a lack of grain for personal consumption on those collective farms....

In the village of Voronivka in Novo-Ukraina raion, a group of collective farmers presented themselves to the collective-farm administration and declared: "We will not go to work until you give us bread. Stop fooling us: we will not go to work hungry."....

In the village of Moskalivka in Vovchansk raion, a group of up to sixty collective farmers, mostly women, presented themselves in orderly fashion to the village council and demanded that bread be distributed. There were shouts: "Give us bread, we're hungry."....

Vice Chairman, GPU, UkrSSR, [Karl] Karlson

Resolution of the Politburo of the CC CP(B)U "On Measures to Intensify Grain Procurement"

In *Tragediia sovetskoi derevni* (2001). Excerpts, pp. 227–28. Translated by Bohdan Klid.

29 December 1931

The Politburo of the CC CP(B)U, having heard and considered the report of the representative of the CC AUCP(B), Comrade [Viacheslav] Molotov, acknowledges that the complete fulfillment of the grain-procurement plan established for Ukraine (510 million poods) is absolutely necessary and dictated to the USSR by the overall political and, particularly, the international situation.

Further to this, the Politburo of the CC CP(B)U affirms that, notwithstanding the complete feasibility of fulfilling the grain-procurement plan established for Ukraine, progress toward its fulfillment is so unsatisfactory that it threatens the collapse of a significant portion of the Bolshevik organizations of the UkrSSR in one of the decisive sectors of socialist construction....

1. The CC [CP(B)U] demands that Party, Soviet, and Komsomol organizations immediately mobilize all forces and organizations of collective farmers, especially the vanguard [elements], to fulfill as soon as possible the current year's grain-procurement plan, for which the CC declares January to be a month of intensive struggle to complete the grain procurements.

Telegram from the secretary of the Zinovivsk [Kirovohrad] City Committee, AUCP(B) [*sic*], Mykheienko, to V. M. Molotov on the course of grain procurement

In *Tragediia sovetskoi derevni* (2001). Excerpts, pp. 239–41. Translated by Bohdan Klid.

1 January 1932
For delivery in a sealed packet

Kharkiv, CC CP(B)U to Comrade Molotov
Copy: Comrade Stroganov

Resolution of the bureau of the Zinovivsk committee of the CC CP(B)U of 31 December on the course of grain procurement, based on the resolution of the CC CP(B)U of 29 December 1931 and directives of Comrade Molotov...:

1. To oblige all authorized officials of the city Party committee, in the course of three days, to ensure the removal for grain procurement of all basic seed stocks held for spring sowing from those collective farms that have not fulfilled the grain-procurement plan...the removal of the seed stocks to be used as a means of educating every collective farmer and elevating his sense of responsibility for the welfare of the collective farm and the fulfillment by the collective farm of its obligations toward the proletarian state;
2. During the removal of seed stocks, to oblige all authorized officials of the city Party committee and secretaries of collective-farm Party cells to intensify their political work among the masses even more in order to mobilize [the return of] squandered and stolen grain, taking into account that this is required both to fulfill the annual grain-procurement plan and to secure seed-stock material for spring sowing....

Secretary of the City Party Committee, Mykheienko

Political summary of unpublished letters from the "Reading Office" of the newspaper *Izvestiia TsIK SSSR i VTsIK* (News of the Central Executive Committee of the USSR and of the All-Russian Central Executive Committee, Moscow) for February–March 1932

In *Tragediia sovetskoi derevni* (2001). Excerpt, p. 312. Translated by Bohdan Klid.

[Not before 31 March 1932]
Not for publication....

Novyi Oskol raion, Central Black Earth Region, village of Lobovka, Nikolaev village council, Ivan Litvinov:

Every day whole caravans of hungry Ukrainian peasants—collective and individual farmers—ride the length and breadth of our raion. For any piece of bread they give up all their belongings, such as shoes, clothing, and anything else they might have with them. When asked why they are hungry, they reply: "Our harvest was good, but Soviet power 'procured' our grain, carrying through to us its plans and tasks to the point where we were left without a pound of grain." When they are asked who is responsible for this, they reply: "Soviet power, which took away our grain to the last kernel, condemning us to hunger and poverty—worse than under serfdom."

I am a worker, a member of the Komsomol since 1928, and I am astonished: can it be that Ukraine would hunger during a good harvest? We also have collective farms, and there is enough bread, so why is there such a situation precisely in the Central Black Earth Region? I am bringing this phenomenon to the attention of *Izvestiia* because the "hungry caravans," wherever they go, bring panic and spread hostile talk against Soviet power.

Internal memorandum from the Deputy People's Commissar of Agriculture of the USSR, A. V. Grinevich, to the People's Commissar of Agriculture of the USSR, A. Ya. Yakovlev, on the situation in Zinovivsk [Kirovohrad] raion, Ukrainian SSR

In *Tragediia sovetskoi derevni* (2001). Excerpts, pp. 363–65. Translated by Bohdan Klid.

---

3 May 1932
Top Secret

To the People's Commissar of Agriculture of the USSR, Comrade Yakovlev....

1. Zinovivsk raion is 98 percent collectivized. As a result of the past production year, the collective farmers, on the basis of information from seventy collective farms, received on average 76 kg of grain per person, and that was to be their nourishment for the whole year. There were a number of cases of swelling from hunger. At present, according to information received from workers in the county and the observations that I have had occasion to make in the villages, there is almost no grain on the collective farms. By March there were many in the raion who were starving....
2. Since 1 January 1932, according to information from village councils, 28.3 thousand persons (out of a population of 100 thousand) have left the raion, and it is the adult inhabitants, the healthier ones, who are leaving....
3. As of 1 July 1931, according to agricultural tax records, there were 18,908 horses. According to census records, as of 1 February 1932 there were 11,934 horses. According to information from the village councils, as of 25 April 9,026 horses were left, that is, in less than a year more than 50 percent of the stock of horses has disappeared. Moreover, of the remaining horses, no less than 50 percent should be removed from work very soon, as working them will soon lead to the demise of that portion because of their extreme exhaustion....

Deputy People's Commissar of Agriculture of the USSR, Grinevich

Letter from Hryhorii Petrovsky to Molotov and Stalin on the grave food situation and famine in the Ukrainian SSR

In *Holodomor of 1932–33 in Ukraine* (2008). Excerpts, pp. 33–36.

10 June 1932

During the sowing campaign in Pryluky, Lokhvytsia, Varva, Chernukhy, Pyriatyn, and Mala Divytsia raions, I came face to face, so to speak, with the village....

We knew beforehand that fulfilling state grain procurements in Ukraine would be difficult, but what I have seen in the countryside indicates that we have greatly overdone it.... I was in many raion villages and saw a considerable part of the countryside engulfed in famine. There are not many, but there are people swollen from starvation, mainly poor peasants and even middle farmers.... At large meetings in villages, I am cursed furiously; old women cry, and men sometimes do so as well. At times, criticism of the situation created goes very deep: "Why did they create an artificial famine? After all, we had a harvest. Why did they take away the seed grain? That did not happen even under the old regime. Why should Ukrainians make difficult journeys for grain to non-grain-producing areas? Why is grain not being brought here?" And so on....

...In response to the desperate cry for relief [in the form of] seed grain and grain for food, I promised something with regard to seed grain but told the farmers to find seed in their own regions.... Mass thefts are occurring in the villages because of the famine, mainly of poultry: they steal chickens, ducks, take potato scraps, and butcher calves and cows during the night and eat them.

Right now, the men are sowing millet and buckwheat. The days for sowing millet are ending, but not for buckwheat, and the villagers are expecting it from us.... There will be insufficient sowing in these raions compared to last year's area. There is still a month or a month and a half before the new crop. This means that famine will intensify. Therefore, I am asking you directly: Would it not be possible to send relief to the Ukrainian countryside in the amount of two, or, if worse comes to worst, one and a half million poods of grain?....

Because of the general famine, as you know, villagers have started flocking to the Dno station, the Central Black Earth Oblast, Belarus, and the North Caucasus. In some cases, two-thirds of all men have left their villages in search of grain.... Naturally, there is mayhem at the stations and in transports.... Tickets are not being issued to villagers, or are being issued in very limited numbers. Peasants have asked me: Why are trips for grain prohibited?....

...In closing, I once again request that you consider all methods and resources available to provide urgent food relief in the form of grain to the Ukrainian countryside and to supply buckwheat for sowing as quickly as possible in order to make up for what has not been sown.

H[ryhorii] Petrovsky

Letter from Vlas Chubar to Molotov and Stalin on agricultural affairs in the Ukrainian SSR

In *Holodomor of 1932–33 in Ukraine* (2008). Excerpts, pp. 36–38.

10 June 1932

In two trips (with a small break), I spent fifteen days in the hardest-hit raions and villages of Kyiv and Vinnytsia oblasts.... [T]he main facts in all these raions and villages are similar enough that some general conclusions can be made....

...Along with the general weakness of the state grain-procurement plan, caused primarily by lower harvests across Ukraine and colossal losses during harvesting...a system of requisitioning of all grain, including seed reserves, from private farmers was introduced, and almost everything of value was confiscated from collective farms. Even if collective farms met their plan targets, they received an extra second and often third [grain quota target]. In many cases, grain issued to collective farmers as advance payment for work was confiscated by brigades for state grain procurement. As a result, the majority of collective farms in those raions were left without grain, without animal feed concentrate for livestock, without food for the disabled, for teachers, etc....

Cases of malnutrition and starvation were noted in December and January both among private farmers (particularly those whose farms and belongings were sold for failing to meet grain targets) and among collective farmers, especially those with large families.... In March and April there were tens and hundreds of malnourished, starving, and swollen people dying of hunger in every village; children abandoned by their parents and orphans appeared....

In addition to grain procurements, the same methods were applied to potato and, especially, meat procurements....

The proper functioning of agriculture has been impaired in the Ukrainian SSR over such a large area that special adjustments are required to state grain and meat procurement targets and other agricultural goals....

V[las] Chubar

Resolution of a joint meeting of the Bureau of the Poltava City Committee of the CP(B)U and the City Party Control Commission at a closed session on the speech by CP(B)U member Poltavets containing a declaration on the famine and the oppression of peasants and workers in the Ukrainian SSR

In *Holod-henotsyd 1932–1933 rokiv v Ukraïni* (2005). Excerpts, pp. 94–95, 97.
Translated by Maksym Motorenko and Bohdan Klid.

11 June 1932

Having discussed the information of the Party commission (Comrades Rohal, Hrekov, Ahranovych) on the nature and circumstances of the anti-Party and anti-Soviet statement of Poltavets, a Party member since 1929, at a closed session of the Party Center of the Institute of Meat Technology, following discussion of the restricted letter of the Oblast Committee of 16/V–1932 and the explanation of Poltavets himself, the Joint Meeting of the C[ity] P[arty] C[ommittee] and the Presidium of the C[ity] C[ontrol] C[omission] finds:

1. The speech by Poltavets, which contained the following assertions:

a) "The center and its representatives are to blame for deviations in Party policy during grain procurements"; "someone named [Mykola Nestorovych] Demchenko came to Poltava, hammered with his fist on the table, and ordered us to fulfill the grain-procurement plan, but they blame the lower strata [of the Party for this]."
b) "Socialism has been built in Russia, but in Ukraine there is famine."
c) "Not only people eat white bread in Leningrad and Moscow; they even feed horses with white bread, but in Ukraine and in Poltava there is famine."
d) "All the peasantry is against socialism."....
   There are cases of kulak and Ukrainian national chauvinist provocative activities against the Party and its central and local authorities, with unprecedented slander of general Party policy and of the successful construction of socialism. Poltavets's outrageous anti-Party and anti-Soviet statement reflects the resistance of the defeated and generally liquidated—on the basis of total collectivization—but not yet completely eliminated enraged Ukrainian kulak....

Accordingly, the CPC bureau and the Presidium of the CCC resolve:

1. To expel Poltavets, Party member since 1929, a middle peasant, FROM THE RANKS OF THE PARTY AND FROM STUDY AT THE INSTITUTE as a kulak agent....

Secretary of the CPC, Malii
Head of the CC, Kuliashov....

Letter from Stalin to Kaganovich on appeals from Ukrainian SSR leaders to the CC AUCP(B)

In *Holodomor of 1932–33 in Ukraine* (2008). Excerpt, p. 40.

---

15 June 1932

I did not like the letters from Chubar and Petrovsky.[1] The former spouts "self-criticism" in order to secure millions more poods of bread from Moscow; the latter is feigning sainthood, claiming victimization by the "CC AUCP directive" in order to reduce grain-procurement levels. Neither one nor the other is acceptable. Chubar is mistaken if he thinks that self-criticism is required for securing outside "help" and not for mobilizing forces and resources in Ukraine. In my opinion, Ukraine has been given more than enough....

Regards,
J. Stalin

---

1 The letters of 10 June 1932 from Petrovsky and Chubar. See pp. 230–31.

Resolution of the Politburo of the CP(B)U on sending a telegram to the CC AUCP(B) about the provision of food aid to Ukraine

In *Holod 1932–1933 rokiv na Ukraïni* (1990), p. 183. Translated by Maksym Motorenko and Bohdan Klid.

17 June 1932

To send the following telegram to the CC AUCP(B), addressed to Comrades Kaganovich and Molotov: "[Vlas] Chubar, on the instructions of the CC CP(B)U, initiated a request to send food aid to Ukraine for regions in difficult circumstances. We urgently request an additional 600,000 poods [of grain], in addition to the 220,000 poods of food aid already assigned for beet cultivation."

Letter from Stalin to Kaganovich and Molotov on organizing the 1932 grain-procurement campaign

In *The Stalin-Kaganovich Correspondence 1931–36* (2003). Excerpts, pp. 138–39.

To Kaganovich and Molotov (for members of the Politburo)

...The principal error of our grain-procurement work last year, especially in the Ukraine and the Urals, was that the grain-procurement plan was allocated among districts and collective farms and was carried out not in an organized manner but spontaneously, based on the equalizing "principle," it was carried out mechanically, without taking account of the situation in each individual district, on each individual collective farm. This mechanical equalizing approach to the matter has resulted in glaring absurdities, so that a number of fertile districts in the Ukraine, despite a fairly good harvest, have found themselves in a state of impoverishment and famine.... The results of these errors are now having an effect on the sowing situation, especially in the Ukraine, and several tens of thousands of Ukrainian collective farmers are still traveling around the entire European part of the USSR and are demoralizing our collective farms with their complaints and whining.

What must be done to avoid repeating last year's errors?

The districts and collective farms must get a revised plan, but revised with reference to the distinctive features of each district and each collective farm rather than in a mechanical and equalizing manner. Since the present condition of our organizations does not allow for absolutely precise record of these features, we should add an extra 4–5 percent to the plan in order to cover inevitable errors in the records and fulfill the plan itself at any cost....

J. Stalin, 18 June 1932

Telegram from the AUCP(B) and the CPC USSR to the CC CP(B)U and the CPC UkrSSR on ensuring the fulfillment of grain requisitions by collective farms and individual peasant homesteads

In *Holod 1932–1933 rokiv na Ukraïni* (1990), pp. 186–87. Translated by Maksym Motorenko and Bohdan Klid.

21 June 1932
Two addresses: Kharkiv, CC CP(B)U, [Stanislav] Kosior
Copy: CPC, [Vlas] Chubar

In accordance with the resolution of the CPC and CC of 20 and 21 June, the CPC USSR and the CC AUCP(B) propose that you ensure at all costs:

First. The delivery, in fulfillment of the annual grain requisition, by collective farms and individual peasant homesteads according to Ukraine's allocated obligations: 14,500,000 poods in July; 72,400,000 poods in August; 71,200,000 poods in September....

Second.... No manner of evasion should be allowed under any circumstances for collective farms and individual peasant homesteads with regard to grain procurement or for grain delivery by state farms, or for the delivery schedules established for your region according to the resolutions of 20 and 21 June.

Molotov, Stalin

Resolution of the Politburo of the CC AUCP(B) on sending food aid to Ukraine

In *Holod 1932–1933 rokiv na Ukraïni* (1990), p. 190. Translated by Maksym Motorenko and Bohdan Klid.

23 June 1932

Do not go beyond the resolutions already adopted by the CC, and do not undertake additional grain deliveries to Ukraine.

Letter from Stalin to Kaganovich and Molotov commenting on the leadership of the Ukrainian SSR

In *The Stalin-Kaganovich Correspondence 1931–36* (2003). Excerpts, p. 152.

2 [July1932]
To Kaganovich, Molotov.

1) Give <u>the most serious</u> attention to the Ukraine. [Vlas] Chubar's corruptness and opportunistic essence and [Stanislav] Kosior's rotten diplomacy (with regard to the CC of the VKP) and criminally frivolous attitude toward his job will eventually

ruin the Ukraine. These comrades are not up to the challenge of leading the Ukraine today. If you go to the Ukrainian conference (I insist on it), take every measure in order to improve the functionaries' mood, isolate the whining and depraved diplomats (no matter who they are!) and ensure genuinely Bolshevik decisions by the conference. I have formed the impression (probably even the conviction) that we will have to remove both of them from the Ukraine—Chubar and Kosior. Maybe I am mistaken. But you have an opportunity to check this situation at the conference.

Regards, J. Stalin

Letter from Kaganovich to Stalin on the participation of Kaganovich and Molotov in the All-Ukrainian Party Conference

In *The Stalin-Kaganovich Correspondence 1931–36* (2003). Excerpts, pp. 152–54.

2 [July 1932]
Greetings, Comrade Stalin....

2) We have sent you the draft resolution on the grain-procurement and harvest campaign. I think it conforms with your standpoint, and our speeches at the conference also fully adhere to your counsel that we direct the main thrust against the Ukrainian demobilizers....

...At their conference [in the Ukraine] they will discuss only one topic: agriculture. We will have to use specific examples to develop the question of the leadership's being out of touch with agriculture and the uneven distribution of grain procurements, due to a lack of familiarity with the districts, which has led to unhappy consequences....

Regards. Yours, L. Kaganovich

Telegram from Molotov and Kaganovich to Stalin on the need to remain silent about the true situation in the Ukrainian SSR

In *Holodomor 1932–1933 rokiv v Ukraïni* (2007), p. 232. Translated by Maksym Motorenko and Bohdan Klid.

6 July 1932
To Com[rade] Stalin

Criticism should be undertaken at the Ukrainian conference of the work of the CC CP(B)U, whose shortcomings have brought about a difficult situation in some regions. The question arises of how this should be explained in the press. In order not to give fodder to the foreign press, we deem it necessary to expound on this criticism in our press in moderate tones, without printing facts about the situation in the bad regions.

Please relay your opinion to Kharkiv.

Molotov, Kaganovich

Letter from Molotov and Kaganovich to Stalin on the Ukrainian Party Conference and grain-procurement plan

In *Holodomor of 1932–33 in Ukraine* (2008). Excerpts, pp. 42–43.

6 July 1932
To Comrade Stalin

Today we discussed the draft of the resolution and the conference with the Politburo CC CP(B)U. We said the draft resolution was unacceptable in its weak criticism of CC CP(B)U leaders for affairs in the countryside.... All Politburo members, including [Mykola] Skrypnyk, spoke for reducing the plan....

We categorically rejected a revision of the plan.... We think that the resolution should express dissatisfaction with the CC CP(B)U for affairs in the countryside in the last while. Please provide your thoughts.[2]

Molotov, Kaganovich

Mykola Skrypnyk, "III Vseukraïns'ka partiina konferentsiia. Obhovorennia dopovidi tov. Kosiora. Promova tov. M. O. Skrypnyka" (III All-Ukrainian Party Conference. Discussion of Comrade [Stanislav] Kosior's Speech. Comrade M. O. Skrypnyk's Speech)

Visti VUTsVK (News of the All-Ukrainian Central Executive Committee, Kharkiv), 11 July 1932. Excerpts, pp. 5–6. Translated by Bohdan Klid.

...[I]n speaking about the situation in which Ukraine finds itself, we cannot allow for any underestimation of that which exists.... That which exists is a consequence of our struggle, our leadership, our ability to organize the class struggle, and that is why we cannot by any means downplay the difficulties and cover up the failures that exist here. Is it worthwhile to engage in equilibration and downplay the failures in the sowing of spring crops, grain, and so on? This is not acceptable. We need to know the situation as it exists. We need to know that we have a huge, shameful failure, that in the sowing of spring grains we have a huge failure; the same applies, in general, to the sowing of winter and spring crops.

Also, we absolutely cannot downplay the food situation that exists in some districts. We cannot downplay the very difficult situations on some collective farms and in a number of districts....

2 The following day Stalin agreed to an expression of dissatisfaction with the work of CC CP(B)U leaders.

We have to say straightforwardly that the situation is difficult. We had failures in the grain-procurement campaign last year; we fell short by 70 million poods; we have failures in the food situation in a whole series of collective farms and villages in a whole row of districts....

What is the reason for our current failures, our current situation?....

Since January I have driven through more than thirty districts and many dozens of collective farms, state farms, and Machine-Tractor Stations, and I say firmly that this question of the reason behind the current state of affairs stands before each of us.

And so, I heard the following answer in certain localities. I was in a district where there are great food difficulties: this was in Moldavia, the Okniansk district, the village of Novokrasne: "The reason is that everything was swept away from us with a broom, a 'leftist' deviation; they clamped down and crushed us." That is the reason they give for this situation. In other words, this explanation goes: "The communists are at fault for the nonfulfillment of the grain-procurement plan, for the poor food situation; the communists took the grain, and that is why there is no grain to live on; that is why there is a difficult food situation; that is why there is famine in certain localities." This same village of Novokrasne is an example of certain social roots of that explanation.... I saw the fields of that village in the condition in which they were. And when I came and heard that supposedly the communists were responsible for the difficult situation, I said: "This is not true; this is a lie, a shameful kulak lie, because I saw the fields; I saw the fallen grain growing there; that there were certainly more than six, considerably more than eight poods sown there. Grain was poorly harvested there, and that spoke for the causes of the present state of affairs. If the whole harvest had been properly gathered in this village, there would have been enough for the complete fulfillment of the grain-procurement plan; there would have been enough for food until the next harvest; and there would even have been a surplus for sale.

The Party has given us directives. The XVI Party Conference and the Politburo of the CC AUCP(B) have clearly indicated that the main task before us is that of strengthening the organization and management of the collective farms....

The main cause of our failures lies in not fulfilling the tasks of our Party with regard to strengthening the management of the collective farms....

Now, in the harvesting campaign, we will again have a savage class struggle, and again the kulak will go to battle under the slogan: don't break your backs, be sure to take care of yourself, take [grain] for yourself, do not be concerned about the general good, put whatever you can in your own pocket, hide it in a pit. That is why the harvesting campaign stands before us as the most important campaign. In the class struggle, organizing the broad masses of millions of collective farmers and the poor and middle peasants for battle means, on the one hand, defeating the kulak, destroying him and finishing him off, and, on the other hand, ensuring that we leave our failures behind and further guarantee the broad socialist development of our country....

Addendum to special report of the OGPU Secret Political Division on the anti-collective farm movement and famine in Belarus, Kazakhstan, Ukraine, and individual regions of the USSR

In *Tragediia sovetskoi derevni* (2001). Excerpts, pp. 420–21. Translated by Bohdan Klid.

[Not before 20 July 1932]....

The spring sowing campaign in Ukraine proceeded in extremely tense circumstances (failures in gathering seed stocks, a difficult situation with fodder and draught animals, extremely slow tempos and poor quality of repair work, and acute difficulties with food supplies). Difficulties with food supplies affected 127 raions and the whole territory of the A[utonomous] M[oldavian] SSR, where the number of starving families was more than twenty thousand. In these raions, numerous instances were observed of eating surrogates and carrion, swelling, and death from starvation. In some raions, cases of cannibalism and suicide owing to hunger were registered. These incidents had a negative effect on the tempo and quality of spring sowing....

As of 20 May, in 21 raions alone, 116,000 people left in unorganized fashion, compared to 11,900 as of 15 February.... In some raions, up to 50 percent of the population has left to search for food.

As a rule, departures from the collective farms have been accompanied by the sorting out and division of property, animals, and agricultural equipment.... In the first ten days of July 70 disturbances were observed in connection with the sorting out of property and animals. Up to 200–300 people took part in some of the disturbances. The decline in labor discipline on collective farms affected by [the mass] departures is striking. On 150 collective farms selected here, as many as 30 to 70 percent [of the collective farmers] are not showing up for work.

Kulaks and anti-Soviet elements have noticeably increased their activities. Ukraine stands in first place when it comes to mass anti-Soviet incidents.

In the period from 1 January to 15 July 1932, 923 mass actions were registered in the UkrSSR. A whole series of disturbances accompanying the [mass] departures from the collective farms are not counted here. Noteworthy are the disturbances caused by food shortages, which are accompanied in some cases by demonstrative declarations by the mobs about leaving for Romania and on heading for the banks of the Dnister [River] to request assistance from the Romanians....

From 1 January to 1 July 1932, 118 kulak counterrevolutionary organizations, with an overall number of 2,479 participants, were uncovered. Besides this, 35 national c[ounter]r[evolutionary] groups with 562 participants were uncovered. In the main, the counterrevolutionary organizations are of an insurgent character, and their practical activity is characterized by the recruitment of insurgent cadres and preparations for an armed uprising.

Resolution "On Safekeeping Property of State Enterprises, Collective Farms and Cooperatives and Strengthening Public (Socialist) Property"[3]

In *Holodomor of 1932–33 in Ukraine* (2008). Excerpts, pp. 46–47.

7 August 1932....

II

1) Make all property belonging to collective farms and cooperatives (harvests in the fields, public reserves, livestock, cooperative stock and stores, etc.) equivalent to state property and fully strengthen the protection of this property against theft.
2) Use judicial repressions of the highest degree as measures of social protection against theft of collective farm and cooperative property: execution by shooting and confiscation of all property, commutable under mitigating circumstances to ten years' imprisonment with confiscation of all property.
   Amnesty cannot be granted to criminals sentenced in cases involving theft of collective farm and cooperative property....

Head, USSR Central Executive Committee, M[ikhail] Kalinin
Head, Council of People's Commissars, V[iacheslav] Molotov (Skriabin)
Secretary, USSR Central Executive Committee, A[vel] Yenukidze

Letter from Stalin to Kaganovich on changing the Ukrainian SSR leadership

In *Holodomor of 1932–33 in Ukraine* (2008). Excerpts, pp. 47–49.

11 August 1932....

3) The main issue now is Ukraine. Matters in Ukraine are currently extremely bad. Bad from the standpoint of the Party line. They say that, in two oblasts of Ukraine (Kyiv and Dnipropetrovsk, I believe), nearly 50 raion Party committees have spoken out against the grain-procurement plan as unrealistic. They say the matter is no better in other raion committees. What does this look like? This is not a Party but a parliament, a caricature of a parliament. Instead of directing the raions, [Stanislav] Kosior is always waffling between CC AUCP directives and the demands of raion committees, and now he has waffled himself to the end. Lenin was right when he said that a person who lacks the courage to go against the flow at the right moment cannot be a real Bolshevik leader. Bad from the standpoint of the Soviet line. [Vlas] Chubar is no leader. Bad from the standpoint of the GPU. [Stanislav] Redens is incapable of leading the battle against counterrevolution in such a large and unique republic as Ukraine.

3 This law made collective farm property equal to state property and provided extremely severe punitive measures for encroaching on the harvest. In popular lore, this resolution became known as the "law of five ears of wheat."

If we do not correct the situation in Ukraine immediately, we could lose Ukraine.... Also keep in mind that within the Communist Party of Ukraine (500,000 members, ha, ha) there is no lack (yes, no lack!) of rotten elements, active and latent Petliurites and direct agents of [Józef] Piłsudski. As soon as the situation gets worse, these elements will not hesitate to open a front within (and outside) the Party, against the Party. Worst of all, the Ukrainian leadership does not see these dangers.

Things cannot continue this way any longer.

It is necessary:

a) to remove Kosior from Ukraine and replace him with you [Kaganovich]. You will retain the post of secretary of the CC AUCP(B);
b) after this, transfer [Vsevolod] Balytsky to Ukraine as chairman of the Ukrainian GPU...and he will remain deputy chairman of the [All-Union] OGPU; make Redens deputy to Balytsky in Ukraine;
c) in a few months, replace Chubar with another comrade....
d) Set yourself the goal of turning Ukraine into a fortress of the USSR, a real model republic, within the shortest possible time. Do not spare money for this purpose. Without these and similar measures (economic and political strengthening of Ukraine, starting with the raions along the border, etc.), I repeat once again, we may lose Ukraine.

What do you think in this matter?

This requires attention as soon as possible, immediately after [your] arrival in Moscow.

Regards, J. Stalin....

Letter from the leadership of the Secret Political Division of the GPU Ukrainian SSR to the head of the SPD OGPU, Georgii Molchanov, on an attempt by Ukrainian scholars to inform the historian Mykhailo Hrushevsky about the famine in the Ukrainian SSR

In *Rozsekrechena pam'iat'* (2007). Excerpts, pp. 291–92. Translated by Bohdan Klid.

10 September 1932

PERSONAL

To the Head of the SPD OGPU
Comrade [Georgii] Molchanov
Moscow

We hereby inform you that at the behest of the Special Division of the OGPU an agent of the Secret Political Division of the Kyiv Oblast Department of the GPU has left...for Moscow.

Before leaving Kyiv, [the agent] spoke with students close to M. S. HRUSHEVSKY, the scholarly associates of the All-Ukrainian Academy of Sciences [Vasyl] DENYSENKO and [Sylvestr] HLUSHKO, informing them that he would be going to Moscow for several days to study materials related to his scholarly work.

DENYSENKO and HLUSHKO entrusted me…to convey the following to HRUSHEVSKY: "Upon my question of what to convey to the old man, DENYSENKO said the following:…

6) As to the political situation, say that a real famine prevails in Ukraine, that entire villages and districts are dying out; emphasize especially the horrific death rate among children. Explain this as a policy intended to break the Ukrainian nation once and for all as the only national force capable of serious resistance [to the regime]. Some will die, while others will be scattered across the endless expanses of Russia."

[The agent] promised to pass on all this….

ACTING HEAD, SPD GPU UkrSSR [Boris] KOZELSKY

ACTING HEAD, SECOND DEPARTMENT, SPD [Sergei] PUSTOVOITOV

Resolution of the Politburo of the CC AUCP(B) on grain procurement in Ukraine and the North Caucasus[4]

In *Holodomor of 1932–33 in Ukraine* (2008). Excerpts, p. 53.

22 October 1932

In order to strengthen grain procurement, dispatch for two ten-day periods:

Comrade Molotov to Ukraine….

Comrade Kaganovich to the N[orth] Caucasus….

Resolution of the Politburo of the CC CP(B)U on measures to strengthen grain procurement

In *Holodomor of 1932–33 in Ukraine* (2008). Excerpts, pp. 55–60.

18 November 1932….

III. On Grain Procurements from Collective Farms

On collective farm reserves

In accordance with the resolution of the CC AUCP(B) stating that "the fulfillment of the grain-procurement plan is the highest-priority mission for collective farms, state farms, MTS [machine-tractor stations], and private farmers," the Central Committee of the Communist Party (Bolshevik) of Ukraine expressly points out to all Party organizations in Ukraine that the full delivery of grain-procurement plans is the principal duty of all collective farms and MTS to the Party and the working class, the highest-priority task to which all other collective-farm tasks are subordinate, including the formation of various collective-farm reserves: seed grain, fodder, food supplies, and others.

4 Distrustful of local leaders, Stalin dispatched his emissaries to these major grain-producing areas. Using wide-ranging repressions, they managed to extort all grain and food reserves, resulting in millions of deaths.

In accordance with the above, the CC CP(B)U instructs Party organizations that....

2. A ban be instituted immediately on expending any reserves in kind stored on collective farms that are unsatisfactorily fulfilling grain-procurement plans....
3. Raion executive committees be authorized to transfer to grain-procurement reserves all reserves in kind accumulated by collective farms that are most unsatisfactorily fulfilling grain-procurement plans.
4. Where seed-grain reserves are concerned, paragraph 3 be implemented only with the prior consent of oblast executive committees with regard to every individual collective farm....

On in-kind advances and combating abuses on collective farms

1. Upon receipt of this decree, the distribution of any in-kind grain advances to all collective farms unsatisfactorily fulfilling grain-procurement plans shall be discontinued....
3. The seizure of grain stolen from collective and state farms during crop harvesting, threshing, transportation, storage, etc. by collective and private farmers...shall be organized immediately in all raions....
4. On collective farms unsatisfactorily fulfilling grain-procurement plans, all grain harvested by collective farmers from their home garden plots shall be counted as their in-kind payment for workdays; any excess grain issued to them shall be collected toward grain procurements.
5. Fines shall be levied on those collective farms that permitted the stealing of grain and are maliciously undermining grain-procurement plans in the form of additional meat-procurement targets: they are to supply a 15-month quota of meat from both collectivized and privately owned livestock....

On measures to combat kulak influence on collective farms and in village Party organizations

For the purposes of overcoming kulak resistance and the fulfillment of grain-procurement plans, the CC CP(B)U resolves the following:

1. Collective farms that are most maliciously sabotaging state grain-procurement plans shall be blacklisted.

The following measures shall be imposed upon blacklisted collective farms:

a) Immediate suspension of delivery of goods and of cooperative and state commerce in these villages and the removal of all available goods from cooperative stores;
b) Full prohibition of collective-farm commerce both for collective farms and collective farmers and for private farmers....

IV. On Grain Procurement from Private Farmers

1. Fines shall be levied on those private farmers who are maliciously undermining grain-procurement plans...in the form of an additional meat-procurement target amounting to a 15-month quota of meat....
   ...[V]illage councils shall establish deadlines and amounts of fines for each household within the limits of 15-month meat and one-year potato quotas....

The imposition of fines shall not release the farms from their duty of complete fulfillment of the grain-procurement plan....

3. Seed-grain and foodstuff loans given to private farmers by collective farms in their raions shall be collected immediately, without recourse to appeal....
4. Brigades consisting of collective-farm activists shall be organized...to assist in the complete fulfillment of grain-procurement plans by the private farming sector.

By 1 December, no fewer than 1,100 of these collective-farmer brigades shall be organized throughout Ukraine....

"Pro robotu z kolhospnym aktyvom. Postanova TsK KP(b)U vid 18 lystopada 1932" (On Work with Collective-Farm Activists. Resolution of the CC CP(B)U of 18 November 1932)

Komunist (Kharkiv), 20 November 1932, p. 1. Translated by Bohdan Klid.

...Under current conditions, the principal and basic task of collective-farm activists is the struggle with the kulak, with Petliurism and other counterrevolutionary elements that undermine the fulfillment of the grain-procurement plan, and rendering active assistance to the Party and the working class in fulfilling the established grain-procurement plan and strengthening of the collective farms on this basis....

CC CP(B)U

"Postanova TsK i TsKK KP(b)U vid 18 lystopada 1932" (Resolution of the CC and CCC CP(B)U of 18 November 1932)

Komunist (Kharkiv), 21 November 1932, p. 1. Translated by Bohdan Klid.

Given that in a number of village Party organizations, especially in the grain-procurement period, a coalescence has been uncovered of whole groups of communists and individual leaders of Party centers with kulakdom, Petliurism, and so on, which is turning those communists and Party organizations into de facto agents of the class enemy and is visible proof of the complete break of those centers and communists with the poor and middle strata of the collective-farm masses, the CC and CCC CP(B)U resolve to conduct an immediate purge of a number of village Party organizations that are openly sabotaging the fulfillment of the grain-procurement plan and undermining trust in the Party in the ranks of the workers....

CC and CCC CP(B)U

From a speech by Lazar Kaganovich at a joint meeting of the enlarged bureau of the North Caucasus Territorial Committee of the AUCP(B) and the bureau of the city committee and activists of Rostov-on-the-Don

In *Komandyry velykoho holodu* (2001). Excerpts, pp. 286–89, 291–92. Translated by Bohdan Klid.

23 November 1932

Tasks of the North Caucasus Bolsheviks in the struggle for grain and for the strengthening of collective farms....

At the end of October the CC AUCP(B) sent a group of its representatives to the North Caucasus, including members of the CC and the CCC, having established it as their main task, together with the Party's territorial committee, to draw up and put into effect "measures to crush sabotage in sowing and grain procurement organized by counterrevolutionary kulak elements in the Kuban."....

What brought forth this decision of the CC? As of 25 October, only 56 million poods of grain had been collected throughout the territory, as against 128 million poods collected by the same date last year....

Three *stanitsy* [settlements] of the Kuban—Novo-Rozhdestvenskaia, Medvedovskaia, and Temirgoevskaia—were blacklisted.... All goods were taken out of the blacklisted *stanitsy* and transferred to districts and *stanitsy* that were doing well in fulfilling the plan for sowing and procurements.... About 25–30 percent of the staff have already been purged from the ranks of the *stanitsa* organizations. The purge revealed great corruption in the Party organizations consisting of hostile class elements (kulaks and their agents, formerly active White Guardists, and others).... We will deport those purged from the Party beyond the borders of the territory to the northern oblasts as traitors to the working class and as politically dangerous.

In ten districts of the Kuban, delivery of goods to cooperative and state stores was halted, and in another ten districts that most shamefully failed in sowing and procurements, in addition to stopping deliveries, all goods were removed. Residents of the blacklisted *stanitsy* were warned that in the event sabotage continued in sowing and grain procurements, they would be deported beyond the borders of the territory to the northern oblasts, and these *stanitsy* would be settled by conscientious collective farmers....

We had materials available in the CC concerning protest actions of a number of communists and administrators of collective farms against grain procurements, of underground meetings of communists convoked in the *stanitsy* for collusion on how best to mislead the state and hide grain....

First of all, concerning individual peasant households....

How can this refusal of sowing and procurements be explained? It is undoubtedly the result of sabotage tactics organized by kulak elements....

In the village, especially in the Kuban, representatives of the kulaks still remain.... They are: first, some of the kulaks who were not deported; second, prosperous farmers developing into kulaks and closely associated with them; third, those who have escaped from exile and are hiding with their relatives, and sometimes also with "bleeding-heart" Party members who have a membership card in their pocket but are in fact traitors to the working class. And, finally, representatives of the bourgeois, White Guard, and Cossack intelligentsia.... Some of the Petliurists who moved from Ukraine in the spring joined this intelligentsia.

They carry on counterrevolutionary agitation....

Here is one example of counterrevolutionary activity by kulak elements in the Poltavskaia *stanitsa* of the Slaviansk district.

A counterrevolutionary kulak White Guard organization was uncovered in this *stanitsa*. It was associated with the former *stanitsa* ataman Omelchenko, a member of the Kuban Rada and one of the most active White Guard émigrés. Having penetrated the state economic apparatus with the aim of undermining it, the organization engaged in wrecking in the collective farms and organized the sabotage of grain procurements and sowing.

Operations bulletin of the GPU Ukrainian SSR on matters concerning the exposure of anti-collective farm groups and grain procurements

In *Rozsekrechena pam'iat'* (2007). Excerpts, pp. 430–31. Translated by Maksym Motorenko and Bohdan Klid.

6 December 1932
TOP SECRET

An effective blow against anti-Soviet groups within collective farms is continuing at a rapid rate.

The c[ounter]r[evolutionary] activities of uncovered and liquidated groups on collective farms consisted essentially in disrupting the main agricultural campaigns, especially of grain procurement; in squandering, hiding, and stealing grain; and in anti-collective farm and anti-Soviet agitation.

In addition, some anti-collective farm groups were involved in insurgent agitation.

The overwhelming majority of liquidated groups in the collective farms were strongly influenced by kulaks and other counterrevolutionaries, especially Petliurite elements that corrupted the collective farms, most notably their administrative apparatus....

This bulletin takes account of 55 internal collective-farm and anti-Soviet groups from 42 regions of five oblasts: 290 members of these groups were arrested, including 28 chairmen of collective farms.

Resolution of the CC AUCP(B) and CPC USSR on grain procurements in Ukraine, the North Caucasus, and the Western Oblast

In *Holodomor of 1932–33 in Ukraine* (2008). Excerpts, pp. 65–68.

14 December 1932

...[T]he CC AUCP(B) and the CPC USSR resolve the following:

1. The CC CP(B)U and the CPC Ukrainian SSR, on the personal responsibility of Comrades [Stanislav] Kosior and [Vlas] Chubar, shall fully complete the grain and sunflower seed procurement plans by the end of January 1933.
2. The North Caucasus regional Party and executive committees, on the personal responsibility of Comrades Sheboldaev and Larin, shall fully complete the procurement plan for grain by 10–15 January 1933 and for sunflower seeds by the end of January 1933....
4. In view of extremely poor efforts and the absence of revolutionary vigilance in a number of local Party organizations in Ukraine and the North Caucasus, a significant number of raions have been infiltrated by counterrevolutionary elements: kulaks, former officers, Petliurites, supporters of the Kuban Rada, and so on. They have managed to find their way into collective farms as directors and other influential administration members.... They have succeeded in infiltrating village councils, land-management bodies, and cooperative societies and are now trying to direct the work of these organizations against the interests of the proletarian state and Party policy, as well as trying to organize a counterrevolutionary movement and sabotage of grain procurements and sowing campaigns. The CC AUCP(B) and CPC USSR order the CC CP(B)U, the North Caucasus regional Party and executive committees, and the CPC of Ukraine resolutely to root out these counterrevolutionary elements by means of arrest and long-term imprisonment in concentration camps, without stopping short of capital punishment for the most malicious elements.
5. The CC and CPC inform all Party and state organizations of the Soviet Union that the worst enemies of the Party, the working class, and the collective-farm peasantry are the saboteurs of grain procurement who have Party membership cards in their pockets.... The CC and CPC order appropriate structures to apply severe repressive measures against these traitors and enemies of Soviet rule and collective farms, who still carry Party membership cards in their pockets: five- to ten-year terms of imprisonment in concentration camps and, under certain circumstances, execution by shooting.
6. The CC and CPC point out that instead of the correct Bolshevik implementation of nationality policy, Ukrainization was carried out mechanically in a number of raions of Ukraine.... This made it easier for bourgeois-nationalist elements, Petliurites and others to create their legal façades and counterrevolutionary cells and organizations.
7. The CC and CPC particularly point out to the Party and executive committees of the North Caucasus region that the irresponsible, anti-Bolshevik "Ukrainization" of nearly half the raions in the North Caucasus did not correspond to the cultural interests of the population. It was carried out with a complete lack of supervision and...provided the enemies of Soviet rule with legal façades for organizing resistance to the measures and tasks of Soviet authorities by kulaks, [tsarist] officers, reemigrating Cossacks, members of the Kuban Rada, etc.

   In order to crush resistance to grain procurement by kulak elements and their "Party" and non-Party flunkeys, the CC and CPC USSR resolve the following:

a) To relocate the entire population of the Poltavskaia *stanitsa* (North Caucasus) as the most counterrevolutionary to the northern oblasts of the USSR in the shortest time possible.... [T]o populate this *stanitsa* with conscientious collective farmers who are Red Army soldiers.... [T]o transfer all lands, winter crops, buildings, inventory, and livestock from the farmers being expelled to these settlers....

b) To prosecute and sentence traitors to the Party who were arrested in Ukraine for organizing the sabotage of grain procurement to terms of 5–10 years' imprisonment in concentration camps: former raion secretaries, chairmen of executive committees, directors of land-management bodies, and chairmen of raion associations of collective farms....

c) To exile all "communists" expelled from the Party for sabotaging grain procurement and sowing campaigns to the northern oblasts on the same basis as kulaks.

To propose that the CC CP(B)U and CPC of Ukraine pay serious attention to the proper implementation of Ukrainization; to eliminate its mechanical implementation; to expel Petliurites and other bourgeois-nationalist elements from Party and state organizations....

e) Immediately to change the language used in state and cooperative agencies in the North Caucasus, as well as all newspapers and magazines in the "Ukrainized" raions, from Ukrainian to Russian, which is more understandable to Kuban residents. Also, to prepare to change the language of school instruction to Russian by autumn. The CC and CPC order the regional Party and executive committees immediately to investigate and improve the staffing of schools in "Ukrainized" raions....

Chairman, CPC USSR, V[iacheslav] Molotov (Skriabin)
Secretary, CC AUCP(B), J[oseph] Stalin

Resolution of the CC AUCP(B) and CPC USSR on Ukrainization in the Far Eastern Region, Kazakhstan, Central Asia, the Central Black Earth Oblast, and other areas

In *Holodomor of 1932–33 in Ukraine* (2008), pp. 68–69.

15 December 1932

The CC AUCP(B) and the Council of People's Commissars of the USSR resolutely condemn the statements and suggestions made by individual Ukrainian comrades on the mandatory Ukrainization of entire areas of the USSR (for example, the DVK [Far Eastern Region], Central Asia, the Central Black Earth Oblast, and so on). Statements of this nature only play into the hands of bourgeois nationalists who, having been chased out of Ukraine as harmful elements, are emerging in newly Ukrainized areas to continue their demoralizing work.

The regional Party and executive committees of the DVK, the oblast Party and executive committees of the Central Black Earth Oblast, the Kazakh regional Party committee, and the [regional] Council of People's Commissars are immediately to discontinue Ukrainization in their regions, change all Ukrainized newspapers, printed materials, and publications to the Russian language and, by autumn 1933, to prepare the transfer of schools and instruction to the Russian language.

Secretary, CC AUCP(B), J[oseph] Stalin
Chairman, CPC USSR, V[iacheslav] Molotov (Skriabin)

Resolution of the CC AUCP(B) and CPC USSR on grain procurement in Ukraine, 19 December 1932

In *Holod 1932–1933 rokiv na Ukraïni* (1990), p. 295. Translated by Maksym Motorenko and Bohdan Klid.

1. The CC AUCP(B) and CPC USSR consider that unless a radical breakthrough in grain procurements is immediately organized in the Dnipropetrovsk, Odesa, and Kharkiv oblasts, Ukraine will be unable to fulfill even the twice-reduced plan that is obviously failing because of the frivolous attitude of Ukrainian workers toward the tasks assigned them by the Party and the government.
2. The CC AUCP(B) and CPC USSR charge Comrades [Lazar] Kaganovich and [Pavel] Postyshev immediately to depart for Ukraine to assist the CC CP(B)U and the CPC of Ukraine; as well as to spend time in the key oblasts of Ukraine as specially authorized by the CC AUCP(B) and the Council of People's Commissars of the USSR, sharing the work with [Stanislav] Kosior, [Vlas] Chubar, and [Mendel] Khataevich, and to adopt all necessary measures of an organizational and administrative nature in order to fulfill the grain-procurement plan.

Secretary of the CC: J[oseph] Stalin
Chairman of the CPC USSR: V[iacheslav] Molotov

Telegram from Kaganovich to Stalin on the need to cancel the CC CP(B)U resolution of 18 November 1932

In *Holodomor of 1932–33 in Ukraine* (2008). Excerpts, p. 70.

22 December 1932

…[T]he resolution of the Politburo of the CC CP(B)U…of November 18 is still in effect….

Although this directive begins with the statement that fulfillment of the grain-procurement plan is the top priority, it nevertheless provides grounds for permitting the creation of all sorts of reserves on collective farms that have failed to fulfill the grain-procurement plan….

The very raising of the issue of creating and securing reserves, as well as prohibiting the transfer of seed reserves to grain procurement, provides the legal grounds and basis for entrenching the established view that the plan cannot be fulfilled, although this is not said openly…. [W]e are convinced that this "preoccupation" with reserves, including seed reserves, is seriously hampering and undermining the entire grain-procurement plan. These views are being reinforced by the resolution of the CC CP(B)U dated 18 November.

For these reasons we consider it necessary to cancel this resolution as well....

[Lazar] Kaganovich, [Mikhail Aleksandrovich] Chernov

Memorandum from Comrade [Vsevolod] Balytsky (Ukraine) to CC AUCP(B) Comrade Stalin

In *Narodna viina* (2011). Excerpts, pp. 230, 233. Translated by Bohdan Klid.

The uncovering of counterrevolutionary organizations and groups establishes:

1. The existence of a broadly ramified Polish-Petliurite insurgent underground encompassing 67 raions of Ukraine, according to incomplete data.
2. The contamination of collective farms, state farms, MTS [Machine-Tractor Stations], MTM [Machine-Tractor Workshops] by Petliurite, kulak, White Guardist and anti-Soviet elements who were actively carrying on seditious activity in the collective farms, misappropriating, squandering and deliberately destroying grain, draft animals, and livestock.
3. The activity of the national-chauvinist part of the Ukrainian intelligentsia, which, in a number of instances, ideologically and organizationally formed and headed the uncovered counterrevolutionary insurgent organizations.
4. The seditious activity of traitors with Party [membership] cards, not only by way of sabotaging and conducting subversive activity to prevent the fulfillment of grain procurements, but, as has been determined in many cases of uncovered insurgency, they are organizers and leaders of counterrevolutionary groups.

In 20 days of December 12,178 persons were arrested.

Of these: 4,204 persons for [belonging to] insurgent c[ounter[-r[evolutionary] organizations. For ruining and sabotaging grain procurements [as members of] 995 liquidated groups. 3,044 persons as kulaks, those subject to firmly established quotas, and those concealing grain....

At the present time we are continuing our work of destroying insurgent organizations and [their] cells, of uncovering and liquidating organizational centers.

The entire Chekist apparatus has been mobilized to render the utmost assistance to Party organizations in fulfilling grain procurements, and a decisive operational blow is being struck at all saboteurs and their lackeys, speculators, and other counterrevolutionary elements who are working against the fulfillment of the grain-procurement plan.

Specially Authorized Operative of the OGPU in Ukraine
V[sevolod] Balytsky

23 December 1932

Telegram of 28 December 1932 from Joseph Stalin to members of the CC and Presidium of the CCC AUCP(B), other Communist Party and OGPU bodies

In *Narodna viina* (2011). Excerpt, p. 234. Translated by Bohdan Klid.

Top secret....

To all members of the CC and the Presidium of the CCC AUCP(B), all secretaries of oblast and provincial committees and national CCs, all Party members of Collegiums of the People's Commissariat of Agriculture and the People's Commissariat of State Farms, and all authorized representatives of the OGPU.

The following are being distributed for your information: a) a memorandum from C[omrade] [Yefim Georgievich] Yevdokimov (North Caucasus) on wrecking in the system of state grain farms; b) a memorandum from C[omrade] [Vsevolod] Balytsky (Ukraine) on the Petliurite organization in Ukraine, which has set as its goal the conducting of sabotage of grain procurements and the preparation of peasant uprisings to separate Ukraine from the USSR and reestablish capitalism. In view of the importance of the documents being distributed, it is recommended that they be treated with serious attention.

Secretary of the CC J[oseph] Stalin

Letter from the CC CP(B)U on the mandatory delivery of all collective-farm grain reserves, including sowing seed, to fulfill the grain-procurement plan

In *Holodomor of 1932–33 in Ukraine* (2008). Excerpts, p. 71.

To: Secretaries of Party raion and oblast committees, persons authorized by the CP(B)U
24 December 1932....

1. All collective farms that failed to fulfill the grain-procurement plan have five days to deliver all collective-farm reserves without exception, including sowing seeds, in order to fulfill grain-procurement quotas.
2. Everyone resisting this measure, including communists, shall be arrested and tried.
3. Warn all collective-farm heads that if any hidden reserves, stores, and the like are found after the set date, the chairmen and other guilty parties will be brought before the courts and severely punished....

[Stanislav] Kosior
Stroganov
Alekseev

Letter from the CC CP(B)U to oblast and raion Party committees on collecting all available reserves for grain procurement

In *Holodomor of 1932–33 in Ukraine* (2008). Excerpts, pp. 73–74.

29 December 1932....

...[T]he CC AUCP(B) has canceled the CC CP(B)U resolution of 18 November on the nonshipment of seed reserves as a decision that weakened our positions in the battle for grain.

The CC CP(B)U orders those collective farms that have not fulfilled the grain-procurement plan immediately to hand over all available reserves, including so-called sowing seed, in the course of five to six days for the fulfillment of the grain-procurement plan....

Any delay in handing over these reserves will be considered by the CC to be sabotage of grain procurement by raion leaders and will be subject to commensurate measures.

Secretary, CC CP(B)U, S[tanislav] Kosior

Resolution of the Politburo of the CC AUCP(B) on grain procurement in Ukraine

In *Holodomor of 1932–33 in Ukraine* (2008). Excerpts, p. 77.

1 January 1933

The CC CP(B)U and CPC UkrSSR shall widely inform village councils, collective farms, collective farmers, and toiling private farmers that....

b) Those collective farms, collective farmers, and private farmers who stubbornly insist on misappropriating and concealing grain will be subject to the strictest punitive measures provided by the USSR Central Executive Committee resolution of 7 August 1932 "On the safekeeping of property of state enterprises, collective farms, and cooperatives and strengthening public (socialist) property."

Secretary, CC AUCP(B), J[oseph] Stalin

Joseph Stalin, "O rabote v derevne. Rech' tov. Stalina na Ob"edinennom plenume TsK i TsKK VKP(b), 11 ianvaria 1933 goda" (On Work in the Countryside: Speech Delivered on 11 January 1933 at a Joint Plenum of the CC and CCC of the AUCP[B])

Pravda, 17 January 1933, p. 1. Modified English translation from Stalin, *Works*, vol. 13, *1930–January 1934* (Moscow: Foreign Languages Publishing House, 1954). Excerpts, pp. 220–24, 226–37.

...What was the main defect in our work in the countryside during the past year, 1932?

The main defect was that our grain procurements in 1932 were accompanied by greater difficulties than in the previous year, in 1931.

This was by no means due to the bad state of the harvest; for in 1932 our harvest was not worse but better than in the preceding year....

What was the matter? What are the reasons for this defect in our work? How is this disparity to be explained?

1) It is to be explained, in the first place, by the fact that our comrades in the localities, our Party workers in the countryside, failed to take into account the new situation created in the countryside by the authorization of collective-farm trade in grain.... There is no need to prove that this circumstance was bound to give rise among the peasants to a certain reluctance to deliver their grain to the state....

   But the unfortunate thing is that our Party workers in the countryside, at all events many of them, failed to understand this simple and natural thing.... Instead of speeding up grain procurements, they began to speed up the formation of all sorts of funds on the collective farms, thus encouraging the grain producers in their reluctance to fulfill their obligations to the state....

   ...[F]or the first commandment is—fulfill the plan for grain procurements; the second commandment is—get the seed stored; and only after these conditions have been fulfilled may collective-farm trade in grain be begun and developed....

2) The second reason for the defects in our work in the countryside is that our comrades in the localities—and not only those comrades—have failed to understand the change that has taken place in the conditions of our work in the countryside as a result of the predominant position acquired by the collective farms in the principal grain-growing areas....

   ...[T]he prime responsibility for conducting the farm has now been transferred from the individual peasants to the leadership of the collective farm, to the leading group of the collective farm.... And what does this mean? It means that the Party...must now take over the direction of the collective farms, assume responsibility for the work....

   The transition from individual farming to collective farming should have led...to an intensification of Communist leadership on the collective farms. In fact, however, what has happened in a number of cases is that the Communists have been quite out of it, and the collective farms have been run by former White officers, former Petliurists, and enemies of the workers and peasants generally....

3) The third reason for the defects...is that many of our comrades...failed to understand that, in spite of being a socialist form of economy, the collective farms by themselves are yet far from being guaranteed against all sorts of dangers and against the penetration of all sorts of counter-revolutionary elements into their leadership; that they are not guaranteed against the possibility that under certain circumstances anti-Soviet elements may use the collective farms for their own ends.

   The collective farm is a socialist form of *economic* organisation, just as the Soviets are a socialist form of *political* organisation.... But collective farms and

Soviets are only a *form* of organisation—a socialist form, it is true, but only a *form* of organisation for all that. Everything depends upon the *content* that is put into this form....

Collective farms, as a socialist form of economic organisation, may perform miracles of economic construction if they are headed by real revolutionaries, Bolsheviks, Communists. On the other hand, collective farms may for a certain period become a shield for all sorts of counter-revolutionary acts if these collective farms are run by Socialist-Revolutionaries and Mensheviks, Petliura officers and other White Guards, former Denikinites and Kolchakites. Moreover, it must be borne in mind that the collective farms, as a form of organisation, not only are not guaranteed against the penetration of anti-Soviet elements, but, at first, even provide certain facilities which enable counter-revolutionaries to take advantage of them temporarily.... Hence, it is not only a matter of the collective farms themselves as a socialist form of organisation; it is primarily a matter of the content that is put into this form; it is primarily a matter of *who* stands at the head of the collective farms and *who* leads them....

...[I]it is precisely because some of our Communists have not understood this simple thing that we now have a situation where a number of collective farms are managed by well-camouflaged anti-Soviet elements who organise wrecking and sabotage in them.

4) The fourth reason for the defects in our work in the countryside is the inability of a number of our comrades in the localities to reorganise the front of the struggle against the kulaks; their failure to understand that the face of the class enemy has changed of late, that the tactics of the class enemy in the countryside have changed, and that we must change our tactics accordingly if we are to achieve success....

...The present-day kulaks and kulak agents, the present-day anti-Soviet elements in the countryside...will never say, "Down with the collective farms!" They are "in favour" of collective farms. But inside the collective farms they carry on sabotage and wrecking work that certainly does the collective farms no good. They will never say, "Down with grain procurements!" They are "in favour" of grain procurements. They "only" resort to demagogy and demand that the collective farm should reserve a fund for the needs of livestock-raising three times as large as that actually required; that the collective farm should set aside an insurance fund three times as large as that actually required; that the collective farm should provide from six to ten pounds of bread per working member per day for public catering, etc. Of course, after such "funds" have been formed and such grants for public catering made, after such rascally demagogy, the economic strength of the collective farms is bound to be undermined, and there is little left for grain procurements....

...The kulaks have been defeated, but they are far from having been crushed yet.... [C]ollective farms can be either Bolshevik *or* anti-Soviet. And if certain collective farms are not being led by us, that means that they are being led by anti-Soviet elements. There can be no doubt about that.

5) Finally, there is one other reason for the defects in our work in the countryside. This consists in underestimating the role and responsibility of Communists

in the work of collective-farm development, in underestimating the role and responsibility of Communists in the matter of grain procurements. In speaking of the difficulties of grain procurement, Communists usually throw the responsibility upon the peasants, claiming that the peasants are to blame for everything. But that is absolutely untrue, and certainly unjust. The peasants are not to blame at all. If we are to speak of responsibility and blame, then the responsibility falls wholly upon the Communists, and we Communists alone are to blame for all this....

Order from the CPC USSR and CC AUCP(B) on preventing the mass flight of starving villagers in search of food

In *Holodomor of 1932–33 in Ukraine* (2008). Excerpts, pp. 85–86.

22 January 1933

The CC AUCP and the CPC USSR have received reports on the mass flight of peasants "for bread" to the Central Black Earth Oblast, the Volga region, the Moscow Oblast, the Western Oblast, and Belarus. The CC AUCP and the Council of People's Commissars of the USSR do not doubt that this flight of villagers, like the exodus from Ukraine last year, have been organized by enemies of Soviet rule.... Last year the Party, Soviet, and Cheka [secret police] agencies of Ukraine missed that counterrevolutionary undertaking by the enemies of Soviet rule. Last year's mistakes cannot be repeated this year.

First. The CC AUCP and the CPC USSR order the Regional Council, the Executive Council, and the Official OGPU Representative in the North Caucasus to prevent the mass flight of peasants from the North Caucasus to other regions and entry into the region from Ukraine.

Second. The CC AUCP and the CPC USSR order the CC CP(B)U, the CPC Ukrainian SSR, [Vsevolod] Balytsky, and [Stanislav] Redens to prevent the mass flight of peasants from Ukraine to other regions and entry into Ukraine from the North Caucasus.

Third. The CC AUCP and the CPC USSR order the Official Representatives of the OGPU in the Moscow Oblast, the Central Black Earth Oblast, the Western Oblast, Belarus, and the Lower Volga and Middle Volga regions to arrest "peasants" fleeing north from Ukraine and the North Caucasus and, after the filtration of counterrevolutionary elements, to return the rest to their places of residence....

Chairman, CPC USSR, V. M. Molotov
Secretary, CC AUCP(B), J[oseph] Stalin

Resolution of the Politburo of the CC AUCP(B) on strengthening the CP(B)U Central Committee and oblast organizations

In *Holodomor of 1932–33 in Ukraine* (2008). Excerpts, pp. 88–89.

24 January 1933

The CC AUCP(B) considers it to be established fact that the Party organizations of Ukraine have failed to perform the tasks assigned to them by the Party in organizing grain procurement and fulfilling the grain-delivery plan....

The CC AUCP(B) considers that the Odesa, Dnipropetrovsk, and Kharkiv oblasts are the critical ones for deciding the fate of Ukraine's agriculture and that they must be secured in the first instance.

The CC AUCP(B) resolves to:

1) Appoint CC AUCP(B) Secretary Comrade [Pavel] Postyshev [to the posts of] Second Secretary of the CC CP(B)U and First Secretary of the Kharkiv oblast Party committee.
2) Appoint Comrade [Mendel] Khataevich First Secretary of the Dnipropetrovsk oblast Party committee while retaining him as one of the secretaries of the CC CP(B)U.

Appoint Comrade [Mikhail] Razumov First Secretary of the Odesa oblast Party committee.[5]

Relieve Comrades Maiorov, Stroganov, and Terekhov of their duties....

From a draft report of the GPU Ukrainian SSR on the progress of repressive operations in the countryside from November 1932 to January 1933

In *Rozsekrechena pam'iat'* (2007). Excerpts, pp. 502–3. Translated by Maksym Motorenko and Bohdan Klid

[Early February 1933]....

As a result of intensifying operative pressure by the organs of the GPU between November and January with the aim of suppressing the activity of organized c[ounter]r[evolutionary] elements on the collective farms, 1,208 groups inside collective farms were uncovered and liquidated and, among these, 6,682 people were arrested.

These groups, according to the basic nature of their activities, are classified as follows:

Kulak insurgent and other c[ounter]r[evolutionary] organizations and groups	71
National c[ounter]r[evolutionary] groups	2
Theft and squandering of grain	757
Theft of other socialist property	97

5 The decision regarding Razumov was canceled; Yevgenii Veger (1899–1938) was confirmed as First Secretary of the Odesa oblast committee of the CP(B)U.

Sabotage of grain procurements	105
Wrecking on collective farms	65
Resistance to grain procurements	119
Other anti-Soviet groups	99

In the process of grain procurement, it also became glaringly apparent that there was organized sabotage on the part of some deviant communists in deference to kulaks, Petliurites, and other counterrevolutionary elements corrupting the Soviet and collective-farm apparatus.

Active resistance to grain delivery was noted on the part of the leadership of village councils, Party cells, collective-farm and district organizations. In particular, attempts were noted on the part of some "communists" to disrupt the removal of seed grain for the fulfillment of grain requisitions from collective farms that maliciously did not fulfill their grain-procurement plans....

From operational order no. 2, GPU Ukrainian SSR, on the need to liquidate the insurgent underground before beginning sowing

In *Rozsekrechena pam'iat'* (2007). Excerpts, pp. 511–12. Translated by Maksym Motorenko and Bohdan Klid.

13 February 1933....
Top Secret....
Kharkiv

The organized sabotage of grain procurement and autumn sowing; organized mass theft on collective and state farms; terror against the staunchest and most steadfast communists and village activists; the transfer of dozens of Petliurite emissaries in the fall of last year; the distribution of counterrevolutionary Petliurite leaflets, especially on the Right Bank; and the analysis of secret-service materials **indicated the undoubted existence of an organized counterrevolutionary insurgent underground in Ukraine associated with foreign powers and foreign intelligence services, mainly with the Polish general staff....**

For the purpose of immediately breaking up and exposing the c[ounter] r[evolutionary] underground, a Shock Operative Group was organized in the GPU Ukrainian SSR. During this period it successfully undertook a series of operations and exposed a counterrevolutionary underground in Ukraine that spanned up to 200 districts, about 30 railway stations and depots, and a number of places in border zones....

An analysis of cases liquidated in this period indicates that we were faced here with an integral, thoroughly developed plan for the organization of an armed insurrection in Ukraine by spring 1933 for the purpose of overthrowing Soviet rule and establishing a capitalist state, the so-called "Independent Ukrainian Republic."....

Special Plenipotentiary in Ukraine
Vice Chairman, OGPU
V[sevolod] Balytsky

Stanislav Kosior, "Ob oshibkakh i nedochetakh v organizatsii khlebozagotovok na Ukraine" (On Errors and Shortcomings in Organizing Grain Procurements in Ukraine)

Pravda, 15 February 1933. Excerpts, p. 3. Translated by Bohdan Klid.

...I now want to focus on our concrete errors directly related to that which Com[rade] Stalin revealed in his speech—the errors and shortcomings in organizing grain procurements in Ukraine....

...[I]n essence, only in November did we actually begin to rouse the Party organization for grain procurement. Until November there were very widespread illusions and easygoing attitudes to the effect that one way or another grain would be procured; that the plan, after all the reductions that we received, would be fulfilled....

...[T]he theft of grain, the squandering of grain, as it is delicately described, was very widespread during this year's grain harvest.... But what is especially characteristic, testifying to the existence of easygoing attitudes and absence of Bolshevik vigilance, is that approximately until November that mass incidence of theft and squandering of grain was not uncovered....

New forms of struggle against grain procurements by our class enemy were overlooked. As before, the class enemy was "sought" outside the collective farm, but he, having made his way into the collective farm in such positions as inventory keeper, accountant, vice chairman, and so on, organized thievery, provided cover for and facilitated the theft and squandering of grain.... [A]ll this was hidden from us by all kinds of pious signs, such as the establishment of various funds for public catering, and so on....

When you come to a district for grain procurements, they begin to take reports out of every pocket for you, statistics about low yields compiled more often than not by hostile elements that have wormed their way into the collective farms, land divisions, and Machine-Tractor Stations. But in these reports you will not find one word about the harvest that was in the field, that was squandered, stolen, hidden. Our comrades...unable to make head or tail of the falsified figures supplied to them, sometimes become kulak advocates, defenders of those numbers. In countless examples it has been shown that this arithmetic is kulak arithmetic, that according to it we not only would not receive the quantity of grain that was procured but would not procure even half of it. In the hands of hostile elements, false figures and inflated balances became a cover for thievery, for the pilfering of grain on a massive scale....

...In order to procure grain it is necessary that every leading official and every communist be imbued with distrust toward false, juggled figures. It is necessary, by means of concrete facts—and there are more than enough of them—to reveal to the collective farmers the true essence of kulak arithmetic....

It is clear that where there was no pressure from our side: where class vigilance was dulled among our comrades, the kulak, the class enemy, was active. In a number of districts quite a few collective farms turned out to be under the influence if not in the hands of kulaks, Petliurites, Makhnovites, and other elements.... This took place because, as a result of complacency, the absence of Bolshevik vigilance and perspicacity, our work became so unsatisfactory that even in good districts kulaks and wreckers managed to worm their way into the leadership of a number of collective farms and organize the sabotage of grain procurements....

We did not uncover these facts in time and did not firmly grasp the reins so as to correct the mistakes of Party organizations in a timely fashion and promptly reorient their work according to the new situation in the countryside. The CC AUCP(B) and Comrade Stalin gave us a number of clear and precise directives in that regard at the appropriate time....

The legacy of last year's mistakes hung over us; the fear of going to extremes, of squeezing too hard was dominant in the districts, and in a number of instances it turned into total inactivity and opportunistic neglect....

At the plenum Comrade Stalin said that the new situation in the countryside created by the appearance of collective-farm trade in grain required that Party organizations speed up and intensify the tempo of grain procurement from the very first days of the harvest.... Instead of directly and firmly facing the collective and individual farmers with their primary obligation of fulfilling the plan, instead of speeding up grain procurement from the very beginning of the harvest, they did not take the appropriate measures, lost time, and did not take the offensive in the most critical period of grain procurement....

...We let matters slip from our grasp and caused irreparable harm to grain procurements—the main task that we were obliged to fulfill, come what may....

If we are to speak about grain procurements themselves, about the methods adopted, about means of putting pressure on weak points, then here as well there were very serious shortcomings this year.

I should first of all recall the attitudes prevailing at the start of the grain procurements...and through June–September. What were those attitudes made up of? Of whining that the plan was difficult, that the plan given was incorrect, and so on.... We spoke about this more than once with district workers of Odesa and Dnipropetrovsk [oblasts]; we posed the question more than once and with great seriousness and were obliged to take severe measures with regard to some leading district workers but, even so, we must frankly admit that we did not bring this matter to an end. We did not strike hard at hidden, masked attitudes; at those who were saying in various quarters that nothing would come of the plan, that one should wait, that it might be reduced, and so on. And at the same time there were discussions that served to demobilize and disarm Party organizations. These demobilizing attitudes in localities can also be explained by the fact that when they were making preparations for grain procurements, they were engaged in conversations about plan reductions, hoping for an easy plan, and raising the expectations of collective farmers in that regard. And then, when the plan was announced; when in Odesa [oblast], for instance, where the harvest was considerably better than last year's, a plan was announced that was greater than last year's, the oblast and district leadership was unable to counteract these attitudes and break these demobilizing attitudes even in the course of the entire campaign....

And finally, the last question, which also played by no means the least role in the unsatisfactory fulfillment of the grain-procurement plan, and which also showed that we allowed a serious error here—I have in mind the policy of the creation of so-called seed funds in Ukraine for storage prior to the fulfillment of the grain-procurement plan.

What is the essence of the question? It is clear that the fulfillment of the grain-procurement plan is the primary obligation of every collective farm. And if in the countryside an opportunist, an agent of the class enemy, comes forward and declares: first of all for me and later, what remains, for the state, then it is easy to figure out this line. Every communist will reject such an obviously opportunistic line; here it is immediately clear that this is not our line but one prompted by the class enemy, even though there were such "communists" among us who themselves defended this line. But there was a second line, similar in its essence, that brought us great harm: it was explained in large measure by the fear of repeating the mistakes of the previous year. It consisted in the policy of creating and storing so-called seed funds while not fulfilling the grain-procurement plan. We stored seed funds, declaring them untouchable....

What was the harm in the policy of untouchable funds? The harm consisted in demoting the interests of the state to second place, and, as a result, our comrades in the districts, instead of turning things around, guaranteeing the fulfillment of grain procurements first and foremost, retreated before the funds. This policy of creating and storing funds prior to the fulfillment of the grain-procurement plan clearly weakened our positions with regard to fulfilling the grain-procurement plan, created plausible cover for saboteurs, and strengthened resistance to grain procurements. Indeed, this policy disoriented the district and village workers, demobilizing them with regard to organizing grain procurements.

In essence, on the one hand we struggled against the kulak and struggled to fulfill the grain-procurement plan, while on the other hand, in the main question—that grain had to be delivered to the state first of all, and funds created afterward—we took the wrong position and found ourselves in the falsest of situations....

I must say directly that we failed to fulfill the plan, notwithstanding all opportunities to fulfill it; we failed because we did not work satisfactorily.

"Vyshe znamia proletarskogo internatsionalizma!" (Raise Higher the Banner of Proletarian Internationalism!)

Lead editorial in *Pravda*, 10 March 1933, p. 1. Excerpts. Translated by Bohdan Klid.

...The growing strength of the Soviet Union is encountering desperate resistance on the part of the shattered counterrevolutionary bourgeois-kulak nationalist groups, which is inevitably being reflected within the Party. On the front of national and cultural development as well, the class enemy, having suffered a resounding defeat in open battle, is now trying in other ways, by other means to throw his last forces, desperate evil and hatred, against us. From open methods of struggle he has turned to camouflaged methods, not encountering determined resistance on the part of local Party and Soviet organizations in a number of instances....

There can be no doubt that in the current period of class struggle and the liquidation of the kulak, local nationalist deviationists, screened by the false national flag, are essentially defending the last positions of the defeated and economically shattered bourgeois-kulak nationalist elements, playing into the hands of the international imperialists, into the hands of the interventionists.

The counterrevolutionary activities of all sorts of chauvinists and deviationists with regard to the nationality question are facilitated and, in a number of instances, made possible primarily by the insufficient revolutionary vigilance and occasional crude errors of local Party and Soviet organizations.... [L]ocal Party and Soviet organizations have not understood the new tactics and new maneuvers of the remnants of the shattered kulaks and have found themselves captive to local nationalist elements and those deviating in their direction.

And then, finally, do we not find testimony to the same effect in outrageous instances of the crudest distortions of Leninist nationality policy in Ukraine? Here, in a number of raions, as a result of the dulling of class vigilance, of not understanding the new maneuvers of the remnants of the shattered classes and underestimating the unbreakable link between the national and peasant questions, there has been a significant weakening of the struggle against deviations in the nationality question. In some raions the nationality policy of the Party was carried out mechanically, without taking account of concrete particularities, without the necessary educational work and necessary controls, without giving enough attention to training Bolshevik cadres. All this, obviously, played into the hands of the bourgeois-kulak and Petliurite elements, making it easier for them to enter into the Soviet apparatus, collective farms, etc.....

The class enemy is desperately resisting the victorious building of socialism, also directing his weapons against Leninist nationality policy.

The task of Party organizations, especially in Ukraine, Belarus, Central Asia, Kazakhstan and other national republics and oblasts, as well as the local press, lies in the timely exposure of the new tactics and machinations of class enemies, in tearing off their masks and showing the masses the true counterrevolutionary face of the bourgeois-kulak nationalist elements, deviationists, and those reconciled to them....

Report from the GPU Ukrainian SSR on problems with food supplies and raions of Ukraine affected by famine

In *Holodomor of 1932–33 in Ukraine* (2008). Excerpts, pp. 100–102.

12 March 1933

According to data reported in February and March, problems with food supplies were registered in 738 population centers of 139 raions, where 11,067 families are starving.

Among the starving, 17,308 people are suffering from acute illnesses owing to malnutrition.

In the same period, 2,487 people died of hunger.

The largest number of famine cases was registered at the end of February and at the beginning of March. In some places this phenomenon has grown massive in scale....

Dnipropetrovsk and Kyiv oblasts and the Moldavian ASSR are most affected by food-supply problems. The number of starving families afflicted by disease and mortality is particularly striking in Dnipropetrovsk oblast.

Collective farmers prevail among the starving....

Starving families eat various food substitutes (corn cobs and stalks, millet pods, dried straw, herbs, rotten watermelons and beetroots, potato peelings, acacia pods, etc.) as food. Incidents of eating the flesh of cats, dogs, and dead horses have been registered.

Twenty-eight incidents of cannibalism have been registered....

Deputy Head, Ukrainian SSR GPU
Secret Political Department, Aleksandrovsky

From a memorandum of the CC CP(B)U to the CC AUCP(B) on progress in preparing spring sowing, some reasons for the difficult food situation in a number of oblasts and raions of the republic, and measures to aid the starving

In *Holod 1932–1933 rokiv na Ukraïni* (1990). Excerpts, pp. 441–44. Translated by Maksym Motorenko and Bohdan Klid.

15 March 1933....

At the present time, along with reports from all oblasts about preparations for sowing, we are receiving reports about the difficult food situation with demands for assistance.

1. Food situation

If in the last year there was silence about the difficult situation in the raions, this year it is the opposite—in every possible way they are trying to overemphasize the worst cases, to collect figures and generalize them. In a great many reports the true purpose of the information is apparent—to obtain assistance from the CC....

The reports available to the CC CP(B)U from the oblast committees and through the GPU on the scale of famine are extremely contradictory....

Information coming in from various sources indicates that the gravest situation is indisputably the one that has developed in Dnipropetrovsk oblast. It must be said that it is precisely from there that we receive most information about famine, deaths, and so on, while, for instance, there is very little information for Odesa oblast, and, if one were to judge only from reports, then Odesa oblast would have to be considered the most fortunate oblast of all. In fact, of course, that is far from being the case.... Out of 49 raions of Dnipropetrovsk oblast, 21 raions are considered to be in dire straits. Kyiv oblast, where 31 raions are considered to be in exceptionally difficult condition, is in second place as to the number of reports concerning starvation. Here we obviously have a very serious recurrence of the starvation that occurred last year on quite a large scale. Further, according to the number of affected raions, we have Vinnytsia [oblast]—17; the Donbas—11 raions; Odesa—14; Kharkiv—9 raions. Altogether, according to GPU registers, 103 raions are affected in Ukraine. But all these data on the number of raions hardly represent the true state of affairs.... Compared to last year, with regard to affected raions, as well as collective farms, we get a much more varied picture. Here the raions with the most dilapidated collective farms and poor management practices are obviously most affected. Most of the starving are those who had few workdays or none at all, especially those with large families, as well as individual farmers.

So-called "returnees," who roamed somewhere with their families during this time and are now returning to their villages and collective farms in significant numbers, are in especially difficult straits.... A significant number of the starving are members of collective farms who earned plenty of workdays but received very little grain in hand. In such raions 75–80 percent of grain issued was allotted for public catering. What is more, it is certainly the good members of collective farms, especially those with large families, who suffered relatively more because of public catering. There were cases when issued bread was taken back. There are also cases in which a great many collective farmers and individual farmers hid grain under the influence of panic and starved at the same time.... The main reason for the famine stands out more prominently and sharply before the masses this year: poor management and an unacceptable attitude toward the public good (losses, stealing, and waste of grain). For in most of the starving raions a negligible amount of grain was taken for procurement, and it is by no means possible to say that "grain was taken.".... Why are people starving in Kyiv oblast, where we took hardly any grain from the major raions for the procurement plan? There was a serious nonfulfillment of the spring crop-sowing plan and a huge loss of winter crops in those raions. And that which was gathered was eaten in public catering—as much as one wanted—and pilfered by those who did not work.... Comrades who have been to the localities say that now there is hardly any talk in the Kyiv region to the effect that "grain was taken" and that people blame themselves for poor work, for not safeguarding grain, for allowing it to be pilfered. In this regard, there is undoubtedly a certain about-face among the masses on the collective farms that manifests itself in their attitude toward those who did not work.

But this is not by any means understood everywhere and by all collective farmers. An exodus from the village took on huge proportions despite measures taken to prevent it. The fact that starvation has not yet knocked sense into the heads of a great many collective farmers is shown by the unsatisfactory preparations for sowing precisely in the most troublesome raions....

There is a need for food aid not only in grain but also other products, vegetables, potatoes, meat, fats, and so on....

Certainly, at the beginning of sowing, extra food assistance will be required for Kyiv oblast, the Donbas, the Moldavian ASSR, and the Dnipropetrovsk, Kharkiv, and Vinnytsia oblasts.

S[tanislav] Kosior

Report of the All-Union Resettlement Committee on resettling collective farmers to Ukraine (with table)

In *Holodomor of 1932–33 in Ukraine* (2008). Excerpts, pp. 121–22.

29 December 1933
Express. Secret.
To: Head of GULAG OGPU, Comrade Berman

The All-Union Resettlement Committee of the CPC USSR...reports that the proposed resettlement plan has been fulfilled by 104.76 percent. In total...117,149 persons...have been relocated....

Deputy Chairman, All-Union Resettlement Committee, CPC USSR Rud

Summary Data on Echelons of Resettlers Sent to Ukraine as of 28 December 1933

Source Oblast	Destination Oblast	Number Households
Gorky	Odesa	2,120
Ivanov	Donetsk	3,527
Belarusian SSR	Odesa	4,630
Central Black Earth Oblast	Kharkiv	4,800
Western	Dnipropetrovsk	6,679

S. V. Kosior, "Results and Immediate Tasks of the National Policy in the Ukraine: Report by Comrade S. V. Kosior to the Joint Plenum of the Central Committee of the Communist Party of the Ukraine, November, 1933"

In *Soviet Ukraine Today* (1934). Excerpts, pp. 34, 72–74.

...The transition to the policy of mass collectivization, the liquidation of the kulaks as a class, and the severe intensification of the class struggle which it entailed could not but activize the nationalist elements. It should never have been forgotten that in the Ukraine in particular, in nine cases out of ten, the struggle of every form of counter-revolution is waged under nationalist slogans, is camouflaged by the nationalist flag, the most cunning, the most harmful and the most despicable flag.

We did not bear this in mind sufficiently in our work; we overlooked the nationalist danger, we did not mobilize ourselves against it, did not rouse the Party to the struggle against it.

In the new situation which arose as a result of the final and irrevocable victory of the collective farm system, and of the almost complete liquidation in the main of the kulaks as a class, the remnants of the defeated class enemy began to adopt new tactics in the fight against the Soviet governments—tactics of "quiet sapping." Camouflaged in all ways, they wormed their way into our factories, our Soviet farms, machine and tractor stations, collective farms, and even into our Party organizations. Several sections of the cultural and economic construction in the rural districts were captured by the kulak, Petliura, nationalist elements. It must be admitted that we, the Communist Party of the Ukraine and its Central Committee, did not in time discover the new methods of struggle the class enemy was adopting in the villages or the manner in which he penetrated into our apparatus....

We must on no account forget that the remnants of the defeated kulaks are becoming active and are being welded together by the Ukrainian nationalists, by the remnants of the former Ukrainian petty-bourgeois parties abroad, which do their mercenary work first for one and then for another capitalist country.

We must discover and unmask before the toilers of the Ukraine all these foul and despicable traitors to the Ukrainian people—the Ukrainian nationalists of all shades.

During the last few years the nationalist elements have been able to penetrate into our institutions in considerable numbers, to place their own people in these institutions, to organize sabotage and wrecking, and to pursue their counter-revolutionary aims under the flag of Ukrainization. Whole counter-revolutionary, nationalist nests were formed in the People's Commissariat of Education, of Agriculture, of Justice, in the Ukrainian Academy of Sciences, the Ukrainian Institute of Marxism-Leninism, the Agricultural Academy, the Shevchenko Institute, etc. More than that, it became particularly clear during the Party purging that in several districts, nationalist elements had wormed their way into the leadership of the district Party organizations as well.

How was it that the enemy succeeded in getting round us....

In this connection we must most particularly emphasize the role of [Mykola] Skrypnik [Skrypnyk]. He, to a certain extent, was the centre of attraction for the different nationalist elements; he acted as a sort of shield for them....

"The Results and Immediate Tasks of the National Policy in the Ukraine. Resolution Adopted by the Joint Plenum of the Central Committee and Central Control Commission of the Communist Party of the Ukraine on the Report of Comrade S. V. Kosior (November 22, 1933)"

In *Soviet Ukraine Today* (1934). Excerpts, pp. 102, 105, 107–11.

...Our Party's adoption of the policy of mass collectivization and the liquidation of the kulaks as a class and the uprooting of the last remnants of capitalism encountered the desperate resistance of the bourgeois nationalist elements, particularly of the Ukrainian kulaks and their agents in the Party.

Forced out of their production base, the bourgeois-kulak elements continued the struggle against the Soviet government and the Communist Party by adopting in the changed situation, the new tactics of quiet sapping, and thus penetrated into our factories and government offices, Soviet farms, machine and tractor stations, collective farms, and even Party organizations, and tried to disrupt them from within....

However, the Communist Party of the Ukraine overlooked and did not in time expose the intensified penetration of Ukrainian national elements, the remnants of the defeated class enemy, into the leading bodies of the collective farms, machine and tractor stations, of various Soviet land departments, and cultural organizations, and even into the Party itself, for the purpose of carrying on their wrecking and counter-revolutionary sabotage of the Party and the Soviet government....

Owing to the relaxation of the Bolshevik struggle against Ukrainian nationalism, the Communist Party (Bolsheviks) of the Ukraine and its Central Committee, which several years ago successfully smashed [Oleksandr] Shumsky-ism, recently overlooked the formation of a new nationalist deviation in the ranks of the Party led by N. A. Skrypnik [Mykola Skrypnyk]....

The nationalist deviation of Skrypnik and the trend that he led facilitated the work of the Ukrainian nationalist[s] that was directed towards separating the Ukraine from the Soviet Union and towards converting it into a colony of Polish fascism or German imperialism....

The decision of the Central Committee of the Communist Party of the Soviet Union of December 14, 1932, and that of January 24, 1933, served as the beginning of serious self-criticism in the ranks of the Communist Party of the Ukraine and of the rectification of the mistakes committed in the leadership of agriculture as well as in the practical pursuit of the national policy....

This Plenum of the Central Committee and Central Control Commission of the Communist Party of the Ukraine sets before the Communist Party of the Ukraine the following main tasks in the sphere of national policy....

As hitherto, Great Russian chauvinism is the principal danger confronting the whole of the Soviet Union and the whole of the Communist Party of the Soviet Union. But this does not in the least contradict the fact that in certain republics of the U.S.S.R., particularly in the Ukraine at the present moment, the principal danger is local Ukrainian nationalism, which has joined with the imperialist interventionists....

To offer determined resistance to all attempts to break or to relax the ties between the Ukraine and the Soviet Union, to strengthen these ties...such are the most important tasks of the Party in the Ukraine.

J. V. Stalin, "Report to the Seventeenth Party Congress on the Work of the Central Committee of the C.P.S.U.(B.)," 26 January 1934

In Stalin, *Works*, vol. 13 (Moscow: Foreign Languages Publishing House, 1955). Excerpts, pp. 368–70.

...It should be observed that the survivals of capitalism in people's minds are much more tenacious in the sphere of the national question than in any other sphere. They are more tenacious because they are able to disguise themselves well in national costume. Many think that [Mykola] Skrypnyk's fall from grace was an individual case, an exception to the rule. This is not true. The fall from grace of Skrypnyk and his group in the Ukraine is not an exception. Similar aberrations are observed among certain comrades in other national republics as well.

What is the deviation towards nationalism—regardless whether it is a matter of the deviation towards Great-Russian nationalism or the deviation towards local nationalism?.... The deviation towards nationalism reflects the attempts of "one's own," "national" bourgeoisie to undermine the Soviet system and to restore capitalism. The source of both these deviations, as you see, is the same. It is a *departure* from Leninist internationalism. If you want to keep both deviations under fire, then aim primarily against this source, against those who depart from internationalism—regardless whether it is a matter of the deviation towards local nationalism or the deviation towards Great-Russian nationalism. (*Stormy applause.*)

There is a controversy as to which deviation represents the chief danger: the deviation towards Great-Russian nationalism, or the deviation towards local nationalism. Under present conditions, this is a formal and, therefore, a pointless controversy. It would be foolish to attempt to give ready-made recipes suitable for all times and for all conditions as regards the chief and the lesser danger. Such recipes do not exist. The chief danger is the deviation against which we have ceased to fight, thereby allowing it to grow into a danger to the state. (*Prolonged applause.*)

In the Ukraine, only very recently, the deviation towards Ukrainian nationalism did not represent the chief danger; but when the fight against it ceased and it was allowed to grow to such an extent that it linked up with the interventionists, this deviation became the chief danger. The question as to which is the chief danger in the sphere of the national question is determined not by futile, formal controversies, but by a Marxist analysis of the situation at the given moment, and by a study of the mistakes that have been committed in this sphere....

Pavel Postyshev, Speech delivered at the Seventeenth Congress of the AUCP(B), 27 January 1934

In *XVII s"ezd Vsesoiuznoi Kommunisticheskoi partii (b)* (1934). Excerpts, pp. 65–67, 69, 71. Translated by Bohdan Klid.

...Comrades, the full power and full significance of the day-to-day leadership of the CC AUCP(B) and of Comrade Stalin personally are particularly apparent in the example of the correction of errors and blunders in the work of the CP(B)U.

You are well aware that in the period 1931–33 the CP(B)U committed gross errors and blunders in the management of agriculture and in carrying out the Leninist nationality policy of the Party in Ukraine....

What were the root causes of all these errors, blunders, and failures?....

The CP(B)U did not take into account all the distinctive characteristics of the class struggle in Ukraine and the peculiarities of the internal situation in the CP(B)U.

What are those characteristics?....

The first characteristic is that in Ukraine the class enemy masks his activity against socialist construction with the nationalist banner and chauvinist slogans.

The second characteristic is that the Ukrainian kulak underwent a lengthy schooling in struggle against Soviet power, for in Ukraine the civil war was especially fierce and lengthy, given that political banditry was in control of Ukraine for an especially long period.

The third characteristic is that splinter groups of various counterrevolutionary organizations and parties settled in Ukraine more than elsewhere, being attracted to Ukraine on account of its proximity to western borders.

The fourth characteristic is that Ukraine proves to be an object of attraction to various interventionist centers and finds itself under their especially diligent observation.

And, finally, the fifth characteristic is that the deviationists in the CP(B)U in all-Party questions usually allied and continue to ally themselves with the nationalist elements in their ranks, with the deviationists on the nationality question....

The CP(B)U should have crushed the nationalist elements, increased substantially the vigilance of all Party organizations in relation to those forms and methods of struggle that the class enemy has used and continues to use in Ukraine, mobilized the Party organizations even more in the spirit of intolerance toward the slightest manifestations of opportunism and nationalist deviations in particular, secured all important sectors of work in the city and especially in the countryside with reliable Bolsheviks, and, most important of all, more firmly adjusted methods of Bolshevik leadership according to the new situation and the directives of Comrade Stalin on the new tasks.

Unfortunately, the CP(B)U did not draw all those conclusions in full measure. There lies the explanation of its errors and failures both in agriculture and in carrying out Leninist nationality policy in Ukraine....

In those years of failure we had a situation in which Ukraine's agricultural capacity increased consistently, but the grain-procurement situation, the best indicator of the state of agriculture and class struggle in the village, deteriorated from one year to the next....

What was the grain-procurement situation in 1931? If by December 1930 Ukraine fulfilled its grain-procurement plan, by December 1931 only 74 percent was fulfilled; grain procurement stretched into May [1932], and only 90 percent was fulfilled in the rural sector....

If we look at the grain-procurement plan for 1932, the picture looks even worse than in 1931. Instead of 400 million poods procured by December 1930, and 380 million by December 1931, by December 1932 only 195 million poods were procured....

The question arises: What was the matter?....

This can be explained, first of all, by the lack of Bolshevik vigilance, by the failure to hone Party organizations and conduct due struggle with the class enemy.

It is to be explained, secondly, by the fact that the CP(B)U's methods of work and leadership in agriculture were inappropriate to the new situation and new tasks of developing collectives....

What solved the problem of overcoming the breakdown in Ukrainian agriculture?

The problem was solved above all by the day-to-day management of the CC AUCP(B) and of Comrade Stalin personally and by the tremendous material and technical assistance provided to Ukraine by the CC AUCP(B). The problem was solved, secondly, by the Bolsheviks of Ukraine giving battle—decisive battle—to the class enemy. The problem was solved, thirdly, by the Bolsheviks of Ukraine radically reforming the methods of managing agriculture according to the historic directives of Comrade Stalin at the January plenum of the CC and CCC and by the subsequent day-to-day directives of the CC AUCP(B) and Comrade Stalin personally....

As you know, the CP(B)U also committed extremely serious errors and blunders in carrying out Leninist nationality policy.

Where did these errors and blunders lie?

The error lay, first of all, in overlooking the activities of the nationalist counterrevolution, notwithstanding such serious signals as the trial of the Union for the Liberation of Ukraine in 1929 and the Ukrainian National Center affair in 1931.

The error lay, secondly, in overlooking the escalation of [Mykola] Skrypnyk's particular nationalist errors into a system of national-opportunistic views, into a nationalist deviation, which took place roughly in 1930–31.

You see, therefore, that the roots of these errors lie in the failure of the CP(B)U to draw all the necessary conclusions from the directives of Comrade Stalin at the Sixteenth Congress of our Party concerning the threat of the activation of nationalist elements, the threat of the revival of deviations on the nationality question in connection with the full-scale advance of socialism on all fronts and the increasing acuteness of class struggle in the country....

The decisions of the CC AUCP(B) of 14 December [1932] and 24 January [1933] roused the CP(B)U to battle to correct the errors and blunders in carrying out the Party's nationality policy in Ukraine.

The past year was the year of the defeat of the nationalist counterrevolution, the uncovering and defeat of the nationalist deviation headed by Skrypnyk, and the exertion of great creative effort in the sphere of the development of Soviet Ukrainian culture....

Stanislav Kosior, Speech delivered at the Seventeenth Congress of the All-Union Communist Party (Bolshevik), 30 January 1934

In *XVII s"ezd Vsesoiuznoi Kommunisticheskoi partii (b)* (1934). Excerpts, pp. 197–99.
Translated by Maksym Motorenko and Bohdan Klid.

...The period from the Sixteenth to the Seventeenth Congress is distinguished particularly by the fact that in the course of it the Party achieved tremendous victories, achieved them in fierce class struggle against the remnants of the capitalist elements....

...[I]n this period the CC AUCP(B) paid exceptional attention to the task of directing socialist construction in Ukraine.... The situation was extremely complicated. The completion of total collectivization and the liquidation on that basis of the kulaks as a class required increased attention and better management of collective farms, which was absolutely necessary in that period, when the collective farms became the decisive force in the countryside, when there was need for an even more decisive struggle with the remnants of the defeated kulaks and all kinds of counterrevolutionary elements that were attempting to demolish the collective farms from within and to corrupt them. And it turned out that at this very moment there was a lack of vigilance among us in the CP(B)U....

Only after the historic speech of Comrade Stalin at the January plenum of the CC and the CCC, following the severe criticism of our errors by Comrade Stalin—the errors of our leadership; after his Bolshevik instructions, extraordinary in their strength and simplicity, on how to get out of the situation that had developed and how to conduct our further work—only then did the true reorganization of our work begin. To that end the CC AUCP(B) had to take additional measures in relation to Ukraine. I have in mind the resolution of 24 January 1933—the resolution on strengthening the leadership of the CP(B)U and the main oblasts of Ukraine by sending to us entire ranks of first-rate workers....

The example of Ukraine gives only a partial but nevertheless a quite striking illustration of the titanic work carried out by the Central Committee and of the results we had all across the Soviet Union. All this bears witness to the highest quality of leadership. Here, again and again, we want to speak of the role of Comrade Stalin....

When referring to Ukraine, we cannot but dwell on the nationalist deviation in the CP(B)U, which played an exceptional role in creating and intensifying the lag in agriculture. We cannot but say that after the Sixteenth Congress the CP(B)U did not conduct a decisive struggle against nationalist deviations. Here, Comrade Stalin was absolutely correct in pointing this out. In Ukraine, where the class situation is the most complicated, where the activities of the remnants of the defeated class enemy attain the highest level of acuteness, the national flag plays an exceedingly important role for the class enemy. Moreover, the predominant coloring of the class enemy, with which he masks himself, is above all the national flag, nationalist clothing....

Only in 1933, under the direct control of the CC AUCP(B), of Comrade Stalin, according to his instructions, did we conduct a struggle in Ukraine to unmask the nationalist deviation of the CP(B)U, a struggle with counterrevolutionary nationalist elements, with nationalism in general....

...And the fact that we destroyed nationalism, and the fact that we took up work in the countryside properly, determined our successes in 1933....

BRITISH FOREIGN OFFICE DOCUMENTS

"Mr. Cairns' Investigations in Soviet Union." Andrew Cairns to E. M. H. Lloyd, 3 August 1932

In *The Foreign Office and the Famine* (1988). Excerpts, pp. 104–9, 111.

Dear Lloyd,

I left Moscow on June 15th and returned July 30th. During my six weeks absence I saw a good sample of the Ukraine, Crimea and Northern Caucasus....

...At a station close to the Ukrainian border the peasants I spoke to in the bazaar all cursed collectivisation... Every station had its crowd—from scores to several hundred, depending on the size of the town—of rag-clad hungry peasants, some begging for bread, many waiting, mostly in vain, for tickets, many climbing on to the steps or joining the crowds on the roof of each car, all filthy and miserable and not a trace of a smile anywhere.... I did not see a single good crop until we got very close to Kiev. The autumn sown crops were generally badly winter-killed, spindly, weedy and short, and the spring sown crops were choked by weeds. But all crops were of good colour, indicating that they had ample moisture.... At the depot in Kiev many people asked for bread.

In the morning of June 17th, I went for a walk and soon came across a small street bazaar.... I finally got one woman alone and made her stop talking and answer my questions. She said there was practically no bread because the Government had collected so much grain and exported it to England and Italy; that the collective farms around Kiev were very bad; that all the members were hungry and many were leaving; she had left her village with many others because she could not get food and that some were dying of starvation; she had a job in Kiev but it was impossible to keep from being hungry as she could not buy much food with her small salary....

...While climbing up a very steep hill to get a good look at the beautiful Dnieper [Dnipro] River, I came across two women pulling what at first I thought was dandelions or young leeks for greens, but upon examination it turned out to be tender grass. I asked them what they were going to do with the grass and they said "make soup." They were third category workers and got only 125 roubles per month and only 200 grammes of bread per day.... On the way back to my hotel I saw a horrible sight—a man dying on the street. He was apparently insane as he was going through all the motions of eating and rubbing his stomach with apparent satisfaction.... Further on I took advantage of a foreigner's privilege and took my place at the head of a long queue.... Outside the store were swarms of people.... I asked several people why things were so dear, and, seeing I did not understand a word of Ukrainian, they pulled in their cheeks, pretended to vomit, drew their finger's across their throat, and said, in Russian, "Kushat' nyet, nichevo nyet" (there is nothing to eat, nothing at all)....

[T]he next day, June 18th....

In the evening I found one of the largest bazaars in Kiev and had a most interesting time. Men's soft leather top boots, 300 roubles; ladies' split leather shoes, 120 roubles; a few small squares of sugar at 2/3 of a rouble each; butter 10 roubles per pound; eggs 6 roubles for 10; very small tins of fish 7 roubles; old scabby potatoes 1 rouble, and very small new ones 1½ roubles per pound; bread 10½ roubles per loaf; a policeman offering a pair of completely worn out top boots for 5 roubles; pigs feet 4 for 10 roubles; and scores of men and children, with badly swollen tummies, in rags, asleep on the ground (while flies by the thousand crawled over them) or begging or picking up scraps of vegetables and fish scales to eat. A terrific rain storm broke and I had to stand under a roof for 2 hours, during which time many people crowded around to try and make me understand them. Many of them were quite young, and nearly all were town workers. They were unanimous that things had never been so bad, that nearly everybody was hungry, that the peasants would not work, because they were all hungry, and were moving into the towns by the thousands, that less than 80% of the crop had been sown by collective farms and that the individual peasants had eaten their seed.... On my way home I stopped to give coins to 3 small girls (they were all nearly dead with hunger and the smallest one certainly could not have lived more than a few days longer) and a crowd gathered around to tell me there were many such children in Russia....

June 20th....

...On the way home I saw a truck load of rye meal being unloaded into a big bakery. The men carrying the bags told me the meal would cost over 100 roubles a pood in the bazaar. As usual, a crowd soon gathered around and all agreed that conditions were very bad, that people were hungry because there was no bread or anything else, that the peasants were not working so there would be less bread next winter, and that the collective farms were in a very bad condition. One man followed me all the way back to the hotel. He said he was a second category worker and got 180 roubles per month and 525 grammes of bread per day, that first category workers got 600 grammes of bread per day and street car conductors only 400 and absolutely nothing else. What surprised me most in Kiev was not what the people said (although conditions there seemed to be worse than in any place I visited in the next five weeks), but that they should all—young, middle-aged and old alike—be unanimous and that none of them seemed to care what they said or who heard them, even the police and G.P.U....

"Situation in Soviet Union." Sir Edmund Ovey (Moscow) to the Foreign Office, 5 March 1933

In *The Foreign Office and the Famine* (1988). Excerpt, p. 215.

Conditions in Kuban have been described to me by recent English visitor as appalling and as resembling an armed camp in a desert—no work no grain no cattle no draught horses, only idle peasants or soldiers. Another correspondent who had visited Kuban was strongly dissuaded from visiting the Ukraine where conditions are apparently as bad although apathy is greater. In fact all correspondents have now been "advised" by the press department of Commissariat for Foreign Affairs to remain in Moscow. Expulsions and arrests are the order of the day and this morning names of forty officials arrested for agricultural sabotage have been published in the press....

"Conditions in Northern Caucasus in Spring of 1933." Report by Otto Schiller, German Agricultural Attaché in Moscow, 23 May 1933. Forwarded to Anthony Eden by the Duchess of Atholl, July 1933

In *The Foreign Office and the Famine* (1988). Excerpts, pp. 258–59, 262–63.

In the spring of 1933 I visited the following districts of the Northern Caucasus: The Kuban Province (Kubanskaya Oblast) from Kropotkino to Krasnodar; the Districts of Stavropol and Armavir; and the Povolye territories up to Salska-Bieloglina—a stretch, altogether of 1,200 kilometres by car.

The chief problem of North Caucasian agriculture is the famine, which since the late Autumn of 1932 has reached appalling dimensions. This time, in contrast to the preceding year, it is not only a matter of semi-starvation which then caused a fall in the productivity of labour, and of morale. It has reached the point of actual death from starvation, thanks to which, in whole districts, the population is rapidly disappearing, and agricultural activity, therefore, at an almost complete standstill.

There are two factors which are simultaneously causing the diminution in the population of the Northern Caucasus, now so clearly apparent. Firstly, the measures for the deportation and transplanting of large masses of the population, carried out on a large scale since last Autumn in connection with the State grain collection, and the fight against Kulak sabotage (a fight which is still proceeding), and secondly the extinction of the population through famine, now in full swing.

The policy of expulsion and deportation was put into force principally against the Cossacks of the Kuban Territory. The Kuban Cossacks by tradition and mentality were the most resolute antagonists of agricultural collectivism.... During last Autumn they exercised passive, and also, in some cases active, resistance to the measures of the Government.... The greater part of that particular Cossack population was forcibly uprooted from their villages and deported to the Ural territories, thus practically annihilated. The Cossack population remaining in their native districts was considerably thinned through famine....

Populations have diminished, not only in those villages against which measures of expulsion and other punitive measures have been applied, but in almost all the villages visited by me during my journey....

The famine is not so much the result of last year's failure of crops as of the brutal campaign of State Grain Collection....

A distinctive feature of this famine is that the authorities have not acknowledged and do not now acknowledge that famine exists. They even officially deny it.... [A]t present no foreign help is possible. And the Soviet Government itself does nothing. I was told of many cases when sufferers, swollen from famine, implored help from the village soviets, only to be told that they should eat the bread which they had got hidden away, and that no famine at all existed. In fact the authorities explain the present situation by insisting that there is no lack of grain, that the peasants hide it....

There is no doubt that last Spring grain was concealed in many cases. *The Government at that time formed special permanent committees of Komsomoltsy* (young Communists, male and female) *who, carrying iron rods, went prodding the soil in the peasant courtyards, thus revealing large quantities of grain.* These Committees still continue to visit the villages in many places seeking freshly dug spots which might prove to be hiding places for grain....

...It may very well be that the extermination of the Cossack population was advantageous and desirable to the Soviet Government....

"Conditions in Union of Soviet Socialist Republics." William Strang (Moscow) to Sir John Simon, 17 July 1933

In *The Foreign Office and the Famine* (1988). Excerpts, pp. 255–56.

Moscow, July 17, 1933

Sir,

It is hardly necessary to confirm the notorious fact that on the eve of the harvest conditions of semi-famine still continue to obtain over large areas of the Soviet Union. Unauthorised estimates of the number of people who have died, either directly or indirectly, from malnutrition in the past year vary up to as much as the fantastic figure of 10 million. It is, I think, quite impossible to guess what the figure may be. I am told by a member of the German Embassy that in the German Agricultural Concession in the North Caucasus, five men have been employed in gathering and burying the corpses of peasants who have come in from outside this oasis of plenty in search of food and have died. One of the erectors employed by Metropolitan-Vickers in the Ukraine says that people died of starvation in the block of apartments in which he lived, one of them outside his door. He says that he refused to believe the stories he heard of conditions in the villages outside and walked out to see for himself; he found, as he had been told, that some villages were completely deserted, the population having died or fled, and that corpses were lying about the houses and streets. His Majesty's consul in Moscow is occasionally visited by Canadians of Russian origin settled in the Ukraine who tell him the same dreary, if less lurid, story of want, hopelessness and desolation.

2. Great indignation has been expressed in the Soviet press at the establishment of a fund in Germany for the assistance of starving Germans in the Soviet Union, and the columns of the Moscow newspapers are full of resolutions from collective farms and other organisations in the Volga and other regions inhabited by colonists of German race, protesting against these stories of starvation as "Fascist lies" and inviting unemployed Germans from the Reich to come and see for themselves or to send their children to the Volga collective farms to be fed and educated. It is, of course, true that there are prosperous and productive collective farms in the Volga German Republic and that a part of the population has enough to eat, but it is also true, as we know from Volga German servants of the Embassy, that the conditions prevalent in the Ukraine also obtain, to a milder degree and less widely perhaps, in the Volga German Republic....

"Tour by Mr. W. Duranty in North Caucasus and the Ukraine." William Strang (Moscow) to Sir John Simon, 26 September 1933

In *The Foreign Office and the Famine* (1988). Excerpts, pp. 309–13.

Moscow, September 26, 1933

Sir,

...I have the honour to inform you that Mr. Walter Duranty, the Moscow correspondent of the *New York Times,* returned to Moscow a few days ago after a ten days' trip in the North Caucasus and the Ukraine....

According to Mr. Duranty, the population of the North Caucasus and the Lower Volga has decreased in the past year by 3 million, and the population of the Ukraine by 4–5 million. Estimates that he had heard from other foreigners living in the Ukraine were that approximately half the population had moved either into the towns or into more prosperous districts....

From Rostov Mr. Duranty went to Kharkov, and on the way he noticed that large quantities of grain were in evidence at the railway stations, of which a large proportion was lying in the open air. Conditions in Kharkov were worse than in Rostov. There was less to eat, and the people had evidently been on very short commons.... During the year the death rate in Kharkov was, he thought, not more than 10 per cent above the normal. Numerous peasants, however, who had come into the towns had died off like flies....

...The Ukraine had been bled white. The population was exhausted, and if the peasants were "double-crossed" by the Government again no one could say what would happen. It was all very well, Mr. Duranty said, to call the U.S.S.R. a pacific country. It had to be, for, if a war occurred within the next five years, before the peasants had had time to forget the winter of 1932 and the spring of 1933, it would be impossible to mobilise the peasants....

According to Mr. Duranty, Postyshev is the real force in the Ukraine. He and his "boys" in the political departments now run the country....

Mr. Duranty thinks it quite possible that as many as 10 million people may have died directly or indirectly from lack of food in the Soviet Union during the past year....

William Strang

GERMAN FOREIGN OFFICE DOCUMENTS

German Consulate, Kyiv, 15 January 1934, "Politischer Jahresbericht 1933" (Political Report for 1933)

In *Holodomor v Ukraïni 1932–1933 rokiv* (2008). Excerpts, pp. 172–82, 187–88. Translated by Alexander J. Motyl.

The Internal Political Situation

The internal political situation in the jurisdictional area [*Amtsbezirk*] was characterized by famine, which, according to cautious estimates, took some 2.5 million lives from among the approximately 12 million inhabitants of the provinces of Kyiv, Chernihiv, and Vinnytsia. The condition and mood of the population were, like the measures of the Party and administrative agencies, decisively influenced by the catastrophe.... Hunger and want created a condition of despair not only among peasants; the workers, who are politically more important to the Soviet authorities, are deeply embittered as a result of bad food conditions, delayed and inadequate payment [of wages], and all kinds of privations in general. After all the disappointments, villagers no longer believed government promises that state organs would not demand more grain than already established in quotas at the beginning of the year and would not tolerate alternative plans from local authorities. Often the population even desired a worsening of the catastrophe, which they hoped might soon lead to the downfall of Bolshevik rule.

When, in order to guarantee the harvest, state authorities wanted and needed to squeeze enormous labor efforts out of people in this physically and spiritually weakened condition, the solution of this task could only be attempted by force. It was applied in the villages first and foremost by the "political sections" in the Machine-Tractor Stations, which thereby performed undeniable services for Soviet power.... In the cities, tens of thousands of workers and other inhabitants had to take part "voluntarily" in the harvest, without regard for their responsibilities at work and their suitability and under terrible housing and food conditions; they were received with suspicion and rejection by the peasants. Refusal led to loss of job or to denial of passport and thus to resettlement. Such a feudal system necessarily produced an intensification of anti-Soviet attitudes, which, in addition to a generally growing anti-Semitism, led to many acts of violence by the peasants, who went so far as to set on fire the living quarters of the urban agricultural workers....

The Party

If the Soviet authorities have finally succeeded in gathering the grain they need for their purposes, despite great difficulties and at the cost of destroying countless lives, that is due to the vigor with which the Party has asserted its will in its own ranks and thus also in all state agencies....

Only extraordinary measures could mobilize the internally weakened Party and state apparatus for the grain battle. This happened as a result of further developing the competitive and shock-brigade systems, sending thousands of tested Party members to the countryside, establishing the already mentioned "political sections," and above all ruthlessly weeding out elements considered unreliable. This vigorous approach was a clear warning to the majority of Party members. Fear of punishment and defamation, more than persuasion and conscience, was the cause of a more serious execution of their duties. Many officials, including just the chairmen of some 130 raion executive committees and city councils in the jurisdictional area, were administratively removed from their positions as a result of professional lapses or "opportunistic" behavior, and some were arrested. By the same token, the purge of the Party has been conducted since the beginning of the year with constantly growing vigor. Falling victim to it in the jurisdictional area were some 120 secretaries of raion Party committees, i.e., 60 percent of the total, and about 70 chairmen of raion control commissions....

Further evidence of the fall in confidence in the Communist Party is the large contraction of the young communist movement, whose membership in Kyiv fell from 9,600 in 1928 to 2,600 in the year under report....

The Ukrainian Question

The development of the Ukrainian question during the year under report can also be evaluated only in relation to the famine. As a result of this catastrophe, for which the people hold Moscow's policies responsible, the old chasm between Ukrainians aspiring to independence and the unitary leanings of Moscow must naturally have become greater. Characteristic of the population's mood is the widespread view that the Soviet government promoted the expansion of the famine so as to force the Ukrainians to their knees. The frequently heard cynical comment made by individual communists—"We do not fear the hungry; it is the well-fed who are dangerous to us!"—has contributed to strengthening this feeling, even if it hardly corresponds to the view of the Party leadership.

Moscow has recognized the tenseness of the situation and has even artificially increased it by the claim of German and Polish attempts at separating Ukraine. Even so, it is true that the prospect of liberation appeared to Ukrainians to be closer after the change in Germany [Hitler's accession to power]. These hopes, newly revived without German involvement, were politically dangerous to the Soviet state. In addition, the Communist Party of Ukraine had not only failed in the execution of agrarian policy but also lacked the vigor demanded by Moscow in the struggle against Ukrainian tendencies—defined as chauvinist—in its own ranks and in the country. The supreme Party leadership was not mistaken in seeing fruitful soil for Ukrainian national development in the difficult economic and food situation.

The man who was supposed to eliminate these dangers was [Pavel] Postyshev, Stalin's confidant, sent to Kharkiv with unlimited powers. As a result of the already mentioned measures within the Party, he produced the preconditions for an assault on the Ukrainian front. The signal was the removal of Education Commissar [Mykola] Skrypnyk, who had long been a representative of an emphatically Ukrainian communist orientation. He was followed by high officials in the central apparatus in Kharkiv and by leading personalities in the provinces. In the jurisdictional area professors of the Academy of Sciences and of Kyiv University, directors of the Institute of Linguistics and the Kyiv Film School [*Lehrkombinat*], school directors, many employees of the "education front," and officials lost their positions and sometimes their freedom. They were all accused of working on behalf of the counterrevolution by promoting Ukrainian chauvinism—be it in language, scholarship, or literature, or be it in administrative regulations. Secret organizations with supposed ties to "German and Polish fascism" were uncovered in ways that enabled the GPU [secret police] to demonstrate once again its talent for constructing highly treasonous intrigues. With regard to the jurisdictional area, only the head of cultural propaganda in Chernihiv province, Skarbek, was named by [Stanislav] Kosior in a speech to the CC and the CCC of the Communist Party of Ukraine. He [Skarbek] is supposed to have admitted to being the head of the "Polish Military Organization" in Soviet Ukraine for more than ten years. Revelations of so-called organizations must be regarded with skepticism. They serve above all as a deterrent against *any* Ukrainian tendency and remind the people of the intensified vigilance of the GPU. A new phase in the struggle against Ukrainianism has begun with the well-known November resolutions of the supreme Party leadership in Kharkiv. While they also mention the danger of "Great Russian chauvinism" in addition to "Ukrainian chauvinism," this should be regarded as only a theoretical concession to the Ukrainian masses. In reality, a continually intensifying "Great Russian communist chauvinism" is the current rule for Soviet policy in Ukraine....

Concluding Remarks

In conclusion, one may state that in the jurisdictional area the Soviet government had to deal with extraordinary difficulties and that serious manifestations of crisis are still present in all internal political spheres. Nevertheless, there is currently no evidence that this situation represents an immediate danger to the survival of the system, at least as long as the workers can be protected from immediate hunger. All in all, a vigorous and ruthless state leadership, which is still strong enough to assert its will in decisive moments, and an intact GPU stand opposed to a passive and unorganized popular mass that—as much as it may reject and even hate the Bolsheviks—has neither the strength nor the will to fight. It therefore seems to be true that the communist cynics with the above-mentioned saying—"We do not fear the hungry; it is the well-fed who are dangerous to us!"—are at present not incorrect in their evaluation of the people, at least in the countryside....

German Consulate, Kyiv, May 1936, "Bericht auf Grund von persönlichen Eindrücken bei einer mehrwöchigen Reise durch die Ukraine: Ukrainische Ukraine?" (A Report Based on Personal Impressions from a Multi-week Trip through Ukraine: Ukrainian Ukraine?)

In *Holodomor v Ukraïni 1932–1933 rokiv* (2008). Excerpts, pp. 326–28. Translated by Alexander J. Motyl.

Ukrainian Ukraine has been destroyed. According to approximate estimates, *one-fifth* of its 30-million population, or about 6 million, died from famine in 1932–33. The people were now sufficiently weak to suffer the final blows of Moscow's centralism: the elimination of the hitherto obligatory Ukrainian-language examination for officials and administrators, the "reorganization" of the Ukrainian Academy of Sciences, the "purge" of higher education, the destruction of millions of books and other printed materials of the pre-Postyshev era that, "in their insolence and openness as uniquely nationalist products, filled libraries and bookstores for many years and thereby infused individual groups of workers and collective farmers with the poison of chauvinism" (Postyshev), the "inclusion of tested Bolshevik elements in all spheres" (Postyshev), and the construction of a "Ukrainian Soviet culture."

What is the situation in Ukraine today, now that Stalin's prefect has already had two and one-half years for the "construction of a Ukrainian Soviet culture"? Here are several examples:

I am standing at the counter of the Main Telegraph Office of the city of Kyiv. I request a telegraph form. I receive a printed form in the Ukrainian language. I write something (drafted for me for this purpose in the German consulate) in Ukrainian on the form. The woman at the counter gives me a blank look. "This sort of thing" is unacceptable. I excuse myself hypocritically and in Russian. I am a foreigner and had assumed that it was better to use the "national language" in Kyiv. "One speaks Russian in the Soviet Union," the woman comrade instructs me. I take another form and write something in German. After checking with the boss, the *German* telegram is accepted....

I have the opportunity to visit the highest foreign-policy official of Ukraine. He speaks no Ukrainian. In the People's Commissariat of Ukraine, as I learn from him, Russian is spoken.

In the cities one hears almost nothing but Russian. Whoever speaks Ukrainian thereby shows that he is from the countryside and is backward.

Neither in Kyiv, nor in Stalino [Donetsk], nor in Kharkiv could I acquire a Russian-Ukrainian or Ukrainian-Russian dictionary. "This sort of thing" is no longer available.

The Ukrainian press is rarely bought. Russian newspapers are snapped up completely. There is no Ukrainian literature. There is hardly a Ukrainian book that is not a translation from the Russian. There are no longer any Ukrainian history books.

The signs on the streets and in the offices are in Ukrainian. But the man who sits behind the door bearing a Ukrainian sign rarely speaks Ukrainian. Only Jews speak both Russian and Ukrainian with their notorious accent. In the Stalino city council I saw that an official, to whom a little old woman had made her request in Ukrainian, did not even understand the petitioner, despite the closeness of the languages.

I visited schools in various places. The impression is everywhere the same. The schools mostly consist of parallel classes. Class A has Russian as the language of instruction; class B has Ukrainian as the language of instruction. Parents may choose the language of instruction for their children. Completely Ukrainian schools are very rare, as Ukrainians also frequently send their children to Russian schools. The sections with Russian as language of instruction devote 5 hours per week to Russian-language instruction and 3 to Ukrainian. The Ukrainian section has 5 hours per week of Ukrainian-language instruction and 3 hours of Russian-language instruction. This parallel system is intentionally constructed to enable Russian to dominate as the children's conversational language. Moreover, the teachers in the Ukrainian section are primarily Russians, and in the Russian section they are often Ukrainians. I made this observation in 6 of 8 schools that I visited. The writing abilities of the pupils in the Ukrainian classes are noticeably bad.... Hardly a child completes school with adequate knowledge of Ukrainian orthography. The closeness of the languages [Ukrainian and Russian] usually results in a horrible gibberish.... That the majority of even the urban Ukrainian population still chooses the Ukrainian language of instruction for their children, despite obvious discrimination against Ukrainian, shows how deeply rooted the consciousness of linguistic and cultural specificity still is in the people. Lectures in the universities of Kyiv and Kharkiv and in the higher educational institutions of Stalino are almost exclusively in Russian....

A future, just historiography will perhaps one day establish that the Ukrainian people's moral spine was broken in the terrible years of 1932 and 1933, certainly for decades, perhaps forever. Although the Ukrainian folk song has been "rehabilitated" today thanks to Postyshev's mercy, although the Ukrainian opera today appears with Ukrainian performances in Moscow, and although dancers in Ukrainian folk costumes again appear today in Moscow film theatres, this is nothing but a grotesque parody of Ukraine's fate.

ITALIAN FOREIGN OFFICE DOCUMENTS

Report by the Novorossiisk royal vice consul, L. Sircana, 8 April 1933, "Re: Developments in the agricultural season"

In *Investigation of the Ukrainian Famine, 1932–1933* (1988). Excerpts, p. 417.
Original text in *Lettere da Kharkov*, ed. Andrea Graziosi (Turin, 1991), pp. 157–64.

Vice-Consulate of Italy
Novorossiisk (U.S.S.R.)

April 8, 1933–Year XI

Ref. No. 223/24
Reference: Telex No. 549/11 of February 1, 1932/X.

Royal Embassy of Italy, Moscow and copy to the Royal Consulate of Italy, Tbilisi (224/44)

Re: *Developments in the agricultural season*

Dear Ambassador:

I should like to refer once again to the situation in the Northern Caucasus....

...[T]he appointment in the Northern Caucasus of a special committee invested with unlimited powers to resolve the situation by force and at whatever cost, shows just how serious things have become.

The main measures adopted by the committee may be summarized as follows:

> the peasants have been prohibited from leaving their farms or villages (serfdom!?). In practical terms, this fastening to the land is obtained by suspending sales of rail tickets (tickets can only be obtained by submitting a special permit from the political authorities, who of course systematically refuse to give these to the peasants); by not admitting peasants at offices and factories, etc., and by expelling them from the cities; by seizing the products which the peasants have been trying to bring onto the markets, and keeping them out of the markets themselves;
>
> the registration of entire villages or collective farms on the "blackboard," followed by severe penalties; for example: suspension of any laying in of stock; the withdrawal of goods, however few, already available at the co-operatives; an absolute ban on leaving the boundaries of one's village or farm; searches and seizures of products; expulsion *en masse* from the territory of the Northern Caucasus of all or part of the population, unless they show an immediate change of heart;
>
> the holding of summary trials in three days flat, with no chance of appeal, and sentencing to maximum penalties, which may be increased at the court's discretion.

These three groups themselves bear eloquent testimony to the desperate struggle to which the once fertile lands of the Northern Caucasus are now playing host....

Report by the Kharkiv consulate royal consul, Sergio Gradenigo, 31 May 1933, "Re: The Famine and the Ukrainian Question"

In *Investigation of the Ukrainian Famine, 1932–1933* (1988). Excerpts, pp. 424–25, 427.
Original text in *Lettere da Kharkov*, ed. Andrea Graziosi (Turin, 1991), pp. 168–74.

Royal Consulate of Italy
Kharkiv

May 31, 1933

Ref. No. 474/106

Embassy of Italy, Moscow

Re: The Famine and the Ukrainian Question

The famine continues to wreak havoc among the people, and one simply cannot fathom how the world can remain so indifferent to such a catastrophe and how the international press, which is so quick to bring international condemnation upon Germany for its so-called 'atrocious persecution of the Jews,' can stand quietly by in the presence of this massacre organized by the Soviet government, in which the Jews play such a major role, albeit not the leading one.

For there is no doubt: 1) that this famine is primarily caused by a contrived scarcity designed 'to teach the peasants a lesson,' and 2) that there is not one Jew among the famine victims; on the contrary, they are fat and well fed under the fraternal wing of the GPU.

The 'ethnographic material' must be changed, cynically stated one Jew who is a high ranking official in the local GPU. One can already foresee the final fate of this 'ethnographic material,' which is destined for replacement....

Through barbaric requisitions...the Moscow government has effectively engineered not so much a scarcity...but rather a complete absence of every means of subsistence throughout the Ukrainian countryside, Kuban, and the Middle Volga.

Three considerations can be taken into account as having dictated such a policy:

1) the peasantry's passive resistance to collectivized agriculture;
2) the conviction that the 'ethnographic material' can never be reduced to an integral communist prototype;
3) the necessity or expediency, more or less openly acknowledged, of denationalizing those regions in which Ukrainian or German consciousness have reawakened, threatening possible political difficulties in the future, and where, for the sake of the unity of the empire, it is better that a preponderantly Russian population reside....

This calamity, which is claiming millions of lives, is destroying the infancy of an entire nation and is really affecting only Ukraine, Kuban, and the Central Volga. Elsewhere it is felt much less or not at all....

In conclusion: The current disaster will bring about a preponderantly Russian colonization of Ukraine. It will transform its ethnographic character. In a future time, perhaps very soon, one will no longer be able to speak of a Ukraine, or a Ukrainian people, and thus not even of a Ukrainian problem, because Ukraine will become a *de facto* Russian region.

Sincerely yours,
The Royal Consul, Gradenigo

Report by the Kharkiv consulate royal consul, Sergio Gradenigo, 10 July 1933, "Re: The Famine and the Sanitation Situation"

In *Investigation of the Ukrainian Famine, 1932–1933* (1988). Excerpts, pp. 439–40.
Original text in *Lettere da Kharkov*, ed. Andrea Graziosi (Turin, 1991), pp. 189–91.

Royal Consulate of Italy
Kharkiv

July 10, 1933

Ref. No. 570/74

Royal Embassy of Italy, Moscow
and for the information of the
Royal Italian Ministry of Foreign Affairs

Re: The Famine and the Sanitation Situation

Today Ukraine presents one of the saddest of portraits. Except for regions that are in the immediate vicinity of cities...and the major cities themselves, the country has fallen victim to famine, typhus, dysentery, supposedly even cholera, and finally the plague....

When last year the possibility of famine first presented itself, the government became preoccupied with the political situation that would emerge from it and, faithful to Lenin's doctrine that famines provoke revolutions, had taken action. It is now possible to explain why some of the measures have been adopted. The danger of a revolution or, better, counterrevolution because of hunger could be serious only in the large industrial centers. Thus it was necessary to think first of them and supply them as best possible.... [T]he countryside was less threatening and could thus be left to its fate.... [N]ow one can explain the reason for the revival of passports and the exclusion of hundreds of thousands of people...outside the 50 km. (or 100 km. for Moscow) so as to facilitate the task of supplying the major centers and to prevent any uprisings or even protests. The purge of the Party is connected with the food situation, or rather with the feared prospective reaction to the famine.

This famine has destroyed half the rural population of Ukraine.

This explains the savaqery with which all the peasants are inexorably picked up by the police (I have observed that the urban population, out of an obscure sense of defensiveness, deliberately promote hatred, or an unconquerable desire to tyrannize, willingly collaborate with this peasant hunt...and this explains why doctors have been given orders not to treat peasants who show up in town)....

The doctors are forbidden to mention typhus and deaths from starvation, nor can they even collect those observations which would be of great interest to them from a scientific point of view....

Very frequent is the phenomenon of hallucinations, in which people see their children only as animals, kill them, and eat them. Later some, having recuperated with proper food, do not remember wanting to eat their children and deny even being able to think of such a thing....

Sincerely yours,
The Royal Consul
Gradenigo

Report by the Kharkiv consulate royal consul, Sergio Gradenigo, 19 July 1933, "Re: After the Suicide of Mykola Skrypnyk"

In *Investigation of the Ukrainian Famine, 1932–1933* (1988). Excerpts, pp. 446–47.

Royal Consulate of Italy
Kharkiv, U.S.S.R.

Kharkiv, July 19, 1933–XI

Confidential
Ref. No. 608/88

Royal Embassy of Italy, Moscow
and for the information of the
Royal Ministry of Foreign Affairs, Rome

Re: After the Suicide of Mykola Skrypnyk.

I can now add the following details on the death of the above-specified individual....

The dying man was carried to the university clinic, where he regained consciousness during the blood transfusion. He told [Pavel] Postyshev, who had come by, that the real danger for Communism lay in Russian imperialism, which was on the rise....

Proceeding at all speed at present is the reform of Ukrainian spelling (it has been stripped of the vocative which Russian, unlike Ukrainian, does not have). In government offices the Russian language is once again being used, in correspondence as well as in verbal dealings between employees....

[W]e can only conclude that the Ukrainian people are about to go into an eclipse, which could well turn out to be a night without end, because Russian imperialism, with its present tender mercies (i.e., tender communist mercies), is capable of wiping a nation—nay, a civilization—right off the face of the earth if we aren't very careful.

Sincerely yours,
The Royal Consul

Letter from the royal consul general in Odesa to the Italian ambassador in Moscow, 19 February 1934

In *Investigation of the Ukrainian Famine, 1932–1933* (1988). Excerpts, p. 475.

Royal Consulate of Italy
Odesa

February 19, 1934–XII

Confidential
Ref. No. 262/42

Dear Ambassador:....

It has also been clear for quite some time that the Moscow Government intends to settle the Ukrainian problem once and for all.

The persecutions conducted against the Ukrainian intellectuals accused of sympathizing with their colleagues and brothers in Galicia and Poland; the suicide of [Mykola] Skrypnyk, the Ukrainian Commissar for Public Education; the incarceration of numerous Germans accused of sympathizing with the Ukrainians; the withholding of the grain reserves from the peasants, which has turned Ukraine over the spring of last year into the site of an unprecedented famine, which according to reliable evidence has sent 7,000,000 people to their deaths; all of these things betoken the Moscow Government's intention to use every means at their disposal to crush every last vestige of Ukrainian nationalism....

Ukraine used to be the sole major population center endowed with some degree of ethnic, linguistic and historical cohesiveness that was resisting Moscow's centralization program. This obstacle may now be said to have been overcome.

Sincerely yours,
The Royal Consul General

"The Holy Father and News of the Famine in Russia" (Polish Catholic Press Agency, no. 196, Vatican City, 28 August 1933)

In *The Holy See and the Holodomor: Documents from the Great Famine of 1932–1933 in Soviet Ukraine*, ed. Athanasius D. McVay and Lubomyr Y. Luciuk ([Kingston, Ont.]: The Kashtan Press and Chair of Ukrainian Studies, University of Toronto, 2011), p. 57.

A special emissary of the pope has recently returned to Rome from Russia. He presented to the Holy Father a detailed report on his time in Russia where, as is already known from other sources, a terrible famine is raging. The pope's emissary reported, among other things, that the death of close to 12,000,000 people can be expected during the coming winter. Listening to this, the Holy Father had tears in his eyes. He said: "We must find, at all costs, any sort of way to stop this."

It is generally supposed that the pope wants to send to Russia, if the Soviet authorities will permit, an aid expedition like that sent several years ago.

POLISH FOREIGN OFFICE AND INTELLIGENCE SERVICE DOCUMENTS

Report on the nationality question in the U[kr.]SSR prepared by the head of the consulate general in Kharkiv for a consular meeting in Moscow

In *Hołodomor 1932–1933* (2008). Excerpts, pp. 251, 264, 276. Translated by Bohdan Klid.

Secret

The nationality question in Soviet Ukraine as of I.V.1933....

The economic exploitation of Ukraine by the central authorities is most glaringly apparent in the agricultural sector. Ukraine has always been and still remains the most important producer of grain in the Soviet Union, which always provided produce for export or to serve the needs of cities and regions with shortages in the country. For this reason, according to the general line of Soviet rural policy, forced collectivization has begun there as well, and there it has also fallen hardest on the shoulders of the peasants. Nowhere else, with the sole exception of the North Caucasus, has "grain procurement" been carried out with such ruthlessness and, indeed, constituted de facto confiscation of almost all the farmers' produce.

The frequent warnings and protests of local officials had no effect, for the central authorities, citing the interests and needs of the state as a whole, ruthlessly continued the policy of stripping bare the Ukrainian countryside. Any disobedience to the directives of the central authorities, or even criticism on the part of local government, which understood the danger of that policy, was mercilessly punished and characterized as giving in to the influence of kulak ideology.

The result of this predatory management was a great famine in the spring of 1932, which, after a brief respite in the autumn of last year, resumed last winter and continues to this day. The ruin and destitution of the Ukrainian village cannot easily be described; moreover, it is telling that this condition does not apply to southern Russia as such, but specifically to Ukraine, for, on crossing the northern border of the U[kr.]SSR, the picture changes quite radically. In the Central Black Earth Province, which differs little from Ukraine in climate and economy, the condition of the peasantry is incomparably better. This attests that the economic policy of the central government with regard to Ukraine has been much more ruthless and predatory than toward the neighboring provinces of the RSFSR, with the sole exception of the North Caucasus....

Reported by: J. Karszo-Siedlewski
Kharkiv, 8 May 1933

Description of a car trip to Moscow by the head of the Polish consulate general in Kharkiv

In *Hołodomor 1932–1933* (2008). Excerpts, pp. 294–95. Translated by Bohdan Klid.

Kharkiv, 31 May 1933

To the Ambassador of the R[epublic] of P[oland] in Moscow....

On 5 May at 11:30 I left the Consulate General in Kharkiv in a Buick automobile for a consular meeting in Moscow, where I reached the building of the Embassy of the R[epublic] of P[oland] the next day at 14:30....

What struck me most in the whole journey was the difference in the appearance of the villages and fields of Ukraine as compared with the neighbouring CB-EO (Central Black Earth Oblast), or even the infertile area near Moscow. The Ukrainian villages are in an obvious state of decline, standing empty, abandoned, and destitute. Cottages are half-ruined, often with roofs torn off; new dwellings are nowhere to be found; children and elders look like skeletons; livestock is nowhere to be seen. There is something growing on barely one-fifth of the cultivated fields; only about two-fifths have been plowed; the remaining two-fifths lie fallow. Although this is prime time for spring work in the fields, one sees very few people working, and still fewer tractors; sowing is conducted in the most primitive manner, mainly by hand.

Finding myself immediately afterward in the CB-EO (mainly in the area of Kursk and Orel), I felt as if I had crossed from the land of the Soviets into Western Europe. There were considerably more plowed and sown fields; the villages were cleaner and more orderly, the cottages kept in good repair, and the people relatively better off. Cattle could be seen grazing and, especially in the Orel region, there were plenty of sheep....

Head of the Consulate General
(J. Karszo-Siedlewski)

Letter from a correspondent of PAT (Polish Telegraph Agency) to the editor in chief of *Gazeta Polska* concerning unofficial conversations with Karl Radek and the prohibition on admitting foreign correspondents to Ukraine

In *Hołodomor 1932–1933* (2008). Excerpts, pp. 296–98. Translated by Bohdan Klid.

Moscow, 1.VI.33

Dear Mr. Minister....

[Y]esterday I saw [Karl] Radek...., who touched on the Ukrainian problem, declaring that "any activity of yours on that territory will be commented on by us as deliberate or unconscious carrying out of German plans in the East."....

Immediately after your departure, the press division of Narkomindel [People's Commissariat of Internal Affairs], in the form of my "initial request" of fifteen months ago, forbade my entry into Ukraine. [Konstantin] Umansky gave me clearly to understand that this is a confidential instruction of the GPU applicable to all correspondents....

Jan Otmar Berson

Article in the bulletin *Polska a Zagranica* (Poland and the Outside World), 10 October 1933, about the pacification of Ukraine by the Soviet authorities

In *Hołodomor 1932–1933* (2008). Excerpts, pp. 396–98. Translated by Bohdan Klid.

...According to the latest information obtained from reliable sources, the situation in Ukraine can now be seen as basically under control.

This is due to a combination of two factors: the decisive and consistent policy of the Communist Party, which has unscrupulously managed to break the passive resistance of the countryside and shatter the decentralizing nationalist tendencies of the Ukrainian intelligentsia, and the unexpectedly favorable yield of this year's harvest. It is another matter at what great cost this victory was achieved—considering the deaths of at least 5,000,000 people and the devastation of the Ukrainian village, whose residents fled en masse to the cities or other Soviet republics—so that there is now talk of the need to settle certain parts of Ukraine with people from other, less fertile parts of the USSR....

From the political viewpoint, what should be emphasized in the situation in Ukraine is the growth in the power of [Pavel] Postyshev, Stalin's second deputy in the Secretariat of the CC of the Party, who has become the de facto dictator of Ukraine.

The CC CP(B)U adopted a resolution on 25 September asserting that the Commissariat of Agriculture [equivalent to the ministry of agriculture] and the district agricultural administrations did no real work on the organization of agriculture and did not manage it; hence it has resolved to dismiss a number of people.... The agricultural academies in Kharkiv and Kyiv have been closed down, inasmuch as most of the professors have been dismissed and many of them arrested on charges of harmful anti-state activities.

The above-mentioned arrests, like those still going on in other Ukrainian institutions, are related to Postyshev's consistent effort aimed at the total destruction of the Ukrainian intelligentsia that supports nationalist ideas. It should be emphasized that among those arrested there are quite a few Ukrainians from Eastern Little Poland [Galician Ukraine]....

Report of the vice consul in Kyiv on Bolshevik policy toward the Polish minority in Ukraine

In *Hołodomor 1932–1933* (2008). Excerpts, pp. 404–5, 407, 409–12. Translated by Bohdan Klid.

13 October [193]3
CONFIDENTIAL
To the ambassador of the R[epublic of] P[oland]
in Moscow

Re: Nationality policy in Ukraine with regard to the Polish minority

The course of official nationality policy with regard to the Polish minority found its expression at the all-Ukrainian meeting of Polish newspaper editors that took place in Kyiv this summer.... R. Maksymowski, the editor of *Trybuna Radziecka* [Soviet Tribune], also attended this gathering as the main speaker. J[ózef] Teodor, the head of the nationality section of the Kharkiv government, participated on behalf of the government, [as did] the head of the so-called Kultprop [Department of Culture and Propaganda], Kilerog, from the CC CP(B)U....

Kilerog...emphasized in the course of his speech that dangerous tendencies had been uncovered within the bosom of the CP(B)U: they were exaggerating the significance of nationality questions and creating a theory of so-called "national Bolshevism." In his opinion, these tendencies belonged to the category of initiatives that had served to promote a challenge to the integrity of the USSR.... The current leadership recognized in time the rise of dangerous deviations and is undertaking a struggle with all that was harmful and showing solicitude for all that was hitherto oppressed. In particular, attention will be paid to the Polish minority, which was especially wronged by the former leadership of the C[ommissariat] of P[eople's] Education....

The editor of *Trybuna Radziecka*, R. Maksymowski, characterized the situation in the sphere of nationality affairs as follows:

"This gathering of Polish editors is proof of the special attention that the leadership of the CP(B)U is devoting to the Polish problem, and it is closely related to the declaration of struggle against Petliurism, Ukrainian nationalism, and its allies in Polish circles."....

In his speech, J. Teodor condemned the principle of assigning children to schools of the nationality into which they were born without regard to the language that the child actually speaks as "unlawful" and as directed against the Russian minority in Ukraine, having as its goal the "robbing" of children who would undoubtedly choose a Russian school....

After such harsh criticism of the results of nationality policy practiced in Ukraine to date, one might have hoped that the new authorities in the Commissariat of Education would make every effort to eliminate the noted errors and help create firm foundations for developing the cultural life of the Polish minority. Information received from the field and from the Polish press, however, completely contradicts this supposition....

In the sphere of economic policy, the tactic of the Soviet authorities...aims at the breakup and destruction of the Polish minority in Ukraine.... On the Polish collective farms, almost all of which fulfilled their "grain procurement" quotas in timely fashion, only husks of grain remained for distribution [among the collective farmers]. The high level of assigned quotas, as well as the obligatory quantity of vegetables to be sown, [both] invariably detrimental to Polish collective farms as compared to Ukrainian ones, deserve special emphasis. This leads to the frequent incidence of peasants leaving Polish collectives for Ukrainian ones.

"Individual farmers" find themselves in especially difficult circumstances. Here, as a rule, the "grain procurement" quota exceeds the entire annual yield [of the farm]....

Individuals unable to fulfill the "grain procurement" plan are accused of political sabotage and "kulak" tendencies....

Dozens of families alleged to be "kulaks" have been expelled from their homes and villages and, with winter approaching, find themselves in a tragic situation, stripped completely of reserves of food and clothing. Their situation, as compared with that of previous years, is worsened by the fact that they are unable to seek salvation in the cities (the passport system): they are condemned to death by starvation....

The overall nationality policy in Ukraine can be defined as a function of the growing internal strength of the Soviet state and its military might, as well as its international situation. As these factors gain strength, nationality policy in Ukraine, still outwardly cloaked in liberal slogans, is in fact becoming more ruthless in its predatory instincts.

If we are concerned with shedding light on the tactic used with regard to the Polish population, then, in my opinion, that tactic was never the same throughout the existence of the [Soviet] Union. Its first stage consisted in the notion of creating here, beyond the borders of the R[epublic] of P[oland], a strong Polish center organized along communist lines. This center had two tasks to fulfill: 1) It was to become a tool of communist propaganda for the entire Polish population.... [and] also serve as proof of the liberal policy of the [Soviet] Union in the treatment of its minorities.... 2) The creation on the Soviet side of a kind of Piedmont for the Polish communist movement and the organization of Polish revolutionary cadres that would ignite and direct the communist revolution in Poland....

After a few years of effort, these concepts proved illusory....

A new concept has therefore been adopted: with regard to the revolutionary movement in Poland, it accepts the premise that its focus must be within Poland, while the role of the Soviets is to be strictly limited to supporting that movement. Accordingly, in the understanding of authoritative Soviet officials, the Polish minority in Ukraine is completely bereft of its initial importance....

Every reason for maintaining the distinctness of the Polish national minority has therefore disappeared....

And now we are witnesses to the process of the destruction of that distinctness, carried out by way of physical and economic ruination.

Piotr Kurnicki
Vice Consul, R[epublic of] P[oland]

A conversation between the Polish ambassador in Ankara and Kliment Voroshilov: his surprise that "Poland is so lenient with the Ukrainians... in Soviet Russia Ukrainians are kept on a tight leash"

In *Hołodomor 1932–1933* (2008). Excerpts, pp. 680–81. Translated by Bohdan Klid.

6 November [193]3

To the Ministry of Foreign Affairs....

I had the opportunity to converse with Voroshilov at a reception at the Soviet embassy.... He made reference, with some irritation, to the Ukrainians, and to the fact that in Lviv there had been a murderous assault on the Soviet consulate. In this connection, he expressed surprise that Poland is so lenient with the Ukrainians and has not dealt with them severely enough, inasmuch as in Soviet Russia they are kept on a tight leash....

Ambassador of the R[epublic of] P[oland]
Jerzy Potocki

Excerpt of a report from Napoleon Nalewajko to Jerzy Niebrzycki about the situation prevailing in Ukraine

In *Pomór w "Raju Bolszewickim"* (2009). Excerpts, pp. 131, 134. Translated by Bohdan Klid.

18.XI.[19]33.

My Dear One!....

...There is no situation from which the Bolsheviks cannot manage to gain an advantage for themselves. The secret of their behavior, in my opinion, lies above all in their total disregard for the means used and the sacrifices whereby they achieve their goals.

So it is that they have managed to take advantage of this year's famine in Ukraine.

I assert most categorically that by taking advantage of the peasant's hunger alone, they have managed, by flinging him scraps as to a hungry dog, to force him to carry out a whole range of agricultural work and then compel that same peasant to express his appreciation to them for their humanitarian provision of the food that he lacked. Through the use of systematic terror they have managed to break the mass of peasants to such an extent that despite the tragic experience of the past year they have obtained the fulfillment of the entire grain-procurement plan, again confiscating almost the entire harvest. All this has been accomplished by throwing huge cadres of newly trained communists who, in the first place, had no connection with the local populace or were influenced to such a degree by theoretical conclusions that they became almost fanatics, carrying out any and all instructions while closing their eyes to all the effects on the populace....

N. Nalewajko [pseudonym of Piotr Kurnicki, Polish vice consul in Kyiv]

Note of the head of the Polish consulate general in Kharkiv on the reasons for the reversal of Bolshevik policy in Ukraine

In *Hołodomor 1932–1933* (2008). Excerpts, pp. 495–97. Translated by Bohdan Klid.

Kharkiv, 6 January 1934

Top Secret

...[L]ast November's resolutions of the plenum of the CC CP(B)U, as well as the mass persecutions and arrests still taking place, can neither be understood nor justified by the threat of the Ukrainian national movement. In the most recent period there have been absolutely no developments indicating the growth or even the further normal development of that movement, to say nothing of any mass nationalist or separatist manifestations. The reasons for this action should be sought, in my opinion, in the systematic, planned, and perspicacious policy of the Muscovite rulers, calculated for the long term: they are becoming more and more great-power politicians, strengthening their regime and the borders of their state, sacrificing to that end the ideals hitherto upheld by the Communist International. The emissaries of Moscow in Ukraine, [Pavel] Postyshev and [Vsevolod] Balytsky, for their part, are merely the scrupulous and devoted executors of the instructions given them from the top....

Head of the Consulate General
J. Karszo-Siedlewski

Letter from the student Buczak, 12 January 1934, delivered to the Polish consulate in Kyiv

In *Pomór w "Raju Bolszewickim"* (2009). Excerpts, pp. 141–42. Translated by Bohdan Klid.

...The spring of 1933 will be remembered by grandchildren and great-grandchildren. Workers who could not find work were also dying of hunger in the cities of Ukraine. In 1933 there was a series of layoffs in enterprises. Laid-off workers were deprived of ration cards for bread, swelled from hunger, and died. Many also died of hunger in hospitals and prisons. Bodies were removed from prisons and hospitals by freight trucks. Families of the deceased were not informed, and no one asked the names or titles [of the deceased]. Parents who received miserly wages were unable to feed their children; [hence] they took them to the bazaars and abandoned them there. They froze from cold and hunger [*sic*]. Some of them were taken by orphanages, but this was only a tactical game on the part of the authorities. To avoid embarrassment, the authorities removed them from public view. [However] in the orphanages [the children] were also starved and died all the same....

In Ukraine the main component of nourishment is bread. All that the farmer and the worker now dream about is bread. The people of Ukraine have forgotten about oils and other products. For the last four years the workers have been living on money that has no value. The peasant does not have even that. He produces grain but does not see it. For nourishment, he has to eat linden leaves, chaff, and all kinds of weeds. This was a mass phenomenon in the Ukrainian countryside in the spring of 1933. From this one can infer just what the attitude of the Ukrainian population is to Soviet Power in Ukraine. That is the source of Ukrainian nationalism in the Party, which is now feared more than the kulaks were three years ago. Ukrainian nationalism is now treated by Jewish communists and Great-Power Russian chauvinists as the main internal danger. They know that they have sinned [*sic*] and realize that if the peasants could be awoken from their slumber, their situation would not be a happy one. They would pay with their lives.

At present the communists are frightened of Ukrainian nationalism, which has raised its head to free the Ukrainian people and separate Ukraine, a de facto Russian colony, from Russia. As of now, the second five-year plan makes no provision at all for construction in Ukraine. The communists are afraid that the time will come and, with the help of other peoples, Ukraine will begin to free itself, and all that has been built will become the property of the Ukrainian people.

Kyiv, 12 January 1934
Buczak

REACTION TO THE FAMINE BY NGOs AND UKRAINIANS OUTSIDE THE SOVIET UNION

[Appeal by] the Ukrainian Catholic Episcopate of the Galician Church Province concerning events in Greater Ukraine, to all people of good will

Dilo (Lviv), 27 July 1933 and *Pravda* (Lviv), 30 July 1933. Reprinted in *Natsiia v borot'bi za svoie isnuvannia* (1985), p. 84. Translation in *Svoboda* (Jersey City, N. J.), 20 September 1933, p. 1. Revised by Bohdan Klid.

UKRAINE IS IN ITS PRE-DEATH CONVULSIONS! — Its population is dying of starvation. Based on injustice, fraud, godlessness and depravity, the cannibalistic system of state capitalism has reduced this recently rich country to complete ruin. Three years ago the Head of the Catholic Church, His Holiness Pope Pius XI, protested energetically against everything in Bolshevism that is contrary to Christianity, God, and human nature, warning against the terrible consequences of such crimes—and the whole Catholic world, and we with it, joined in that protest. We now see the consequences of the Bolshevik actions: the situation becomes more terrible with every passing day. The enemies of God and humanity have cast aside religion, the basis of social order; suppressed liberty, mankind's greatest good; made slaves of free peasant citizens; and do not have enough sense to feed them for their hard slave labor in the sweat of their brows.

In the face of these crimes, human nature grows numb, and the blood chills in one's veins.

Powerless to provide our dying brethren with any material assistance, we call upon Our faithful, through prayers, fasting, nation-wide mourning, sacrifices, and all possible good works of Christian life, to beseech aid from heaven at a time when there is no hope of human assistance.

And before the whole world we again protest against the persecution of the little ones, the poor, the weak, and the innocent, and accuse the persecutors before the Most High for Judgment.

The blood of the workmen who tilled the black earth of Ukraine as they starved cries out to heaven for vengeance, and the voice of the hungry reapers has reached the ears of Almighty God.

We ask all Christians throughout the world, all who believe in God, and especially all workers and peasants, and above all our compatriots, to join us in our voice of protest and pain and to disseminate it to the remotest corners of the world.

We ask all radio stations to broadcast Our voice to the whole world; perhaps it will reach the poor cottages where the peasants are dying of hunger.

May it be at least some consolation to those facing a terrible death in the severest of suffering to surmise that their brethren knew of their terrible fate, empathized and suffered, and prayed for them.

And you, our suffering, starving, and dying brethren, call on our Merciful God and Savior, Jesus Christ. You are enduring severe suffering—bear it for your sins, for the sins of all our people, and repeat after Jesus Christ: "Thy will be done, Heavenly Father!" Death accepted as the will of God is a holy sacrifice, which, united with the sacrifice of Jesus Christ, will bring you the Kingdom of Heaven, and salvation to all our people.

Our hope is in God!

Issued in Lviv, on the day of St. Olha, 24 July1933 AD.
[Signed] Andrei Sheptytsky, Metropolitan [and six bishops of the Ukrainian Catholic Episcopate of Galicia]

"Byimo u velykyi dzvin na trivohu!" (Let Us Strike the Great Bell to Raise the Alarm!)

Dilo (Lviv), 14 August 1933, p. 1. Reprinted in *Natsiia v borot'bi za svoie isnuvannia* (1985), pp. 80–83. Excerpts. Translated by Bohdan Klid

Let Us Strike the Great Bell to Raise the Alarm!

Ukrainian people!

Greater Ukraine, your mainland, this richest of lands in Europe, is now contorted in pains of hunger and torment and suffering unbearable national oppression.

The Russian communist Bolsheviks, who destroyed the Ukrainian State on the Dnipro with fire and sword, who imposed their dictatorship on our land with bayonets, are now crucifying the Ukrainian people. They are destroying its finest sons by firing squads, tormenting them with imprisonment and exile, and starving the entire population of Ukraine en masse.

This is not rumor or gossip but the honest truth! The whole world is now speaking out about this terrible truth; our brothers from over there are telling this painful truth in many letters to relatives and friends; and numerous refugees from Bolshevik captivity are speaking about this horrible truth. However, communists are covering up this tragic truth. From all the letters from our unfortunate brethren and from all the accounts of the refugees we hear the desperate cry: "Save us, for we are perishing from violence and famine!"

Ukrainian people!

Wherever you may be living beyond the bounds of Greater Ukraine...nowhere can you calmly observe the great tragedy and torments of your enslaved and starved brothers.

You must do all you can to save the threatened existence of 35 million brothers in order to save yourself, your national life, from annihilation. For the communist Muscovite dictators are now bent on destroying the very life of the Ukrainian people, which finds itself under their rule. They have destroyed all the riches of the Ukrainian land; they have destroyed the economy of the Ukrainian people; through forced collectivization they have completely destroyed agriculture and reduced the Ukrainian people to starvation. The broad, fertile Ukrainian fields are now mainly overgrown with weeds, and the Ukrainian farmer, tormented by starvation, has descended to cannibalism in some instances. On the Ukrainian lands, where recently abundant ears of wheat rolled like waves on fields without end, cannibalism prevails as a result of communist management. This is the most horrific phenomenon under the sun. That in an agrarian land brother should eat brother because of hunger—this the world has never heard of, and our land has never known....

The communists have decided to ship all grain north from Ukraine, to the Muscovite industrial centers, and thereby to consign the Ukrainian population to death by starvation en masse. For resisting this pillage of the country and starvation, the communists are destroying the people by merciless executions and blaming the poor harvest entirely on Ukrainian national consciousness, and that is why the Ukrainian people are suffering political persecution worse than under the Muscovite tsars. They are abolishing all remnants of the political autonomy of Soviet Ukraine, destroying all Ukrainian cultural achievements, and rooting out Ukrainization. By means of terror, they are inflicting political oppression unheard of and unseen in the history of any people on the organism of the nation, exhausted by hunger.

Ukrainian people!

The limits of your patience have been broken. Silence is no longer possible! Wherever a Ukrainian heart beats, one must not only protest all communist oppression but also stir the conscience of all humanity, bring the whole world to its feet so that it pays attention to your situation and renders you assistance.

The Ukrainian Parliamentary Representation and all central Ukrainian institutions have established in Lviv the Ukrainian Civic Committee to Save Ukraine. Similar Ukrainian committees should be formed around the world; their work should be coordinated and joint efforts directed toward easing the fate of our enslaved brethren in Greater Ukraine.

Ukrainian people!

Wherever you may be living...rise together in solid columns for battle with tyranny. Mobilize world opinion against the communist horrors in Greater Ukraine. Help your brethren in Greater Ukraine with whatever you can and however you can. The Lviv Civic Committee will conduct a mass aid action in this country and abroad, and will announce details of its plan in the immediate future. The Committee is counting on general, mass support for its work. With complete faith in the success of the action undertaken, the Committee calls for harmonious cooperation on the part of all Ukrainians who sincerely wish to unite in pain with their oppressed brethren along the Dnipro.

And you, unfortunate Brethren from the Dnipro, Kuban, and Don regions, swollen with hunger, accept from us expressions of admiration for your courage in adversity; accept from us expressions of deepest sympathy in your great misfortune; and rest assured that sooner or later your suffering will end, and from beyond the communist clouds and darkness hanging over Ukraine the sun of Freedom will shine forth.

Lviv, 25 July 1933
[Signed by the leadership of the Ukrainian Parliamentary Representation and of 34 organizations, institutions, and associations in Lviv]

"To the Christian World! Appeal of the Cardinal and Archbishop of Vienna on Behalf of the Hungry in Soviet Russia"

Published in the Austrian press on 19 August 1933. Reprinted in *Holodomor Studies* 1, no. 1 (2009). Full text, pp. 102–3. Translated by Alexander J. Motyl.

At a time that with its profound seriousness awakens the consciousness of responsibility of civilized humanity, there arises the duty to appeal to the world public to engage in relief work. No attempts at denial can contravene the fact that hundreds of thousands, indeed millions, of people have in the last few months perished of hunger in Soviet Russia. Hundreds of moving letters from the famine areas of the Soviet Union, especially from Ukraine and the North Caucasus, provide reports, while eyewitnesses about whose competence there is no doubt have depicted horrible details of the tragedy taking place in Russia. I draw your attention to the appeal of the Metropolitan of Galicia, Count Andrei Sheptytsky, which reports on the terrible suffering of the population in the Ukrainian region of the Soviet Union. The Englishman Gareth Jones also confirms this; indeed, he establishes on the basis of enquiries on the ground that in some areas of the Soviet Union a quarter of the population has already died of hunger. In a memorandum that incorporates authentic information from the various people dying in Russia, Dr. Ewald Ammende, the General Secretary of the Congress of European Nationalities, reports that the famine catastrophe has horribly affected, besides the Russians and Ukrainians, members of all other ethnic groups living in the Soviet Union. Famine in the Soviet Union is killing the members of all religions and nationalities in equal measure.

It is already certain that the catastrophe is continuing even now, at the time of the new harvest. In order to supply industrial centers, the grain output is, as the Soviet press openly admits, being forcibly taken from the peasants in Ukraine, the North Caucasus, and elsewhere. The Russian famine catastrophe will therefore reach a new high point in a few months, and then millions of human lives will be destroyed. To remain silent any longer means to raise the responsibility of the civilized world for the mass death in Russia to the level of unacceptability; it means bearing the guilt for the fact that, at a time when large areas of the world are choking on too much grain and foodstuffs, people in Soviet Russia are starving miserably and falling victim to such terrible accompanying phenomena of every mass hunger as the killing of children and cannibalism.

In the name of the eternally valid laws of humanity and love of neighbor, the author therefore raises his voice and appeals to all, especially to those organizations and agencies of the world whose work stands in the service of humanity and justice, to conduct, before it is too late, general relief work in an effective manner on the basis of supranational and interconfessional principles, on behalf of the people threatened by death from hunger in Russia. This appeal applies above all to the international Red Cross and its world-wide organizations; it is also directed toward all those actors who are today negotiating the expansion of economic relations with the Soviet Union, so that the principle be maintained that these negotiations be made dependent on a general clarification of the aid requirements in various parts of Russia and on the acceptance by the Soviet Union of a so-called humanitarian clause.

In order also to promote this relief work from Vienna, I will invite representatives of various confessions to create a committee. This invitation will be sent out in the next few days. To common fraternal work, before it is too late! God wills it!

Theodor Cardinal Innitzer, Archbishop

Letter from the Liaison Committee of Women's International Organisations to the President of the Council of the League of Nations

In *The Foreign Office and the Famine* (1988). Excerpts, pp. 326–27.

Liaison Committee of Women's International Organisations
Hon. Secretary:
Miss Elsie M. Zimmern,
26, Eccleston Street
London, S.W.1

Member Organisations:
World's Woman's Christian Temperance Union
International Council of Women
World's Young Women's Christian Association
International Alliance of Women for Suffrage and Equal Citizenship
Women's International League for Peace and Freedom
World Union of Women for International Concord
International Federation of University Women
Equal Rights International
International Federation of Women Magistrates, Barristers
and Other Branches of the Legal Profession
St. Joan's Social and Political Alliance

September 26th, 1933

His Excellency Monsieur Joh[an] L. Mowinckel,
President of the Council,
League of Nations

Excellency,

On behalf of the above Committee of Women's International Organisations may I beg you to bring to the notice of the Council of the League the desperate condition of the famine stricken population of Soviet Ukraine.

Again and again the League has rendered invaluable services to the cause of humanity and we entreat Your Excellency as President to submit to the Council the present need for League action in any form which you may think wise.

The Committee was unanimous in their decision to appeal to you....
On behalf of the Committee I have the honour to remain,

Your Obedient Servant,
(signed) Margery Corbett Ashby
President of one of the Organisations
Int. Alliance for Suffrage & Equal Citizenship

Letter from the Ukrainian National Council in Canada to Prime Minister of Canada R. B. Bennett

In *Natsiia v borot'bi za svoie isnuvannia* (1985), p. 118. Excerpts.

October 2nd, 1933

Right Honourable R. B. Bennett.
Prime Minister of Canada,
Ottawa, Ont.

Sir:

We are taking the liberty of directing your attention to the deplorable fact that for a considerable time the population of Eastern Ukraine (now under a military Bolshevik occupation) are being systematically starved by the Moscow authorities.

The tragedy of the great famine of 1921–22, when nearly ten million people died from hunger, is being repeated, but in all probability on a still larger scale. Thousands of letters are being received in Canada continuously, containing gruesome details of the vast number dying; there are settlements in Ukraine where only one-third—sometimes only one-fourth—of the original population are still alive.

Crop failure is not the reason for this famine, but the brutal policy of the Moscow rulers who, needing grain for export to balance their budget, pitilessly take everything from the farmers, already proletarized. Especially in Ukraine, where the peasants are opposed to the foreign Russian rule, are they being deprived of literally everything, being left without even the smallest ration for daily meals, under the excuse that they are hiding food. With such tactics, even a bumper crop, of huge yield, could not save these people from starvation.

Having in mind the tragic plight of their compatriots, and realising their moral duty in the matter, the Ukrainian National Council in Canada turn to you, as to a leader of a great civilized nation, with an urgent request to take the necessary steps to arrange for an immediate neutral investigation of the famine situation in Ukraine, with a view to organizing international relief for the stricken population. Any private action, even on the largest scale, would prove inadequate owing to the magnitude of the calamity. We are prepared to supply you, if necessary, with original documents and information giving details of the famine conditions.

We trust that your Excellency will take this, our appeal, under most serious consideration.

We remain,
Yours faithfully,
Ukrainian National Council in Canada
[Signed] President, S. Skoblak; Secretary, J. M. Boyduck;
Chairman of Advisory Board, L. Biberovich

"Memorandum of Ukrainian Organizations to the President of the United States Concerning the Recognition of the Union of Socialist Soviet Republics"

Svoboda (Jersey City, N.J.), 30 October 1933, no. 252, p. 1.

The President,
Washington, D.C.

Sir,

The time has come when you shall decide one of the most important problems of America's foreign policy: the question of the official recognition by the United States of the Union of Socialist Soviet Republics.

Hitherto this question of recognition has been decided negatively, for the United States Government had no desire to have any official connection with a state whose rule over the Russian people, as well as over its subjugated and enslaved peoples such as the Ukrainians, was based upon direct force alone. We have grown accustomed to regard the Soviet Republic as a state whose main purpose is the wholesale destruction throughout the entire world of those principles of democracy upon which our Constitution is based. We have come to regard the Soviet Republic as a state which through the medium of its subservient tool, the Third International, disseminates Bolshevist propaganda throughout the United States for the purpose of overthrowing by violent means our democratic institutions and our social order.

The truth of this assertion has been repeatedly confirmed by the investigations of our government. It has been the motivating cause of the recent resolution of the American Legion—a body whose members fought to defend our democratic institutions—to oppose the recognition of the Soviet Republic by the United States Government.

The American Federation of Labor has recently also expressed its opposition to this proposed recognition, basing its action upon the ground that in no other country in the world is the laboring class so mercilessly exploited as in Soviet Russia. The Federation has repeatedly pointed out that the recognition of Soviet Russia by America would give the former an unprecedented opportunity of gaining American credit and loans by means of which Soviet trade would greatly increase, as a result of the further and greater exploitation of their enslaved workers, and the underselling of their competitors, including America. And finally, as the American Federation of Labor points out, the recognition of the Soviets by America would automatically open America's door to the hordes of Bolshevik propagandists who, as already has been proven, would stoop to any means to create dissensions and troubles among the American workers, seek to dominate the labor unions, and thus retard the progress of American reconstruction and make impossible the cooperation between Capital and Labor, towards which goal the National Recovery Administration is striving today.

And it is because of these reasons that we, American citizens of Ukrainian descent, are also strongly and unequivocally opposed to the recognition of the Union of Socialist Soviet Republics by the United States Government.

And in addition to these very pertinent reasons as brought out by the American Legion and by the American Federation of Labor, we beg leave to add one more, to wit:

During the past year several millions of inhabitants of Soviet Ukraine, the land of our ancestors, have died from starvation. The existence of this terrible famine in Ukraine has been repeatedly proven by the leading European and American press. It is impossible to give the exact figures as to the total number of deaths from this great famine, principally because of the rigid censorship in Soviet Russia. Just recently the Associated Press correspondent during his interview in Kharkiv with Alexander Asatkin, a Moscow political overlord in Ukraine, managed to obtain some official figures as to the number of famine victims in Ukraine, only to have these figures, which were considerably lower than reported in the outside world, refused transmission to America by the censor in Moscow.

It will be sufficient for us, however, to affirm the well authenticated reports of impartial American and European newspaper correspondents that during the past year several million inhabitants of Ukraine have died a terrible death from starvation, and that even cannibalism was discovered in several sections of the country; all of this in a land which is regarded as one of the most fertile in the world.

As to the cause of this terrible famine in Ukraine, even the foreign correspondents in Soviet Russia do not attempt to hide the fact any longer that the famine is a result of Soviet policy. They regard the famine as another step taken by Moscow directed towards the breaking down of the opposition of the Ukrainian peasantry, which at all times was and still is, uncompromisingly hostile to the Communistic system, as well as to the occupation of Ukraine by Moscovschena (Russia proper).

The American-Ukrainian press is filled with reprinted letters from Ukraine which somehow managed to elude the strict Soviet censorship, and which contain pathetic appeals for help against this terrible foe—hunger. They implore us and others to appeal to the American sense of humanity and justice and have America aid the stricken Ukraine once more, as it did back in 1921.

All of these foregoing reasons have led us to send a delegation to the President of the United States, in order to inform the United States Government of our opinion concerning the recognition of the Union of Socialist Soviet Republics by the United States Government. We regard this task of expressing our unprejudiced opinion on this most important problem as our patriotic duty. And because of the reasons already cited, we respectfully recommend to the President to conduct any further necessary negotiations with the Soviets on the subject of the recognition only on the condition that the Soviet Republic permits the sending of an impartial Special American Mission to Soviet Russia, particularly to Ukraine, for the purpose of investigating the conditions therein, and to ascertain the direct cause of this terrible famine which during the past year mowed down millions of victims in Ukraine.

We are firmly convinced that the famine in Ukraine is not a result of poor crops or drought, but on the contrary, is a result of the political and cultural conflict between Ukrainian nationalistic aspirations and Moscow's imperialistic and centralizing designs; and also because of the Ukrainian peasants' opposition to Moscow's economic exploitation of Ukraine and to its forcibly imposed collectivization and other Communistic experiments practiced upon the Ukrainian people. The famine is the culmination of that unremitting and ferocious persecution of the Ukrainian people by Moscow dictatorship, which beginning back in 1918—when the Bolsheviks forcibly seized Ukraine, which in accordance with the will of its inhabitants and their desire for self-determination had been formed into the Ukrainian National Republic—has continued with unabated force to this day.

The Bolshevik dictatorship over Ukraine, from its very beginning up to the present time, has always and without any interruptions whatsoever been maintained by brutal force alone against the will and wishes of the Ukrainian people. And in order to break this opposition, and to quell forever the unceasing struggle of the Ukrainian people to free themselves, the Soviets fostered during the past year this famine which has taken such a terrible toll of human life.

And therefore, in view of all of these circumstances, we believe that at least from the standpoint of humanity an investigation of these terrible conditions in Ukraine under the Soviets be immediately undertaken by this proposed Special American Mission.

Only after a thorough investigation of these conditions—as enunciated by the American Legion and American Federation of Labor, and finally by Ukrainian people—can the question of the official recognition of the Union of Socialist Republics by the United States Government be finally decided in accordance with the world renowned American principles of justice and humanity.

In view of the fact, that the Ukrainian people have repeatedly declared, thru their legal representatives, that they do not recognize the Russian occupation of Ukraine nor treaties and obligations entered into by the Moscow government concerning Ukrainian territories,

And in view of the fact, that under present Soviet Russian oppression the Ukrainian people are unable to express themselves freely upon questions vitally affecting them,

We owe it to the American Government as loyal citizens to call its attention to those facts.

Respectfully submitted,
United Ukrainian Organizations of the United States:
Emil Revyuk, President; D-r Luke Myshuha, Secretary [and others].

73rd Congress, 2nd Session. H. Res. 399

In the House of Representatives, May 28, 1934. Resolution. Reprinted in *Famine in Ukraine* (1934). Full text, pp. 3–4.

Mr. [Hamilton] Fish submitted the following resolution; which was referred to the Committee on Foreign Affairs and ordered to be printed.

Whereas several millions of the population of the Ukrainian Soviet Socialist Republic, the constituent part of the Union of Soviet Socialist Republics, died of starvation during the years of 1932 and 1933; and

Whereas the Government of the Union of Soviet Socialist Republics, although being fully aware of the famine in Ukraine and although having full and complete control of the entire food supplies within its borders, nevertheless failed to take relief measure designed to check the famine or to alleviate the terrible conditions arising from it, but on the contrary used the famine as a means of reducing the Ukrainian population and destroying the Ukrainian political, cultural, and national rights; and

Whereas intercessions have been made at various times by the United States during the course of its history on behalf of citizens of states other than the United States, oppressed or persecuted by their own governments, indicating that it has been the traditional policy of the United States to take cognizance of such invasions of human rights and liberties: Therefore be it

RESOLVED, That the House of Representatives express its sympathy for all those who have suffered from the great famine in Ukraine which has brought misery, affliction, and death to millions of peaceful and law-abiding Ukrainians; be it further

RESOLVED, That the House of Representatives express its earnest hope that the Government of the Union of Soviet Socialist Republics will speedily alter its policy in respect to the famine in Ukraine, take active steps to alleviate the terrible consequences arising from this famine, and undo so far as may be possible the injustices to the Ukrainian people; and be it further

RESOLVED, That the House of Representatives express its sincerest hope that the Union of Soviet Socialist Republics Government will place no obstacles in the way of American citizens seeking to send aid in form of money, foodstuffs, and necessities to the famine-stricken regions of Ukraine.

SOVIET DENIALS (1930S TO 1980S)

Letter from Maksim Litvinov, People's Commissar of Foreign Affairs, to Herman P. Koplemann, U.S. Congressman, 3 January 1934

In *Famine in Ukraine* (1934), p. 6.

I am in receipt of your letter of the 14th inst. and thank you for drawing my attention to the Ukrainian pamphlet. There is any amount of such pamphlets full of lies circulated by counter-revolutionary organizations abroad, who specialize in the work of this kind. There is nothing left for them to do but to spread false information or to forge documents.

However, I am instructing Mr. Skvirsky in Washington to supply you with data on the real situation in the Ukraine.

Yours sincerely,
M. Litvinoff

Letter from B. Skvirsky, Counsellor of the Embassy of the USSR, to Herman P. Koplemann, U.S. Congressman, 3 February [1934]

In *Famine in Ukraine* (1934), pp. 6–8.

My dear Representative Koplemann:

Commissar Litvinoff has forwarded to me your inquiry in regard to a pamphlet ostensibly published by the "Ukrainian National Women's League of America." In effect these anonymous ladies (I use the word anonymous because no name nor address is given in the pamphlet) accuse the Soviet Government of deliberately killing off the population of the Ukraine.

The idea is wholly grotesque. The population of the Ukraine is somewhat over 30,000,000. During the period of the first Five-Year Plan, concluded a year ago, the population increased at the rate of 2 per cent per year. The death rate was the lowest of that of any of the seven constituent Republics composing the Soviet

Union, and was about 35 per cent lower than the pre-war death rate of Tsarist days. The death rate in the larger Ukrainian cities is the lowest among the cities of the Soviet Union. More than three times as many children are in school today in Ukraine as in 1913. The Ukrainian language is used in the schools as well as Russian, and in the literature and the theatre. It was banned in the Tsarist days. So much for the general charge.

Fortunately we can check up on one or two specific things mentioned in the pamphlet. They show that the authors were not particularly scrupulous about facts.

1. The pamphlet states that in the N.Y. Times of August 24, 1933, Duranty stated that three to four million persons in the Ukraine died the same year. Duranty, writing from Moscow on that date, actually stated that from information he had received he estimated that owing to the poor harvest of 1932 possibly three million persons died during 1932, not in Ukraine alone but in Ukraine, North Caucasus and lower Volga region together, an area roughly triple the size of the Ukraine. The pamphlet does not add that in the Times, September 13, writing from Rostov-on-Don in the course of a personal inspection trip through these sections, Duranty stated that his estimate of July 24, before he had made his personal inspection, was exaggerated. He said that the poor harvest of 1932 had made for difficult conditions in certain sections, but there had been no famine. Writing from Kharkov, capitol of Ukraine, Sept. 18, 1933 on the conditions of that year, he said:

"'The writer has just completed a 200 mile trip through the heart of the Ukraine and can say positively that the harvest is splendid and all talk of famine now is ridiculous.' The A.P. correspondent made a similar first hand report."

[**Interpolation by editors of** *Famine in Ukraine*: The letter then proceeds to disqualify the report of Frederic T. Birchall appearing in the New York Times of August 25, 1933, in which that correspondent states that three or four million people starved to death in Ukraine—by saying that Mr. Birchall was not in Ukraine but used as a basis for his article information received from persons who came from Ukraine. The letter then concludes as follows:]

3. The pamphlet quotes "The Ukrainian Daily Dilo" published in Lemberg "in the western part of the Ukraine"? as authority for the statement that six million Ukrainians had starved to death. Here apparently we have a newspaper published in the Ukraine itself apparently admitting this horrible fact. Unfortunately, however, the pamphlet is a little bit misleading. Lemberg, as you can readily see from any standard atlas, is not in Ukraine at all, but in Poland. The "Dilo" is not a Ukrainian publication. It is an organ issued by an émigré group in Poland by former feudal landlords of the Ukraine, now living abroad. The question is whether one should credit this émigré source or credit the two American newspaper men, representing respectively the N.Y. Times and the Associated Press, who made a personal inspection of the territory in question.

Sincerely yours,
B. Skvirsky,
Counsellor of the Embassy.

News release, Press Office of the USSR Embassy in Canada, no. 60, 28 April 1983

Copy in the possession of the editors supplied by Marco Carynnyk.

On the So Called 'Famine' in the Ukraine

Recent stories in the Western news media try to create an impression that there was an artificially created famine in the Ukraine in 1932–33 because Ukrainian farmers, allegedly, resisted collective farming.

Indeed, the situation in the Ukraine as well as in other parts of the USSR in 1932 was quite difficult. Yet it was not as critical as it is portrayed in the West. And of course it was not because somebody wanted to make it bad, but because of a number of reasons, drought being the major one.

Many Canadians of Ukrainian origin know from their mothers and fathers that the Ukraine had chronically suffered from crop failures, and though there were good years the bad ones came nearly as often. In fact many of them left their country exactly because of the famines that occurred in the Ukraine in the 19th as well as in the early 20th century.

In 1931, 27 million hectares of land in the Ukraine (nearly 60 million acres, more than all the cultivated area of Saskatchewan) were hit by the most severe drought. In 1932 major grain producing areas in the Ukraine and in the Russian Federation were affected by the drought again. As a result the 1932 harvest in the Ukraine was 14.7 million metric tons, 3.9 million less than the year before.

Specialists in anti-Soviet propaganda say that Moscow allegedly imposed "Draconian quotas" on the Ukraine, which made the situation worse. In actual fact, history carries quite a different record.

The reasons for the crop failure were considered at the 3rd Conference of the Communist Party of the Ukraine (July, 1932) and measures were taken to lessen the effect of the poor year on the population. As a result, government quotas were drastically reduced to 6.6 million metric tons. Later even this figure was cut and the actual Ukrainian quota was 4.7 million tons.

In other words, 10 million tons of grains out of the 14.7 million tons harvested in 1932 remained in the Ukraine. Of course distribution of grain was not absolutely even, some areas were better off than the others, but the overall situation in the country was far from that described by some Canadian media.

The agricultural difficulties in the Ukraine happened to take place during one of the most crucial periods in the history of farming. The transition to large scale collective farming was completely new and untried. Farmers, as well as the party and government officials lacked the experience as to how to organize their work better, hence there were mistakes and omissions. Tractors or other agricultural machinery were scarce at the time and yet at many collectivized farms the stake was made on machinery while draught horses and oxen were neglected, which resulted in a mass loss of cattle. That misjudgement frustrated to great extent the sowing and harvesting campaigns in 1932.

Another reason for the difficulties the new collective way of farming experienced was that it was violently opposed by the wealthy landowners called the Kulaks and not by peasants, as it is sometimes claimed here. The overwhelming majority of peasants immediately saw the advantages of collective farming which among other things was able to increase farmers' security against crop failures and put an end to the Kulaks' tyranny. The Kulaks who did not want to lose their control over poor peasants or to share a piece of bread with them tried every possible means to hamper the progress of collective farming. For this purpose they organized gangs that poisoned the cattle, set fire to collective farmers' houses and office buildings, exercised terror and murder.

In 1929 alone when collective farming was just starting on a mass scale, the Kulaks killed about 10,000 activists, communists, leaders of the farms or those who agreed to try to farm collectively. In the first six months of 1930 they committed over 1500 acts of terrorism in the Ukraine.

The acts of sabotage were multiple. The Kulaks, using blackmail, terror or other means managed to make their way into collective farms' management, where they delayed or ruined field work, damaged machinery, etc. Western authors admit that in 1931 in the Ukraine arson committed on 24.7 per cent of the collective farms, machinery damaged in 9.6 per cent, cattle poisoned in 8.8 per cent, activists attacked in 44 per cent.

All this could not but tell on the results of the agricultural production and on the overall situation in the republic.

The masters of the new anti-Soviet campaign which fits so perfectly into the recently pronounced crusade against communism, finding it hard to oppose the facts, or bring any evidence in support of their allegations, tend to concentrate on the emotional side of the story, overplaying human sufferings. Some even say that collectivization resulted in a smaller population in the Ukraine. Of course, many families were badly affected, some did suffer, especially those whose husbands or sons were murdered by the Kulak bandits. Some villages felt a terrible strain after their grain reserves were burned, or cattle poisoned. Nevertheless, the whole picture in the Ukraine was not that of a nearly complete collapse with a smell of a nation-wide tragedy as it is portrayed by the most zealous anti-Soviet writers in the media in Canada. On the contrary, the atmosphere of vigorous work and unparalleled enthusiasm prevailed as the nation embarked on great economic and social programs. Collective farming proved extremely effective as 22.3 million tons of harvest were harvested in 1933.

As to the alleged decrease in the Ukrainian population, the argument is as groundless as the whole man-made-hunger campaign. The fact is that in 1929 the Ukraine had a 30.2 million population. Throughout 1932–1933 the population remained at a level of 32 million, which has nothing to do with the widely circulated and televised lie that some 10 million Ukrainians were starved to death.

The early thirties in the USSR witnessed an historic drive of the whole country to build its own industry, and many huge construction projects were started across the country. There were big schemes in the Ukraine, like the world famous Lenin hydro-power station on the Dnieper river. But a great number of them were built in the Urals and in Siberia, in Central Asia and the Caucasus, in the Far East and in the North. Hundreds of thousands of people from the Western part of the country left their homes for those industrial projects because there they found jobs and new professional and career opportunities. One of the major social results of the first years of industrialization in the USSR was that it created the conditions for the first time ever to achieve full employment. Economic and political consequences of an unprecedented construction boom in the USSR in the early thirties were no less important. It was then that Soviet industry was consolidated which made it possible in a few years' time to face and eventually defeat the most powerful Nazi war machine.

This argument is hard to find in the new round of slanders against the USSR, because some of the emigrants' organizations and their leaders who are behind this campaign participated in or actively supported Nazi atrocities against their Ukrainian compatriots.

And finally, if the hard times of 1932–33 are to be remembered, there is one solid reason for that. The droughts in the early thirties were the last to have such an effect on the Ukraine or the USSR. Since farming in the country became collectivized fifty years ago Soviet people, including Ukrainians, no longer fear that poor crops may result in human suffering. We may have a good year or a bad year, but on the whole collective farming indisputably resulted in steady and continuous growth of grain production.

These are the most important social, economic and political results of collectivized farming and they are the prime target of the new slanderous anti-Soviet campaign under the pretext of the so-called "man-made famine" in the Ukraine.

6

LITERATURE: PROSE, PLAYS, POETRY

INTRODUCTION

The final section of the *Reader* contains a variety of excerpts—most never before translated into English—from novels, stories, plays, and poems dealing with the Holodomor. Many of the writings are based on the personal experiences of the authors. Most prominent among them are two selections by non-Ukrainian authors: George Orwell's savage satire *Animal Farm* and Vasily Grossman's painfully honest *Forever Flowing*. The other selections, by Ukrainian writers, perfectly complement the writings of Orwell and Grossman. Many of the authors explicitly use the theme of mass death as an opportunity to reflect on the meaning of life, the existence of God, and other existential questions.

All the selections convey the pervasive sense of doom that became an everyday component of the Ukrainian peasantry's existence and nonexistence. Unsurprisingly, a constant theme is food and the desperate efforts of starving Ukrainians to find, cook, and digest it. As a variety of folk verses and folk rhymes demonstrate, however, Ukrainian peasants were fully aware of Stalin's murderous campaign against their country, sought to retain their dignity to the end, and engaged in "passive resistance" by making fun of the authorities. Serhii Kokot-Lediansky's play, *Nineteen Hundred Thirty-Three*, is also notable for employing black humor to depict a scene in which a famine survivor is being carted away by gravediggers who have no time to return for him when he is dead.

Of particular interest are Vasyl Barka's important novels *Paradise* and *The Yellow Prince*, which pull no punches in confronting the reader with some of the most horrific descriptions of life and death in the Ukrainian countryside. Samchuk, Ponedilok, Zvychaina, and Chaplenko describe the tragic circumstances surrounding the acquisition, or loss, of food. Wira Wowk's poem "Iconostasis of Ukraine" manages to convey the unimaginable suffering of the Ukrainians with sparse images and a minimum of words. Natalia Vorozhbyt's *The Granary* opened to critical acclaim on 10 September 2009, when it was first performed in English by the Royal Shakespeare Company at the Courtyard Theatre in Stratford-upon-Avon.

The prose and theater excerpts have been arranged not alphabetically by author but thematically. They begin with depictions of incipient hunger and scavenging for food, proceed through the darkest period of mass famine and its consequences, such as cannibalism, and end with the aftermath of the disaster—emptiness, hopelessness, and death.

PROSE

George Orwell, *Animal Farm*

(New York: Harcourt, Brace & World, Inc., 1946). Excerpts, pp. 82–86.

George Orwell was the pen name of Eric Arthur Blair (1903–1950), an uncompromising critic of totalitarianism and one of the most prominent English writers of the twentieth century. He is best known for the dystopian novel *Nineteen Eighty-Four* (1949), the allegorical novella *Animal Farm* (1945), and an essay collection about the Spanish Civil War, *Homage to Catalonia* (1938)

Chapter VII

It was a bitter winter. The stormy weather was followed by sleet and snow, and then by a hard frost which did not break till well into February. The animals carried on as best they could with the rebuilding of the windmill, well knowing that the outside world was watching them and that the envious human beings would rejoice and triumph if the mill were not finished on time.

Out of spite, the human beings pretended not to believe that it was Snowball who had destroyed the windmill: they said that it had fallen down because the walls were too thin. The animals knew that this was not the case. Still, it had been decided to build the walls three feet thick this time instead of eighteen inches as before, which meant collecting much larger quantities of stone. For a long time the quarry was full of snowdrifts and nothing could be done. Some progress was made in the dry frosty weather that followed, but it was cruel work, and the animals could not feel so hopeful about it as they had felt before. They were always cold, and usually hungry as well. Only Boxer and Clover never lost heart. Squealer made excellent speeches on the joy of service and the dignity of labour, but the other animals found more inspiration in Boxer's strength and his never-failing cry of "I will work harder!"

In January food fell short. The corn ration was drastically reduced, and it was announced that an extra potato ration would be issued to make up for it. Then it was discovered that the greater part of the potato crop had been frosted in the clamps, which had not been covered thickly enough. The potatoes had become soft and discoloured, and only a few were edible. For days at a time the animals had nothing to eat but chaff and mangels. Starvation seemed to stare them in the face.

It was vitally necessary to conceal this fact from the outside world. Emboldened by the collapse of the windmill, the human beings were inventing fresh lies about Animal Farm. Once again it was being put about that all the animals were dying of famine and disease, and that they were continually fighting among themselves and had resorted to cannibalism and infanticide. Napoleon was well aware of the bad results that might follow if the real facts of the food situation were known, and he decided to make use of Mr. Whymper to spread a contrary impression. Hitherto the animals had had little or no contact with Whymper on his weekly visits: now, however, a few selected animals, mostly sheep, were instructed to remark casually in his hearing that rations had been increased. In addition, Napoleon ordered the almost empty bins in the store-shed to be filled nearly to the brim with sand, which was then covered up with what remained of the grain and meal. On some suitable pretext Whymper was led through the store-shed and allowed to catch a glimpse of the bins. He was deceived, and continued to report to the outside world that there was no food shortage on Animal Farm.

Nevertheless, towards the end of January it became obvious that it would be necessary to procure some more grain from somewhere. In these days Napoleon rarely appeared in public, but spent all his time in the farmhouse, which was guarded at each door by fierce-looking dogs. When he did emerge, it was in a ceremonial manner, with an escort of six dogs who closely surrounded him and growled if anyone came too near. Frequently he did not even appear on Sunday mornings, but issued his orders through one of the other pigs, usually Squealer.

One Sunday morning Squealer announced that the hens, who had just come in to lay again, must surrender their eggs. Napoleon had accepted, through Whymper, a contract for four hundred eggs a week. The price of these would pay for enough grain and meal to keep the farm going till summer came on and conditions were easier.

When the hens heard this, they raised a terrible outcry. They had been warned earlier that this sacrifice might be necessary, but had not believed that it would really happen. They were just getting their clutches ready for the spring sitting, and they protested that to take the eggs away now was murder. For the first time since the expulsion of Jones, there was something resembling a rebellion. Led by three young Black Minorca pullets, the hens made a determined effort to thwart Napoleon's wishes. Their method was to fly up to the rafters and there lay their eggs, which smashed to pieces on the floor. Napoleon acted swiftly and ruthlessly. He ordered the hens' rations to be stopped, and decreed that any animal giving so much as a grain of corn to a hen should be punished by death. The dogs saw to it that these orders were carried out. For five days the hens held out, then they capitulated and went back to their nesting boxes. Nine hens had died in the meantime. Their bodies were buried in the orchard, and it was given out that they had died of coccidiosis. Whymper heard nothing of this affair, and the eggs were duly delivered, a grocer's van driving up to the farm once a week to take them away.

Vasyl Barka, *Rai* (Paradise)

(Jersey City, N.J.: Svoboda, 1953). Excerpts, pp. 60–64. Translated by Alexander J. Motyl.

Vasyl Barka (pseudonym of Vasyl Ocheret, 1908–2003) was a Ukrainian poet, writer, literary critic, and translator. He settled in the United States in 1949. He was the author, in Ukrainian, of collections of poetry, *Pathways* (1930), *Guilds* (1932), *Apostles* (1946), *The White World* (1947), *The Rose Novel* (1957), *The Psalm of the Dovelike Field* (1958), *Ocean* (1959, 1979, 1992), *The Witness for the Sun of Seraphims* (1981), and *Steppe of Judgment* (1992); translations of William Shakespeare and Dante; and novels, *Paradise* (1953), *The Yellow Prince* (1962, 1968), and *The Penitent and the Keys to the Earth* (1992).

There were few corrections to be made to the text. He crossed out the first sentence: "The winter of 1933 was severe." The manuscript began with dreary images.

"The slush froze into hard, black lumps like a killer's fists. From the Kremlin to the Caucasus, the biting wind, armed with millions of thin, long needles resembling insidious thoughts, pierced the tattered clothing of the exhausted people, pressed their heads, gray faces, and huddled shoulders—down, to the very ground, provoking suffering similar to that experienced in prehistoric times. The snowy expanse was terrifying, a bottomless pit into which one was fated to fall and die in pain....

"One could imagine an invisible sphinx standing behind the leadership—a sphinx more powerful than death. His icy eyes observed the unworldly evil all around. He watched and remained silent.

"The farmers who fed half of Europe were going to town for the bit of bread that had been taken from them and given in miserly rations to everyone but them—simply because they had refused to agree to become ants in this modern-day serfdom. City dwellers received a daily ration to enable them, despite their hunger-induced yellow complexions, to power the economic machine on which the state rested. They too died, though proportionately in fewer numbers, but with the same agonies as the peasants who trundled to town in hope of getting at least some of their leftovers. The famine turned the cold village huts into huge coffins with bloated corpses on the floors and benches. There was no one to collect them; they lay for days on end, and even the neighbors didn't know what had happened to them. They too awaited the same fate or were looking down at the huts from the next world, where there is 'neither grieving nor sighing.' The straw roofs had been stripped for fuel, while the fruit trees had been chopped down for firewood to heat the soup made of weeds and the ribs of the last remaining village dogs and cats. The healthier peasants, who managed to reach town through the snowstorm, past the weaker ones lying dead, their bodies twisted, in the snowdrifts along the roads, wandered about the streets, peering hopelessly into the windows of the empty stores. With time, they too lost strength, swelled up, stomped around with legs as thick as logs and wrapped in filthy rags, leaned against the brick walls, and fell onto the snow, where they expired silently. Only the children, resting on the stones, whimpered like birds expelled from their nests. Soon they too fell silent. The city streets were abundantly littered with corpses. At first, the dead were immediately gathered; afterwards, one became indifferent to them, and they turned black, lying for a long time on the sidewalks, streets, and yards. Meanwhile, the new, so-called 'passenger' cars of the 'responsible workers' (whose work consisted in carrying out strict orders), their sirens blaring, dashed past the corpses. Through the windows one could see the arrogant faces of the thick-necked and evil-eyed Party, state, and political-police administrators. They didn't cast a single glance at the corpses! They drove past them with the heightened speed of people who must save humanity from the accursed old world and replace it with the harmonious, sunny, and happy classless society....

"Every day there was talk of cannibalism. A band of thieves was uncovered not far from the small train station; they had set up a factory that made sausages from children's flesh. One day some passersby accidentally saw crows picking through piles of little bones and tugging at some colored rags. They chased the birds away and, after looking at their booty, noticed tiny fingers. They began looking around and found a trash can with the torn remains of a child's clothes and a large number of children's fingernails. Close by stood a building that had once been an old shed. In the basement they found several children's corpses, two vats with salted meat, crates of sausages, and some bones in the corner near the stove with cooking utensils. The attic contained piles of children's shirts and shoes. The owner of the building, a nondescript 40-year-old woman, had come here last fall from Kazakhstan, where she had settled from Kuibyshev in 1930. She said she knew nothing. She had sat quietly in the house and had been afraid to step out while they puttered about in the basement at night. Finally, she did name a few names, but try catching the wind! Naturally, the woman was sent away—who knows where. The case was 'hushed up,' as we say.

"There were also such cases. Mothers with several children would kill the smaller ones and feed the older ones with cutlets made of their flesh. That saved them.

"The sphinx watched and remained silent. It was only when the honest foreign press began to speak of the famine that he snarled and swore, shouting that the capitalist lackeys were trying to tarnish the paradise of the worldwide socialist proletariat....

"Once the sphinx even spoke to the people. He said that 'dying has become better, dying has become happier.' That's how everyone understood him, even though he had said 'living.'

"Sometimes a peasant who saw the inevitability of death by starvation for himself and his family would seize an axe and smash the head of the 'plenipotentiary' taking the last kernels in his yard. A military court would promptly order him to be 'executed.'"

Vasily Grossman, *Forever Flowing*

(New York: Harper and Row, 1972). Excerpts, pp. 156–57, 159–60, 162–66. Translated by Thomas P. Whitney.

Vasily Grossman (1905–1964) was a Soviet Jewish writer, journalist, and dissident. He published several literary works in the 1930s and was nominated for the Stalin Prize for the novel *Stepan Kol'chugin* (1937–40). He served as a war correspondent for the Red Army newspaper *Krasnaia zvezda* (Red Star) and covered the battles of Moscow, Stalingrad, Kursk, and Berlin. He became a critic of the Soviet regime in the late 1940s. He was the author, in Russian, of *The Black Book: The Ruthless Murder of Jews by German-Fascist Invaders Throughout the Temporarily Occupied Regions of the Soviet Union and in the Death Camps of Poland during the War, 1941–1945* and of the novels *Life and Fate* (1959) and *Forever Flowing* (1961).

It was when the snow began to melt that the village was up to its neck in real starvation.

The children kept crying and crying. They did not sleep. And they began to ask for bread at night too. People's faces looked like clay. Their eyes were dull and drunken. They went about as though asleep. They inched forward, feeling their way one foot at a time, and they supported themselves by keeping one hand against the wall. They began to move around less. Starvation made them totter. They moved less and less, and they spent more time lying down. And they kept thinking they heard the creaking of a cart bringing flour, sent to them by Stalin from the district center so as to save the children....

No dogs and cats were left. They had been slaughtered. And it was hard to catch them too. The animals had become afraid of people and their eyes were wild. People boiled them. All there was were tough veins and muscles. And from their heads they made a meat jelly.

The snow melted and people began to swell up. The edema of starvation had begun. Faces were swollen, legs swollen like pillows; water bloated their stomachs; people kept urinating all the time. Often they couldn't even make it out of the house. And the peasant children! Have you ever seen the newspaper photographs of the children in the German camps? They were just like that: their heads like heavy balls on thin little necks, like storks, and one could see each bone of their arms and legs protruding from beneath the skin, how bones joined, and the entire skeleton was stretched over with skin that was like yellow gauze. And the children's faces were aged, tormented, just as if they were seventy years old. And by spring they no longer had faces at all. Instead, they had birdlike heads with beaks, or frog heads—thin, wide lips—and some of them resembled fish, mouths open. Not human faces. And the eyes. Oh, Lord! Comrade Stalin, good God, did you see those eyes? Perhaps, in fact, he did not know. After all, he was the one who wrote the essay on "dizziness from success."

And now they ate anything at all. They caught mice, rats, snakes, sparrows, ants, earthworms. They ground up bones into flour and did the same with leather and shoe soles; they cut up old skins and furs to make noodles of a kind, and they cooked glue. And when the grass came up, they began to dig up the roots and eat the leaves and the buds....

The village moaned as it foresaw its approaching death. The whole village moaned—not out of logic, but from the soul, as leaves moan in the wind or straw crackles. And I myself saw red; why were they moaning so plaintively? One had to be of stone to hear all that moaning and at the same time eat one's own ration of bread. I used to go outdoors with my bread ration, and I could hear them moaning. I would go farther, and then it would seem as if they had fallen silent. And then I would go on a little farther, and it would begin again. At that point, it was the next village down the line. And it seemed as if the whole earth were groaning, together with the people on it. There was no God. Who could hear them?....

And the peasants kept crawling from the village into the city. All the stations were surrounded by guards. All the trains were searched. Everywhere along the road were roadblocks—troops, NKVD. Yet despite all this the peasants made their way into Kiev. They would crawl through the fields, through empty lots, through the swamps, through the woods—anywhere to bypass the roadblocks set up for them. They were unable to walk; all they could do was crawl. People hurried about on their affairs, some going to work, some to the movies, and the streetcars were running—and there were the starving children, old men, girls, crawling about among them on all fours. They were like mangy dogs and cats of some kind. And they had the nerve to want to be treated like human beings!....

And this is what I came to understand. In the beginning, starvation drives a person out of his house. In its first stage, he is tormented and driven as though by fire and torn both in the guts and in the soul. And so he tries to escape his home. People dig up worms, collect grass, and even make the effort to break through and get to the city. Away from home, away from home! And then a day comes when the starving person crawls back into his house. And the meaning of this is that famine, starvation, has won. The human being cannot be saved. He lies down on his bed and stays there. Not just because he has no strength, but because he has no interest in life and no longer cares about living. He lies there quite quietly and does not want to be touched. And he does not even want to eat. He keeps urinating constantly and he has continuous runs and he becomes sleepy. All he wants is to be left alone, and for things to be quiet....

What I found out later was that everything fell silent in our village. The children were no more to be heard. They didn't need any cultural toys, nor any chicken soup either. They no longer moaned. There was no one left to moan. I found out that troops were sent in to harvest the winter wheat. The army men were not allowed to enter the village, however. They were quartered in their tents. They were told there had been an epidemic. But they kept complaining that a horrible stink was coming from the village. The troops stayed to plant the spring wheat too. And the next year new settlers were brought in from Orel Province. This was the rich Ukrainian land, the black earth, whereas the Orel peasants were accustomed to frequent harvest failures. The new settlers left their women and children in temporary shelters near the station, and the men were brought into the village. They were given pitchforks and told to go through the huts and drag out the corpses. The dead men and women still lay there, some on the floor and some in their beds. The stink in the huts was still frightful. The new settlers covered their noses and mouths with kerchiefs and began to drag out the bodies, but the bodies fell apart in pieces. Then they buried the pieces outside the village. And it was then that I understood what was meant by the phrase "a hard-school cemetery." When they had removed the corpses from the huts, they brought in the womenfolk to clean the floors and to whitewash the walls. Everything was done as it was supposed to be done. But the stink remained. They whitewashed a second time, and they spread new clay on the floors, but the stink remained. They were unable either to eat or sleep in those huts, and they returned to Orel Province. But of course the land did not remain empty. It is rich land.

Olena Zvychaina, "Socialist Potatoes"

In *A Hunger Most Cruel*, ed. Sonia Morris (Toronto: Language Lantern Publications, 2002). Excerpts, pp. 254–56. Translated by Roma Franko.

Olena Zvychaina (early 1900s–1985) was a Ukrainian writer. After being interned in a Nazi labor camp in Austria during World War II, she settled in the United States in the late 1940s. Her stories describe life in Ukraine under Soviet oppression and Nazi occupation, as well as the experiences of people displaced by war. In an autobiographical novel written in collaboration with her husband, she described the fate of the unfortunate millions accused by the Soviet secret police of being "enemies of the people."

It is December... The fierce winter of 1932–1933 imperiously comes into its own...

The wind, sharp as a razor blade, stings my face and nimbly searches out the tiniest gaps in my clothing, forcing its way into the very marrow of my bones and painfully pinching my toes. In the predawn darkness, I am running as fast as I can to the mustering point—it is no joking matter to lose not only your own ration card but also those of your family members. My legs speed me on my way like an arrow... Finally, gasping for breath and drenched in sweat, I make it to the designated spot at the very moment that our group leaves for the station.

A forty-minute ride on the suburban train, and we arrive at our destination, the state storage cellars for potatoes. There are ever so many of them! And they are all numbered and laid out in neat rows on a huge field in the form of a chessboard. We are received expeditiously, counted off like cattle, formed into brigades of six people, and lowered by means of ladders into the ground—deep down into the storage cellars...

Now the ladder disappears, and the lid covering the opening above us slams shut. We—the six of us—find ourselves in a cavernous grave... An acrid, penetrating stench winds its way like a snake through our nostrils into our stomachs, our brains, our very souls...

We feel nauseated and terrified. We want to shout: "Help! Save us!" But a huge lamp conscientiously shows us the mountainous heaps of potatoes that seem to undulate before our eyes; the heaps that are the source of that putrid smell, and that patiently await the labor of our hands....

Donning the aprons that we brought with us from home, we get down to work, separating the undamaged potatoes from those that are slightly spoiled, and dropping the rotted ones into a large vat that has been lowered into the hole on thick ropes. Klava, a Komsomol member, starts singing a Komsomol song, but, choking on the vile odor, she breaks off abruptly in the middle of a word, saying that singing makes the stench "go right to your gut."

The two men—K., a young engineer and former aristocrat, and B., an elderly stooped man who was formerly employed as an office manager—work silently, gloomily immersed in the task at hand. There is not a sound out of them!

Why is this so? Is it the effect of the stench on one's psyche? Or is it, perhaps, something else? Why is it that the talkative young engineer—so saccharinely sweet in his dealings with all young women—is not showering the well-built and dark-eyed Zoia with his customary honeyed compliments, even though he is standing right next to her as he scoops up the rotten potatoes?

The six of us working here say nothing at all about the potatoes and the stench, but, at the same time, other topics seem out of place, because we are all—I am convinced of this—thinking only about the potatoes... About the peasants that they were taken from, and why they were dumped into storage cellars before they were dry, and why they are rotting in December...long before the coming of spring. And why grain is rotting in huge piles under the open sky near railroad stations, and why it is that this year there is so much grain that the state storage bins are unable to accommodate it all!

And these questions inevitably lead to other questions: how many hungry peasants would not be starving for how long a time if these potatoes and that grain—rotting in full public view—had not been taken away from them by force.

The rotten corpses of the potatoes fall with a soft thud into the yawning depths of the vat that, every now and then, is pulled up on its heavy ropes, to be replaced by another one—an empty one. During this exchange of vats, a narrow streak of fresh, frosty air filters into the fetid bowels of our grave, and, for a brief moment, we see a patch of sky overspread with clouds...

We pick over the potatoes in silence, like worms gnawing at a corpse. Thoughts about corpses are on the tip of everyone's tongue, but...we have all learned only too well the "truth" that has been pounded into us so energetically: "there is no famine," notwithstanding the fact that ever increasing numbers of starving farmers appear daily on our city streets—farmers terrifyingly disfigured by hunger, and reduced to shouting and begging: "Bread! Just a crumb! A tiny crust of bread!"

We know that down here, in this storage cellar oozing with putridness, Klava is the watchful eye of the Communist Party, and there might be someone else as well... Who can say for sure?

There is good reason for the popular proverb created by Soviet reality: "Wherever three people are gathered, one of them is a secret agent for the Party." And there are six of us here!

We do not talk at all. It is only the tottering mounds of half-rotten potatoes that speak. It is only the noxious stench that shouts. And thus the hours pass...

Yevhen Pashkovsky, "Five Loaves and Two Fishes"

In *From Three Worlds: New Writing from Ukraine*, ed. Ed Hogan (Boston: Zephyr, 1996). Excerpts, pp. 90–91, 93. Translated by Volodymyr Hruszkewycz. English style-editing by Ed Hogan.

Yevhen Pashkovsky (b. 1962) is a Ukrainian writer currently living in Ukraine. He is the author, in Ukrainian, of the novels *Holiday* (1989), *Wolf's Star* (1991), *Abyss* (1992), *Autumn for the Angel* (1994), and *Daily Baton* (2001), for which he was awarded the Shevchenko Prize.

In the fall military transports snaked through the village, everyone knew that this did not bode well, as they took our horses, collectivized the land, plowed up the graveyard so that we had to break the corpses' knees with a blow to lay them properly into their coffins. The orphaned land remembered the creaking of wagons, the thunder of a drum and the moaning of a harmonica, we put out the lamp, lay down to sleep, the poorest peasants raced headlong down the road, with cornflower wreaths they bedecked the heads of the supply detail, who chased off horseflies with their Red Army caps, with bayonets affixed on perforated tubes they spread dung behind the barns; spread the white rot in the cellar bin, the caked straw in the loft, from then on they slapped our boots with their bayonets, to knock loose any grains that might have lodged in the soles and sank their claws into the landowner in the name of the Revolution; the faded flag tangled whitely around its staff on the porch of the town hall, and they promised to mount a radio loudspeaker on a post. Now it was the domestic fowls' turn, in just a few days they had slaughtered all the roosters, and the white feathers swirled fiercely in the wind like a snowstorm, stuck to the sweaty napes of the mangy horses, to the officers' tunics, to the black grease on the wheel axles....

The soldiers took Father, rode the horses into the ground, tied my brothers' arms behind their backs, "You'll live off the fat of the land in the new settlement, kulak viper," only one whip was left free on the harrows in the cattle shed. With no one to feed them, Mother set out for Western Ukraine, ground rye, tended other people's children and gathered grain in a little sack for her own bluelipped ones, kernel by kernel, dried crust by dried crust, she couldn't raise a spoon to her mouth without crying, the little ones hung on my sister's neck. Mother would faint from despair and pray that there be no famine; grandpa and grandma grew ill on the journey, so they just threw them off the railroad car, Father ended up in the mines....

It was quiet, oh so quiet, but before, whenever our mother burst into song, the boys in the next village would begin to dance. Sister was the first to fall asleep forever under the coarse linen, for me the table still held the aroma of wheat flour on the rolling pin in Grandmother's hands, with which she rolled out the dough for pies, the aroma of smoked sausage with Christmas horseradish, of potato cakes in a bowl with fried onions and crackling, of beet soup spilled onto the oaken boards. I dreamed about a mustached peasant: he spat on the stone, gave the scythe a good sharpening, knocked his pipe out against the scythe handle, preparing to mow the river, milky in the fog, to crop the brooklime in the river shallows, the ripples running before a heavenly breath, that splashing woke me, and I saw: a granite darkness of clouds hanging over the windows, some sort of scratching struck my ear, as if heaven and earth, turned to stone by the cruelty, were grinding the rest of the living. There was a commotion under the table, I looked, two glowing coals flashed, the rat leaped back....

Ulas Samchuk, *Mariia. Khronika odnoho zhyttia* (Maria: The Chronicle of One Life)

(Buenos Aires: Mykola Denysiuk, 1952). Excerpts, pp. 264–66. Translated by Alexander J. Motyl.

Ulas Samchuk (1905–87) was a Ukrainian writer and journalist. He settled in Canada in 1948. He was the author, in Ukrainian, of the trilogy *Volhynia* (1932–37), the novels *Kulak* (1932), *Maria* (1934), *The Hills Are Speaking* (1934), *The Youth of Vasyl Sheremeta* (1946–47), the trilogy *East* (1948–82), the novel *What Fire Does Not Heal* (1959), and the memoirs *Five after Twelve* (1954), *On a White Horse* (1965), *On a Black Horse* (1975), and *The Planet of the DPs* (1979).

Kornii is looking for food. His wife, daughter, and small granddaughter are on his mind. They all want to eat; they are all waiting for him at home. He walked through the forest, looking at the birds, the trees, and the plants.... What will he find here? None of it was made to be eaten. He gathered a few buds and cut off some birch bark. Then he went to the edge of the forest....

He went straight through unplowed fields. And then there occurred a stroke of luck, quite unexpected and quite extraordinary. In a small rut in which there still was snow lay a dead rabbit. Kornii came upon it and stopped. And he stood for a long time. How could one possibly believe that this was really a rabbit, dead and ready to be taken, torn to bits, and eaten? Kornii felt joy and, without bending over, looked to see whether there was anyone around and then expressed his satisfaction. Yes! That means I'll have something to eat. That means I'll get home and, showing the rabbit, say, "Look, Maria! Here's something for you to eat. I found it today, on this joyous sunny day."

Kornii picks up the rabbit. It hasn't even begun to rot. It's quite whole and quite fresh. He cut it open with a sharp axe and, after finding a dry spot, sat down to rest and get some nourishment. You think he's had something to eat today? Hardly. What could he have eaten? He got up and set out. It was good that Maria was still asleep.

He thought of Maria. "If I only knew that I'd make it back home, I wouldn't start on this rabbit. The child could then have it. The thing is that I won't make it. How can I, when my legs buckle and refuse to move? Do what you may, they refuse to move, and that's that. You may as well sit down and cry."

And then there's the wind. It's pushing the man wherever it wants to. There's always a wind in the spring, but he can't remember so strong and insistent a wind. No, no...he can't remember anything like it—something that would keep him from walking and knock him off his feet like a child.

He ate a few pieces of the rabbit, got back on his feet, and again began fighting the wind. The sun kept on shining, burning brightly and mercilessly. Kornii walked for a long time—for a very long time. Then he turned around and saw that the forest was just behind him. Before he reached the mill, his stomach hurt, he writhed with pain, and then, unable to hold it in, puked.

"Did I have to go that far?" he asked himself. "You shouldn't have gone that far. You won't drag your feet back. See what you've become? No. But you did go. You just up and went. Now your legs are shaking, and just try walking."

As Kornii was deliberating, he looked at the meat he had just rejected. A shame. He bent over and slowly ate it again. Maybe the same thing won't happen a second time. Maybe, God willing, it won't happen…

As he walked through the village, he carried his rabbit and axe hidden beneath his coat. The streets were empty, but it was better not to tempt anybody. Who knows? Anything could happen in these times.

The first thing he said when he got home was: "Maria, are you still alive? Look, I brought a rabbit…."

Vasyl Chaplenko, "Zoik" (The Cry)

In *Zoik ta inshi opovidannia* (The Cry and Other Stories) (The Bronx, N.Y., and Buenos Aires: Peremoha, 1957). Excerpts, pp. 34–35. Translated by Alexander J. Motyl.

Vasyl Chaplenko (1900–90) was a Ukrainian writer, linguist, and publicist. He settled in the United States after World War II. He was one of the founders of the Ukrainian Academy of Arts and Sciences in the U.S. and the founder and first chairman of the Vynnychenko Commission at the Ukrainian Academy, which strove to preserve the legacy of the writer Volodymyr Vynnychenko. He was the author, in Ukrainian, of several novels, collections of stories and poems, and of such scholarly works as *Ukrainisms in Gogol's Language* (1948), *Bolshevik Language Policy* (1956), and *The Ukrainian Literary Language: Its Origins and Development* (1955, 1962).

Silently I started untying the bundle with the bread that I had brought from town. My back ached with a dull pain, and I was completely exhausted: I had come on foot. I was ashamed to show my eyes: my belly was full, but I had entered the house and forgotten to give them the bread immediately. For some reason my hands shook, and I couldn't untie the bundle.

What a knot! I might as well gnaw on it with my teeth!

"Use your teeth," Maksym said quietly. "It's faster with your teeth." His eyes glistened strangely. "Give it to me. I'll do it with my teeth..."

And he leapt up from the bench. His movements were more agile than a furry cat's. What a jump! He sank his jaws into the knot with inhuman force.

There was a deathly stillness in the house. It was a morgue. From the oven there dangled sinewy legs, with veins like black leeches: that was my mother. On the oven was another pair of limbs, the unnaturally sprawled corpse-like legs of my feverish and disheveled sister, lying face down. And on the floor my father, a rough gray woolen coat beneath his head, was writhing in his death throes, like a fish on land, jabbering away.

Father has had nothing at all to eat, I thought feverishly, my veins throbbing in my temples. And Mother and Hashka probably haven't eaten in a long time.

"More," pleaded Maksym with childlike insistence. He had eaten the bread I had given him. "Give me more..."

I held the rest of the bread, the end piece, and was trying to decide, without putting it away, whom to give it to—the sick people or him.

Maksym understood my hesitation. He fell to the floor and seized my knees with his hands, speaking swiftly, fearfully.

"Give it to me! Give it! They don't want it. They won't eat it..."

I gave him the end piece.

There was famine in the village, and I came from town to save my family. There was no need for much food anymore, as only Maksym and I had to eat. The other three didn't have a clue that their son and brother had come from town, where he had survived on American food, and that he had bought some buckwheat and millet from the aid committee, which he could grind up at a mill, and, after making hard wafers from the meal, could feed them.

"Papa, Mama, Hashka, I'm here. Don't be afraid."

But I was afraid to look into my father's face. I knew that I'd see something terrible. I'd see death. I was going to lose my father....

Mykola Ponedilok, "Chorna khustka" (The Black Kerchief)

In *Hovoryt' lyshe pole* (None but the Land May Speak) (Toronto: Homin Ukraïny, 1962). Excerpts, pp. 131–38. Translated by Alexander J. Motyl.

Mykola Ponedilok (1922–76) was a Ukrainian writer, satirist, dramatist, and translator. He settled in the United States in 1949. He was a founding member of the Slovo Association of Ukrainian Writers in Exile and a member of the Ukrainian Literary-Artistic Club in New York. He was the author, in Ukrainian, of the plays *The Misfortunate*, *Lieutenant Fliaiev*, and *And We Will [Raise] That Red Viburnum*; and collections of short fiction, *The Black Kerchief* (1947), *Vitamins* (1957), *Pan-Ukrainian Borshch* (1960), *None but the Land May Speak* (1962), *Funny Tears* (1966), *Shooting Stars* (1969), *Save My Soul!* (1973), and *A Marvel in the Sieve* (1977).

Katria was busy at the stove as she asked her father: Was it hard to carry the flour? How did he manage to find such fine, thinly ground flour in town and exchange the kilim for it? Did he take all the flour from town, or was there still a bit left over for later, when they use up this little sack for baking and cooking and need more?....

"Papa, is this enough salt for the dumplings?"

"Add some more."

"That's all there is. We have no more."

"Then it's enough. Maybe we'll get some later."

The food was almost ready. Just another minute, and they can be poured out....

He jumped up as soon as he sat down. Katria froze, the ladle in her hand...

"They're coming."

"Who, Papa?"

"The Soviets are coming, the commission. Now they're really going to extremes! They make me sick and tired. They're going too far this time. They're looking for grain again."

"But we have no grain."

"There's flour. They'll see it and take it, the cursed devils. Katria, we have to trick them."

"We'll trick them later, Papa. I want to eat. Let's eat, and then we'll trick them."

"There's no time, child. Climb up on the oven. Lie down and stay there quietly. You're sick. And we'll hide the little sack of flour beneath your pillow. Maybe they won't go digging around among the pillows."

"But the dumplings will get cold. When will we eat?"

"We'll still get to eat them. Lie down. Cover yourself with the sackcloth. And place the flour over there...underneath...lower...lower...near the hearthstone. And place the pillow on top... That's right... Now, quickly... Lie down without a peep... Yes, that's right, my smart little girl."

Three dumb giants stormed into the house....

"Proletarians of all countries, unite! Isn't that right, Andrii?" Their old acquaintance drummed out the beloved slogan he had learned in political literacy class.

"Hello!" the man of the house replied, as if he were throwing a stone.

"And why don't you answer in Soviet style? Go ahead, say it, don't be afraid, you won't break your tongue: 'Proletarians, unite.'"

"We're uniting, don't you see? We're all uniting in the graveyard."

"So that's how much you love the state!"

"As much as it loves me. You get what you give."

The three of them stood two steps away from the man. One had a shovel; one was leaning against a hook, as if it were a cane; while the acquaintance was, as usual, holding some crumpled orders instead of tools.

"Let's talk. But sensibly," said the one with the hook to Andrii.

"Did you really come here to talk? You came here to quarter me. To bury me and my child."

"Do you have bread? Just answer. Without beating around the bush. Yes or no?"

"We had some."

"And where is it now?"

"It's gone."

"Gone where?"

"In the devil's gut."

"Tell the truth, or things'll just get worse."

"It can't get any worse."

"Why are we bothering with him?" cried the old acquaintance disdainfully and imperiously. "Let's start searching! We'll turn the house upside down, but we'll find it! We'll shake it down, we'll root it all up."....

Finally, red-faced, out of breath, and angry from the futile search, they returned to the house. They looked angrily at the man, almost as if they were about to eat him.

"You moneybags! I swear you're rich. Where did you hide it?"

"Where?" the old acquaintance shouted furiously at the man, who was standing near the window, motionless and pale, like a statue.

The man didn't respond.

"I'd really like to take a look on top of the oven. The grain or flour has to be somewhere, after all. Look, the dumplings are still steaming. I'll go look on top of the oven."

"Why bother? These parasites are clever. They wouldn't hide the grain in full view. They took it outside and hid it in the field."

At that moment, Katria moved and embraced the pillow tightly.

Three pairs of eyes immediately glued themselves to the girl, and their harsh, punishing gaze made her cry and mumble something.

"Suspicious."

"Da, something isn't quite right."

"Should I climb up?"

"Go ahead! But I doubt you'll find anything."

The old acquaintance was getting ready to climb when Katria quickly sat up and, scared stiff, began chattering:

"There isn't any! We have no flour! I won't give it! It's ours! Father bought it for the dumplings, and not for you."

"It's all clear now! Didn't I say it looked suspicious?" And the old acquaintance cast aside the pillow and the sackcloth and, espying the sack, seized hold of it as if it contained not flour but silver and gold.

"I found it! See how he hid it? He threw some rags and even placed the child on top. You're a smart devil, but, as you can see, Soviet power is smarter."

"Don't take our last remnants!" The man rushed toward the oven, but the two men with the hook and the shovel got in his way. "What'll we have left? We need…"

"The Soviet state needs it. There's only one state, while you, the enemies of the people, are many."

Terrified, Katria huddled in a corner and, like a small animal forced into a cage, shook and watched as the huge and odious hands pulled the little sack of flour from the hearthstone.

She cast a glance at her father. He wants to say something to her, but what? She can't hear, but she sees his lips moving… He's showing her something with his finger… Suddenly—why did Papa do it?—a pocket knife rolled toward her. Why did he take the knife from his pocket and throw it toward her?

"Why? I don't understand, Papa."

"Fool!"

Her father is very angry. Why? If she could only figure out what to do with the knife. Meanwhile, her father is looking at her so intensely that he's almost ready to leap into her eyes.

Finally, Katria figured it out. He threw her the knife so that she could defend herself. She'll wave it about, and the men will surely be frightened to death and withdraw from the oven, maybe even run away.

But, to Katria's surprise, the men took no fright at all. She held the knife in her little fist and threatened them, while they, the attackers, became even more insolent and laughed.

"Hey, you, soldier girl!" And the old acquaintance shoved Katria's hand, and the knife slid out of her fist and fell behind the sackcloth.

A moment later and the sack of flour, thrown across the shoulder of the man with the hook, disappeared from the house forever.

On the oven, Katria whimpered, both because her hand hurt from the man's shove and because the flour—there was enough for so many more dumplings!—was suddenly lost… And then there's her father, looking at her with hostility….

"Are they gone, Papa?"

"They're gone. Stop sniveling, or I'll let you have it."

"But what did I do? I was protecting it." The girl shed still bitterer tears.

"Quiet, I say. It's your fault... You've got a screw loose up there. You're as dumb as an ox. Fool."

"Papa, I'm not stupid. I'm hungry."

"Quiet—stop bothering me. Or else I'll feed you right away. I'll give you so much to eat that you won't be able to sit down!"

"Go ahead, feed me..."

"You dare talk back to me!!" He struck his daughter, blind with rage, and with every blow he said, "Wise up, wise up... Understood?"

"What's that for, Papa?"

"Why did I throw you the knife? You were supposed to cut open the sack. And then a little flour would have poured out! And then we'd have some! Now do you know why, you fool? You were supposed to cut it open. What did you think?"

"I was scaring them off, Papa..."

"You made them laugh. You didn't scare them. And now what? Because of you, you idiot, we don't even have a speck of flour. What will you wolf down now? You can feast on the devil—then you'll see!"

Completely exhausted, he fell face down on the bed. But he immediately understood, and his face burned with shame. Why did he attack his daughter like an animal? Is it her fault that those damned men took the last morsel from their mouths?....

Frantically, he rushed toward his daughter, the only and most important thing that still remained in the once buoyant house of his grandfather.

"Katria, the dumplings are waiting. Maybe we'll eat them?"

"Let's eat them. You won't beat me anymore?"

"I won't. These bad times are beating us. Oh, how they're beating us!" It was as if an ocean of sorrow had suddenly broken through, and he shook as he wept. Except that there were no tears; tiny silver beads froze in the corners of his eyes.

"Don't cry, Papa. Look, I'm no longer crying either. I've already stopped."

"My head got mixed up. I'm a fool, Katria."

"And I'm a fool."

"You're my smart little girl. Do me a favor. Forgive me."

"How should I forgive you?"

"Just say: I forgive you, Father, for being so mad, for being such an animal... Forget that I beat you. Does it hurt, my child?"

"Of course it hurts. And I want to eat...and I forgive you."

Marsha Forchuk Skrypuch, "The Rings"

In *Kobzar's Children: A Century of Untold Ukrainian Stories*, ed. Marsha Forchuk Skrypuch (Toronto: Fitzhenry and Whiteside, 2006). Excerpt, pp. 48–51.

Marsha Forchuk Skrypuch (b. 1954) is a Ukrainian-Canadian children's writer living in Brantford, Ontario. She is the author of *Silver Threads* (1996), *The Best Gifts* (1998), *The Hunger* (1999), *Enough* (2000), *Hope's War* (2001), *Nobody's Child* (2003), *Aram's Choice* (2006), *Kobzar's Children: A Century of Untold Ukrainian Stories* (2006), *Dear Canada: Prisoners in the Promised Land: The Ukrainian Internment Diary of Anya Soloniuk* (2007), *Daughter of War* (2008), *Call Me Aram* (2009), *Stolen Child* (2010), and *Making Bombs for Hitler* (2012).

Danylo's sharpest memory was of hunger.

When his father had refused to sign the papers handing over their tiny farm to the state, his family earned the label *pidkurkul*—or poor farmer who sympathizes with the kulaks.

His father knew that the communists would send in the Red Army to confiscate their grain, so he had mixed some wheat with the chaff and hidden it in the loft. He had also put the best wheat, for sowing, up in the rafters. Danylo's mother had hidden a sack of grain in the chimney.

The soldiers who came were a rough and brutal lot. They were not from the village, and they spoke Russian, not Ukrainian. They brought with them a stabber—a device made of a sharp-pronged stick with a bag on the end—to collect evidence of grain.

As one of the soldiers carried an armful of his father's hidden grain to the waiting cart, Danylo rushed forward and grabbed back some stalks of wheat. "Why are you doing this?" he cried.

The man said something in Russian that sounded like a curse. Another Red Army soldier opened the *pich* (oven) and confiscated the fresh loaves of bread baking there. They loaded all the food into the cart and took it away.

A few pieces of stale bread on the rubbish pile had somehow been missed. Danylo's family—his father, his mother, and three younger brothers—survived on these crusts and water for a couple of days. His baby sister Larissa was still at his mother's breast—one less mouth to feed.

Danylo watched as those around him appeared to shrink. His mother remarked one day, as she washed her face, that she could feel every bone in her skull. Later, when Danylo carried the soapy basin of water outside to empty it, he found her wedding ring, which had slipped off. She had not noticed. His mother had not been able to get the silver band past her knuckle for years. Danylo dried it on his shirt and brought it back in to her. From then on, she wore it on a cord of leather around her neck.

When the crusts of bread were gone, one day passed with no food at all, just water. Danylo's feet and stomach began to swell with the first signs of starvation. His father caught and skinned a stray cat, which sustained them a few more days. But Danylo's four-year-old brother, Anatoly, swelled up and died. Danylo caught a hedgehog, and the remaining family survived on that for a while.

As winter set in, the rats, cats, dogs, and birds in the village disappeared. Danylo learned, like everyone else, that one must eat at least one morsel, each and every day, to keep oneself from swelling. If the swelling set in, your feet and belly would get so huge that you wouldn't be able to move. At that point, you could only sit and wait to die. When his mother began to starve, Danylo couldn't bear to look at her body, ballooning out grotesquely, as if it were about to burst. Her swelling caused what little milk she had been able to produce to stop. And so Larissa died. His mother died the next day. Then ten-year-old Vasyl, and then seven-year-old Ivan.

Danylo and his father said prayers for the dead. His father reverently removed the cord that held her wedding ring from around his wife's neck. Before putting it around his own neck, he slipped off his own wedding ring and strung it on the cord.

In their small home, Danylo and his father sat with their dead loved ones for hours, perhaps days. What was time, anyway? It wasn't until the corpses began to stink that they dragged their family beyond the threshold. The village authorities had dug a huge pit in the graveyard. Each morning they sent a cart around to all the houses, collecting the bodies. They dumped the bodies into the pit until it was full. And then they dug a new one.

Yevhen Hutsalo, "Holodomor: Murder by Starvation"

In *A Hunger Most Cruel*, ed. Sonia Morris (Toronto: Language Lantern Publications, 2002). Excerpts, pp. 141–47. Translated by Roma Franko.

Yevhen Hutsalo (1937–95) was a Ukrainian writer and poet. He was one of the *shestydesiatnyky*—the generation of the sixties—who rejected Stalinist norms in culture. He was the author, in Ukrainian, of *People among People* (1962), *Apples from an Autumn Orchard* (1964), *The Stag Avhust* (1965), *The Horses Flew By* (1966), *The Family Hearth* (1968), *Hunting with a Hound* (1980), *Stories from Ternivka* (1982), and the trilogy *The Borrowed Man* (1982), *The Private Life of a Phenomenon* (1982), and *Parade of Planets* (1984).

Perhaps old man Hnylokvas is not so old, but he looks like an aged, hoary man.

And he looks like an old man because he is badly stooped, because his hands drag along the ground, and his straggly hair resembles a mound of riddled March snow sprinkled with reddish manure. His disheveled hair falls down over his forehead, obscuring his eyes, and so it seems that Hnylokvas never looks either to the left, or to the right, but rather, always stares down at his feet.

He is forever searching and looking for something. As he makes his way through the village, he hangs on to the reins of a small mouse-grey horse with protruding ribs that plods along beside him; and behind the horse creak the ungreased wheels of a funeral cart. Hnylokvas could ride in that cart, but he does not want to do that because he makes many stops, and it would mean that he would have to get in and out a lot.

He stops the cart in front of a yard, knocks on the gate, raps on the window, and calls out: "Are you still alive?"

An old woman comes out of the cottage: "Have you come for my soul already?"

"There's time enough for me to come for your soul… What's happening in your neck of the woods? Has anyone died?"

"How am I to know? I sit in my cottage, and no one comes to see me," the old woman mumbles. "There are times when I myself no longer can tell if I'm still in this world, or if I've already gone on to the next one."

"Oh, you're still in this one…"

"Then why is this world so much like that one?"

"Ask the village head, not me… So, when should I come to pay you a visit, granny?"

"To pay me a visit? Why pay me a visit?"

"To haul you off to the cemetery. I only want to help you."

"How am I to know?"

"Well, who's supposed to know if you don't? I have a job to do. Do you think I'd be doing this for nothing? I haul someone off to the pit, and I get half a pound of bread."

"How much?" the old woman can hardly believe her ears.

"Half a pound of bread. And they'll give me the same amount for you, as well."

"So much? They'd do better to give it to me; I haven't eaten any bread for ever so long. I might even live a little longer."

"They don't give you bread for just living."

After chatting for a while with the old woman who still yearns for bread and does not want to die—she does not even want to mention death—old man Hnylokvas moves slowly onward, and the ungreased wheels of his cart creak with a dry, hungry whine.

"Oh, I almost forgot," the old man says, slapping his forehead. "Why, to be sure, this is the cottage and plot owned by Marko Hrusha. We haven't seen each other for ages, and there's no one out in the yard just now. Should I drop in, or shouldn't I? Yes, I think I will."

Hnylokvas walks into the cottage, sees granny Yavdokha on the sleeping bench, and greets her dully: "Good day to you, Yavdokha."

Granny Yavdokha is lying on a pillow; she does not stir.

"Where's Marko?" Hnylokvas asks her.

Granny Yavdokha does not reply—she seems to be asleep. And then Hnylokvas glances up and notices bare legs sticking out from the oven bed.

"Marko, do you hear me?" he calls.

Marko Hrusha remains silent.

"Both of them," Hnylokvas mutters, "they're both dead. Let's see, half a pound of bread for Yavdokha, and half a pound for Marko—that's a pound already. Even though it's hard to do this work by myself, I don't want to share it with anyone. Lots of people have wanted to help me, but I wouldn't let them. Because what if I did? Would I have to give away my half pound of bread? And who is going to give me a half pound? Is someone rushing to give it to me?"

He touches the old woman's forehead. It is cold.

"You're a goner. And why? Because you were foolish. You didn't want to marry me back then—you married Marko instead. Well, has he managed to feed you? He hasn't fed either himself or you. If you'd been with me, you'd still be living. But now, I'll have half a pound of bread because of you."

He removes a blanket from the plank bed, spreads it on the earthen floor, and shoves granny Yavdokha onto it from the sleeping bench.

"How light you are… I never held you in my arms, but I'm holding you now."

The old woman's heels thud on the floor, and her body thumps dully. Seizing the corners of the blanket tightly with both hands, old Hnylokvas drags it through the cottage, and then from the porch into the yard and to the cart. The old woman's head dangles, and her eyes are bulging.

"I'll haul you to the pit; I won't leave you in the cottage. Because you're so foolish…"

When he reaches the funeral cart, he once again has to embrace the old woman to lift her off the ground. But he has lifted heavier bodies than this—and Yavdokha is like a feather.

"And now I'll go get the old man, so that you'll be together, like a couple… I'll haul you away like a couple, and the two of you can marry the damp earth. But what a wedding you had back then—in a church, with a priest. I didn't go to your wedding, but that's what people said…"

Walking back into the cottage, Hnylokvas looks around at the bare walls.

"The two of you lived out your lives, but you didn't amass any wealth. The Lord didn't even give you children."

Gasping, he leans on the sleeping bench and growls at Marko's unmoving heels: "What a man! You couldn't die on the sleeping bench—you had to crawl up on the oven bed so that I'd have more trouble with you."

He grabs a leg with both hands, and just as he gives a good tug a feeble voice gasps: "Is that you, Karpo? Why are you yanking my leg?"

By now Hnylokvas is used to all manner of things, and so even this does not faze him. "So, you're still alive? You haven't died yet? I was pulling you down from the oven bed, but now you can get down by yourself… What's there for you to do on this oven bed?"

"What's there to do? I want to die, but I just can't… Yavdokha crossed over into the other world this morning, but I just can't," he says, straining to pull his feeble voice out of his chest. "Yesterday the two of us had a talk… We said that we'd die together. And she's over there already, but I'm still here. She did what she said she'd do, but I deceived her. Where is she?"

"I've carried her out to the cart."

Marko Hrusha closes his eyes and falls silent. Then he opens them again and says: "I just can't. I want to die—but I can't."

"You aren't trying hard enough."

"I want to die so badly…along with Yavdokha, so that we can be together… And I didn't know that you were such a fine fellow. You'll help us. You'll help us be together… You've taken Yavdokha to the cart, so lug me out to it too. To the cemetery."

"It's to the pit, not the cemetery."

"Let it be to the pit, as long as we're together… I'll die along the way. My heart tells me that I'll die along the way."

"And what if you don't die along the way?"

"Then I'll die in the pit."

"Just to be with Yavdokha?"

"Just to be with her."

Hnylokvas stands on the sleeping bench and looks up at the oven bed. Does Marko Hrusha still have his wits about him? Imagine babbling such nonsense. Maybe he's still conscious, but he's not in his right mind.

"Oh, I'm sorry to lose my half pound of bread," he sighs.

"Huh?" Marko Hrusha tries to open the soggy eyelids on his swollen face.

"I said that I'm sorry to lose my half pound of bread."

"You lost your bread?"

"I will lose it… I won't haul you to the pit. Don't even ask me to do it."

"Then help me get up, and pull me down from the oven bed, and I'll crawl to the pit myself."

"I won't help you."

"Take pity on me…"

"No, I won't. I don't want you to die at Yavdokha's side. It's enough that you lived your life out with her on this earth. And now you want to be together in the next world? And you're begging me to help you? Well, I won't."

Wheezing and gasping, Hnylokvas slides off the sleeping bench on his stomach. Marko Hrusha groans, moves about on the oven bed, and jerks his feet. But he cannot raise himself.

"You better die first… And then I'll haul you away."

Holding the reins in his hand and walking beside the funeral cart, he mutters angrily, and his words buzz like wasps: "Do you hear, Yavdokha? I've taken you away from Marko at last… Do you know how long I suffered without you? My whole life. Now let him suffer for a while without you… Oh, who is that over there under the apple tree?"

On a nearby hillock, a girl with her head slumped on her shoulder is sitting under an apple tree.

"Is she sleeping in the sun, or has she given her soul to God?"

Leaving the funeral cart on the road, Hnylokvas shuffles to the tree on the hillock.

"Are you alive, or are you dead?" he asks the girl who is leaning against the trunk.

The girl does not stir.

"Listen, who are you?" he peers at her. "Oh, it's Pavlo Muzyka's child. Her head is still warm—she isn't stiff yet. Should I wait here until she stiffens? But do I have the time to go back and forth? Well, my girl, I'll haul you away right now."

Hnylokvas takes a couple of small steps, bends over, grabs the unconscious Halia under the arms and, backing up, pulls her off the mound.

"She hasn't even lived as yet; she wasn't even married, and she's died already… Oh, she seems to be moaning… What are you saying, huh?"

Another moan escapes from the girl's chest.

"You don't want an old man to embrace you? But where is one to find young men to hug you? There are no young ones, so you just have to put up with me."

He drags the unconscious girl to the road and lifts her in his arms to put her in the cart.

Just then, as luck would have it, Pylyp the teacher appears out of the blue. His head sticks out from the collar of his unbuttoned embroidered shirt like a golden sunflower from behind a fence.

"Granddad!" he calls.

And he holds his hands in front of himself as if he were warding off an evil spirit.

"Help me, my boy," Hnylokvas says hoarsely.

"Where are you taking her?"

"To the cart, and then I'll take her away to the pit."

"But she's still alive!" Pylyp shouts. "Can't you hear her? She's groaning. Where are you taking her? She's still alive!"

"She'll die soon anyway... Come on, help me."

"Let go of her. Let her be."

"My boy, of what use to you is a living corpse? How much time does she have left to live? And I'm supposed to make another trip for her later? My horse can scarcely lift its legs. But if you're so keen on the dead girl, take her, may you go berserk. No one wants to understand what my job is like."

Leaving the unconscious Halia with the infuriated, wild-eyed teacher, Hnylokvas snaps the reins.

"Giddy-up! Let's go... Just try and please these people. You see, a defender has shown up. He sways in even the slightest breeze, but yet... And I've just lost half a pound of bread! Well, I'll haul you out to the pit before long, and then I'll get it back. Giddy-up! The day is long, the village is big, and there's so much work that it's hard to get it all done. Our people are so ignorant. Oh, how ignorant they are!"

Olena Zvychaina, "'Lucky' Hanna"

In *A Hunger Most Cruel*, ed. Sonia Morris (Toronto: Language Lantern Publications, 2002). Excerpts, pp. 262–69. Translated by Roma Franko.

Olena Zvychaina (early 1900s–1985) was a Ukrainian writer. After being interned in a Nazi labor camp in Austria during World War II, she settled in the United States in the late 1940s. Her stories describe life in Ukraine under Soviet oppression and Nazi occupation, as well as the experiences of people displaced by war. In an autobiographical novel written in collaboration with her husband, she described the fate of the unfortunate millions accused by the Soviet secret police of being "enemies of the people."

She was tall and sturdy, with strong, calloused hands and surprisingly heavy legs... Her stony face was slightly marred by pockmarks, and spongy pouches hung under her wide-open hazel eyes... Her feet were bare, and she wore a few wretched remnants of traditional peasant clothing—clothing that was, however, carefully washed and ingeniously patched. Her persona bore the stamp of ongoing abuse and violence, and the distinguishing marks of long-endured hunger.

She was over forty, and her name was Hanna.

It was in our courtyard—a long corridor joining several buildings heavily populated in the Soviet manner—that Hanna first appeared unexpectedly as someone's servant toward the end of May in 1933.

On my way to and from work, or simply hurrying through the yard, I often saw Hanna, and I always found myself looking into the depths of her large staring eyes—eyes that drew me to them like a magnet and, at the same time, terrified me.

The pupils of her eyes were truly strange. Unnaturally dilated, frozen into a state of immobility, and haunted—to the point of shrieking insanely—by something incomprehensible and starkly unique that they had witnessed. They appeared to have captured on their retinas a veridical photograph of a ghastly horror. And, adding to that photograph the question: "Why?" they screamed and pleaded for succor.

Whenever I came across Hanna, I plunged into the terrifying depths of her pupils and…I often caught myself brooding over them. Through an odd association, those pupils made me think of a person who had been murdered and whose retinas retained the imprint of the murderer's face, thereby providing the justice officials with an unexpected weapon against the criminal who, adroitly covering his tracks, had hoped to avoid being caught and punished.

I was pleased to notice that Hanna differentiated me from the bustling swarms of residents who lived in the buildings of our complex. I often caught her looking at me with those staring eyes of hers that seemed incapable of smiling. And I was deeply convinced that Hanna's eyes had stopped smiling on the very day that a horrific crime had been imprinted on the retinas of her pupils....

I looked at her in some confusion as I struggled to find the words, the right words to soothe this unfortunate woman.

"Don't worry, Hanna! You'll get through this difficult year in one way or another, and then, in the future, fate might smile at you! You're lucky, Hanna, that you've managed to stay alive!"

"Me? Lucky?" And, like a horse that bolts from the blow of a whip after being kept in the stable too long, Hanna's sturdy, muscular body jerked abruptly. With a sharp movement of her right hand, she shoved aside the bowl of food and dropped her head on the table. Ragged, spasmodic wails tore out of her breast—but she was not weeping. It is a mortally wounded animal that howls like that.

At that moment, I would have given anything to take back the truly inopportune word that, flying so unexpectedly out of my mouth, had seared Hanna like a flame.

"So you say…I'm lucky?" she asked in a strange voice that was tense and distraught. And as she slowly raised her head, her kerchief slipped, revealing her prematurely grey hair. "I've been proclaimed a *kurkul* [well-to-do peasant]! I was chased out of my village! You probably didn't know that!"

I did know. I was deeply convinced that what she said was true, but I remained silent. I just gently caressed her gray hair, and this tender gesture found its way to the depths of Hanna's soul—to those mysterious retinas of her pupils that were imprinted with someone's heinous crime…

A silence, heavy with words that were, as yet, unspoken, descended on the room; the silence was like an impenetrable cloud from which, at any moment, a long-awaited rain is about to fall in torrents. The stove went out; the food grew cold. The unfinished laundry lay in forgotten white heaps in the tub. But was this the time to think about that?

"They chased all of us out of our house—me, my husband, and our ten-year-old daughter. We're from a distant village…you know? By the time we finally made our way on foot to Kharkiv, the three of us had almost died on the road. We hoped to find work in Kharkiv. But it was no use! There was no work for the likes of us…

"Then one night, just after we had fallen asleep under a fence in Moskalivka, I heard a noise...and before we knew what was happening to us, strong hands had thrown us into a truck on top of a pile of ice-cold corpses. Thank God that they did not throw anyone else on top of us... And we were driven far away from Kharkiv. And it was out there, out in the fields, that my husband died under a tree. He died peacefully... I saw that he was near death, and so I folded his hands on his chest and prayed for his soul. I bent down to his ear and called him for the last time: 'Ivan!' And he answered, so he heard me, and..."

Hanna's pupils widened with pain, with an insane scream, and she fell silent, staring intently into a corner with her frozen, unmoving eyes. Those eyes of hers most certainly did not see anything that was directly in front of her. They saw something different and, staring fixedly into that corner, she continued.

"And so I left my Ivan under that tree for the rooks to feast on... It's a sin! Don't you think so? And, taking my child by the hand, I slowly made my way back to Kharkiv... And, with every step, I kept thinking... And that's when I decided to abandon my Yustynka—my only child!—in the marketplace... Grief was breaking my heart into tiny pieces, but...what was I to do? My child was very weak, and I could not wait until her swollen belly crowded in on her heart. My heart, a mother's heart, sensed that unless she got some food, she would close her eyes for good at any moment... And what beautiful eyes she had—before the famine—if only you could have seen them! You mustn't think that my Yustynka had a face like mine—pockmarked by smallpox. No! No! She was a lovely and wise little girl! Do you know what I mean?"

"Yes, I do, Hanna..."

"You see, at that time there was a rumour that the authorities were picking up orphaned peasant children and taking them to shelters. And so, I thought that if I abandoned her in the market and made her an orphan, well...she would get to a shelter, and they would feed her..."....

"When I came back to the marketplace, I hid behind the gate of a big building and watched my Yustynka from there. I could see her, but she couldn't see me. Standing in the very same spot where I had left her, she was looking around in all directions, searching for me with her eyes...and wiping away her tears with her tiny fists... An old woman gave her a chunk of bread, and I saw her swallow it without even chewing it. And then she cried more loudly, as loudly as she could...

"I don't know how many hours I waited there. And then I saw that people were beginning to leave the marketplace. A large crowd, all kinds of people, shuffled past the gate where I was hidden. They blocked my view of Yustynka, as a cloud blocks the sun. I couldn't see her, and I was fainting with despair... Finally, all the people passed by, and I saw that the marketplace was empty except for several dozen abandoned peasant children. Crying piteously, they gathered together and nestled against each other—the younger ones to the older ones—just like little chicks that are suddenly left without a mother hen. But my Yustynka was crying the loudest of all of them. Do you know what I mean?"

"I know, Hanna..."

"I swear that among all the children, I could hear *her* cry, *her* shout: 'Mummy, where are you?' I saw her—so small and terrified, with her bloated belly and blond hair... I saw her look all around, looking for *me*... She could not be searching for her father, because she knew that we had left him lying under a tree…left him there for the rooks to eat…

"And just at that moment I remembered that I had promised her that I would come back with some bread. I had promised her…and I had deceived her! Yustynka already knew that her mother had tricked her! I leapt up from behind the gate as if I had been scalded and flew like a bird toward my child.

"I did not have much farther to go, and I was just about to call out to her; 'Yustynka, don't cry. Your mummy's here!' But just then, at that very moment, a truck drove up between me and the children. I had to stop; I thought it would go by, but then I saw that it was turning toward the children. So I dashed back to the gate and hid behind it once again. I watched three militiamen jump down from the vehicle and toss the children, like kittens, into the back of the truck. My Yustynka was the last to be thrown in. A tall, red-headed militiaman grabbed her by her linen shirt…and I saw her hovering in his hand above the truck that was already filled with children, and I heard her shriek when her chest hit the edge of the truck as she fell…"

Vasyl Barka, *Zhovtyi kniaz'* (The Yellow Prince), 2 vols.

(New York and Kharkiv: Ukrainian Academy of Arts and Sciences in the U.S., 2008). Excerpts, vol. 2, pp. 295, 299–303. Translated by Alexander J. Motyl.

Vasyl Barka (pseudonym of Vasyl Ocheret, 1908–2003) was a Ukrainian poet, writer, literary critic, and translator. He settled in the United States in 1949. He was the author, in Ukrainian, of collections of poetry, *Pathways* (1930), *Guilds* (1932), *Apostles* (1946), *The White World* (1947), *The Rose Novel* (1957), *The Psalm of the Dovelike Field* (1958), *Ocean* (1959, 1979, 1992), *The Witness for the Sun of Seraphims* (1981), and *Steppe of Judgment* (1992); translations of William Shakespeare and Dante; and novels, *Paradise* (1953), *The Yellow Prince* (1962, 1968), and *The Penitent and the Keys to the Earth* (1992).

The steppe appeared to the small wanderer as an empire of death: depopulated and without animals and birds, which, like some people, had been caught and eaten. The very road made walking difficult, since it was overgrown with wildly growing vegetation that hid even the deepest ruts made long ago by heavy carts.

There was no one! Neither the echo of human voices nor the cry of winged creatures....

As he approached the village, he remembered its appearance from over a year ago, when he had visited Lavryk: its cleanliness and the decorations on the village huts and yards.

He had become accustomed to the destruction of his own village, gradually accepting its transformation into ruin and death, but what he unexpectedly saw in Horodnytsia horrified him almost to the point of tears: he suddenly lost all hope of finding any help.

Immediately upon entering the village, he was struck by the realization that he almost failed to recognize it: he saw not one tree, neither in the streets nor in the yards. Gone were the orchards, the hedges, the garden walls, the latticed fences. There was nothing next to the earthen huts and brick buildings. The village was completely bare, with no fruit trees, no poplars, no willows, no acacias, and no bushes. And Andriiko immediately guessed why: as in Klenotoch, everything had been burned up for making grassy broth just before one died.

The straw roofs had been removed from many houses, and one could see the pointed rafters and joints. In some places the doors and doorposts, the windows and windowsills, as well as the thresholds had disappeared—into the fire, for one last use. The walls, of various sizes, remained: they had grown dark and were peeling, seeming on the verge of collapse and covered with stains. Often they had holes, the result of searches by the armed commissions that plundered the food in the hiding places.

On a few equally tattered stone buildings in the center of the village there still remained tin roofs. The frightening emptiness was filled with weeds—quite thick in some places, creating the impression of densely overgrown little islands, with various kinds of smaller undergrowth scattered in between. All in all, the hopeless absence of human beings terrified the boy with an inhuman force.

This impression quickly dissipated and changed into fear after he saw the dead peasants. The corpses were rotting and turning black amid the thick grasses all along the street. And the boy, timidly glancing in their direction, made a large detour around them—at first with great and painful anxiety, and then, after calming down and quickening his step, he remained in a state of unusual alarm called forth by their deathliness and an oftentimes unbearable stench. It was easier for him to endure such things, as he had already begun to contain his emotions upon seeing the dead at home.

Here, along the streets that Andriiko slowly traversed, the corpses appeared in various states depending on when they had died. They breathed their last breath and fell with empty bags—some setting out to find a piece of bread, others returning to their native village without anything and then giving up the ghost to heavenly care.

Those who had died longer ago were completely decomposed, resembling skeletons covered with leaflike rags. Those who had died more recently had, while decaying, partly retained their physical features, even though their bodies experienced accelerated decomposition during the warmer days and produced an intolerable stench that forced the boy to make a detour around them.

The dead were found everywhere—on the streets and in the orchards, near the dilapidated houses.

Crossing the square in the center of the village, the boy saw a large black board attached to posts and, involuntarily, with childlike curiosity, glanced at the crookedly hanging paper covered with print.

He could only make sense of one part of the official decree: that the village of Horodnytsia had been placed, together with many others, on the "blacklist," and that the supply to it of foodstuffs, kerosene, salt, matches, and other necessities had ceased.

Going farther, he noticed a pole high up on a bare wall. One end of the pole was stuck into a hole in the wall, while the other end was attached to a black cloth similar to a flag. The boy remembered having heard at home that this sign meant that the entire village had died, down to the very last human soul.

As in the steppe, there were no birds in the village, and one couldn't hear the sound of living creatures: an ominous quiet reigned amid the ruins of their existence.

It occurred to Andriiko that the officials who were leaving the village by car had been the last people here: they had come to the village to make certain that their deadly work had reached its conclusion and that they would be able to report complete success in carrying out their orders.

Despite all his fears, the boy greatly desired to get to Lavryk's house, as if it were a safe haven from the gloomy devastation that oozed out of and was exhaled by all the ruined, weed-covered yards without portals, wicket gates, and fences and all the houses stripped down to their skeletal earthen structures.

He hastened his step, as if driven by a dark storm, feeling completely lost: cry as much as you like, no one will help you in your time of need, for no one is alive, even the transporters whose job was to deposit the corpses in the common grave. They had probably died.

Moreover, visitors from neighboring villages had stopped coming around because of their hopelessness and the vastness of their troubles with their own dead at a time of mass extinction.

He retained a spark of hope that, perhaps, some miracle might have preserved the house of Lavryk's family....

The closer he came to Lavryk's address, the more horribly was the boy's spirit affected by the all-pervasive deathliness of the village. All the houses on both sides of the street he was looking for resembled a horrible void surrounded by wild brush. The absence of human beings was complete....

One house, larger than the others, was more or less intact.... The boy wanted to glance inside, through the nearest window opening on the side of the building.

When his eyes became accustomed to the dark, the boy saw a sight that caused him to freeze with fright.

The man of the house lay on an iron bed near the second window. The thick eyebrows on his decomposed face had, in life, hung over his eye sockets. Now they had fallen from the bare bone of the forehead and, like leaves, covered them completely. The nasal cavity also lay exposed, the white teeth glistened beneath the decomposed flesh, and the clothes sank unto the bones they covered. The ribs peered out from beneath the disheveled shirt and decomposed flesh. Tiny toe bones extended from the tips of the feet.

In addition to the horror, the boy was struck by such an intolerable, almost poisonous smell that he proved unable to examine the other, equally decomposed family members who lay scattered throughout the house, like rotting corpses thrown to the bottom of a grave. An overwhelming sense of despair drove the boy out of the house and down the overgrown street toward Lavryk's home.

At last he came face to face with a weed-covered wasteland containing the ruined remnants of a homestead, darkened by the walls of the house and the collapsed roof. And here, as everywhere, black holes gaped out from where the windows and door had been. Andriiko immediately went toward it, wading through the thick knee-high overgrowth, while restraining the growing alarm in his soul that he might encounter the same devastation he had seen in the house of the hunter.

He even hesitated a moment before stepping inside the doorless building. He walked through the darkened corridor and stood at the entrance to the room. It was difficult to manage the strikingly thick odor that hung in the air.

Eventually he mustered up the courage to look around—what was inside?—and saw nearby, lying face down on the earthen floor, a man in rags. His gray hair had fallen from the decomposed crown of his head, turned slightly to the side, and laid bare his skull. Bones protruded from his decomposed heels.

His arms looked broken; indeed, he looked completely battered, as if he had fallen to the floor from some great height.

Two of the dead man's sons, both much older than Lavryk, were on the floor, stiff, near the wall. The larger one lay on his side, his hands pressed to his chest, seemingly trying to stop the searing pain, his mouth wide open, as if madly shrieking from the onset of his woes to his death. His white teeth, protruding from beneath his rotting flesh, were spread fully apart.

The smaller one, just as decomposed as his brother, had sat down near the wall so as to lean against it in his weakened state. He appeared to have fallen to the right. He was completely twisted, while his teeth, set loose from the rotting flesh, were tightly closed. The bones of his fingers were also twisted: they remained in that position after having been placed on the earthen floor, although the skin and connective tissue with nerves were long gone.

Neither the woman of the house nor Lavryk was there! The boy couldn't imagine where they were until he glanced into a corner and saw a photograph of a women's monastery. It hung crookedly, beneath glass and in frames, once white, but now darkened and covered with mold.

The thought of that monastery inspired the boy to surmise that the sister of Lavryk's mother was a nun there and that he frequently visited her, sayinq that his auntie gave him all kinds of gifts.

PLAYS

Mykola Kowshun, *The Black Vulture: A Drama in 3 Acts*

In *Epiloh pryide* (Epilogue To Come) (Canada [place not specified], 1975). Excerpts, pp. 144–52. Trans. I. Lewis.

Mykola Kowshun (pen name of Mykola Kovshyk, 1901–99) was a Ukrainian writer and professor. After fleeing from Ukraine, he settled in Canada. He was the author, in Ukrainian, of a collection of dramatic works, *Epilogue To Come* (1975), short stories, and a novel, *Mavra the Avenger* (1993).

Act I, Scene II

A strange woman gravely enters the room, a living skeleton, with grey, pallid skin. She is dressed in an old torn wrapper. At the shoulder, through the ripped fabric, an embroidered sleeve of a blouse is peering out. Her head is covered by an old rag. She cowers from exhaustion, cold and hunger. Crossing her arms on her chest, she fixes her glassy eyes somewhere to the left. She sees the fire, leans over the stove, as if trying to embrace the warmth. Her eyes are closed, and it seems as if the warmth of the stove melts her soul and heavy tears start rolling from her eyes. In a while the stranger opens her heavy lids and her eyes meet Oksana's. There is a grave, oppressive pause. The stranger takes a couple of labouring steps and stretches out her trembling hand. Oksana takes a piece of bread and places it in the thin bony hand. Biting into the bread, the stranger leaves the room. Oksana D[idenko] closes the door behind her, putting the latch on.

OKSANA D.: What are they doing to our people? They walk about like death. No voice, no strength left. And nobody sees it, and there is no help from anywhere. Just gnawing hunger. (*Sigh.*) A terrible, inhuman horror. (*Walks up to the stove. You can hear a dog howling.*) Hm… A dog's howling again, perhaps proclaiming death. His own? Or maybe ours?

Scene III

DIDENKO [Oksana's husband]: (*Knocking on the door.*) Open up, Oksana.

OKSANA D.: Glory to God, you came, and where are the children?

DIDENKO: (*Stepping in.*) They are coming. (*Takes off his hat and coat.*) (*He is tall, his face is puffy. Has abrupt nervous gestures. His posture reflects mental depression and resignation.*) And you, Oksana, why did you lock the door?

OKSANA D.: To keep it tighter. It's soooo…cold today.

DIDENKO: The classes are melting away like spring snow. From the three grades only eleven youngsters showed up, and these were like living corpses. Just skin and bones.

OKSANA D.: And how could they learn?

DIDENKO: They can't at all. In every child's soul there is fixed only one feeling and one thought—something to eat. In these times nobody's able to think of anything else—just food. It's stamped in their every movement, their eyes, their voice. You write the problems on the blackboard, and they suck their fingers, crunch acorns, chew old corn cobs, rummage under their desks for lost crumbs.

OKSANA D.: Starvation would lead to anything.

DIDENKO: And today…

OKSANA D.: What today? Why did you stop? Tell me, Leonid.

DIDENKO: Something frightful has happened today in class.

OKSANA D.: Someone died?

DIDENKO: No. By now, we are used to that.

OKSANA D.: But what, then?

DIDENKO: (*Fixing his look to one spot, as if in his memory he is reliving the same episode.*) I was reading a story about…Comrade Stalin… And one boy gets up from his desk, asking: "Leonid Stepanovych…does Comrade Stalin, like us, gather wheat-ears for food? I just shook... The book fell out of my hands... And my soul shrieked out... (*With every phrase his voice rises.*) Children... Stalin doesn't gather wheat-ears... Stalin sips your blood... Stalin devours the labour of your parents' hands...

OKSANA D.: Leonid...

DIDENKO: Stalin drinks your mothers' tears.

OKSANA D.: (*In panic.*) Leonid, did you say that? (*In agony.*) What are we to do now?

DIDENKO: (*Sitting down at the table, speaking with a broken voice.*) No, Oksana... I didn't... It seemed from the shrieking of my soul the window panes would shatter, but in my mind appeared your face, our children's faces, and I wilted.

OKSANA D.: (*Embracing Didenko's head and pressing it to her breast.*) Thank God... Don't do it... Never say it...anywhere.

DIDENKO: I don't even remember how I left the class. I don't remember, Oksana. Something strange is happening with my memory.

OKSANA D.: Stop thinking that.

DIDENKO: I would like to, but I can't. The more I try to chase these thoughts away, the more relentlessly they press upon me and settle in my mind. They stick to me like glue... Like savage bees they sting me... Even in my dreams they swarm around my soul. And now, the district is pestering me to give them a report on the children's socialist contest. (*Bitterly.*) Hm... What shall I report? How they are struggling with their death?

OKSANA D.: Write, Leonid... Report anything...so they will not bother you... It may be that somehow all this will pass...

DIDENKO: Well, maybe, something... Coming home from school, I saw a woman lying under our fence with a piece of bread near her mouth.

OKSANA D.: Still alive?

DIDENKO: No, dead. Right there in the snow.

OKSANA D.: And this one died too.

DIDENKO: You know her?

OKSANA D.: No, not really.

DIDENKO: (*Getting up, heavily shuffles his legs, takes a few steps.*) Ah...

OKSANA D.: Leonid, stop tormenting yourself.

DIDENKO: (*Walks up to his wife, embraces her.*) Tell me, perhaps you remember better than I, if you've ever read that somewhere in any other country, hungry, starved people dropped dead in the streets, under fences?

OKSANA D.: No, Leonid, this I have never read.

DIDENKO: Neither have I. But this I remember well, how one fall a small, thin horse fell down in the soup-like mud. The villagers gathered around, unhitched the horse, and they themselves pulled the wagon to the owner's place.

OKSANA D.: Those people had human hearts.

DIDENKO: Yes, yes. You tell the truth, Oksana. I often think about this. This new system has torn the hearts out of our people. Has shaken out their souls… Reports, numbers, competitions, obligations have devoured human beings… They have taken everything away…bread, strength, joy… Have stamped out the right to self-defence. They have locked our mouths with fear… Have smothered people to death. And then have turned humanity into a compost pile… With men's bones they are laying roads, cementing canals… All this, as a duty for the glory of our great Party in Moscow… And where is the world? Where are its eyes? Dear wife, I fail to understand it.

OKSANA D.: My dear, don't ask these questions. You can't think about all this.

DIDENKO: And what shall I do? Just think about death? Alright, Oksana, I'll stop. Now, tell me honestly, is my body swollen very badly?

OKSANA D.: That's a silly question. I think you look better.

DIDENKO: Then why are my legs so heavy, as if loaded with lead? And my head, bells keep ringing, many, many bells. They are racing like horses, and ringing, ringing. Nearer and nearer, stronger and stronger… And then as if pouring into one great big wave, they engulf me and shatter my skull into a thousand pieces.

OKSANA D.: You are tormenting yourself. It's time for dinner. Have something to eat, then rest, and you will feel much better....

Scene V

OKSANA D.: Have a little rest, Leonid, before you go.

DIDENKO: Go where?

OKSANA D.: To the village soviet. There is a summons from the chairman. (*Takes out a piece of paper and hands it to Didenko.*)

DIDENKO: What sort of summons? (*Takes the notice and reads it.*) "You are to appear at the village soviet at 3:00 p.m." (*Firmly.*) No, I am not going.

OKSANA D.: You must not stay away.

DIDENKO: I am not going, that's all there is to it.

OKSANA D.: You must, if the village soviet chairman sends for you.

DIDENKO: I know why they are summoning me, to rob the people!

OKSANA D.: Maybe it has something to do with school business.

DIDENKO: There is no business now but systematic robbery. Inspection, with a crow-bar and a shovel. This is the business. And then, through the homes, like thieves, rummaging in the corners, looking for bitter bread… No, I am not going…

OKSANA D.: One cannot disobey an order from the authorities.

DIDENKO: And to grab the last crumb of bread, one can?

OKSANA D.: Leonid!

DIDENKO: Push people to their destruction…

OKSANA D.: Leonid!

DIDENKO: To their death!

OKSANA D.: Calm down, Leonid…

DIDENKO: In every seed I see human tears; in the rustling of wheat-ears I hear the murmur of the dying… Every crow-bar blow echoes with sighs from the grave. Dead men's eyes are eating into my soul… They will curse me.

OKSANA D.: (*Finally catches up with Didenko, who is rushing about disconsolately.*) No, no, Leonid! They will not curse you…they know you are innocent…they know you are forced to it.

DIDENKO: It's no help to them.

OKSANA D.: They'll understand that you have absolutely no rights.

DIDENKO: Oh, dear, dear Oksana, but how can my broken heart hold all this? Or my shredded soul? Not to be deprived of a piece of bread, we snatch crumbs from starved children. Not to lose your own corner, we must throw out the unfortunate ones into the snow… I cannot bear it any longer. No, no—I cannot go, and I will not go. Do you hear me? I'm not going.

OKSANA D.: (*Whispering.*) Leonid, what are you saying? You can't be serious? You will not listen to the authorities? The order from Moscow? You want them to come and get you at night? Be shipped away? Have us thrown out of our home? What shall I do with the children? Where shall I go? Where, Leonid? (*Embraces her husband, silently crying. Didenko stiffens up. Behind the window a few silhouettes flash by.*)….

Scene VI

DIDENKO: Oksana, do you hear? Someone is coming…

(*The chairman Hrabchenko of the village soviet and a communist agent, Laptev, enter the room. Hrabchenko is wearing a warm sheepskin coat, a Persian lamb hat and a good pair of boots; the agent a black leather coat, a leather peak-cap, black leather boots and black trousers.*)

HRABCHENKO: Good day. I told you that our comrade teacher would be home. Get acquainted. (*Pointing to the agent.*) This is our new representative from Moscow. Direct from Comrade Stalin. (*Turning to the agent.*) And this is our village activist—comrade teacher.

LAPTEV: (*Offering his hand.*) Glad to meet you—Laptev.

DIDENKO: (*Forlorn.*) Didenko.

HRABCHENKO: We waited and waited for you, and then, not to lose any more time, decided to drop in ourselves.

OKSANA D.: He's just been getting ready.

HRABCHENKO: Naturally, we understand that comrade teacher is very busy, checking homework, soviet contests, and so on.

LAPTEV: Yes, yes... Activists are the base of our socialist village rebuilding.

OKSANA D.: Please sit down and get warmed up.

LAPTEV: Do not trouble yourself, comrade. Our soldiers of the Revolution can sleep even standing up, but for a moment or two we will sit down. (*Sits down, and the chairman follows suit.*)

HRABCHENKO: Our Central Committee representative spoke like a genius. Yes, we are all now soldiers of the most crucial front.

LAPTEV: Yes, our Stalinist front in the fight for bread.

HRABCHENKO: Yes, the fight for bread is the fight for socialism. Our whole village is aware of this.

LAPTEV: Theoretically it may be aware, but practically, comrade chairman, your village is lagging behind and is very far from the front line. It's even breaking up the front, thus disrupting the plan of our ultimate stage of socialism in our country.

HRABCHENKO: Well, no doubt, comrade, your criticism is right, but under the leadership of our genius Stalin and under direct supervision of our new representative, we will certainly straighten out all broken lines, pull up the lagging ones, and in the end will achieve the victory.

LAPTEV: Well, then, let's go.

HRABCHENKO: Yes, we had better go. (*Hands Didenko a list of all the villagers that will have to be canvassed.*) Here it is, comrade, your list of the river district for you to watch and what is necessary for you to note.

DIDENKO: (*Takes the list and quickly scans the names.*) What? Oryna Stohnii again on the list? But her husband died, lately, from starvation...

LAPTEV: (*Threatening.*) What? What did you say? A man died from starvation, famine? Is there a famine in Ukraine?

HRABCHENKO: Oh, that's just a village talk... What famine? Where? The lazy are always hungry.

LAPTEV: (*Gets up determinedly.*) Let's not waste our time. (*Everyone gets up.*) Put on your coat, comrade teacher, and let's get on with it...

(*Oksana D. grabs her husband's hat and coat, helping him to get dressed.*)

OKSANA D.: Get dressed, Leonid. Button up your coat. It's terribly cold outside.

HRABCHENKO: Don't worry, comrade, going from house to house, we won't notice the cold. So long, good health...

(*Laptev leaves with the chairman, Didenko following him.*)

OKSANA D.: Good health to you... (*Grabs the list from the table and calls Didenko.*) Leonid, you forgot the list. Here it is, take it. (*Whispering.*) Don't say anything, please. (*Her husband lingers, then leaves.*) He's gone...to the people's tortures...to his own ruin... (*She leans on the door and closes her eyes.*)

Serhii Kokot-Lediansky, *Tysiacha dev'iatsot trydtsiat' tretii rik: drama na 5 kartyn* (Nineteen Hundred Thirty-Three: A Drama in 5 Acts)

In *Holodomor: Dvi p'iesy* (Holodomor: Two Plays), ed. Larissa Zaleska Onyshkevych (Kyiv: Smoloskyp, 2008). Excerpts, pp. 50–57. Translated by Alexander J. Motyl.

Serhii Kokot-Lediansky (1906–2000) was a Ukrainian writer and dramatist. He settled in the United States in the late 1940s. He was the author, in Ukrainian, of the prose collection *Your Brother Cain* (1951) and of the plays *A Directive from the Center* (1943), *Beneath the Scythe* (1944), *The Resident* (1944), *After Happiness* (1944), and *The Land beneath Khmel* (1945). The play *Nineteen Hundred Thirty-Three* was written in Lviv in 1942.

Act Four

A desolate peasant house. The oven occupies one-fourth of the space. A bench and a bed. A woman lies on the bed, a man on the bench. They are covered with sackcloth. The house exudes emptiness. It is quiet. The door opens. A WOMAN enters.

Scene 1

(*The WOMAN and those who are lying motionlessly.*)

WOMAN: Good day to you. (*Quiet. No one responds. The woman looks all around: there are no signs of life.*) So the Tomashuks are also dead. In the name of the Father, and of the Son, and of the Holy Spirit… May the Heavenly Kingdom be theirs… So they never got to see their daughter. O God! O God! (*She crosses herself and leaves.*)

MAN: (*Until now he has been lying motionlessly on the bench; he raises his head.*) Who's that? Is that you, Halochka? (*Listens. It's quiet.*) Mariika! Mariika! Did you hear someone come to us just now? Maybe it was our daughter? (*No one answers.*) I guess I thought I heard something. (*Tries to get up.*) No, it's not going to work. My head's spinning, and I can't breathe… (*To his wife, who is lying motionlessly on the bed.*) Mariika, do you feel as bad as I do? I tried to get up but couldn't. I saw black, everything started going round. I guess the end is near. And our daughter, Halynochka, hasn't come, after all. Maybe that Olenka didn't write to her? After all, if Halya knew about us, she'd walk here. I don't want anything anymore, just to see her before I die, to stroke her head—and then to die… (*A pause.*) Somewhere near you was a photograph of her. Give it to me. I'll look at it one last time. You hear, Maria? Maria! (*Raises himself.*) Give me the photograph of our Halochka, and I'll take a look at it. Are you sleeping? Maria! Maria! (*He pushes aside the sackcloth covering his wife, but she shows no signs of life.*) So what gives? Are you, heaven forbid, dead? (*He musters all his strength, drags himself to the bed, looks, and touches her face with his hand.*) She's cold! Cold as ice! So she's dead. Our Mama died, Halochka. Lord, Lord… (*Looks all around.*) And there's no one here… (*Looks through the window.*) Maybe someone's coming? Someone! Anyone! No one, nowhere. The street's dead. So what am I supposed to do on my own? In the name of the Father, and of the Son… Grant repose, O Lord, to the soul of your recently departed servant Maria…

(*He whispers a prayer.*) Take her soul into the Heavenly Kingdom… Oh, how awful I feel. I feel faint. I guess it's time for me to follow her… In that case, accept me too into Your Kingdom. I've committed no sins. All my life I've labored, I've worked the earth and watered it with my sweat. And it's not my fault, Lord, that I haven't any bread today… And that we must die now…

(*He bends over and falls silent. A pause. The door opens, and two gravediggers enter.*)

Scene 2

(*GRAVEDIGGERS.*)

FIRST GRAVEDIGGER: They're ready to go here too. (*Approaches the bed and touches the woman.*) Hard as a rock. The Tomashuks are ready to go.

SECOND GRAVEDIGGER: Looks like these are the last ones on this street. Let's have a smoke. You got paper?

FIRST GRAVEDIGGER: No, I don't. But there's fine paper near those icons. (*Stands on the bench, tears off a piece of the paper, climbs down, tears off a bit for the cigarette and starts rolling it.*) This paper's very good, better than newspaper.

SECOND GRAVEDIGGER: Did that old man Gudz ever stink! If it weren't for the cigarettes, we'd have to put a clasp on our noses.

FIRST GRAVEDIGGER: He was probably lying there for a week. It got warm, and he began to stink.

SECOND GRAVEDIGGER: That's for sure. But then that Ryhorets woman lay dead for over a week, and there was no smell. It's like she fell asleep.

FIRST GRAVEDIGGER: I suppose it depends on the person. They say some people can lie dead for a year, and they look like they've fallen asleep.

SECOND GRAVEDIGGER: Well, I can't believe that. Even a tree rots after a year. While a person… That lucky bastard Klymchak had some good luck. He found two gold coins in Myronka's braids! We should pat them down too. Maybe we'll find something.

FIRST GRAVEDIGGER: You won't find anything. Did you hear that the Urativ village council even gives corpse collectors two days' worth of vodka? Did you hear?

SECOND GRAVEDIGGER: No, I hadn't heard. Maybe we'll get some too?

FIRST GRAVEDIGGER: They'll give it… Like hell they will. They'll drink it themselves. I know them. Take her. (*They approach the woman, lift her, and take her outside. They return and grab hold of the man, but he opens his eyes and speaks.*)

MAN: Who are you? What do you want?

FIRST GRAVEDIGGER: Look, he's still alive!? Good day to you! Haven't you died yet?

SECOND GRAVEDIGGER: We thought…

MAN: What do you guys want?

FIRST GRAVEDIGGER: We came for you. We came to take you.

SECOND GRAVEDIGGER: Uh-huh, for you.

MAN: What do you mean? Where are you taking me?

SECOND GRAVEDIGGER: We thought you'd already died. We wanted to take you to the graveyard.

FIRST GRAVEDIGGER: Your wife's already dead.

MAN: My wife? Dead? (*Looks around and then remembers.*) Oh, yes, she died.

FIRST GRAVEDIGGER: We're from the village council. We're taking the dead to the graveyard.

MAN: From the village council? Are you getting something for this?

SECOND GRAVEDIGGER: Sure. Bread, sausage, herring…

MAN: They've got all that? They've got bread, sausage, and herring?

SECOND GRAVEDIGGER: It's brought in from the district.

MAN: Oh, that's good. You've got a good job. You won't die of hunger. You've got a good job.

FIRST GRAVEDIGGER: We have to. It's necessary.

MAN: I'll probably die. My old lady is already dead. It's a pity about my daughter. Our daughter's a student in Kyiv.

SECOND GRAVEDIGGER: Uh, so why didn't you let your daughter know? Whoever can goes there. They've got as much bread as you want. One and a half karbovantsi a kilo.

MAN: Isn't that something? We asked the secretary, Olena, to write to her, but she probably forgot.

FIRST GRAVEDIGGER: You should've asked her to send a telegram!

MAN: A telegram? Yes, a telegram. Too bad. Our only child. She'll become an orphan. Hey, maybe there's a job for me at your place?

FIRST GRAVEDIGGER: What do you mean?

MAN: I'm saying maybe they could find something for me to do where you work. And maybe I could get some sausage or herring…

SECOND GRAVEDIGGER: Are you kidding? Why, we barely got the job.

FIRST GRAVEDIGGER: There's no food. Even the bosses get it from the district.

MAN: Too bad. I guess I've got to die. (*Looks around the house.*) And where's my wife?

SECOND GRAVEDIGGER: We already took her outside. She's already on the wagon.

MAN: On the wagon? Why on the wagon?

FIRST GRAVEDIGGER: We'll take her to get buried.

MAN: To get buried?

SECOND GRAVEDIGGER: Uh-huh.

MAN: Where did you get the coffin?

FIRST GRAVEDIGGER: There's no coffin, old man. We have to bury forty people a day. How could one make so many coffins? Besides, there are no boards.

SECOND GRAVEDIGGER: And even if there were, who'd make them? Rokh died, Klymko died, Fedosyk died—all the carpenters are dead.

FIRST GRAVEDIGGER: Only the ones who fled last winter to the Donbas or to town may still be alive.

MAN: So you just bury them without coffins?

FIRST GRAVEDIGGER: That's right.

SECOND GRAVEDIGGER: This isn't the time for coffins, old man.

MAN: And who digs the pits?

SECOND GRAVEDIGGER: Pits? What pits? There's one pit for everybody, old man.

MAN: For everybody?

FIRST GRAVEDIGGER: Uh-huh.

MAN: God, O God, so our daughter won't know where her Mama is buried!

SECOND GRAVEDIGGER: (*To the first.*) So what will we do with him?

FIRST GRAVEDIGGER: How should I know?

MAN: What's going on? What are you saying?

SECOND GRAVEDIGGER: What will we do with you? There's no one left in the whole street; they're all dead. We won't come back just for you.

MAN: Are you saying you want to take me alive to the graveyard? You want to bury me alive?

SECOND GRAVEDIGGER: No, we don't, but…

MAN: But what?

SECOND GRAVEDIGGER: After noon we're going over to the new settlement. If you die, you'll lie here a long time. There'll be no one to bury you.

FIRST GRAVEDIGGER: It's your call.

SECOND GRAVEDIGGER: I think you should be buried together with your wife. After all, you won't live past the evening.

MAN: What?

SECOND GRAVEDIGGER: I said you won't live past the evening. I tell you, you'll die before evening.

FIRST GRAVEDIGGER: You'll die today.

MAN: Good God, fellas, so you want to bury me alive?

SECOND GRAVEDIGGER: Not at all!

FIRST GRAVEDIGGER: We place those who haven't died yet separately, under a tree, on the grass, until they kick the bucket.

SECOND GRAVEDIGGER: And then, when they're dead, we bury them.

FIRST GRAVEDIGGER: You see, we can't come here again for you alone. There's no time.

SECOND GRAVEDIGGER: That's right, there's no time. We have until evening to go down all the roads outside the village and collect the dead. The people are constantly on the move, and they just drop along the roads and die like flies.

FIRST GRAVEDIGGER: Meanwhile, the militia goes around and causes a ruckus at the village council, saying there's no order.

MAN: Well, in that case, take me too. (*Tries to get up but cannot.*)

SECOND GRAVEDIGGER: See? You can't even get up.

MAN: You're right, fellas, you're quite right. But will I really die by evening?

SECOND GRAVEDIGGER: You'll die, absolutely.

FIRST GRAVEDIGGER: We've seen guys like you. You'll be dead by evening for sure.

MAN: Then let me say good-bye to the house. (*They lift him. He faces the pictures and looks at both sides.*) There's a photo of my daughter someplace on the bed. Let me take it with me.

(*The FIRST GRAVEDIGGER goes to the bed, where the woman lay, searches and finds the photograph.*)

FIRST GRAVEDIGGER: Is this her?

MAN: Uh-huh, that's her. (*Takes the photograph, looks at it, and hides it on his chest.*) I do have one request: place me near my old lady. We'll lie together, and our daughter will be between us. Alright?

SECOND GRAVEDIGGER: Very well, very well. We'll do that. That's no problem. (*They hold him by his arms and take him from the house. A pause. After a while, they nail boards over the windows. Voices are heard: "Maksym, I need nails!" And the response: "They're in the wagon." The empty house grows dark.*)

Bohdan Boychuk, *Holod 1933* (Hunger 1933)

In *An Anthology of Modern Ukrainian Drama*, ed. Larissa Zaleska Onyshkevych (Edmonton: Canadian Institute of Ukrainian Studies Press, 2012). Excerpts, pp. 418–20. Translated by Vera Rich.

Bohdan Boychuk (b. 1927) is a Ukrainian poet, dramatist, writer, and translator. He settled in the United States after World War II. He was cofounder of the New York Group of avant-garde Ukrainian writers and poets. He is the author, in Ukrainian, of several collections of poetry and novels, eight plays, and many translations. He served on the editorial board of the journal *Suchasnist'* (The Present) and coedited an anthology of modern Ukrainian poetry, *Coordinates* (1969).

Scene Six

From the back of the stage on the left, a silent funeral procession advances. In it is an OLD WOMAN. On her left shoulder she holds a spade as if it were an icon on a pole.

With her right arm she supports the corpse of a youth. She is barely able to drag him along, and his legs leave furrows in the field. A MAN IN UNIFORM…observes her every movement, intently....

THE MAN: Do you see something, too?

THE WOMAN: Where?

THE MAN: Over there.

THE WOMAN: Yes, some people, it seems.

THE MAN: Do you think they're real?

THE WOMAN: Yes, they're coming this way.

As the OLD WOMAN approaches the center of the stage, the MAN IN UNIFORM makes a gesture with his hand. The OLD WOMAN reacts in fear instantly and changes direction. She goes to the right side of the stage, glancing back constantly at the MAN IN UNIFORM.

OLD WOMAN (*lamenting*):
Grant peace to his young soul,
he brought me fruit
from the orchards... my grandson,
and cover the valley gently
with linen cloth
and lay there Thy servant's
and my grandson's soul…
grant him peace… under the warm
palm of Thy right hand,
Grant him peace, O Christ our—

Dissatisfied, the MAN IN UNIFORM makes a stern gesture with his hand, and the OLD WOMAN breaks off her lament. THE WOMAN kneels down.

THE MAN: What are you doing?

The OLD WOMAN drops the spade from her trembling hand. Unable to bear the weight of the corpse, her legs buckle, and she slumps to the ground. She whispers something in her grandson's ear, caresses him, is overcome with grief, and again whispers something and caresses him.

THE WOMAN (*praying*):
Receive our
ardent prayers,
which flow from our hearts
as if from great wounds
in our breast;
receive them from us
like warm milk…

THE MAN: That's beginning to turn sour! Ha, ha, ha.

THE WOMAN:
That will drench
with our supplication
Thy hands
pierced with compassion…

THE MAN: Hands petrified from compassion!

THE WOMAN: O receive our love…

THE MAN: Born of fear!

THE WOMAN:
Like the blood of entreaty
from our hearts,
and leave us not
in fields
Where children's voices
do not grow
and which cast dew
like a chill;
and leave not
old women
at the end of the day
with the bodies of their children
who wish not to speak to them;
and send us
plenitude
between sunset and sunrise,
and send us our
daily bread
so that our children
need not die.

THE MAN (*shouting*): Give them bread!

THE WOMAN: Give us our daily bread.

THE MAN: This day!

THE WOMAN: So that our children…

THE MAN: Will have bread!

THE WOMAN:
Our daily bread,
our daily bread,
our dai...ly

The MAN IN UNIFORM makes an angry gesture with his hand: in his opinion, the OLD WOMAN has rested long enough. Trembling in fear, the OLD WOMAN picks up the spade, lifts her grandson's body, and drags him off the stage....

Natalia Vorozhbyt, *Zernokhranilishche* (The Granary)

A Two-Act Play (2009). Excerpt. Translated by Halyna Klid.

Natalia Vorozhbyt (b. 1975) is a Ukrainian playwright and screenplay writer currently living in Kyiv. She graduated from the Gorky Institute of Literature in Moscow in 2000. She is the author, in Russian, of the plays *The Life of Ordinary People* (1994), *The Little Match Girl* (1995), *The Superboom and Other Gifts* (1997), *The Screen* (1999), *Galka Motalko* (2002), *What Do You Want, Ukrainian God?* (2004), *Demons* (2004), and *I Am Joining* (2005).

Act Two

Characters

Mokryna Starytska
Arsei Pechorytsia
Mortko the bookkeeper — county official
The corpse of Feodosii, Mokryna's father, in the grave
Izbach — manager of the village library or reading room
Havrylo and Yukhym — village activists
Artiukh — gravedigger and corpse collector

16 April 1933

A cemetery on a hill. Many freshly dug graves. Crosses have been erected on some of them. But overall the graves are unmarked. Only mounds of fresh soil indicate burial sites. It is beautiful at the cemetery. Sour-cherry trees are in bloom. Birds are singing.

MOKRYNA and ARSEI are sitting by one of the graves, kissing. The grave has no cross. Just a fresh pile of soil. There are many similar ones here. There are more and more large graves for common burials. A freshly dug pit is not yet full; hence it has not been covered.

The corpse collector ARTIUKH approaches the common burial site on his horse-driven cart. He dumps several bodies from his cart into the pit.

MOKRYNA tears herself away from the kiss, sighing wearily and happily.

MOKRYNA: What have you brought?

ARSEI unties a rag and spreads it out. It contains bread, sow fat, and an onion. ARSEI slices everything very thinly. MOKRYNA tries to grab something, but he gently pushes her aside and feeds her from his hands.

ARSEI: I'll do it. You could get full again and get sick.

MOKRYNA: Thank you, thanks... If it were not for you... Oh, how I love you, Arsei...

ARSEI: My beloved sweetheart, my cherry blossom.

He kisses her on the lips as she chews. MOKRYNA laughs. She snuggles up to him.

With great difficulty, the corpse collector ARTIUKH tries to throw off the last body. He loses his balance and falls with the body into the pit. His weak cries are heard....

MOKRYNA: Oh! There is someone out there, walking...

ARSEI: Leave, Mokryna, 'cause my lads are coming. Looks like Mortko has sent for me. There is no need for them to see me with you.

MOKRYNA: Damn your Mortko, and damn your lads!

MOKRYNA rises and walks away with a staggering gait. YUKHYM and IZBACH appear on horseback.

IZBACH: Here you are! Hanky-panky? Mortko asked that you be sent for.

ARSEI: What's so urgent out there?

IZBACH: (*With agitation*) It's urgent, it's urgent. We have been informed by the county, and they were notified by the district. And they—directly from Moscow. This is the scoop. An American journalist is coming to us.

ARSEI: Where? To our village? From America? Have they gone completely mad out there?

IZBACH: Well, this is not up to us. This journalist is writing about Soviet achievements for all the American people. He had an interview with Stalin himself. He is coming here to see with his own eyes...that (*in astonishment*) there is no famine.

ARSEI: You guys! Have you already been drinking this morning? What are you talking about? What do these people look like, lying in the pits? Are they drunk?

YUKHYM: That... That is the directive from the top. We can't disgrace ourselves.

ARSEI: Well, maybe he'll go elsewhere.

YUKHYM: But it's the same everywhere.

ARSEI: I don't even know what to call this. Some kind of fairy tale.

IZBACH: In short, Arsei, Mortko has made us responsible for this. If we manage it, he said, we'll be sent to the city right away. Out of this hell. He'll be here in a week.

ARSEI angrily spits in front of himself.

ARSEI: Couldn't he come in a year? There will be paradise, and nothing but, right here.

IZBACH: So there should be no corpses. No starving people. A Soviet village with a cultural center, dancing, and an eatery. With progressive youth. The center will send us everything we need. The clothes and the food. We have to find the agitprop team. Have you heard where they are now?

ARSEI: I heard they got stuck right in Bairak. Their horses were stolen and eaten. So they're stuck.

The corpse collector ARTIUKH struggles out of the pit, evidently easing his way out by stacking corpses. He gets into the cart. The sickly, emaciated nag slowly pulls the cart out of the cemetery.

IZBACH: Very well. We need to send for them. Yukhym, you'll go. And you'll find horses for them.

YUKHYM: Where will I get them?

IZBACH: Dekulakize and expropriate someone. There, take Artiukh's horse. It only looks like it's at death's door.

YUKHYM: What?! And how is Artiukh supposed to work?

IZBACH: Just joking. Mortko will give you a car. We'll put on such a show here that the American won't want to leave.

ARSEI: Curse that tongue of yours!

YUKHYM: And what are we going to tell the folks?

IZBACH: Mortko will think of something. He said it's not our problem.

ARSEI: I can't understand one thing. Why did they decide to bring him here? Why are we saddled with this curse?

IZBACH (*Genuinely astonished*): How come? Well, look around you! Is there a better village than ours? Just take a look at our Psel. What a river! It winds like a serpent through the meadows. And how picturesque the banks are alongside it! Too bad I'm not an artist, or I'd paint it... And what fine sheatfish are in the river! Like this (*stretches out his arms, showing the size of the fish*). No kidding! It used to be, sometimes you would walk into the meadow at dawn, and the beauty of the place would make you stop in your tracks: a soft fog floating along the ground, and white geese sleeping in it like in a blanket. And the forest in our parts is like the Kremlin Wall. Nothing scares you if you have such a forest! No need to say any more! When I look at the village from this hill, I forget everything for joy. Even if there is a better village out there somewhere, it is definitely not in Ukraine. There is definitely no such place in America. And the folks here are good. And the soil is bountiful... Stick a pole into it, and it will bloom.

He sticks his pole instead of a cross onto the grave of FEODOSII. ARSEI and YUKHYM look dumbly at the pole, as if expecting it to start blooming immediately.

You'll see, in three springs the sparrows will build their nests in it.

POETRY

Wira Wowk, *Ikonostas Ukraïny* (Iconostasis of Ukraine)

(Rio de Janeiro and New York: Companhia Brasileira de artes gráficas, 1988). Excerpts, pp. 38–40. Translated by Alexander J. Motyl.

Wira Wowk (pen name of Vira Selianska, b. 1926) is a Ukrainian poet, literary scholar, and translator. After World War II she settled in Rio de Janeiro, where she currently lives. Her Ukrainian-language poetry collections include *Youth* (1954), *The Leading Star* (1955), *Elegies* (1956), *Black Acacias* (1961), *Love Letters of Princess Veronica to Cardinal Giovannibattista* (1967), *Kappa of the Cross* (1969), *Meanders* (1979), *Mandala* (1980), *Women's Masks* (1993), *A Supplication to the Mother of God* (1997), *Painted Stove Tiles* (1999), *Viola in the Evening* (2000), and *Poetry* (2000).

LAMENTATION ON THE GREAT FAMINE

Grass stubble.

WOMAN'S VOICE:
the forlorn
field cries
famine
the Golgotha
of a home without a roof
distant are the storks
how many years of woe
did the cuckoo announce?
how many eclipses of the sun
how many scarecrows amidst poppies?
a stream of blood
flows through the fields
a bleached skull in the black earth
ravens circle above corpses
the shadows of children
along the fence
blinded by tears
the dark church
its zinc cupola nodding
where are you mallows
near the multicolored walls
where is the spindle of the song
where is the wreath of the dance?
death dances on the grass stubble
the zither's strings
snapped from the lament
of millions of innocents

MAN'S VOICE:
o land of cries
you were sown
with grain and sweat
now you demand
our flesh
and the plow of death
plows our eyes
and soul in despair
what countless passions
sunsets on the farms!
the moon drives nails
into the sunken chest
leaving black burns
whose are the claws
that grab
the last crumb from the mouth?
sun—but no sunflower

the mornings—in a mist
not yet awakened have
the pupils of the world
to our sorrows
where are you, dews
for our wounds?
speak up, you breezes!
rise up, you greenery,
shine with fruit!
may the dead, gladdened,
become the earth

Mykola Rudenko, "Khrest" (The Cross, written 1976)

In Wasyl Hryshko, *The Ukrainian Holocaust of 1933* (Toronto: Bahriany Foundation, 1983). Excerpts, pp. 135–36. Translated by Marco Carynnyk.

Mykola Rudenko (1920–2004) was a Ukrainian poet, writer, and philosopher. Although initially a supporter of the Soviet regime, he became a critic after World War II and eventually a political dissident. In 1976 he founded the Ukrainian Helsinki Group. He was the author, in Ukrainian, of the novels *The Last Sabre* (1959), *The Magic Boomerang* (1966), and *The Eagle's Ravine* (1970), the philosophical treatise *The Energy of Progress* (1974), and the memoir *The Greatest Miracle Is Life* (1998).

The rye is beginning to ripen,
But—and his hair stands on end—
Not many have survived
To see the new harvest.
The nights, oh these infernal nights!
He won't fall asleep till dawn.
Some woman's robust hands
Are trying to strangle him to death.
Then his mother approaches
And says with sorrow,
"My son, it's time to get up,
The sun has risen over the field.
We cannot lie peacefully in our graves,
We, the dead, are unable to rest.
Who will care for the precious ears of grain
In the fields, my dear son?"
The little ones with their fair heads,
Totally emaciated, keep whining.
"Please, Mama, a crumb of bread,
A tiny piece of bread!"—and their cry is dying.
And where the collective's pantry stands,
Khrystia, a widow gone mad,

Comes running on the porch in the morning
And starts dancing her cannibal dance:
"Why, I slaughtered my children,
I cooked them before sunrise.
I prepared some jellied meat
For the tractor driver, that brave man."

Vasyl Holoborodko, "Shukachi mohyl" (Grave Seekers, published 1990)

In *Icarus with Butterfly Wings and Other Poems* (Toronto: Exile Editions, 1991), p. 39. Translated by Myrosia Stefaniuk.

Vasyl Holoborodko (b. 1945) is a Ukrainian poet currently living in Ukraine. He was one of the *shestydesiatnyky*—the generation of the sixties—who rejected Stalinist norms in culture. He is the author, in Ukrainian, of *The Flying Window* (1970), *A Green Day* (1988), *Icarus with Butterfly Wings* (1990), *A Viburnum Tree on Christmas* (1992), *Nightingale, You Match-Maker...* (2002), and *We Are Going On* (2006). He was awarded the Shevchenko Prize in 1994.

For Ihor Kalynets

We stare into each other's eyes,
as if our existence were threatened at this moment,
we call out crucial words, through the thick air
pressed into heavy ocean water,
instead of words we hear mutual silence:
—where is our voice?—
We stand in front of peepholes at prison gates
in endless lines, pleading for a visit,
a chance to bring a parcel—but are told
that those we're looking for are not here:
—where are our poets?—
We roam the world's cemeteries
pressing our ears to silent nameless
graves in forests, taigas, tundras
and listen at the barrows of our brothers
ravaged in thirty-three by famine
(perhaps we'll hear the sound of flutes, reed pipes,
floiarkas and sopilkas buried
together with the dead)
like divers we descend to the grave on the ocean floor,
the sunken barge with the condemned,
with horror, we approach the lime-filled hole
barely covered with dirt:
—where are the graves of our poets?—
(We light a candle
before the world's wasteland
covered with cherry blossoms)....

Vasyl Symonenko, "Chuiu" (I Hear, written 1961)

Previously unpublished translation by Michael M. Naydan. Original in Vasyl Symonenko, *Bereh chekan'* (The Shore of Expectations), ed. Ivan Koshelivets, 2nd ed. (Munich: Suchasnist', 1973), p. 115.

Vasyl Symonenko (1935–63) was a Ukrainian poet and journalist. He was one of the leading *shestydesiatnyky*—the generation of the sixties—who rejected Stalinist norms in culture. He published only one collection of poetry during his lifetime, *Silence and Thunder* (1962). His Ukrainian-language works appeared posthumously as *The Shore of Expectations* (1965, 1973), *Earth's Gravity* (1964), and *Poems* (1966).

I hear, earth, your breathing,
I understand your quiet grief,
As cold dawns shed the dew
In handfuls on you.

I know the downpours and violent storms,
And dew in the rustle of boughs—
First an orphan's, then a widow's tears,
Then the sweat of our tortured ancestors.

You collected them without number
On the expanse of fields and forests of oak
In order that human tears and human love
Might nourish you for eternity.

Maksym Rylsky, "Zhaha" (Thirst, published 1943)

In *Autumn Stars: The Selected Lyric Poetry* (Lviv: Litopys, 2008). Excerpts, pp. 253–55. Translated by Michael M. Naydan.

Maksym Rylsky (1895–1964) was a highly celebrated Ukrainian poet and translator who experienced repression in the 1930s and then returned to the Soviet regime's favor. His best poetry appeared in the 1920s: *The Blue Distance* (1922), *Poems* (1924), *Through Storm and Snow* (1925), *The Thirteenth Spring* (1926), *The Resonance and the Echo* (1929), and *Where the Roads Meet* (1929). He translated Adam Mickiewicz, Paul Verlaine, William Shakespeare, and Aleksandr Pushkin.

"Don't throw away bread, for it's sacred!"
  In tender severity,
It happened, says the old man
  To curly-headed toddlers.

"Don't play with bread, for it's a sin!"
  Still talking to the infant,

Restraining happy laughter,
It happened, says mother.

The children grew, from infants
They were made into grown-ups,
And what was heard
Ten years ago is forgotten later,

And with good reason we entered
The word "sin" into the archive,
Having begun curly-headed childhood
With the new words.

Nevertheless there remains for us
(And this is not an oversight)
A deep veneration always—
Yes!—for the *sacred* bread!

For labor is beautiful, though sweat is abundant,
For the honey spirit of rye
Carries life to the people of the world
And gives birth to human tongues.

He who sows a golden kernel
Into the fiery strength of the earth
Himself will grow as wheat
On the field common to mankind.

Yurii Klen, *Prokliati roky* (The Accursed Years)

(Lviv: Vistnyk, 1937). Excerpts, p. 26. Translated by Alexander J. Motyl.

Yurii Klen (pseudonym of Oswald Burghardt, 1891–1947) was a Ukrainian writer, poet, literary scholar, and translator. He emigrated to Germany in 1931. His only collection of Ukrainian-language poetry appeared as *Caravels* (1943). He was the author, in Ukrainian, of *Memoirs about the Neoclassicists* (1947) and coauthor of the literary parody *Diabolic Parabolas* (1947).

The dumb Hrytskos, Opanases
Died like mosquitoes in the rain.
Human flesh was eaten in the villages
And bread was baked from ground bark.
Hungry children looked greedily
On the bloated body of their dead sister.

And we, though we'd abandoned the caves,
Became cannibals in the twentieth century.

Mustering what famished strength remained,
They removed the corpses secretly,
Which recently they'd buried in the graves.
The pillagers ripped off their clothes.
Didn't they collect carrion in barrels
And cook the dead to extract fat?
The bumpkin went to town for bread
Dropping to the pavement, dead.

Valerii Prokoshin, "Liudoedy" (Cannibals)

From a verse cycle titled "Russkoe kladbishche" (Russian Cemetery), part 3.
Online at http://www.solovki.ca/camp_20/cannibals.php. Translated by Halyna Klid and Jars Balan.

Valerii Prokoshin (1959–2009) was a poet, prose writer, and journalist from the Kaluga region of Russia. His poems were published in the collections *Povodyr' dushi* (Leader of the Soul, 1991), *Borovsk. Provintsiia* (Borovsk. Province, 1992), *Mezhdu Pushkinym i Brodskim* (Between Pushkin and Brodsky, 2006), and elsewhere. He also wrote children's literature under the pseudonym Evgenii Kozinaki.

Why are you crying, Ukraine,
In the midst of lifeless snows?
Without any daughter or any son,
Any old women or old men.

The thirty-third year, a biblical number.
Cold. Hunger. Corpses.
But in the village Red Army fighters
Are gorging themselves like beasts.

Twenty-five Red Army scrappers
Have devoured infants alive.
While a commissar, like his comrades,
Polishes off someone's mother.

With his side cap cocked over his ear,
The old cook lit a fire:
From brothers and sisters
He cooks a tasty porridge.

Without a devil or a God,
Without a heart or human face,

Only a terrifying road
With no beginning and no end.

Marching alongside the ruins
Are the Red Army's sons.
At their head is Joseph Stalin
With the corpse of his own wife.*

The thirty-third year—a biblical number.
And peering with a grin
From behind the smoke screen
Is an embalmed corpse.

*Nadezhda Sergeevna Allilueva, Stalin's second wife (almost 23 years his junior), died on 8 November 1932 under mysterious circumstances. Most evidence points to suicide, for which Stalin was indirectly responsible. (Translators' note)

Lesia Roi, "Lullaby 33." Song from the CD *Ishov ia nebom* (I Walked the Heavens, 2010)

Music by Dmytro Dobryi-Vechir. Performed by Vii. Translated by Halyna Klid and Jars Balan.

Lesia Roi (Olesia Vitaliivna Roi) was born in 1980 in Illichivsk (Odesa region, Ukraine) into a family of musicians. At the age of five she began playing the flute; at six, the violin; afterward she took to playing the guitar, piano, accordion, domra, and other instruments. She started writing her own songs at the age of 17. She has been with the band Vii since 2006, singing and playing the violin, flute, keyboards, and percussion.

Rock-a-bye, rock-a-bye, sweet dreams, my little angels,
The moon is already on its watch, and the dark night will soon fall upon the earth.
I stand over the cradle: what am I to feed you?
For three days hunger has haunted our home, while mother says:

Why are you rocking them? You should take them into the forest—
Let the night rock them on its black wing!
God will show you mercy—if not through salvation, then by damnation.
If we are so much ash, then let dust go unto dust.

Let them wander through the dew on their little bare feet,
Shimmering in the grass from spring to fall in green luminescence,
And when it turns cold, snow will spread like linen....
You are not going to live anyway—you'll die of hunger, and mother says:

Why are you rocking them? You should take them into the forest—
Let the night rock them on its black wing!
And toss leaves over them—I don't have the strength:
We are all ash—let dust go unto dust.

My sweet nestlings, to cradle you once more...
You won't cry from hunger anymore—I alone shall weep:
Thanks to your father, you became *poterchata*,*
You will cry out beneath windows at night, but I will tell you:

Rock-a-bye, rock-a-bye, sweet dreams, my little angels,
May the night carry you on its black wing
It no longer matters whether you forgive me:
We are all ash—let dust go unto dust.

*According to folk beliefs in Ukraine (similar to myths in Norway and Sweden), *poterchata* were the souls or ghostly spirits of children who died unbaptized and could be heard crying out to be christened. Demonic beings, the *poterchata* flew about for seven years begging for "the Cross." (Translators' note)

Vasyl Riabko, "The Communards." Song from the CD *Mova, seks ta rok-n-rol* (Language, Sex, and Rock 'n' Roll, 2012)

Music by Vasyl Riabko. Performed by P@p@ Karlo. Translated by Halyna Klid.

Vasyl Riabko was born in 1975 in the Ukrainian city of Kharkiv. By education he is a musician and specialist in cultural studies. In 1997 he and Oleksandr Molchanov founded the rock group P@p@ Karlo, in which Riabko plays guitar and sings backup vocals. He began to write lyrics in Ukrainian in the year 2000.

Open the gate! Come on—cheerfully!
Don't you see, you son of a bitch,
That to you and your village have come
The mind and conscience of the working class.

Hand over your grain. Come on—quietly!
Take your belongings out of the house,
It's for you we'll shed the blood
Of those who don't want to die of hunger…

Refrain
Commune-commune-communards,
Some get cocaine, some get plank beds,
Some go to the collective farm, some go to war.
We'll drive the old world into a coffin.

Let's blow up the day, let's shoot the night.
Let the nation shudder.
Our law is a gun, our Christ is Illich,
Our testament is collectivization.

We'll sprinkle this kulak rye with blood,
We'll slaughter all the manorial livestock.
If you want to eat and live well,
Then grab a rifle and let's hurry
To the commune–commune–communards....

FOLK VERSES

V. Pakharenko, "Slovo, shcho zdolalo smert'" (The Word That Overcame Death)

Literaturna Ukraïna (Kyiv), 7 May 1992. Translated by Alexander J. Motyl.

Lenin's sitting on a mount,
While Stalin's in the mud—
What they did to the kurkul
Will also happen to the poor.

They croaked or died—
Their hooves hold up the sky:
The butter and grain
Were taken abroad,
While the barley and oats
Rotted in the machine-tractor station.

Don't be surprised, good people,
If the same befalls you tomorrow.

They rolled and swept the bread—
The whole people's sad,
While the great head
Appears not to hear.

Dozhylasia Ukraïna...: Narodna tvorchist' chasiv holodomoru i kolektyvizatsiï na Ukraïni (Ukraine Has Come Down to This...: Folklore in the Times of Famine and Collectivization in Ukraine)

ed. I. Buhaievych (Kyiv: Ukraïns'kyi pys'mennyk, 1993), pp. 7, 11–12, 15. Translated by Alexander J. Motyl.

Clothes in rags, two sacks of grain—
They make you into a kurkul,
All your pots are registered
And off you go to Solovki.

Mother's in the co-op, Father's in the co-op,
The children cry along the way,
There's no bread, there's no fat,
Only movies and shows,
Just one sheaf's in the house,
And they still say you're a kurkul.

Father's in the co-op, Mother's in the co-op,
Our house is made of twigs,
There's just one sheaf in the house—
And they all cry you're a kurkul.

The pigs aren't squealing today,
The cattle aren't lowing—
There's nothing to eat,
So go lie down in the grave.

I used to be a farmer during NEP,
But the co-op's like a trap:
They drive you as they will,
'Cause they take you for a fool.

When the land was mine,
I met the stars in the field,
Now I sleep until the time
The brigade leader wakes me up.

Work or sit—
The co-op'll give you nothing to eat.

The old man's sitting in the stubble
And is patching his pants,
The stubble pricks him from behind,
While he curses the collective farm:
—I worked twelve days,
But they recorded one workday.

The old woman had one goat
That she gave the collective farm,
She sat down at the table
And began counting her workdays.

The old woman's sitting in the weeds
And is counting her workdays.
She counted three hundred days:
—Give me bread for just one day.

She worked all summer,
Earned a kilo of buckwheat,
One of buckwheat, two of barley,
Now I'm worried where I'll grind it.

The old woman asked the old man:
—Will the collective farm give us bread?
—They'll give you bread as well as flat cakes,
We'll eat them without a knife.

Drink the water, eat the chaff—
Go fulfill the Five-Year Plan!
Empty belly, pants in rags—
Go fulfill the Five-Year Plan!

Why's the village so lamenting?
The confiscator's now in charge:
Takes the bread from the people—
Lets the whole village die out.

The lentils and the peas,
The potatoes and the beets—
The confiscators take it all,
Let the peasants croak.

Father's in the co-op, Mother's in the co-op,
The children cry along the way,
There's no bread, there's no fat,
'Cause the local authorities took it all.

Don't look for the coffin—
The father ate his child.
The brigade leader carries a whip—
Drives people to Siberia.

There's hunger and cold in our house,
There's nothing to eat, nowhere to sleep,
Our neighbor already went crazy
And ate his children.

Where the confiscator's in charge,
The whole village'll feel it:
There'll be screams and tears
And the whining of dogs.

Oh, when the Kochubeis were princes,
There was enough bread,
But when the pantless ones came,
Then it ran out.

Oh, my millstones,
My little chatterboxes,
Grind the bark into flour
For little doughnuts.

Let the guts growl—
They want to eat.
The eyes don't sleep,
'Cause they don't want to eat.

Get up, Taras, from your grave,
Look at Ukraine's woes—
People swell, they die like beasts,
They die 'cause of the co-ops.

Get up, Lenin, and take a look
At what we've come to:
The barn's down, the house's down,
The collective-farm horse has one eye
There's no cow, there's no pig—
Only Stalin's on the wall.

Lenin said to Stalin:
—After I'm gone, issue these orders:
Don't give much bread,
Don't show any meat.

There's no cow, there's no pig,
Only Lenin's on the wall,
And he shows with his hand
Where to go for nettles.

Stalin's hanging on the wall,
Smiling down at me,
And he shows with his hand
Where to go for flour:
To Romny, to Sencha?
Better for me to pound the mortar!

There's no bread, there's no milk,
While we clap our hands.
Do get up, Lenin, take a look

At how well the collective farms are living:
The cart's down, the tractor's down
And the mare's got only one side.

Stalin's riding a dried fish,
With two herrings in his pocket,
He drives it forward with an onion
And catches up with America.

On the house is a hammer and sickle,
While in the house are death and famine.

Get up, Lenin, and take a look
At what we've come to:
We catch and pound mice—
And bake flat cakes.

Krupskaia's playing the accordion,
Stalin's dancing a mean hopak,
That's what Ukraine's come to—
A hundred grams a head.

Oh, thank you, Ilich,
That I'm not baking bread,
I'll have to ask Stalin
Not to cook anything.

Father Stalin, take a look,
How well we're living in the co-op:
The house's down, the barn's down,
There are three horses with one eye.

Stalin's sitting on his throne
Playing a violin.
At fertile Ukraine
He looks suspiciously.

Oh, the violin's of walnut,
The bow's of rue,
When he plays his commands,
They can be heard in Ukraine.

Oh, Stalin played,
Oh, Stalin played,
He began looking closely:
They'd so fleeced Ukraine
That its ribs were visible.

Oh, Stalin played,
Oh, Stalin played,
So that the strings broke.
In Ukraine the people died,
Only some remained…

Don't be surprised, brother,
That we're communists—
The peasants'll make the bread,
And we'll eat it.

The communists bring
A dark cloud to Ukraine—
And famine—a savage punishment
To the innocent farmers.

Hey, Postyshev, you son of a bitch,
May your hands wither
For delivering Ukraine
To famine-filled torments.

If only Father Makhno'd rise up—
He wouldn't let the communists
Take the peasants' bread
And eat it in their communes.

—Where're you going, where're you going,
Where are you limping?
—To the district committee for my ration,
Don't you know?!

Oh, I won't marry Pylyp,
I'll marry the "confiscator"
Because he's got lots of bread
And butter and cheese.

Yu. Semenko, *Narodne slovo: Zbirnyk suchasnoho ukraïns'koho fol'kloru*
(The Word of the People: An Anthology of Contemporary Ukrainian Folklore)

(Lviv: Vechirnia hodyna), 1992, no. 6: 37–39, 41–43. Translated by Alexander J. Motyl.

Don't worry, Hapka,
That we're communists:
The peasants'll work
While we eat!

The girl's sitting on sackcloth
And is counting her workdays.
The workdays, the workdays.
Father walks around with no pants,
While Mother has no skirt.

The old woman's sitting on sackcloth
And is counting her workdays.
She has forty days plus one,
Give me bread for just one!

Stalin's walking, and he asks
What don't children have enough of.
—There's no bread, there's no salt,
And besides that they're naked.

Lenin's playing the accordion,
Stalin's dancing a mean hopak,
'Cause in our collective farm
They've given a hundred grams a head.

I worked ten days
And earned one workday.
And thanks to that workday,
I'm hungry every day.

The rye and wheat
Are sent abroad,
While the scraps and weeds
Are for workers and peasants.

I collected ears of wheat
On the collective-farm field
And for that they gave me
Ten years of bondage.

O, my Ukraine,
You producer of grain,
You gave Moscow your bread
And became hungry yourself.

In the year 1932
People ate goosefoot.
In the year 1933
They began to die on foot.

Hey, Stalin, you torturer,
What've you made of us today,
The bandits have come to rule,
While Father and Mother are in Siberia.

H. Hryn, "Chorno-chervona kosa 33-ho" (The Black-and-Red Scythe of '33)

Holos Ukraïny (Voice of Ukraine, Kyiv), 5 July 2003. Translated by Alexander J. Motyl.

The blue cornflowers have blossomed
In the steppe near the road.
But my children have died
Of hunger in the "co-op."

"Narodni prymovky pro 'Shchaslyve kolhospne zhyttia'" (Folk Rhymes about "Happy Collective-Farm Life")

Holos Ukraïny (Voice of Ukraine, Kyiv), 10 September 1993. Translated by Alexander J. Motyl.

Mama, I'm hungry!
Papa, I'm hungry!—
The little ones cry hysterically.
The activists took everything—
There's famine in the village.

As Lenin was dying,
He ordered Stalin
Not to give people bread,
Not to show them any fat.

BIBLIOGRAPHIC NOTE AND GUIDE TO FURTHER RESEARCH

Compiling a bibliography for a book such as this presented us with a few unexpected problems. We realized that, at best, we could offer readers only a select bibliography. As this volume already contains important selections to which readers can refer, repeating those entries in a bibliography seemed pointless. Moreover, readers can easily refer to the original works from which excerpts have been reprinted here. Most important, it made no sense to provide print sources for further research when existing digital sites list much of this literature. We therefore decided to direct readers to some important bibliographies and to a number of online sites as guides to further reading or research.

The best and most comprehensive published bibliography to date is the second edition of *Holodomor v Ukraïni 1932–1933 rr. Bibliohrafichnyi pokazhchyk* (The Holodomor in Ukraine, 1932–33: A Bibliographic Guide), compiled by L. M. Bur'ian et al. (Odesa: Studiia Nehotsiant, 2008). The first edition, under the same title, was published in Odesa and Lviv by M. P. Kots in 2001. A select bibliography appears in Wsevolod W. Isajiw, ed., *Famine-Genocide in Ukraine, 1932–1933: Western Archives, Testimonies and New Research* (Toronto: Ukrainian Canadian Research and Documentation Centre, 2003). Also useful is Andrew Gregorovich, *Holodomor Bibliography: Ukrainian Famine-Genocide 1932–33 in English Language Resources* (Toronto: Ucrainica Research Institute, 2011).

There are many Internet sites comprising bibliographies and other resources. A bibliography by Cheryl A. Madden including many English-language titles may be found on the website of the Shevchenko Scientific Society: http://www.shevchenko.org/famine/index.htm. Students may also wish to consult the online *Wikipedia* entries for "Holodomor" and "Soviet famine of 1932–1933" for references. The French historian Nicolas Werth appends a brief bibliography to his article on the Ukrainian famine on the *Encyclopedia of Mass Violence* website: http://www.massviolence.org/The-1932-1933-Great-Famine-in-Ukraine?artpage=5. Also useful is the bibliography posted on the website of the Ukrainian Canadian Congress, Toronto Branch: http://faminegenocide.com/resources/bibliogr.html.

In Ukraine, the State Committee of Archives of Ukraine has established a site with a massive amount of mainly Ukrainian- and Russian-language materials and publications: http://www.archives.gov.ua/Sections/Famine/index-eng.php. The main section of this site contains important documentary publications that can be read online or downloaded: http://www.archives.gov.ua/Sections/Famine/Publicat/. Another useful page on this site is the online bibliography based on Bur'ian et al., *Holodomor v Ukraïni 1932–1933 rr.*: http://www.archives.gov.ua/Sections/Famine/Documents/Bibliogr.php#Y1933.

Readers should also see the section of the site established by the Institute of Ukrainian History, National Academy of Sciences of Ukraine, dedicated to research on the Holodomor: http://www.history.org.ua/index.php?urlcrnt=projects/select.

php&seriaName=golod&lnProject=Holod. This section contains the bibliography that was published in *Holod v Ukraïni 1932–1933 rokiv v Ukraïni: prychyny ta naslidky* (Holodomor in Ukraine: Causes and Consequences. Kyiv: Naukova dumka, 2003): http://www.history.org.ua/LiberUA/Book/Golodor/72.pdf. Also useful to readers of Ukrainian is the webpage featuring back issues of *Ukraïns'kyi istorychnyi zhurnal* (Ukrainian Historical Journal), which contains many articles by leading Ukrainian historians on the famine of 1932–33: http://www.history.org.ua/index.php?urlcrnt=JournALL/select.php&seriaName=journal. Those who want to conduct archival research on the Ukrainian famine should also look at the article by Hennadii Boriak in *Harvard Ukrainian Studies*: "Sources and Resources on the Famine in Ukraine's Archival System" (vol. 27 [2004–5]: 117–47).

Articles on the Ukrainian famine can be found in many academic journals worldwide. Many university libraries offer online versions of these journals. Searches by keywords, authors' names, and article titles will turn up many articles on the famine. We should note here that, to date, there is only one specialized journal in English, *Holodomor Studies*, dedicated specifically to the Ukrainian famine. The journal, which began appearing semiannually in 2009, publishes scholarly articles and book reviews, including contributions from scholars in Ukraine and Russia, as well as documents, some previously unpublished, all related to the Ukrainian famine. Unfortunately, an online version of this journal is not yet available.

The Ukrainian famine has been a controversial topic since the appearance of the first scholarly monograph in English, Robert Conquest's *Harvest of Despair* (1986). Frank Sysyn discusses reactions to the appearance of Conquest's study in his article "The Ukrainian Famine of 1932–3: The Role of the Ukrainian Diaspora in Research and Public Discussion," in *Studies in Comparative Genocide*, ed. Levon Chorbajian and George Shirinian (London and New York: Macmillan and St. Martin's, 1999), pp. 182–215.

Mention should also be made of the pro-Soviet apologist tract by Douglas Tottle, *Fraud, Famine and Fascism: The Ukrainian Genocide Myth from Hitler to Harvard* (Toronto: Progress Books, 1987). Although the book was issued in Canada by a pro-communist publisher, the text was prepared with assistance from collaborators in the Soviet Union. In it Tottle denied that the famine was the result of deliberate policies and actions on the part of the Soviet authorities. He also attempted to deflect attention from discussion of the famine toward issues of Nazi collaboration, World War II-era war criminals, Ukrainian nationalism, and the Ukrainian diaspora.

The journal *Europe-Asia Studies* published a series of articles in response to a monograph by R. W. Davies and Stephen G. Wheatcroft, *The Years of Hunger: Soviet Agriculture, 1931–1933* (2004), in which the authors emphasized their disagreement with Conquest's conclusion that the famine was the result of deliberate policy. The first article to appear in the *Europe-Asia Studies* debates was Michael Ellman, "The Role of Leadership Perceptions and of Intent in the Soviet Famine of 1931–1934" (vol. 57, no. 6, September 2005: 823–41). Davies and Wheatcroft replied in "Stalin and the Soviet Famine of 1932–1933: A Reply to Ellman" (vol. 58, no. 4, June 2006: 625–33). Ellman responded with "Stalin and the Soviet Famine of 1932–1933 Revisited" (vol. 59, no. 4, June 2007: 663–93). Earlier, Mark B. Tauger wrote "Arguing from Errors: On Certain Issues in Robert Davies' and Stephen Wheatcroft's Analysis of the 1932 Soviet Grain Harvest and the Great Famine of 1931–1933" (vol. 58, no. 6, September 2006: 973–84). Wheatcroft replied in "On Continuing to Misunderstand Arguments: Response to Mark Tauger" (vol. 59, no. 5, July 2007: 847–68). Hiroaki Kuromiya joined the debate with "The Soviet Famine of 1932–1933 Reconsidered" (vol. 60, no. 4, June 2008: 663–75), and David Marples wrote "Ethnic Issues in the Famine of 1932–1933 in Ukraine" (vol. 61, no. 3, May 2009: 505–18).

Much of the English-language scholarly literature on the Ukrainian famine has tended to focus on the policies and police-administrative decisions and actions of the Soviet government and Communist Party, mainly in the context of the pan-Soviet famines of the period. Readers interested in exploring these perspectives should refer to the study by Davies and Wheatcroft, *The Years of Hunger*, and the above-mentioned debates in *Europe-Asia Studies*. The excellent essay by Andrea Graziosi, "The Great Soviet Peasant War: Bolsheviks and Peasants, 1917–1933," in his *Stalinism, Collectivization and the Great Famine* (2009), treats the famine in the context of Bolshevik policies and actions, generally hostile to the peasantry, from 1917 to 1933.

The Ukrainian famine also lends itself to consideration in wider contexts, such as the study of famines worldwide. Cormac Ó Gráda, *Famine: A Short History* (Princeton and Oxford, 2009) includes a chapter on "The Violence of Government" in which the Soviet and Ukrainian famines are briefly treated. Steven Devereaux, *Theories of Famine* (New York, London et al.: Harvester Wheatsheaf, 1993), examines the Soviet famines, including the famine in Ukraine, as a case study in the chapter "Famine and Government Policy." In his book *Development as Freedom* (New York: Knopf, 1999), Amartya Sen has looked at the relationship between the occurrence of famine and the lack of democracy and colonial status in the chapter on "Famines and Other Crises."

Finally, there have been three books of note published recently in which the Ukrainian famine has been treated in broader European contexts. Timothy Snyder, *Bloodlands: Europe between Hitler and Stalin* (New York: Basic Books, 2010), contains a chapter on "The Soviet Famines" that focuses largely on Ukraine and treats the famine as one of the episodes of mass killings by Hitler and Stalin in the expanse of east-central Europe that he calls the "bloodlands." Norman M. Naimark's short book *Stalin's Genocides* (Princeton and Oxford: Princeton University Press, 2010) treats the Ukrainian famine of 1932–33 as one of Stalin's acts of genocide. Finally, Claus Leggewie and Anne Lang place the Ukrainian famine within the context of ongoing attempts to define European identity and memory in a chapter on "Holodomor: die Ukraine ohne Platz im europäischen Gedächtnis" in *Der Kampf um die europäische Erinnerung: Ein Schlachtfeld wird besichtigt* (Munich: C. H. Beck, 2011).

ACKNOWLEDGMENTS OF COPYRIGHTS AND SOURCES

COLLECTIONS

Documents from *The Foreign Office and the Famine* (1988) reprinted by permission of the Kashtan Press.

Documents from *Holodomor of 1932–33 in Ukraine* (2008) reprinted by permission of the Kyiv Mohyla Academy Publishing House and Ruslan Pyrih.

Document from *The Holy See and the Holodomor:Documents from the Great Famine of 1932–1933 in Soviet Ukraine* reprinted by permission of the Kashtan Press.

Documents from *The Stalin-Kaganovich Correspondence 1931–36* (2003) reprinted by permission of Oleg Khlevniuk.

Letters from *We'll Meet Again in Heaven* (2001) reprinted by permission of the Germans from Russia Heritage Collection, North Dakota State University Libraries, Fargo, N.D., www.ndsu.edu/grhc.

OTHER PUBLICATIONS

Robert Conquest, *The Harvest of Sorrow: Soviet Collectivization and the Terror-Famine.* Reprinted by permission of Robert Conquest.

Terry Martin, *The Affirmative Action Empire: Nations and Nationalism in the Soviet Union, 1923–1939.* Reprinted by permission of Cornell University Press.

Liudmyla Hrynevych, "Stalins'ka 'revoliutsiia zhory' ta holod 1933 r. iak faktory polityzatsiï ukraïns'koï spil'noty." Translated and published by permission of the Ukrainian Historical Journal.

R. W. Davies and Stephen G. Wheatcroft, *The Years of Hunger: Soviet Agriculture, 1931–1933.* Reprinted by permission of Palgrave Macmillan.

Andrea Graziosi, "The Soviet 1931–1933 Famines and the Ukrainian Holodomor: Is a New Interpretation Possible, and What Would Its Consequences Be?" Reprinted by permission of the President and Fellows of Harvard College.

Stanislav Kulchytsky, "Why Did Stalin Exterminate the Ukrainians? Comprehending the Holodomor. The Position of Soviet Historians." Reprinted by permission of the Ukrainian Press Group.

Yurii Shapoval, "Understanding the Causes and Consequences of the Famine-Genocide of 1932–1933 in Ukraine: The Significance of Newly Discovered Archival Documents." Reprinted by permission of the Shevchenko Scientific Society, Inc.

Nicolas Werth, "The Great Ukrainian Famine of 1932–33." Reprinted by permission of Nicolas Werth and the editorial board of the Online Encyclopedia of Mass Violence.

Viktor Kondrashin, "Hunger in 1932–1933—A Tragedy of the Peoples of the USSR." Reprinted by permission of the journal *Holodomor Studies*.

David R. Marples, *Holodomor: Causes of the 1932–1933 Famine in Ukraine*. Reprinted by permission of David Marples.

Jacques Vallin, France Meslé, Serguei Adamets, and Serhiy Pyrozhkov, "The Great Famine: Population Losses in Ukraine." Reprinted by permission of the Kashtan Press.

Oleh Wolowyna, "The Famine-Genocide of 1932–33: Estimation of Losses and Demographic Impact." Reprinted by permission of the Shevchenko Scientific Society, Inc.

International Commission of Inquiry into the 1932–33 Famine in Ukraine, *Final Report*. Reprinted by permission of Jacob W. F. Sundberg, Director of Studies, Stockholm Institute of Public and International Law.

Kyiv Court of Appeal Ruling of 13 January 2010 on the Famine in Ukraine. English translation by Victor Rud, Myroslaw Smorodsky, and Volodymyr Vasylenko, published with their permission.

Raphael Lemkin, "Soviet Genocide in Ukraine." Reprinted by permission of Oxford University Press.

Roman Serbyn, "The Ukrainian Famine of 1932–1933 and the United Nations Convention on Genocide." Reprinted by permission of the Shevchenko Scientific Society, Inc.

Volodymyr Vasylenko, *The Ukrainian Holodomor of 1932–33 as a Crime of Genocide: A Legal Assessment*. Reprinted by permission of Volodymyr Vasylenko, Serhiy Medintsev, and Peter T. Smilsky.

Yevhen Zakharov, "Pravova kvalifikatsiia Holodomoru 1932–1933 rokiv v Ukraïni ta na Kubani iak zlochynu proty liudianosti ta henotsydu." Translated and published by permission of the Kharkiv Human Rights Protection Group.

Malcolm Muggeridge, "The Soviet's War on the Peasants." Reprinted by permission of the Malcolm Muggeridge Society and the Malcolm Muggeridge Literary Estate.

Suzanne Bertillon, "L'effroyable détresse des populations de l'Ukraine." Digital copy accessed at http://gallica.bnf.fr/ark:/12148/cb328123058/date.r=.langFR.

Suzanne Bertillon, "La Famine en Ukraine." Digital copy accessed at http://gallica.bnf.fr/ark:/12148/cb328123058/date.r=.langFR.

Harry Lang, "Seen and Heard in the Villages of the Ukraine." Reprinted by permission of the journal *Holodomor Studies*.

Harry Lang, "A Trip to the Jewish *Kolkhozy* of Ukraine and White Russia." Reprinted by permission of the journal *Holodomor Studies*.

Louis Fischer, *Soviet Journey*. Reprinted by permission of Kathy Baxter and Victor Fischer.

Ewald Ammende, *Human Life in Russia*. Reprinted by permission of John T. Zubal, Inc., Publishers.

Eugene Lyons, *Assignment in Utopia*. Reprinted by permission of Transaction Publishers.

Victor Kravchenko, *I Chose Freedom: The Personal and Political Life of a Soviet Official*. Reprinted by permission of Andrew Kravchenko.

Extract from *The Invisible Writing* by Arthur Koestler reprinted by permission of Peters Fraser & Dunlop (www.petersfraserdunlop.com) on behalf of the Estate of Arthur Koestler.

Khrushchev Remembers. Reprinted by permission of Andrew Nurnberg Associates.

Lev Kopelev, *The Education of a True Believer*. Reprinted by permission of HarperCollins Publishers.

Molotov Remembers: Inside Kremlin Politics. Conversations with Felix Chuev. Reprinted by permission of Rowman & Littlefield Publishing Group.

Miron Dolot, *Execution by Hunger: The Hidden Holocaust*. Reprinted by permission of W. W. Norton & Company, Inc.

Anastasiia Lysyvets, *Spomyny*. Translated and published by permission of Natalka Bilotserkivets.

Pavlo Makohon, *Svidok: Spohady pro Holod 33-ho roku*. Translated and published by permission of Tamara Makohon.

F. P. Burtiansky, "The Famine: A Pogrom of the Ukrainian Peasantry." Reprinted by permission of the Ukrainian Orthodox Brotherhood of St. Volodymyr.

Vasyl Zaiika [Zaïka], "The Secrets of the Famine (Where the NKVD-OGPU Buried Thousands of Bodies)." Reprinted by permission of the Ukrainian Orthodox Brotherhood of St. Volodymyr.

"Survivor Transcript: Victor Tkacz," *The Famine in Ukraine, 1932–1933*. Reprinted by permission of Yuri Tkacz.

Tetiana Nykytiuk, "A Candle Lit in Memory and Hope." Reprinted by permission of the Ukrainian Press Group.

Tamara Orlova, "My Beloved Unhappy Mother a Murderer?" Reprinted by permission of the Ukrainian Press Group.

Vladimir Keis, "Moi zhiznennyi put' i zhiznennye perezhivaniia moei molodosti na rodnoi ukrainskoi zemle do 1929 goda i Vtoraia Mirovaia Voina." Translated and published by permission of Vladimir Keis.

George Orwell, *Animal Farm*. Reprinted by permission of Bill Hamilton as the literary executor of the estate of the late Sonia Brownell Orwell and Secker & Warburg Ltd.

Vasyl Barka, *Rai*. Translated and published by permission of Svoboda Press.

Vasily Grossman, *Forever Flowing*. Reprinted by permission of HarperCollins Publishers.

Olena Zvychaina, "Socialist Potatoes." Reprinted by permission of Roma Franko.

Yevhen Pashkovsky, "Five Loaves and Two Fishes." Reprinted by permission of Zephyr Press and Victoria Hruszkewycz-Moll.

Mykola Ponedilok, "Chorna khustka." Translated and published by permission of Homin Ukraïny (Ukrainian Echo).

Marsha Forchuk Skrypuch, "The Rings." Reprinted by permission of Marsha Forchuk Skrypuch.

Yevhen Hutsalo, "Holodomor: Murder by Starvation." Reprinted by permission of Roma Franko.

Olena Zvychaina, "'Lucky' Hanna." Reprinted by permission of Roma Franko.

Vasyl Barka, *Zhovtyi kniaz'*. Translated and published by permission of the Ukrainian Academy of Arts and Sciences in the U.S., Inc.

Mykola Kowshun, *The Black Vulture: A Drama in 3 Acts*. Reprinted by permission of Idea Lewis.

Serhii Kokot-Lediansky, *Tysiacha dev'iatsot trydtsiat' tretii rik: drama na 5 kartyn*. Translated and published by permission of Larissa Zaleska Onyshkevych.

Natalia Vorozhbyt, *Zernokhranilishche*. Translated and published by permission of Natalia Vorozhbyt.

Wira Wowk, *Ikonostas Ukraïny*. Translated and published by permission of Wira Wowk.

Mykola Rudenko, "Khrest." Reprinted by permission of the Bahriany Foundation, Inc.

Vasyl Holoborodko, "Shukachi mohyl." The poem originally appeared in the collection *Icarus With Butterfly Wings & Other Poems* (1991) and is reprinted by permission of Exile Editions and Myrosia Stefaniuk.

Vasyl Symonenko, "Chuiu." Translated by and published by permission of Michael Naydan.

Maksym Rylsky, "Zhaha." Reprinted by permission of Michael Naydan.

Valerii Prokoshin, "Liudoedy." Translated and published by permission of Marina Prokoshina.

Lesia Roi, "Lullaby 33." Translated and published by permission of the rock group Vii.

Vasyl Riabko, "The Communards." Translated and published by permission of Vasyl Riabko.

INDEX